ENCYCLOPEDIA
OF
LOUISIANA MUSICIANS

ENCYCLOPEDIA OF LOUISIANA MUSICIANS

JAZZ ⁞ BLUES ⁞ CAJUN CREOLE ⁞ ZYDECO ⁞ SWAMP POP ⁞ GOSPEL

GENE TOMKO

LOUISIANA STATE UNIVERSITY PRESS BATON ROUGE

Published by Louisiana State University Press

Manufactured in the United States of America
First printing

Designer: Michelle A. Neustrom
Typeface: Sentinel
Printer and binder: Sheridan Books, Inc.

Library of Congress Cataloging-in-Publication Data

Names: Tomko, Gene, author.
Title: Encyclopedia of Louisiana musicians : jazz, blues, cajun, creole, zydeco, swamp pop, and gospel / Gene Tomko.
Description: Baton Rouge : Louisiana State University Press, 2020. | Includes bibliographical references.
Identifiers: LCCN 2019040503 | ISBN 978-0-8071-6932-2 (cloth)
Subjects: LCSH: Musicians—Louisiana—Encyclopedias.
Classification: LCC ML101.U6 T66 2020 | DDC 780.92/2763 [B]—dc23
LC record available at https://lccn.loc.gov/2019040503

The paper in this book meets the guidelines for permanence and durability of the Committee on Production Guidelines for Book Longevity of the Council on Library Resources. ♾

Every strand of American music comes directly from Congo Square.

—Wynton Marsalis

CONTENTS

PHOTOGRAPHS

following page 8

ACKNOWLEDGMENTS

A book of this scope would have never come to fruition without the invaluable help of countless musicians and their families, music scholars, researchers, and writers who have graciously shared their time and knowledge with me to help get things as accurate as possible.

To the many people who have helped and supported me throughout the years, I am sincerely grateful to all, including Lynn Abbott, Ray Abshire, Deirdre Adams, Dean Alger, Johnnie Allan, Bobby Allen, Joyce Ambrose of the Southwest Louisiana Genealogical & Historical Library, Doug Ardoin, Sean Ardoin, Classie Ballou Sr., Scott Barretta, Larry Benicewicz, Shane K. Bernard, Camille Bob, Scott M. Bock, Brett Bonner, A. J. Brooks, Millie and Jeffery Broussard, John Broven, Chris E. Brown, Kerry Brown, Wayne "Blue" Burns, Chuck Bush, Wes Carroll, Brandon K. Carter, Roscoe Chenier, Mary and Chester Chevalier, Henry Clement, Dominick Cross, Phil Daigle, Andrew Dansby, Eliza Dasher and Eliza Bledsoe, Albert Davis, Judy Domingue, Jimmy Dotson, Shelton Dunaway and Bryan James, Bob Eagle, Thomas Wayne Emery, Clarence "Jockey" Etienne, Wade Falcon, Bruce Flett, Carol Fran, Bridget Fuselier of the St. Martin Parish Library, Herman Fuselier, Henry Gray, Major Handy, Jeff Hannusch, Joseph Hardin, Amanda Hawk at Special Collections at Louisiana State University, Martin Hawkins, Zydeco Ray Hébert, Lawrence Hoffman, Terry Huval, Bruce Iglauer, Matthew "Boogie Jake" Jacobs, Greg Johnson at the Blues Archives at the University of Mississippi, Moriba Karamoko, Chad Kassem, Harvey Knox, Tee Don Landry, Lazy Lester, Eric LeBlanc, Peter B. Lowry, Dr. Horace J. Maxile Jr., Bill Millar, Mark Miller, S. J. Montalbano, Kevin Naquin, Paul Natkin, Jim O'Neal, Todd Ortego, Guy Owens, David "Ozy" Ozenbaugh, Ira "Dr. Ike" Padnos, Philip Paulin, Guitar Gable Perrodin, Dan Phillips, Mary and John Potier, David Rachou, Robby "Mann" Robinson, Howard W. Rye, Clayton Sampy, Ben Sandmel, Becky Schexnayder, John "Pudd" Sharp, Paul "Lil' Buck" Sinegal, Floyd Soileau, Nick Spitzer, Bill Stafford of the Louisiana State Archives, Philliper "Phlip" Stewart of the Buddy Stewart Memorial Foundation and Rhythm Museum, Warren Storm, Eddie Stout, Jodi Stovall and Wallace "Red" Touchet, Jude Taylor, Melvin W. Tezeno, Lee Tillman, John Wirt, Roger Wood, and Lee Allen Zeno. My apologies to anyone who was inadvertently omitted.

In addition to all of the primary research that went into this work, this book also greatly benefited from the exemplary research and writings of Lynn Abbott, Mary Katherine Aldin, Johnnie Allan, Dr. Barry Jean Ancelet, Larry Benicewicz, Pete Bergeron, Shane K. Bernard, Scott M. Bock, John Broven, Chris E. Brown, Ron Brown, Samuel B. Charters, Bob Eagle, Les Fancourt, Kevin S. Fontenot, Robert Ford, Herman Fuselier, Marv Goldberg, Lawrence Gushee, Peter Hanley, Jeff Hannusch, Martin Hawkins, Michael Hurtt, Dr. Karl Koenig, Eric LeBlanc, Nick Leigh, John and Alan Lomax, Kip Lornell, Donald M. Marquis, Mack McCormick, Bob McGrath, Kevin Nutt, Jim O'Neal, Paul Oliver, Dan Phillips, Lauren C. Post, Fred Ramsey, Susan Roach, Al Rose, Bill Russell, Tony Russell, Howard W. Rye, Ben Sandmel, Ann Allen Savoy, Dr. Edmond Souchon, Chris Strachwitz, Michael Tisserand, Sherrie Tucker, Brice White, John Wirt, Stefan Wirz, Roger Wood, and Ron Yule.

I would also like to extend my sincere gratitude to everyone at LSU Press who helped make this book possible. Foremost, to acquisitions editor Margaret Lovecraft who initially reached out to me about her interest in my work several years ago and who has consistently been one of the most considerate and supportive professionals that I've had the good fortune to work with. Also to managing editor Catherine Kadair and freelance editor Stan Ivester for all of their invaluable expertise and insight, and to senior designer Michelle Neustrom for her very imaginative and beautiful cover design and layout.

Most of all I would like to thank my wife, Carol, without whose unlimited love and support this book would not have been at all possible, and whose passion for Louisiana music and culture matches my own. And to my mother, who has always been there for me from day one, and my father, who also shared a deep love of music and history, and to whose memory this book is dedicated.

ENCYCLOPEDIA OF LOUISIANA MUSICIANS

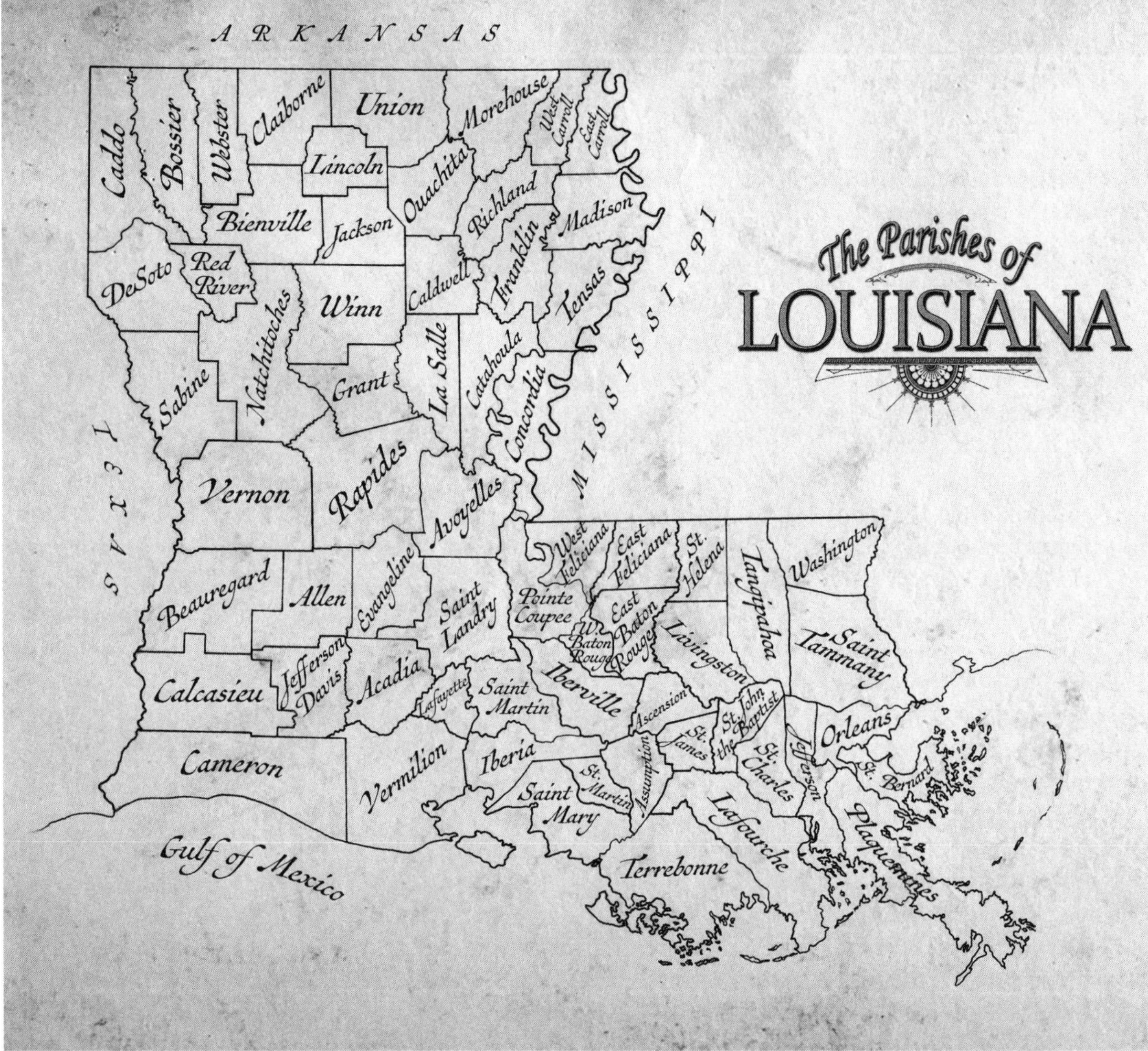

ARKANSAS
TEXAS
MISSISSIPPI
The Parishes of
LOUISIANA
Caddo
Bossier
Webster
Claiborne
Union
Morehouse
West Carroll
East Carroll
Lincoln
Ouachita
Richland
Madison
Bienville
Jackson
DeSoto
Red River
Caldwell
Franklin
Tensas
Winn
Natchitoches
Sabine
Grant
La Salle
Catahoula
Concordia
Vernon
Rapides
Avoyelles
Beauregard
Allen
Evangeline
Saint Landry
West Feliciana
East Feliciana
St. Helena
Tangipahoa
Washington
Pointe Coupee
W. Baton Rouge
East Baton Rouge
Livingston
Saint Tammany
Calcasieu
Jefferson Davis
Acadia
Lafayette
Saint Martin
Iberville
Ascension
St. John the Baptist
Orleans
Cameron
Vermilion
Iberia
St. James
St. Charles
Jefferson
St. Bernard
Assumption
St. Martin
Saint Mary
Lafourche
Plaquemines
Terrebonne
Gulf of Mexico

INTRODUCTION

Of all the extraordinary gifts Louisiana has given the world, its single greatest contribution is undoubtedly its music. And Louisiana's music is America's music. In fact, one could quite effectively argue that Louisiana is the most important of all the United States in the development of its indigenous music. Simply put, without its immeasurable contributions, American music would not exist as we recognize it today.

Louisiana has also produced more distinct styles of music than any other state. Jazz, Cajun, Creole, and zydeco all originated from within its borders before spreading throughout the country and then the world. Jazz took off like wildfire in the first decades of the twentieth century and quickly migrated to Chicago, New York City, Los Angeles, Kansas City, and all parts in-between while also spreading throughout Europe and eventually to all corners of the world. Cajun, Creole, and zydeco's international exposure took several more decades to occur, but the music did finally reach mass global destinations.

In addition to these indigenous styles for which the state is most famously known, the region also served as an incubator for early forms of blues and gospel, and in turn, their offspring rhythm and blues, rockabilly, and rock and roll. Although today many around the country and throughout the world more closely associate the state with its exquisite cuisine, Louisiana's most profound and influential cultural legacy is unquestionably its music.

Place and Peoples

The Bayou State's remarkable musical legacy is a product of both its geographic location and its rich multicultural history. Claimed as part of the Louisiana Colony in 1682 by the French, whose deep influence can still be strongly felt today, the Mississippi River port that several decades later became New Orleans served as a vital gateway of commerce, trade, defense, and transportation, making New Orleans the most important city in the South for centuries to come. This preeminent status attracted an extremely diverse immigrant population along with a massive influx of involuntary arrivals—African and West Indian slaves who reached a population so great that they would ultimately outnumber the prevailing white ruling class. Although the first European explorers to reach the area were led by Spanish conquistadors Pánfilo de Narváez when he discovered the mouth of the Mississippi River in 1528, and Hernando de Soto during his famed expedition on the river in 1542, the region remained virtually untouched by Europeans for almost a century and a half. The French explorer René-Robert Cavelier, Sieur de La Salle, claimed the river and its basin for France in 1682, naming the territory La Louisiane in honor of King Louis XIV.

Adding to this populace, of course, were the original inhabitants of the land, who also played an ongoing role in the development of Louisiana's unique culture—the indigenous Native Americans. These tribes included the Caddo Indians of northwest and west-central Louisiana; the Tunica Indians of northeast Louisiana; the Natchez Indians of central and upper-east Louisiana; the Choctaw Indians of the region from central Louisiana directly east across the vast expanse encompassing present-day Baton Rouge, Kentwood, and Bogalusa; the Atakapa Indians of southwest Louisiana from the Atchafalaya Basin west to the Texas border; and the Chitimacha Indians, who inhabited all of southeast Louisiana from the Atchafalaya

Basin east to the mouth of the Mississippi River and the surrounding lower coastal parishes. Another important tribe was the Houma Indians of the Choctaw Nation, who by the early 1700s were driven from central Louisiana near present-day West Feliciana Parish south to coastal southeast Louisiana, where they later shared the region with the arriving Acadian settlers in Terrebonne and Lafourche Parishes.

After control of much of what is now Louisiana was ceded to Spain from France near the end of the Seven Years War through the secret Treaty of Fontainebleau in 1762, a large influx of Spanish immigrants also began arriving, including those from Spain's Canary Islands, who provided Louisiana with another one of its major cultural influences. Under Spanish rule the region began flourishing economically, which in turn attracted other distinct and culturally influential immigrant populations to the region, such as the recently expulsed French-speaking Acadians from what is now Nova Scotia, Canada, and Haitian refugees fleeing the Haitian Revolution of the 1790s and early 1800s. Adding to this was the arrival of Anglo-Americans and black slaves from the United States to the north, which had recently gained its independence.

Spanish rule was decidedly less harsh in its treatment of enslaved people than its American or even French counterpart, allowing them opportunities to gain their freedom by self-purchase or through grants following good deeds, such as saving the master's life or reporting treason. This, in turn, led to a sizable population of free people of color, a great majority of whom were Creoles—those of mixed-race heritage consisting of French, Spanish, and African (and sometimes Native American) lineage, and largely French-speaking. (Although there are many different meanings of the word "Creole," this definition will be used in this work to refer to the people of this ancestry, and in rural southwest Louisiana, also to the distinctive style of fiddle-and-accordion-based music that they created.)

After Spain transferred control of the region back to France in 1800 during Napoleon's secret Third Treaty of San Ildefonso, the United States secured the Louisiana Territory from France through the Louisiana Purchase of 1803. Stretching from the Mississippi River west to the Rocky Mountains, the territory gained effectively doubled the size of the country. Less than a decade later, on April 30, 1812, Louisiana was officially admitted as the eighteenth state of the Union.

Musical Roots

Throughout the nineteenth century Louisiana's population enjoyed a rich diversity of traditional folk and classical music and dance from the homelands of its immigrants and slaves, and their descendants: opera and classical music of the French, Italians, and New Orleans Creoles; traditional drumming and dance celebrations of the African and Afro-Caribbean slaves; French ballads, lullabies, and historical songs, dubbed "home music," of the Acadians/Cajuns and rural southwest Louisiana Creoles; *décima* ballads of Spain's *Isleños* from the Canary Islands; as well as mazurkas, polkas, quadrilles, contra dances, jigs, reels, two-steps, waltzes, and other popular European ethnic musical styles.

European-styled military marching bands also had a major impact on Louisiana's music at this time, especially in and around New Orleans, whose strategic location required a strong and ongoing military presence. Adding to all of this was the growing popularity of minstrelsy with Caucasians performing in blackface, openly lampooning the black population and their culture. These traveling shows and their songs became an extremely popular form of entertainment by the mid-1800s. One of its earliest musical inspirations was **Old Corn Meal**, a black New Orleans street vendor who sang and danced in the streets while selling his Indian cornmeal. His popularity became so widespread he was invited to perform at New Orleans's prestigious St. Charles Theatre in the late 1830s.

By the century's end minstrelsy was to be replaced by vaudeville, with black vaudeville singers such as Ma Rainey, Bessie Smith, **Lizzie Miles**, **Edna Hicks**, and **Esther Bigeou** gaining national recognition in the 1910s and 1920s. Often accompanied both on stage and recording sessions by some of New Orleans's finest early jazz musicians such as **King Oliver**, **Louis Armstrong**, and **Sidney Bechet**, many of these early female black vaudeville performers would be later defined as "classic blues" singers.

Perhaps most important of all to the development of Louisiana's indigenous music was what took place on the edge of the French Quarter, where Louis Armstrong Park is located today. Throughout much of the first half of the 1800s slaves were allowed to congregate on Sundays in New Orleans's Congo Square to perform drumming, dance, and spiritual celebrations such as the seminal ring shout. Starting out in an area which was considered "back o' town," this hallowed ground eventually became the cultural center of the French Quarter for both slaves and free Creoles and served as the pulse of New Orleans music. It was a place unlike anywhere else in the United States, where the African drum and other instruments as well as self-expression were systematically banned. The archetypical Africa-meets-Europe music created in Congo Square would profoundly influence subsequent generations of black and Creole families and, in a much broader sense, all American music.

The Emergence of Jazz

After the Civil War ended in 1865, newly emancipated black New Orleanians began teaching themselves a variety of brass-band instruments which were widely available, discarded by military band members after the war. Performing classical pieces, marches, quadrilles, waltzes, and other popular styles of the day early on, by the 1890s the music of some of the prevalent black marching bands started evolving into something completely unique, completely American, with its incorporation of blues, ragtime, spirituals, minstrel and vaudeville songs, and West African–rooted second-line drumming (from Congo Square) into a looser rhythmic form which progressively featured improvisation. Among such early pioneers was **Buddy Bolden**, who was performing around New Orleans by the mid-1890s and within a few short years reached unprecedented local success, becoming the new music's first "king" well over a decade before it would finally become known as jazz.

In the first decade of the twentieth century the music was gaining such popularity in New Orleans that local classically trained Creole musicians who had previously thought of this new music as primitive and beneath their considerable talents began to reconsider their positions. Renowned Creole musicians such as **Manuel Perez**, **Alphonse Picou**, and members of the prestigious **Baquet** and **Tio** families who had been leading and/or performing in societal dance orchestras and marching bands such as the Excelsior, Onward, and Imperial, began contributing their highly refined talents in joining their fellow black musicians and performing this emerging new style on the bandstands and parade lines. Younger Creole musicians also fell under its spell, most notably **Jelly Roll Morton**, who became a key central figure in its early development. It was when these distinguished, classically trained Creole musicians from the "Downtown" section of New Orleans (areas north and east of Canal Street) began collaborating with the often self-taught, emotionally driven and improvisational black musicians of "Uptown" (areas south and west of Canal), jazz fully transformed into a true American art form.

The music's mass appeal quickly crossed racial boundaries, both within its audience and on the bandstand. Local white musicians and white society dance orchestras started incorporating this new style, taking inspiration from some of the finest black and Creole musicians of the day such as **King Oliver**, **Freddie Keppard**, and **Kid Ory**. The enamored musicians, many of Italian American lineage, caught these early jazz performances in various venues and street parades throughout New Orleans, including inside the city's notorious red light district, Storyville, where its brothels, dance halls, saloons, and streets often featured early black and Creole jazz musicians until its closure in Nov. 1917. **Tom "Red" Brown**, **Nick LaRocca**, **Larry Shields**, and others, most of whom began in the preceding years performing in **Papa Jack Laine**'s Reliance Brass Band, became the music's first noted white proponents in the mid- to late 1910s, with LaRocca's Original Dixieland Jass Band credited as making the first jazz recording in 1917. (The band and LaRocca himself also falsely promoted themselves as "the Creators of Jazz.")

Throughout the first decades of the 1900s this new music was also spreading throughout other parts of Louisiana, including the Acadiana region of southwest Louisiana where trumpet player **Evan Thomas** of Crowley led his band the Black Eagles. Popular from the late 1910s until his tragic murder in the early 1930s, Thomas's exemplary band was regarded as an equal to the finest groups in New Orleans and included at times such early jazz greats as **Bunk Johnson**, **George Lewis**, and **Lawrence Duhé**. Other noted early rural bandleaders included New Iberia's **Gus Fontenette**, who led his popular Banner Orchestra for several decades, and Professor **Claiborne**

Williams from the Donaldsonville area, a highly revered music teacher who led his orchestras from the late 1880s through the 1940s.

Cajun and Creole Music

While jazz was starting to flourish in the first decades of the twentieth century, so was the indigenous music for which southwest Louisiana would become most famous, that of the white Cajuns and black Creoles. Now settled for well over a century in the region's bayous and prairies, the majority of the Cajuns descended from the French-speaking Acadians who were driven from their land in Canada by the British starting in the latter half of the 1700s, but they also included a faction who migrated directly from France, notably the northern coastal regions surrounding Brittany and Normandy from where much of the original Acadia settlers hailed. In time their Cajun descendants would adapt to their unique and often isolated surroundings and develop their own distinct culture—one which included their own music, food, dialect and *joie de vivre* spirit.

As European musical instruments such as the French violin/fiddle, the German accordion, the Spanish guitar, and the English triangle (or *'tit fir*) eventually became locally available, Cajun music steadily developed over the generations from its traditional European-based ballads, jigs, and waltzes into an original American musical style dominated by fast two-steps and slow waltzes and characterized by high, emotionally charged singing and wails—all created for the primary purpose of dancing. Retaining their native language well into the twentieth century, their songs were all sung strictly in French, a tradition which continued unabated until the mid- to late 1930s when occasional English-language Cajun recordings began appearing as an attempt to broaden its audience. Traditional Cajun music is still sung almost exclusively in French to this day.

The music of the rural black Creoles of southwest Louisiana shared much of the same instrumentation and language with their Cajun neighbors using fiddles and later accordions as the main rhythm and lead instruments and also singing in French, but instead of the triangle, a washboard (or *frottoir*) was more commonly employed as a percussive instrument. Economically, the two groups also shared the lowest rung of society as the poorest of the poor. But because both musical styles have similar instrumentation and throughout their history Cajun and Creole musicians have influenced each other, they are often mischaracterized as being interchangeably "Cajun" despite significant differences. Creole music, or French la la as it was more often called, was strongly influenced by the blues and African rhythms and melodies in contrast to its Cajun equivalent which retained more Eurocentric traditions.

The earliest form of this rural black Creole music was juré, an intense, ritualized chant with heavy syncopation which featured improvised lyrics, hand-clapping, and foot-stomping along with specialized dance steps. Mostly performed without instrumentation (or occasionally with basic makeshift percussion such as spoons, mule jawbone, or washboards), these "testifying shouts" were very African in nature and served as early Creole spirituals during the Catholic season of Lent, a religion shared by the vast majority of Creoles and Cajuns alike.

The very practice of Roman Catholicism itself, which dominated much of south and southwest Louisiana's black and white populations from New Orleans to Lake Charles, also played a significant role in the development of Louisiana's music. In stark contrast with most other areas of the Deep South (including central and north Louisiana), where the vast majorities were strict Baptists, many Catholics not only shared a more lenient and liberal view of such "sinful" activities as drinking, dancing, and playing secular music, but unabashedly celebrated them.

In the late 1920s the recording industry finally discovered the musical treasures of rural southwest Louisiana when **Joe Falcon** and his future wife **Cléoma Breaux** made the first commercial Cajun recording, "Lafayette," on April 27, 1928. The extraordinary regional success of its release quickly ushered in the first Cajun and Creole recording era with **Douglas Bellard** and **Kirby Riley** claiming the honor of making the first French la la recording the following year. Throughout the next several years many important early Cajun and Creole musicians would record, but none more significant than **Amédé Ardoin** and **Dennis McGee**. Performing and recording both separately and as a mixed-race duo, the black Creole accordion player and white Cajun fiddler laid the very foundation of both Cajun and Creole music in their subsequent historic recordings from 1929 through 1934—a canon which would continue to influence every generation of Cajun and Creole musician to this day.

By the mid-1930s the new popular wave of Western swing from Texas began having a tremendous impact on Cajun music, causing the accordion to be replaced by the fiddle and later steel guitar as lead instruments. This, combined with America's involvement in World War II, which enforced a ban on German imports such as the accordion as well as an increasing public distaste for anything associated with Germany, all but eliminated the instrument from most Cajun performances and recordings for more than a decade. Cajun string bands such as **Luderin Darbone** and **Edwin Duhon**'s Hackberry Ramblers, **Happy Fats**'s Rayne-Bo Ramblers and **Leo Soileau**'s various groups continued to dominate bandstands and record sales until the late 1940s when **Iry LeJeune** and **Nathan Abshire** ushered the accordion back into popularity and ignited the Cajun dance-hall heyday of the 1950s and 1960s.

Blues, Gospel, and Rhythm and Blues

Also from Louisiana's long and storied musical legacy come some of the earliest historical references to the blues, the most fundamental of all American musical forms, whose exact birthplace is all but impossible to precisely narrow down. Although Mississippi has long claimed it as its own, and unquestionably the vast majority of its early rural exponents and recording artists of the 1920s and 1930s hailed from there, a more likely scenario of its origins is that it developed contemporaneously in the cotton fields and plantations in pockets across the Deep South, born out of the spirituals, work songs, and field hollers of its severely mistreated slaves.

Those same oppressive conditions and sociopolitical factors that produced the blues and which notoriously existed in the Mississippi Delta also thrived on the cotton fields and sugar plantations further south across Louisiana, especially along its own Mississippi River delta land. Although later known as pioneers of jazz, performers such as **Buddy Bolden**, **Freddie Keppard**, **Jelly Roll Morton**, **King Oliver**, and **Tony Jackson** were just some of the musicians who had either played the blues in some form or fashion, or vividly recalled hearing it (and were greatly inspired by it) throughout New Orleans and the surrounding areas in the late decades of the 1800s and early 1900s. Notable early blues recording artists who hailed from Louisiana include **Lonnie Johnson**, **Richard "Rabbit" Brown**, **Papa Charlie Jackson**, **Oscar "Buddy" Woods**, and **Little Brother Montgomery**.

And from those same cotton fields and plantations that birthed the blues also came an even earlier form of healing music—the Negro spiritual. From the earliest days of slavery when its African captives began converting to Christianity, singing these spirituals while working in the fields became their only outlet of self-expression. Deeply rooted in African culture, rhythms, and melodies, this sacred oral tradition expressed the slaves' unwavering Christian faith and enduring quest for freedom, often using coded language to communicate messages and deeper meanings which would escape the master's ear. Gospel music, or black sacred music, began taking form after the Civil War as African American churches began incorporating more modern hymns and arrangements into their services and eventually started adding instrumentation. Many of gospel music's finest and most influential figures hailed from Louisiana, and New Orleans in particular, including **Mahalia Jackson**, who is often cited as its greatest voice, as well as **Bessie Griffin**, **Linda Hopkins**, and the "Two-Winged Preacher," guitar evangelist **Elder Utah Smith**, who was originally from Shreveport.

As the blues eventually evolved and modernized, becoming more urbane in the 1930s, early rhythm and blues started taking on a recognizable form by the early 1940s with various jump- and swing-influenced bands. Among those at the forefront was one led by Louisiana-born **Saunders King**, who was also among the first to record with an electric guitar. Several years later it was another Louisiana native who made an even larger impact when in 1947 **Roy Brown** recorded his immortal hit "Good Rocking Tonight," often cited as the very first rock and roll record. This groundbreaking recording marked the beginning of an unprecedented era of New Orleans rhythm and blues, which made the Crescent City a dominating force on the American popular music scene for two decades with countless hits emanating from **Cosimo Matassa**'s famed New Orleans studios by **Fats Domino**, **Dave Bartholomew**, **Paul Gayten**, **Lloyd Price**, Little

Richard, **Guitar Slim**, **Huey "Piano" Smith**, **Smiley Lewis**, and countless others.

Although most likely lost on the vast majority of his millions of fans, Domino played an important role in carrying on New Orleans's rich piano tradition into the rock and roll era. This important musical legacy included such key early practitioners as **Tony Jackson** and **Jelly Roll Morton** as well as its more recent masterful players such as **Tuts Washington** and **Professor Longhair**, the latter of whom brought the city's strong Latin and Caribbean influences which Morton had introduced decades earlier into full bloom with his many New Orleans and Mardi Gras classics. It would be the supremely multitalented **Allen Toussaint** as well as the brilliant **James Booker** who would then take this defining piano tradition into the 1960s and beyond.

Zydeco, Swamp Blues, and Swamp Pop

The popular rhythm and blues of the late 1940s and early 1950s of course also had a direct and dramatic impact on the musicians of southwest Louisiana, both white and black. In the Creole community, the younger musicians began adding structural elements of current rhythm and blues as well as its instrumentation to the older French la la style of their parents. Musicians from Opelousas to Lake Charles as well as natives who had recently migrated across the border to the Houston and Port Arthur/Beaumont area during the region's oil boom began performing in this more modern style, eventually adding drums, electric guitar, bass, and saxophone to accompany the ubiquitous accordion and rubboard (and leaving the fiddle behind). Among those most responsible for creating and shaping this new form of Creole music, which would become known as zydeco, it would be **Clifton Chenier**, who would have the most profound impact on the music and be universally hailed as the "King of Zydeco" by both fans and musicians alike.

New Orleans rhythm and blues also had a tremendous influence on other musicians of southwest Louisiana who wanted to perform the music more faithfully than the new zydeco trailblazers. Both young Cajuns and Creoles were infatuated with this sound, particularly Fats Domino's loping rhythms and driving piano triplets, and began forming their own groups by the mid-1950s. **Bobby Charles**, **Cookie** and the Cupcakes, **Guitar Gable** and **King Karl**, **Warren Storm**, **Johnnie Allan**, **Roy "Boogie Boy" Perkins**, **Rod Bernard**, and the band the Boogie Kings were just some of its early practitioners. Initially known to most performers and their fans simply as Louisiana rhythm and blues or Louisiana rock and roll, by the late 1960s this Cajun- and Creole-influenced rhythm and blues had acquired the name swamp pop, and for better or worse, the label stuck.

Also during this time another influential musical offshoot was taking shape in the clubs, taverns, and juke joints around Baton Rouge; a style which would eventually come to define the blues of Louisiana—swamp blues. Inspired greatly by the laid-back shuffles of Chicago bluesman Jimmy Reed and the deep, gut-bucket guitar style of Lightnin' Hopkins, the music was pioneered early on by such artists as **Lightnin' Slim**, **Lazy Lester**, and **Slim Harpo**. Crowley studio owner **J. D. Miller** was responsible for producing virtually every classic swamp blues recording of its heyday from the mid-1950s through the mid-1960s, which were then issued almost exclusively on Nashville's Excello label. Miller also played a major role in shaping its signature sound with his inventive engineering which featured moody, reverb-laden production and imaginative makeshift percussion, often creatively supplied by **Lazy Lester** or **Jockey Etienne**. Although the majority of swamp blues musicians hailed from the Baton Rouge area, southwest Louisiana also produced a number of notable artists including **Guitar Gable**, **Leroy Washington**, and **Rudy Richard**.

Sounds from Shreveport

Located much farther north in the Ark-La-Tex region of northwest Louisiana, Shreveport also played an important role in the development of the state's music. Although known primarily as the home of the *Louisiana Hayride,* Louisiana's version of Nashville's *Grand Ole Opry,* the city's rich musical landscape encompassed much more than country music. It was also a hotbed for early blues, rockabilly, gospel, and southern soul. **Lead Belly**, who was among the most important musical figures of the first half of the twentieth century, was born on a plantation just northwest of Shreveport, and the early folk-blues icon performed often in Shreveport's red light district along Fannin Street in the first decade of the 1900s and later in the mid- to late 1920s. Fannin Street as well as the

African American business and entertainment district which ran along Texas Avenue and the nearby Blue Goose neighborhood were all magnets for many other early blues musicians, such as brothers **Jesse "Babyface"** and **Willard "Ramblin'" Thomas** and **Oscar "Buddy" Woods**, as well as barrelhouse piano players like **Black Ivory King**.

Although most famous for its role as a launching pad for country musicians in the late 1940s and 1950s, Shreveport's *Louisiana Hayride* radio program also played a significant role in the early development and popularization of rockabilly, where country and western twang combined with a heavy dose of rhythm and blues. Besides famously giving Elvis Presley his first major break in 1954, the show also featured many Louisiana-born early rockabilly performers such as **Werly Fairburn**, **Joe Clay**, **James Burton**, **Al Ferrier**, and Cajun brothers **Rusty** and **Doug Kershaw**. In 1957, aspiring local singer-songwriter **Dale Hawkins** cut his classic hit "Suzy-Q" backed by Burton's brilliant guitar work. Shreveport also played a supporting role in the development of southern soul with local producers **Dee Marais** and **Stan "the Record Man" Lewis** recording such exceptional north Louisiana talent as **Reuben Bell**, **Eddie Giles**, and **Bobby Rush** in the 1960s and 1970s.

Using the Encyclopedia

This *Encyclopedia of Louisiana Musicians* is devoted to accurate and concise biographical entries of the musicians who created, recorded, innovated, and carried on the tradition of Louisiana music in all its eclectic indigenous forms: jazz, blues, Cajun, Creole, zydeco, swamp pop, and gospel. It also includes important subgenres such as rhythm and blues and its derivatives soul, funk, rockabilly, and early rock and roll. With few exceptions, the scope of this book does not include musicians who mainly performed modern rock, pop, country, bluegrass or rap/hip-hop. Country artists who performed and/or recorded a significant amount of Cajun or rockabilly music in their career are generally included.

Each entry lists the musician's name and/or stage name, style(s) of music performed, instrumentation, whether they were a composer and/or bandleader, and birth and death dates and places. This is followed by a succinct but informative summary of their career and/or musical contributions. Because of the book's vast scope, sentences were written to be as concise as possible with limited use of pronouns or the musician's name. Any names that appear in bold indicate an entry of their own in one of the volume's three sections.

Entries are generally listed alphabetically by the musician's given last name. In cases where a musician was primarily known by a pseudonym, such as **Slim Harpo**, those entries will be listed alphabetically under the first name, with Slim Harpo appearing in the S section. When a stage name appears as it could be a given name, such as **Bobby "Boogas" Page** (who was born Elwood Dugas), the entry will be listed under the last name (such as under P for Page), and the given name will be indicated afterwards. In many cases cross-references for given names and pseudonyms are provided in the main section.

Places of birth and death are where the actual event took place, such as a nearby larger town where the hospital was located, and not necessarily where the family resided at the time. Along with the community, town, or city, the parish (Louisiana's designation for county) is also listed for all Louisiana births and deaths, with a parish map located at the beginning of this introduction for reference. Instrumentation listed does not necessarily include all instruments performed, but ones in which the musician was most proficient, with the first most often indicating the performer's main instrument. The style of music listed refers to the genre that the musician performed for a substantial period of time and for which he or she is best known. Other styles may be listed for performers of multiple genres, but such lists do not necessarily include all applicable genres.

Although jazz did not take on a completely recognizable form until the first decades of the twentieth century and the actual name jazz (or jass) did not start being commonly used until the mid- to late 1910s, there were many musicians in the late decades of the 1800s such as **John Robichaux**, **Manuel Perez**, **Charley Galloway**, and others who performed in a style that foreshadowed what was to come, which some may refer to as pre-jazz. Although these musicians in such ragtime, brass, and society dance bands and orchestras were technically not jazz musicians during that time period (although many would later perform jazz), they will be classified in this work under the jazz label.

The term "hit" in regard to popular recordings can

have a variety of meanings. In general, this book uses "hit" to refer to a recording that attained an appreciable level of popularity though not always one that reached the national charts. A "local hit" refers to a recording whose popularity was confined to a specific city and/or nearby surrounding area, usually where the artist was based. A "regional hit" includes a much wider area of popularity and can encompass multiple states. A "minor hit" is a recording that peaked lower in the charts than a "hit" or "major hit." On recordings prior to the late 1930s (before music charts existed), a "hit" strictly refers to a recording that sold exceedingly well for the artist at the time.

The term "postwar" when describing a musician or musical style refers to the period following World War II, an era which saw significant changes in musical styles and instrumentation, particularly in blues, Cajun, and Creole music. "Prewar" refers to the period preceding World War II, particularly the 1920s and 1930s, before electric amplification became prevalent.

This book does not include entries for bands, but often includes notable members of prominent bands. In general, commercial awards and inductions into honorary foundations were not cited as this was beyond the scope of the book and can be easily referenced online.

Following the main section of Louisiana-born musicians, there is a section of musicians who have made an impact on Louisiana music or who are essentially considered Louisiana artists but were born elsewhere. These include such noteworthy musicians as early New Orleans rhythm and blues tenor saxophonist **Lee Allen** from Pittsburg, Kansas; early jazz pianist **Billie Pierce** from Marianna, Florida; and influential blues singer, guitarist, and composer **Eddie "Guitar Slim" Jones** from Greenwood, Mississippi. Musicians who have been incorrectly reported as being natives of Louisiana but were later found to have been born elsewhere through historical records or newly discovered documents, such as Memphis Minnie, were generally not included.

And finally there is a regional survey of important Louisiana-based record producers, along with their labels and/or studios, who provided the audio canvas for the musicians to create their art. By no means exhaustive, the list highlights the prominent (mostly) nonmusicians who played a key role in capturing and preserving Louisiana music for future generations to enjoy.

While creating the *Louisiana Music Map* and the *Southwest Louisiana Music Map,* which together visually document the birthplaces of nearly two thousand native musicians who performed the music indigenous to Louisiana, I have collected a significant amount of data. Research included thousands of hours combing through books, magazines/periodicals, newspapers, and other reliable published sources; conducting hundreds of personal interviews and correspondence with musicians and surviving family members; and examining thousands of historical documents such as census data, military records, Social Security Administration files, birth, marriage, and death certificates, prison and arrest records, city directories; and other invaluable resources. Through this process I have been able to document many musicians' birth and death dates and places for the first time and ascertain more accurate information where there have been conflicting or incorrect published accounts. I cite sources for new information published for the first time and for information that conflicts with and corrects previously published accounts. When information has been verified with historical documents and found to be consistent with multiple previously published findings, no source is cited.

Although Louisiana's celebrated music is currently enjoying its largest global audience, many of its highly influential musicians are still not immediately identified with the state from which they came. Even some of its most famous musicians such as **Lead Belly**, **Jerry Lee Lewis**, and **Mahalia Jackson** often fail to be recognized as Louisiana-born artists, sadly even among many of the Bayou State's own residents. From the late 1940s into the 1960s, the music coming out of New Orleans dominated rhythm and blues and early rock and roll, yet in recent years Memphis, Detroit, and even Cleveland(!) seem to be much more closely associated with its legacy.

The *Encyclopedia of Louisiana Musicians* aims to help rectify this situation as well as educate its readers about the truly astounding number of important musicians who hail from this unique state—an area that has produced more influential musicians than anywhere else in the United States, and perhaps the world.

Gene Tomko
October 2019

Amédé Ardoin

About 1912. Public domain.

Louis Armstrong

New York City, 1946. Courtesy of William P. Gottlieb/Ira and Leonore S. Gershwin Fund Collection, Music Division, Library of Congress.

Clarence "Gatemouth" Brown
King Biscuit Blues Festival, Helena, Arkansas, 2004. Copyright Gene Tomko.

Clifton Chenier

Chicago, 1984. Alligator Records promo. Courtesy of photographer Paul Natkin/Photo Reserve and the Blues Archives, University of Mississippi.

Dr. John

Arkansas Blues & Heritage Festival, Helena, 2010. Copyright Gene Tomko.

Cléoma and Joe Falcon

Rayne, Louisiana, around 1934. Lauren Chester Post, "Joe and Cléoma Falcon," Box 1, Photographic Negatives, Lauren Chester Post Papers, Mss 2854, Louisiana and Lower Mississippi Valley Collections, Louisiana State University Libraries, Baton Rouge.

Buddy Guy
Baton Rouge Blues Festival, 2016. Copyright Gene Tomko.

Mahalia Jackson

1962. Courtesy of Library of Congress, Prints & Photographs Division, Carl Van Vechten Collection, reproduction no. LC-USZ62-54231.

Left to right, **George Lewis, Bunk Johnson, Alcide "Slow Drag" Pavageau, and Lead Belly**
New York City, 1946. Courtesy of William P. Gottlieb/Ira and Leonore S. Gershwin Fund Collection, Music Division, Library of Congress.

Lazy Lester
Blue Moon Saloon, Lafayette, Louisiana, 2014. Copyright Gene Tomko.

D. L. Menard

Festivals Acadiens et Creoles, Lafayette, Louisiana, 2013. Copyright Gene Tomko.

Jelly Roll Morton
Possibly Storyville District, New Orleans, around 1906. Public domain.

Warren Storm with James Burton

Ponderosa Stomp, New Orleans, 2009. Copyright Gene Tomko.

Irma Thomas
Chicago Blues Festival, 2007. Copyright Gene Tomko.

Allen Toussaint with Art Neville

Crescent City Blues & BBQ Festival, New Orleans, 2015. Copyright Gene Tomko.

I

LOUISIANA MUSICIANS

ABSHIRE, FERNEST "MAN" *Cajun.* Drums, vocals. Composer. (Born Dec. 26, 1934, Crowley, Acadia Parish; died Feb. 27, 1965, New Iberia, Iberia Parish.) Noted early postwar Cajun drummer and singer-songwriter started playing drums before his teens and in the early 1950s performed with **Lawrence Walker**. In 1953 joined **Aldus Roger**'s Lafayette Playboys and performed and recorded with group through the mid-1960s, handling many of the vocal duties with his impeccable singing. Also worked and recorded with **Belton Richard**'s Musical Aces throughout the early 1960s. Composed several Cajun standards including "One Scotch, One Bourbon, One Beer." Died of Leukemia at age 30.

ABSHIRE, LEO *Cajun.* Fiddle, accordion, guitar, vocals. Bandleader. (Born July 27, 1933, Kaplan, Vermilion Parish; died May 31, 2005, Gueydan, Vermilion Parish.) Renowned Cajun fiddle player and master instrument maker started playing in his youth and first performed with **Joe Bonsall**, whom he stayed with for twenty years. In the following decades recorded with **August Broussard** and **John Oliver** and worked with numerous artists including **D. L. Menard**, **Doug Kershaw**, **Milton Adams**, **Eddie LeJeune**, and **Horace Trahan**. In later years performed as leader of the Ole Tymers Cajun Band. Cousin of **Nathan Abshire** and **Ray Abshire**.

ABSHIRE, NATHAN *Cajun.* Accordion, vocals. Composer. Bandleader. (Born June 27, 1913, Gueydan, Vermilion Parish; died May 13, 1981, Basile, Acadia Parish.) Highly influential early Cajun recording artist who along with **Iry LeJeune** was primarily responsible for the revival of accordion-based Cajun music in the late 1940s and 1950s. Greatly influenced by Creole musicians, began playing accordion at age six and performed in the 1930s with **Lionel LeLeux** and **Amédé Ardoin**. Recorded for Bluebird with **Happy Fats**'s Rayne-Bo Ramblers in 1935. Throughout following decades led or performed in some of the most popular bands in Cajun music, notably the Pine Grove Boys. In 1949 released his popular signature recording "Pine Grove Blues" on the O.T. label and through the late 1950s had numerous singles on O.T., Hot Rod, Khoury, and Lyric. Throughout the 1960s and 1970s recorded for Kajun, Swallow, Arhoolie, Sonet, and La Louisianne, often with the **Balfa Brothers**, and served as a Cajun cultural ambassador by performing at festivals and colleges throughout the country. Appeared in several documentaries, including *The Good Times Are Killing Me* in 1975. Performed sporadically in final years, working by day maintaining city salvage yard in Basile until his death. Cousin of **Leo Abshire** and **Ray Abshire**.

ABSHIRE, RAY (Emerson Ray Abshire) *Cajun.* Accordion, vocals. Bandleader. (Born Apr. 17, 1951, Gueydan, Vermilion Parish.) Noted traditional Cajun accordionist and singer began playing in the mid-1960s, mentored by cousin **Nathan Abshire**. From 1969 to 1975 performed and toured with the **Balfa Brothers** and also worked with **Will Kegley** and **Robert Bertrand**. After an 18-year hiatus from performing, joined cousin **Leo Abshire**'s Ole Tymers Cajun Band in the early 1990s and continued performing with various groups. In the early 2000s began performing with his own group and released several acclaimed recordings on Swallow through 2010s, including *All Night Long* in 2013.

ACOSTA, KENNY *Blues.* Guitar, vocals. Composer. Bandleader. (Born Nov. 9, 1949, Baton Rouge, EBR Parish.) Baton Rouge blues guitarist and singer-songwriter spent much of his early music career based in Austin, Texas, in the 1970s. In 1978 returned to Baton Rouge and formed band the House Reckers. Toured throughout the South in the 1980s and 1990s and released self-titled debut album on Skratch in 1984. Released two more albums in the 2000s and continued to be active on the Baton Rouge blues scene in the 2010s.

ADAMS, AMADUS *Cajun.* Accordion. Composer. (Born Feb. 11, 1899, Leleux, Vermilion Parish; died May 30, 1966, Crowley, Acadia Parish.)[1] Early Cajun accordionist and leader of the Midnight Playboys in the 1940s and 1950s. Also worked with various area musicians including **Doris Matte** and **Fernest "Man" Abshire**. Reportedly composed Cajun standard "Johnny Can't Dance" but did not record it.

ADAMS, DOLLY DOUROUX *Jazz.* Piano, trumpet, bass, guitar, drums. Bandleader. (Born Jan. 11, 1904, New Orleans, Orleans Parish; died Nov. 6, 1979, New Orleans, Orleans Parish.) Born into a family of prominent jazz musicians, noted early New Orleans jazz multi-instrumentalist started playing piano at age seven and by age 13 joined her uncle **Manuel Manetta**'s band which included at times **Louis Armstrong**, **King Oliver**, and **Kid Ory**. Worked with **Papa** and **Lorenzo Tio Jr.**, **Alphonse Picou**, and **Peter Bocage** before forming her own group in the early 1920s. Retired from music for 15 years to raise a family before returning in the late 1930s, leading a band with her three sons, Gerald, **Justin,** and **Placide Adams Jr**. In the 1960s performed at Preservation Hall with her family band as well as with other groups until sidelined by a stroke in 1967. Made occasional appearances after a recovery period into the 1970s.

ADAMS, JOHNNY *Rhythm and blues.* Guitar, vocals. (Born Jan. 5, 1932, New Orleans, Orleans Parish; died Sept. 14, 1998, Baton Rouge, EBR Parish.) Known as "The Tan Canary," regarded as one of New Orleans's greatest soul singers for his impeccable but powerful delivery. Spent first ten years in gospel groups before recording for Ric in 1959 and gaining initial success with "I Won't Cry" and later "A Losing Battle" in 1962. Recorded country-tinged soul ballad "Reconsider Me" on SSS International in 1969 which became his biggest hit. Returned to the national spotlight in the mid-1980s with long series of recordings for Rounder, including LP *Room with a View of the Blues* in 1988, and continued to record and perform until succumbing to cancer at age 66.

ADAMS, JUSTIN *Rhythm and blues, jazz.* Guitar. (Born June 1, 1923, Algiers, Orleans Parish; died July 4, 1991, New Orleans, Orleans Parish.) New Orleans guitarist began performing during his teens in his mother **Dolly Douroux Adam's** band with brothers Gerald and **Placide Adams Jr**. Later appeared on numerous New Orleans rhythm and blues recording sessions from the early 1950s into the 1970s with **Fats Domino**, **Smiley Lewis**, Little Richard, **Eddie Bo**, **Roy Brown**, **Dave Bartholomew**, **Professor Longhair**, **Ernie K-Doe**, **Shirley & Lee**, **Roy Brown**, **Clarence "Frogman" Henry**, **Cousin Joe**, and others.

ADAMS, MARIE HERPIN *Cajun.* Vocals. (Born Aug. 16, 1922, Kaplan, Vermilion Parish; died Aug. 12, 2007, Kaplan, Vermilion Parish.) Noted Cajun *a cappella* singer of "home songs" which consisted of traditional ballads of French Louisiana, some of which dated back centuries. Wife of **Milton Adams**.

ADAMS, MILTON *Cajun.* Accordion, vocals. Composer. Bandleader. (Born Oct. 26, 1918, Kaplan, Vermilion Parish; died July 12, 2002, Kaplan, Vermilion Parish.) Respected traditional Cajun musician began playing accordion around age 10, influenced by his musician uncles and later **Lawrence Walker**, and by age 12 was performing at local house dances. Started performing in dance halls in the mid-1940s, and in the 1960s recorded for La Louisianne and Cajun Classics with his band the Midnite Playboys. In 1992 released *Milton Adams Plays Traditional Cajun Music* on Swallow. Mentored several young accordion players throughout the years, including **Wayne Toups**. Husband of **Marie Herpin Adams**.

ADAMS, PLACIDE, JR. *Jazz, rhythm and blues.* Bass, drums, vocals. Bandleader. (Born Aug. 30, 1929, New Orleans, Orleans Parish; died Mar. 29, 2003, New Orleans, Orleans Parish.) Prominent proponent of New Orleans traditional jazz and a founding member of Preservation Hall. Began performing in mother **Dolly Douroux Adams**'s band at age 13 with brothers Gerald and **Justin Adams** and later worked with many noted jazz figures including **Papa Celestin**, **Louis Cottrell**, **Paul Barbarin**, and **George Lewis** and blues musicians Big Joe Turner, **Roy Brown**, and B.B. King. Also led Onward Brass Band and Original Dixieland Hall Jazz Band.

ALBERT, DON (Albert Anité Dominique) *Jazz.* Trumpet. Bandleader. (Born Aug. 5, 1908, New Orleans, Orleans Parish; died Mar. 4, 1980, San Antonio, Texas.) Respected early jazz trumpeter and bandleader, began learning cornet at age nine, tutored by **Louis "Papa" Tio** and **Manuel Perez**. Worked in New Orleans with Perez's band as teenager. Recorded as soloist in the late 1920s and led his own touring band throughout the 1930s which recorded for Vocalion in 1936 and was called "America's Greatest Swing Band." Settled in San Antonio in 1950 and performed with small ensembles through the mid-1970s. Nephew of **Natty Dominique**.

ALBERT, TOM *Jazz.* Trumpet. Bandleader. (Born Dec. 23, 1877, Algiers, Orleans Parish; died Dec. 12, 1969, New Orleans, Orleans Parish.) Noted early New Orleans jazz trumpeter who led his band from 1904 through 1929. Also was an original member of Eureka Brass Band in the 1920s.

ALCORN, ALVIN *Jazz.* Trumpet. Bandleader. (Born Sept. 7, 1912, New Orleans, Orleans Parish; died July 10, 2003, New Orleans, Orleans Parish.) Began playing professionally in his teens and worked with **Armand Piron**, **Red Allen**, and Excelsior Brass Brand early in career. Toured with **Don Albert**'s band throughout the 1930s and later worked with **Sidney Desvigne**, **Alphonse Picou**, **Papa Celestin**, **George Lewis**, and **Kid Ory** (in California), with whom he made some of his finest recordings. Recorded as leader and toured Europe with New Orleans Jazz All Stars in the 1960s and toured as soloist in the 1970s. Brother of **Oliver Alcorn**.

ALCORN, OLIVER *Jazz, blues.* Saxophone, clarinet. (Born Aug. 3, 1910, New Orleans, Orleans Parish; died Mar. 21, 1981, New Orleans, Orleans Parish.) Older brother of **Alvin Alcorn**, whom he taught music theory, worked with **Lee Collins** and **Papa Celestin**'s Original Tuxedo Jazz Band, among others. Later relocated to Chicago and worked (and often recorded) with numerous jazz and blues musicians, including **Sidney Desvigne**, **Natty Dominique**, **Lonnie Johnson**, **Little Brother Montgomery**, and Sunnyland Slim.

ALEXANDER, ADOLPHE, JR., "TATS" *Jazz.* Cornet, clarinet, saxophone, baritone horn. (Born July 15, 1898, New Orleans, Orleans Parish; died Dec. 30, 1968, New Orleans, Orleans Parish.) Son of **"Old Man Taton" Alexander Sr.**, performed as member of **Papa Celestin**'s Tuxedo Brass Band in the 1910s and 1920s and also worked with **Sidney Desvigne**. Later performed with **Kid Thomas**'s Brass Band and the Eureka Brass Band and recorded with **Bunk Johnson**'s Brass Band in 1945.

ALEXANDER, ADOLPHE, SR., "OLD MAN TATON" *Jazz.* Cornet, baritone horn. (Born July 1874, New Orleans, Orleans Parish; died July 30, 1932, New Orleans, Orleans Parish.)[2] Father of **Tats Alexander**. Early 1900s orchestra musician performed as member of several noted bands including Golden Rule Orchestra around 1905 and Imperial Orchestra and Superior Orchestra from 1909 to 1912. Worked as arranger in the late 1920s for several **Papa Celestin** recordings.

ALEXANDER, CLIFFORD "HUMPY" *Zydeco.* Rubboard. (Born Sept. 3, 1959, St. Martinville, St. Martin Parish.) Renowned zydeco rubboard player best known for his long association with **C. J. Chenier**'s Red Hot Louisiana Band which he performed and recorded with for more than twenty years. Also worked in bands of **Nathan Williams**, **Jude Taylor**, and others. Continued performing in 2010s, working often with **Curley Taylor**.

ALEXANDER, DAVE *See* Sharriff, Omar, *and* Black Ivory King [Notable Musicians Born outside Louisiana].

ALEXANDER, DUDLEY *Creole.* Accordion, vocals. Bandleader. (Born July 13, 1914, Cecilia, St. Martin Parish; died Feb. 22, 2000, Houston.)[3] Creole singer and accordion player moved from New Iberia to Houston in the 1940s where he was recorded by folklorist Mack McCormick in 1959. His washboard band's Creole version of Big Joe Williams's "Baby, Please Don't Go" sung in both English and French was included on McCormick's double LP *A Treasury of Field Recordings* on Candid in 1960, which established the now-standard spelling of "zydeco" for the first time in McCormick's lyric transcription in the album's notes.

ALEXANDER, JAMES *Rhythm and blues.* Vocals, drums. (Born May 11, 1939, Lafayette, Lafayette Parish.) Lafayette soul singer began performing in his late teens and worked with several groups in the 1960s including **Rockin' Dopsie**'s Twisters. In the mid-1960s joined **Little Buck Sinegal**'s Top Cats and performed with group as vocalist for five years, recording single "Don't Make Me Cry" on La Louisianne with band. Retired from performing in the early 1970s but made occasional special appearances in the 2010s.

ALEXIS, RICARD *Jazz.* Cornet, trumpet, bass. (Born Oct. 16, 1891, New Orleans, Orleans Parish; died Mar. 15, 1960, New Orleans, Orleans Parish.)[4] Played trumpet in early brass bands including Imperial, Onward, and Tuxedo brass bands in 1910s and 1920s. Recorded with **Papa Celestin** in 1927. Switched to upright bass after jaw injury in late 1927.

ALFRED, EUGENE *Blues.* Guitar, vocals. Composer. Bandleader. (Born May 27, 1949, Carencro, Lafayette Parish; died Jan. 27, 2015, Lafayette, Lafayette Parish.) Lafayette-based blues guitarist and singer recorded single "All I Wanted (Was Your Love)" on Vidrine in 1991, followed by self-titled full-length release for the label in 1996. Continued performing with his own blues and soul group around Lafayette area, often with daughter Cynthia Lee on vocals, until his death at age 65.

ALI, BARDU *Jazz, rhythm and blues.* Guitar, vocals. Bandleader. (Born Sept. 23, 1906, New Orleans, Orleans Parish; died Oct. 29, 1981, Los Angeles.) Served as frontman for Chick Webb in the 1930s and discovered 16-year-old Ella Fitzgerald. Led his own band later that decade. Relocated to Los Angeles in the 1940s and worked with Johnny Otis and Redd Foxx.

ALLAN, JOHNNIE (John Allen Guillot) *Swamp pop, Cajun, country.* Vocals, guitar, steel guitar. Composer. Bandleader. (Born Mar. 10, 1938, Rayne, Acadia Parish.) Internationally renowned early swamp pop singer, bandleader, and author best known for his regional hits "Lonely Days and Lonely Nights," "South to Louisiana," and "Promised Land." Raised in a musical family, began learning guitar at age six and in his teens performed as guitarist with **Walter Mouton**'s Scott Playboys and as steel guitarist in **Lawrence Walker**'s Wandering Aces. Inspired by **Fats Domino** and Elvis Presley, formed swamp pop group the Krazy Kats in the late 1950s and recorded regional hit "Lonely Days" for Jin in 1958. After several more singles for Jin, recorded for Viking from 1960 to 1963 and had minor hit with "South to Louisiana" in 1962. In the mid-1960s returned to Jin and throughout following decades released numerous singles and albums, including 1971 gold-selling cover of Chuck Berry's "Promised Land" which led to international acclaim and numerous tours overseas in the following years. In 1989 recorded album *Cajun Born* on La Louisianne with **Warren Storm** and **Clint West**. Continued performing at clubs and festivals through 2010s. Great-nephew of **Joe Falcon** and **Cléoma Breaux Falcon**.

ALLEMAN, PHILLIP *Cajun.* Guitar, drums, vocals. Composer. (Born Jan. 2, 1940, Rayne, Acadia Parish; died Mar. 5, 2005, Eunice, St. Landry Parish.) Renowned postwar Cajun steel guitarist and singer best known for his long tenure with **Aldus Roger**'s Lafayette Playboys. Raised in a musical family, began playing guitar and singing at age nine and started performing with Roger's band at age 11. Soon switched from guitar to drums before settling on steel guitar by age 15. Performed and recorded with Roger through the early 1970s. After a hiatus from music from the late 1970s through 1980s, performed with Roger, **Blackie Forestier**, Louisiana Cajun Heat, and other groups in the 1990s and early 2000s. Brothers Clarence and Ellis were also Cajun musicians.

ALLEN, BOBBY *Rhythm and blues.* Vocals. Composer. Bandleader. (Born Feb. 8, 1943, Crowley, Acadia Parish.) Southwest Louisiana deep soul singer began spending time at **J. D. Miller**'s studio as a teenager and befriending area blues musicians, sitting in regularly with **Lazy Lester** on local gigs. In the mid-1960s formed the Hurricanes which soon included **Johnny Truitt** on colead vocals and recorded behind Truitt on session with Miller for A-Bet. Inspired by **Little Bob**, formed the Exceptions and had local hits "Please Santa (Bring My Baby Back to Me)" and "Soul Chicken" on Soul Sound in 1969–70. In 2011 recorded with Big Jay McNeely for APO Records and continued performing around Lafayette area in the 2010s, often with **Lil' Buck Sinegal**.

ALLEN, HENRY, SR. *Jazz.* Cornet. Bandleader. (Born around 1877, Algiers, Orleans Parish; died Jan. 11, 1952, New Orleans, Orleans Parish.) Early New Orleans jazz cornetist and music teacher who led his popular Allen Brass Band of Algiers for more than four decades from 1907 to the early 1950s. Father of **Red Allen**.

ALLEN, RED (Henry Allen Jr.) *Jazz.* Trumpet, vocals. Composer. Bandleader. (Born Jan. 7, 1908, Algiers, Orleans Parish; died Apr. 17, 1967, New York City.) Highly regarded and innovative New Orleans jazz trumpeter whose six-decade career influenced several generations of jazz musicians. Learned trumpet from his father **Henry Allen Sr.**, and by age eight was performing in his brass band. While still in his teens worked with **George Lewis**, **Captain John Handy**, **Sidney Desvigne**, and Excelsior Brass Band. In the late 1920s and 1930s worked and recorded with **King Oliver**, **Louis Armstrong**, **Jelly Roll Morton**, Fletcher Henderson, and Luis Russell in New York. Led his own bands in the 1940s and 1950s in New York, Chicago, and California and recorded extensively as a leader and with Morton, **Sidney Bechet**, **Kid Ory**, Coleman Hawkins, and others. Toured Europe multiple times in the 1960s.

ALLEN, TONY (Anthony Penia Allan) *Rhythm and blues.* Piano, vocals. Composer. Bandleader. (Born Aug. 13, 1932, New Orleans, Orleans Parish; died Apr. 2, 2018, Downey, California.) Raised in the Ninth Ward and began playing piano at age six in church. Moved to Los Angeles in the early 1940s and later worked with Big Jay McNeely. Recorded "Nite Owl" for Specialty in 1955 and had releases on Ebb, Dig, Aladdin, Imperial, Dot, Jamie, Kent, and others throughout the 1950s and 1960s.

ALMERICO, TONY *Jazz.* Trumpet. Bandleader. (Born Aug. 16, 1905, New Orleans, Orleans Parish; died Dec. 5, 1961, New Orleans, Orleans Parish.) Noted New Orleans jazz trumpeter began leading his own band in the mid-1930s and worked as sideman throughout the 1940s. Recorded in the 1950s with **Lizzie Miles** as well as his own bands. From 1948 to 1960 ran the Parisian Room on Royal Street which featured live jazz on weekly national radio broadcast.

AMOS, IRA "NEW ORLEANS SLIM" *Rhythm and blues.* Vocals. Composer. (Born Feb. 10, 1924, New Orleans, Orleans Parish; died Apr. 17, 1963, Los Angeles.) Early rhythm and blues singer with a crooning style who recorded for Octive and Modern in 1951, including single "What You Been Doin' to Me?"

ANCKLE, FLO (Himas Floyd Anckle) *Jazz, rhythm and blues.* Saxophone. Composer. Bandleader. (Born Sept. 14, 1927, New Orleans, Orleans Parish; died May 16, 1994, New Orleans, Orleans Parish.) New Orleans saxophonist worked in both brass bands and rhythm and blues groups, influenced early on by Louis Jordan. Recorded with **Earl King** in 1960 and worked with **Doc Paulin** before forming Majestic Brass Band in 1977. Cowrote New Orleans Mardi Gras classic "Second Line Parts 1 & 2."

ANDERSON, ELTON *Blues, swamp pop.* Guitar, vocals. Composer. Bandleader. (Born Feb. 9, 1930, Ville Platte, Evangeline Parish; died Nov. 13, 1984, Eunice, St. Landry Parish.)[5] Noted early blues and swamp pop singer-guitarist began performing around Opelousas area with the Sid Lawrence Combo in the mid-1950s and had minor regional hit with "Shed So Many Tears" in 1958 on Vin. Following year recorded two singles for Trey, including swamp pop classic "Secret of Love," which made *Billboard*'s Hot 100 in 1960 when leased to Mercury. In the early 1960s recorded several singles for Lanor, including **King Karl**'s "Life Problem," which was a minor regional hit in 1962 and leased to Capitol. Later relocated to California but eventually returned to southwest Louisiana where he died at age 54.

ANDERSON, ROSHELL *Rhythm and blues.* Vocals. Composer. Bandleader. (Born Sept. 16, 1952, Bogalusa, Washington Parish.) Raised in New Orleans, southern soul singer-songwriter began career as radio disc jockey in the early 1970s after earning degree in broadcasting. In 1973–74 had national hits "Know What You're Doing When You Leave" and "Grapevine Will Lie Sometimes" on Sunburst. Also released singles on Excello and Jerri. In the late 1970s began career as television newscaster under name Mike Anderson but continued to record with numerous releases on Ichiban throughout the late 1980s and 1990s.

ANDREWS, GLEN DAVID *Jazz.* Trombone, vocals. Composer. Bandleader. (Born Apr. 27, 1980, New Orleans, Orleans Parish.) Born and raised in Tremé in a prominent musical family, began playing trombone at age 12, mentored by **Tuba Fats**, and later worked with New Birth, Lil Rascals, and Tremé brass bands, and others before forming own group. Known as "Crown Prince of Tremé." Cousin of **Trombone Shorty**.

ANDREWS, JAMES "12" *Jazz.* Trumpet, vocals. Composer. Bandleader. (Born Jan. 12, 1969, New Orleans, Orleans Parish.) Born and raised in Tremé and older brother and mentor of **Trombone Shorty**. Worked in various brass bands, including Junior Olympia, Tremé, and New Birth Brass Band, which he founded. Known as "Satchmo of the Ghetto."

ANDREWS, REVERT "PEANUT" *Jazz.* Trombone. (Born May 13, 1971, New Orleans, Orleans Parish.) Cousin to **Trombone Shorty**, **James** and **Glen David Andrews**. Began playing trombone in Tremé street parades, mentored by **Danny Barker**. Worked with Dirty Dozen and Rebirth brass bands as well as with cousin **Glen David Andrews**.

ANDREWS, TERRENCE *Jazz.* Bass drum. (Born Dec. 12, 1975, New Orleans, Orleans Parish.) Part of extended Andrews family of Tremé which includes **Glen David**, **Revert**, **James**, and **"Trombone Shorty" Andrews**. Worked with various brass bands from the late 1980s onward including Rebirth, New Breed, and Lil Rascals.

ANDREWS, TROY *See* Trombone Shorty.

ANDRUS, FRANK *Creole.* Accordion, vocals. (Born Jan. 10, 1926, Port Barre, St. Landry Parish; died Apr. 30, 2012, Opelousas, St. Landry Parish.) Early Creole accordion player who was a mentor of a young **Clifton Chenier**. Learned accordion from his father as a child and began performing at age 11. Performed primarily at la la house dances in Port Barre area through the early 1950s.

ANGEL FACE (Elsie Mae Kenley) *Rhythm and blues.* Vocals. (Born Dec. 6, 1930, New Orleans, Orleans Parish; died May 16, 1991, New Orleans, Orleans Parish.) Powerful vocalist who began career with **Papa Celestin**'s Tuxedo Brass Band before relocating to Washington, D.C., in the early 1950s. Worked regularly with trumpeter Frank Motley's band in the mid-1950s with singles on Gem, Big Town, DC, Hollywood, and OKeh. Recorded with own group the Swingmasters in 1959 for DC label and with Jimmy Davis Combo for Specialty in 1960. Returned to New Orleans by the early 1960s and continued performing locally.

ANGELLE, DONNA (Donna Charles) *Zydeco, rhythm and blues.* Accordion, piano, bass, flute, vocals. Composer.

Bandleader. (Born Oct. 10, 1951, Cypress Island, St. Martin Parish.) Noted zydeco multi-instrumentalist and singer began playing various instruments in high school and in the 1970s performed with **Bobby Price**, Cosmic Sky, and her own group Chapter IV. After being sidelined for several years due to a car accident, began performing again in 1994 and released debut album *Zydeco Soul* on Bad Weather in 1995. Two releases followed on Maison de Soul in the late 1990s, including *Old Man's Sweetheart* in 1997. In the 2000s had releases on Master-Trak and J&S, and continued performing with her band Zydeco Posse in the 2010s.

ANGRUM, STEVE *Jazz.* Clarinet. (Born July 4, 1895, New Roads, Pointe Coupee Parish; died Nov. 26, 1961, New Orleans, Orleans Parish.) Early New Orleans jazz clarinetist moved to the city around 1904 and began performing in the mid-1910s. Throughout the 1920s worked with **Kid Thomas**, **Kid Howard**, **Charlie Love**, **Joe Gabriel**, and others. In the 1940s and 1950s performed with **George Williams** and Young Tuxedo Brass Band, **De De Pierce**, and **Albert Jiles** and recorded as a leader in 1961 for Jazzology backed by **Kid Sheik**'s Storyville Ramblers.

ANSELMI, HARRY/"HARRY SELMA" *Cajun.* Guitar, steel guitar, vocals. Composer. Bandleader. (Born Mar. 31, 1931, Golden Meadow, Lafourche Parish; died Aug. 29, 2012, Golden Meadow, Lafourche Parish.) Cajun guitarist, singer, and songwriter began performing in the mid-1940s with **Dudley Bernard**'s Southern Serenaders. After working with country artists in the 1950s such as **Jimmie Davis** and **Jimmy C. Newman**, recorded with **Vin Bruce** for Jin and began long association as his guitarist and cowriter. Also worked extensively with **Leroy Martin**. In 1966 recorded as leader for Jin as "Harry Selma." In 2000 released *Hello Sunshine* on Louisiana Red Hot Records and continued to perform occasionally through the early 2010s.

ANTHONY, VINCE (Vincent Guzzetta) *Swamp pop, rockabilly.* Vocals, guitar. Composer. Bandleader. (Born June 27, 1936, Berwick, St. Mary Parish.) Noted early swamp pop singer-songwriter recorded singles for Hilton and Viking in the late 1950s with his band the Blue Notes, notably "Too Hot to Handle" and "Sneakin' Home." In later years released more than a dozen albums of largely original material and continued to perform in south Louisiana in the 2010s.

ARCENEAUX, FERNEST *Zydeco, rhythm and blues.* Accordion, guitar, vocals. Composer. Bandleader. (Born Aug. 27, 1940, Carencro, Lafayette Parish; died Sept. 4, 2008, Lafayette, Lafayette Parish.) Renowned traditional zydeco accordionist and bandleader began playing the instrument as a child and performed with his father Ferdinand at la la house parties. Later switched to guitar and played rhythm and blues and rock and roll with his band the Thunders from the late 1950s through the early 1970s. In the mid-1970s switched back to accordion and began playing zydeco upon urging from **Clifton Chenier** and released numerous singles on Blues Unlimited. Hailed as the "New Prince of Zydeco" for his instrumental prowess, began touring Europe regularly in the late 1970s with the Thunders, which included **Jockey Etienne** and **Chester Chevalier**. In following years released LPs on Ornament, JSP, Greybeard, and CMA. In the 1990s performed nationally and abroad with **Lil' Buck Sinegal** replacing Chevalier and recorded two CDs for Mardi Gras, including *Old School Zydeco* in 2000. Continued performing through the mid-2000s until succumbing to complications from diabetes. Uncle of zydeco accordionist and bandleader Corey Arceneaux.

ARCHIBALD (John Leon Gross) *Rhythm and blues.* Piano, vocals. Composer. (Born Sept. 14, 1916, New Orleans, Orleans Parish; died Jan. 8, 1973, New Orleans, Orleans Parish.)[6] Influential barrelhouse piano player began performing around New Orleans in the 1930s as "Archie Boy," inspired by **Tuts Washington** and **Burnell Santiago**. After serving in World War II, returned to performing in New Orleans and signed with Imperial in 1950. Made a series of influential recordings in the next two years with producer **Dave Bartholomew**, including "Stack-A-Lee" which reached number ten on *Billboard*'s R&B charts in 1950. Continued performing in New Orleans throughout the 1960s, battling ill health until succumbing to a fatal heart attack at age 56.

ARDOIN, ALPHONSE "BOIS SEC" *Creole.* Accordion, vocals. Composer. (Born Nov. 16, 1915, near Duralde, Evangeline Parish; died May 16, 2007, Eunice, St. Landry Parish.) Highly influential early Creole accordionist and singer best known for his four-decade partnership with master fiddle player **Canray Fontenot**. Started playing on his older brother's accordion at age seven and soon began playing triangle with cousin **Amédé Ardoin**, closely studying his accordion style. Throughout the 1930s performed at la la house dances on weekends, occasionally with Ardoin, while working as sharecropper during the day. In the late 1940s formed duo with Fontenot called the Duralde Ramblers and continued performing at local house dances together in following years, playing Creole standards as well as originals such as "Bonsoir, Moreau" and "Joe Pitre a Deux Femmes." In 1966 appeared at Newport Folk Festival with Fontenot and recorded LP *Les Blues du Bayou* on Melodeon which is regarded as the first newly recorded album devoted to Creole music. Continued performing and touring internationally with Fontenot through the early 1990s, making several recordings including 1974 Arhoolie LP *La Musique Creole* with sons **Morris** and **Black Ardoin** and 1981 Sonet LP *A Couple of Cajuns* with sons and **Dewey Balfa**. After Fontenot's death in 1995, recorded CD *Allons Danser* on Rounder in 1997 with **Christine Balfa**'s Balfa Toujours and continued performing into the 2000s, often with son Morris and grandson **Dexter Ardoin**.

ARDOIN, AMÉDÉ *Creole.* Accordion, vocals. Composer. (Born Mar. 11, 1898, L'Anse Rougeau, Evangeline Parish; died Nov. 3, 1942, Pineville, Rapides Parish.)[7] Profoundly influential but enigmatic early Creole accordionist and singer-songwriter whose late 1920s and early 1930s recordings helped lay the foundation of Cajun and Creole, and later, zydeco music. His innovative and groundbreaking style of blending Cajun, Creole, blues, and early French Louisiana ballads significantly influenced countless Cajun and Creole musicians from **Iry LeJeune** to **Clifton Chenier**. Raised speaking only Creole French on a farm near Basile, began playing accordion as a small child and by his teens was working as an itinerant musician. Throughout the 1920s performed extensively at house dances and dance halls across the region, playing regularly with **Douglas Bellard** as well as **Nonc Adam Fontenot** and **Sady Courville**. By the late 1920s was working regularly with Cajun fiddler **Dennis McGee** and was extremely popular with both white and black audiences. In Dec. 1929 became the second Creole musician to record French la la music and through 1934 cut 34 sides on sessions for Columbia, Brunswick, Bluebird and Decca (often with McGee), including such classics as "Two Step de Eunice," "Blues de Basile," "Two Step de la Prairie Soileau," and "Les Blues de Voyage." Continued performing throughout the region in the 1930s, occasionally accompanied by cousins **Bois Sec Ardoin** and **Canray Fontenot**. In the late 1930s was a victim of a brutal racial attack after performing at a dance near Eunice and beaten to near-death. Although he survived, he suffered serious physical and mental injuries and was eventually committed to Central Louisiana State Hospital in Sept. 1942, where he died six weeks later.

ARDOIN, CHRIS *Zydeco.* Accordion, guitar, bass, drums, piano, vocals. Composer. Bandleader. (Born Apr. 4, 1981, Lake Charles, Calcasieu Parish.) High-energy contemporary zydeco accordion player and singer began performing at age four, mentored by his father **Black Ardoin** and grandfather **Bois Sec Ardoin**. In the early 1990s joined his father's band Lagniappe with brother **Sean Ardoin** and made recording debut at age 10. Three years later formed band Double Clutchin' with brother and recorded debut CD *That's the Lick* in 1994 on Maison de Soul. Through the early 2000s had multiple releases on Rounder and J&S, including *Turn the Page* in 1998. In 2005 dissolved band and formed NuStep which added a strong contemporary rhythm and blues influence, releasing CD *Sweat* later that year. Toured nationally and overseas and recorded prolifically in following years with numerous releases on his NuStep4Lyfe label and Maison de Soul, including chart-topping *Back Home* and *Zydeko Fever* in 2014 and 2015. Continued performing extensively in the late 2010s. Distant cousin of **Amédé Ardoin**.

ARDOIN, DEXTER (Ernest Dexter Ardoin) *Creole, zydeco.* Accordion, drums, vocals. Composer. Bandleader. (Born Nov. 2, 1980, Duralde, Evangeline Parish.) Noted Creole multi-instrumentalist learned accordion from his grandfather **Bois Sec Ardoin** and father **Morris Ardoin**, performing with both in the years preceding Bois Sec's death in 2007. Also worked regularly as drummer with cousin **Chris Ardoin**, **Sheryl Cormier**, **Willis Prudhomme**, and others. In the 2000s performed with his band Creole Ramblers and recorded CD *What You Come to Do* on Louisiana Radio label in 2003. Continued performing in the 2010s. Distant cousin of **Amédé Ardoin**.

ARDOIN, DOUG/"DOUG CHARLES" *Swamp pop.* Guitar. Bandleader. (Born Apr. 12, 1940, Eunice, St. Landry Parish.) Early swamp pop guitarist and bandleader best known as a founding member of the Boogie Kings. Formed band in 1956 with **Harris Miller** and **Bert Miller**, being among the first white groups to play New Orleans–influenced rhythm and blues. Performed and recorded with the Boogie Kings (often billed as "Doug Charles") through the mid-1960s, then left band and joined Bert Miller in the Swing Kings. Worked and recorded with the Swing Kings through the late 1960s before retiring from music and relocating to Houston. In the 1990s reunited with several original members of Boogie Kings and continued performing with group into the 2010s.

ARDOIN, LAWRENCE "BLACK" *Creole, zydeco.* Accordion, drums, vocals. Composer. Bandleader. (Born Nov.

17, 1946, Duralde, Evangeline Parish.) Renowned Creole multi-instrumentalist formed the Ardoin Brothers Band as drummer with brothers Gustave, Russell, and **Morris Ardoin** in 1966 to back up their father **Bois Sec Ardoin**, who was gaining national prominence. Performed and recorded with group through the mid-1970s, taking up accordion after Gustave's death in 1974. In the early 1980s formed his French Band which included son **Sean Ardoin** on saxophone, **Edward Poullard** on fiddle, and **Clarence Leday** on guitar and recorded acclaimed self-titled LP on Arhoolie in 1984. In the early 1990s formed zydeco band Lagniappe featuring 10-year-old son **Chris Ardoin** and released self-titled LP on Maison de Soul. Performed and recorded as member of Creole United with son Sean, Poullard, and **Jeffery Broussard** in the mid-2010s. Distant cousin of **Amédé Ardoin**.

ARDOIN, MORRIS *Creole, zydeco.* Fiddle, accordion, guitar, vocals. Composer. Bandleader. (Born Sept. 21, 1935, Duralde, Evangeline Parish; died Dec. 1, 2017, Eunice, St. Landry Parish.) Oldest son of master Creole accordionist **Bois Sec Ardoin**, renowned Creole multi-instrumentalist began playing triangle with his father at house dances at age nine. In 1966 formed Ardoin Brothers Band with brothers Gustave, Russell, and **Black Ardoin** and toured and recorded with group through the mid-1970s, performing several times at Carnegie Hall. In the 1980s operated zydeco dance hall Cowboy Club in Duralde and in the 1990s began performing with son **Dexter Ardoin**, recording *Cajun Creole Music of Louisiana* for PlayaSound in 2000. Also continued working with father Bois Sec during this time. Released CD *La Tracas de Morris* with Dennis Stroughmatt in 2005 and continued performing into the 2010s, often with Dexter. Distant cousin of **Amédé Ardoin**.

ARDOIN, SEAN *Zydeco, Creole.* Accordion, drums, saxophone, vocals. Composer. Bandleader. (Born July 10, 1969, Eunice, St. Landry Parish.) Contemporary zydeco accordionist and singer-songwriter began playing drums as a child, learning from his father, **Lawrence "Black" Ardoin**. In the early 1990s joined his father's band Lagniappe with younger brother **Chris Ardoin** and performed and recorded as drummer and vocalist with group for several years, changing band name to Double Clutchin' in the mid-1990s. In the late 1990s formed band Zydekool and released numerous CDs into 2000s, including *Pullin'* in 2001 on Tomorrow. After a hiatus from music in mid-2000s released zydeco gospel CD *How Great Is Your Love* in 2009. Formed traditional band Creole United with father Lawrence, **Jeffrey Broussard**, **Ed Poullard**, and Andre Thierry and released *Non Jamais Fait* in 2014. Continued performing with Zydekool in the late 2010s and founded Creole Hall of Fame to honor Creole culture and music. Grandson of **Bois Sec Ardoin** and distant cousin of **Amédé Ardoin**.

ARMSTRONG, LOUIS "DIPPERMOUTH"/"POPS"/ "SATCHELMOUTH"/"SATCHMO" *Jazz.* Trumpet, vocals. Composer. Bandleader. (Born Aug. 4, 1901, New Orleans, Orleans Parish; died July 6, 1971, Queens, New York.) Widely regarded as one of the most influential and innovative musicians in the history of jazz and one of the greatest musical and cultural figures of the twentieth century. Often cited as the first great soloist in jazz. Began singing on street corners at age eight and learned cornet by ear, inspired by top current players **King Oliver**, **Freddie Keppard**, and **Bunk Johnson**. Performed with and led Colored Waif's Home band in 1913–14 after being incarcerated on a minor violation, being tutored by music professor **Peter Davis**. Worked with various groups in the mid- to late 1910s and was mentored by Oliver, whom he eventually replaced in **Kid Ory**'s band when Oliver left for Chicago around 1918. Also worked regularly with **Fate Marable** on riverboats through 1921. In the following year moved to Chicago to join Oliver's Creole Jazz Band and made recording debut with group in 1923. In 1924 relocated to New York and joined Fletcher Henderson's orchestra and recorded extensively backing Henderson, Ma Rainey, Bessie Smith, **Sidney Bechet**, **Clarence Williams**, Alberta Hunter, and others. Returned to Chicago in 1925 and through 1928 made some of the most important and influential recordings in jazz during his Hot Five/Hot Seven sessions for OKeh. In the late 1920s and 1930s recorded extensively and toured nationally and overseas, quickly becoming an international sensation. Appeared in several dozen films, starting in 1930, including *Pennies from Heaven* with Bing Crosby in 1936. A highly influential vocalist and pioneering scat singer, he expanded his repertoire outside of jazz and made numerous recordings which greatly impacted popular music around the world with hits such as "Mack the Knife," "Hello Dolly," and "What a Wonderful World." Recorded popular duets with Crosby, Billie Holiday, Louis Jordan, and others, and made numerous television and radio appearances. From the mid-1940s through mid-1960s toured extensively with his All Stars, performing throughout the world and routinely working more than 300 dates per year. Suffered from ill health in remaining years and gave final public performance in Mar. 1971 at New York City's Waldorf Astoria Hotel.

ARODIN, SIDNEY (Sidney Arnondin) *Jazz.* Clarinet, saxophone. Composer. Bandleader. (Born Mar. 29, 1901, Westwego, Jefferson Parish; died Feb. 6, 1948, Westwego, Jefferson Parish.)[8] Noted early New Orleans jazz musician and composer best known for his composition "Lazy River." Performed on riverboats in the early 1920s and worked with New Orleans jazz bands in New York and San Antonio in the mid-1920s. Returned to New Orleans and performed with Halfway House Orchestra and appeared on renowned Jones-Collins Astoria Hot Eight session in the late 1920s. In the 1930s worked with **Louis Prima**, **Wingy Manone**, and New Orleans Rhythm Kings in New York. Led his own band in the late 1930s and early 1940s before health issues forced retirement.

ASSUNTO, FREDDIE *Jazz.* Trombone. Composer. Bandleader. (Born Dec. 3, 1929, Jennings, Jeff. Davis Parish; died Apr. 21, 1966, Las Vegas.) New Orleans jazz trombonist learned the instrument from his father, **Papa Jac Assunto**, as a child and formed his first Dixieland jazz band with his younger brother Frank (1932–1974) on trumpet in New Orleans in 1946. In 1949 formed Dukes of Dixieland with Frank which became popular in New Orleans through three-year residency at the Famous Door on Bourbon Street. By the mid-1950s band was playing in New York and Las Vegas and was joined by Papa Jac as featured soloist on trombone and banjo. In 1957 became the first band to release a record in stereo with LP *You Have to Hear It to Believe It* on High Fidelity. Released numerous recordings on multiple labels in the following years, including LP *Louie and the Dukes of Dixieland* with **Louis Armstrong** in 1960. Continued to perform with band until sidelined by illness in the mid-1960s.

ASSUNTO, PAPA JAC (Jacinto A. Assunto) *Jazz.* Trombone, banjo, drums. (Born Nov. 1, 1905, Lake Charles, Calcasieu Parish; died Jan. 5, 1985, New Orleans, Orleans Parish.) New Orleans jazz trombonist began playing drums in groups around Jennings area before settling in New Orleans. In the late 1940s and early 1950s taught music until joining sons Frank and **Freddie Assunto** in their band Dukes of Dixieland in 1955. Toured and recorded with group until Freddie's death in 1966, then resumed working as music teacher.

AUGUST, JOE "MR. GOOGLE EYES"/"MR. G" *Rhythm and blues.* Vocals. Composer. (Born Sept. 13, 1931, New Orleans, Orleans Parish; died Aug. 9, 1992, New Orleans, Orleans Parish.) Began performing as a teen in New Orleans and made recording debut on Coleman in 1946 with "Young Boy," billed as "World's Youngest Blues Singer." Recorded for Columbia in the late 1940s and toured nationally. After releases on Domino and Lee, recorded with Johnny Otis for Duke in 1953–54. Singles on Flip and Dot followed before making final recording for **Allen Toussaint** on Instant in 1961. Worked occasionally with **Earl King** and **Deacon John** in later years.

AUGUST, LYNN *Zydeco, rhythm and blues.* Piano, accordion, drums, vocals. Composer. Bandleader. (Born Aug. 7, 1948, Lafayette, Lafayette Parish.) Noted blind zydeco and rhythm and blues multi-instrumentalist began playing drums in his early teens with Esquerita (Eskew Reeder Jr.), **Jay Nelson**, and later Stanley Dural Jr. (**Buckwheat Zydeco**). In the mid-1960s started playing piano and through the 1970s had singles on Tamm, Banner, Maison de Soul, and other local labels. After working with **Marcel Dugas** for several years, began playing accordion in the early 1980s and formed zydeco band Hot August Knights, recording debut album *It's Party Time* for Maison de Soul in 1988. Releases followed on Rounder, Black Top, and AIM, including *Sauce Piquant* in 1993, and made several tours overseas including five-week tour of Africa. After recovering from health issues in the late 1990s, continued performing into the 2010s and appeared on CD *Legends Making Memories* with **Willie Tee** & Cypress on Jin in 2012.

AUSTIN, SANDY *See* Manuel, Abe, Sr.

AVERY, JOSEPH "KID" *Jazz.* Trombone. Bandleader. (Born Oct. 3, 1892, Waggaman, Jefferson Parish; died Jan. 9, 1956, New Orleans, Orleans Parish.)[9] Early New Orleans jazz trombonist began performing in the early 1910s and in the mid-1910s joined **Amos Riley**'s Tulane Orchestra. In the 1920s toured with **Evan Thomas**'s Black Eagles. Led his own band in the 1930s and 1940s and also performed with Young Tuxedo Brass Band. Recorded as leader in 1954 for Southland. Succumbed to liver cancer at age 63.

B

BABINEAUX, PERCY *Cajun.* Fiddle, vocals. Composer. (Born Apr. 17, 1907, Lafayette, Lafayette Parish; died Jan. 7, 1962, Lafayette, Lafayette Parish.)[1] Early Cajun fiddle player and singer who recorded eight sides for Victor and Bluebird with accordionist **Bixy Guidry** in Nov. 1929, including "Elle a Plurer Pour Revenir (She Cried to Come Back But She Couldn't)." After Guidry's death in 1938, continued performing with various local musicians through the late 1940s.

BABINEAUX, SIDNEY *Creole.* Accordion, vocals. (Born Feb. 25, 1896, Iota, Acadia Parish; died Dec. 28, 1967, Rayne, Acadia Parish.)[2] Influential early Creole accordionist who recorded one of the earliest versions of the traditional Creole song known as "Zydeco Sont Pas Salé" for Arhoolie in 1962. Influenced many area musicians including **Clifton Chenier**, **Al Rapone**, **Thomas "Big Hat" Fields**, and his great-nephew **Boozoo Chavis**. Father Oscar Babineaux (1853–1923) played accordion and fiddle and performed Creole and blues as early as the first decade of 1900.

BABINEAUX, WILTON "T-BAB" *Cajun.* Fiddle. (Born Aug. 21, 1936, Iota, Acadia Parish; died Oct. 20, 2018, Jennings, Jeff. Davis Parish.) Noted Cajun fiddle player was raised in a large musical family which included his father, Arthur; aunt Ophelia; and uncle Joe, who were all accordion players. Began playing fiddle as a child and soon started playing local house dances. Later worked and recorded with numerous bandleaders including **Happy Fats**, **Joe Turner**, **Camey Doucet**, **Phil Menard**, **Wayne Toups**, and others. Brother of Cajun guitarist Charlie Babineaux and father of Cajun steel guitarist Murnel Babineaux.

BABINO, ALFRED *See* Lil' Alfred.

BADEAUX, ELIAS "SHUTE" *Cajun.* Accordion, fiddle, guitar. Bandleader. (Born Feb. 25, 1910, Bayou de la Petite Anse, Iberia Parish; died May 5, 1978, New Iberia, Iberia Parish.) Renowned Cajun accordionist and bandleader of Badeaux and the Louisiana Aces who were best known for their 1962 Cajun classic "The Back Door," sung and written by band member **D. L. Menard**. Began playing accordion in his youth, mentored by brother-in-law **Dewey Segura**. Formed the Louisiana Aces in 1950 and recorded four singles for Swallow in the early to mid-1960s before disbanding by 1969. Reunited with the Louisiana Aces for the 1973 National Folk Festival in Washington, D.C., and recorded self-titled LP with band for Rounder in 1974.

BADIE, PETER "CHUCK" *Rhythm and blues, jazz.* Bass. Bandleader. (Born May 17, 1925, New Orleans, Orleans Parish.) Noted New Orleans bass player began performing in local clubs such as the Dew Drop Inn in the late 1940s. Performed and recorded with **Roy Brown**, **Paul Gayten**, and **Dave Bartholomew** in the early 1950s and toured with Lionel Hampton from 1953 to 1956. Recorded as session musician for Instant with **Allen Toussaint** and was original member of A.F.O. Executives in the early 1960s. Relocated to Los Angeles in 1963 and recorded with Sam Cooke before returning to New Orleans the following year. Worked outside music from the mid-1970s through 1990 but returned to performing and recording into the late 2010s.

BAILEY, JUNE BUG *Rhythm and blues.* Vocals. (Born around 1947, presumably Shreveport, Caddo Parish.) Unidentified Shreveport singer who recorded single "Lee Street Blues"/"Louisiana Twist" on Jo in 1962 at age 15 and was a daughter of a waitress at a barbecue restaurant located near **Mira Smith**'s recording studio. Smith later released single as by "June Bug Bailey" unaware of the singer's real name.

BAKER, GUITAR GEORGE *Blues.* Guitar, vocals. Composer. Bandleader. (Born Apr. 5, 1938, New Roads, Pointe Coupee Parish.) Blues guitarist and singer performed with various rhythm and blues groups throughout the 1960s including the Drifters and the Flamingos before playing in house band of Harlem's Apollo Theater in the late 1960s. Served as bandleader for Marvin Gaye for several years and eventually settled in New Haven, Connecticut in the mid-1980s. Influenced later in career by **Buddy Guy** and Albert King, continued performing on local club scene through the 2010s with releases *Mojo Lady* in 2006 and *A Night to Remember* in 2015.

BAKER, VICKIE *Rhythm and blues.* Vocals. Composer. Bandleader. (Born Mar. 10, 1961, Shreveport, Caddo Parish.) Noted southern soul singer and songwriter was raised in Belcher and began singing in church as a child. Toured as backup singer in the 1990s with **Ernie Johnson** and Willie Clayton before starting solo career in 1997 and releasing debut CD *Don't Gimme No Lip* on Paula. In the early 2000s released two CDs on her own So Fly label and in 2007 recorded *I Could Show You* on FaLife, produced by brother and recording artist Luster Baker. Continued to tour on southern soul circuit in the 2010s while serving as high-school band director in Vicksburg, Mississippi.

BALFA BROTHERS *See* Balfa, Dewey.

BALFA, CHRISTINE *Cajun.* Guitar, triangle, vocals. Composer. Bandleader. (Born June 28, 1968, Basile, Evangeline Parish.) Internationally renowned Cajun singer-songwriter and guitarist began playing triangle as a child with her father **Dewey Balfa**'s band, touring extensively with group which also included older sister Nelda. After her father's death in 1992, formed traditional Cajun band Balfa Toujours with Nelda and husband Dirk Powell on fiddle and toured internationally, recording several albums on Swallow and Rounder including *La Pointe* in 1998. In 2006 cofounded Cajun band Bonsoir, Catin and continued performing and recording with both groups in the 2010s. In 2009 released CD *Christine Balfa Plays the Triangle* on Valcour.

BALFA, DEWEY *Cajun.* Fiddle, vocals. Composer. Bandleader. (Born Mar. 20, 1927, near Mamou, Evangeline Parish; died June 17, 1992, Eunice, St. Landry Parish.) Highly regarded and influential Cajun fiddle player and cultural ambassador/preservationist who popularized Cajun music with international audiences in the 1960s, 1970s, and 1980s with his family band. Born into a large musical family, started playing fiddle as a child, learning on a borrowed instrument from older brother Will (1917–1979). In the mid-1940s began performing with Will at Hicks Wagon Wheel Club near Ville Platte and in 1951 made recording debut backing **Elise Deshotel** on three singles for Khoury's. Also began performing and recording with **Nathan Abshire** with whom he'd work extensively for several decades. Performed at 1964 Newport Folk Festival with **Gladius Thibodeaux** and Vinesse LeJeune to national acclaim. In following years toured extensively with Balfa Brothers Band, which included Will on second fiddle, brothers Rodney (1934–1979) on guitar, Harry (1931–1995) or Burkeman (1936–2004) on triangle, and **Hadley Fontenot** on accordion. Through the 1970s released numerous recordings for Swallow, including influential 1967 LP *The Balfa Brothers Play Traditional Cajun Music,* as well as albums for Arhoolie and Sonet. After the death of Will and Rodney in a 1979 automobile accident, continued performing through the early 1990s, often with daughters Nelda and **Christine Balfa** and nephew Tony Balfa. Mentored many young Cajun musicians, including **Robert Jardell**, **Steve Riley**, **David Greely**, **Kevin Wimmer**, and others.

BALLOU, CLASSIE, JR. *Zydeco.* Bass, guitar. (Born Nov. 17, 1954, Lake Charles, Calcasieu Parish.) Influential zydeco bass player best known for his long tenure with **Boozoo Chavis**'s Magic Sounds and credited with introducing funk bass lines into zydeco. Inspired by his father **Classie Ballou Sr.** and raised by his grandparents, began playing guitar in garage bands as a teen before switching to bass. Performed with various rhythm and blues groups before joining Chavis's band in the late 1980s. Toured and recorded extensively with Chavis until Chavis's death in 2001. Continued performing with various zydeco groups into the 2010s, notably with **Jeffrey Broussard**. Brother of musicians Cedric Ballou and uncle of Cedryl Ballou.

BALLOU, CLASSIE, SR. *Blues, zydeco.* Guitar, vocals. Composer. Bandleader. (Born Aug. 21, 1937, Elton, Jeff. Davis Parish.) Veteran blues guitarist began playing at age 10 and during his mid-teens started performing around Lake Charles after moving there with family, working early on with **Simon "Kee-Dee" Lubin**. In the next several years led his popular band the Tempo Kings, which included at times **Carol Fran** and **Shelton Dunaway**. In 1954 recorded behind **Boozoo Chavis** on the first zydeco regional hit "Paper in My Shoe" for Goldband. From 1956 to 1958 had singles on Goldband,

Excello, and Nasco, including "Crazy Mambo" and "Hey! Pardner." Relocated to Dallas in the late 1950s and in following years toured with his band backing numerous national artists including Big Joe Turner, Rosco Gordon, Joe Tex, Chuck Berry, and many others. In the mid-1960s settled in Waco and recorded instrumental classic "Classie's Whip" on Soulsville U.S.A. in 1968. In following decades performed throughout region with occasional tours overseas, leading his family band which included sons **Classie Ballou Jr.** and Cedric, daughter CaCean, and later grandsons Cedryl and Cam'ron. Released recordings on Lanor, Krazy Kat, and his own Yeah Baby label and continued performing into his 80s.

BAMBURG, LARRY/"LARRY LINCOLN" *Rockabilly, country.* Fiddle, bass, vocals. Composer. Bandleader. (Born Aug. 26, 1931, Coushatta, Red River Parish; died July 3, 2011, Shreveport, Caddo Parish.) Early rockabilly and country fiddle and bass player moved to Shreveport in 1949 and performed on the *Louisiana Hayride* through 1951 with country artists Webb Pierce, Faron Young, and others. In the mid- to late 1950s recorded as session player for **Mira Smith**'s RAM label, often with **James Burton**, and released country single "Cheatin' On Me" in 1956. In 1959 cut rockabilly single "That'll Hold You"/"My Baby Went Away" under name Larry Lincoln on Fido before retiring from music soon afterwards.

BANISTER, IRVING, SR. *Rhythm and blues.* Guitar, bass, vocals. Bandleader. (Born Feb. 16, 1933, New Orleans, Orleans Parish.) Early New Orleans rhythm and blues guitarist who worked and recorded with **James "Sugar Boy" Crawford**, **Danny White**, **Eddie Bo**, and the Sha-Weez in the 1950s and 1960s. In the early 1970s performed and recorded with **Willie Tee**'s funk group the Gaturs and remained the longtime bandleader of Irving Banister's All Stars. Continued performing in New Orleans clubs into the late 2010s. Father of musician Irving "Honey" Banister Jr.

BAQUET, ACHILLE *Jazz.* Clarinet, saxophone. Composer. (Born Nov. 15, 1885, New Orleans, Orleans Parish; died Nov. 20, 1955, Los Angeles.)[3] Early New Orleans Creole jazz reedman was tutored by his father, **Theogene Baquet**, and **Louis "Papa" Tio** and later performed with **Papa Jack Laine**'s Reliance Brass Band and Original Dixieland Jazz Band. Relocated to New York in 1915 and worked and recorded with Jimmy Durante. Settled in California around 1920. Brothers Harold and **George Baquet** were also jazz musicians.

BAQUET, GEORGE *Jazz.* Clarinet, saxophone. Composer. Bandleader. (Born July 22, 1882, New Orleans, Orleans Parish; died Jan. 14, 1949, New Orleans, Orleans Parish.)[4] Regarded as the first great clarinetist of jazz and was a major influence on **Sidney Bechet**. Began performing in 1897 with father **Theogene Baquet**'s Lyre Club Symphonic Orchestra and worked with Onward Brass Band and **Manuel Perez**'s Imperial Orchestra in the early 1900s. Reportedly performed with **Buddy Bolden**. Also worked with **John Robichaux** and Magnolia and Olympia brass bands before moving to California in 1914 with **Freddie Keppard** to join the Original Creole Band. Recorded with Bessie Smith and **Jelly Roll Morton** in the 1920s. Spent much of remaining years in Philadelphia and recorded with his band the Swingsters and with Bechet. Brother of Creole jazz musicians Harold and **Achille Baquet**.

BAQUET, THEOGENE V. *Jazz.* Cornet, clarinet. Bandleader. (Born Apr. 1850, Ascension Parish, Louisiana; died Sept. 26, 1923, Los Angeles.)[5] One of the earliest important figures in New Orleans jazz and longtime bandleader of Excelsior Brass Band from the early 1880s through 1904. Later conducted Lyre Club Symphonic Orchestra, which included sons **Achille** and **George Baquet**. Relocated to Los Angeles in the late 1910s.

BARBARIN, ISIDORE *Jazz.* Cornet, alto horn. Bandleader. (Born Sept. 24, 1871, New Orleans, Orleans Parish; died June 12, 1960, New Orleans, Orleans Parish.) Patriarch of noted New Orleans jazz family, performed in various early brass bands from the late 1890s through 1910s including Onward, Excelsior, and **Papa Celestin**'s Tuxedo Brass Band. Recorded with **Bunk Johnson** in 1945 and with Original Zenith Brass Band in 1946. Father of **Paul**, **Louis**, Lucien (drums, 1905–1955) and William Barbarin (cornet, about 1906–1973). Grandfather of **Danny Barker**.

BARBARIN, LOUIS *Jazz.* Drums, vocals. (Born Oct. 24, 1902, New Orleans, Orleans Parish; died May 11, 1997, New Orleans, Orleans Parish.) Began performing with Onward Brass Band with **Manuel Perez** in 1918 and also worked with **Kid Rena** and **Punch Miller**. Worked and recorded with **Papa Celestin** from 1937 through the early 1950s. Performed with various traditional jazz and brass bands in the 1960s and 1970s and toured regularly. Appeared at Preservation Hall in later years. Son of **Isidore Barbarin**.

BARBARIN, LUCIEN *Jazz.* Trombone, drums. Bandleader.

(Born July 17, 1956, New Orleans, Orleans Parish.) Influenced by great-uncle **Paul Barbarin**, began playing snare drum in the early 1970s with second cousin and mentor **Danny Barker**'s Fairview Baptist Church Brass Band and continued with group as Hurricane Brass Band. Switched to trombone and went on to work with **Wynton Marsalis**, **Kermit Ruffins**, **Dr. Michael White**, Preservation Hall Jazz Band, and others. Longtime band member with **Harry Connick Jr.** and recorded and toured extensively as sideman and leader.

BARBARIN, PAUL *Jazz.* Drums. Composer. Bandleader. (Born May 5, 1899, New Orleans, Orleans Parish; died Feb. 17, 1969, New Orleans, Orleans Parish.) Highly regarded early New Orleans jazz drummer and bandleader began playing professionally in 1915 and joined Young Olympia Brass Band with **Buddy Petit** and **Jimmie Noone**. Relocated to Chicago in the late 1910s and worked with Noone, **Sidney Bechet**, **King Oliver**, and **Freddie Keppard**. Returned to New Orleans in 1923 but spent extended time in Chicago and New York and worked (and often recorded) with **Barney Bigard**, Luis Russell, **Louis Armstrong**, **Jelly Roll Morton**, **Red Allen**, and others. Performed mainly around New Orleans in the 1950s and 1960s with own group and recorded extensively as leader and sideman. Composed jazz standard "Bourbon Street Parade." Son of **Isidore Barbarin**.

BARBEROT, LADNER "PAT" *Jazz.* Saxophone. Bandleader. (Born Mar. 17, 1926, New Orleans, Orleans Parish; died May 5, 2007, Bush, St. Tammany Parish.) Founder and bandleader of Pat Barberot Orchestra from 1940 until his death in 2007. Subject of PBS documentary *A Place to Dance.*

BARKER, DANNY (Daniel Moses Barker) *Jazz, blues.* Guitar, banjo, clarinet, ukulele, vocals. Composer. Bandleader. (Born Jan. 13, 1909, New Orleans, Orleans Parish; died Mar. 13, 1994, New Orleans, Orleans Parish.) Highly influential jazz multi-instrumentalist, cultural ambassador and educator who helped revive the New Orleans brass-band tradition in the 1960s and 1970s. Raised in the home of grandfather **Isidore Barbarin** and learned multiple instruments including banjo. In the 1920s worked with **Little Brother Montgomery**, **Willie Pajeaud**, **Lee Collins**, and others. Switched from banjo to guitar in the 1930s and performed regularly with **Sidney Bechet**, James P. Johnson, **Red Allen**, and wife **Blue Lu Barker**, and recorded extensively. Worked with Lucky Millinder and Cab Calloway in the late 1930s and 1940s. Founded Fairview Baptist Church Brass Band in the late 1960s to engage neighborhood youth in traditional brass bands, giving **Branford** and **Wynton Marsalis**, **Lucien Barbarin**, **Dr. Michael White**, **Kirk Joseph**, and many others their start.

BARKER, LOUISE "BLUE LU" *Jazz, blues.* Vocals. (Born Nov. 13, 1913, New Orleans, Orleans Parish; died May 7, 1998, New Orleans, Orleans Parish.) Began singing in her teens and in 1930 married **Danny Barker**, whom she worked with her entire career. Signed with Decca in 1938 and made series of recordings, notably "Don't You Make Me High," which featured her signature double-entendre lyrics and girlish vocal delivery. Recorded for Apollo and Capitol in the late 1940s and had hit with "A Little Bird Told Me" in 1948. Performed sporadically in the 1970s and 1980s before retiring due to ill health in the 1990s.

BARNES, EMILE *Jazz.* Clarinet. (Born Feb. 18, 1892, New Orleans, Orleans Parish; died Mar. 1, 1970, New Orleans, Orleans Parish.) Older brother of **Paul "Polo" Barnes**, early New Orleans jazz clarinetist known for his bluesy, expressive style. Studied with **Lorenzo Tio Sr.**, **Alphonse Picou**, **George Baquet**, and **Big Eye Louis Nelson** and worked with **Buddy Petit**, **Chris Kelly**, and **Wooden Joe Nicholas** from the late 1910s through 1920s. Recorded as a leader in the 1950s and with **Peter Bocage** in 1954, which is regarded as some of his finest work. Performed with Superior and Olympia brass bands and at Preservation Hall.

BARNES, HARRISON *Jazz.* Trombone, baritone horn, cornet. (Born Jan. 13, 1889, Magnolia Plantation, Plaquemines Parish; died June 8, 1960, New Orleans, Orleans Parish.) Began taking cornet lessons with **Professor Jim Humphrey** around 1905 and was soon performing with the Eclipse and Allen brass bands. Moved to New Orleans in the mid-1910s and switched to trombone. From the mid-1910s to late 1920s worked with **Chris Kelly**, **John Robichaux**, and Excelsior Brass Band. Recorded with Zenith Brass Band in the late 1940s and **Kid Thomas** in 1951.

BARNES, PAUL "POLO" *Jazz.* Clarinet, saxophone. Composer. Bandleader. (Born Nov. 22, 1901, New Orleans, Orleans Parish; died Apr. 13, 1981, New Orleans, Orleans Parish.)[6] Renowned early New Orleans jazz multi-instrumentalist cofounded Original Diamond Band in 1919 and performed with **Kid Rena** in the early 1920s. Worked and recorded with **Papa Celestin**'s Tuxedo Jazz Band, **Jelly Roll Morton**, and **King Oliver** in the

1920s. Led his own band in Lake Charles in 1932 and also worked with **Chester Zardis** and **Kid Howard**, among others. Later performed with **Paul Barbarin** and worked and recorded with **Kid Thomas** and Eureka Brass Band in the 1960s. Toured Europe and appeared at Preservation Hall and Dixieland Hall before retiring in the late 1970s. Younger brother of **Emile Barnes**.

BAROCCO, DOMINICK *Jazz.* Banjo, guitar, piano, trumpet. Bandleader. (Born Oct. 5, 1893, New Orleans, Orleans Parish; died Jan. 1970, New Orleans, Orleans Parish.) Started early jazz band with brother **Joe Barocco** in 1912 and led Susquehanna Band on steamship of same name in the 1920s.

BAROCCO, JOE *Jazz.* Tuba. Bandleader. (Born Oct. 16, 1891, New Orleans, Orleans Parish; died 1947, New Orleans, Orleans Parish.) Started performing with brother **Dominick Barocco** in 1912 and later worked with Reliance Brass Band and with brother Dominick in Susquehanna Band.

BARREL HOUSE WELCH *See* Welsh, Nolan.

BARRETT, SWEET EMMA *Jazz.* Piano, vocals. Bandleader. (Born Mar. 25, 1897, New Orleans, Orleans Parish; died Jan. 28, 1983, New Orleans, Orleans Parish.) Noted self-taught barrelhouse and jazz pianist began performing publicly at age 12 and was known as the "Bell Gal" for the bells attached to her garters which jingled with her foot tapping. Worked with **Papa Celestin**'s Original Tuxedo Jazz Band, **Bebé Ridgley**, **Sidney Desvigne**, **John Robichaux**, and **Armand Piron** in the 1920s and 1930s. After a period of inactivity, led her own band in the late 1940s and 1950s with **Willie** and **Percy Humphrey**. Began performing regularly at Preservation Hall from 1961, becoming one of its most popular and beloved stars throughout the following two decades. In 1965 appeared in the film *The Cincinatti Kid* with Steve McQueen. Recorded for Riverside, Southland, and Preservation Hall in the 1960s. Despite suffering a stroke in 1967 which paralyzed her left side, she continued to perform and occasionally record until her death at age 85.

BARRO *See* Boudreaux, Barro.

BARRON, RONNIE (Ronald Barrosse) *Rhythm and blues.* Piano, vocals. Composer. Bandleader. (Born Oct. 9, 1943, Algiers, Orleans Parish; died Mar. 20, 1997, Orange County, California.) Rhythm and blues singer and keyboardist partnered with Mac Rebennack in the late 1950s and early 1960s and had singles issued as Ronnie Barron, Drits and Dravy, and Ronnie and the Delinquents. Also performed as Reverend Ether which would later inspire Rebennack's **Dr. John** persona. Relocated to California in 1965 and worked as session musician. Released LP *Reverend Ether* on Decca in 1971. Throughout the 1970s and 1980s appeared on recordings with Dr. John, **Tony Joe White**, Paul Butterfield, Ry Cooder, B.B. King, Tom Waits, Canned Heat, and others. Released several albums as leader in the late 1970s and early 1980s.

BARRY, JOE (Joseph Barrios Jr.) *Swamp pop.* Guitar, vocals. Composer. Bandleader. (Born July 13, 1939, Cut Off, Lafourche Parish; died Aug. 31, 2004, Houma, Terrebonne Parish.) Renowned early swamp pop singer best known for his 1961 hit "I'm a Fool to Care." Influenced by Ray Charles and the rhythm and blues coming out of New Orleans, began performing with bands around south Louisiana in the mid-1950s. In 1960 recorded for Jin with little success. Following year had major hit with "I'm a Fool to Care" on Smash, followed by minor hit "Teardrops in My Heart." In the mid-1960s recorded for Huey Meaux's Princess label and worked clubs in Houston and New Orleans, often with Mac Rebennack (**Dr. John**) and **Joey Long**. After singles on Houma and Nugget in the late 1960s, worked mainly outside music in following decades except for a country and gospel release in 1976 and 1980. Struggled with health issues during later years and released final recording *Been Down That Muddy Road* in 2003 shortly before his death from a heart condition. Cousin of **Leroy Martin**.

BARTHOLOMEW, DAVE (Davis Bartholomew) *Rhythm and blues, jazz.* Trumpet, vocals. Composer. Bandleader. (Born Dec. 24, 1918, Edgard, St. John the Baptist Parish; died June 23, 2019, New Orleans, Orleans Parish.) Profoundly influential musician, bandleader, songwriter, producer, arranger, and talent scout who was one of the most important figures in New Orleans rhythm and blues and early rock and roll. Began playing trumpet and tuba as a child and moved to New Orleans with family in the early 1930s. Worked with **Fats Pichon**, **Papa Celestin**, **Claiborne Williams**, and **Jimmy Lunceford** before serving in World War II. In 1946 formed his premier horn-driven band which became the foundation of countless hit recordings throughout the 1950s and early 1960s and included such top musicians as **Earl Palmer**, **Red Tyler**, **Lee Allen**, **Ernest McLean**, **Herb Hardesty**, and **Frank Fields**. Signed with DeLuxe in 1947 and had only hit as leader with "Country Boy" in 1949. Later that year switched to Imperial and began extremely successful and long-running partnership with **Fats Domino** as producer, bandleader, and cowriter which resulted in Domino's nearly 40 Top 40 hits. In the early 1950s recorded for King, Decca, and Specialty and produced **Lloyd Price**'s early hits. Throughout the 1950s was responsible for many dozens of hits by numerous artists including **Smiley Lewis**, **Shirley & Lee**, **Earl King**, **Chris Kenner**, **Archibald**, the Spiders, and many others. Left Imperial in 1963 and worked with Trumpet, Mercury, and his own Broadmoor label through the early 1970s. In the 1970s and 1980s led a traditional New Orleans jazz band which appeared regularly at Preservation Hall and continued to work sporadically with Domino. Released two albums in the 1990s including *New Orleans Big Beat* in 1999 and continued to make occasional appearances into 2010s.

BARZAS, MAURICE (Maurice Berzas) *Cajun.* Accordion, vocals. Composer. Bandleader. (Born Feb. 2, 1909, near Ville Platte, Evangeline Parish; died July 23, 1985, Mamou, Evangeline Parish.)[7] Locally popular Cajun accordionist who led his band the Mamou Playboys for nearly four decades in the Mamou, Basile, and Ville Platte area with son Vorance (1938–) on drums and vocals. Formed band in the early 1950s which soon became one of area's most popular dance-hall groups performing in local venues, including a weekly engagement at Snook's in Ville Platte for over three decades. Also performed and recorded with **Elise Deshotel**'s Louisiana Rhythmaires with **Dewey Balfa** in the early 1950s. In the early 1960s recorded two singles as leader on Swallow, notably "Mamou Hot Step." After band dissolved in 1985 after his death, **Steve Riley** later continued using Mamou Playboys name in tribute.

BAT THE HUMMING BIRD *See* Robinson, James.

BATISTE, ALVIN *Jazz.* Clarinet. Composer. Bandleader. (Born Nov. 7, 1932, New Orleans, Orleans Parish; died May 6, 2007, Baton Rouge, EBR Parish.) Avant-garde jazz clarinetist began playing bebop in the early 1950s and worked with **Ed Blackwell**, **Ellis Marsalis**, **Harold Battiste**, Ornette Coleman, Ray Charles, and Cannonball Adderly, among others. Member of A.F.O. Executives in the early 1960s and was jazz educator at Southern University with students who included **Branford Marsalis** and **Henry Butler**. Released five albums as leader, including *Songs, Word and Messages, Connections* in 1999 on SLM.

BATISTE, DAVID (RUSSELL), SR. *Rhythm and blues.* Keyboards, vocals. Composer. Bandleader. (Born Sept. 26, 1947, New Orleans, Orleans Parish.) Leader of early funk group the Gladiators which he formed with brothers in 1962 and recorded "Funky Soul Parts 1 & 2" in 1970 on Soulin'. Father of **Russell Batiste Jr**.

BATISTE, JON *Jazz.* Piano, melodica, drums, bass, accordion, vocals. Composer. Bandleader. (Born Nov. 8, 1986, Kenner, Jefferson Parish.) Renowned jazz multi-instrumentalist and composer best known as the bandleader of Stay Human, which also serves as house band of CBS's *The Late Show with Stephen Colbert.* Member of the prestigious **Batiste** family of New Orleans jazz, began playing drums in Batiste Brothers family band at age eight before switching to piano three years later. Released first recording at age 17 and received master's degree from Juilliard. Formed Stay Human in the mid-2000s and continued to tour nationally and overseas with group through the 2010s. Appeared in several seasons of the HBO television series *Treme* in the early 2010s and scored several television and film soundtracks. In 2015 began working as bandleader on *The Late Show.*

BATISTE, MILTON "BAT"/"HALF A HEAD" *Rhythm and blues, jazz.* Trumpet, vocals. Bandleader. (Born Sept. 5, 1934, New Orleans, Orleans Parish; died Mar. 29, 2001, New Orleans, Orleans Parish.) Began playing trumpet in teens, inspired by Louis Jordan. Worked with **Professor Longhair** in the 1950s and toured with Little Richard, **Eddie Bo**, **Clarence "Frogman" Henry**, **Smiley Lewis**, and Big Joe Turner. Recorded with **Earl King** and **Champion Jack Dupree**. Led **Harold Dejan**'s Olympia Brass Band in the 1960s and later formed Young Olympia Brass Band to foster young musicians. Recorded three albums as leader in the mid-1990s, including *Embraceable Melodies,* and performed regularly at Preservation Hall.

BATISTE, (DAVID) RUSSELL, JR. *Rhythm and blues.* Drums, bass, guitar, keyboards, vocals. Composer. Bandleader. (Born Dec. 12, 1965, New Orleans, Orleans Parish.) Noted percussionist started playing drums at age four and by age seven was performing in family band the Batiste Brothers. Joined the Funky Meters in 1989 and performed regularly with Joe Krown and **Walter "Wolfman" Washington**, among others. Recorded two solo albums and led Russell Batiste Group. Son of **David Russell Batiste Sr**.

BATISTE, UNCLE LIONEL *Jazz.* Drums, piano, banjo, guitar, kazoo, vocals. Bandleader. (Born Feb. 11, 1932,

New Orleans, Orleans Parish; died July 8, 2012, New Orleans, Orleans Parish.) Beloved longtime bass drummer, vocalist and coleader of Tremé Brass Band. Regarded as the "Face of Tremé" for his ever-present exuberance and impeccable fashion style, remained a fixture in parades and on the streets in various brass bands from the 1940s until his death, starting with Olympia Brass Band.

BATTISTE, HAROLD *Jazz, rhythm and blues.* Saxophone, piano, clarinet. Composer. Bandleader. (Born Oct. 28, 1931, New Orleans, Orleans Parish; died June 19, 2015, New Orleans, Orleans Parish.) Important musician, arranger, producer, label owner, and educator who worked in jazz, rhythm and blues, and pop. Cofounded American Jazz Quintet in the mid-1950s with **Ellis Marsalis**, **Alvin Batiste**, **Ed Blackwell**, and **Richard Payne**. Founded A.F.O. Records in 1961, New Orleans's first black-owned record label. Relocated to Los Angeles in 1964 and worked as session musician. Also served as arranger for Sam Cooke and musical director for pop group Sonny and Cher. Produced and arranged **Dr. John**'s first album in 1968. Returned to New Orleans in the late 1980s and joined faculty of jazz studies at University of New Orleans. Also formed Next Generation Band to mentor young musicians. *See also Battiste's entry as producer.*

BAUDUC, RAY *Jazz.* Drums. Composer. (Born June 18, 1906, New Orleans, Orleans Parish; died Jan. 8, 1988, Houston.)[8] Influential drummer of swing era, performed with Scranton Sirens, Joe Venuti and Eddie Lang, Ben Pollack, and Bob Crosby (which garnered him national fame.) Cowrote with Bob Haggart hits "South Rampart Street Parade" and "Big Noise from Winnetka" in the late 1930s.

BAYERSDORFFER, JOHNNY *Jazz.* Cornet. Composer. Bandleader. (Born Aug. 4, 1899, New Orleans, Orleans Parish; died Nov. 14, 1969, Metairie, Jefferson Parish.)[9] Popular bandleader of Jazzola Novelty Orchestra in the 1920s which recorded for OKeh in 1924. Also worked with **Happy Schilling** and **Tony Parenti**.

BAZLEY, TONY "OULABULA" *Jazz.* Drums. Bandleader. (Born Sept. 10, 1934, New Orleans, Orleans Parish; died Dec. 16, 2015, Toronto.) Distinguished bebop drummer for more than six decades, began playing drums at age 13, turned professional at age 14, and performed with various bands including **Plas Johnson**'s Johnson Brothers. Worked in jazz clubs in California after being discharged from Air Force in the mid-1950s and joined Eric Dolphy's band. Recorded with Wes Montgomery, Roy Ayers, Les McCann, Teddy Edwards, and others throughout the late 1950s and 1960s. Returned to New Orleans in 1989 and worked with **Ellis Marsalis** and **Earl Turbinton**, among others, and toured regularly overseas as bandleader.

BEARB, EDDIE *Cajun.* Accordion, vocals. (Born Aug. 27, 1915, Bristol, St. Landry Parish; died Jan. 9, 1990, Opelousas, St. Landry Parish.) Early Cajun accordionist began teaching himself how to play the instrument at age 10 and by the late 1920s was playing professionally at local dances. Later formed his band the Bristol Ramblers, which he led for many years while influencing numerous local musicians.

BEARB, RICKY *Cajun.* Accordion, vocals. Composer. Bandleader. (Born Jan. 15, 1959, Church Point, Acadia Parish.) Noted Cajun accordion player and leader of the Cajun Ramblers. Recorded several singles for Kajun and Swallow in the late 1970s and early 1980s, notably "That's What Makes the Cajuns Dance" and "Mom, She'll Never Replace You." Father of acclaimed fiddle player Jamey Bearb, who performed with High Performance, **Jimmy Breaux**, **Don Montoucet**, and others.

BEAU JOCQUE (Andrus Joseph Espre) *Zydeco.* Accordion, guitar, tuba, vocals. Composer. Bandleader. (Born Nov. 1, 1953, Duralde, Evangeline Parish; died Sept. 10, 1999, Kinder, Allen Parish.) Highly influential contemporary zydeco accordionist and bandleader who helped usher in a new sound influenced by funk, rock, and rap in the early 1990s. Nicknamed Beau Jocque, which is Creole French for "Big Guy" due to his imposing six-foot-six-inch stature. The son of an accordion player, began playing tuba in a rhythm and blues combo with **Warren Ceasar** during his teens. After serving in the Air Force, worked outside music as an electrician until suffering serious back injury from a fall on a job in 1987. During his recovery, began learning to play his father's accordion, inspired greatly by **Boozoo Chavis**. By 1990 was performing with his band Zydeco Hi-Rollers, which quickly became one of the most popular bands in local dance halls. In 1992 recorded debut CD *My Name is Beau Jocque* on Lanor before signing with Rounder and releasing *Beau Jocque Boogie* in 1993 which contained signature songs "Richard's Club" and "Give Him Cornbread," both of which would become zydeco standards. Numerous releases followed on Rounder, including *Gonna Take You Downtown* in 1996. Toured extensively nationally and overseas as one of the leading zydeco acts of the 1990s. Also held numerous shows featuring "zydeco battles" with Chavis as documented in 1994 film *The Kingdom of Zydeco*. At peak of popularity suffered fatal heart attack at his home at age 45.

BECHET, SIDNEY *Jazz*. Clarinet, soprano saxophone. Composer. Bandleader. (Born May 14, 1897, New Orleans, Orleans Parish; died May 14, 1959, Paris.)[10] Profoundly influential and virtuosic New Orleans jazz musician who was the first celebrated jazz soloist and established the soprano saxophone as a prominent instrument in jazz. Widely regarded as one of greatest musicians of New Orleans jazz along with **Louis Armstrong** and **King Oliver**. A child prodigy, studied clarinet with **Lorenzo Tio Jr.**, **Big Eye Louis Nelson**, and **George Baquet**. Turned professional by age 13 and worked with **Jack Carey**, **Buddy Petit**, **Bunk Johnson**, **Frankie Duson**, Imperial and Superior brass bands, **Freddie Keppard**, **Red Allen**, and others. Toured throughout the South and Midwest at age 16 with **Clarence Williams** and worked with Oliver and Petit in Olympia Brass Band. Relocated to Chicago in 1919 and joined Southern Syncopated Orchestra to tour Europe. Worked throughout Europe with several jazz groups to critical acclaim. In 1920 began playing soprano saxophone, which became his main instrument. Returned to United States in 1922 and recorded with blues singers Sara Martin and Mamie Smith, and also worked with Duke Ellington. In 1924–25 made a series of recordings with Armstrong in Williams's Blue Five which are regarded as among the most important recordings of New Orleans jazz. In the late 1920s toured Europe with Josephine Baker and others. Recorded with **Tommy Ladnier** in New Orleans Feetwarmers and Willie "The Lyon" Smith in the 1930s, and recorded extensively for Blue Note and Victor as leader and sideman. Resided and worked in Brooklyn in the mid-1940s before moving permanently to Paris in 1949. Recorded and performed throughout Europe and United States in remaining years before succumbing to lung cancer at age 62. Older brother Dr. Leonard Bechet (1886–1952) was an early jazz trombonist.

BELL GAL *See* Barrett, Sweet Emma.

BELL, WARREN, SR. *Jazz, rhythm and blues*. Saxophone. (Born Apr. 2, 1929, New Orleans, Orleans Parish; died Nov. 22, 2006, New Orleans, Orleans Parish.) Early New Orleans rhythm and blues saxophonist was influenced early on by bebop musicians and began performing in his teens in **Dooky Chase**'s band. Worked with **Dave Bartholomew**'s band extensively in the 1950s and 1960s and appeared on numerous recordings with **Fats Domino**, **Professor Longhair**, **Lloyd Price**, Ray Charles, and others.

BELLARD, DOUGLAS *Creole*. Fiddle, vocals. Composer. (Born Nov. 6, 1905, Ville Platte, Evangeline Parish; died Jan. 4, 1946, Ville Platte, Evangeline Parish.)[11] Influential but enigmatic early Creole fiddle pioneer who along with partner **Kirby Riley** were the first Creole musicians to record French la la music. Performed throughout Acadia and Evangeline Parish in the 1920s, often with **Amédé Ardoin**, and was a major influence on **Freeman** and **Canray Fontenot**, **Wade Frugé**, and **Lynn Dozart**. In Oct. 1929 recorded four sides with Riley for Vocalion, including "Valse de la Prison" and "Mon Camon la Case Que Je Sui Cordane," the latter of which would become the Cajun and Creole standard "Les Flammes D'Enfer." Continued performing locally in the 1930s and working as a farmer, but other details remain unclear. Struck by a car crossing a street in Ville Platte and succumbed to multiple injuries in a local hospital four days later.

BENOIT, CEDRIC *Cajun*. Accordion, vocals. Composer. Bandleader. (Born Oct. 9, 1958, Kaplan, Vermilion Parish.) Contemporary Cajun accordionist and singer-songwriter with zydeco and rock influences began performing in the 1980s and released debut *Cajun! Cajun!! Cajun!!!* in 1988. Relocated to Branson, Missouri, and remained popular act on local music scene with his band Cajun Connection for over 25 years with several more releases, including *Louisiana* in 2013.

BENOIT, LEE (Bradley Dale Joseph Benoit) *Cajun*. Accordion, guitar, organ, vocals. Composer. Bandleader. (Born July 14, 1959, Abbeville, Vermilion Parish.) Noted Cajun singer-songwriter was raised in Crowley and began playing organ and guitar as a child, performing in rock and country bands in his teens and 20s. In the late 1980s began playing accordion, inspired by **Wayne Toups**, and released several CDs throughout 1990s on Master-Trak, including acclaimed debut *Avec Amis* in 1993. Also recorded with **Doug Kershaw** and **Hadley J. Castille**. Continued performing through 2010s with several more releases, including *Pour Les Générations À Venir* in 2014, which contained all original compositions.

BENOIT, TAB *Blues*. Guitar, vocals. Composer. Bandleader. (Born Nov. 17, 1967, Baton Rouge, EBR Parish.) Born in a Baton Rouge hospital but a lifelong resident of Houma, renowned blues guitarist and singer-songwriter began playing guitar in his teens, often sitting in at **Tabby**

Thomas's Blues Box with Thomas, **Raful** and **Kenny Neal**, **Henry Gray**, and others. Formed first band in 1987 and released debut album *Nice and Warm* in 1992 on Justice which brought national recognition. In the 1990s toured extensively and had numerous releases on Vanguard, Telarc, and Rykodisc through the early 2010s, including *Wetlands* in 2005 and *Medicine* in 2011. In 2004 founded nonprofit Voice of the Wetlands Foundation to raise awareness of the continuing loss of Louisiana's coast which featured an annual festival and the Voice of the Wetlands All-Star band with Benoit, **Cyril Neville**, **Johnny Vidacovich**, **Big Chief Monk Boudreaux**, and others. Continued touring extensively with own group and occasionally with All-Stars in the 2010s.

BENOIT, TAN (Clifton Tan Benoit) *Cajun.* Accordion, fiddle, drums, vocals. Composer. Bandleader. (Born Jan. 12, 1915, Gueydan, Vermilion Parish; died Mar. 1, 1992, Jennings, Jeff. Davis Parish.)[12] Early postwar Cajun multi-instrumentalist relocated to Jennings area early on and performed with several area bands through the 1960s on accordion and fiddle including Travelers Playboys and Tan Benoit French Band. Made recording debut with "Iowa Two Step" on Hot Rod in the late 1940s. In the early 1950s performed and recorded as drummer with Sundown Playboys and also worked regularly with **Will Kegley**. Continued performing through the 1980s with various musicians and bands including **Ervin LeJeune**, Calcasieu Cajuns, Jennings Playboys, and others.

BENOIT, VALMONT "JUNIOR" *Cajun.* Guitar, steel guitar, fiddle, accordion, vocals. (Born Apr. 25, 1930, Lake Charles, Calcasieu Parish; died Oct. 25, 2008, Ragley, Beauregard Parish.) Noted Cajun guitarist and multi-instrumentalist performed and recorded as steel guitarist with **Lawrence Walker**'s Wandering Aces from 1946 to 1951. From the early 1950s through early 1970s performed and recorded as member of **Nathan Abshire**'s Pine Grove Boys, appearing on numerous recordings including as vocalist on Abshire's "Crying Heart Waltz" on Kajun in 1962. Also worked and recorded with the **Balfa Brothers** and many others.

BERARD, AL "PYOOK" *Cajun.* Fiddle, guitar, mandolin, bass, vocals. Composer. Bandleader. (Born June 26, 1960, Cecilia, St. Martin Parish; died Feb. 26, 2014, Lafayette, Lafayette Parish.) Highly regarded and beloved fiddle and guitar player and songwriter best known for his work as leader of Cajun band the Basin Brothers. Began playing guitar at age 11 and, after performing with local rock band in his late teens, joined **Hadley J. Castille**'s band and began learning Cajun fiddle, which he would ultimately master. In 1983 formed the Basin Brothers and performed throughout south Louisiana for several years before signing with Flying Fish in the late 1980s and releasing *Let's Get Cajun* in 1991. Numerous acclaimed recordings followed with both the Basin Brothers and solo projects including *Al Berard and Friends Play Cajun Music from the Heart* on Swing Cat in 1999. Continued performing and producing until his sudden death from meningitis at age 53. Father of musicians Laura Huval and Maegan Berard.

BERGERON, ALPHÉE *Cajun.* Accordion. Composer. Bandleader. (Born Aug. 8, 1912, Church Point, Acadia Parish; died Oct. 15, 1980, Church Point, Acadia Parish.) Early Cajun accordionist and bandleader began performing at house dances at age 13 and in 1947 joined **Bill Matte**'s Veteran Playboys and soon took over leadership. In 1948 made recording debut with "Eunice Waltz"/"-Chinaball Special" on Feature. Joined that year by son **Shirley Bergeron** on steel guitar and vocals, continued performing with band in local dance halls through the 1970s with numerous releases on Lanor, notably LP *The Sounds of Cajun Music* in late 1960s.

BERGERON, JAMIE *Cajun.* Accordion, vocals. Composer. Bandleader. (Born Sept. 24, 1974, Rayne, Acadia Parish.) Popular contemporary Cajun accordionist and singer-songwriter with zydeco and country influences formed his band the Kickin' Cajuns in the late 1990s, inspired to play accordion by his musician father, Kermit. Released debut CD *Traditionally Untraditional* in 2000 and through the 2010s released several more recordings including *Your New CD!* in 2010 which featured signature songs "RCA (Registered Coonass)" and "10 to a 2." Continued performing as popular act on regional club and festival circuit in the late 2010s.

BERGERON, PETE/"PETE/PETO MARLOWE" (Joseph Hilton Bergeron) *Swamp pop, Cajun.* Fiddle, vocals. Composer. Bandleader. (Born Nov. 9, 1939, Eunice, St. Landry Parish.) Noted Cajun and early swamp pop singer began playing in Cajun-country band the Salty Dogs with brother Nelson in the mid-1950s. From 1956 to 1960 led swamp pop group Pete Marlowe and the Rhythm Rockers with Nelson and recorded several sides for **J. D. Miller**, including "Rock and Roll Beat." In the 1980s and 1990s made several Cajun recordings, notably 1995 CD *Une Deuxième Chance* with **Helen Boudreaux** on Swallow. Also worked for several decades in public radio, including hosting the acclaimed Cajun French weekday morning program *Bonjour Louisiane* for over 30 years.

BERGERON, SHIRLEY RAY *Cajun.* Steel guitar, guitar, vocals. Composer. Bandleader. (Born Nov. 16, 1933, Church Point, Acadia Parish; died Nov. 20, 1995, Church Point, Acadia Parish.) Highly renowned Cajun steel guitarist and singer-songwriter began performing in his father **Alphée Bergeron**'s band the Veteran Playboys in 1948. From 1960 through the early 1970s recorded numerous singles for Lanor, including Cajun classics "J'ai Fait Mon Edée," "Quel Etoile," and groundbreaking 1962 Cajun-rocker "French Rockin' Boogie." Also recorded LP *Cajun Style Music* in 1969 for Lanor with **Marc Savoy**. In the mid-1980s recorded on session backing **Paul Daigle** for Bee.

BERNARD, ALFRED "AL" *Rhythm and blues.* Saxophone. (Born Sept. 5, 1935, New Orleans, Orleans Parish; died Apr. 19, 2012, Baton Rouge, EBR Parish.) Performed and recorded as member of the Sha-Weez as well as with bandmate **James "Sugar Boy" Crawford** in the 1950s. Later earned Master of Music Education degree and served as band director at several high schools.

BERNARD, DUDLEY *Cajun.* Guitar, vocals. Bandleader. (Born July 17, 1924, Golden Meadow, Lafourche Parish; died Dec. 4, 2000, Golden Meadow, Lafourche Parish.) Influential Cajun musician, bandleader, and broadcaster who led his band Southern Serenaders in the mid- to late 1940s which included at times **Vin Bruce**, **Harry Anselmi**, **Leroy Martin**, and **Uncle Pott Folse**. Also hosted a popular Cajun radio show in Lafourche Parish for four decades beginning in the mid-1940s. In later years his Cajun band included son **Wade Bernard**.

BERNARD, ROD (Rodney R. Bernard) *Swamp pop.* Guitar, vocals. Composer. Bandleader. (Born Aug. 12, 1940, Opelousas, St. Landry Parish.) Popular early swamp pop singer and bandleader best known for his 1959 hit "This Should Go On Forever." Began playing guitar at age eight, inspired by Cajun performers at his uncle's nightclub. By age 10 was performing on radio with the Blue Room Gang and toured with the Cajun band for several years, making recording debut with "Jambalaya" around 1953. In 1956 began hosting local rhythm and blues radio show and formed band the Twisters, releasing two singles on Carl in 1957. Following year recorded **King Karl**'s "This Should Go On Forever" for Jin which became national hit when leased to Argo. After minor hit "One More Chance" for Mercury in 1960, recorded several singles on Hall-Way including swamp pop classics "Fais Do Do" and "Colinda" in 1962. Also performed and recorded with the Shondelles with **Warren Storm** and **Skip Stewart** in the 1960s. Through the late 1970s released singles and albums on numerous labels, including Teardrop, Copyright, Scepter, Crazy Cajun, and Jin, notably 1976 LP *Boogie in Black & White* with **Clifton Chenier**. After a long recording hiatus, released *A Louisiana Tradition* on CSP in 1999 and continued working mainly outside music with occasional appearances at swamp pop reunions and festivals into the 2010s. Not to be confused with zydeco musician **Rodney Bernard**.

BERNARD, RODNEY *Zydeco.* Drums, rubboard, vocals. (Born Mar. 25, 1937, Lafayette, Lafayette Parish.) Early zydeco multi-instrumentalist began playing rubboard as a child at local la la house dances and from the 1960s through late 1980s worked as drummer with **Fernest Arceneaux**, **Rockin' Dopsie**, **Hiram Sampy**, and others. In the 2010s continued performing on rubboard and as vocalist with **Horace Trahan**. Not to be confused with swamp pop singer **Rod Bernard**.

BERNARD, WADE *Cajun, swamp pop.* Guitar, bass, vocals. Composer. Bandleader. (Born Dec. 15, 1953, Thibodaux, Lafourche Parish.) Raised in Golden Meadow, began performing with Cajun and swamp pop bands while in his teens. In the 1970s recorded singles for Jin and Dominion. Relocated to Nashville in 1981 and performed and recorded with **Jimmy C. Newman**, **Jo-El Sonnier**, and **Rufus Thibodeaux** as well as numerous country and rock and roll artists including George Jones, Conway Twitty, **Jerry Lee Lewis**, and Carl Perkins. Performed throughout United States and Europe and released a dozen recordings as a leader into 2010s, including *Down in Cajun Country.* Son of Cajun bandleader **Dudley Bernard**.

BERRY, RICHARD *Rhythm and blues.* Piano, vocals. Composer. Bandleader. (Born Apr. 11, 1935, Extension, Franklin Parish; died Jan. 23, 1997, Los Angeles.) Early rhythm and blues singer-songwriter best known for his composition "Louie Louie," one of the most covered songs in rock and roll history. Raised in Los Angeles since a baby, began singing in gospel and doo-wop groups in his teens, inspired by singer Jesse Belvin. In the mid-1950s recorded extensively for Modern as a leader and member of various doo-wop groups including the Flairs and appeared on sessions with the Robins, the Crowns, Etta

James, and others. In 1957 recorded "Louie Louie" with his band the Pharoahs for Flip which became a regional hit. In 1963 the Kingsmen's cover of the song became an international hit. Continued writing, performing, and recording in relative obscurity throughout the next two decades until a career resurgence in the mid-1980s and early 1990s brought national exposure and recognition.

BERTRAND, HOBO (Oscar "Coteaux" Bertrand) *Cajun.* Accordion, vocals. Composer. (Born Feb. 6, 1911, Elton, Jeff. Davis Parish; died July 1, 1996, Elton, Jeff. Davis Parish.)[13] Cajun accordionist began performing at dances in the 1930s with **Percy Fuselier** and later recorded one single, "Starvation Waltz"/"Tite Villian Manniere," on Goldband in the late 1950s. Later performed and recorded a single with Longshoremen Playboys in the early 1970s.

BERTRAND, JAKE *Cajun.* Fiddle. (Born Oct. 4, 1915, Hathaway, Jeff. Davis Parish; died Feb. 13, 1972, Lake Charles, Calcasieu Parish.) Noted Cajun fiddler played local house dances early on and performed with **Lionel Cormier**'s Elton Playboys in the late 1940s. In the early 1950s relocated to Lake Charles and in 1955 formed Lake Charles Playboys, which included son **Robert Bertrand** on fiddle and drums and **Bobby Leger** on accordion. Worked with various groups through the 1960s and in 1969 formed Calcasieu Cajuns, which included **Ervin LeJeune**, **Atlas Frugé**, and **Tan Benoit**. Performed with group until his death, recording single "Calcasieu Playboys Waltz" on Buck in 1971.

BERTRAND, JOHN H. (John Homer Bertrand) *Cajun.* Accordion, fiddle, vocals. Composer. (Born June 18, 1891, Prairie Ronde, near Opelousas, St. Landry Parish; died Sept. 10, 1942, near Opelousas, St. Landry Parish.)[14] Early Cajun accordionist and singer taught himself how to play the instrument while in his late teens. In the late 1910s and early 1920s lived near Avoyelles Parish border, possibly associating with **Blind Uncle Gaspard** at the time. Returned to Opelousas area in the mid-1920s and in Jan. 1929 recorded six sides for Paramount with local guitarist Milton Pitre, notably "Miserable" and "Cousinne Lilly." Several months later recorded six more sides for Paramount with guitarist Roy Gonzales and son Anthony on fiddle. Continued performing in Opelousas area until his death at age 51 from heart complications.

BERTRAND, ROBERT *Cajun.* Fiddle, drums, guitar, accordion, vocals. Composer. Bandleader. (Born July 27, 1937, Hathaway, Jeff. Davis Parish; died Feb. 8, 1974, Lake Charles, Calcasieu Parish.) Renowned Cajun multi-instrumentalist began playing fiddle as a child, mentored by his father, **Jake Bertrand**. After relocating to Lake Charles in the early 1950s, joined his father and **Bobby Leger** in Lake Charles Playboys and also worked with **Iry LeJeune** as drummer. In the 1960s performed and recorded with **Nathan Abshire**'s Pine Grove Boys. Formed Louisiana Ramblers in the late 1950s and led group until his death, recording prolifically through the early 1970s for numerous labels, including Goldband where he also served as session musician. Noted members who performed and recorded with Louisiana Ramblers include Leger, **Jo-El Sonnier**, **John Oliver**, **Geno Thibodeaux**, and **Nolan Cormier**. In the late 1960s performed and recorded with **Phil Menard**'s Louisiana Travelers.

BERZAS, JAMIE *Cajun.* Accordion, guitar, drums, vocals. Bandleader. (Born Feb. 1, 1958, near Mamou, Evangeline Parish.) Renowned traditional Cajun accordionist and bandleader began playing the instrument at age 10, learning from his father. Formed his band Cajun Tradition in 1979 based in Mamou and throughout following decades toured nationally and overseas, recording a single for Bee in 1986 and highly acclaimed CD *À La Vieille Façon* on Swallow in 1988. Continued performing with Cajun Tradition in the 2010s, including regular gigs at Fred's Lounge in Mamou. Wife, Madeline, is drummer with band.

BIG CHIEF JOLLY (George Landry) *Rhythm and blues, jazz.* Piano, vocals. Composer. (Born Apr. 4, 1917, New Orleans, Orleans Parish; died Aug. 9, 1980, New Orleans, Orleans Parish.) Founder and leader of Mardi Gras Indians tribe Wild Tchoupitoulas, recorded landmark album of same name in 1976 with nephews **Neville Brothers** and coproduced by **Allen Toussaint**.

BIG CHIEF TAKAWAKA *See* Clement, Henry.

BIG IKE (Isaac Martin) *Blues.* Vocals. Composer. (Born July 28, 1949, Lake Charles, Calcasieu Parish; died Aug. 31, 2003, Lake Charles, Calcasieu Parish.)[15] Blues and southern soul vocalist began singing in church as a child and in high school formed soul band the Episodes. Renamed group Lake City Show Band in the mid-1970s and continued performing around Lake Charles area, often opening for national rhythm and blues acts. In the late 1980s recorded single "I'm Not the Man" on Master-Trak and performed in southwest Louisiana and east Texas, eventually expanding onto southern soul circuit. Shortly before death recorded CD *Teddy Bear* for Mardi Gras, the title cut of which gained some success on southern soul radio when released posthumously in late 2003.

BIG SAM (Williams) *Jazz.* Trombone, vocals. Composer. Bandleader. (Born Feb. 20, 1981, New Orleans, Orleans Parish.) Popular New Orleans brass bandleader studied with **Kidd Jordan** and was founding member of Stooges Brass Band while in his teens. Later worked with Dirty Dozen Brass Band and recorded with **Allen Toussaint** in 2006. In the 2010s continued touring with his own group, Big Sam's Funky Nation, releasing multiple CDs, including *Feet on the Floor* on Ropeadope in 2015.

BIGARD, ALEX *Jazz.* Drums. Bandleader. (Born Sept. 25, 1898, New Orleans, Orleans Parish; died June 27, 1978, New Orleans, Orleans Parish.)[16] Brother of **Barney Bigard**, studied drums in his late teens with **Louis Cottrell Sr.** and by 1919 was a member of Excelsior Brass Band and Maple Leaf Orchestra. Worked with **Buddy Petit**, **Chris Kelly**, **Sidney Desvigne**, and **John Robichaux** in the 1920s and 1930s and **Kid Rena** in the early 1940s. Formed the Mighty Four in the early 1950s and recorded with **Kid Clayton** in 1962. In the 1960s performed regularly at Preservation Hall and recorded with **Punch Miller**, **Kid Howard**, **Harold Dejan**, and **De De** and **Billie Pierce**.

BIGARD, BARNEY *Jazz.* Clarinet, saxophone. Composer. Bandleader. (Born Mar. 3, 1906, New Orleans, Orleans Parish; died June 27, 1980, Los Angeles.) One of the premier clarinetists of jazz who first gained prominence as a tenor saxophonist. In the early 1920s worked with various bands around New Orleans and moved to Chicago in 1924 where he worked and recorded with **King Oliver** from 1925 to 1927. While with Oliver, began performing on clarinet, which soon became his primary instrument. Recorded with **Jelly Roll Morton**, **Johnny Dodds**, and **Louis Armstrong** in the late 1920s. From 1928 to 1942 performed and recorded extensively with Duke Ellington. Worked with **Kid Ory** and Freddie Slack in the early 1940s and toured and recorded with Armstrong's All Stars from 1947 to 1955. Semiretired in 1962 but continued to perform and record sporadically through the 1970s. Younger brother of **Alex Bigard**.

BIGEOU, ESTHER *Blues, jazz.* Vocals. (Born 1893, New Orleans, Orleans Parish; died Nov. 15, 1934, New Orleans, Orleans Parish.)[17] Classic blues singer and dancer began performing on vaudeville circuit in 1913 and appeared in *Broadway Rastus Revue* in Philadelphia and New York in 1917. Recorded for OKeh in 1921 and 1923, often with **Clarence Williams** and during one session with **Armand Piron**'s Orchestra which included **Peter Bocage**, **Lorenzo Tio Jr.**, and **Louis Cottrell Sr.** Toured country on T.O.B.A. black vaudeville circuit throughout the 1920s and settled back in New Orleans by 1930, retiring from music. Died of pulmonary congestion accompanied by marked emaciation and dehydration. Cousin of **Paul Barbarin**.

BLACK BENNY (Williams) *Jazz.* Drums. (Born 1892, New Orleans, Orleans Parish; died July 6, 1924, New Orleans, Orleans Parish.)[18] Regarded as one of the greatest drummers in early jazz by musicians such as **Louis Armstrong** and **Sidney Bechet**, although remained unrecorded. Performed regularly with Onward Brass Band in the 1910s and later with Tuxedo Brass Band around 1920. Worked with numerous early jazz musicians, including Armstrong, Bechet, **Kid Ory**, **Bunk Johnson**, and **Johnny Dodds**. Succumbed to complications following experimental emergency surgery at Charity Hospital at age 32 after being stabbed in the heart by a woman in a bar fight on Gravier Street.

BLACK BILLY SUNDAY (Rev. Dr. James Gordon McPherson) *Gospel.* Vocals. (Born 1869, New Orleans, Orleans Parish; died Apr. 9, 1936, New Orleans, Orleans Parish.)[19] Noted African American Baptist preacher and traveling evangelist who recorded sermons with singing for Paramount in 1931, including "The High Cost of Sin" and "This Old World's in a Hell of a Fix." Toured the country, particularly in California and Washington area, for decades lecturing and preaching. A character in the Pulitzer Prize–winning play and movie *The Green Pastures* was based on him. Died of a stroke at age 67 after a long illness.

BLACK, JAMES *Jazz, rhythm and blues.* Drums, trumpet. Composer. Bandleader. (Born Feb. 1, 1940, New Orleans, Orleans Parish; died Aug. 30, 1988, New Orleans, Orleans Parish.) Highly influential and accomplished jazz and early funk drummer. Appeared on sessions with **Fats Domino** and also recorded with **Ellis Marsalis** and Nat and Cannonball Adderly in the early 1960s. Performed with Yusef Lateef and Lionel Hampton in the mid-1960s. Worked and recorded with **Eddie Bo** in the late 1960s (notably on hit "Hook and Sling") and continued performing and recording with **Marsalis** family in the 1970s and 1980s as well as leading the James Black Ensemble.

BLACKWELL, ED *Jazz, rhythm and blues.* Drums. (Born Oct. 10, 1929, New Orleans, Orleans Parish; died Oct. 7,

1992, Hartford, Conn.) Greatly influenced by jazz drummer Max Roach, began performing around 1950 with **Plas Johnson** and toured with Ray Charles. Relocated to California in the early 1950s and worked with Ornette Coleman. Recorded with **Ellis Marsalis**, **Harold Battiste**, **Richard Payne**, and **Alvin Batiste** as American Jazz Quintet in New Orleans in 1956. Moved to New York in 1960 and worked and recorded with Ornette Coleman through the early 1970s. Also recorded with Eric Dolphy, Don Cherry, and Archie Shepp. Toured internationally and had long affiliation as educator with Wesleyan University.

BLADE, BRADY L., JR. *Rhythm and blues, country, rock.* Drums. (Born June 10, 1965, Shreveport, Caddo Parish.) Highly accomplished and renowned drummer began performing gospel in his father **Brady L. Blady Sr.**'s church while in his teens. In the 1990s and 2000s performed and/or recorded with numerous artists, including Emmylou Harris, Steve Earle, Jewel, Solomon Burke, Dave Matthews, and many others. In the 2010s continued working as producer, songwriter, and label and studio owner.

BLADE, BRIAN *Jazz.* Drums, guitar, vocals. Composer. Bandleader. (Born July 25, 1970, Shreveport, Caddo Parish.) Internationally renowned jazz drummer began playing violin as a child before switching to drums, inspired by older brother **Brian L. Blade Jr.** At age 18 moved to New Orleans and while attending Loyola University worked with **Johnny Vidacovich**, **Herlin Riley**, **Ellis Marsalis**, and others. In the late 1990s formed Fellowship Band and recorded five albums through the 2010s, including *Body and Shadow* on Blue Note in 2017, and toured internationally. As a session musician has appeared on numerous recordings by Bob Dylan, Emmylou Harris, Joni Mitchell, Nora Jones, and many others. In 2009 released CD *Mama Rosa* showcasing talents as singer-songwriter and guitarist. Continued to work as in-demand session musician and bandleader in the 2010s. Son of **Reverend Brady L. Blade Sr.**

BLADE, REVEREND BRADY L., SR. *Gospel.* Vocals, bass. Composer. (Born May 23, 1939, Shreveport, Caddo Parish.) Pastor of Zion Baptist Church in Shreveport for more than five decades who recorded several gospel singles and an LP on Paula in 1973–74. In 1982 released single "By His Grace We've Come a Long Way" on his own B.L.B. label. Father of drummers **Brian** and **Brady L. Blade Jr.**

BLAKE, CLIFFORD, SR. *Field hollers, blues.* Vocals. (Born July 7, 1909, Natchitoches, Natch. Parish; died Mar. 20, 1992, Natchitoches, Natch. Parish.) Worked "calling the press" at local cotton-processing plant from 1927 until being seriously injured on job in 1967, using call-and-response blues and spiritual chants and hollers to lead and encourage workers on the dangerous bale compresses. Recorded LP *Cornbread for Your Husband, Biscuits for Your Man,* a collection of work songs, hollers, and folktales for Louisiana Folklife Recording Series in 1980.

BLAKES, RAYMOND *Blues.* Guitar, vocals. (Born Mar. 10, 1934, Mira, Caddo Parish.) Locally renowned Shreveport blues singer and guitarist began playing on a homemade one-string instrument as a child. In the 1960s performed in clubs around Osceola, Arkansas, with wife, Ernestine, on drums, and worked with Albert King. Returned to Shreveport in the 1970s and continued performing in following decades with his own group as well as stints with various area bands including A-Train and the Bluebirds.

BLANCHARD, EDGAR *Rhythm and blues.* Guitar, banjo, vocals. Composer. Bandleader. (Born Aug. 17, 1924, Grosse Tete, Iberville Parish; died Sept. 16, 1972, New Orleans, Orleans Parish.) Highly regarded rhythm and blues guitarist, arranger, and session player whose group the Gondoliers was one of the top bands in Louisiana in the late 1940s and 1950s. Raised in New Orleans since childhood, started playing professionally in his early teens. Formed the Gondoliers in the mid-1940s and soon began performing in New Orleans's most popular clubs. Recorded for Peacock in 1949 and in 1950–51 toured and recorded with **Roy Brown**. Continued to perform with band throughout the 1950s and recorded extensively on sessions with Big Joe Turner, Ray Charles, Little Richard, Papa Lightfoot, **Professor Longhair**, **Clarence "Frogman" Henry**, **Bobby Charles**, **Eddie Bo**, **Tommy Ridgley**, and many others. Recorded several instrumental singles as a leader on Specialty and Ric in 1956 and 1958. Continued to lead the Gondoliers through mid-1960s before semiretiring from music due to health reasons. In the early 1970s performed sporadically with jazz groups in the French Quarter before suffering fatal heart attack at age 48.

BLANCHARD, TERENCE *Jazz.* Trumpet. Composer. Bandleader. (Born Mar. 13, 1962, New Orleans, Orleans Parish.) Inspired by **Alvin Alcorn**, highly acclaimed jazz musician and composer began playing trumpet at age eight. During the 1980s toured with Lionel Hampton and Art Blakey and coled jazz quintet with **Donald Harrison**, which recorded five albums. Launched solo career in 1990 and began decades-long association scoring films for director Spike Lee, including *Jungle Fever, Malcom X,* and *BlacKKKlansman.* From the 1990s through 2010s recorded numerous solo albums for Columbia, Sony Classical, and Blue Note, including *Flow* in 2005. Continued to score films and perform and record with his group E-Collective in the late 2010s.

BLAZER BOY (George Stevenson) *Rhythm and blues.* Vocals, piano. Composer. Bandleader. (Born June 6, 1930, New Orleans, Orleans Parish; died Apr. 13, 1973, New Orleans, Orleans Parish.)[20] Son of a Baptist preacher, early New Orleans rhythm and blues singer and piano player was performing in local clubs by the early 1950s and recorded three singles for Imperial in 1952 and 1961, notably "Mornin' Train" and "New Orleans Twist," the latter having local success in 1962. In 1954 released single "Meet Me at Grandma's Joint" on Savoy. Continued performing around New Orleans area through the 1960s. Not to be confused with James "Blazer Boy" Locks, who recorded for Regal in 1949–50.

BLEDSOE, JIM *See* Country Jim.

BO, EDDIE (Edwin Joseph Bocage) *Rhythm and blues, jazz.* Piano, vocals. Composer. Bandleader. (Born Sept. 20, 1929, New Orleans, Orleans Parish; died Mar. 18, 2009, Picayune, Mississippi.)[21] Influential New Orleans rhythm and blues and early funk piano player, songwriter, and producer. Inspired by jazz pianists Art Tatum and Oscar Peterson, led own group Spider Bocage Orchestra before switching to rhythm and blues in the early 1950s, largely influenced by **Professor Longhair**. Toured country backing **Lloyd Price**, **Smiley Lewis**, **Guitar Slim**, and others. From 1955 to 1970 recorded extensively and released more singles than any other New Orleans artist except **Fats Domino**, notably "Check Mr. Popeye" and "Hook and Sling." Also wrote and produced recordings for many others, including **Irma Thomas**, **Chris Kenner**, **Johnny Adams**, and **Art Neville**. After 10-year break starting in the mid-1970s, continued to perform, record, and produce throughout remaining decades. Nephew of **Peter Bocage**.

BO, PHIL (Phillip Boudreaux) *Swamp pop.* Vocals. Composer. Bandleader. (Born Aug. 30, 1940, Chauvin, Terrebonne Parish; died Apr. 7, 2017, Bourg, Terrebonne Parish.) Swamp pop singer best known for his 1961 single "Don't Take It So Hard" on Jin. Also had singles on Som, Shane, T. and K., and Smash in the late 1950s and early 1960s, working often with producer Huey Meaux.

BOB, CAMILLE *See* Little Bob.

BOCAGE, PETER *Jazz.* Trumpet, violin, guitar, trombone. Composer. Bandleader. (Born July 31, 1887, Algiers, Orleans Parish; died Dec. 3, 1967, New Orleans, Orleans Parish.)[22] Highly respected early New Orleans jazz multi-instrumentalist began performing on violin around 1904 with **Tom Albert**'s band and through the mid-1910s worked with **Frankie Duson**, Superior Orchestra, **Bab Frank**, and Onward, Tuxedo, and Excelsior brass bands, and in Storyville with **Papa Celestin** and **King Oliver**. Switched to trumpet in the mid-1910s and performed regularly with **Armand Piron**'s orchestra through the late 1920s, recording with group in 1923–24. In the late 1920s formed the Creole Serenaders and performed regularly with group through the early 1940s. Recorded with Original Zenith Brass Band and **Emile Barnes** in 1940s and 1950s. In the 1960s worked and recorded as leader and as member of Eureka Brass Band and appeared regularly at Preservation Hall. Brothers Henry and Charles were also jazz musicians and members of Creole Serenaders. Uncle of **Eddie Bo**.

BOLDEN, BUDDY (Charles Bolden) *Jazz.* Cornet, vocals. Composer. Bandleader. (Born Sept. 6, 1877, New Orleans, Orleans Parish; died Nov. 4, 1931, Jackson, E. Feliciana Parish.) Regarded as the first "king" of New Orleans jazz and a key figure in its early development in the late nineteenth century. Largely self-taught, began playing cornet in his mid-teens with small string bands, including **Charley Galloway**'s group. Around 1895 started leading his own band and performed in a raw, aggressive style which combined ragtime, blues, and gospel influences within the brass-band framework and which featured a loose rhythmic feel and improvisation. By the first years of the 1900s was known as "King" Bolden for his unique style, unrivaled showmanship, and immense popularity and performed regularly throughout New Orleans with his band which included at times Galloway, **Willie Cornish**, **Bob Lyons**, **Albert Glenny**, **Ed Garland**, **Henry Zeno**, and **Frankie Duson**. Known as a charismatic, flamboyant performer and celebrated for his extremely loud and powerful, clear tone with deep blues inflections, he directly influenced **King Oliver**, **Freddie Keppard**, **Bunk Johnson**, and many other prominent early jazz musicians. In 1906 and at the height of his popularity he started showing signs of severe mental illness and alcoholism and declined rapidly. He collapsed while performing at a Labor Day parade in 1906 and the following spring was committed to a state mental hospital where he remained until his death. He is believed to have made phonograph cylinder recordings in the late 1890s, but they were reportedly accidently destroyed in the early 1960s.

BONANO, JOSEPH "SHARKEY" *Jazz.* Trumpet, vocals. Bandleader. (Born Apr. 9, 1898, New Orleans, Orleans Parish; died Mar. 27, 1972, New Orleans, Orleans Parish.)[23] A powerful trumpeter with impeccable tone, began performing professionally during his teens around New Orleans and worked with Wolverine Orchestra, Original Dixieland Jazz Band, **Norman Brownlee**, Jimmy Durante, and **Leon Prima** in the 1920s and early 1930s. Performed and recorded with his band the Sharks of Rhythm in the mid- to late 1930s. Toured overseas in the 1940s and held successful residencies in New York and Chicago. In the 1950s and 1960s recorded for various labels, including Capitol, Southland, Storyville, and GHB and was a very popular draw at New Orleans clubs due in part to his outgoing stage performances. Continued performing throughout the 1960s until illness forced retirement in 1971.

BONSALL, JOE *Cajun.* Accordion, fiddle, guitar, vocals. Composer. Bandleader. (Born June 3, 1921, Lake Arthur, Jeff. Davis Parish; died Oct. 14, 1996, Vinton, Calcasieu Parish.) Renowned Cajun multi-instrumentalist and bandleader learned accordion, fiddle, and guitar as a child and during his early teens played professionally with **Joe Falcon** and **Lawrence Walker**. In 1937 relocated with family near Vinton and performed at local house dances. Formed the Orange Playboys in the early 1950s, which soon became the most popular Cajun band in east Texas. From 1962 to 1964 recorded numerous sides for Goldband, including "Bayou Pon-Pon" in 1964. Later that year began recording for producer **Floyd Soileau** and had numerous releases on Swallow and Cajun Jamboree through the mid-1970s, including regional hits "Step It Fast," "Your Picture," and "Grand Prairie Waltz." In the mid-1970s quit music to recuperate from heart surgery but by 1977 formed Cajun Ramblers with **Wallace Derouen**, recording a single for Swallow in 1979. In the early 1980s recorded two singles for Swallow and continued performing with his Orange Playboys until plagued by ill health in the mid-1980s. Performed sporadically in the late 1980s with Louisiana Cajuns until retiring due to illness by 1990.

BOO *See* Boulet, V. J.

BOOGIE JAKE (Matthew Jacobs) *Blues.* Guitar, vocals. Composer. Bandleader. (Born Aug. 2, 1927, Marksville, Avoy. Parish; died Dec. 6, 2013, Marksville, Avoy. Parish.) Noted early Baton Rouge blues singer and guitarist best known for his 1959 recording "Bad Luck and Trouble" on Chess. Began playing guitar in his teens, inspired by Lightnin' Hopkins and local guitarist Ernest Barron. In the early 1950s performed with cousin **Little Walter** who was touring Louisiana and shortly afterwards began performing on Baton Rouge blues scene with his band the House Rockers. Recorded several unissued sides for **J. D. Miller** in 1957 and appeared on **Slim Harpo**'s "I'm a King Bee" hit record. In 1959–60 recorded two singles on Minit, with "Bad Luck and Trouble" leased to Chess. Relocated to northern California in 1961 and worked outside music until the early 1970s when he began performing on Bay Area blues scene, occasionally with **Schoolboy Cleve**. Recorded a single for Blues Connoisseur in 1976. Retired from performing in the mid-1980s and eventually returned to Louisiana.

BOOGIE WOOGIE RED (Vernon Harrison) *Blues.* Piano, vocals. Composer. (Born Oct. 18, 1925, Rayville, Richland Parish; died July 2, 1992, Detroit.) Detroit barrelhouse blues piano player and singer moved to the city with his family at age two and at age eight began teaching himself piano, influenced by Big Maceo Merriweather. From the mid-1940s through the 1950s worked local clubs, often with **Baby Boy Warren**, Sonny Boy Williamson (Rice Miller), and John Lee Hooker and recorded as sideman with Warren, Hooker, Eddie Kirkland, and others. In 1960 recorded as leader for Decca and in the 1970s toured nationally and overseas, with recordings for Trix, Big Bear, and Blind Pig. Continued to perform in local clubs until suffering health issues in the late 1980s.

BOOKER, BEA *Rhythm and blues.* Vocals. (Born Aug. 10, 1929, New Orleans, Orleans Parish; died Aug. 30, 1997, New Orleans, Orleans Parish.)[24] Rhythm and blues singer recorded a single each for Imperial in 1953 and Peacock in 1957, including "Comfort in My Heart." Married pianist **Melvin Dowden**.

BOOKER, JAMES (James Carroll Booker III) *Rhythm and blues, jazz, classical.* Piano, organ, vocals. Composer. (Born Dec. 17, 1939, New Orleans, Orleans Parish; died Nov. 8, 1983, New Orleans, Orleans Parish.) Regarded as one of the most virtuosic piano players to emerge from New Orleans. A child prodigy, began playing piano as a boy, often performing in his father's church. Studied classical and also took lessons from **Tuts Washington**. In his early teens started his first band, which included

Aaron Neville. Through local radio broadcast was discovered by **Dave Bartholomew** and recorded for Imperial in 1954. Worked on sessions for **Earl King**, **Smiley Lewis**, and **Fats Domino**, among others, and in late 1960 recorded hit instrumental "Gonzo" for Peacock. Performed throughout the 1960s with various rhythm and blues acts, including life-long friend **Dr. John**. His notoriety spread in the 1970s and he made several acclaimed recordings and performed overseas. Also mentored a young **Harry Connick Jr.** His health and quality of performances rapidly declined in 1982 due to persistent drug and alcohol abuse, which claimed his life the following year.

BOUDREAUX, BARRO (Hubert Joseph Boudreaux) *Cajun*. Accordion, vocals. Composer. Bandleader. (Born Nov. 9, 1918, Creole, Cameron Parish; died Apr. 15, 2002, Lake Charles, Calcasieu Parish.) Noted Cameron Parish Cajun accordion player and bandleader performed at local house dances for many years around Creole and Grand Chenier area. Later formed Barro and the Teardrops and performed with group from the early 1970s through 2000, recording several singles on Swallow and Tamm, including "Cameron Two Step" and "La Tete Fille de Grand Chenier" in the 1970s.

BOUDREAUX, BIG CHIEF MONK *Rhythm and blues, jazz*. Vocals. Composer. Bandleader. (Born Dec. 7, 1941, New Orleans, Orleans Parish.) Joined Mardi Gras Indians tribe the Wild Magnolias led by **Big Chief Bo Dollis** in the late 1960s and worked and recorded with group throughout next three decades. Continued to lead and record with the Golden Eagles Mardi Gras Indians, as well as Voice of the Wetland All-Stars, among others. Received National Endowment for the Arts National Heritage Fellowship in 2016.

BOUDREAUX, BUDDY (John Landry Boudreaux) *Jazz*. Saxophone, clarinet. Bandleader. (Born Dec. 27, 1917, Donaldsonville, Ascension Parish; died June 13, 2015, Baton Rouge, EBR Parish.) Locally renowned jazz musician and bandleader who led several prominent Baton Rouge–area jazz and dance bands from 1939 to 2014. Performed first professional gig at age 14 and by age 22 was leading his first band. Later toured as member of swing bands of Bob Crosby, Jimmy Dorsey, and Tommy Dorsey. In 1973 cofounded 16-piece Buddy Lee Orchestra. Recorded six albums in the 1980s and continued performing until age 96. Father of **Jeff Boudreaux**.

BOUDREAUX, HELEN *Cajun*. Vocals, guitar. Composer. (Born Mar. 14, 1939, Catahoula, St. Martin Parish.) Noted Cajun singer-songwriter began singing with local bands in her early teens and performed with **Belton Richard**, **Blackie Forestier**, **Johnnie Allan**, Larry Brasso, and others. In the 1990s and early 2000s released four CDs, including *Pour Tout Mon Famille* in 1993.

BOUDREAUX, JEFF *Jazz*. Drums. (Born Jan. 26, 1959, Baton Rouge, EBR Parish.) Highly regarded jazz percussionist started playing drums at age eight and turned professional at age 12 performing in the band of his father, **Buddy Boudreaux**. Based in New Orleans in 1980s, worked with numerous jazz and rhythm and blues musicians and performed regularly with New Orleans Philharmonic Orchestra. Relocated to Vienna in 1990 and settled in Paris in 1995 where he continued to perform with various jazz and classical ensembles through the 2010s.

BOUDREAUX, JOHN *Rhythm and blues, jazz*. Drums, saxophone. Composer. Bandleader. (Born Dec. 10, 1936, New Roads, Pointe Coupee Parish; died Jan. 14, 2017, Los Angeles.) Highly influential New Orleans rhythm and blues and early funk drummer who appeared on numerous classic recordings in the 1950s and 1960s. Moved to New Orleans with family as a child and began playing drums in early teens. Worked with **Professor Longhair** in the early 1950s and later joined the Hawkettes, appearing on their classic recording "Mardi Gras Mambo" in 1955. In the late 1950s and early 1960s worked extensively as session drummer at **Cosimo Matassa**'s famed studio and performed on countless hit recordings by **Irma Thomas**, **Ernie K-Doe**, **Chris Kenner**, **Lee Dorsey**, **Johnny Adams**, **Barbara George**, and many others. In 1963 relocated to California and worked on sessions with **Harold Battiste**, Sam Cooke, **Dr. John**, and others. Released modern jazz album *Past, Present and Future* in 2002 and later switched to saxophone due to nerve damage in elbow.

BOULET, V. J. "BOO" *Swamp pop*. Piano, vocals. Composer. Bandleader. (Born Feb. 4, 1939, Rayne, Acadia Parish.) Early swamp pop piano player and singer-songwriter performed and recorded with **Bobby Page** and the Riff Raffs in the mid- to late 1950s and early 1960s. In the 1970s released single "Gratefully"/"Where Did You Stay" as "Boo" on Jin, operated Boo Boo's Nite Club in Breaux Bridge and ran the Booray record label with releases by **T. K. Hulin** and others. Continued hosting a local weekly swamp pop radio show and performing with his band Swamp Pop Express in the 2010s. His composition and original recording "I Love My Baby" with the Riff Raffs appeared in the 2018 award-winning film *Green Book.*

BOURG, SONNY (Ludwill Bourg) *Swamp pop, Cajun.* Drums, vocals. Bandleader. (Born Aug. 3, 1940, New Iberia, Iberia Parish; died Dec. 27, 2011, Florida.) Popular Lafayette area swamp pop singer, drummer, and bandleader began career as original member of **Randy** and the Rockets in 1957–58. After performing with various groups, formed his Bayou Blues Band and had singles on La Louisianne before releasing self-titled CD on Master-Trak in 1997. Performed throughout south Louisiana and made numerous appearances at New Orleans Jazz & Heritage Festival until his death from natural causes while on a hunting trip.

BOUTTÉ, JOHN *Jazz.* Vocals, cornet, trumpet. (Born Nov. 3, 1958, New Orleans, Orleans Parish.) Younger brother of **Lillian Boutté**, noted jazz vocalist began performing in marching bands in high school and with an a cappella group on streets. Turned professional in the 1990s and continued performing into the late 2010s, releasing multiple recordings, including *All About Everything* in 2012.

BOUTTÉ, LILLIAN *Jazz, gospel, rhythm and blues.* Vocals. (Born Aug. 6, 1949, New Orleans, Orleans Parish.) A dynamic singer and performer, began professional career in the early 1970s working with **Allen Toussaint**, **Neville Brothers**, and **Dr. John**, among others. In the late 1970s starred in musical *One Mo' Time* and toured overseas, where she remained working and recording with various jazz groups throughout the next three decades. Resettled in New Orleans in 2017 for health reasons. Older sister of **John Boutté**.

BOWLES, EDDIE *Blues.* Guitar, vocals. Composer. (Born Apr. 15, 1884, Lafayette, Lafayette Parish; died Oct. 3, 1984, Cedar Falls, Iowa.)[25] Early Louisiana country blues singer-guitarist performed with various groups in New Orleans in the early 1900s before settling in Cedar Falls by 1920. In the 1970s began performing at local folk festivals and became mentor to many area musicians. Known for his composition "Bowles' Blues," continued performing into his late 90s.

BRADLEY, MARTEE *Blues.* Vocals, guitar. Composer. (Born Aug. 25, 1926, Columbia, Caldwell Parish; died May 19, 1995, Detroit.)[26] Down-home blues singer and guitarist who was billed as "The Hastings Street Hill-Billy" and made two records for Citation in the early 1950s in Detroit, including "Now I'll Have to Sing the Blues"/"Winter Time is Coming."

BRADY, EVERETT *Swamp pop.* Vocals, piano, trumpet. (Born Jan. 17, 1948, Melville, St. Landry Parish.) Popular swamp pop vocalist made recording debut in 1970 with single "Pin Ball Machine" on Goldband and in 1975 had single on Phillips Cash & Carry Records. Later worked with Dale & **Grace** and was longtime member of the Boogie Kings. In 2006 released CD *Swamp & Roll with Soul* on Master-Trak and continued to perform in the 2010s until sidelined by illness in early 2018.

BRASSEAUX, DANNY *Cajun.* Accordion, vocals. Composer. Bandleader. (Born Apr. 5, 1959, Carencro, Lafayette Parish.) Highly skilled Cajun accordionist began playing the instrument at age seven and as a teenager won Church Point Cajun Days accordion contest. Led several bands in following years and released acclaimed debut CD *Memories of Mama* in 1992 with his band Cajun Express.

BRAUD, WELLMAN *Jazz.* String bass, violin. Composer. Bandleader. (Born Jan. 25, 1891, St. James Parish; died Oct. 27, 1966, Los Angeles.)[27] Early New Orleans jazz bass pioneer and innovator who was among the first to incorporate slap bass and walking bass lines in jazz. Began performing in Storyville on various stringed instruments around 1910, often with **Armand Piron**. Relocated to Chicago in 1917 and worked with **Lawrence Duhé** and **Charlie Elgar**. After touring Europe moved to New York and worked and recorded with Duke Ellington from 1927 to 1935. Through the mid-1940s led his own band and recorded with the Spirits of Rhythm, **Jelly Roll Morton**, **Sidney Bechet**, **Louis Armstrong**, **Blue Lu Barker**, **Jimmie Noone**, Hot Lips Page, and others. In 1956 toured Europe with **Kid Ory** and then relocated to California. In the 1960s worked with **Joe Darensbourg**, Barbara Dane, and briefly reunited with Duke Ellington. Distant relative of **Marsalis** brothers on mother's side.

BRAY, JOHN "BIG NIG" *Blues, folk.* Guitar, vocals. Composer. (Born Dec. 25, 1888, Royal Ville, St. Mary Parish; died Mar. 4, 1967, New Orleans, Orleans Parish.)[28] Singer and guitarist who recorded four songs for folklorists John and Alan Lomax in Amelia in 1934, notably "Trench Blues," which detailed his experiences as an African American soldier during World War I. Also recorded "Cypress Logging Holler" as an example of work songs he sang as leader of a logging team recovering cypress in St. Mary Parish swamps. Succumbed to sepsis at VA Hospital in New Orleans after month-long stay.

BRAZLEE/BRAZLEY, HARRISON *Jazz.* Trombone. (Born Oct. 25. 1888, New Orleans, Orleans Parish; died Mar. 22, 1955, New Orleans, Orleans Parish.)[29] Early New Orleans jazz trombonist was raised in Mississippi and performed with brass bands around Mobile, Jackson (Mississippi), and Texas in the late 1910s and 1920s. Also traveled with Rabbit Foot Minstrels. Settled in New Orleans in the 1930s and worked and recorded with **Emile Barnes** and **De De Pierce** in the 1940s and 1950s.

BREAUX, AMÉDÉE *Cajun.* Accordion, vocals. Composer. Bandleader. (Born Sept. 1, 1900, Crowley, Acadia Parish; died May 18, 1973, Rayne, Acadia Parish.)[30] Highly influential early Cajun accordion player, singer-songwriter, and leader of Breaux Fréres. Learned accordion as a child and began playing at house parties in his early teens. By the 1920s was performing regularly with brothers **Ophy** and **Clifford Breaux** and sister **Cléoma Breaux Falcon** in local dance halls. Recorded several sides with Ophy and Cléoma on Columbia and OKeh in Apr. 1929, including "Ma Blonde Est Partié," the forerunner of the Cajun standard "Jolie Blon." In 1934 recorded 18 sides with brothers as Breaux Fréres for Vocalion, including "Crowley Breakdown." In the early 1950s recorded several sides for **J. D. Miller**'s Feature label. Father August Breaux was also noted local accordion player but remained unrecorded.

BREAUX, CLÉOMA *See* Falcon, Cléoma Breaux.

BREAUX, CLIFFORD *Cajun.* Guitar, fiddle, vocals. Composer. (Born Oct. 10, 1904, Crowley, Acadia Parish; died Oct. 3, 1960, Crowley, Acadia Parish.)[31] Member of renowned family of early Cajun musicians began playing multiple instruments as a child. Recorded with brothers **Amédée** and **Ophy Breaux** as Breaux Fréres in 1934 and two sides as leader in 1937 on Decca, notably "Continuez de Sonner (Keep A' Knockin' (But You Can't Come In)." Brother of **Cléoma Breaux Falcon** and son of noted local accordionist August Breaux.

BREAUX, GARY *Cajun, swamp pop.* Drums, accordion. (Born Oct. 20, 1953, Arnaudville, St. Martin Parish.) Noted Cajun and swamp pop drummer and accordionist and member of renowned Breaux family of Cajun musicians. Began playing drums and accordion as a child and recorded several singles with brother **Pat Breaux** on Swallow and Cajun Jamboree. Later performed and recorded with numerous musicians, including brother **Jimmy Breaux**, **Johnnie Allan**, **Ed Gary**, and others. Son of Cajun guitarist Preston Breaux and grandson of **Amédée Breaux**.

BREAUX, JIMMY *Cajun.* Accordion, drums, vocals. (Born Nov. 18, 1967, Breaux Bridge, St. Martin Parish.) Renowned Cajun accordionist best known for his long association performing and recording as member of Cajun band BeauSoleil from the late 1980s through 2010s. Also released two acclaimed CDs as a leader, notably *Un 'Tit Peu Plus Cajun* on La Louisianne in 1991. Son of Cajun guitarist Preston Breaux, brother of **Gary** and **Pat Breaux**, and grandson of **Amédée Breaux**. Stepson of **U. J. Meaux**.

BREAUX, LYON "BEBE" *Cajun.* Accordion, vocals. (Born Aug. 1, 1912, Jennings, Jeff. Davis Parish; died Dec. 4, 1992, Bell City, Calcasieu Parish.)[32] Locally renowned Cajun accordionist began playing house dances and church halls around Jennings and Hathaway area in 1930. Around 1936 relocated to Sweetlake area and continued performing in Calcasieu and Cameron parishes.

BREAUX, OPHY *Cajun.* Fiddle. (Born Mar. 22, 1908, Crowley, Louisiana; died Apr. 5, 1968, Crowley, Acadia Parish.)[33] Noted early Cajun fiddler recorded with brother **Amédée Breaux** and sister **Cléoma Breaux Falcon** in 1929 for Columbia and OKeh and with brothers **Amédée** and **Clifford Breaux** as Breaux Fréres in 1934 for Decca. Son of accordionist August Breaux.

BREAUX, PAT *Cajun, swamp pop.* Saxophone, accordion. (Born Mar. 30, 1958, Arnaudville, St. Martin Parish.) Highly accomplished multi-instrumentalist and member of renowned Breaux family of Cajun musicians. Recorded several Cajun singles with brother **Gary Breaux** on Swallow and Cajun Jamboree and later performed and recorded with numerous artists and bands, including **Bobby Charles**, **Zachary Richard**, **Warren Storm**, **Kevin Naquin**, **Rosie Ledet**, BeauSoleil, Red Beans and Rice Revue, Lil' Band O' Gold, and many others. Son of Cajun guitarist Preston Breaux, brother of **Jimmy Breaux**, and grandson of **Amédée Breaux**.

BRIDGES, EUGENE "HIDEAWAY" *Blues.* Guitar, vocals. Composer. Bandleader. (Born Mar. 30, 1963, New Orleans, Orleans Parish.) Contemporary blues guitarist and singer began playing around age five and performed in church early on. Formed teenage gospel group with brothers before relocating to Texas. Worked with various gospel groups around Houston before forming his own blues band in 1990s. Toured nationally and overseas throughout following decades and had multiple releases on Armadillo Records, including *Rock and a Hard Place* in 2011. Son of blues guitarist Othineil "Hideaway Slim" Bridges.

BRIMMER, CHARLES *Rhythm and blues.* Vocals. (Born Oct. 10, 1948, New Orleans, Orleans Parish.) Classic New Orleans deep soul singer began performing with group the Ravens in high school and recorded a single produced by **Wardell Quezergue** on ABS which sold well locally. After a stint with **David Batiste**'s Gladiators, recorded for **Dave Bartholomew**'s Broadmoor label. In the 1970s worked with producer **Senator Jones** and had minor hit with Al Green cover "The New God Blessed Our Love" on Chelsea. Made several more recordings through the early 1980s before retiring from music for several decades. Made occasional special appearances in the 2010s.

BRISCOE, BABY (Neliska Briscoe) *Jazz.* Vocals, trumpet. Bandleader. (Born Apr. 7, 1914, New Orleans, Orleans Parish; died Aug. 25, 1994, Cleveland, Ohio.)[34] Pioneering female bandleader began working as dancer in a cabaret as a young girl and became a well-known entertainer in New Orleans by her teens. Worked with **Joe Robichaux**'s New Orleans Rhythm Boys in the 1930s as tuxedo-dressed band director and also performed with Lil Armstrong. Toured country as bandleader of all-female band Harlem Play Girls in the late 1930s. Retired from music in the early 1940s.

BRISCOE, BRAZELLA *Gospel.* Vocals. Bandleader. (Born July 20, 1948, Gretna, Jefferson Parish.) Lead singer and bandleader of New Orleans's longest-running gospel group, the Zion Harmonizers, which formed in 1939 in the Zion City neighborhood. Joined group in 1987 and took over leadership in 2011 after the death of **Sherman Washington** and continued to lead group through the late 2010s.

BROOKS, JUANITA *Jazz, rhythm and blues, gospel.* Vocals. (Born Aug. 17, 1954, New Orleans, Orleans Parish; died Sept. 10, 2009, Baton Rouge, EBR Parish.) Powerful traditional jazz and gospel singer was raised in a musical family and began career performing with **Eddie Bo** in the late 1970s. In the 1980s starred in hit musicals *One Mo' Time* and *Staggerlee* and portrayed title character in *Ma Rainey's Black Bottom* in 1999. In the 1990s and 2000s toured Europe, recorded behind **Irma Thomas** and **Kermit Ruffins**, and performed regularly in local clubs with numerous artists including **George** and **Bob French**. As a leader released album *More Jazz* in 2007. Daughter of gospel musician George A. Brooks and sister of jazz musicians Mark and Detroit Brooks.

BROOKS, LONNIE/"GUITAR JR." (Lee Baker Jr.) *Blues, swamp pop.* Guitar, vocals. Composer. Bandleader. (Born Dec. 18, 1933, Dubuisson, St. Landry Parish; died Apr. 1, 2017, Chicago.) Internationally renowned Chicago blues singer-guitarist and early swamp pop musician began performing in the early 1950s after moving to Port Arthur, Texas, influenced largely by **Long John Hunter**, **Ervin Charles**, and B.B. King. After working with **Clifton Chenier** and **Lonesome Sundown**, started solo career as Guitar Jr. and in the late 1950s had several swamp pop singles on Goldband and Mercury, including regional hit "Family Rules" and "The Crawl." In 1960 relocated to Chicago and began performing and recording as Lonnie Brooks with singles on Midas, USA, Palos, and Chirrup and in 1969 recorded LP *Broke an' Hungry* for Capitol as Guitar Jr. After touring Europe in the mid-1970s, began long association with Alligator Records with LP *Bayou Lightning* in 1978. Throughout the 1980s and 1990s toured extensively and released numerous recordings on Alligator, including *Lone Star Shootout* in 1999 with Hunter and **Phillip Walker**. Remained highly popular on the blues club and festival circuit into the 2010s and continued performing into his 80s. Father of Chicago blues guitarists Ronnie Baker and Wayne Baker Brooks.

BROTHER CORNBREAD *See* Thomas, Joseph.

BROTHER RANDOLPH *See* Randolph, Percy.

BROTHER TYRONE (Tyrone Anthony Pollard) *Rhythm and blues.* Vocals. Composer. Bandleader. (Born Feb. 21, 1957, New Orleans, Orleans Parish.) Deep soul and blues vocalist began singing at age eight, inspired by James Brown. Started performing in New Orleans clubs in his teens and worked with various bands throughout the 1980s. Made several recordings starting in 1999, including critically acclaimed *Mindbender* in 2008.

BROUSSARD, AL *Jazz, blues.* Piano, vocals. (Born Apr. 30, 1906, New Orleans, Orleans Parish; died Aug. 4, 2001, New Orleans, Orleans Parish.) Beloved longtime New Orleans piano player and singer began playing piano at age five and started working professionally in the early 1920s performing at house parties. Led his own orchestra in the mid-1920s but mainly performed as a soloist in taverns and clubs in the French Quarter. Recorded LP *The Music of a Lifetime* in 1984 and held a long-running gig at the 711 Club (later Tricou House) on Bourbon Street until his death at age 95.

BROUSSARD, ALDUS "POPEYE" *Cajun.* Fiddle, vocals. (Born Sept. 6, 1908, Rayne, Acadia Parish; died Jan. 6, 1967, Rayne, Acadia Parish.) Early Cajun fiddle player and singer performed with **Lawrence Walker** and **Cleveland Mire** in the 1930s. In the mid-1940s joined **Aldus Roger**'s Lafayette Playboys and recorded and performed with group through 1950s. Also recorded with **Lee Sonnier** for Fais-Do-Do in late 1940s and released single "Hole in the Wall" on Folk-Star/Goldband in 1956.

BROUSSARD, ALEX *Cajun.* Guitar, banjo, vocals. Composer. (Born Aug. 19, 1926, Maurice, Vermilion Parish; died Nov. 2, 2010, Alexandria, Rapides Parish.) Locally popular Lafayette-area Cajun guitarist and singer-songwriter best known for his regional hit single "La Sud de la Louisianne" on La Louisianne in 1959. Also recorded and performed with **Happy Fats** in the Bayou Buckaroos in the 1950s and early 1960s as well as appearing with Happy Fats on radio broadcasts and weekly television program *The Mariné Show* in Lafayette. Recorded LP *Cajun & Country Songs* with Happy Fats for Swallow in 1964.

BROUSSARD, ALLEN "CAT ROY" *Zydeco.* Saxophone. (Born Jan. 3, 1943, Carencro, Lafayette Parish; died Oct. 31, 2006, Scott, Lafayette Parish.) Noted zydeco saxophonist best known as longtime member of **Nathan Williams**'s Zydeco Cha Chas from the 1990s through early 2000s. Recorded single "Two For One"/"Lovely Lady" as Cat Roy on Blues Unlimited in 1984. In the 1970s worked with **Little Bob** and the Lollipops and performed and recorded with **Fernest Arceneaux**, **Morris Francis**, and **J. J. Caillier** in the 1980s.

BROUSSARD, AUGUST *Cajun.* Accordion, guitar, steel guitar, fiddle, harmonica, vocals. Composer. Bandleader. (Born Aug. 3, 1946, Westlake, Calcasieu Parish.) Lake Charles–area Cajun accordionist and singer-songwriter began performing at house parties around Lake Arthur at age 20, inspired by his cousin **Leroy Broussard**. Within several years began performing with **Tan Benoit** after filling in for him on several gigs. In the early 1970s formed Calcasieu Ramblers and led group for several decades, cutting several singles for Swallow, including "Hardship Waltz." Also performed with **John Oliver**, **Bobby Leger**, and Hicks Wagon Wheel Ramblers, and in the 1990s and 2000s performed and recorded with **Lionel Cormier** and the Sundown Playboys. Continued performing through the late 2010s.

BROUSSARD, CLINTON *Zydeco.* Accordion, guitar, vocals. Bandleader. (Born Sept. 13, 1952, Arnaudville, St. Martin Parish.) Noted zydeco accordionist began playing at age eight, mentored by his father, **Delton Broussard**. From the mid-1960s through late 1970s performed and recorded with his father in Lawtell Playboys and led his own band the Zydeco Machines from 1979 to 1985. Also worked with **Marcel Dugas** and **Lil' Buck Sinegal**. In 2011 recorded self-titled EP for APO. Oldest brother of **Jeffery** and **Shelton Broussard**.

BROUSSARD, DELTON *Creole, zydeco.* Accordion, vocals. Composer. Bandleader. (Born Sept. 24, 1927, Arnaudville, St. Martin Parish; died Apr. 20, 1994, Sunset, St. Landry Parish.) Renowned Creole accordionist and bandleader who took over leadership of the famed Lawtell Playboys in the 1970s, and patriarch of noted zydeco family with sons **Clinton**, **Jeffery**, and **Shelton Broussard**. Learned accordion in his youth from **Eraste Carrière** and in the mid-1960s joined Carrière's band the Lawtell Playboys. In the 1970s began leading band with recordings on Swallow, Rounder, and Maison de Soul through 1976.

BROUSSARD, GRACE *Swamp pop.* Vocals. Bandleader. (Born Feb. 5, 1939, Prairieville, Ascension Parish.) Acclaimed swamp pop singer best known for her 1963 hit "I'm Leaving It Up to You" as part of duo Dale & Grace. Began singing with brother **Van Broussard** while in her mid-teens around Baton Rouge area and recorded for Montel in the early 1960s. In 1963 teamed up with singer Dale Houston and had number-one hit with "I'm Leaving It Up to You" and toured nationally. After several more singles on Montel and Hanna-Barbera, including the 1964 hit "Stop and Think It Over," split with Houston in 1965. Recorded several singles with Van in the late 1960s and 1970s and briefly reunited with Houston in the mid-1990s. Continued to perform with Van and as solo artist at swamp pop reunions and festivals in the 2010s.

BROUSSARD, JEFFERY *Zydeco.* Accordion, fiddle, drums, guitar, bass, vocals. Composer. Bandleader. (Born Mar. 10, 1967, Lafayette, Lafayette Parish.) Renowned zydeco accordion player and bandleader known for his work as cofounder of highly influential contemporary zydeco band Zydeco Force in the late 1980s, which included brother **Shelton Broussard**. Began playing drums in his father **Delton Broussard**'s band the Lawtell Playboys at age eight and with brother **Clinton Broussard**'s band in his teens. In the 1980s started playing accordion, inspired by his father and **Boozoo Chavis**. Cofounded Zydeco Force in the late 1980s with **Robby**

"Mann" Robinson and through the mid-2000s released numerous acclaimed recordings on Maison de Soul. In the late 2000s launched solo career with his band the Creole Cowboys and released two recordings on Maison de Soul, including *Keeping the Tradition Alive!* in 2011.

BROUSSARD, JULES *Jazz, rhythm and blues.* Saxophone. Composer. Bandleader. (Born Mar. 21, 1937, Marksville, Avoy. Parish.) Highly accomplished jazz saxophonist began playing at age 12, inspired by Louis Jordan and his musician uncle. Formed first band at age 16 and performed in clubs around Alexandria. After a stint in the Air Force, settled in California Bay Area in 1960 and began performing on local music scene. In the 1960s and 1970s worked with Ray Charles, Alice Coltrane, Carlos Santana, Johnny Otis, and others, and led house band at popular Bay Area nightclub Sweetwater for seven years. Known for his extroverted playing style, continued leading his own band into the 2010s with several releases as a leader, including *With Strings Attached* in 2007.

BROUSSARD, LAURA *Cajun.* Vocals. Composer. (Born Aug. 19, 1923, Rayne, Acadia Parish; died May 24, 1989, Duson, Lafayette Parish.) Early postwar Cajun singer who was among the first female Cajun recording artists after **Cléoma Breaux Falcon**. Performed with **Lee Sonnier**'s Acadian All Stars in the late 1940s and 1950s and appeared as vocalist on her composition "War Widow Waltz" with Sonnier for Fais-Do-Do in 1950, which became producer **J. D. Miller**'s first big-selling release.

BROUSSARD, LEROY *Cajun.* Accordion, vocals. Composer. Bandleader. (Born June 8, 1921, Rayne, Acadia Parish; died Nov. 5, 1991, Carencro, Lafayette Parish.) Influential early Cajun accordionist and singer-songwriter began playing at age eight and by age 15 was performing in local bands in Winnie, Texas, where his family had relocated. Returned to Louisiana in the early 1940s and performed with **Pee Wee Broussard**'s Melody Boys. In the 1950s performed and recorded with **Cleveland Crochet** and recorded several sides as a leader in 1957 for Goldband, including "Lemonade Song," "B.O. Sparkle Waltz," and "Café Chaud." In the early 1960s recorded single "Brasse Dons le Cush Cush Cush" on La Louisianne. Formed the Lagniappe Gang in the late 1970s and recorded self-titled LP on Kajun in 1983. Continued performing in Lafayette area until a few days before his death at age 70. Cousin of **August Broussard**.

BROUSSARD, MARC *Rhythm and blues.* Guitar, vocals. Composer. Bandleader. (Born Jan. 14, 1982, Carencro, Lafayette Parish.) Noted blue-eyed soul singer-songwriter began performing in the early 2000s with local Christian band before recording debut CD *Momentary Setback* on Ripley in 2002. In 2004 released major-label debut *Carencro* on Island and had minor hits with "Where You Are" and "Home." Began touring extensively and through the mid-2010s had multiple releases on Vanguard and Atlantic, including *A Life Worth Living* in 2014. Continued performing nationally and abroad in the late 2010s with several releases on G-Man, including *Easy to Love* in 2017. Son of Boogie Kings guitarist Ted Broussard.

BROUSSARD, MARY JANE *Creole.* Accordion, vocals. Composer. Bandleader. (Born Aug. 23, 1942, Duralde, Evangeline Parish.) One of the genre's few female practitioners, noted Creole accordionist and singer began learning the instrument in the 1970s, mentored by her uncle **Bois Sec Ardoin**. In the late 1970s cofounded Magnolia Sisters with **Ann Savoy** and Jeanie McLerie. Continued performing based in Jennings area, and in the 1990s and 2000s performed often with son Bryant Keith's (**T-Broussard**) band Zydeco Steppers. In the early 2010s formed band Sweet La La and released debut CD *Creole Royalty* in 2011. Niece of **Carlton Frank**.

BROUSSARD, PEE WEE (Chester Isaac Broussard) *Cajun.* Accordion, fiddle, guitar, vocals. Composer. Bandleader. (Born Nov. 12, 1920, Breaux Bridge, St. Martin Parish; died Mar. 23, 2014, Maurice, Lafayette Parish.)[35] Highly regarded early postwar Cajun recording artist began playing accordion at house dances in his early teens. In the early 1950s recorded several sides with his band the Melody Boys for Feature, notably "The Pee Wee Special," and in the late 1950s and early 1960s had singles on Khoury's and La Louisianne. Also worked with various Cajun bands, including with **Cleveland Crochet**, **Leeman Prejean**, and **Aldus Roger**, and recorded singles for Bee. Father Sosthene and brothers Jules and Jim were also Cajun musicians.

BROUSSARD, SAM *Cajun, Americana, swamp pop.* Guitar, vocals. Composer. (Born Aug. 17, 1951, Lafayette, Lafayette Parish.) Renowned guitarist and singer-songwriter began performing in 1970 and throughout following decades worked and recorded with numerous artists, including **Bobby Charles**, Linda Ronstadt, Michael Martin Murphey, **Sonny Landreth**, and James McMurtry. In the 2000s and 2010s toured and recorded as member of **Steve Riley**'s Mamou Playboys and Lil' Band O' Gold as well as performing as solo artist, releasing two albums as leader, *Geeks* and *Veins*. Continued performing in the late 2010s and recorded acclaimed CD *Broken Promised Land* for Swallow with Cajun folklorist Dr. Barry Jean Ancelet in 2016.

BROUSSARD, SHELTON *Zydeco.* Guitar. (Born Sept. 14, 1962, Lafayette, Lafayette Parish; died Nov. 6, 2012, Opelousas, St. Landry Parish.) Noted zydeco guitarist who was a founding member of Zydeco Force and performed and recorded with group from the late 1980s through mid-2000s. In the 1970s performed and recorded with his father **Delton Broussard** in the Lawtell Playboys. Died in a house fire at age 50. Brother of **Clinton** and **Jeffery Broussard**.

BROUSSARD, SIDNEY, SR. *Cajun.* Fiddle. (Born Sept. 4, 1892, Welsh, Jeff. Davis Parish; died Sept. 28, 1946, Lake Arthur, Calcasieu Parish.)[36] Early Cajun fiddler and patriarch of revered Lake Arthur family of musicians which included son Sidney Jr. (1916–1986) on guitar and vocals, daughters Lena Mae (1912–1999) and Evelyn (1924–2003) on vocals and triangle, and brother-in-law Theogene Broussard (1890–1980) on accordion. Performed at local house dances and dance halls throughout the 1930s and early 1940s and appeared at the 1936 National Folk Festival in Dallas as the Acadian Band with **Lawrence Walker** and at the 1937 National Folk Festival in Chicago.

BROUSSARD, TROY LEE *Blues.* Guitar. Composer. Bandleader. (Born June 18, 1940, Lake Providence, E. Carroll Parish.) Arkansas-based blues guitarist began performing with swing bands throughout Louisiana and Mississippi while in his teens. In the early 1960s worked and recorded with Willie Cobbs and toured with Earl Hooker. Continued performing with his own bands for several years and recorded with the Soul Superiors with Sherman Willis around 1970. Later was a member of John Weston's band Blues Force and appeared on three of his releases in the 1990s.

BROUSSARD, VAN *Swamp pop.* Guitar, vocals. Composer. Bandleader. (Born Mar. 29, 1937, Prairieville, Ascension Parish.) Popular early swamp pop singer and guitarist best known for his regional hits "Feed the Flame" and "Lord I Need Somebody Bad Tonight." As a teenager began playing with a local Dixieland jazz group and formed his first band, the Hearts, in 1954 playing current rhythm and blues hits. Performed around Baton Rouge area, often with sister **Grace Broussard**, and released debut single "I Can't Complain" on Rex in 1961. Throughout the 1960s and 1970s had releases on Montel, Heartco, Mala, Red Stick, International City, Bayou Boogie, and other labels. Also released singles with sister as Van and Grace. In the early 1990s began recording for CSP Records and had numerous releases, including *The Final Curtain* in 2014. Continued to perform with his band Bayou Boogie and occasionally with sister Grace in 2010s.

BROWN, CLARENCE "GATEMOUTH" *Blues, jazz, country.* Guitar, fiddle, drums, mandolin, harmonica, vocals. Composer. Bandleader. (Born Apr. 18, 1924, Vinton, Calcasieu Parish; died Sept. 10, 2005, Orange, Texas.) Internationally renowned blues singer, songwriter, and master multi-instrumentalist whose idiosyncratic and innovative guitar style influenced several generations of blues and rock musicians such as **Guitar Slim**, Albert Collins, and Johnny "Guitar" Watson. Raised in Orange, Texas, after family relocated from Vinton, learned fiddle as a child from his musician father and soon began playing drums and guitar, inspired early on by T-Bone Walker, Louis Jordan, and Count Basie. In the mid-1940s worked as drummer with several touring bands before settling in Houston. While filling in for an ailing Walker in 1947 he was discovered by label and club owner Don Robey. After two singles on Aladdin, signed with Robey's Peacock label in 1949 and through 1961 cut numerous singles including "My Time is Expensive," "Dirty Work at the Crossroads," and his signature instrumental "Okie Dokie Stomp." Throughout the 1960s recorded for several small labels and led house band on Nashville's syndicated black music television show *The !!!! Beat* in 1966. In the 1970s and 1980s toured extensively nationally and overseas with numerous releases on domestic and European labels, including highly acclaimed LPs *Makin' Music* on MCA in 1979 with country star Roy Clark and *Alright Again!* on Rounder in 1981. Continued touring internationally through the mid-2000s with releases on Alligator and Verve, including *American Music, Texas Style* in 1999. Succumbed to cancer shortly after evacuating to Orange from his Slidell home just prior to Hurricane Katrina. Brother of blues musicians Bobby (1935–) and James "Widemouth" Brown (1930–1971).

BROWN, CLARENCE "JUNIE BOY"/"MULE" *Rhythm and blues.* Drums. (Born June 10, 1940, New Orleans, Orleans Parish; died Apr. 9, 2003, New Orleans, Orleans Parish.)[37] Longtime drummer for **Fats Domino** for three decades and also worked and recorded with **Chris Ken-**

ner, **Roy Montrell**, **Allen Toussaint**, and **Willie Tee**, among others. Retired in the early 1990s due to health reasons.

BROWN, ELGIE *Blues.* Saxophone, vocals. Composer. (Born Feb. 14, 1938, Bossier City, Bossier Parish.) Noted Shreveport saxophonist began playing during his teens and in the 1950s and early 1960s performed with Bobby Bland and Junior Parker and toured with Rosco Gordon and Freddie King. Recorded several sides for **Mira Smith**'s RAM label as a leader with **Banny Price**, including "Let Me Feel It." Also backed Price on recordings for Jewel in the mid-1960s.

BROWN, KERRY *Rhythm and blues, jazz.* Drums, piano. (Born Aug. 12, 1954, New Orleans, Orleans Parish.) Inspired by **Earl Palmer**, veteran blues and jazz drummer began performing in church as a child and started professional career touring regularly with **Clarence "Gatemouth" Brown** in the 1970s. Throughout following decades worked and/or recorded with dozens of jazz and blues musicians, including **Champion Jack Dupree**, **Danny Barker**, **Ironing Board Sam**, Freddie King, Koko Taylor, **Little Freddie King**, and Albert King, as well as with Tuxedo, Olympia, and Tremé brass bands. In the 2010s continued to perform regularly including at Preservation Hall.

BROWN, RICHARD "RABBIT" *Blues.* Guitar, vocals. Composer. (Born around 1880, possibly in or near New Orleans, Orleans Parish; died around 1937, possibly New Orleans, Orleans Parish.) Influential but enigmatic early prewar blues guitarist and songster who lived and performed around New Orleans's notorious Battlefield area. Performed on street corners and in local taverns throughout the early decades of the 1900s, occasionally with **Papa Lemon Nash**, and is widely regarded as among the first to employ a twelve-bar blues pattern. Known for his compositions about local and national news and events such as "Sinking of the Titanic." Recorded six sides for Victor in 1927, including "James Alley Blues" which referenced Battlefield's Jane Alley. Possibly recorded two gospel sides as "Blind Willie Harris" in 1929 on Vocalion, but remains unconfirmed.

BROWN, ROY *Rhythm and blues.* Vocals, piano. Composer. Bandleader. (Born Sept. 10, 1920, Kinder, Allen Parish; died May 25, 1981, Los Angeles.)[38] Highly influential rhythm and blues pioneer best known for his 1947 landmark recording "Good Rocking Tonight," which is regarded as one of the first rock and roll records. His gospel-drenched melismatic vocal style influenced countless singers, including B.B. King, Bobby Bland, Elvis Presley, James Brown, Junior Parker, Nappy Brown, Little Richard, and many others. Began singing in church as a child and in his teens formed a gospel group and began writing songs. In the early 1940s worked as a professional boxer in Los Angeles before winning local talent contest which eventually led to engagements in Galveston and Shreveport in the mid-1940s. After a single on Gold Star, had national hit in 1948 with "Good Rocking Tonight" on Deluxe, which would be covered by countless artists. Recorded prolifically for Deluxe through 1951 and had more than a dozen hits, including "Rockin' at Midnight," "Hard Luck Blues," "'Long about Midnight," "Cadillac Baby," and "Miss Fanny Brown." Continued touring extensively with his band the Mighty Men and from 1952 to 1960 recorded numerous sides for King and Imperial, working with producer **Dave Bartholomew** while with Imperial and which produced 1957 hit "Let the Four Winds Blow." After several singles on Home of the Blues in the early 1960s, settled in Los Angeles and worked outside music throughout much of decade with occasional singles on local labels. Enjoyed career resurgence in the 1970s with several album releases, appearances at major festivals, and two European tours.

BROWN, SIDNEY *Cajun.* Accordion. Composer. Bandleader. (Born Oct. 28, 1906, Church Point, Acadia Parish; died Aug. 6, 1981, Lake Charles, Calcasieu Parish.) Early postwar Cajun accordionist and bandleader and renowned pioneer Cajun accordion maker. Began playing accordion as a child and by his early teens was playing local house dances. Relocated to Lake Charles in the 1940s and in late 1940s formed the Traveler Playboys. In the mid- to late 1950s recorded numerous singles on Goldband, including "Highball Two Step," "Traveler Playboy Special," and "Pestauche ah Tante Nana." Retired from performing due to health issues in 1963 but continued building accordions, regarded as the first and possibly finest accordion maker from Louisiana. Not to be confused with jazz musician **Sidney "Jim Little" Brown**.

BROWN, SIDNEY "JIM LITTLE"/"LITTLE JIM" *Jazz.* Bass, tuba, violin. (Born July 19, 1894, Deer Range, Plaquemines Parish; died Nov. 8, 1968, New Orleans, Orleans Parish.) Early New Orleans jazz multi-instrumentalist moved with family to New Orleans in 1912 and began playing with **Sam Morgan**'s band as violinist in 1916. Learned bass in France during World War

I and in the 1920s worked as bassist with **Isaiah Morgan**'s band and later Sam Morgan's Jazz Band through the early 1930s, recording with group in 1927 for Columbia. In 1940s recorded with **Bunk Johnson** and **George Lewis** and performed and recorded with **Papa Celestin**'s Tuxedo Brass Band through the early 1950s. Nephew of **Big Jim Robinson**. Not to be confused with Cajun musician **Sidney Brown**.

BROWN, STEVE (Theodore Brown) *Jazz.* Bass, tuba. (Born Jan. 13, 1890, New Orleans, Orleans Parish; died Sept. 15, 1965, Detroit.)[39] An early practitioner of the upright slap-bass style, began performing with **Papa Jack Laine** before joining brother **Tom "Red" Brown**'s band in the early 1910s. In the early 1920s worked and recorded with New Orleans Rhythm Kings and Jean Goldkette Orchestra in Chicago and developed influential percussive upright bass style later known as slap bass. Settled in Detroit in 1930 and continued performing into the 1950s.

BROWN, TOM "RED" *Jazz.* Trombone, bass. Bandleader. (Born June 3, 1888, New Orleans, Orleans Parish; died Mar. 25, 1958, New Orleans, Orleans Parish.) Began performing with **Papa Jack Laine**'s Reliance Brass Band in the early 1900s. Around 1910 formed Brown's Ragtime Band, followed by Tom Brown's Band from Dixieland, which performed in Chicago in 1915, among the first New Orleans bands to do so. Soon began advertising as Brown's Dixieland Jass Band, being among the first to use the term "jass" publicly. Continued performing in Chicago and New York before returning to New Orleans to record with **Johnny Bayersdorffer**. Worked with various bands throughout the next several decades and recorded as a leader in the mid-1950s. Older brother of **Steve Brown**.

BROWNLEE, NORMAN *Jazz.* Piano, string bass. (Born Feb. 7, 1896, Algiers, New Orleans, Orleans Parish; died Apr. 9, 1967, Pensacola, Florida.) Noted New Orleans jazz bandleader and musician led his orchestra from 1920 to 1930. Recorded two sides as leader in 1925 for OKeh. Relocated to Pensacola in the early 1930s and served as president of local musicians' union.

BRUCE, VIN (Ervin Bruce) *Cajun.* Guitar, vocals. Composer. Bandleader. (Born Apr. 25, 1932, Cut Off, Lafourche Parish; died June 8, 2018, Cut Off, Lafourche Parish.) Popular Cajun-country singer and songwriter who was among the first Cajun artists to receive national attention and one of the first Cajun musicians to appear on the *Grand Ole Opry* and *Louisiana Hayride*. Began playing guitar at age 10 and by age 14 was performing with local bands. After being discovered while a member of **Gene Rodrigue**'s band, made recording debut in 1951 for Columbia and through 1956 had several major hits, including "Dans La Louisianne." In the early 1960s recorded for Swallow and had hit with "Jole Blon," produced by **Leroy Martin** and featuring **Doc Guidry** and **Harry Anselmi**. Known as the "King of the Cajun Singers," continued to perform and release recordings on Swallow, La Louisianne, Cajun Sound, Mardi Gras, and Louisiana Red Hot Records through 2000s, and made occasional appearances in the 2010s.

BRUNIES, ALBERT "ABBIE" *Jazz.* Cornet. Bandleader. (Born Jan. 19, 1900, New Orleans, Orleans Parish; died Oct. 2, 1978, Biloxi, Mississippi.) Member of noted early jazz family which included brothers **George**, **Henry**, and **Merritt**. Led Halfway House Orchestra from 1919 to 1927 which recorded for OKeh in 1925. Performed with various brass bands before relocating to Biloxi in the mid-1940s and working with Brunies Brothers Dixieland Jazz Band with brother Merritt through the 1960s.

BRUNIES, GEORGE *Jazz.* Trombone. (Born Feb. 6, 1902, New Orleans, Orleans Parish; died Nov. 19, 1974, Chicago.) Influential early trombonist began playing at age eight in **Papa Jack Laine**'s Reliance Brass Band before joining brother **Abbie Brunies**'s Halfway House Orchestra. In 1919 traveled to Chicago with **Ragbaby Stephens**'s band and worked and recorded in 1920s with New Orleans Rhythm Kings where his tailgate style was greatly influential. Worked with Ted Lewis, **Louis Prima**, Muggsy Spanier, and others through the late 1940s and continued performing through the early 1970s. Brother of **Henry** and **Merritt Brunies**.

BRUNIES, HENRY "HENNY" *Jazz.* Trombone. Composer (Born Oct. 19, 1891, New Orleans, Orleans Parish; died Dec. 11, 1932, New Orleans, Orleans Parish.)[40] Second oldest brother of the prominent early jazz family. Was considered by brother **George Brunies** as best musician of family. Worked with various brass bands in New Orleans and toured Mississippi Gulf Coast and California with brother **Merritt Brunies**'s Five Jazz Babies in the early 1920s. In the mid-1920s worked and recorded with Merritt's Friars Inn Orchestra in Chicago, billed as "world's greatest jazz trombonist."

BRUNIES, MERRITT *Jazz.* Cornet, trombone. Bandleader. (Born Dec. 25, 1895, New Orleans, Orleans Parish;

died Feb. 5, 1973, Biloxi, Mississippi.)[41] Began playing in family band and went on to lead Original New Orleans Jazz Band in New Orleans and Chicago from 1916 to 1918. In the early 1920s formed Merritt Brunies and His Five Jazz Babies and toured California and Mississippi Gulf Coast with brother **Henry Brunies**. From 1924 to 1926 led and recorded with Friars Inn Orchestra. After a brief return to New Orleans in the late 1920s, settled in Biloxi and later formed Brunies Brothers Dixieland Jazz Band with brother **Abbie Brunies**.

BRUNIOUS, JOHN, JR. *Jazz.* Trumpet, vocals. (Born Oct. 12, 1940, New Orleans, Orleans Parish; died Feb. 12, 2008, Casselberry, Florida.) Inspired by father **John "Pickey" Brunious Sr.**, Dizzy Gillespie, and Maynard Ferguson, traditional jazz trumpeter initially played bebop and performed with rhythm and blues bands early in his career. Joined Preservation Hall in 1987 and performed there for two decades. Displaced by Hurricane Katrina, spent remaining years in Florida as flood-related illnesses delayed a comeback. Older brother of **Wendell Brunious**.

BRUNIOUS, JOHN "PICKEY," SR. *Jazz.* Trumpet, piano, vocals. Composer. Bandleader. (Born Oct. 17, 1920, New Orleans, Orleans Parish; died May 7, 1976, New Orleans, Orleans Parish.) Father of **John Jr.** and **Wendell Brunious**, studied at Juilliard in the mid-1930s and subsequently worked with Billy Eckstine, Cab Calloway (also as composer and arranger), and Jay McShann through the 1940s. Recorded with **Paul Barbarin**, Young Tuxedo Brass Band, and others in following decades.

BRUNIOUS, WENDELL *Jazz.* Trumpet, flugelhorn, vocals. Composer. Bandleader. (Born Oct. 27, 1954, New Orleans, Orleans Parish.) Youngest son of **John "Pickey" Brunious Sr.**, began playing trumpet at age 11, inspired by his father. Performed with rhythm and blues and dance bands in the late 1960s and early 1970s. Worked with **Albert "Papa" French**, Lionel Hampton, **Louis Hall Nelson**, and **Kid Thomas** regularly at Preservation Hall. Assumed leadership of Valentine's band after his death in 1987. Made recording debut as leader in 1986 and continued appearing at Preservation Hall into the 2000s before relocating to Sweden for seven years. Returned to live and perform in New Orleans in the early 2010s. Younger brother of **John Brunious Jr.**

BUCKWHEAT ZYDECO (Stanley Joseph Dural Jr.) *Zydeco, rhythm and blues.* Accordion, piano, organ, vocals. Composer. Bandleader. (Born Nov. 14, 1947, Lafayette, Lafayette Parish; died Sept. 24, 2016, Lafayette, Lafayette Parish.) Internationally renowned zydeco accordionist and bandleader who incorporated elements of blues, funk, and rock and became the most popular zydeco artist for three decades. Son of a Creole accordion player, began playing piano as a child and in the 1960s toured as organist with **Little Buck Sinegal**, **Clarence "Gatemouth" Brown**, Little Richard, Barbara Lynn, and others. In 1971 formed 15-piece soul and funk band Buckwheat and the Hitchhikers and performed throughout Lafayette area for several years. From 1975 to 1977 toured extensively as organist with **Clifton Chenier** before taking a year off to learn accordion. In the late 1970s formed Buckwheat Zydeco's Ils Sont Partis Band and through 1983 recorded several LPs for Blues Unlimited, including *One for the Road.* In following years released LPs on Black Top and Rounder, notably *Turning Point* and *Waitin' for My Ya Ya,* before signing with Island and becoming first zydeco artist on a major label. In 1987 released acclaimed label debut *On a Night Like This* and began touring extensively nationally and overseas. After several more releases on Island as well as albums on Charisma, Music for Little People, Mesa, and his own Tomorrow label, released award-winning *Lay Your Burdon Down* on Alligator in 2009. Despite suffering from serious health issues in later years, continued performing into the mid-2010s with support from son **Reggie Dural** until losing battle with cancer at age 68.

BURBANK, ALBERT *Jazz.* Clarinet, vocals. (Born Mar. 25, 1902, New Orleans, Orleans Parish; died Aug. 15, 1976, New Orleans, Orleans Parish.) Regarded as among the upper tier of New Orleans clarinetists. Studied with **Big Eye Louis Nelson** and began performing around New Orleans in the 1920s with **Chris Kelly**, **Buddy Petit**, **Punch Miller**, and others. After World War II worked with Eureka Brass Band and **De De Pierce** and recorded with **Paul Barbarin**, **Kid Clayton**, and **Wooden Joe Nicholas**. Toured California in the mid-1950s and worked with **Octave Crosby** and **Kid Ory** and performed and recorded with **Kid Thomas** in the 1960s and early 1970s, appearing regularly at Preservation Hall. In 1973 worked briefly with **Percy Humphrey** until illness forced retirement.

BURKE, RAYMOND *Jazz.* Clarinet, saxophone. Bandleader. (Born June 6, 1904, New Orleans, Orleans Parish; died Mar. 21, 1986, New Orleans, Orleans Parish.) Began playing homemade instruments at age nine and started learning clarinet at age 16. Worked with various groups throughout the 1930s and led bands in the late 1940s and early 1950s which included **Wooden Joe Nicholas** and **Johnny Wiggs**. Recorded with his Speakeasy Boys in the late 1930s and 1940s and also worked with **Sharkey Bonano**, **Johnny St. Cyr**, and others. Regularly performed at Preservation Hall for 20 years starting with its inception in 1961.

BURNS, WAYNE "BLUE" *Blues, zydeco.* Guitar, bass, trombone, vocals. Bandleader. (Born Aug. 11, 1947, Jeanerette, Iberia Parish.) Highly accomplished zydeco bassist began playing guitar as a child but switched to bass and trombone to work with **Lonesome Sundown** and **Jay Nelson** during his teens. In the late 1960s performed and recorded as trombonist with **Little Buck Sinegal**'s Top Cats but returned to bass to join Stanley Dural's (**Buckwheat Zydeco**) group in the early 1970s. Also led his own band the Invaders as singer-guitarist in the late 1960s. Throughout the next several decades recorded and toured internationally as zydeco bassist with **Clifton Chenier**, **Fernest Arceneaux**, **C. J. Chenier**, **Nathan Williams**, **Lynn August**, and many others. In the early 2010s began leading his blues trio as singer-guitarist in the Lafayette area. Cousin of jazz trumpeter Cootie Williams.

BURRELL, ALEXANDER "DUKE" *Rhythm and blues, jazz.* Piano, vocals. Composer. Bandleader. (Born July 9, 1920, New Orleans, Orleans Parish; died Aug. 5, 1993, Los Angeles.) Led his French Quarter Trio around New Orleans in the late 1940s and did session work for Mercury behind **Theard Johnson**, **Little Joe Gaines**, and others. Relocated to Hawaii in 1950 and worked local clubs before returning to New Orleans. Eventually settled in Los Angeles in 1963 and formed Louisiana Shakers Band in 1974, which recorded and toured the United States and Europe. Also recorded with Louis Jordan's Tympany Five and **Barney Bigard**'s Pelican Trio in the 1970s.

BURTON, JAMES *Rockabilly, rock and roll, country.* Guitar. Composer. (Born Aug. 21, 1939, Dubberly, Webster Parish.) Highly influential and accomplished early rockabilly guitar player best known for his work with Elvis Presley, **Dale Hawkins**, and Ricky Nelson. Raised in Shreveport, began playing guitar as a child and by age 14 was playing professionally on the *Louisiana Hayride.* Following year began recording extensively as session guitarist for **Mira Smith**'s RAM Records and performing with various bands around Shreveport. In 1957 appeared on Hawkins's rockabilly classic "Susie-Q." After touring and recording with Bob Luman in the late 1950s, relocated to Hollywood and performed and recorded with Ricky Nelson's band through 1965. Continued working as in-demand session musician in Los Angeles, appearing on hundreds of recordings. In 1969 joined Presley's band and performed and recorded with band until Presley's death in 1977. Continued recording and touring extensively in the 1980s with numerous artists, including Johnny Cash, **Jerry Lee Lewis**, John Denver, Elvis Costello, and Roy Orbison. Returned to Shreveport in 1990 and continued performing and recording into the 2010s, having appeared on more than 350 albums throughout career.

BUSH, CHUCK *Zydeco.* Bass, guitar, vocals. (Born Mar. 13, 1958, Lafayette, Lafayette Parish.) Renowned zydeco bass player best known for his influential work as member of **Beau Jocque**'s Zydeco Hi-Rollers. Raised in Rosa, learned guitar and bass as a child and performed as guitarist in various local rhythm and blues bands through the early 1990s, including his own group Flashback. Joined Beau Jocque's band in 1992 as guitarist before quickly switching to bass. Influenced by **Classie Ballou Jr.**, he was among the first to incorporate heavy funk bass lines in zydeco and which greatly shaped Beau Jocque's sound. After Beau Jocque's death in 1999, continued performing and recording with numerous zydeco artists including **Chubby Carrier**, **Geno Delafose**, **Rosie Ledet**, André Thierry, and **Terry Domingue**.

BUTERA, SAM *Jazz, rhythm and blues.* Saxophone, vocals. Composer. Bandleader. (Born Aug. 17, 1927, New Orleans, Orleans Parish; died June 3, 2009, Las Vegas.) Highly talented saxophonist best known for his raucous performances during his very successful twenty-year collaboration with **Louis Prima**. Began playing saxophone at age seven and during his mid-teens worked with bands in strip clubs along Bourbon Street. In the late 1940s toured with Tommy Dorsey and **Paul Gayten**. Relocated to Las Vegas in 1954 to become saxophonist and arranger in Prima's band, gaining international fame as member of the Witnesses and performing and recording extensively with Prima throughout following 20 years. After Prima's death in the late 1970s worked with Frank Sinatra, Sammy Davis Jr., and many others. Recorded as leader throughout his career and led his popular band the Wildest in Las Vegas and other cities throughout the swing revival of the 1990s. Retired from music due to poor health in the mid-2000s.

BUTLER, HENRY *Jazz, blues.* Piano, trombone, drums, vocals. Composer. Bandleader. (Born Sept. 21, 1948, New Orleans, Orleans Parish; died July 2, 2018, New York City.) Blinded from glaucoma since infancy, internationally renowned New Orleans rhythm and blues pianist began playing at age six and by age 12 was composing and playing professionally, influenced by local piano greats **Professor Longhair**, **Tuts Washington**, and **James Booker** as well as classical composers. After graduating college taught music and performed locally. Gained national acclaim in the late 1980s with release of recording debut *Fivin' Around.* Continued to record and perform in the United States and abroad throughout following decades, regarded as among the finest exponents of the New Orleans piano tradition. Based in Colorado and then New York in years following his evacuation during Hurricane Katrina in 2005, he continued to perform until weeks before his death from cancer at age 68.

BUTLER, JOSEPH "KID TWAT" *Jazz.* String bass, piano, vocals. Composer. (Born Dec. 26, 1905, Algiers, Orleans Parish; died June 19, 1982, New Orleans, Orleans Parish.) Traditional New Orleans jazz bassist best known for his later work with **Kid Thomas** and his numerous appearances at Preservation Hall. Began performing in his teens, often with childhood friend **Red Allen**. Early on worked in bands of **Armand Piron**, **Sidney Desvigne**, and **Papa Celestin**. In the 1960s and 1970s worked and recorded regularly with Kid Thomas's Algiers Stompers. Also recorded with **Billie** and **De De Pierce**. Performed at Preservation Hall throughout the 1960s and 1970s with Kid Thomas, **Sweet Emma Barrett**, and others.

BYRD, ROY *See* Professor Longhair.

C

CAESAR, SISTER PENOLA *Gospel.* Vocals. (Born Oct. 8, 1943, Thatcher Plantation, Philip, Ouachita Parish; died Oct. 14, 2006, Monroe, Ouachita Parish.) Noted gospel singer and advocate who gave workshops teaching older traditional gospel songs and hymns of the African American Baptist church. Released album *Old Timers Church Songs Featuring Penola Caesar* which was recorded live at Piney Grove Baptist Church in West Monroe in 2004.

CAFFREY, ROBERT "CATMAN" *Rhythm and blues.* Saxophone. (Born Feb. 4, 1925, New Orleans, Orleans Parish; died Jan. 2, 2002, New Orleans, Orleans Parish.)[1] Member of Dew Drop Inn house band in the 1950s and worked and/or recorded with **Huey "Piano" Smith**, **Bea Booker**, **Earl King**, **Guitar Slim**, **James Booker**, and others.

CAGNOLATTI, ERNIE "CAG"/"LITTLE CAG" *Jazz.* Trumpet. (Born Apr. 2, 1911, Madisonville, St. Tammany Parish; died Apr. 7, 1983, New Orleans, Orleans Parish.) Noted early New Orleans jazz trumpeter moved to New Orleans in 1919 to join his brother Claiberre, who was a drummer with **Bunk Johnson** around 1917. Inspired by Johnson, began playing trumpet and in the 1930s worked with **Papa Celestin**, **Sidney Desvigne**, and Herb Leary's society dance band. In the 1940s and 1950s worked with **Paul Barbarin**, **Bill Matthews** and Eureka, Onward, and Tuxedo brass bands. Performed regularly with **Big Jim Robinson** and **Harold Dejan** in the 1960s and appeared on numerous recordings with Robinson, Barbarin, and others. Performed regularly at Preservation Hall throughout the 1970s before retiring from music in 1980 after suffering a stroke.

CAILLIER, J. J. (John Jules Caillier Sr.) *Zydeco, rhythm and blues.* Vocals. Composer. (Born Feb. 2, 1945, Lafayette, Lafayette Parish; died Apr. 1987, Lafayette, Lafayette Parish.) Lafayette funk and zydeco singer, producer, disc jockey, and label owner who helped usher in the zydeco boom of the 1980s. After releasing several singles as vocalist on Reynaud and Maison de Soul in the early 1960s and 1970s, formed Caillier Records in the mid-1970s and produced releases by **Boozoo Chavis**, **(Hiram) Sampy** and the Bad Habits, **Clifton Chenier**, **Major Handy**, **Morris Francis**, **Terrance Simien**, and others. Also recorded LP *Zydeco Train Revue* as vocalist backed by **Fernest Arceneaux** and hosted popular local zydeco radio show in the 1980s. Father of **J. J. Caillier Jr.**

CAILLIER, J. J., JR. (John Jules Caillier Jr.) *Zydeco.* Accordion, piano, vocals. Composer. Bandleader. (Born Oct. 27, 1967, Lafayette, Lafayette Parish.) Contemporary zydeco accordionist and bandleader and son of **J. J. Caillier Sr.**, recorded his first single, "Candy Kiss," on his father's Caillier label in 1987. In the mid-1990s launched solo career inspired by **Clifton Chenier** and **Beau Jocque** and formed band Zydeco Knockouts. Continued performing with group into the 2010s, releasing numerous CDs, including *Bad as I Wanna Be* in 2017.

CAITON, RICHARD *Rhythm and blues.* Vocals, piano. Composer. Bandleader. (Born Dec. 26, 1944, New Orleans, Orleans Parish.) New Orleans soul singer made recording debut in 1964 with single on GNP/Crescendo produced by **Dave Bartholomew**. Recorded several singles for Up Tight in the late 1960s, including "Take a Hold, Brothers and Sisters," which sold well in New Orleans. Released singles on Malaco, Caiburt, and JB's in the 1970s before retiring from music. Made occasional special appearances in the 2010s.

CAMPBELL, JOHN *Blues, rock.* Guitar, vocals. Composer. Bandleader. (Born Jan. 20, 1952, Shreveport, Caddo Parish; died June 13, 1993, Manhattan, New York.) Raised in Shreveport, blues-rock guitarist and singer-songwriter began performing in the early 1970s in a trio around Corpus Christi and released first solo album *Street Suite* in 1975. In the late 1970s and early 1980s performed in clubs around east Texas and New Orleans before relocating to New York City in 1985. Recorded *A Man and His Blues* on CrossCut in 1988 and began gaining national attention in the early 1990s with two releases on Elektra, *One Believer* and *Howlin' Mercy.* Died of heart failure at his home at age 41.

CAPELLO, LENNY *Rhythm and blues.* Guitar, vocals. Composer. Bandleader. (Born Sept. 22, 1942, New Orleans, Orleans Parish.) Began playing guitar in 1952 just before family relocated to Baton Rouge. In 1957 joined local rhythm and blues band the Dots as lead singer and guitarist. In the late 1950s and early 1960s had several releases on Ric, including "Cotton Candy," recorded at **Cosimo Matassa**'s famed studio in New Orleans. In 1969 and 1970 had singles on Silver Fox and Jubilee, the latter under the name Lenny Damon. Continued to perform and teach music into the 2010s.

CARBO, HAYWARD "CHUCK" *Rhythm and blues, gospel.* Vocals. Composer. Bandleader. (Born Jan. 11, 1926, Houma, Terrebonne Parish; died July 11, 2008, New Orleans, Orleans Parish.) Highly regarded early rhythm and blues singer best known for his work as lead vocalist with premier New Orleans vocal group the Spiders. Family moved to New Orleans in the early 1930s and after serving in World War II, joined gospel group Zion City Harmonizers with brother **Chick Carbo** in 1947, which later became the Delta Southernaires. Upon studio owner **Cosimo Matassa**'s recommendation, gospel group began recording rhythm and blues in 1954 as the Spiders for Imperial and had a string of major hits, including "I Didn't Want to Do It," "I'm Slippin' In," and "Witchcraft." Left group in 1957 and released two more singles on Imperial. In the early 1960s cut singles for Teem, Rex, Ace, and ETAH, working often with Mac Rebennack (**Dr. John**), and in the late 1960s and early 1970s had releases on Fire Ball (with **Eddie Bo**) and Superdome. After working largely outside music for more than a decade, made comeback album *Life's Ups and Downs* on 504 label in 1988, which included local hit "Meet Me with Your Black Drawers On." In the mid-1990s recorded two albums for Rounder. Younger brothers Hank and Claude Carbo relocated to Los Angeles in the late 1960s and recorded soul and funk singles for several local labels in following years.

CARBO, LEONARD "CHICK" *Rhythm and blues, gospel.* Vocals. Bandleader. (Born Dec. 28, 1927, Houma, Terrebonne Parish; died Aug. 18, 1998, New Orleans, Orleans Parish.) Early rhythm and blues singer known for his work as bass and lead vocalist with archetypal 1950s New Orleans vocal group the Spiders. Relocated with family to New Orleans in the early 1930s and in late 1940s joined gospel group the Zion City Harmonizers with brother **Chuck Carbo**. Group later changed name to the Delta Southernaires and recorded for Imperial in 1953. Under producer **Dave Bartholomew**, group recorded rhythm and blues as the Spiders and produced five major hits, including "You're the One" and "21" in the mid-1950s. After Spiders disbanded in 1957, recorded singles for Atlantic and Vee-Jay. In the early 1960s worked with **Allen Toussaint** on two releases for Instant and in the late 1960s cut a single for International City. Succumbed to a fatal heart attack at age 70. Brothers Hank and Claude Carbo were also musicians.

CAREY, JACK *Jazz.* Trombone. Composer. Bandleader. (Born around 1889, Hahnville, St. Charles Parish; died around 1935, New Orleans, Orleans Parish.) Early New Orleans jazz trombonist who was among the first to play in the tailgate style. Began playing with Allen Brass Band around 1910 and in 1912 formed popular Crescent Orchestra which included brother **Mutt Carey** and later **Punch Miller**. Noted for performing song that became known as "Jack Carey" and which would later evolve into jazz standard "Tiger Rag." After Miller took over leadership of band in the early 1920s, continued to perform with **Papa Celestin**'s Tuxedo Brass Band and other groups through the late 1920s.

CAREY, THOMAS "MUTT"/"PAPA MUTT" *Jazz.* Cornet. Bandleader. (Born Sept. 17, 1890, Hahnville, St. Charles Parish; died Sept. 4, 1948, Elsinore, California.)[2] Highly regarded early New Orleans jazz cornetist whose musicianship rivaled **King Oliver**'s and who was among the first to use horn mutes. Began performing in brother **Jack Carey**'s Crescent Orchestra in 1912 and worked regularly in Storyville, often with **Kid Ory**. In 1917 toured with **Mary Mack** along with **Johnny Dodds** to Chicago and performed there with **Lawrence Duhé**. Relocated to California in 1919 to join Ory's band and appeared on their historic recordings in 1922. Took over leadership of group after Ory's departure to Chicago in 1925 and continued performing until beginning of Great Depression. In the mid-1940s began performing again and worked and recorded with Ory's Creole Jazz Band. In 1946–47 recorded with Hociel Thomas as well as his band the New Yorkers, which included **Albert Nicholas**, **Baby Dodds**, and **Danny Barker**.

CARL, JOE (Nolan Duplantis) *Swamp pop.* Vocals. Composer. Bandleader. (Born Mar. 19, 1937, Houma, Terrebonne Parish; died Apr. 20, 2016, Marrero, Jefferson Parish.) Swamp pop singer best known for his work with the Dukes of Rhythm in the late 1950s and early 1960s after replacing **Joe Barry** as vocalist. Released two singles on Rocko in 1959–60, including "Don't Leave Me Again," which was leased to Top Rank for national distribution and became a regional hit. Also had a single on Zynn. Later cofounded popular swamp pop dance hall the Old Scorpio Lounge in Marrero.

CARNAHAN, CLIFF (Joseph Clifford Carnahan) *String band, Cajun.* Fiddle, guitar. Composer. (Born Dec. 25, 1914, Chopin, Natch. Parish; died Apr. 22, 2001, Cloutierville, Natch. Parish.) Highly regarded country and Cajun fiddle player and prolific songwriter best known for his composition "Ocean of Diamonds." Raised in a musical family and played guitar in family string band as a child. Began performing in the 1930s with **Joe Falcon** and in the late 1930s and early 1940s worked with Cajun bands around Lake Charles. Continued performing with string and country bands into his 80s and composed more than two hundred songs, several of which were recorded by Hank Williams, Willie Nelson, Jimmy Martin, and others.

CARRIER, CHUBBY (Joseph Roy Carrier Jr.) *Zydeco.* Accordion, drums, bass, vocals. Composer. Bandleader. (Born July 1, 1967, Church Point, Acadia Parish.) Nationally renowned zydeco accordionist and bandleader began playing drums in his father **Roy Carrier**'s band the Night Rockers at age 12, picking up accordion several years later. In his late teens toured for several years as drummer with **Terrance Simien** before forming his own group the Bayou Swamp Band with brothers **Troy Carrier** on drums and Kevin on bass. Through the 2010s toured extensively nationally and overseas with releases on numerous labels including Jewel, Flying Fish, Blind Pig, Louisiana Red Hot Records, and Swampadelic, notably highly acclaimed CD *Zydeco Junkie* in 2010.

CARRIER, ROY (Joseph Roy Carrier Sr.) *Zydeco.* Accordion, guitar, drums, vocals. Composer. Bandleader. (Born Feb. 11, 1947, Lawtell, St. Landry Parish; died May 4, 2010, Opelousas, St. Landry Parish.) Noted blues-influenced zydeco accordionist and dance-hall owner began performing on rubboard, then guitar and drums, as a child with his father at la la house dances. From 1961 through early 1970s performed locally with his band the Night Rockers, soon switching to accordion as main instrument. In 1980 opened Offshore Lounge dance hall in Lawtell which would serve as training ground for many young zydeco musicians, including **Beau Jocque**; **Geno Delafose** and sons Kevin, **Chubby**, and **Troy Carrier**. From the late 1980s through mid-2000s had releases on Lanor, Paula, Zane, Right On Rhythm, Severn, and Mardi Gras, including *Offshore Blues & Zydeco* in 2000. Toured extensively with the Night Rockers until succumbing to fatal heart attack at age 63. Distant relative of **Carrière Brothers**.

CARRIER, TROY "DIKKI DU" *Zydeco.* Accordion, drums, rubboard, vocals. Composer. Bandleader. (Born June 22, 1969, Church Point, Acadia Parish.) Zydeco multi-instrumentalist began playing rubboard while in his teens with his father **Roy Carrier** and **C. J. Chenier** and performed as drummer in his brother **Chubby Carrier**'s band in the late 1980s and 1990s. Began playing accordion during his mid-20s and formed his band the Zydeco Krewe. Continued performing in the 2010s with releases on Lanor, Swampadelic, and his own private label.

CARRIÈRE BROTHERS *See* Carrière, Eraste "Dolon," *and* Carrière, Joseph "Bébé."

CARRIÈRE, CALVIN *Creole, zydeco.* Fiddle, accordion, vocals. Composer. Bandleader. (Born Sept. 10, 1921, Lawtell, St. Landry Parish; died Mar. 3, 2002, Lawtell, St. Landry Parish.) Renowned Creole fiddle player learned the instrument from his uncle **Bébé Carrière** and accordion from his father, **Eraste Carrière**, in his youth and later joined their band the Lawtell Playboys in the late 1960s. Continued performing and recording with band in remaining years with **Delton Broussard** and later **Goldman Thibodeaux**. Also worked regularly with **Nolton Semien** and appeared on LP *John Semien and his Opelousas Playboys* on La Louisianne in the 1970s, which is often cited as among his finest work.

CARRIÈRE, ERASTE "DOLON" *Creole.* Accordion, vocals. Composer. Bandleader. (Born Sept. 17, 1900, Prairie Ronde, St. Landry Parish; died Aug. 15, 1983, Mallet, St. Landry Parish.) Noted early Creole accordion player and singer best known for his work with brother **Bébé Carrière** in the Lawtell Playboys. Began learning accordion as a child by his Creole musician father, Ernest, and was soon performing for both white and black audiences. In the 1920s and 1930s played la la house dances with Bébé, traveling as far as Lake Charles. From the 1940s through late 1960s led Lawtell Playboys with Bébé, which later included son **Calvin Carrière** and daughter Beatrice. Retired from Lawtell Playboys in the late 1960s but recorded with Bébé for Arhoolie, Rounder, Folkways, and Maison de Soul in the 1970s.

CARRIÈRE, JOSEPH "BÉBÉ" *Creole.* Fiddle, vocals. Composer. Bandleader. (Born Aug. 7, 1908, Opelousas, St. Landry Parish; died Apr. 22, 2001, Port Arthur, Texas.) Influential early Creole fiddle player and singer who cofounded the famed Lawtell Playboys with older brother **Eraste "Dolon" Carrière** and known for his classic fiddle compositions such as "Blue Runner" and "Blues à Bébé." Began learning fiddle as a boy, mentored by his father, Ernest, who played accordion, and by his teens was performing with Eraste at la la house dances. In the 1940s formed Lawtell Playboys and performed with group through the late 1960s, often at famed dance hall Slim's Yi-Ki-Ki in Opelousas. In the 1970s made recordings with Eraste for Arhoolie, Rounder, Folkways, and Maison de Soul before retiring from music.

CARSON, BIG AL (Alton Carson) *Rhythm and blues.* Vocals, tuba, trumpet. Composer. Bandleader. (Born Oct. 2, 1953, New Orleans, Orleans Parish.) Popular French Quarter blues singer and bandleader began music career performing in brass bands around New Orleans. Held residency at Bourbon Street's Funky Pirate for more than 20 years with his band the Blues Masters and recorded several albums, including "Take Your Drunken Ass Home" on Mardi Gras in 2002. Continued performing on Bourbon in late 2018 after several-year hiatus due to health issues.

CARTER, FRED, JR. *Rockabilly, country.* Guitar, bass, mandolin, vocals. Composer. Bandleader. (Born Dec. 28, 1933, Winnsboro, Franklin Parish; died July 17, 2010, Nashville.)[3] Highly regarded and influential early rockabilly guitarist and songwriter who later worked for decades as one of Nashville's premier session musicians. Began performing professionally in the 1950s and appeared regularly on the *Louisiana Hayride.* In the late 1950s and early 1960s worked with Roy Orbison and Ronnie and **Dale Hawkins**. Settled in Nashville in the early 1960s and throughout following decades recorded extensively as session guitarist, appearing on hundreds of recordings with artists such as Simon & Garfunkel, Joan Baez, Bob Dylan, Marty Robbins, and Waylon Jennings. In the 1960s had singles as a leader on Monument, Viking, and Nugget. Continued writing, producing, and recording into the 2000s. Father of country singer Deana Carter.

CARTER, JOE L. *See* Joe L.

CASIMIR, JOHN *Jazz.* Clarinet. Bandleader. (Born Dec. 17, 1898, New Orleans, Orleans Parish; died Jan. 3, 1963, New Orleans, Orleans Parish.)[4] Early New Orleans jazz clarinetist performed with **Red Allen** from 1918 to 1922 and worked with Eureka, Tuxedo, and WPA brass bands through the 1930s. In 1938 founded Young Tuxedo Brass Band, which he recorded with and led until his death at age 64.

CASTILLE, HADLEY J. *Cajun.* Fiddle, vocals. Composer. Bandleader. (Born Mar. 3, 1933, Leonville, St. Landry Parish; died Oct. 25, 2012, Opelousas, St. Landry Parish.) Internationally renowned Cajun fiddle player and singer-songwriter began playing at age nine, inspired early on by **Harry Choates**. Performed with various local groups throughout next several decades and gained national prominence in the late 1970s after several major festival appearances. From the 1980s through 2000s toured internationally with his Sharecroppers band, which included son Blake on guitar, and released numerous albums on Kajun and Swallow, notably *200 Lines: I Must Not Speak French* in 1991. Continued performing and recording until being diagnosed with an inoperable brain tumor several months before his death. Grandfather of Cajun musician Sarah Jayde Williams.

CAT ROY *See* Broussard, Allen "Cat Roy."

CATALON, INEZ *Creole.* Vocals. (Born Sept. 23, 1913, Kaplan, Vermilion Parish; died Nov. 23, 1994, Kaplan, Vermilion Parish.)[5] Noted Creole a cappella singer who as a child began learning from her mother a vast repertoire of traditional French ballads, lullabies, and historical songs which were sung at home for many generations. Performed at numerous national festivals, including 1976 Festival of American Folklife in Washington, D.C., and appeared on LPs *Louisiana Creole Music* on Folkways in 1978 and *Zodico: Louisiana Creole Music* on Rounder in 1979.

CAUSEY, CLYDE *Blues.* Harmonica, vocals. (Born Apr. 14, 1939, Clinton, E. Feliciana Parish; died Sept. 22, 2010, Baton Rouge, EBR Parish.) Baton Rouge blues harmonica player worked with **Clarence Edwards** in the early

1950s. Appeared on recordings with Smoky Babe in 1960–61 produced by folklorist Harry Oster.

CAYOU, JOSEPH "RED" *Jazz, blues.* Piano. (Born Aug. 4, 1904, New Orleans, Orleans Parish; died Sept. 7, 1947, Oakland, California.)[6] Influential early barrelhouse piano player who mentored **Tuts Washington** and was regarded by some peers as the finest pianist in New Orleans. Began playing piano around age five and by his teens was performing in saloons. Worked with small groups and as solo performer through the 1920s and performed with **Louis Armstrong**, **Tio Lorenzo Jr.**, and others. Relocated to Oakland in 1928 and quickly established himself as top pianist in city. In the early 1940s toured with Helen Humes and continued performing until his death at age 43.

CEASAR, WARREN *Zydeco, rhythm and blues.* Trumpet, flute, vocals. Composer. Bandleader. (Born Feb. 29, 1952, near Basile, Evangeline Parish; died May 11, 2000, Lafayette, Lafayette Parish.) Soul- and reggae-influenced zydeco singer and trumpeter began teaching himself the instrument at age seven and by his mid-teens was performing in clubs around Opelousas with **Guitar Gable**. After stints in Houston and Memphis in the early 1970s, toured with Isaac Hayes before returning to Lafayette area and working with **Little Bob**, **Zachary Richard**, and others. From 1979 to 1987 toured and recorded with **Clifton Chenier** and released solo LPs *Bayou Trash* and *Cotton Pickin' Blues* on Big Note in 1987. In 1990 appeared on Rounder's *Zydeco Shootout at El Sid O's* and followed with CD *The Crowd Pleaser* on Sound of New Orleans in 1995. Continued performing with his Creole Zydeco Snap Band until his death at age 48.

CELESTIN, OSCAR "PAPA" *Jazz.* Trumpet, vocals. Bandleader. (Born Jan. 1, 1884, Napoleonville, Assumption Parish; died Dec. 15, 1954, New Orleans, Orleans Parish.) Important early New Orleans jazz bandleader who founded the Original Tuxedo Jazz Band, the longest-running jazz band in history and whose members included dozens of prominent early jazz musicians, including **Louis Armstrong**, **King Oliver**, and **Mutt Carey**. Studied music with Professor **Claiborne Williams** as a child and soon began performing with local bands. In 1906 moved to New Orleans and worked with **Henry Allen**'s brass band, **Jack Carey**, **Bunk Johnson**, and others. In 1910 joined the band at Storyville's Tuxedo Dance Hall and shortly afterwards took over leadership. Continued using Tuxedo name after dance hall's closure and coled a separate Tuxedo orchestra and brass band with **Bebé Ridgley** after Storyville's closure in late 1917. Recorded for OKeh in 1925 and then split with Ridgley and continued to record as Celestin's Original Tuxedo Jazz Orchestra for Columbia through 1928. Throughout Depression years worked sporadically but had major comeback after World War II with reformed Tuxedo band and became nationally renowned during the current jazz revival. In the late 1940s and early 1950s held popular residency on Bourbon Street, appeared on radio and television broadcasts and at the White House, and made several recordings. Tuxedo Jazz Band continued after his death under the leadership of **Eddie Pierson**, **Albert "Papa" French**, **Bob French**, and most recently, **Gerald French**, who succeeded his uncle in 2011, a hundred years after the band's formation.

CHAMBERS, HENDERSON *Jazz.* Trombone. (Born May 1, 1908, Alexandria, Rapides Parish; died Oct. 19, 1967, New York City.) Highly accomplished jazz trombonist got his start playing in Morehouse College band and performed with several regional jazz bands in the early to mid-1930s. In 1937–38 toured with Tiny Bradshaw before relocating to New York and working at Savoy Ballroom with Chris Columbus. Between 1941 and 1943 performed and recorded with **Louis Armstrong** and through the 1950s worked with **Edmond Hall**, Lucky Millinder, Cab Calloway, Count Basie, Duke Ellington, Doc Cheatham, and others. In the 1960s toured with Ray Charles and Basie for several years. Recorded extensively throughout career and appeared on sessions with Hall, Basie, Charles, Wynonie Harris, Frank Sinatra, Billie Holiday, Ella Fitzgerald, Gene Ammons, and many others.

CHAMPION, MICKEY (*born* **Mildred Sallier**) *Blues.* Vocals. Composer. Bandleader. (Born Apr. 9, 1925, Lake Charles, Calcasieu Parish; died Nov. 24, 2014, Los Angeles.) Powerful West Coast–based blues vocalist began singing in church as a child and relocated to Los Angeles in 1945. Soon began performing on local blues and jazz club scene and in the late 1940s and early 1950s worked with Johnny Otis, **Percy Mayfield**, and future husband Roy Milton. From 1950 through the early 1960s had releases on Modern, Aladdin, Dootone, and Lilly, notably "I'm a Woman"/"Bam-A-Lama" (with Milton) in 1956. Also recorded with Jimmy Witherspoon as "Girl Friday" and with vocal group the Nic Nacs, both in 1950. After several decades of relative inactivity, began performing regularly again in the late 1990s and released CDs *I Am Your Living Legend!* and *What You Want* on Tondef in the early 2000s. Continued performing around Los Angeles area until illness forced retirement by end of decade.

CHANCLER, LEON "NDUGU" *Jazz, rhythm and blues.* Drums, vibes. Composer. Bandleader. (Born July 1, 1952, Shreveport, Caddo Parish; died Feb. 3, 2018, Los Angeles.) Highly renowned jazz and funk drummer and educator began playing drums in his early teens. After graduating college worked and recorded with numerous artists, including Miles Davis, James Brown, Herbie Hancock, Frank Sinatra, Freddie Hubbard, George Duke, Kenny Rogers, Michael Jackson, and John Lee Hooker. Formed band Chocolate Jam Co. in the late 1970s and released two albums on Epic and in 1988 recorded *Old Friends New Friends* as a leader for MCA. Worked as producer and session musician in the 1980s and 1990s and later worked and recorded with Stanley Clarke in trio Jazz Straight Up. Continued performing, recording, and serving as adjunct assistant professor at University of Southern California until his death from cancer at age 65.

CHANDLER, EDWARD "DEE DEE" *Jazz.* Drums. (Born Jan. 17, 1867, New Orleans, Orleans Parish; died Jan. 13, 1918, New Orleans, Orleans Parish.)[7] Highly influential and innovative early New Orleans jazz drummer who is widely credited as the first to use a makeshift pedal to play a bass drum with his foot and freeing up his hands to simultaneously play other percussion instruments such as snare, toms or cymbals, thereby becoming the first jazz musician to use a trap drum set in the 1890s. Throughout decade worked regularly with **John Robichaux**'s band as well as in street parades with various brass bands, including occasional jobs with **Buddy Bolden**. Reportedly served in the Spanish-American War in 1898 and performed only sporadically in following years. Died of tuberculosis.

CHAPMAN, TOPSY (Gladys T. Chapman) *Jazz, gospel.* Vocals. Composer. Bandleader. (Born Aug. 9, 1947, Kentwood, Tangipahoa Parish.) Internationally renowned jazz and gospel vocalist began singing as a child in church. In her late teens moved to New Orleans and founded gospel group the Chapman Singers and toured internationally. In the late 1970s performed as original cast member of hit musical *One Mo' Time.* Released several acclaimed albums throughout the 1990s and 2000s, including *My One and Only Love* on GHB in 2001. In the 2010s continued to perform and record as soloist and with several jazz and gospel groups, including Solid Harmony with daughters Yolanda Windsay and Jolynda Phillips. Also appeared in several films, including *12 Years a Slave* in 2013.

CHARLES, BOBBY (Robert Charles Guidry) *Swamp pop, rhythm and blues, rock.* Guitar, vocals. Composer. Bandleader. (Born Feb. 21, 1938, Abbeville, Vermilion Parish; died Jan. 14, 2010, Abbeville, Vermilion Parish.) Highly regarded and influential singer-songwriter known for his numerous compositions, including "See You Later, Alligator," "Walkin' to New Orleans," "Jealous Kind," and "Tennessee Blues." Formed his first band the Cardinals at age 14, inspired by **Fats Domino**. In 1955 began recording for Chess with producer **Paul Gayten** and recorded debut "Later, Alligator"/"On Bended Knee," which is regarded as among the first swamp pop records. Numerous singles followed on Chess and Imperial through 1960, and his compositions were recorded by other artists such as Domino, Bill Haley, and **Clarence "Frogman" Henry**. In the early to mid-1960s had singles on Jewel and his own Hub-City label and in 1972 released acclaimed self-titled LP on Bearsville backed by members of the Band and **Dr. John**. In following years his compositions were covered by Etta James, Ray Charles, **Johnny Adams**, **Clarence "Gatemouth" Brown**, **Dr. John**, Kris Kristofferson, Joe Cocker, and many others. After a ten-year hiatus began recording again in the late 1980s and in the following two decades released several recordings on Stony Plain and his own Rice 'n Gravy label, including *Last Train to Memphis* in 2004 and *Homemade Songs* in 2008.

CHARLES, DOUG *See* Ardoin, Doug.

CHARLES, ERVIN *Blues.* Guitar, vocals. Composer. Bandleader. (Born Jan. 3, 1932, Port Barre, St. Landry Parish; died Apr. 5, 2000, Houston.) Influential Texas-based blues guitarist relocated to Beaumont, Texas, in his late teens and began performing in local clubs, influenced greatly by T-Bone Walker. In 1953 taught **Long John Hunter** guitar and performed with Hunter in the Hollywood Bearcats. Continued performing in Beaumont/Port Arthur clubs throughout following decades with various groups, including Big Sambo and the Housewreckers, influencing many area guitarists, including **Lonnie Brooks**, **Phillip Walker**, Barbara Lynn, and Johnny Winter. After working mainly outside music in the 1980s, began performing again and appeared on 1999 Alligator CD *Lone Star Shootout* with Hunter, Brooks, and Walker. Recorded his only full-length release, *Greyhound Blues,* which was released posthumously on Dialtone in 2000.

CHARLES, ERVING, JR. *Rhythm and blues.* Bass. (Born Aug. 28, 1941, New Orleans, Orleans Parish; died Feb. 26, 2003, New Orleans, Orleans Parish.) Noted rhythm and blues bass player who performed and recorded with **Fats Domino**, **Dave Bartholomew**, **Snooks Eaglin**, **Irma Thomas**, **Clarence "Frogman" Henry**, and others. Son of bassist Erving Charles Sr.

CHARLES, HYPOLITE *Jazz.* Cornet. Bandleader. (Born Apr. 18, 1891, Parks, St. Martin Parish; died Nov. 29, 1984, Slidell, St. Tammany Parish.)[8] Renowned early New Orleans jazz cornetist and bandleader formed his first marching band in Parks area while in his teens. In 1908 relocated to New Orleans and studied music with **George Moret**'s brother Eugene. Through 1920 worked with **Manuel Perez**, Silver Leaf, Excelsior, and Maple Leaf Orchestra, and **Papa Celestin**'s Tuxedo Brass Band. In the early 1920s led his own orchestra until health condition forced retirement from music in 1925. Returned to Parks in the early 1940s and worked outside music in remaining years. Father August Charles (1880–1933) was a baritone horn player.

CHARLES, ROCKIE (Alfred Charles Merrick) *Rhythm and blues.* Guitar, vocals. Composer. Bandleader. (Born Nov. 13, 1939, Boothville, Plaquemines Parish; died Mar. 12, 2010, New Orleans, Orleans Parish.)[9] New Orleans rhythm and blues singer and guitarist known as "The President of Soul." Learned guitar from his father and moved to New Orleans at age 13. Formed first band at age 18, inspired by **Guitar Slim**. Released debut single "Riccasha"/"Sinking Like a Ship" on **Senator Jones**'s Black Patch label in 1968 and in the late 1960s toured with **Irma Thomas**, Little Johnny Taylor, and others. In the 1970s recorded several singles on his own Soulgates label, including "The President of Soul." Released first album, *Born for You,* on Orleans in 1996 and continued to perform and record through the late 2000s.

CHARLIE, FRED *Cajun.* Guitar, vocals. Composer. Bandleader. (Born Oct. 5, 1948, Chataignier, Evangeline Parish.) Noted Cajun-country singer-songwriter and guitarist performed extensively nationally and abroad with his Acadiana Cajuns since forming band in the early 1980s. Released recordings on Lanor, Crazy Cajun, Swallow, and his own Acadiana label, including CD *Je Rêvé Heir au Soir* in 2003. In the 2010s continued performing with band, hosting weekly Cajun French radio show and long-running local jam session as well as operating recording studio in Eunice.

CHARLO (Charles Guilbeau Jr.) *Swamp pop, Cajun.* Piano, vocals. Composer. Bandleader. (Born Sept. 8, 1948, Carencro, Lafayette Parish.) Swamp pop singer-songwriter released several singles for Jin in the 1980s, including "She Walks By (All Dressed in White)" and "I'll Be Hurting (the Rest of My Life)." In 2003 recorded CD *History of the Cajuns in Story and Song* on Swallow and continued performing around Lafayette area with his bands Southern Tradition and the Swampers through the 2010s. His compositions have been recorded by **Johnnie Allan**, **Don Rich**, **Warren Storm**, the Boogie Kings, and others.

CHASE, EDGAR "DOOKY" *Jazz.* Trumpet. Bandleader. (Born Mar. 23, 1928, New Orleans, Orleans Parish; died Nov. 22, 2016, New Orleans, Orleans Parish.) Owner and namesake of famed New Orleans Creole restaurant Dooky Chase's with wife Leah, jazz trumpeter began performing in high school and formed his first band at age 16. Led 16-piece Dooky Chase Orchestra in the 1940s which toured throughout the Southeast and gave many young area jazz musicians their start.

CHAVIS, BOOZOO (Wilson Anthony Chavis) *Zydeco.* Accordion, harmonica, vocals. Composer. Bandleader. (Born Oct. 23, 1930, Dog Hill, Lake Charles, Calcasieu Parish; died May 5, 2001, Austin, Texas.)[10] Highly influential and innovative early zydeco accordionist and singer-songwriter whose 1954 single "Paper in My Shoe" is widely regarded as the first zydeco record. Born in the small farming community of Dog Hill near Lake Charles, began playing accordion around age 10, inspired by his father and several local musicians, including **Ambrose "Potato" Sam**. By the late 1940s and early 1950s was playing at local house dances. In 1954 recorded "Paper in My Shoe" backed by **Classie Ballou** for producer **Eddie Shuler**'s Folk-Star label which became a regional hit. After several more singles failed to produce a hit and discouraged by lack of royalties from "Paper in My Shoe," worked mainly outside music in the 1960s and 1970s, raising race horses and farming. After hearing of a Boozoo Chavis impersonator in the early 1980s, began performing again and recorded four LPs for Maison de Soul through 1990, which included signature songs such as "Leona Had a Party," "Dance All Night," "Dog Hill," and "Uncle Bud," all which became zydeco standards. In the 1990s began touring nationally with his band the Magic Sounds and had high-profile releases on Rounder, Electra, and Discovery, adding many more standards to the zydeco repertoire, including "Lula Lula Don't You Go to Bingo," "You're Gonna Look Like a Monkey," and "I Got a Camel." Shortly after completing what would become his final studio album, died of complications after suffering a heart attack following a performance in Austin at age 70. Sons Charles, Rellis, and Poncho Chavis were members of Magic Sounds. Great-nephew of **Sidney Babineaux**.

CHAVIS, JOSEPH "COOKIE" *Guitar.* (Born Nov. 25, 1967, Lake Charles, Calcasieu Parish.) Noted zydeco guitarist best known for his tenure performing and recording with **Beau Jocque**'s Zydeco Hi-Rollers in the 1990s. Also performed and recorded with **Buckwheat Zydeco**, **Geno Delafose**, **Sean Ardoin**, **Rosie Ledet**, **Curley Taylor**, and others.

CHAVIS, LEON *Zydeco.* Accordion, trumpet, vocals. Composer. Bandleader. (Born June 18, 1981, Lawtell, St. Landry Parish.) Contemporary zydeco accordionist began performing in college on trumpet in Southern University's famed marching band. In the mid-2000s formed the Zydeco Flames and remained popular act on the Louisiana and east Texas zydeco club and trail ride circuit into the 2010s with several noted releases, including *The Champ is Here* in 2014. Distant cousin of **Boozoo Chavis**.

CHENIER, CLEVELAND *Zydeco.* Rubboard. (Born June 11, 1921, Leonville [near Opelousas], St. Landry Parish; died May 7, 1991, Lafayette, Lafayette Parish.)[11] Influential zydeco rubboard pioneer began performing with brother **Clifton Chenier** in the mid-1940s and early 1950s in Lake Charles and east Texas and helped design the first modern over-the-shoulder rubboard instrument which was then crafted by Port Arthur metalworker Willie Landry. Continued performing with Clifton from the mid-1950s until his brother's death in 1987, recording and touring extensively nationally and overseas. Also worked with cousin Lightnin' Hopkins in the 1960s. Continued performing with band after his brother's death under the leadership of **C. J. Chenier** until retiring from music in 1990.

CHENIER, CLIFTON *Zydeco.* Accordion, harmonica, vocals. Composer. Bandleader. (Born June 25, 1925, Leonville [near Opelousas], St. Landry Parish; died Dec. 12, 1987, Lafayette, Lafayette Parish.) Profoundly influential Creole accordionist and singer-songwriter whose pioneering style of combining elements of rhythm and blues with the traditional black Creole music of rural southwest Louisiana in the 1950s defined what would soon become known as zydeco. Universally regarded as "The King of Zydeco" and responsible for introducing the large piano accordion to black Creole music. Raised in a musical family speaking Creole French, began playing accordion as a child, influenced greatly by his accordion-playing father, **Claude Faulk**, and the recordings of **Amédé Ardoin**. From the mid-1940s through mid-1950s spent time living in Lake Charles, Port Arthur, and Houston, and performing with brother **Cleveland Chenier**, occasionally working with **Clarence Garlow** and **Lonnie Brooks**. In 1954 made first recordings on Elko and Imperial/Post with uncle **Morris "Big" Chenier** on guitar. Signed with Specialty the following year and recorded a series of early zydeco classics, including label debut "Ay-Tete Fee," which led to national tours with artists such as Etta James and Jimmy Reed. In the next several years released singles on Argo and Zynn before starting long association with Arhoolie Records in 1964, which resulted in numerous notable recordings throughout the next two decades, including zydeco standard "Zydeco Sont Pas Salé" and acclaimed LPs *Louisiana Blues and Zydeco* and *Bogalusa Boogie.* Continued touring extensively nationally and abroad in 1970s with his Red Hot Louisiana Band, which included brother Cleveland, **Robert St. Julien**, **Lil' Buck Sinegal**, **Jumpin' Joe Morris**, and **John Hart**. In 1982 recorded highly acclaimed LP *I'm Here* with producer Sam Charters and continued performing despite suffering serious health problems due to diabetes in final years. Father of **C. J. Chenier**, nephew of **Peter King**, and second cousin of **Roscoe Chenier**.

CHENIER, MORRIS "BIG" *Blues, Creole.* Guitar, fiddle, vocals. Composer. Bandleader. (Born July 10, 1915, Opelousas, St. Landry Parish; died Jan. 8, 1978, Lake Charles, Calcasieu Parish.)[12] Opelousas blues singer and guitar and fiddle player performed at local house parties before relocating to Lake Charles in the late 1940s. In 1954 recorded behind nephew **Clifton Chenier** on singles for Elko and Post before cutting several sides for Goldband from 1957 to 1960, including "Let Me Hold Your Hand." In the 1960s played fiddle on Arhoolie session for Clifton Chenier but continued working mainly outside music, operating a barbecue restaurant.

CHENIER, ROSCOE (Joseph Roylton Chenier) *Blues.*

Guitar, vocals. Composer. Bandleader. (Born Nov. 6, 1941, Prairie Basse, St. Landry Parish; died Feb. 7, 2013, Opelousas, St. Landry Parish.) Noted Opelousas blues guitarist and singer-songwriter began playing guitar at age 16, inspired by B.B. King and **Clarence "Gatemouth" Brown** and mentored by **Lonesome Sundown** and **Leroy Washington**. After performing with a cousin's band, formed his own group the Blue Runners in the late 1950s and recorded single "I Broke the Yo Yo"/"Born for Bad Luck" for Reynaud in 1962 which became a local hit. Throughout the 1960s and 1970s performed with numerous blues and zydeco musicians, including Lonesome Sundown, **Roy Carrier**, **Little Bob**, **Good Rockin' Bob**, and others. After forming his Inner City Blues Band in the 1980s, recorded two CDs on Vidrine in the 1990s, including *Roscoe Chenier*, which was distributed nationally on Avenue Jazz, and began touring Europe. Releases followed on Black & Tan and APO. Continued performing in area clubs into the early 2010s. Second cousin of **Cleveland** and **Clifton Chenier**.

CHERAMIE, C. J. *See* Clay, Joe.

CHESTER D. (Chester D. Wilson) *Blues.* Guitar, vocals. Composer. (Born Sept. 1, 1915, Shreveport, Caddo Parish; died Dec. 9, 1998, Coushatta, Red River Parish.) Louisiana Delta blues guitarist and singer began playing in his youth on a homemade instrument, inspired by Blind Lemon Jefferson, and while in his 20s performed in clubs and juke joints around Shreveport. Quit performing after being shot in left hand during a performance and relocated to San Francisco in 1943 to work in shipyards. Eventually relearned how to play guitar by fretting with right hand and began performing around Bay Area blues scene. In the late 1980s recorded *Going Back Home* for local Blue Jazz label, performed at San Francisco Blues Festival, and toured Europe. Relocated back to North Louisiana shortly before his death at age 83.

CHEVALIER, ALBERT *Zydeco.* Accordion, vocals. (Born Mar. 20, 1913, Scott, Lafayette Parish; died Oct. 3, 1965, Houston.)[13] Early zydeco accordionist who was among the first to perform the black Creole music of Louisiana in Houston. The son of an accordion player, relocated to Port Arthur in 1943 before settling in Houston in the early 1950s. Performed mainly at house parties and other social gatherings and made numerous field recordings for Arhoolie in 1961.

CHEVALIER, CHESTER *Zydeco, blues.* Guitar, bass. (Born Feb. 7, 1943, Arnaudville, St. Landry Parish.) Traditional blues and zydeco guitarist began playing as a child, inspired by B.B. King and Wayne Bennett. In the mid-1960s joined **Fernest Arceneaux**'s band and toured and recorded extensively with group as bassist and guitarist through the late 1980s. In 1989 formed Creole Zydeco Farmers with **Jockey Etienne** and recorded and toured internationally with group through the early 2010s. Also worked with **Donna Angelle**, **Roscoe Chenier**, and Corey Arceneaux in the 2010s. Retired from performing in early 2018.

CHEVALIER, JAY *Rockabilly.* Guitar, vocals. Composer. Bandleader. (Born Mar. 4, 1936, Lecompte, Rapides Parish; died Mar. 30, 2019, Kenner, Jefferson Parish.) Noted early rockabilly singer-songwriter best known for his topical and political songs such as "The Ballad of Earl K. Long," "Khrushchev and the Devil," and "Castro Rock." Began playing guitar at age 10 and by age 17 was hosting his own local radio show. After a stint in the military, recorded debut single "Rockin Roll Angel" on Cajun, inspired by Gene Vincent. In 1959 had regional hit with "The Ballad of Earl K. Long" on Recco, which reportedly sold 100,000 copies. Following year recorded "Castro Rock" on Goldband. In 1962 performed in Las Vegas with cousin **Tommy Strange**'s band and made several recordings as leader on Crest. Continued working in Vegas through 1968 with several more releases, including regional hit "Come Back to Louisiana" in 1963. In the late 1960s returned to Louisiana and in following decades divided his time between music and running political campaigns. In 2006 was designated Louisiana's official state troubadour and continued to perform into 2010s.

CHEVIS, WILFRED (Joseph Wilfred Chavis) *Zydeco.* Accordion, vocals. Composer. Bandleader. (Born May 6, 1945, Church Point, Acadia Parish; died May 8, 2010, Houston.) Texas-based accordion player and bandleader began learning the instrument as a child from his father. Relocated with family to Houston in the late 1960s and in 1970s began performing in local clubs and formed the Texas Zydeco Band. In 1982 recorded a single for Caillier and released two LPs on Maison de Soul through the early 1990s, including *Foot Stompin' Zydeco* in 1985. Continued performing in Houston-area clubs through the 2000s with self-titled CD on Master-Trak in 2004.

CHISM, CHICO (Napoleon Chisolm) *Blues.* Drums, vocals. Composer. Bandleader. (Born May 23, 1927, Shreveport, Caddo Parish; died Jan. 28, 2007, Phoenix, Arizona.) Highly regarded and beloved Chicago blues musician, best known as Howlin' Wolf's last drummer. Began playing drums in his early teens and made first recordings in 1957 on Shreveport's Clif label with single "Hot Tamales and Bar-B-Cue" as a leader and backing **T.V. Slim** on regional hit "Flatfoot Sam." Worked with numerous musicians throughout the 1960s including Rosco Gordon, **Clifton Chenier**, **Classie Ballou**, and Big Joe Turner, and by the early 1970s was settled in Chicago and performing regularly with Howlin' Wolf. Continued working extensively on Chicago blues scene and in 1979 toured Europe with American Blues Legends package. Started Cher-Kee label and released singles by his own band, Eddie Shaw, Johnny Christian, and others. In 1986 relocated to Phoenix for health reasons and continued to be active on the local blues scene as a performer and session musician until suffering a stroke in 2002 which limited appearances in his remaining years.

CHOATES, HARRY (Harry Henry Choate) *Cajun.* Fiddle, guitar, vocals. Composer. Bandleader. (Born Dec. 26, 1922, Cow Island, Vermilion Parish; died July 17, 1951, Austin, Texas.)[14] Highly influential and innovative Cajun fiddle player and singer best known for his 1946 hit "Jole Blon," which brought Cajun music to national prominence for the first time. Raised in Port Arthur, Texas, from a child, began playing fiddle and guitar and by age 12 was performing locally for tips, influenced early on by Western swing fiddler Cliff Bruner. Joined **Happy Fats**'s Rayne-Bo Ramblers in the late 1930s and made recording debut with group in 1940. In the early to mid-1940s worked with various bands, including as guitarist with **Leo Soileau**. In 1946 recorded Cajun swing version of "Jole Blon (Pretty Blond)" for Gold Star with his band the Melody Boys and had major hit which inspired countless covers and answer songs nationwide. Throughout next several years recorded numerous sides for Gold Star, including "Poor Hobo" and "Devil in the Bayou," as well as for O.T., Macy's, Cajun Classics, and Humming Bird, and performed regularly throughout southwest Louisiana and east Texas. Plagued by chronic alcoholism, which eventually led to the dissolution of his band, relocated to Austin, Texas, in 1950 and worked with local group Jessie James and His Gang. After being arrested for nonpayment of child support, died in a jail cell under unclear circumstances at age 28. Cousin of Pete and **Jimmy Choates**.

CHOATES, JIMMY (James Marvin Choate) *Cajun.* Fiddle, guitar, vocals. Composer. Bandleader. (Born Nov. 23, 1921, Perry, Vermilion Parish; died Mar. 29, 1990, Vermilion Parish.)[15] Noted Cajun swing fiddle player and bandleader began performing early on with the Abbeville Playboys. In the late 1940s and early 1950s recorded for Fais-Do-Do and Khoury's with his band the Melody Boys, which included brother Pete on bass. Continued performing on Gulf Coast through the 1960s with several more singles on Goldband, Cajun Classics and O'Day. Cousin of **Harry Choates**.

CHRISTIAN, BUDDY (Narcisse Joseph Christian) *Jazz.* Banjo, guitar, piano. Bandleader. (Born July 21, 1885, New Orleans, Orleans Parish; died Sept. 2, 1958, New York City.)[16] Known primarily as a pianist in early career, began performing around New Orleans in 1910 and worked with **Peter Bocage** and **King Oliver**. Relocated to New York in the late 1910s and worked as banjo and piano player. In the mid-1920s recorded with **Clarence Williams** on various sessions which also included **Louis Armstrong** and **Sidney Bechet**. Recorded as leader with his Creole Five and Jazz Rippers in 1926 and worked in banjo duo in the late 1920s.

CHRISTIAN, EMILE *Jazz.* Trombone, double bass, clarinet. Composer. (Born Apr. 20, 1895, New Orleans, Orleans Parish; died Dec. 3, 1973, New Orleans, Orleans Parish.) Began performing with brothers Charles and **Frank Christian** in various bands in the 1910s, including with **Papa Jack Laine**. In the late 1910s worked with **Merritt Brunies** and his Original New Orleans Jazz Band in Chicago. Performed throughout Europe in the 1920s and 1930s with several bands, including Original Dixieland Jazz Band. Resettled in New Orleans in the 1940s and performed through the late 1960s with **Johnny Wiggs**, **Leon Prima**, **Sharkey Bonano**, and others, also recording as leader and sideman.

CHRISTIAN, FRANK *Jazz.* Cornet, trumpet, tuba, violin. Bandleader. (Born Sept. 3, 1897, New Orleans, Orleans Parish; died Nov. 27, 1973, New Orleans, Orleans Parish.) Youngest brother of Charles and **Emile Christian**, worked mainly as cornetist in various groups in the 1910s and led Frank Christian's Ragtime Band. After a brief stint in Chicago, moved to New York in 1918 and worked and recorded with Jimmy Durante's Jazz Band. Returned to Chicago and continued as bandleader.

CHRISTIAN, POLITE "FRENCHY" *Jazz, blues.* Cornet. Bandleader. (Born Aug. 10, 1891, New Orleans, Orleans Parish; died Dec. 12, 1944, Fort Worth, Texas.)[17] Early blues and jazz cornetist performed on the streets throughout Deep Ellum section of Dallas throughout the 1910s and 1920s and remembered for his loud playing. Recorded two notable sides for Columbia in 1928, "Texas and Pacific Blues" and "Sunshine Special," with his group Frenchy's String Band which featured **Percy Darensbourg** and **Octave Gaspard**. Settled in Fort Worth in the 1920s and continued performing in DFW area until suffering fatal stroke at age 53.

CHURCHILL, SAVANNAH *Rhythm and blues.* Vocals. Composer. (Born Aug. 21, 1915, Colfax, Grant Parish; died Apr. 19, 1974, Brooklyn, New York.) Noted early rhythm and blues singer and songwriter who had several hits in the late 1940s and early 1950s, including "I Want to Be Loved (But Only By You)." Raised in Brooklyn from an early age, began singing professionally in the early 1940s and made recording debut with "Fat Meat Is Good Meat" on Beacon in 1942. In the mid-1940s toured and recorded with bandleader Benny Carter for Capitol before signing with Manor and having four hits from 1945 to 1948, including "Daddy, Daddy" and "I Want to Be Loved." From 1949 through the early 1950s released singles on Regal, RCA, and Decca and had pop hits with "(It's No) Sin" in 1951 and "Shake a Hand" in 1953. Also appeared in several films, including *Miracle in Harlem.* After signing with Argo in 1956, was seriously injured while on stage, which ended her performing career. Made final recordings in 1961 for Jamie before retiring from music due to declining health.

CLANTON, CLYDE "IKE" *Swamp pop.* Bass, vocals. (Born Dec. 11, 1939, Golden Meadow, Lafourche Parish; died June 9, 2004, Jackson, E. Feliciana Parish.)[18] Younger brother of **Jimmy Clanton**. Had minor hits with "Down the Aisle" on Ace and "Sugar Plum" on Mercury in early 1960s. Also performed as bassist in bands with **John Fred** and guitarist Duane Eddy in the late 1950s.

CLANTON, JIMMY *Swamp pop.* Guitar, vocals. Composer. Bandleader. (Born Sept. 2, 1938, Cut Off, Lafourche Parish.) Popular swamp pop vocalist best known for his late 1950s and early 1960s hits such as "Just a Dream" and "Venus in Blue Jeans." Influenced by **Fats Domino**, Little Richard, and Elvis Presley, joined Dick Holler's band the Rockets while attending high school in Baton Rouge. In 1957 signed with Ace and had major hit with "Just a Dream" in 1958. Released six more Top 40 hits through the early 1960s and starred in Alan Freed's rock and roll film *Go Johnny Go.* Through the early 1970s had releases on several labels, including Philips, Imperial, and Laurie. Relocated to Pennsylvania in the 1970s and worked as radio disc jockey. From the 1990s through 2010s continued performing in theaters and on oldies circuit.

CLARK, JOSEPH "RED" *Jazz.* Trombone, sousaphone. (Born Feb. 12, 1894, New Orleans, Orleans Parish; died Nov. 30, 1960, New Orleans, Orleans Parish.) Early New Orleans jazz trombonist started performing in the late 1920s with Tonic Triad Band and worked with Masonic Brass Band in the 1930s. Later performed with Eureka Brass Band from 1947 to 1960, often on sousaphone.

CLARK, OCTA (Octave Brien Clark) *Cajun.* Accordion, vocals. Composer. Bandleader. (Born Apr. 30, 1904, Judice, Lafayette Parish; died Sept. 11, 1998, Scott, Lafayette Parish.) Highly renowned early Cajun accordionist known for his long association with fiddler **Hector Duhon**. Began performing at local house dances and dance halls at age 14 and by the mid-1920s was regarded by peers as among the finest accordion players of the era. In 1928 started performing with Duhon and his cousin Jesse Duhon on guitar and worked with group into the mid-1930s. After two decades of working outside music, began performing again in 1950s with Duhon and recorded a single for Swallow in the early 1970s, followed by albums for Rounder and Arhoolie in the early 1980s, notably *Old Time Cajun Music* in 1982. Recorded final CD *You Can't Go Wrong If You Play It Right* in 1993 and continued performing into his 90s.

CLARK, THAIS *Jazz, blues.* Vocals. Composer. Bandleader. (Born May 23, 1942, New Orleans, Orleans Parish.) Powerful classic blues and jazz vocalist in the tradition of Ma Rainey and Bessie Smith. Began as a dancer and actress before turning to career in singing. Toured internationally and released several recordings as leader, including *An Affair with the Blues* on Jazz Foundation of America in 2014.

CLAY, JOE (Claiborne Joseph Cheramie Jr.) *Rockabilly, swamp pop.* Guitar, drums, vocals. Bandleader. (Born Sept. 9, 1938, Harvey, Jefferson Parish; died Sept. 26, 2016, Gretna, Jefferson Parish.) Veteran rockabilly singer began playing drums in his early teens in local clubs with country and western bands. Inspired by **Fats Domino**, began incorporating rhythm and blues shuffles and beats and led trio as C. J. Cheramie. Appeared on the *Louisiana Hayride* in 1955 as leader and also backed Elvis Presley on drums. In 1956 signed with RCA subsidiary Vik and recorded several sides as Joe Clay, including rockabilly classics "Duck Tail," "Cracker Jack," and "Sixteen Chicks," and appeared on television program *The Ed Sullivan Show.* In 1962–63 released several swamp pop records on Samter under the name Russ Wayne. Retired from music in the early 1970s but made comeback in 1986 during rockabilly revival and continued to perform nationally and overseas through the mid-2010s. Released *The Legend Is Now* on El Toro in 2004.

CLEM, EDWARD *Jazz.* Cornet. Bandleader. (Born Aug. 6, 1873, Convent, St. James Parish; died Jan. 27, 1925, New Orleans, Orleans Parish.)[19] Noted early New Orleans jazz cornetist best known for replacing **Buddy Bolden** after **Frankie Duson** took over leadership of Bolden's band. Moved to New Orleans around 1893 and, after working with **Charley Galloway**'s group, began leading bands of his own from 1903 through the early 1910s. Often substituted for Bolden during his last year performing before replacing him. Through the early 1920s worked with the Johnny Brown Orchestra and Onward and Excelsior brass bands. Younger brother Jesse was an early jazz bassist and reported to be among the first to employ slap-bass style.

CLÉMENT BROTHERS *See* Clément, Terry.

CLEMENT, HENRY "LITTLE CLEM"/"LITTLE HENRY" "BIG CHIEF TAKAWAKA" *Rhythm and blues, zydeco.* Piano, accordion, harmonica, drums, vocals. Composer. Bandleader. (Born Nov. 8, 1935, Crowley, Acadia Parish.) Versatile rhythm and blues and zydeco multi-instrumentalist was raised speaking Creole French and began playing boogie-woogie piano at age seven. While attending Southern University, started working as session musician for producer **J. D. Miller** and recorded on harmonica backing **Lightnin' Slim** in 1954. In following years recorded with **Lazy Lester**, **Charles Sheffield**, and others on various instruments and recorded singles as a leader and with his groups the Dew Drops, the Drops of Joy, and the Trojans on Zynn and Spot, notably "Trojan's Walla." In 1970 relocated to Oakland and performed throughout Bay Area with his popular Gumbo Band through the early 2010s, with several releases on Blues Unlimited, Master-Trak, and his own Gumbo label, including *Bar-Be-Cueing in the Front Yard* in 2007. Also performed and recorded as Mardi Gras Indian "Big Chief Takawaka."

CLÉMENT, TERRY *Cajun, swamp pop.* Accordion, vocals. Composer. Bandleader. (Born May 5, 1934, Evangeline, Acadia Parish; July 5, 2019, Evangeline, Acadia Parish.) Noted early postwar accordionist, singer-songwriter, and leader of the Clément Brothers with siblings Purvis (1936–2004) on fiddle and Grant (1940–) on guitar, best known for their 1954 regional hit "Diggy Liggy Lo." Raised in a large musical family whose father, Laurent, played fiddle and reportedly taught **Will Kegley**, began playing accordion as a child, inspired greatly by **Nathan Abshire**. In 1949 formed the Rhythmic Five with brothers and performed throughout region. Recorded his composition "Diggy Liggy Lo" for **J. D. Miller**'s Feature label in 1954 which became a Cajun standard and in 1957 recorded one of the earliest versions of "La Chanson de Mardi Gras" for folklorist Harry Oster. In the late 1950s and 1960s performed swamp pop as the Tune Tones with pianist Everett Daigle and released numerous swamp pop and Cajun singles on Miller's Zynn, Rocko, and Cajun Classics labels. Also recorded two LPs on Kajun in the 1980s, including *A Tribute to Nathan Abshire from the Clément Brothers.* Continued performing occasionally into the 2010s.

CLINTON, TERRY (Clinton J. Thierry) *Swamp pop.* Vocals. Composer. Bandleader. (Born Apr. 23, 1940, Roanoke, Jeff. Davis Parish; died Feb. 4, 1967, Lake Charles, Calcasieu Parish.)[20] Rhythm and blues singer moved to Lake Charles in 1952 and joined **Simon "Kee-Dee" Lubin**'s band the Berry Cups in the late 1950s, a group patterned after brother **Huey "Cookie" Thierry**'s popular swamp pop band **Cookie** and the Cupcakes. In 1959 recorded single "Hurt By a Letter"/"Dolores Darlin'" with group for Khoury's.

COLAR, GEORGE *See* Kid Sheik.

COLE, SLIM (Samuel Cole) *Blues.* Guitar, vocals. Composer. Bandleader. (Born Nov. 2, 1934, Levert–St. John Plantation, St. Martinville, St. Martin Parish; died Jan. 15, 1998, Denver.)[21] Blues singer and guitarist was influenced by **Guitar Slim** and performed around St. Martinville and Lafayette area in the 1950s and early 1960s. Recorded single "They Call Me Slim Cole" on Webb around 1960. Incarcerated for robbery in the early 1960s and upon release from prison performed locally for several more years before retiring from music.

COLLET, DANNY *Cajun, swamp pop.* Accordion, guitar, vocals. Composer. Bandleader. (Born Mar. 10, 1969, Breaux Bridge, St. Martin Parish.) Noted Cajun multi-instrumentalist performed and recorded as member of the Basin Brothers with **Al Berard** in the late 1980s and early 1990s before forming his band Louisiana Swamp Cats. Released self-titled debut on Flying Fish in 1994.

In the 2000s released several recordings, including *It Wasn't Supposed to Happen* on Acadiana. Continued performing in area clubs in the 2010s.

COLLINS, BIG ROGER (Freddie Collins) *Blues.* Drums, vocals. Composer. Bandleader. (Born July 15, 1935, Ville Platte, Evangeline Parish; died Oct. 2, 2001, Crosby, Texas.) Longtime Houston-based blues singer began playing drums early on and moved to Berkeley, California, in the 1950s, performing in area clubs with Sonny Rhodes, J. J. Malone, Cool Papa Sadler, and other Bay Area blues musicians. Relocated to Houston in 1975 and became fixture on local blues scene until his death, releasing singles on Palladium and Gritz as well as LP *Houston Blues* on Lunar #2 in the early 1980s. In later years also worked as radio disc jockey.

COLLINS, JAY (Joseph Aloysius Collins Jr.) *Swamp pop.* Guitar, vocals. Composer. Bandleader. (Born Dec. 19, 1940, Church Point, Acadia Parish; died Jan. 17, 1995, Church Point, Acadia Parish.) Swamp pop guitarist and singer-songwriter of Jay and the Traveliers, who performed throughout Lafayette area in the 1970s and 1980s. Recorded singles for Tamm and One Way, including "Tell Me Why"/"Low Down Ways."

COLLINS, LEEDS "LEE" *Jazz.* Trumpet. Composer. Bandleader. (Born Oct. 17, 1901, New Orleans, Orleans Parish; died July 3, 1960, Chicago.) Highly renowned early New Orleans jazz trumpeter began working in his early teens with various bands such as Young Tuxedo Orchestra, tutored early on by **Professor Jim Humphrey**. In the late 1910s and early 1920s worked with **Chris Kelly**, **Buddy Petit**, **Papa Celestin**, **Lorenzo Tio Jr.**, **Alphonse Picou**, and others. While in Chicago in 1924 worked with **King Oliver** and recorded with **Jelly Roll Morton**. Returned to New Orleans and led his own band in the late 1920s, making historic recordings with his Jones-Collins Astoria Hot Eight in 1929 with **Davey Jones**. Worked in New York with Luis Russell in 1930 before settling in Chicago, where he continued to perform as leader and sideman.

COLLOM, WAYNE "TOOKIE" *Blues.* Harmonica, bass, vocals. (Born June 30, 1937, Vivian, Caddo Parish.) Noted blues harmonica player began playing the instrument in 1960 and later formed a blue-eyed soul band. While living in Rayville in the late 1980s formed duo Po' Henry and Tookie with guitarist **Henry Dorsey** and throughout the next two decades performed at numerous prestigious folk, jazz, and blues festivals throughout the country.

COMEAUX, RICHARD "T-COE" *Cajun.* Steel guitar, guitar. (Born June 1, 1961, Rayne, Acadia Parish.) Master Cajun pedal steel guitarist began performing at age 15 with **Terry Huval**'s Jambalaya Cajun Band, recording with group on LP *Buggy Full of Cajun Music* on Swallow in 1979. Later worked in several country bands, including Southbound with Sammy Kershaw and River Road, which toured nationally with several hits in the 1990s. Also recorded as session musician for numerous artists and groups, including **Roddie Romero**, **Warren Storm**, **Rod Bernard**, **Larry Garner**, **Pat Savant**, Ani DiFranco, Bonsoir, Catin, Feufollet, and others. In the 2000s and 2010s performed and recorded as member of several noted groups, including Lil' Band O' Gold and High Performance as well as in a duo with **Yvette Landry**.

CONN, STEVE *Rhythm and blues, Cajun, Americana.* Piano, accordion, vocals. Composer. Bandleader. (Born July 10, 1952, Pineville, Rapides Parish.) Noted pianist and singer-songwriter began performing in the early 1970s, inspired greatly by **Professor Longhair** as well as soul artists such as James Brown. Performed with band Clear Creek in New Orleans and toured with **Clarence "Gatemouth" Brown** before relocating to Colorado in 1980. Throughout next 15 years spent time in Denver and Los Angeles, where he performed with his band Gris Gris, appeared on sessions with artists such as Bonnie Raitt, and served as musical director for weekly NPR program. In the mid-1990s relocated to Nashville and worked as session musician and songwriter. Also released solo albums *River of Madness* in 1994 and *Beautiful Dream* in 2011. Continued to perform as a leader and collaborator with other artists, including **Sonny Landreth**, into the 2010s.

CONNER, ADLAR *Cajun.* Fiddle. Composer. (Born Feb. 20, 1887, Lake Arthur, Jeff. Davis Parish; died Dec. 15, 1957, Lafayette, Lafayette Parish.) Early Cajun fiddle player who recorded two influential sides with **Julian "Bee" Crader** for Brunswick in 1929. Raised in a large musical family, began playing fiddle as a child and in the 1920s performed regularly around Lake Arthur with Crader and also on second fiddle with cousins Valsin, Murphy, and **Varise Conner**. In Oct. 1929 recorded "La Valse de Boscoville" and "Lake Arthur Two-Step" with Crader for Brunswick. Continued performing into the late 1940s in the Morse area, where he later relocated, often with nephew **Cliff Conner**.

CONNER, CLIFF (Harry Cliff Conner) *Cajun.* Fiddle, vocals. (Born Dec. 15, 1921, Elton, Jeff. Davis Parish; died Sept. 2, 1997, Lake Arthur, Calcasieu Parish.)[22] Cajun fiddler began playing at age eight, mentored by uncle **Adlar Conner** while living in Lake Arthur and within a few years was performing at house dances with Adlar. In the 1930s relocated to Sweet Lake area and later performed with **Crawford Vincent**, **Phil Menard**, **Wallace Derouen**, **Buford Galley**, and others.

CONNER, VARISE *Fiddle, vocals.* Composer. (Born Oct. 21, 1906, Lake Arthur, Jeff. Davis Parish; died June 19, 1994, Jennings, Jeff. Davis Parish.) Highly revered and influential early Cajun fiddle player was raised in a large musical family and was inspired to play as a child by his father, Arsen (1859–1938), and grandfather Octave (1835–1924), who were both respected local fiddlers. In later years was greatly influenced by unrecorded Vermilion Parish Cajun fiddler Bascom Mouton (1898–1983), who performed in the 1920s and 1930s. Purchased his first fiddle from cousin **Adlar Conner** and soon began performing around Lake Arthur area with brothers Valsin (1900–1972) on fiddle and Murphy (1908–1968) on guitar as the Conner Boys. Eventually became known for performing his influential composition "Lake Arthur Stomp," which would become a Cajun standard. In the early 1930s also performed with **J. B. Fuselier**. Quit playing music in 1935 but slowly started performing again with Murphy in 1956. In the 1970s began appearing at folk festivals, occasionally partnering with **Lionel Leleux**. In following years also served as mentor to young fiddle players such as **Michael Doucet**, **Ken Smith**, and **David Greely**. Between 1975 and 1977 made a series of field recordings for folklorist Barry Jean Ancelet for the University of Louisiana at Lafayette, which were later released on 2004 CD *Louisiana Folk Masters.*

CONNICK, HARRY, JR. *Jazz.* Piano, vocals. Composer. Bandleader. (Born Sept. 11, 1967, New Orleans, Orleans Parish.) A child prodigy, began playing piano at age three and first performed in public at age five. Made his first recording at age 10 and performed duet with Eubie Blake on a Japanese documentary. During this time developed a friendship with **James Booker**, who provided piano lessons and opportunities to sit in on local gigs. Also studied under **Ellis Marsalis Jr.** and attended New Orleans Center for Creative Arts while in his teens. Moved to New York in the late 1980s and was signed to Columbia Records. In 1989 scored soundtrack for film *When Harry Met Sally* and the following year began acting in films. Continued to record, perform, act, and host television talk show in subsequent years.

CONNIE G (Connie Garrett) *Rhythm and blues.* Vocals. Bandleader. (Born September 12, 1965, Lafayette, Lafayette Parish.) Lafayette rhythm and blues singer was raised in a musical family and began performing in the mid-1980s, working early on as lead vocalist with local group Krossfire. Continued performing nationally and abroad through the 2010s with her band Creole Soul, releasing several recordings, including *Bold Soul Sista* in 2015. Father Guitar George (Alexander) was a locally renowned blues guitarist in the 1950s and 1960s, and brother Danny Alexander is a blues singer-guitarist and bandleader based in New Orleans.

CONNOR, CHARLES *Rhythm and blues.* Drums. (Born Jan. 14, 1935, New Orleans, Orleans Parish.) Highly influential early New Orleans rhythm and blues drummer and pioneer of the seminal "choo choo train" style of playing successive eighth notes with a heavy back beat. Began playing at age five and during his mid-teens started working with **Professor Longhair**, **Smiley Lewis**, **Guitar Slim**, and others. In 1953 joined Little Richard's band the Upsetters and toured and recorded with group throughout the 1950s, propelling such hits as "Keep a Knockin'" and "She's Got It." Also worked and/or recorded with James Brown, Big Joe Turner, **Shirley & Lee**, Sam Cooke, Jackie Wilson, Papa Lightfoot, and many others.

COOK, ANN *Blues.* Vocals. Composer. (Born Apr. 1886, Fazendeville, St. Bernard Parish; died Sept. 29, 1962, New Orleans, Orleans Parish.)[23] Known as "Bad Ann" for her rough character, powerful early New Orleans barrelhouse blues singer was raised in New Orleans's notorious Battlefield neighborhood and became one of Storyville's most popular singers in the 1910s. After Storyville's closure in 1917, continued performing in local clubs throughout the 1920s. In 1927 recorded "He's the Sweetest Black Man in Town" and "Mamma Cookie" on **Louis Dumaine**'s historic Jazzola Eight session for Victor. In the 1940s denounced blues and devoted herself to the church but made one final gospel recording for **Bill Russell** on American Music with **Wooden Joe Nicholas**'s band in 1949.

COOK, ROLAND "COOKIE" *Rhythm and blues.* Bass, vocals. Composer. (Born Oct. 19, 1935, New Orleans, Orleans Parish; died Sept. 10, 2000, New Orleans, Orleans Parish.) Noted bassist recorded with **Jessie Allen**, **Ed-**

die Bo, **Paul Gayten**, **Earl King**, **Big Boy Myles**, **Huey "Piano" Smith**, and others in the 1950s. Recorded one single "That's What You Do to Me" as "Cookie" for RCA/Victor in 1958.

COOKIE *See* Cook, Roland, *and* Thierry, Huey "Cookie."

COOPER, SELWYN *Blues, zydeco.* Guitar, vocals. Composer. Bandleader. (Born Jan. 3, 1954, Baldwin, St. Mary Parish.) Blues and zydeco singer-guitarist began performing in the early 1970s with Buckwheat and the Hitchhikers and later worked in zydeco bands of **Clifton Chenier**, **Rockin' Dopsie**, **Buckwheat Zydeco**, and the Zydeco Hurricanes with **John Wilson**. In the 1990s formed his Hurricane Blues Band and released CD *Louisiana Swamp Blues* on Sound of New Orleans in 1999. Continued performing in clubs and festivals throughout the South in the 2010s.

COPELAND, JOHNNY "CLYDE" *Blues.* Vocals, guitar. Composer. Bandleader. (Born Mar. 27, 1937, Haynesville, Claiborne Parish; died July 3, 1997, Manhattan, New York.) Internationally renowned blues guitarist and singer-songwriter was raised in Houston's Third Ward from his early teens. Influenced by T-Bone Walker and **Clarence "Gatemouth" Brown**, formed Dukes of Rhythm at age 13 with guitarist Joe Hughes and began performing around Houston. In 1958 released debut single "Rock and Roll Lilly" for Mercury and had regional hit with "Down on Bending Knee" for Golden Eagle in 1963. Throughout the 1960s and early 1970s continued developing his intense soul-blues style and had singles on numerous labels, including Wand, Suave, Jet Stream, Atlantic, Wet Soul, Zephyr, Kent, and Brown Sugar. Relocated to Harlem in 1975 and after several years of constant performing on the East Coast signed with Rounder and released LP *Copeland Special* in 1981. Toured nationally and overseas throughout the 1980s with five more releases on Rounder as well as the critically acclaimed LP *Showdown!* with Albert Collins and Robert Cray on Alligator in 1985. In the 1990s recorded three CDs for Gitanes/Verve, notably *Flyin' High* in 1992, and continued touring despite being diagnosed with heart disease in 1993 and enduring multiple surgeries. Six months after receiving a heart transplant succumbed to complications after a reparative procedure on heart valve. Father of blues singer Shemekia Copeland.

CORMIER, ALFRED "DUCKHEAD" *Cajun.* Guitar, drums. (Born May 7, 1931, Lake Charles, Calcasieu Parish; died Sept. 25, 1999, Lake Charles, Calcasieu Parish.) Highly accomplished Cajun guitarist performed with the Musical Aces in the late 1940s with **Earl Demary** and **Wilson Granger**, which also occasionally featured **Iry LeJeune**. In the early to mid-1950s performed with Lake Charles Playboys with LeJeune, Demary, Granger, and **Crawford Vincent**, recording with LeJeune on his famed last session for Goldband in 1954. In following decades worked with numerous musicians, including **Nathan Abshire**, **Bobby Leger**, **J. B. Fuselier**, **Sidney Brown**, **Joe Bonsall**, **Phil Menard**, **Aldus Roger**, and **Doc Guidry**.

CORMIER, ANDREW *Cajun.* Accordion, vocals. Bandleader. (Born July 13, 1936, Church Point, Acadia Parish; died June 2, 2019, Eunice, St. Landry Parish.) Cajun accordionist and bandleader moved to east Texas at age 18 and formed his band the Rambling Aces several years later, recording multiple singles on Jin and Crazy Cajun, including "Two Step de Vieux Temps," from the late 1950s through mid-1960s with band which often included **Rodney LeJeune** and **Dallas Roy**. Continued performing based in Texas until retiring from his day job as a truck driver in the early 1990s and relocating to New Orleans. Performed with **Allen Fontenot** and the Country Cajuns for several years before retiring from music in 1999 and returning to Church Point. Older brother of **Nolan Cormier**.

CORMIER, ELTON "BEE" *Cajun.* Guitar, steel guitar, fiddle, vocals. Bandleader. (Born Feb. 18, 1934, near Sunset, St. Landry Parish; died Apr. 22, 2018, Church Point, Acadia Parish.) Noted Cajun multi-instrumentalist and label owner learned to play fiddle, guitar, and steel guitar in his youth and in 1949 formed the Church Point Playboys. Performed with group for several decades and mentored many young aspiring musicians, including **Reggie Matte**, **Jimmie Venable**, **Terry Cormier**, **Felton LeJeune**, and **Jason Frey**. In the early 1970s started Bee label and throughout next two decades recorded numerous musicians and bands, including **Phil Menard**, **Ambrose Thibodeaux**, **Paul Daigle**, and the Church Point Playboys. Brother of Cajun musician Melvin Cormier.

CORMIER, JAY *Cajun.* Accordion, vocals. Composer. Bandleader. (Born June 20, 1954, Ossun, Lafayette Parish.) Traditional Cajun accordionist and bandleader recorded debut single "My Toot Toot" with **Rodney Miller** in the mid-1980s on Kajun. In 2001 released CD *Deux Vies pour de Donner (Two Lives to Give You)* on La Louisianne and continued performing with his band Cajun Born in the Lafayette area in the 2010s.

CORMIER, JOE WARREN *Cajun.* Accordion, vocals. Composer. Bandleader. (Born Apr. 12, 1945, Church Point, Acadia Parish; died Oct. 8, 2007, Opelousas, St. Landry Parish.) Cajun accordionist and singer-songwriter best known for his 1986 single "T Beck Do," which became a Cajun and zydeco standard. Released LP *Pure Cajun!* on Swallow in 1990 which included "Cinquante Piastres," which also became a bandstand favorite.

CORMIER, LESA *Cajun.* Drums, accordion, guitar, vocals. Composer. Bandleader. (Born Aug. 30, 1930, Gueydan, Vermilion Parish; died Aug. 17, 2019, Lafayette, Lafayette Parish.) Renowned Cajun drummer, singer-songwriter, and longtime bandleader of the Sundown Playboys was raised in Elton and learned accordion from his father, **Lionel Cormier**, as a child. Relocated to Lake Charles and in the late 1940s joined his father's band the Elton Playboys, which would soon be renamed the Sundown Playboys, as drummer and vocalist. Appeared on the band's vast majority of recordings on Feature, Goldband, Cajun Classics, Kajun, Swallow, and Apple through the early 1970s. After his father's death in 1971, took over leadership of band and through the early 1990s had releases on Swallow, Bee, and La Louisianne, including LP *Saturday Night Cajun Music!* in 1988. Continued leading and performing with Sundown Playboys into the late 2010s. Father of Sundown Playboys bass and steel-guitar player Danny Cormier.

CORMIER, LIONEL *Cajun.* Accordion. Composer. Bandleader. (Born Feb. 26, 1913, Rayne, Acadia Parish; died June 5, 1971, Lake Charles, Calcasieu Parish.) Early post-war Cajun accordionist and bandleader began learning the instrument as a child from his father Arvillien and by his early teens was playing local house dances. In 1947 formed the Elton Playboys with **Percy Fuselier**, which was soon to be joined by son **Lesa Cormier** and renamed the Sundown Playboys. Recorded debut single "Welcome Club Waltz"/"Sundown Playboys Special" for Feature in 1952. Releases followed on Goldband and Cajun Classics through the late 1960s, including "Big Boy Bounce" and "Waltz of My Heart." Continued performing with group until suffering fatal heart attack at age 58 while performing at the Bamboo Club in Lake Charles. Grandfather of bass and steel-guitar player Danny Cormier.

CORMIER, LOUIS *Cajun.* Accordion. Composer. Bandleader. (Born Oct. 8, 1908, Mire, Acadia Parish; died July 18, 1970, Lafayette, Lafayette Parish.) Cajun accordionist and leader of the Moonlight Playboys who recorded several singles for Swallow and La Louisianne in the late 1950s and mid-1960s, notably "Drunkard's Blues"/"One Step de Duson" in 1959.

CORMIER, NOLAN *Cajun.* Accordion, guitar, steel guitar, bass, vocals. Composer. Bandleader. (Born Sept. 20, 1951, Church Point, Acadia Parish.) Cajun multi-instrumentalist and singer-songwriter began performing at age 14 and in 1970 formed the Louisiana Ramblers. In the early 1970s recorded singles for Goldband and Swallow, notably "Hee Haw Breakdown," which would become his signature song and a Cajun and zydeco standard. Also recorded with **Robert Bertrand** in the early 1970s. Later formed the Cajun Hee Haws and continued performing in the 2010s, with releases on Kajun and Bee. Father of Cajun fiddler Chad Cormier and brother of **Andrew Cormier**.

CORMIER, SHERYL *Cajun.* Accordion. Composer. Bandleader. (Born Mar. 15, 1945, Grand Coteau, St. Landry Parish.) Pioneering female Cajun accordionist and bandleader began playing accordion at age seven and performed early on in her father Andrew Guilbeau's band the Sunset Playboys. In the late 1970s and early 1980s performed in all-female Cajun band and also began performing with **Blackie Forestier**, which led to her debut single on Kajun in 1979. In the mid-1980s formed her band the Cajun Sounds with husband Russell Cormier on vocals and released debut CD *La Reine de Musique Cadjine* on Swallow in 1990. Continued to perform through the 2010s with numerous European tours, often billed as the "Queen of Cajun Music."

CORMIER, TERRY *Cajun.* Accordion, vocals. Bandleader. (Born Feb. 22, 1951, Church Point, Acadia Parish.) Cajun accordionist and bandleader got his start performing with **Bee Cormier**'s Church Point Playboys and recorded several singles and LP *Church Point Playboys Produce Four Accordion Players* in the early 1970s on Bee. In 1975 recorded two singles with **D. L. Menard** and the Louisiana Aces for Swallow. In the 1990s formed band Louisiana Cajun Heat and released *Une Vielle Memoire Cajine* on Acadiana. Performed with Louisiana Pride in the 2000s.

CORNISH, WILLIE *Jazz.* Valve trombone. Composer. (Born Aug. 1, 1875, New Orleans, Orleans Parish; died Jan. 12, 1942, New Orleans, Orleans Parish.) Very influential early jazz trombonist and member of **Buddy Bolden**'s band from 1897 to 1903. Performed with various brass bands through the early 1920s, including Eureka Brass Band.

COTTON, LAWRENCE "KING" *Rhythm and blues, jazz.* Piano. Composer. (Born Feb. 2, 1927, New Orleans, Orleans Parish.)[24] Early rhythm and blues pianist was inspired by his father, who was also a pianist. In 1950 joined **Lloyd Lambert**'s band and from 1953 to 1958 toured and recorded with group behind **Guitar Slim**. In the 1960s and 1970s worked with **Edgar Blanchard**, **Danny White**, and **Dave Bartholomew**. From the 1980s through 2000s performed regularly with **Wallace Davenport** and the group Bourbon Street Five in the French Quarter, among others. Continued performing regularly in New Orleans into his 90s.

COTTRELL, LOUIS, JR. *Jazz.* Clarinet, saxophone. Bandleader. (Born Mar. 7, 1911, New Orleans, Orleans Parish; died Mar. 21, 1978, New Orleans, Orleans Parish.) Son of **Louis Cottrell Sr.**, studied clarinet with **Barney Bigard** and **Lorenzo Tio Jr.** In the late 1920s and 1930s worked with **Chris Kelly**, **Kid Rena**, and **Sidney Desvigne**, and toured North America with **Don Albert**. In following decades worked and recorded with **Paul Barbarin**, **Alphonse Piron**, **Peter Bocage**, and **Sweet Emma Barrett**, among others. Led Heritage Hall Brass Band in the 1970s.

COTTRELL, LOUIS, SR. *Jazz.* Drums. (Born Dec. 25, 1878, New Orleans, Orleans Parish; died Oct. 17, 1927, New Orleans, Orleans Parish.) Highly influential early jazz drummer who is widely regarded as one of New Orleans's greatest percussionists. Performed with **John Robichaux** and Olympia Orchestra from the early 1900s through mid-1910s. Between 1916 and 1918 worked in Chicago with **Manuel Perez**. Performed and later recorded with **Armand Piron** from the late 1910s until his death. Father of **Louis Cottrell Jr.**

COUNT ROCKIN' SIDNEY *See* Rockin' Sidney.

COUNTRY JIM (James Bledsoe) *Blues.* Guitar, vocals. Composer. (Born May 28, 1930, Mansfield, DeSoto Parish; died Oct. 15, 1988, Houston.)[25] Louisiana Delta blues guitarist and singer-songwriter performed around Shreveport in the late 1940s and early 1950s and made recording debut with single on local Pacemaker label in 1949 as Hot Rod Happy. Although inspired early on by T-Bone Walker, he recorded in a rural style that evoked John Lee Hooker and Lightnin' Hopkins and cut four singles for Imperial in 1950, including "Old River Blues" and "Avenue Breakdown." In 1951–52 recorded nearly 20 sides for Specialty, most of which remained unissued. Signed with Don Robey's Peacock label in late 1951, but no known sessions for the label followed. Relocated to Houston in 1952 and performed as lead guitarist in bands in various area clubs, including Robey's famed Bronze Peacock Dinner Club. Continued performing in Houston clubs into the late 1950s before retiring from music. Succumbed to lung cancer at age 58.

COURVILLE, SADY *Cajun.* Fiddle. Composer. Bandleader. (Born Nov. 15, 1905, Chataignier, Evangeline Parish; died Jan. 3, 1988, Eunice, St. Landry Parish.) Highly regarded early Cajun fiddle pioneer best known for his long musical partnership with **Dennis McGee**. Hailing from a long line of fiddlers which spanned several generations, began playing around age 10, learning his twin-fiddle style from his father, Eraste Courville (1879–1954), and uncle Arville Courville (1882–1929), both renowned local players. By the late 1910s was playing professionally and began partnering with McGee in 1922. Throughout the 1920s also performed with **Leo Soileau**, **Amédé Ardoin**, and **Angelas LeJeune**. In Mar. 1929 recorded eight historic duets with McGee for Vocalion, including "Mon Chère Bébé Crèole" and "Courville and McGee Waltz," which documented the Cajun twin-fiddle style for the first time on record. Retired from music to support family in late 1929 and in the 1960s began performing regularly again, often appearing on Revon Reed's radio broadcast from Fred's Lounge in Mamou. Also continued working regularly with McGee, appearing at national festivals throughout the 1970s. Made several recordings in the 1960s and 1970s with McGee, **Nathan Abshire**, **Cursey Fontenot**, and **Shirley Bergeron** as well as his Mamou Hour Cajun Band, notably 1977 Swallow LP *La Vieille Musique Acadienne* with McGee.

COUSIN JOE (Pleasant Joseph) *Blues, jazz.* Piano, guitar, vocal. Composer. Bandleader. (Born Dec. 20, 1907, Wallace, St. John the Baptist Parish; died Oct. 2, 1989, New Orleans, Orleans Parish.) Internationally renowned blues and jazz multi-instrumentalist and songwriter was raised in New Orleans from age two. Began performing as a street dancer and ukulele player in the 1920s and in the 1930s worked as guitarist and singer with **Joe Robichaux**, **Billie** and **De De Pierce**, **Paul Barbarin**, **Harold Dejan**, **Armand Piron**, and others. Relocated to New York in the 1940s and recorded extensively for numerous labels, including King Jazz, Savoy, Gotham, Signature, and Decca and became popular on the thriving Harlem music scene with his jazz-inflected jump blues recordings such as "Box Car Shorty (and Peter Blue)." Also recorded with **Sidney Bechet**, Sam Price, Mezz Mezzrow, and Earl Bostic. Returned to New Orleans in the late 1940s and had releases on Decca, Imperial (often as Smilin' Joe), and Flip through the mid-1950s. In 1964 toured England as member of popular Blues & Gospel Train program which prompted major career resurgence. Through the early 1980s toured Europe regularly and appeared on major U.S. festivals with recordings on Big Bear, Black and Blue, and Bluesway. Released last recording, *Relaxin' in New Orleans,* on Great Southern in 1985.

COVINGTON, BLIND/BOGUS BEN *See* Curry, Ben.

COYCAULT, ERNEST "NENNY" *Jazz.* Cornet. (Born June 23, 1885, Violet, St. Bernard Parish; died July 1, 1940, Los Angeles.)[26] Early New Orleans jazz cornetist worked with the Peerless and Superior orchestras as well as **Gaspard** brothers and **Emile Barnes** from the mid-1900s through 1914. Relocated to Los Angeles and worked and recorded with Sonny Clay's orchestra. Older brother of jazz clarinetist Phil Coycault, who worked regularly with **Buddy Petit** in the early 1920s.

CRADER, JULIEN "BEE" *Cajun.* Accordion, vocals. Composer. (Born Jan. 2, 1892, Rayne, Acadia Parish; died Feb. 26, 1946, New Orleans, Orleans Parish.)[27] Very early Cajun accordionist and singer who recorded two sides with **Adlar Conner** for Brunswick in Oct. 1929, "Valse de "Boscoville" and "Lake Arthur Two-Step," both considered important early Cajun recordings. Began learning accordion in his youth and performed at dance halls in Lake Arthur area after family relocated there around 1908. Later moved to New Orleans in 1924 and spent remainder of life working mainly outside music as a chef.

CRAWFORD, JAMES "SUGAR BOY" *Rhythm and blues.* Vocals, piano, trombone. Composer. Bandleader. (Born Oct. 12, 1934, New Orleans, Orleans Parish; died Sept. 15, 2012, New Orleans, Orleans Parish.) Early New Orleans rhythm and blues pianist and singer-songwriter joined his first band while in high school in 1950 with **Big Boy Myles** which recorded as the Sha-Weez for Aladdin. In 1953 wrote and recorded "Jock-A-Mo" for Chess Records, which became a New Orleans and Mardi Gras classic. Continued recording for Chess and also had releases on Imperial, Montel, and Ace through the early 1960s. In 1963 was brutally beaten by police during a traffic stop and retired from performing. Made rare occasional appearances in the 2000s singing gospel, preferring to sing only in church. Grandfather of jazz pianist and singer Davell Crawford (1975–).

CRAWFORD, VINCENT *See* Vincent, Crawford.

CREDEUR, ANATOLE *Cajun.* Accordion, vocals. Composer. Bandleader. (Born Sept. 6, 1898, near Church Point, Acadia Parish; died Sept. 11, 1944, Black Bayou, Calcasieu Parish.)[28] Early Cajun accordionist settled with family in Black Bayou, south of Lake Charles, in the early 1920s and formed the Black Bayou Band with wife, Ada (1900–1988), on triangle; Sidney Granger (1908–1977) on fiddle; and **Theo Young** on guitar. In Nov. 1929 recorded four sides for Brunswick (mis-credited as "Anatole Credure") with Young and Granger, including "Black Bayou One Step" and "Lake Charles Waltz." Continued performing, often with son Pierre (1919–2003) and Granger and his brother **Wilson Granger**, into the early 1940s.

CREDEUR, LEON "CRIP" *Cajun.* Fiddle, vocals. Composer. (Born Apr. 7, 1896, Carencro, Lafayette Parish; died Mar. 13, 1959, Lafayette, Lafayette Parish.)[29] Early Cajun swing fiddle player and singer performed with the Jolly Boys of Lafayette with brothers Red and **Joe Fabacher** in the 1930s and recorded 10 sides with group for Decca in 1937, including "Jolly Boys' Breakdown," "Abbeville," and "Old Man Crip." In the 1950s performed as member of **Pee Wee Broussard**'s Melody Boys.

CREDO, WILLIAM "CHUCK," JR. *Jazz.* Clarinet. Bandleader. (Born Aug. 6, 1926, New Orleans, Orleans Parish; died Nov. 11, 2010, New Orleans, Orleans Parish.) Longtime bandleader of the Skylarks and later Basin Street Six which performed throughout New Orleans and toured overseas.

CREDURE, ANATOLE *See* Credeur, Anotole.

CROCHET, CLEVELAND *Cajun.* Fiddle. Composer. Bandleader. (Born Jan. 30, 1919, near Jennings, Jeff. Davis Parish; died Nov. 28, 2011, Lake Charles, Calcasieu Parish.) Popular Cajun fiddle player best known for his 1961 blues-influenced hit "Sugar Bee," which was the first Cajun record to make *Billboard*'s Top 100. Formed his band Hillbilly Ramblers in 1950 and in following years members included nephew **John Crochet**, **Sidney Brown**, **Pee Wee Broussard**, and others. After singles on Folk-Star and Khoury's, recorded "Sugar Bee" for Goldband in late 1960, featuring **Jay Stutes** on vocals and steel guitar and **Shorty LeBlanc** on accordion, which became a national hit and Cajun standard. After song's success, renamed band the Sugar Bees and recorded several more singles before leaving group around 1962. Brothers Clenny and Clarence were also fiddle players, and brother Edgar played accordion.

CROCHET, JOHN *Cajun, country.* Steel guitar, fiddle, guitar, drums. Bandleader. (Born Sept. 20, 1932, Pine Island, Calcasieu Parish; died Nov. 22, 2013, Nacogdoches, Texas.) Cajun multi-instrumentalist learned fiddle from his father, Clenny, and uncle **Cleveland Crochet** and performed as guitarist in his father's band during his early teens. In the 1950s performed and recorded as drummer and steel guitarist with Cleveland's Hillbilly Ramblers and **Sidney Brown**'s Traveler Playboys. Relocated to Nacogdoches, Texas, in 1970 to work as barber and continued performing, later forming country bands Hard Country and Midnight Express, the latter of which included **Manson Manuel**.

CROKER, JAMES "GLEN" (James Glenwood Croker) *Cajun.* Steel guitar, guitar, vocals. (Born Feb. 28, 1934, Lake Charles, Calcasieu Parish; died Aug. 23, 2011, Lake Charles, Calcasieu Parish.) Noted Cajun steel guitarist and singer best known for his long tenure performing and recording with the Hackberry Ramblers with **Luderin Darbone** and **Edwin Duhon** from 1959 through the early 2000s. Often served as lead vocalist, and expanded band's repertoire to include rhythm and blues and swamp pop songs. Also performed with producer **Eddie Shuler**'s All Star Reveliers in the 1950s.

CROSBY, OCTAVE *Jazz.* Piano. Bandleader. (Born June 10, 1898, New Orleans, Orleans Parish; died Oct. 1, 1971, New Orleans, Orleans Parish.) New Orleans jazz pianist began performing in the early 1920s with **Herb Morand**. Led his own band on Bourbon Street in the 1950s and early 1960s.

CRUMB, EARL *Jazz.* Drums. Bandleader. (Born Apr. 30, 1899, New Orleans, Orleans Parish; died Feb. 1979, Rochester, New York.)[30] Early New Orleans jazz drummer worked with the Invincibles and Six and Seven Eights String Band in the late 1910s and early 1920s. Later performed and recorded with the popular New Orleans Owls throughout the 1920s.

CRUTCHFIELD, JAMES *Blues.* Piano, vocals. Composer. Bandleader. (Born May 25, 1912, Baton Rouge, EBR Parish; died Dec. 7, 2001, St. Louis, Missouri.) Early barrelhouse blues piano player and singer moved with his mother to Bogalusa in the 1920s and began teaching himself piano during his early teens. In the late 1920s and 1930s traveled throughout Louisiana, Mississippi, and Texas and performed at juke joints and lumber camps, often crossing paths with early mentors **Champion Jack Dupree** and **Little Brother Montgomery**. Also worked regularly with blues singer Joe Pullum in the 1930s and Elmore James in the mid-1940s. In 1948 settled in St. Louis and became a fixture on the local blues scene through the 1960s, making recording debut in 1957. After a decade working outside music, began performing again in the early 1980s and toured Europe, recording LP *Original Barrelhouse Blues* for Swingmaster in 1983. Continued performing regularly in St. Louis until his death, often accompanied in later years by guitarist Bennie Smith.

CUPID (Bryson Bernard) *Rhythm and blues.* Vocals. Composer. Bandleader. (Born Dec. 22, 1982, Lafayette, Lafayette Parish.) Popular contemporary rhythm and blues singer and songwriter best known for his 2007 hit "Cupid Shuffle," which inspired a national line-dance craze. Began singing in church choir as a child and in the late 1990s performed in local rhythm and blues group Fifth Element. In the early 2000s launched solo career and released self-titled debut recording in 2002. Several releases followed through 2010s, including *Time for a Change* on Atlantic, which featured double-platinum hit "Cupid Shuffle," in 2007. Continued touring and recording in the 2010s.

CURRY, BEN *Blues.* Harmonica, mandolin-banjo, vocals. Composer. (Born possibly Apr. 1892, Claiborne Parish, or Arcadia, Bienville Parish; died around 1950, Arcadia, Bienville Parish.) Enigmatic early prewar blues musician who recorded six sides for Paramount around 1932, including "Boodle De Bum Bum" and "Hot Dog." Believed to have recorded under names Bogus Ben Covington for Paramount in 1928, Blind Ben Covington for Banner in 1929, and Memphis Ben on two unissued audition tests for Vocalion in 1928.

DAIGLE, PAUL *Cajun.* Accordion, vocals. Composer. Bandleader. (Born Apr. 2, 1958, Pointe Noire, near Church Point, Acadia Parish.) Renowned Cajun accordion player, singer-songwriter, and cofounder of premier 1980s band Cajun Gold with **Robert Elkins**, best known for their 1986 regional hit "Georgie Lou." Began playing accordion at age 10, inspired by uncle **Wilson Leger**, and while in his teens won several prestigious local accordion contests. In the early 1980s formed Cajun Gold with Elkins and performed and recorded with group through 1990, releasing singles on Bee in 1984, followed by multiple acclaimed LPs on Swallow. Toured nationally and overseas in the next several years before group disbanded in the early 1990s. After working mainly outside music throughout the decade, joined Baton Rouge–based traditional Cajun band Savoir Faire in the late 1990s and performed and recorded with group through the 2000s. In the 2010s continued performing with reformed Cajun Gold.

DAIGLE, PIERRE V. *Cajun.* Vocals. Composer. (Born Nov. 23, 1923, Church Point, Acadia Parish; died May 15, 2001, Church Point, Acadia Parish.) Noted traditional Cajun singer, songwriter, and author of 1972 book *Tears, Love and Laughter: The Story of the Cajuns and their Music.* Appeared on Folkways LP *Cajun Home Music* in 1977. Composed numerous Cajun songs, many of which appeared on **Paul Daigle** and **Robert Elkins**'s Cajun Gold LPs, notably *La Lumière Dons Ton Châssis* on Swallow in 1987.

DAIGLE, WILBERT *Cajun.* Fiddle. (Born Apr. 27, 1936, Pointe Noire, near Church Point, Acadia Parish; died Feb. 15, 1999, Lake Charles, Calcasieu Parish.) Cajun fiddler began performing in the 1950s and worked with **Austin Pitre**, **Bee Cormier**, **Darrel Higginbotham**, and many others. In the early 1970s formed Calcasieu Ramblers with **August Broussard** and recorded a single with group on Buck in 1977. In the 1990s performed with **John Oliver**'s Louisiana Ramblers.

DAIGREPONT, BRUCE *Cajun.* Accordion, vocals. Composer. Bandleader. (Born July 11, 1958, New Orleans, Orleans Parish.) Cajun accordionist and singer-songwriter who helped popularize live Cajun music in New Orleans in the 1980s, performing every Sunday at Tipitina's for thirty years. Son of Cajun French–speaking parents who moved to New Orleans from Avoyelles Parish in the 1950s and began playing guitar and banjo as a child. In 1978 started learning accordion and by 1980 was leading a band. Released multiple recordings on Rounder in the late 1980s and 1990s, including *Paradis* in 1999, and continued recording and touring internationally through the 2010s.

DAMON, LENNY *See* Capello, Lenny.

DARBONE, LUDERIN *Cajun.* Fiddle, vocals. Composer. Bandleader. (Born Jan. 14, 1913, Evangeline, Acadia Parish; died Nov. 21, 2008, Sulphur, Calcasieu Parish.) Influential early Cajun fiddle player and bandleader who cofounded famed Cajun string band the Hackberry Ramblers with **Edwin Duhon** and continued performing with group for more than 70 years. Raised in east Texas and inspired by string bands, relocated to Hackberry with family and soon met Cajun guitarist and accordionist Duhon. Formed Hackberry Ramblers in Mar. 1933 and within months group was performing throughout Lake Charles area and broadcasting on local radio, becoming the first Cajun band to incorporate Western swing and employ the use of electronic stage amplification in dance-hall performances. Between 1935 and 1939 recorded over 80 sides for Bluebird, including the first version of "Jolie Blonde," which was a reworking of **Amédée Breaux**'s 1929 recording "Ma Blonde Est Partié." Band's versatile repertoire also included blues and jazz numbers. Group had releases on Deluxe in the late 1940s and recorded LP *Louisiana Cajun Music* for Arhoolie in 1963. Continued performing with Hackberry Ramblers throughout the next several decades into the mid-2000s, with several overseas tours and two recordings in the 1990s, including acclaimed release *Deep Water* on Hot Biscuits in 1997, produced by drummer and band member Ben Sandmel.

DARBY, HUEY *Swamp pop.* Drums, vocals. Composer. (Born Dec. 28, 1934, Loreauville, Iberia Parish; died Sept. 24, 2003, Lafayette, Lafayette Parish.) Noted swamp pop drummer and singer performed and recorded as member of New Iberia–based band **Randy** and the Rockets in the late 1950s and 1960s and had singles as a leader on N-Joy, Mon-Art, and Tamm, notably "Rockin' Robin" in 1965. Also worked regularly with **Rod Bernard** and as radio broadcaster for more than 40 years.

DARENSBOURG, JOE *Jazz.* Clarinet, saxophone. Composer. Bandleader. (Born July 9, 1906, Baton Rouge, EBR Parish; died May 24, 1985, Van Nuys, California.) Internationally renowned early New Orleans jazz clarinet and saxophone player studied under **Alphonse Picou** and worked with various groups in the mid-1920s, including **Buddy Petit**'s band. In following years traveled extensively with medicine shows and circus bands and worked on riverboats with **Fate Marable** and Charlie Creath. In the late 1920s relocated to Los Angeles and played saxophone in **Mutt Carey**'s Liberty Syncopators. From 1944 through the mid-1950s worked and recorded with **Kid Ory**. Formed band Dixie Flyers in the late 1950s and had national hit with "Yellow Dog Blues" in 1958 on Lark. Toured internationally with **Louis Armstrong**'s All Stars from 1961 to 1964 and performed as member of the Legends of Jazz from 1973 to 1975. His autobiography *Jazz Odyssey* was released posthumously in 1987.

DARENSBOURG, PERCY *Jazz.* Banjo, guitar. (Born Mar. 20, 1902, Killona, St. Charles Parish; died Nov. 12, 1950, Dallas.)[1] Early New Orleans jazz banjo and guitar player who recorded as member of **Polite Christian**'s Frenchy's String Band in 1928. Later operated a tavern in Dallas and was killed by stabbing during a street altercation. Brother Caffery Darensbourg (1901–1942) was also a jazz banjo and guitar player who worked with **Armand Piron** and **Manuel Perez** in the 1920s and died of a gunshot wound in Dallas in 1940.

DAUPHINE, MORRIS *Jazz.* Saxophone, clarinet. (Born Nov. 16, 1906, Parks, St. Martin Parish; died Nov. 1973, New Iberia, Iberia Parish.)[2] Noted early Acadiana jazz saxophonist who performed with the Banner Orchestra in the 1930s and 1940s, often with **Harold Potier Sr.** and **Bunk Johnson**. In 1925 relocated to New Orleans and studied under **Lorenzo Tio Jr.** Worked with **Papa Celestin**'s Tuxedo Brass Band before moving to Baton Rouge in 1927 to perform with the Deluxe Harmony Players dance band. In 1930 returned to Parks and continued performing occasionally with various bands, including **Gus Fontenette**'s Banner Orchestra, while operating a local nightclub.

DAVENPORT, WALLACE *Jazz, rhythm and blues.* Trumpet. Bandleader. (Born June 30, 1925, New Orleans, Orleans Parish; died Mar. 18, 2004, New Orleans, Orleans Parish.) Began playing trumpet at age 13 and worked with Young Tuxedo Brass Band and **Papa Celestin** in the late 1930s and early 1940s. Throughout the 1950s and 1960s worked and/or recorded with Lionel Hampton, Count Basie, Ray Charles, **Lloyd Price**, **Roy Brown**, Mezz Mezzrow, and others. Recorded with Earl Hines and led his own group in the 1970s.

DAVID, RANDY *Swamp pop.* Guitar. Composer. Bandleader. (Born Dec. 18, 1924, Abbeville, Vermilion Parish; died Sept. 1986, New Iberia, Iberia Parish.)[3] Noted bandleader of locally popular New Iberia–based early swamp pop band Randy and the Rockets which he led from 1957 until disbanding in 1972, best known for their 1962 regional hit "Let's Do the Cajun Twist" on Jin. Group also had singles on N-Joy, Viking, and Azalea, including "Genevieve" in 1959. Rockets reunited a final time at Club La Louisiane in New Iberia in 1983 three years before his death from cancer at age 61.

DAVIS, BONNIE (Gertrude Smith) *Rhythm and blues.* Vocals. (Born June 10, 1920, New Orleans, Orleans Parish; died Aug.1976, East Orange, New Jersey.) Raised in Bessemer, Alabama, joined group Piccadilly Pipers in the early 1940s and recorded for several labels through the 1950s including Savoy, where she had the hit "Don't Stop Now" in 1943. Recorded with pianist husband Clem Moorman as Bonnie & Clem in 1966 and performed together as duo through the early 1970s.

DAVIS, GEORGE *Rhythm and blues, jazz.* Guitar, bass,

saxophone, oboe. Composer. (Born Mar. 30, 1938, New Orleans, Orleans Parish; died Sept. 10, 2008, Lilburn, Georgia.)[4] Important and influential rhythm and blues session musician of the 1950s and 1960s. Member of the Hawketts in the mid-1950s and worked extensively with producers **Allen Toussaint** and **Wardell Quezergue** in the 1960s, appearing on hits by **Lee Dorsey**, **Robert Parker**, **Aaron Neville**, **Willie Tee**, and many others. Cowrote Neville's "Tell It Like It Is," which was released on his Par Lo label. In the 1970s relocated to New York and did session work with Sarah Vaughan, Buddy Rich, Duke Ellington, and others.

DAVIS, JIMMIE "THE SINGING GOVERNOR" *Country, gospel, blues.* Vocals, guitar. Composer. Bandleader. (Born Sept. 11, 1899, Quitman, Jackson Parish; died Nov. 5, 2000, Baton Rouge, EBR Parish.) Highly successful singer-songwriter and former two-term Louisiana governor best known for his 1940 recording "You Are My Sunshine." Began recording for Victor in 1929, influenced greatly by Jimmie Rodgers, and through 1932 cut numerous country, blues, and gospel sides for the label, frequently accompanied by **Oscar Woods**, **Snoozer Quinn**, or Buddy Jones. Some of his risqué double-entendre blues recordings would later be used against him by political opponents. In 1934 began decades-long association with Decca and had various hits on label including "Nobody's Darlin' But Mine," "Is It Too Late Now," and "There's a New Moon Over My Shoulder," the latter released in 1945 while serving first term as governor. In the 1950s and 1960s had successful career as gospel recording artist. In the late 1960s married gospel singer Anna Carter Gordon, and the pair continued to perform and record together for various labels through the late 1990s. In 1977 "You Are My Sunshine" was proclaimed an Official State Song of Louisiana.

DAVIS, JOSEPH "JO COOL" *Gospel.* Vocals. (Born Feb. 26, 1953, New Orleans, Orleans Parish; died Aug. 5, 2016, New Orleans, Orleans Parish.) Beloved spiritual singer who was among the first to bring gospel music from the church to New Orleans nightclubs such as Tipitina's in the 1980s. Hosted popular Sunday gospel brunch and appeared at New Orleans Jazz & Heritage Festival for three decades.

DAVIS, OSCAR "HARPO" *Blues.* Harmonica, vocals. Bandleader. (Born Oct. 10, 1943, Glynn, Pointe Coupee Parish.) Baton Rouge swamp blues harmonica player and singer greatly influenced by mentor **Slim Harpo**. Recorded behind **Tabby Thomas** in the mid-1980s and appeared on several tracks as a leader on Wolf's *Louisiana Swamp Blues* series and *Louisiana Blues Live at Tabby's Blues Box* releases. Also worked regularly with **Clarence Edwards**. In the 2010s continued performing locally, widely regarded as one of Baton Rouge's finest traditional swamp blues harmonica players.

DAVIS, PETER *Jazz.* Cornet, piano. (Born Oct. 25, 1887, New Orleans, Orleans Parish; died Apr. 29, 1971, New Orleans, Orleans Parish.) Early New Orleans jazz music professor best known as **Louis Armstrong**'s first teacher at the Colored Waif's Home for Boys in the 1910s. Taught countless young musicians, including **Kid Rena**, **Danny Barker**, **Chester Zardis**, **Willie** and **Percy Humphrey**, and **Dave Bartholomew**. Also performed with various jazz groups in New Orleans through the 1960s.

DAYS, EMMA L. *See* Jackson, Emma L.

DE DROIT, JOHNNY *Jazz.* Trumpet, piano. Composer. Bandleader. (Born Dec. 4, 1892, New Orleans, Orleans Parish; died Feb. 13, 1986, New Orleans, Orleans Parish.)[5] Early New Orleans jazz trumpeter first heard jazz performed in Storyville and by the late 1910s began leading his own band. Throughout the 1920s performed at posh hotels, restaurants and high society functions with his New Orleans Jazz Orchestra, which included younger brother Paul on drums. In 1924–25 recorded nine sides with group for OKeh. Continued leading his popular band in New Orleans for four decades until retiring from music in the 1960s.

DEACON JOHN (John Moore) *Rhythm and blues.* Guitar, banjo, vocals. Composer. Bandleader. (Born June 23, 1941, New Orleans, Orleans Parish.) Raised in a large musical family, veteran New Orleans rhythm and blues singer-guitarist and bandleader began performing with his group the Ivories as house-band at the famed Dew Drop Inn in the late 1950s. Mentored by **George Davis**, recorded extensively throughout the 1960s with producers such as **Dave Bartholomew** and **Allen Toussaint** and appeared on sessions with **Ernie K-Doe**, **Aaron Neville**, **Lee Dorsey**, and others. Also recorded several singles as leader in the 1960s. Continued to perform in New Orleans clubs and at social events throughout following decades. Released two recordings in the 1990s, notably *Live at the 1994 New Orleans Jazz & Heritage Festival* on RedBone, and in 2003 was featured in documentary and companion CD *Deacon John's Jump Blues.* In 2019 released CD single *Crowded Shotgun House.*

Older brother of **Charles Moore**, who performs with his band.

DEAN, GABE (Gabriel Dean Luneau) *Swamp pop.* Vocals. Bandleader. (Born Feb. 17, 1944, Alexandria, Rapides Parish.) At age 16 recorded two swamp pop singles for Goldband in 1960 including "Slop and Stroll Jolie Blonde." Later relocated to California and performed country and pop music under given name.

DEAN, TOMMY *Rhythm and blues.* Piano. Composer. Bandleader. (Born Sept. 6, 1909, Franklin, St. Mary Parish; died Jan. 6, 1965, St. Louis, Missouri.)[6] Noted St. Louis–based early jump blues pianist, songwriter, and bandleader was raised in Beaumont and performed with traveling carnivals and circuses early in career. After touring with swing bands in the 1930s, formed his own group and relocated to St. Louis in the late 1930s. In the mid-1940s began performing around Chicago and made recording debut for Town & Country in 1947. From 1949 to 1952 recorded for Miracle and States before signing with Vee-Jay in 1954, which produced several releases in following years, including "Evenin' Time" and "One More Mile" featuring vocalist Joe Buckner. Continued to perform in the Midwest until succumbing to a fatal heart attack at age 55.

DECLOUET, THADDEUS *Creole, zydeco.* Accordion, vocals. Composer. (Born Sept. 17, 1905, Opelousas, St. Landry Parish; died Aug. 10, 1980, Lake Charles, Calcasieu Parish.)[7] Enigmatic early zydeco accordion player and singer relocated to Lake Charles with family by 1930 and worked as a farmer early on. Recorded several sides for **Eddie Shuler**'s Folk-Star label around 1954, including "Catch that Morning Train" and "Know That Isn't Right," being among the first to record zydeco on his piano accordion.

DECOU, WALTER *Jazz.* Piano. Bandleader. (Born Jan. 27, 1896, New Orleans, Orleans Parish; died Dec. 16, 1966, New Orleans, Orleans Parish.)[8] Early jazz pianist worked in Storyville District in the 1910s and led his own band in the early 1920s which included **Willie Pajeaud**. Recorded with **Sam Morgan** in 1927 and **Bunk Johnson** in 1942.

DEJAN, HAROLD "DUKE" *Jazz.* Saxophone, vocals. Bandleader. (Born Feb. 4, 1909, New Orleans, Orleans Parish; died July 5, 2002, New Orleans, Orleans Parish.) Prominent bandleader and saxophonist who led Olympia Brass Band to international stardom from the 1950s through early 2000s. Began performing during his teens, tutored early on by **Earl Fouché**, and worked with Moonlight Serenaders. Led bands on riverboats and steamers in the late 1920s and 1930s. Later performed regularly at Preservation Hall with Olympia Brass Band and made a number of recordings with group and toured overseas. After suffering a stroke in 1990, continued on as vocalist in band.

DELAFOSE, GENO *Zydeco.* Accordion, drums, guitar, bass, vocals. Composer. Bandleader. (Born Feb. 6, 1971, Eunice, St. Landry Parish.) Popular accordionist and bandleader with both zydeco and Cajun influences began performing on rubboard at age eight in his father **John Delafose**'s band the Eunice Playboys. He soon switched to drums and later began playing accordion in the band, influenced by his father as well as **Clifton Chenier** and **Iry LeJeune**. Performed and recorded with band until his father's death in 1994 and released debut album *French Rockin' Boogie* on Rounder later that year. Toured extensively with his French Rockin' Boogie band in following years with two more releases on Rounder in the late 1990s. In the 2000s released two CDs on Times Square, including the highly acclaimed *Le Cowboy Creole* in 2007. Continued performing extensively in the 2010s as one of southwest Louisiana's most popular zydeco bands. Younger brother of noted zydeco bassist and drummer Tony Delafose, who recorded as leader on Deep South, Zydeco Hound, and his own label. Uncle of **Gerard Delafose**.

DELAFOSE, GERARD *Zydeco.* Accordion, drums, vocals. Composer. Bandleader. (Born Feb. 11, 1984, Eunice, St. Landry Parish.) Traditional zydeco accordion player and singer started out playing drums and began playing accordion at age 12, inspired by his grandfather **John Delafose** and uncle **Geno Delafose**. In the 2010s continued performing with his band the Zydeco Gators in clubs throughout southwest Louisiana and released CD *Can't Make U Love Me!* in 2017.

DELAFOSE, JOHN *Zydeco.* Accordion, harmonica, vocals. Composer. Bandleader. (Born Apr. 16, 1939, Duralde, Evangeline Parish; died Sept. 17, 1994, Lawtell, St. Landry Parish.) Influential traditional zydeco accordionist and bandleader started out playing harmonica at house dances in his late teens. While in his early 30s began learning accordion, inspired by **Clifton Chenier**, and started performing with local bands. Formed the Eunice Playboys in 1975 with Charles and Slim Prudhomme and sons John Jr. and Tony and quickly became a local favorite. In 1980 recorded LP *Joe Pete Got Two Women* for Arhoolie and had regional hit with title track covering **Bois Sec Ardoin**'s Creole composition. Throughout the 1980s and early 1990s toured extensively and released recordings on Arhoolie, Maison de Soul, and Rounder, including *Blues Stay Away from Me* in 1993. Appeared in 1992 film *Passion Fish* and 1994 documentary *The Kingdom of Zydeco*. Throughout the years incorporated several more family members into band, including son **Geno Delafose** on rubboard and later drums and grandson **Gerard Delafose** on rubboard. While appearing at famed zydeco dance hall Richard's Club in Lawtell, suffered a fatal heart attack at age 55.

DELANEY, JACK *Jazz.* Trombone. Bandleader. (Born Aug. 27, 1930, New Orleans, Orleans Parish; died Sept. 22, 1975, New Orleans, Orleans Parish.) New Orleans jazz trombonist worked with **Sharkey Bonano**, **Johnny Reininger**, and **Tony Almerico** in the late 1940s and 1950s. Also recorded with **Lizzie Miles**, **Pete Fountain**, and his band New Orleans Jazz Babies, which included **Lee Collins** and **Raymond Burke**.

DELISLE, JEAN BAPTISTE *Jazz.* Trombone. (Born Dec. 24, 1868, New Orleans, Orleans Parish; died Aug. 25, 1946, New Orleans, Orleans Parish.)[9] Early New Orleans ragtime and jazz trombonist credited as among the first to switch from valve to slide trombone in the 1890s. Performed with Onward Brass Band from 1890 through the Spanish-American War, in which entire group enlisted. Also worked with **John Robichaux** in the mid-1890s. Had mental breakdown in months following the war but recovered and rejoined Robichaux around 1905. Died of coronary artery disease at age 77.

DEMARY, EARL *Cajun.* Guitar, accordion, vocals. Bandleader. (Born Sept. 8, 1919, Grand Lake, Cameron Parish; died July 3, 1977, Lake Charles, Calcasieu Parish.)[10] Lake Charles–area early postwar Cajun guitarist and bandleader formed the Musical Aces with **Wilson Granger** in the mid-1940s and performed with band throughout southwest Louisiana and east Texas through the early 1950s. Also worked and recorded with **Nathan Abshire**'s Pine Grove Boys, appearing on several notable sides, including "Pine Grove Blues" in 1949. In the early 1950s led his group Earl and the Boys and in following years also performed with **Alfred Cormier**'s Lake Charles Playboys, which included Granger, **Iry LeJeune** and **Crawford Vincent**.

DEPASS, ARNOLD *Jazz.* Drums. Bandleader. (Born Feb. 7, 1883, New Orleans, Orleans Parish; died Mar. 10, 1947, New Orleans, Orleans Parish.)[11] Early New Orleans jazz drummer led bands in the 1910s and throughout 1920s worked with **Punch Miller**, **Chris Kelly**, **Jack Carey**, and **Buddy Petit**. In the late 1920s and early 1930s led Onward Brass Band, which included **George Lewis** and **De De Pierce**. Brother Dave DePass was clarinetist who worked with Magnolia Orchestra around 1910 with **King Oliver**.

DEROUEN, WALLACE *Cajun.* Guitar, vocals. Bandleader. (Born May 3, 1929, Hayes, Calcasieu Parish; died Jan. 4, 1987, Hayes, Calcasieu Parish.) Cajun guitarist and bandleader led the Calcasieu Playboys in the 1950s and 1960s and Cajun Ramblers in the 1970s and 1980s. In the late 1970s formed partnership with **Joe Bonsall** in Cajun Ramblers and released several singles, including "Louisiana Is Cajuns' Paradise" on Swallow in 1979. Also performed and recorded with **Robert Bertrand**, **Nolan Cormier**, **Phil Menard**, Tim and Marty Broussard, and others in the 1960s and 1970s.

DESCANT, PIERRE *Cajun.* Fiddle, vocals. Bandleader. (Born Dec. 23, 1925, Evergreen, Avoy. Parish; died Aug. 16, 2016, Kenner, Jefferson Parish.) Popular New Orleans–area Cajun musician known simply as "The Cajun Fiddler," who led his Cajun Fiddler Band in the 1980s and 1990s with wife, Ura V. Released recording *Cajun Favorites* in 1990.

DESHOTEL, ELISE *Cajun.* Guitar. Composer. Bandleader. (Born Aug. 20, 1914, near Basile, Evangeline Parish; died Feb. 25, 1986, Basile, Evangeline Parish.) Early postwar Cajun guitarist began performing occasionally with **Nathan Abshire** in the late 1940s and in the early 1950s formed Louisiana Rhythmaires with wife, Esther (1922–2000), on drums and brother Cleveland on fiddle or bass. In 1951 recorded six sides for Khoury's, including "Two Step de Kindergarden," which featured Rodney and **Dewey Balfa** and **Maurice Barzas**. Also performed with **Percy Fuselier** in Elton Playboys in the 1950s.

DESHOTELS BROTHERS (Elby "Bee" and Edward) *Cajun.* Guitar, fiddle, vocals. Composers. (Born July 6, 1920, Reddell, Evangeline Parish; died [Elby] Jan. 7, 1988, Reddell, Evangeline Parish; [Edward] Sept. 10, 2003, Mamou, Evangeline Parish.) Twin brothers and traditional Cajun musicians whose repertoire included centuries-old French Louisiana ballads and folk songs, some dating back to early France, which they learned from their father. Guitarist and singer Bee recorded several songs for folklorist Harry Oster in the mid-1950s, which were issued on Folk-Lyric LP *Folk Songs of the Louisiana Acadians* in 1959 and later reissued on Arhoolie. In the 1970s Bee and fiddle player Edward recorded several singles and LPs *Chantent de la Vie des Cajuns* and *Cajun Troubadours* on Swallow, which featured original compositions and traditional songs.

DESVIGNE, SIDNEY *Jazz.* Trumpet. Bandleader. (Born Sept. 11, 1893, New Orleans, Orleans Parish; died Dec. 1, 1959, Los Angeles.)[12] Early New Orleans jazz trumpeter studied with **Manuel Perez** and joined Perez's Onward Brass Band around 1914. Worked with various brass bands in the 1920s, including Excelsior and **Papa Celestin**'s Tuxedo Brass Band and recorded with **Fate Marable**. Led bands in the late 1920s and 1930s. Relocated to southern California in the mid-1940s and operated a nightclub.

DIAMOND, BILLY *Rhythm and blues.* Bass, guitar. Bandleader. (Born Oct. 5, 1916, New Orleans, Orleans Parish; died Oct. 20, 2011, Los Angeles.) Bandleader and bassist who was instrumental in launching **Fats Domino**'s career. Hired Domino in summer of 1947 as pianist in his band the Solid Senders and nicknamed him Fats. After Domino's discovery in group by **Dave Bartholomew**, his band backed Domino on the road. Appeared as bassist on several early recordings, including "Ain't It a Shame" and later served as Domino's road manager.

DIAMOND JOE (Joseph Maryland) *Rhythm and blues.* Vocals, bass. Composer. (Born Jan. 24, 1937, Houma, Terrebonne Parish; died Sept. 2, 2010, Houma, Terrebonne Parish.)[13] Highly talented but often overlooked New Orleans deep soul singer and songwriter who made a series of exceptional recordings produced by **Allen Toussaint** in the 1960s. After serving in the Air Force, worked as bassist and occasional vocalist in the house band at Thibodaux's famed club the Sugar Bowl in the late 1950s, often backing **James "Thunderbird" Davis**. In 1961 began recording with Toussaint and through the late 1960s released singles on Minit, Sansu, Instant, and Deesu, including "Moanin' and Screamin'" and "Gossip Gossip." Continued performing sporadically in clubs around Houma and Thibodaux through the 1990s.

DIAMOND, LEE (Wilbert Smith) *Rhythm and blues.* Saxophone, piano, drums, vocals. Composer. Bandleader. (Born Mar. 23, 1917, New Orleans, Orleans Parish; died Feb. 18, 1985, Atlanta.) Multi-instrumentalist backed **Shirley & Lee** in the early 1950s before becoming original member of Little Richard's band the Upsetters. Toured and recorded with Upsetters throughout the 1950s. After Little Richard left band in the late 1950s, performed and/or recorded with Dee Clark, Larry Birdsong, and James Brown. In the late 1950s and 1960s had singles on Vee-Jay, Minit, and Lola. Wrote songs for Little Richard, **Robert Parker**, **Aaron Neville**, and others.

DIAMOND, TINA (Alline T. Godbolt) *Rhythm and blues.* Vocals. (Born June 10, 1955, New Orleans, Orleans Parish; died Oct. 13, 2012, Jackson, Mississippi.) Southern soul singer known as the "Casino Queen," performed throughout the South in the 1990s and released *In the Heart of the City* on Avanti in 2000.

DIGGS, ROBERT *Blues.* Harmonica, guitar, vocals. Composer. (Born Sept. 1, 1910, Shreveport, Caddo Parish; died Dec. 1979, Friars Point, Mississippi.) Blind Delta blues singer began playing the harmonica at age six along with younger sister Mary, who was also blind. Throughout the 1930s and 1940s the pair traveled throughout the South performing on street corners and in taverns. In the late 1940s settled in the Mississippi Delta and performed only occasionally. In 1967 made field recordings for researcher George Mitchell at home in Friars Point.

DIKKI DU *See* Carrier, Troy.

DIXON, DAVE *Rhythm and blues.* Vocals. Composer. (Born Nov. 30, 1929, New Orleans, Orleans Parish; died Sept. 5, 1974, Los Angeles.)[14] New Orleans rhythm and blues singer had minor hit with recording debut "My Plea" on Savoy in 1954. In 1956 joined **Huey "Piano" Smith** as original member of his Clowns and appeared on recording "Little Liza Jane." Also had single as leader on Ace the same year. In the early 1960s while based in Memphis recorded two singles for Home of the Blues before relocating to California.

DIXON, GEORGE *Jazz.* Trumpet, saxophone. (Born Apr. 8, 1909, New Orleans, Orleans Parish; died Sept. 1, 1994, Chicago.) Raised in Natchez, Mississippi, relocated to Chicago in the 1920s and worked and recorded with various bands throughout the 1940s, including with Earl Hines. Led his own band from the early 1950s through the 1980s.

DODDS, JOHNNY *Jazz.* Clarinet. Bandleader. (Born Apr. 12, 1892, New Orleans, Orleans Parish; died Aug. 8, 1940, Chicago.)[15] Widely regarded as one of the finest jazz clarinetists of the 1920s. Studied with **Lorenzo Tio Jr.** and began performing with **Frankie Duson** around 1910. Worked with **Kid Ory** and **Fate Marable** throughout the mid-1910s. In 1918 relocated to Chicago and worked and recorded with **King Oliver** in the early 1920s. Also recorded with **Louis Armstrong** (as member of his Hot Fives and Hot Sevens), **Jelly Roll Morton**, and brother **Baby Dodds** in various bands throughout the 1920s, appearing on some of the most important recordings in early jazz. Recorded extensively as leader of various groups in the late 1920s, often backed by brother Baby on drums. Continued performing in Chicago throughout the 1930s, making his final recordings in 1938 and 1940 for Decca before succumbing to a fatal heart attack at age 48.

DODDS, WARREN "BABY" *Jazz.* Drums. (Born Dec. 24, 1894, New Orleans, Orleans Parish; died Feb. 14, 1959, Chicago.)[16] Considered one of the greatest and most influential drummers in early New Orleans jazz and credited as the first drummer to play breaks or fills between phrases and solos. Younger brother of **Johnny Dodds** with whom he often performed and recorded. Worked with **Bunk Johnson** early on and throughout the 1910s and early 1920s performed with **Papa Celestin** and **Fate Marable**. Moved to Chicago in 1922 and worked and recorded with **King Oliver**. Remained in Chicago throughout following two decades and recorded extensively with **Louis Armstrong**, **Jelly Roll Morton**, Black Bottom Stompers, and Chicago Footwarmers in the late 1920s. Worked and recorded with **Bunk Johnson** and other notable jazz figures in the 1940s and toured Europe. Retired due to ill health in 1957.

DOLLIS, BIG CHIEF BO (Theodore Dollis) *Rhythm and blues.* Vocals. Composer. Bandleader. (Born Jan. 14, 1944, New Orleans, Orleans Parish; died Jan. 20, 2015, New Orleans, Orleans Parish.) Longtime leader of Mardi Gras Indian tribe Wild Magnolias, who helped spread Mardi Gras Indian culture throughout the world. Became "Big Chief" of Wild Magnolias in the mid-1960s. Group released landmark self-titled debut album in 1974. Led Wild Magnolias through the early 2010s until health issues forced retirement.

DOMINGUE, TERRY (Joseph Terry Domingue) *Zydeco.* Accordion, vocals. Composer. Bandleader. (Born Jan. 23, 1983, Ridge, Lafayette Parish.) Contemporary zydeco accordionist and bandleader grew up speaking Creole French and began playing the instrument at age eight, mentored early on by neighbor **Zydeco Ray**. In 2001 formed the Zydeco Bad Boys and released debut CD *Make You Feel Good* on Master-Trak in 2003. Several releases followed, including *Back on Track* in 2014 and *Allons Zydeco* in 2017, the latter of which featured local favorite "Opossum in the Sack." Continued performing on zydeco club and festival circuit in the late 2010s.

DOMINIQUE, ANATIE "NATTY" *Jazz.* Trumpet. (Born Aug. 2, 1894, New Orleans, Orleans Parish; died Aug. 30, 1982, Chicago.) Early New Orleans jazz trumpeter performed in parades with brass bands from around 1907 through the early 1910s. Moved to Chicago in 1913 and in the early 1920s worked with **Jelly Roll Morton**, **Louis Armstrong**, **Jimmie Noone**, and others. Performed and recorded with **Johnny Dodds** through the 1930s. Uncle of **Don Albert**.

DOMINO, ANTOINE "FATS" *Rhythm and blues.* Piano, vocals. Composer. Bandleader. (Born Feb. 26, 1928, New Orleans, Orleans Parish; died Oct. 24, 2017, Harvey, Jefferson Parish.) Profoundly influential New Orleans rhythm and blues singer and piano player who played a major role in the early development of rock and roll. Also a primary influence on swamp pop, and to a lesser extent, Jamaican ska. Began playing piano at age 10 and in his teens was performing in local bars. In 1947 joined **Billy Diamond**'s Solid Senders and was soon discovered by **Dave Bartholomew**, who signed him to Imperial and remained his longtime producer and collaborator. His debut million-selling hit recording "The Fat Man" from 1949 is regarded as among the first rock and roll records. Throughout the 1950s and early 1960s released more than 60 singles on Imperial with 40 songs that reached the Top 10 on R&B charts such as "Ain't It a Shame," "I'm Walkin'," "Blueberry Hill," "Whole Lotta Loving," and "Walking to New Orleans." From 1963 to 1970 recorded for ABC-Paramount, Mercury, BroadMoor and Reprise. Continued to tour nationally and abroad throughout the next two decades but slowed down considerably in the 1990s and made only limited local engagements in following years. A lifelong resident of the Lower 9th Ward, he was displaced by Hurricane Katrina in 2005 and spent remaining years living with family just outside New Orleans. In 2006 released album *Alive and Kickin'* and the following year returned to the stage for one final performance at Tipitina's in New Orleans, which was filmed for a 2008 television broadcast.

DONATTO, L.C. (Alcide Donatto Sr.) *Zydeco.* Accordion, vocals. Bandleader. (Born Mar. 11, 1932, Opelousas, St. Landry Parish; died July 7, 2002, Houston.) Noted early Texas-based zydeco accordionist and bandleader who was among the first to perform Louisiana's black Creole music and early zydeco in Houston clubs. Relocated to Houston's Frenchtown in the mid-1940s and in 1949 began performing at Irene's Café with fellow accordionist Willie Green. Continued performing with Green through late 1960s and then formed his band the Drifters. In the 1970s and 1980s recorded singles for Maison de Soul and Special Edition and remained one of Houston's most popular zydeco musicians. In the 1990s toured overseas and recorded CD *Texas Zydeco* on Blues Encore in 1994. Father of zydeco rubboard player L.C. Donatto Jr.

DOPSIE, DWAYNE (Dwayne Rubin) *Zydeco.* Accordion, vocals. Composer. Bandleader. (Born Mar. 3, 1979, Lafayette, Lafayette Parish.) Youngest son of internationally renowned accordion player **Rockin' Dopsie**. Began learning the instrument at age seven and formed his band the Zydeco Hellraisers in the late 1990s. Toured nationally and abroad through the 2010s and released numerous CDs, including *Calling Your Name* on Sound of New Orleans in 2015. Brother of zydeco musicians **Rockin' Dopsie Jr.**, Alton Jr., and Anthony Rubin.

DORSEY, ANTHONY "BONE" *Rhythm and blues.* Trombone. Composer. Bandleader. (Born Dec. 13, 1939, Houma, Terrebonne Parish.) Rhythm and blues trombonist and arranger toured and recorded with Joe Tex for several years in the late 1960s and worked with Percy Sledge, Clarence Carter, Joe Simon, Al Green, and others through the mid-1970s. Also worked as arranger and A&R rep for Philly Groove and Capricorn Records. Between 1975 and 1980 toured and recorded with Paul McCartney's band Wings. Cofounded band Bone and Holmes with wife Mary and continued to perform through the early 2010s, based in Macon, Georgia.

DORSEY, LEE (Irvin Lee Dorsey) *Rhythm and blues.* Vocals, piano. Composer. (Born Dec. 4, 1926, New Orleans, Orleans Parish; died Dec. 1, 1986, New Orleans, Orleans Parish.)[17] Popular singer who helped define the New Orleans rhythm and blues sound of the 1960s. After working as a professional boxer on the West Coast, returned to New Orleans and began music career in the late 1950s, making recording debut on Rex in 1958. In 1960 began long collaboration with producer-songwriter **Allen Toussaint** and had series of hits including "Ya Ya," "Do-Re-Mi," "Working in the Coal Mine," "Get Out of My Life, Woman," and "Holy Cow." In the 1970s had releases on Polydor and ABC and continued performing into the 1980s before succumbing to emphysema at age 59.

DORSEY, PO' HENRY *Blues.* Guitar, vocals. (Born May 14, 1928, Oak Ridge, Morehouse Parish; died Sept. 3, 2018, Rayville, Richland Parish.)[18] Louisiana Delta blues guitarist and singer began playing on a homemade one-string instrument as a child, inspired by his sharecropping family, who would perform blues at home and at parties. At age 15 received his first guitar and was later greatly influenced by Texas, Delta, and Chicago blues on the radio and recordings, particularly by Lightnin' Hopkins. While living in Rayville formed duo Po' Henry and Tookie with harmonica player **Wayne "Tookie" Collom** in the mid-1980s and through following two decades performed at numerous national folk, jazz, and blues festivals, notably Smithsonian Institute's Festival of American Music in 1997. The pair also appeared in the films *River of Song* and *Rhythm 'n' Bayous.* Duo continued to perform through the early 2010s until health issues forced retirement.

DOTSON, JIMMY "LOUISIANA" *Blues.* Guitar, drums, piano, vocals. Composer. Bandleader. (Born Oct. 19, 1933, Ethel, E. Feliciana Parish; died Mar. 26, 2017, Houston.) Early swamp blues multi-instrumentalist began performing on Baton Rouge blues scene in the mid-1950s as a drummer and performed with **Slim Harpo**, **Lightnin' Slim**, **Silas Hogan**, and others. Recorded as session musician and leader for producer **J. D. Miller** with a single on Rocko and Zynn in 1959–60, including "I Wanna Know" with Hogan and enigmatic harmonica player Sylvester Buckley. Relocated to Memphis in the early 1960s and recorded single for Home of the Blues. After stints in Arkansas and Baton Rouge, settled in Houston area in the early 1990s and performed on the local blues scene through the early 2000s until sidelined by health issues. Recorded self-produced CD in later years which remained unissued. Not to be confused with Baltimore soul singer Jimmy Dotson who recorded for Mercury, Stax/Volt, and several other labels in the 1960s.

DOUCET, CAMEY *Cajun.* Vocals. Composer. Bandleader. (Born Apr. 4, 1939, Crowley, Acadia Parish.) Popular Cajun singer-songwriter best known for his mid-1970s single "Mom, I'm Still Your Little Boy" on Swallow. Performed and recorded with the Crowley Aces, which included a young **Wayne Toups**, in the early 1970s and through 1980s had multiple releases on Swallow and Kajun, including 1981 LP *The Cajun Gentleman.* Also worked for several decades as popular Cajun radio broadcaster in the Crowley, Lafayette, and Beaumont areas.

DOUCET, JOE *Blues.* Guitar, vocals. Composer. (Born Nov. 12, 1942, near Ville Platte, Evangeline Parish; died Nov. 29, 2010, Houston.)[19] Houston-based blues guitarist and singer was raised speaking Creole French and relocated to Houston's Third Ward in 1962. Performed in various bands, including with **Clifton Chenier** and Freddie King until the late 1970s when disco fad gained popularity. In mid-2000s had chance encounter with music writer and historian Roger Wood and recorded CD *Houston's Third Ward Blues* on Dialtone in 2006 but remained relatively inactive as a performer in remaining years.

DOUCET, MICHAEL *Cajun.* Fiddle, guitar, banjo, vocals. Composer. Bandleader. (Born Feb. 14, 1951, Scott, Lafayette Parish.) Internationally renowned Cajun fiddle player and singer-songwriter best known as longtime leader of popular Cajun band BeauSoleil. Raised in a musical family, began playing banjo and guitar as a child and during his teens formed folk-rock band Bayou Drifters with cousin **Zachary Richard**. In the mid-1970s began studying traditional Cajun and Creole music and learning fiddle with numerous prominent musicians, including **Dennis McGee**, **Dewey Balfa**, **Varise Conner**, **Canray Fontenot**, and **Bébé Carrière**. In 1975 co-founded progressive Cajun band Coteau and also formed BeauSoleil, which would remain his main group for decades after Coteau disbanded several years later. In 1977 recorded BeauSoleil's debut LP, *The Spirit of Cajun Music,* on Swallow and by the late 1980s were signed to Rounder and touring internationally, quickly becoming the most recognized Cajun band in the world. In following years also performed and recorded as solo artist and with other side projects, including 1989 release *Beau Solo* and numerous recordings with Savoy-Doucet Cajun Band with **Ann** and **Marc Savoy**. Continued touring and recording with BeauSoleil and as solo performer in the 2010s. Brother Michael Doucet is longtime guitarist with BeauSoleil.

DOUCET, OSCAR "SLIM" *Cajun.* Accordion, vocals. Composer. (Born May 26, 1900, St. Martin Parish; died Jan. 16, 1967, Opelousas, St. Landry Parish.)[20] Early Cajun accordionist who recorded two sides for OKeh in Mar. 1929 and four sides with fiddler **Alius Soileau** in Nov. 1929 which were issued on Victor and Bluebird, including "When I Met You at the Gate." A resident of Opelousas for most of his life, continued performing at local house dances through the late 1940s.

DOUCETTE, SALVADOR *Rhythm and blues.* Piano. (Born Dec. 23, 1932, New Orleans, Orleans Parish.) Early rhythm and blues piano player who worked and recorded with **Dave Bartholomew**'s band in the 1950s and appeared on numerous sessions with **Smiley Lewis**, **Roy Brown**, **Lloyd Price**, **Cousin Joe**, **Chubby Newsom**, **"Snooks" Eaglin**, and many others.

DOUGET, DEREK *Jazz.* Saxophone. Composer. Bandleader. (Born July 20, 1975, Gonzales, Ascension Parish.) New Orleans jazz saxophonist best known for his work as member of **Ellis Marsalis** Quintet from the late 1990s through 2010s. Also performed regularly and recorded with New Orleans Jazz Orchestra. In 2002 released *Perpetual Motion* on Lookout Jazz and continued to perform in New Orleans clubs and tour nationally with his own quartet in the 2010s.

DOUGLAS, JEWELL (of **Jewell** and the Rubies**)** *See* Jewell [Notable Musicians Born outside Louisiana].

DOWDEN, MELVIN *Rhythm and blues.* Piano. (Born May 8, 1934, New Orleans, Orleans Parish; died Apr. 29, 1989, New Orleans, Orleans Parish.) Rhythm and blues pianist appeared on sessions with Little Richard and **Chris Kenner** in the mid-1950s. Married vocalist **Bea Booker**.

DOZART, LYNN *Creole.* Fiddle, vocals. (Born Mar. 28, 1915, Iota, Acadia Parish; died June 18, 1986, Eunice, St. Landry Parish.) Early Creole fiddle player and singer who was influenced by **Douglas Bellard** and made field recordings for French researcher Gerard Dole in the mid-1970s accompanied by accordionist and singer Etienne Lewis (1900–1977). Selections appearing on 1978 Folkways LP *Louisiana Creole Music* included the Bellard-inspired "La Porte de la Prison" and "Hey Tite Mama."

DR. DRIP DROP *See* Owens, Overton.

DR. JOHN (Malcolm John Rebennack Jr.) *Rhythm and blues.* Piano, guitar, bass, vocals. Composer. Bandleader. (Born Nov. 20, 1941, New Orleans, Orleans Parish; died June 6, 2019, New Orleans, Orleans Parish.) Iconic New Orleans rhythm and blues and funk pianist and singer-songwriter best known for his 1973 hit "Right Place Wrong Time" and his hoodoo-themed persona and theatrical stage shows. Began playing guitar in his early teens and befriended **Professor Longhair**, who became a major influence. In the late 1950s and early 1960s worked as songwriter and session guitarist with **Professor Longhair**, **Huey "Piano" Smith**, **Big Boy Myles**, **Tommy Ridgley**, **Ronnie Barron**, and others. Released several singles as leader and had local hit with "Storm Warning" on Rex in 1959. Around 1960 sustained gunshot injury to finger and switched first to bass then piano. In 1965 relocated to Los Angeles and worked as in-demand session musician. In the late 1960s created Dr. John persona based on nineteenth-century New Orleans hoodoo healer of same name, initially inspired by Barron's Reverend Ether alter ego. As Dr. John, the Night Tripper, he combined New Orleans rhythm and blues, funk, and psychedelic rock into an elaborate hoodoo-themed stage show. In 1968 released debut album *Gris-Gris* on Atco, produced by **Harold Battiste**. After several more releases, including landmark New Orleans tribute LP *Gumbo,* worked with **Allen Toussaint** and The Meters in 1973 on LP *In the Right Place* which included signature hit "Right Place Wrong Time." Throughout following decades recorded prolifically as leader and collaborated with numerous artists such as Doc Pomus, B.B. King, Mike Bloomfield, Willie Nelson, Rickie Lee Jones, and others. Continued touring internationally as a leading exponent of New Orleans funk and rhythm and blues until poor health forced retirement in late 2017.

DRAKE, HAMID *Jazz.* Drums. Composer. Bandleader. (Born Aug. 3, 1955, Monroe, Ouachita Parish.) Highly regarded jazz percussionist moved to the Chicago area with family while in his early teens. Began studying music in the early 1970s with Fred Anderson and from the late 1970s through 1995 recorded and toured with trumpeter Don Cherry. Also performed with numerous world music, Latin jazz, and reggae bands and recorded with Pharoah Sanders, Herbie Hancock, William Parker, Scott Fields, **Kidd Jordan**, and others. Continued to record and tour internationally into the 2010s, hailed as one of finest percussionists in jazz and other improvised music of his time.

DRIFTING CHARLES *See* Tyler, Charles.

DuCONGE, ADOLPHUS, JR. *Jazz.* Piano. (Born May 9, 1896, New Orleans, Orleans Parish; died Mar. 2, 1941, St. James Parish, Louisiana.)[21] Early New Orleans jazz pianist worked on riverboats in the 1920s and 1930s with **Sidney Desvigne**'s S.S. Capitol Orchestra, often with brothers **Earl**, **Albert**, and **Peter DuConge**. Son of **Oscar DuConge**.

DuCONGE, ADOLPHUS "OSCAR," SR. *Jazz.* Cornet. Bandleader. (Born Oct. 1872, Napoleonville, Assumption Parish; died Feb. 24, 1933, New Orleans, Orleans Parish.)[22] Patriarch of famed early New Orleans jazz family with sons **Earl**, **Albert**, **Adolphus Jr.**, and **Peter DuConge**. Performed as early member of Onward Brass Band around 1890 and later led band which included **Alphonse Picou**. Performed in military band during Spanish-American War. Grandfather of **Wendell DuConge**.

DuCONGE, PETER *Jazz.* Saxophone, clarinet, vocals. (Born Feb. 17, 1901, New Orleans, Orleans Parish; died June 13, 1966, Pittsburgh.)[23] Renowned early New Orleans jazz saxophone and clarinet player performed in New Orleans nightclubs and on riverboats in the 1920s before relocating to New York City around 1927 and working in local jazz clubs. While on tour in France met and married vaudeville singer and nightclub owner Ada "Bricktop" Smith in 1929 and worked with various bands in her Paris club. Soon separated from Smith but continued performing in Europe through the late 1930s, working with **Louis Armstrong**, Coleman Hawkins, Benny Peyton, and others. Returned to United States by the end of decade and continued performing sporadically in following years, later settling in Pittsburgh area. Succumbed to sepsis caused by ulcerative colitis at age 65. Son of **Oscar DuConge** and brother of **Earl**, **Albert**, and **Adolphus DuConge Jr.**

DuCONGE, WENDELL (Emmett Wendell Fortner) *Rhythm and blues, jazz.* Saxophone. (Born July 4, 1923, New Orleans, Orleans Parish; died Dec. 24, 1972, New Orleans, Orleans Parish.) Rhythm and blues saxophonist best known for his tenure with **Fats Domino** in the 1950s. Worked in the mid-1950s with **Dave Bartholomew**'s band and appeared on numerous sessions with Domino, **Roy Brown**, T-Bone Walker, and others. Son of early New Orleans jazz saxophonist **Earl DuConge** and grandson of **Oscar DuConge**.

DUGAS, ALVIN *Swamp pop.* Bass, vocals. Bandleader. (Born Sept. 24, 1944, St. Martinville, St. Martin Parish; died Feb. 13, 2019, Lafayette, Lafayette Parish.) Noted swamp pop singer and bass player formed his first band Little Alvin and the Chipmunks while still in his teens in the late 1950s. Throughout the 1960s and 1970s worked regularly with **T. K. Hulin**. Continued performing with various swamp pop groups throughout following decades, including Swamp Pop Express in the 2010s.

DUGAS, IVY *Cajun.* Bass, guitar, drums, vocals. Composer. (Born Aug. 23, 1948, Carencro, Lafayette Parish.) Noted Cajun singer-songwriter and multi-instrumentalist began playing music at age 12 and in the 1960s and 1970s performed and recorded with **Joe Bonsall** and the Orange Playboys on drums and steel guitar. From the late 1970s through early 1990s worked and recorded with **Phil Menard** and the Louisiana Travelers before joining **Jackie Caillier** and the Cajun Cousins as bassist, singer, and songwriter. Continued performing and recording with group through the 2010s, writing much of the band's original material, including "Jolie Cadiene," "The Gravel Road," and "Carencro on My Mind."

DUGAS, MARCEL *Zydeco, rhythm and blues.* Accordion, vocals. Composer. Bandleader. (Born Dec. 18, 1914, Duson, Acadia Parish; died Dec. 26, 1988, Crowley, Acadia Parish.)[24] Noted early zydeco accordionist and bandleader recorded behind **Sticks Herman** for Goldband in the late 1950s and with **Leo Morris** in 1962 for Ivory. In 1969 recorded session backing **Wild Bill Pitre** which resulted in a single on Anla and LP issued on Flyright. In the 1970s had releases on Blues Unlimited backing **Gene Morris** and **Bobby Price** with his band the Entertainers, notably Morris's "Going Back to Big Mamou" in 1974. In the 1980s led his band the Swinging Zydeco Entertainers, which included **Chester Chevalier**, **Rodney Bernard**, and **Allen "Cat Roy" Broussard**.

DUGAS, NOLAN *Cajun.* Fiddle, vocals. Composer. Bandleader. (Born Apr. 24, 1937, Lafayette, Lafayette Parish; died June 9, 2018, Carencro, Lafayette Parish.) Respected Cajun fiddle player and singer-songwriter recorded singles with **Patrick** and **Gary Breaux** in the 1960s for Cajun Jamboree, notably "Married to One—In Love with Another," and recorded Cajun classic "Wait Until I Finish Crying" with the Acadian Aces for Swallow in 1976. Later performed and recorded with High Performance. Father of Cajun drummer Kevin Dugas of **Steve Riley**'s Mamou Playboys and High Performance.

DUHÉ, LAWRENCE *Jazz.* Clarinet, saxophone. Bandleader. Composer. (Born Apr. 29, 1887, LaPlace, St. John the Baptist Parish; died Feb. 24, 1963, Lafayette, Lafayette Parish.)[25] Early New Orleans jazz clarinetist began performing in family band with brothers. In 1913 moved to New Orleans as member of **Kid Ory**'s band and took lessons from **Lorenzo Tio Jr.** and **George Baquet**. Relocated to Chicago in 1917 and led his own band, which at times included **King Oliver**, **Sidney Bechet**, and **Willie Humphrey**. Returned to New Orleans in 1923 but soon relocated to Lafayette area and through the early 1930s worked with **Bunk Johnson** and **Evan Thomas** in Banner Orchestra and Black Eagles Band. In 1932 traveled with Rabbit Foot Minstrels before returning to Lafayette, where he performed with a local group until retiring from music in 1945.

DUHON, EDWIN *Cajun.* Guitar, accordion, piano, bass, harmonica, vocals. Composer. Bandleader. (Born June 11, 1910, Youngsville, Lafayette Parish; died Feb. 26, 2006, Westlake, Calcasieu Parish.) Influential early Cajun multi-instrumentalist who cofounded the famed Cajun string band Hackberry Ramblers with **Luderin Darbone**. Raised speaking Cajun French, learned guitar and accordion as a teenager, and formed group with Darbone in early 1933 after relocating to Hackberry. Performed throughout Lake Charles area and appeared on local radio broadcasts before leaving band temporarily in the mid-1930s to work in the oil fields. Rejoined group in the mid-1940s and eventually began performing mainly on accordion. Recorded LP *Louisiana Cajun Music* for Arhoolie in 1963 and also appeared on two releases with group in the 1990s, including *Cajun Boogie.* In 2000 released first recording as leader, *Cajun Legacy,* on Goldband. Continued touring internationally and recording with Darbone and Hackberry Ramblers into his 90s.

DUHON, HECTOR *Cajun.* Fiddle. (Born June 27, 1915, Lafayette, Lafayette Parish; died Mar. 3, 2000, Duson, Lafayette Parish.) Renowned early Cajun fiddle player best known for his long association with **Octa Clark** and the Dixie Ramblers. Raised in a musical family, began playing at dances at age 13 and within months was performing with Clark and cousin Jesse Duhon on guitar at local dance halls. After Clark's departure by the mid-1930s, began performing as the Dixie Ramblers throughout south Louisiana and east Texas and became one of the first Cajun bands to use stage amplification. In 1935–36 recorded numerous sides for Bluebird. After more than a decade hiatus, began performing again in the 1950s with Clark, often with son Bessyl (1938–) on steel guitar. Continued performing with Clark through the 1980s at clubs and festivals with recordings on Swallow, Rounder, and Arhoolie, notably LP *Old Time Cajun Music* in 1982.

DUKE ROYAL *See* Kent, Luther.

DUKE, TODD (Christopher Todd Duke) *Jazz, rhythm and blues.* Bandleader. Guitar. (Born June 2, 1970, New Orleans, Orleans Parish; died Jan. 6, 2019, New Orleans, Orleans Parish.) Influenced by both blues and jazz musicians, began playing professionally around New Orleans in the early 1990s and worked and recorded with **John**

Boutté for two decades. Also performed regularly with **Leroy Jones**, **Bob French**, **Topsy Chapman**, **Wardell Quezergue**, and others. Continued to perform and record with various groups and lead his own trio into the late 2010s until losing battle with cancer at age 48.

DUMAINE, LOUIS *Jazz.* Trumpet, cornet. Composer. Bandleader. (Born July 17, 1889, New Orleans, Orleans Parish; died Sept. 9, 1949, New Orleans, Orleans Parish.)[26] After serving as U.S. Army bugler during World War I, early New Orleans jazz trumpeter worked with **Chris Kelly**, **Buddy Petit**, and **Walter Decou** in the early 1920s. Also performed with **Papa Celestin**'s Tuxedo Brass Band. Recorded for Victor in 1927 with his band Jazzola Eight, one of the earliest Creole jazz bands recorded in New Orleans. Led W.P.A. Brass Band and Dumaine-Houston Jazz Band in the 1930s but performed only sporadically in the 1940s.

DUNAWAY, SHELTON *Swamp pop.* Saxophone, vocals. Composer. Bandleader. (Born Aug. 3, 1934, Monroe, Ouachita Parish.) Noted early swamp pop singer and saxophone player best known for his work as original member and co-vocalist of **Cookie** and the Cupcakes. Moved to Lake Charles with family at age 12 and began playing saxophone. Performed in first band with **Classie Ballou** before joining the Boogie Ramblers with **Simon "Kee-Dee" Lubin** and **Ernest Jacobs**. Recorded for Goldband in the early 1950s and had regional success with early swamp pop classic "Cindy Lou" in 1955. Renamed band **Cookie** and the Cupcakes after member **Cookie Thierry** and released numerous swamp pop classics such as "Mathilda" and "Got You on My Mind" for Lyric in the late 1950s and early 1960s. Also recorded several singles as leader, including "Shake 'Em Up." After Cupcakes broke up in the early 1970s led his own band for several years. From the mid-1990s through early 2000s performed with the reunited Cupcakes and toured overseas before retiring from music.

DUNLAP, GENE *Rockabilly, country.* Piano, guitar, fiddle, saxophone, vocals. Composer. Bandleader. (Born Jan. 26, 1939, Vick, Avoy. Parish.) Early rockabilly piano player and singer began performing in the early 1950s with siblings in string band as the Dunlap Brothers. In 1956 worked with **Johnny Rivers** in Baton Rouge before relocating to Shreveport and joining house band on the *Louisiana Hayride.* In 1958–59 cut three rockabilly records for Hitt with his band the Jokers, notably "Made in the Shade," and backed other artists on label including Rick Harrington, Jimmy Dart, and the Moods. In the 1960s worked with Sleepy LaBeef, **Jay Chevalier**, and Bob Luman. Relocated to Nashville in the early 1970s and worked regularly in Loretta Lynn's band the Coal Miners.

DUNN, FRED *Blues.* Piano, vocals. Composer. (Born Oct. 15, 1914, Monroe, Ouachita Parish; died May 3, 1966, Monroe, Ouachita Parish.)[27] Exceptional boogie-woogie piano player and singer had three releases on Signature in 1947–48, including "Railroad Blues" and "Baby Don't Feel Lowdown." After recovering from throat surgery in the early 1950s, recorded single "Fred's Boogie Woogie" on Monroe-based label Jiffy in 1953. In later years worked as laborer at local sawmill. Succumbed to throat cancer at age 51.

DUPAS, ARNOLD *See* DePass, Arnold.

DUPIN, SONNY (Joseph Ivy Dupin Jr.) *Cajun.* Guitar, vocals. Composer. Bandleader. (Born Oct. 26, 1926, Lake Charles, Calcasieu Parish; died Dec. 20, 1969, Calcasieu Parish.) Lake Charles–area Cajun singer and guitarist recorded singles for Tek, Goldband, Lyric, and Paul in the late 1950s and 1960s, including "My Glass Is Empty." Also hosted a weekly Cajun music radio show in the 1960s. Succumbed to injuries sustained in a car accident on Interstate 10.

DuPLANTIS, CAMILLE *Cajun.* Fiddle. (Born Nov. 30, 1916, Vermilion Parish; died May 24, 1977, Lafayette, Lafayette Parish.)[28] Early Cajun fiddle player who performed with **Dewey Segura** and was recorded with Segura and **D. L. Menard** by musicologist Richard K. Spottswood in Delcambre in 1975.

DUPONT, AUGUST "DIMES" *Rhythm and blues.* Saxophone, vocals. (Born Nov. 28, 1928, New Orleans, Orleans Parish; died Sept. 14, 1997, New Orleans, Orleans Parish.) Longtime saxophonist with **Edgar Blanchard**'s band the Gondoliers. Throughout the 1950s appeared on numerous sessions with Ray Charles, Big Joe Turner, **Earl King**, **Robert Parker**, **Tommy Ridgley**, and others. Recorded a single as coleader with **Big Boy Myles** as Myles and Dupont on Argo in 1958. Nephew of **Danny Barker**.

DUPREE, CHAMPION JACK *Blues.* Piano, drums, guitar, vocals. Composer. Bandleader. (Born July 4, 1910, New Orleans, Orleans Parish; died Jan. 21, 1992, Hanover, Germany.) Influential early barrelhouse piano player and important link to unrecorded early New Orleans blues piano players and their repertoires. Raised in an orphanage, began playing piano as a boy and took lessons from **Tuts Washington** and **Willie "Drive 'Em Down" Hall**.

As a teenager played for tips in the French Quarter and performed throughout New Orleans in the 1920s. Left New Orleans around 1930 and spent time in New York, Chicago, and Indianapolis. Worked as professional boxer and earned nickname Champion Jack. Made a series of classic recordings for OKeh in Chicago in 1940–41, including Hall's unrecorded "Junker Blues," which later inspired **Fats Domino**'s first hit, "The Fat Man." Recorded for numerous labels throughout the 1940s and 1950s and had hit in 1955 with "Walking the Blues" on King. Released landmark LP *Blues from the Gutter* on Atlantic in 1958. The following year toured Europe and in 1960 became the first bluesman to move permanently overseas. Throughout following three decades performed and recorded extensively throughout Europe. In the early 1990s returned several times to the United States and appeared at major festivals, recording enough studio material for several releases on Bullseye Blues, including *Back Home in New Orleans* in 1990.

DURAL, REGGIE "SIR REG" (Reginald Master Dural) *Zydeco, rhythm and blues.* Piano, organ, accordion, rubboard, vocals. Bandleader. Composer. (Born June 21, 1970, Lafayette, Lafayette Parish.) Zydeco and funk singer and multi-instrumentalist began performing in his father **Buckwheat Zydeco**'s band on rubboard in the 1990s. In later years began singing and playing accordion and organ in band during his father's health struggles. After his father's death in 2016, took over leadership of band and continued touring under original band name Ils Sont Partis with longtime members **Lil' Buck Sinegal** and **Lee Allen Zeno**.

DURAL, STANLEY, JR. *See* Buckwheat Zydeco.

DUSENBERY, PAPA GENE *Cajun.* Guitar, mandolin, vocals. Composer. Bandleader. (Born June 13, 1927, Houma, Terrebonne Parish; died Aug. 19, 2015, Houma, Terrebonne Parish.) Internationally renowned Cajun musician and patriarch of the Dusenbery Family Singers. Born during the Great Flood of 1927, began performing in country band the Southern Playboys in his late teens. After serving in Korea, continued performing around the Houma area. In 1964 formed the Dusenbery Family Singers with his 12 children and toured nationally and abroad. In 1973 released LP *Dusenbery Family Sings French-Acadian Songs* on La Louisianne. From 1980 to 2003 family operated La Trouvaille, a Cajun restaurant in Chauvin which became a world-renowned Cajun destination, featuring weekly performances from the Dusenbery family band. Continued to perform occasionally in the 2010s.

DUSON [*often misspelled* **Dusen**], **FRANK** (*or* **Frankie**) *Jazz.* Trombone. Bandleader. (Born July 26, 1878, Algiers, Orleans Parish; died Apr. 1, 1936, New Orleans, Orleans Parish.)[29] Important early New Orleans jazz trombonist and bandleader who played with **Buddy Bolden** and took over leadership of his band in 1907. After working with **Charley Galloway**'s group in the 1890s, joined Bolden's band, replacing **Willie Cornish** around 1903. After Bolden was institutionalized several years later, began leading group and renamed it the Eagle Band. In the early 1910s members included **Bunk Johnson**, **Sidney Bechet**, and **Henry Zeno**. Around 1917 traveled to California with **Buddy Petit** and worked briefly with **Jelly Roll Morton**. Performed sporadically with **Louis Dumaine** in the 1920s and early 1930s and was member of W.P.A. Brass Band and music teacher in years preceding death.

DUTREY, HONORÉ *Jazz.* Trombone. Bandleader. (Born Oct. 18, 1888, New Orleans, Orleans Parish; died July 23, 1935, Chicago.)[30] Early New Orleans jazz trombonist performed with various brass bands in the 1910s including Melrose, Excelsior, and Magnolia (with **King Oliver** and **Pops Foster**) and worked with **Jimmie Noone** and **Buddy Petit**. After World War I, settled in Chicago and rejoined Oliver through 1924 and recorded with group. In the mid- to late 1920s worked with **Freddie Keppard**, **Louis Armstrong**, and **Johnny Dodds**. Retired in the early 1930s due to ill health. Brothers Sam and Pete were also jazz musicians.

EAGLIN, SNOOKS (Fird Eaglin Jr.) *Rhythm and blues.* Guitar, vocals. Composer. Bandleader. (Born Jan. 21, 1937, New Orleans, Orleans Parish; died Feb. 18, 2009, New Orleans, Orleans Parish.) Masterful New Orleans guitar player who was known as "The Human Jukebox" for his vast repertoire. Blind since a small child from glaucoma, began teaching himself guitar at age six and by age 14 was working as a professional musician. In the early 1950s performed as member of **Allen Toussaint**'s Flamingos and recorded behind **James "Sugar Boy" Crawford**. Worked as street singer in the late 1950s and recorded for folklorist Harry Oster from 1958 to 1960. In the early 1960s recorded numerous singles for Imperial with producer **Dave Bartholomew**, notably the powerful b-side "By the Water." In the 1970s recorded as a leader and also with **Professor Longhair** and the Wild Magnolias. In the 1980s and 1990s had multiple releases on Black Top, including *Soul's Edge* in 1995, and performed sporadically in New Orleans through the late 2000s.

EASTERLING, JAMES "SKIP" *Rhythm and blues.* Vocals, keyboards. Composer. (Born July 1, 1945, New Orleans, Orleans Parish; died Nov. 21, 2015, Carriere, Mississippi.) Born in New Orleans but raised in Slidell, signed with label owner **Joe Banashak** at age 14 and had numerous singles in the 1960s and early 1970s on Ron, Reno, Alon, and Instant, including regional hit "I'm Your Hoochie Koochie Man" in 1970, produced by **Huey "Piano" Smith**.

EDWARDS, CLARENCE *Blues.* Guitar, vocals. Composer. (Born Mar. 25, 1933, Lindsay, E. Feliciana Parish; died May 20, 1993, Baton Rouge, EBR Parish.) Noted swamp blues guitarist and singer moved to Baton Rouge with family at age 12 and began learning guitar. In the 1950s performed with several local blues bands and in 1959–60 recorded for folklorist Harry Oster with guitarist brother Cornelius Edwards and **Butch Cage**. In the early 1970s recorded two sides for Arhoolie with **Henry Gray** and appeared on Excello LP *Blues Live from Baton Rouge at the Speakeasy.* Continued performing with Gray's band until 1977 and worked largely outside music through the 1980s. In 1990 recorded LP *Swamp's the Word* on Sidetrack which brought national exposure. Two more recordings followed on New Rose and Wolf before his death at age 60.

EDWARDS, EDDIE "DADDY" *Jazz.* Trombone, violin. Composer. Bandleader. (Born May 22, 1891, New Orleans, Orleans Parish; died Apr. 9, 1963, New York City.) Early New Orleans jazz trombonist began playing in his mid-teens and performed with **Papa Jack Laine**'s Reliance Brass Band in the late 1910s. Cofounded and recorded with Original Dixieland Jass Band with **Nick LaRocca** in 1917. In the 1920s worked with Jimmy Durante and Original Dixieland Jazz Band in New York.

EDWARDS, PIANO KID *Blues.* Piano, vocals. Composer. (Born possibly June 16, 1903, Benton, Bossier Parish; died possibly June 11, 1983, Detroit.)[1] Enigmatic early prewar blues piano player and singer who made four recordings for Paramount in 1930, including "Gamblin' Man's Prayer Blues," "Give Us Another Jug" and "Piano Kid Special." In the early 1960s a man claiming to have recorded under the pseudonym "Piano Kid Edwards" was found living in Minneapolis and working as a physician, but his identity or assertion was never confirmed.

EDWARDS, TIBBY (Edwin Thibodeaux) *Rockabilly, country.* Composer. Bandleader. (Born Mar. 19, 1935, Garland, St. Landry Parish; died Sept. 21, 1999, Baton Rouge, EBR Parish.)[2] Early rockabilly and country singer began playing guitar during his teens, influenced greatly by Lefty Frizzell and later Elvis Presley. In the early 1950s began performing on the *Louisiana Hayride* radio program and recorded numerous honkytonk and early rockabilly sides for Mercury through 1958, including "Flip, Flop & Fly" and "Play It Cool Man." Released singles on D, Starday, Todd, and Jin before retiring from music in the 1960s.

EGAN, DAVID *Rhythm and blues, swamp pop.* Piano, vocals. Composer. Bandleader. (Born Mar. 20, 1954, Shreveport, Caddo Parish; died Mar. 18, 2016, Lafayette, Lafayette Parish.) Renowned songwriter and musician whose compositions have been recorded by numerous artists, including **Irma Thomas**, **Johnny Adams**, Solomon Burke, Joe Cocker, Etta James, and others. Raised in a musical family in Shreveport, spent time in Nashville as a budding songwriter after studying jazz and music composition in college. Eventually returned to Shreveport and worked and recorded with band A-Train with **Buddy** and **Bruce Flett** throughout the 1980s and toured with **Jo-El Sonnier**. In the early 1990s relocated to Lafayette and joined Cajun band Filé, touring and recording with group until launching solo career in 2003 and releasing album *Twenty Years of Trouble* on Louisiana Red Hot Records. In following years released two more solo albums and performed and recorded as member of swamp pop group Lil' Band O' Gold. Succumbed to complications of lung cancer at age 61.

EGAN, WILLIE (*also* Willie Egans) *Rhythm and blues.* Piano, vocals. Composer. Bandleader. (Born Oct. 1, 1933, near Minden, Webster Parish; died Aug. 4, 2004, Los Angeles.) Powerful early West Coast–based rhythm and blues piano player and singer best known for his rollicking 1950s recordings such as "Wow Wow," "Rock and Roll Fever," and "Wear Your Black Dress." At age nine was sent to live with his grandmother in Los Angeles and began learning piano. From 1954 to 1958 had singles on Elko, Dig This, Mambo, Vita, Spry, and Dash. Also recorded with Marvin Phillips's duo Marvin and Johnny in the late 1950s and early 1960s. After 20-year hiatus from music enjoyed brief comeback in 1983 with tour of England and recorded album *Going Back to Louisiana* on Ace in 1984. Lost long battle with cancer at age 70.

ELAM, DAVE ALEXANDER *See* Sharriff, Omar.

ELBERT, DONNIE *Rhythm and blues.* Vocals, guitar. Composer. Bandleader. (Born May 25, 1936, New Orleans, Orleans Parish; died Jan. 31, 1989, Philadelphia.)[3] Raised in Buffalo, New York, joined doo-wop group the Vibraharps in 1955 and made recording debut. Began solo career two years later and recorded for numerous labels, including Deluxe, Parkway, Checker, and Gateway from 1957 through the 1970s. Composed more than 100 songs and had hits with "What Can I Do," "Can't Get Over Losing You," and "Where Did Our Love Go."

ELGAR, CHARLIE *Jazz.* Violin. Bandleader. (Born June 13, 1879, New Orleans, Orleans Parish; died July 30, 1973, Chicago.)[4] Classically trained violinist relocated to Chicago in the early 1900s and later helped facilitate other early New Orleans musicians to move to the city such as **Manuel Perez** and **George Filhe** in the mid-1910s. Led bands through the late 1920s in Chicago, at times including Perez, **Lorenzo Tio Jr.**, and **Barney Bigard** and recorded as leader of Elgar's Creole Orchestra in 1926. Mainly taught music after 1930.

ELKINS, ROBERT *Cajun.* Guitar, vocals. Composer. Bandleader. (Born Aug. 29, 1942, Church Point, Acadia Parish.) Noted Cajun singer-guitarist and cofounder with **Paul Daigle** of the premier 1980s band Cajun Gold, best known for their 1986 single "Georgie Lou" on Swallow. Formed Cajun Gold with Daigle in the early 1980s and released singles on Bee before signing with Swallow and recording four LPs through 1990, including *La Lumière Dons Ton Châssis* in 1987. Toured nationally and abroad with group, which remained one of the region's most popular Cajun dance hall bands until breaking up in the early 1990s.

ELLIOTT, JELLY (Joseph Rodney Elliott) *Cajun, string band.* Guitar, upright bass, vocals. Composer. Bandleader. (Born June 3, 1911, Crowville, Franklin Parish; died Jan. 24, 1996, Oak Grove, W. Carroll Parish.)[5] Popular bandleader and radio broadcaster who performed on KALB in Alexandria in the late 1940s. In 1947 recorded "Devil's Blues"/"Ville Platte Waltz" on Magnolia with Cajun fiddler **Abe Manuel**. Between 1950 and 1953 hosted popular series of national radio programs with his band the Three Knotheads sponsored by the Forest Service for its forest-fire prevention campaign which was broadcast on 900 U.S. stations.

ERNEST, HERMAN "ROSCOE," III *Rhythm and blues.* Drums, vocals. Composer. Bandleader. (Born Aug. 12, 1951, New Orleans, Orleans Parish; died Mar. 6, 2011, New Orleans, Orleans Parish.) Renowned New Orleans rhythm and blues and funk drummer who was a key member of **Dr. John**'s band Lower 911 for over two decades. Performed and recorded with numerous musicians since the 1970s, including **King Floyd**, **Allen Toussaint**, **Lee Dorsey**, **Earl King**, **Irma Thomas**, **Johnny Adams**, **Kermit Ruffins**, and Patti LaBelle, among many others.

ESTHAY, VOYLEN "T-BOY" *Cajun.* Fiddle. (Born Sept. 27, 1924, near Basile, Acadia Parish; died Sept. 15, 1989, Jennings, Jeff. Davis Parish.) Noted early Cajun fiddler began playing at age five and in the early 1930s started performing at local house dances. In the late 1930s and early 1940s worked with **Will Kegley** and **Ernest Thibodeaux** in Lake Charles Playboys. Also worked with Lacassine Playboys and Pine Grove Boys in following years. Performed and recorded with **Blackie Forestier** in the late 1950s and 1960s and recorded singles as leader on Cajun Classics and Kajun in the early 1960s, including "Church Point Breakdown" in 1963. Later worked with numerous area bands, including Hathaway Playboys, **Phil Menard**'s Louisiana Travelers, **John Oliver**'s Louisiana Ramblers, and others.

ETIENNE, CLARENCE "JOCKEY" *Blues, zydeco, swamp pop.* Drums. (Born Nov. 22, 1933, near St. Martinville, St. Martin Parish; died Aug. 16, 2015, Lafayette, Lafayette Parish.)[6] Highly regarded and influential Creole drummer who helped define the early swamp blues sound of the 1950s with his highly innovative playing style. Began professional career as a child racehorse jockey before teaching himself how to play drums, inspired by a local performance by Ray Charles. In the early 1950s formed his own band and performed around Lafayette and New Orleans. In 1955 joined **Guitar Gable**'s Musical Kings and soon began recording at producer **J. D. Miller**'s studio as session drummer. In the next several years appeared on countless Excello recordings by Guitar Gable, **Lightnin' Slim**, **Slim Harpo**, **Lonesome Sundown**, **Lazy Lester**, and many others. In the 1960s toured nationally with soul artists **Joe Simon** and Solomon Burke, and throughout the 1970s and 1980s performed and recorded extensively with **Fernest Arceneaux**. Formed Creole Zydeco Farmers with **Chester Chavelier** in 1989 and performed with group until 2013, recording several albums and touring overseas. Continued performing sporadically in remaining years, occasionally with Lil' Band O' Gold after **Warren Storm**'s departure from band. Older brother of zydeco and blues drummer Leroy Etienne.

EUGENE, WENDELL *Jazz.* Trombone, vocals. (Born Oct. 12, 1923, New Orleans, Orleans Parish; died Nov. 7, 2017, New Orleans, Orleans Parish.) Traditional New Orleans jazz trombonist began playing at age 13 and by age 15 was performing professionally. In the late 1930s and early 1940s worked with **Kid Howard**, **Papa Celestin**, **George Lewis**, **Kid Thomas**, and others. After serving in World War II, toured with Lucky Millinder and **Buddy Johnson** and performed with Olympia, Tuxedo, and Onward brass bands. Continued to perform, record, and teach music into his 90s. Released final recording, *If I Had My Life to Live Over,* on GHB at age 90. Nephew of **Paul Barbarin**,

EVANS, MARGIE *Blues, gospel.* Vocals. Composer. Bandleader. (Born July 17, 1940, Shreveport, Caddo Parish.) Powerful blues and gospel singer and songwriter relocated to Los Angeles in the late 1950s and performed with various local groups throughout the 1960s, inspired by Big Maybelle and Bessie Smith. In the late 1960s and early 1970s toured extensively with Johnny Otis's band and appeared as vocalist on two albums. In the mid-1970s had minor hits with "Good Feeling" on United Artists and "Good Thing Queen, Part 1" on ICA. Also toured as member of Willie Dixon's Chicago All-Stars and with the American Folk Blues Festival packages in Europe. In the 1980s and 1990s had releases on L+R, Marvic, Terra Nova, and Fun Key and performed extensively overseas. Continued touring internationally into the 2010s and released *Unplugged* on Funk House Blues in 2016 with Swiss guitarist Philipp Fankhauser.

FABACHER, JOE *Cajun.* Guitar. Bandleader. (Born Aug. 20, 1912, Iota, Acadia Parish; died Feb. 13, 2000, Carencro, Lafayette Parish.) Early Cajun string-band guitarist who formed the Jolly Boys of Lafayette in the mid-1930s with guitarist brother Francis "Red" (1920–1997) and **Leon "Crip" Credeur**. Band recorded 10 sides for Decca in 1937, including "La Valse a Papa" and "Abbeville." In the 1950s performed and recorded with **Pee Wee Broussard**. Brother Red also performed and recorded with **Harry Choates** and **Jimmy C. Newman** on steel guitar in the late 1940s.

FAIRBURN, WERLY *Rockabilly, rhythm and blues.* Vocals, guitar. Composer. Bandleader. (Born Nov. 27, 1924, New Orleans, Orleans Parish; died Jan. 18, 1985, Glendora, California.) Raised on a farm near Folsom, Louisiana, early rockabilly singer and guitarist began playing the instrument as a child. Later gained fame in New Orleans in the late 1940s as "The Singing Barber" and hosted popular local radio show. Appeared on the *Louisiana Hayride* in Shreveport and in the 1950s and 1960s had releases on Trumpet, Columbia, Capitol, Savoy, and his own Milestone label, including "Everybody's Rockin'" in 1956, which is considered a rockabilly classic. Relocated to California in 1959 and continued performing until his death at age 57.

FAIRCHILD, GENE (Farrell Marcell) *Rhythm and blues.* Vocals. (Born Dec. 7, 1944, Paulina, St. James Parish; died May 21, 2017, Baton Rouge, EBR Parish.) Baton Rouge soul singer best known for his 1965 single "It Must Be Love"/"Another Shoulder to Cry On" on local Bofuz label. Continued performing occasionally on the Baton Rouge blues scene through the mid-2010s.

FALCON, CLÉOMA BREAUX *Cajun.* Guitar, fiddle, accordion, vocals. Composer. (Born May 27, 1906, Crowley, Acadia Parish; died Apr. 8, 1941, Crowley, Acadia Parish.)[1] Highly influential early Cajun singer, songwriter, and guitarist and pioneering female musician in the male-dominated Cajun music scene of the 1920s and 1930s. Raised in a musical family of multi-instrumentalists. Her father, August, was an accordion player, and brothers **Amédée**, **Ophy**, and **Clifford Breaux** were also highly accomplished musicians. In the 1920s performed with her brothers in area dance halls and achieved local fame. Around 1925 started performing with **Joe Falcon**, whom she would later marry. In Apr. 1928 the pair recorded "Allons à Lafayette" for Columbia Records, regarded as the first commercial Cajun record and which ushered in the first era of Cajun and Creole recordings. Composed and recorded many dozens of songs for Columbia, Bluebird, and Decca through the late 1930s with both Falcon and brothers' group Breaux Frères, many of which became Cajun standards, including "Ma Blonde Est Partié," which is considered the origin of the Cajun standard "Jolie Blon." Remained a popular performer throughout the Great Depression due to her powerful high singing, strong guitar playing, and striking beauty. In the late 1930s was involved in a debilitating automobile accident which left her frail until her death at age 34 following a four-month-long illness.

FALCON, JOE (Joseph F. Falcon) *Cajun.* Accordion, vocals. Composer. Bandleader. (Born Sept. 28, 1900, Roberts Cove, Acadia Parish; died Nov. 19, 1965, Rayne, Acadia Parish.) Highly influential early Cajun accordionist and singer who made the first commercial recording of Cajun music, "Allons à Lafayette," in 1928 with future wife **Cléoma Breaux (Falcon)** and together became the music's first stars. Born and raised in a small community just north of Rayne, began playing accordion at age seven and by the 1920s was performing regularly at local dance halls and house dances, occasionally with **Amédée Breaux** and later regularly with Breaux's sister Cléoma. In Apr. 1928 recorded "Lafayette" for Columbia with Cléoma on guitar, which became a huge regional hit and ushered in the first era of Cajun and Creole recordings. Pair recorded numerous sides on sessions for Columbia, Bluebird, and Decca through 1937, including "Aimer au Perdre," "Acadian One-Step," and "Ossun," and remained the most popular dance-hall performers in southwest Louisiana and east Texas until the mid- to late 1930s when Cajun swing music gained dominance. After Cléoma's death in 1941, continued performing through the early 1960s with his Silver Bells String Band, which later included second wife, **Theresa Falcon**, on drums. Shortly before his death, made live recording with band at the Triangle Club in Scott in 1963 featuring **Lionel Leleux** on fiddle, which was later issued on Arhoolie. Uncle of **Marie Falcon** and cousin of early Cajun fiddler Ulysse Falcon.

FALCON, MARIE (Solange Marie Falcon) *Cajun.* Guitar, vocals. (Born Aug. 22, 1920, Rayne, Acadia Parish; died Sept. 25, 2007, Lafayette, Lafayette Parish.) Early postwar Cajun singer-guitarist performed with **Shuk Richard**'s Louisiana Aces in Lake Charles–area dance halls from the mid-1940s through the mid-1950s, recording two singles with group for Khoury's in the early 1950s, notably "Madame Entelle Two Step." Appeared in 1989 film *J'Ai Été au Bal.* Niece of **Joe Falcon**.

FALCON, THERESA (*born* Meaux) Cajun. Drums, vocals. (Born Oct. 15, 1912, Wright, Vermilion Parish; died June 2, 1990, Crowley, Acadia Parish.) Second wife of **Joe Falcon**, who performed as drummer and vocalist in Falcon's Silver Bells String Band in the 1950s and early 1960s. Appeared on band's 1963 live recording issued on Arhoolie LP 5005 in 1968. Sister of **Pappy "Te-Tan" Meaux**.

FARMER, BETTY *Jazz.* Vocals. (Born Oct. 15, 1938, New Orleans, Orleans Parish; died Sept. 11, 2001, Manhattan, New York.) Jazz vocalist began singing with Dixieland jazz bands as a teenager on Bourbon Street and later toured with Duke Ellington in the 1960s and 1970s. Performed at clubs and festivals throughout the United States in 1980s and early 1990s. Moved to New York in 1997 and was among the victims of the terrorist attack on the World Trade Center.

FASNACHT, YVONNE "DIXIE" *Jazz.* Saxophone, clarinet, vocals. (Born July 7, 1910, New Orleans, Orleans Parish; died Nov. 13, 2011, New Orleans, Orleans Parish.) Performed locally with Harmony Maids and toured with all-women groups the Smart Set and Southland Rhythm Girls in the 1930s. Opened famed Dixie's Bar on Bourbon Street in 1939 with sister, where she occasionally performed. In 1960 recorded LP *Dixie and Sloopy* on Golden Crest with pianist Dorothy Sloop.

FAUL, MERVIN *Cajun.* Steel guitar. (Born Sept. 21, 1932, Iota, Acadia Parish.) Veteran Cajun steel guitarist began performing in the 1950s and throughout following decades worked and recorded with **Robert Bertrand**, **Sidney Brown**, **Phil Menard**, **Nolan Cormier**, **John Oliver**, **Ed Gary** and many others. Continued performing into his 80s.

FAULK, CLAUDE *Creole.* Accordion, vocals. (Born Sept. 27, 1908, Lafayette, Lafayette Parish; died Oct. 14, 1985, Scott, Lafayette Parish.) Early Creole accordionist who performed at la la house dances in Lafayette and Opelousas area and greatly influenced **Clifton Chenier**, **Walter "Creole" Polite**, **Herbert Sam** and other early zydeco accordionists. Brother Ernest Faulk was also a respected accordion player.

FAULK, JOHNNY *Cajun.* Upright bass, vocals. (Born Mar. 24, 1925, Creole, Cameron Parish; died Oct. 17, 2004, Lake Charles, Calcasieu Parish.) Cajun bassist joined the long-running Hackberry Ramblers around 1980 and performed with the group until his death. Appeared on releases *Cajun Boogie* and *Deep Water* on Hot Biscuit Records in the 1990s.

FAWVOR, DUDLEY *Cajun.* Fiddle, vocals. Composer. (Born Aug. 24, 1905, Grand Chenier, Cameron Parish; died Mar. 3, 1930, Port Arthur, Texas.)[2] Early Cajun fiddle player and singer who recorded "T'Est Petite a Ete T'Est Meon (You Are Little and You Are Cute)" and "La Valse de Creole" with brother James (1909–1973) on guitar and vocals in Dec. 1928, foreshadowing the coming Cajun swing era of the 1930s. Succumbed to complications from a tonsillectomy shortly afterwards at age 24.

FAZOLA, IRVING "FAZ" *Jazz.* Clarinet, saxophone. (Born Dec. 10, 1912, New Orleans, Orleans Parish; died Mar. 20, 1949, New Orleans, Orleans Parish.) Accomplished clarinetist and early influence of **Pete Fountain**. Began learning clarinet and saxophone at age 13. Worked with **Sharkey Bonano**, **Louis Prima**, and **Armand Hug** in early career and toured with Glenn Miller, Ben Pollack, Bob Crosby, Claude Thornhill, and others in the 1930s and early 1940s. Recorded as a leader and with Bonano, Billie Holiday, and others.

FERBOS, LIONEL *Jazz.* Trumpet. Bandleader. (Born July 17, 1911, New Orleans, Orleans Parish; died July 19, 2014, New Orleans, Orleans Parish.) Traditional New Orleans jazz trumpeter began music career performing with society jazz bands in the early 1930s around New Orleans and also worked with **Captain John Handy**, **Fats Pichon**, and blues singer Mamie Smith. Later performed regularly with **Harold Dejan** and **Danny Barker**. In remaining years held steady gig in the French Quarter when at age 102 was believed to be the world's oldest active jazz musician.

FERRIER, AL (Alfous Glenn Ferrier Sr.) *Rockabilly, gospel.* Guitar, vocals. Composer. Bandleader. (Born Aug. 19, 1934, Olla, La Salle Parish; died Jan. 6, 2015, Natchitoches, Natch. Parish.)[3] Dubbed "the King of Louisiana Rockabilly," noted singer began playing guitar as a child and during his teens formed country band with older brothers Bryan and Warren. In 1955 signed with Goldband and recorded several rockabilly classics, including "No No Baby" and "Let's Go Boppin' Tonight." Also appeared on the *Louisiana Hayride* program. In the late 1950s recorded for producer **J. D. Miller** and had releases on Excello, Zynn, and Rocko. After retiring from performing in the mid-1960s, began recording again in the 1970s and cut LPs for Goldband and Showtime. In the 1980s toured Europe and recorded LPs for Rockhouse and Jin before switching to gospel. Continued performing occasionally at clubs and rockabilly revivals in the United States and Europe into the 2010s.

FIELDS, FRANK *Rhythm and blues, jazz.* Bass. (Born May 2, 1914, Plaquemine, Iberville Parish; died Sept. 18, 2005, New Orleans, Orleans Parish.) Highly regarded early New Orleans rhythm and blues bass player best known for his prolific session work with **Dave Bartholomew**'s band in the 1950s. Began performing in the 1930s with **Claiborne Williams**'s orchestra before joining Bartholomew after serving in World War II. Appeared on hundreds of classic recordings from the late 1940s through 1960s by **Fats Domino**, **Smiley Lewis**, **Roy Brown**, **Huey "Piano" Smith**, **Professor Longhair**, **Cousin Joe**, Little Richard, Elmore James, Ray Charles, T-Bone Walker, and many others. In the 1990s performed as member of Preservation Hall Jazz Band.

FIELDS, THOMAS "BIG HAT" *Zydeco.* Accordion, vocals. Composer. Bandleader. (Born May 10, 1947, Rayne, Acadia Parish.) Noted zydeco accordion player and singer-songwriter played rubboard behind **Claude Faulk** as a child and grew up listening to local Creole musicians such as **Sidney Babineaux**, **Hiram Sampy**, and Paul "Papillon" Harris. At age 43 began learning accordion from Harris and soon formed the Foot Stompin' Zydeco Band with wife, Geneva, on bass, appearing regularly at his Big Hat Club in Grand Coteau. In the mid-1990s had three releases on Lanor, including recording debut *The Big Hat Man* in 1994. Continued performing locally with several national tours through the 2000s, releasing two CDs on Maison de Soul through 2004. Remained musically inactive in recent years.

FILHE, GEORGE *Jazz.* Trombone. (Born Nov. 13, 1872, New Orleans, Orleans Parish; died Oct. 21, 1952, Chicago.)[4] Very early New Orleans jazz trombonist began performing in the early 1890s and worked with Onward Brass Band from 1893 to 1911 and Peerless and Imperial Orchestra from 1903 to 1905. After several years performing with **Papa Celestin**, moved to Chicago in 1913 and in the early 1920s worked with **King Oliver**, **Manuel Perez**, **Sidney Bechet**, and others. Retired from music in the late 1920s.

FILLMORE SLIM (Clarence "Guitar" Sims) Blues. Guitar, vocals. Composer. Bandleader. (Born Nov. 7, 1934, Baton Rouge, EBR Parish.) Noted blues singer and guitarist began playing guitar in his teens, inspired by hearing **Guitar Slim**, **Earl King**, and others at New Orleans's famed Dew Drop Inn. Moved to California in 1955 to pursue music and recorded for Dooto, Kent, and Dore in the late 1950s and 1960s. Settled in Oakland and worked outside music as a pimp in the 1960s and 1970s. Returned to music in the late 1980s and continued to perform through the 2010s with multiple releases on Fedora and Mountain Top, including *The Blues Playa's Ball* in 2010.

FINLEY, ROBERT *Rhythm and blues.* Guitar, vocals. Composer. Bandleader. (Born Feb. 15, 1954, Monroe, Ouachita Parish.) Soulful rhythm and blues singer-songwriter and guitarist was raised in Winnsboro and began playing at age 11 but was forbidden to play blues by his religious father. In 1970 joined the army and performed in bands overseas. After discharge returned to Louisiana and worked as a carpenter while performing in gospel and blues groups part-time based in Bernice, inspired by B.B. King and Bobby Bland. While in his early 60s retired from carpentry due to vision problems and began performing full-time. After being discovered while busking on the streets in Helena, Arkansas, recorded debut album *Age Don't Mean a Thing* on Big Legal Mess in 2016 and began touring internationally. In late 2017 released *Goin' Platinum!* on Easy Eye Sound.

FIZER, CHARLES *Rhythm and blues.* Vocals. (Born June 3, 1940, Shreveport, Caddo Parish; died Aug. 14, 1965, Los Angeles.) Second lead singer of popular rhythm and blues vocal group the Olympics which had several hits in the late 1950s and early 1960s including "Western Movies," "(Baby) Hully Gully," and "Good Lovin'." In 1965 was tragically gunned down by the National Guard while driving to band rehearsals during the Watts riots.

FLETT, BRUCE *Blues.* Bass, vocals. Bandleader. (Born Nov. 28, 1951, Shreveport, Caddo Parish.) Accomplished Shreveport bass player and singer began performing in the mid-1970s on the Bossier Strip with brother **Buddy Flett**. From 1977 to 1987 performed in popular rhythm and blues band A-Train with Buddy and toured the South and abroad. In the following decades performed in the Bluebirds with Buddy and released three albums, including *Swamp Stomp* in 1994. Continued performing and working as booking agent and promoter in the late 2010s, having worked extensively in the past for famed Shreveport producer **Stan Lewis**.

FLETT, BUDDY (Deane Flett Jr.) *Blues.* Guitar, vocals. Composer. Bandleader. (Born June 26, 1953, Shreveport, Caddo Parish.) Noted Shreveport blues guitarist and singer-songwriter began performing in the mid-1970s on the Bossier Strip. In 1977 formed band A-Train with older brother **Bruce Flett** which remained a popular touring act throughout the South through 1987, recording several albums. Also served as writing partner with bandmate **David Egan**. In the late 1980s brothers formed trio the Bluebirds and continued to perform into 2010s with three releases. In 2007 released solo album *Out of the Past* and appeared with **Kenny Wayne Shepherd** on tour and in documentary *10 Days Out*. Continued to perform as solo artist in the 2010s, releasing CD *Rough Edges* in 2013.

THE FLOCK-ROCKER *See* Gabriel the Flock-Rocker.

FLOYD, KING (King Floyd III) *Rhythm and blues.* Vocals. Composer. Bandleader. (Born Feb. 13, 1945, New Orleans, Orleans Parish; died Mar. 6, 2006, Jackson, California.) New Orleans soul singer best known for his 1971 hit "Groove Me." Born King Floyd III in New Orleans, was raised in Kenner and by the early 1960s was singing in clubs on Bourbon Street. Moved to Los Angeles in the mid-1960s and worked with **Harold Battiste**, recording for Original Sound and Pulsar. Back in New Orleans in 1970, worked with producer Wardell Quezergue and recorded number-one hit "Groove Me" for Malaco's Chimneyville label. Through the early 1970s had several more minor hits and also had releases on Atlantic and Dial. Worked in and out of music in following decades with final recording in 2000 on Malaco.

FOLSE, UNCLE POTT (Gatewood Folse) *Cajun.* Accordion, piano, banjo, drums, vocals. Composer. Bandleader. (Born June 12, 1925, Raceland, Lafouche Parish.) Veteran Cajun multi-instrumentalist, singer-songwriter, and patriarch of renowned music family of Raceland. Began performing in the 1940s as member of **Dudley Bernard**'s Southern Serenaders with **Vin Bruce**, **Harry Anselmi**, and **Leroy Martin** and also worked with **Gene Rodrigue**. From the 1960s through 2000s had releases on numerous labels, including Ladd, Barnyard, Houma, Starbarn, and Jin, notably *Bayou Cajun Music* in 1998. Formed the Pott Folse Family Band in the 1970s and continued performing throughout the Raceland area into his 90s.

FONTAINE, RICK *See* Fontenot, Richard.

FONTANA, CARL *Jazz.* Trombone. (Born July 18, 1928, Monroe, Ouachita Parish; died Oct. 9, 2003, Las Vegas.) Highly regarded jazz trombonist known for his fluid, lyrical style. Began performing locally with his father's jazz band in the 1940s. From 1951 to 1953 toured with Woody Herman and in 1954 worked with Lionel Hampton. Performed and recorded for two years with Stan Kenton before relocating to Las Vegas in 1958. In the 1960s and 1970s performed primarily in house orchestras and worked with Benny Goodman, Paul Anka, Sammy Davis Jr., and others. Recorded extensively as a sideman starting in the 1950s but released only one recording as leader, *The Great Fontana,* on Uptown in 1987. Continued performing and recording sporadically into the 1990s.

FONTANA, D. J. (Dominic Joseph Fontana) *Rockabilly.* Drums. (Born Mar. 15, 1931, Shreveport, Caddo Parish; died June 13, 2018, Nashville.) Highly influential early rockabilly drummer best known for his extensive work with Elvis Presley, appearing on more than 450 Presley recordings. Began performing as backup drummer on the *Louisiana Hayride* in 1953 and worked with Johnny Horton, George Jones, **Dale Hawkins**, and others. In

1954 backed Presley on the *Hayride* and joined his band the following year with Scotty Moore and Bill Black. Appeared on vast majority of Presley's recordings in the 1950s and 1960s and toured extensively with band through 1968. Relocated to Nashville in the 1960s and began long career as an in-demand session musician. Continued performing and recording in the decades following Presley's death in 1977 and appeared on critically acclaimed release *All the King's Men* on Sweetfish with Moore in 1997. Made occasional appearances into his 80s.

FONTENETTE, GUS (Gustave Fontenette Sr.) *Jazz.* Trombone. Bandleader. (Born Dec. 25, 1887, New Iberia, Iberia Parish; died June 12, 1967, New Orleans, Orleans Parish.)[5] Important early Acadiana jazz trombonist and longtime bandleader of the Banner Orchestra, the region's largest and most celebrated jazz and dance band of its time. Began playing music professionally in his early teens and formed Banner Orchestra in 1908, which he led for more than 40 years and whose members at times included **Bunk Johnson**, **Evan Thomas**, **Lawrence Duhé**, **Hypolite** and **Harold Potier Sr.**, **Morris Dauphine**, and daughter **Mercedes Potier**. Retired from music in the early 1950s due to illness and disbanded orchestra. Succumbed to complications of heart disease and stroke at New Orleans Charity Hospital at age 79. Father of saxophonist Gus Fontenette Jr. (1912–1994), who worked with **Guitar Slim**, Ray Charles, T-Bone Walker, and others, and grandfather of **John** and **Harold Potier Jr.** Great-grandfather of **Tony Hall**.

FONTENOT, ALLEN *Cajun.* Fiddle, vocals. Composer. Bandleader. (Born Jan. 19, 1932, Plaisance, Evangeline Parish; died July 30, 2013, River Ridge, Jefferson Parish.) Renowned Cajun fiddle player and bandleader who was among the first to perform Cajun music regularly in New Orleans. Began playing on makeshift fiddles made out of ukuleles and cigar boxes as a child. After serving in the military and working outside music for several years, settled in New Orleans in the early 1970s and formed his band the Country Cajuns. Throughout following decades performed regularly in New Orleans area and toured nationally and overseas, releasing albums on Antilles, Delta, PMF, Ralph's, and Lone Star, including *Fais Do Do Songs* in 1980. In the late 1970s and early 1980s operated Cajun Bandstand in Kenner. Appeared 37 consecutive times at New Orleans Jazz & Heritage Festival and continued performing until retiring from music in 2010.

FONTENOT, BEE (Ray B. Fontenot) *Creole.* Accordion. (Born Dec. 8, 1907, near Eunice, St. Landry Parish; died Nov. 24, 1973, Basile, Evangeline Parish.)[6] Noted Creole accordionist and younger brother of **Freeman Fontenot**. Learned to play accordion from **Amédé Ardoin** while in his teens and began playing house dances in the mid-1920s in the Basile area. Performed with various musicians, including **Leo Soileau**, in following years. Appeared in Jean-Pierre Bruneau's acclaimed 1974 film *Dedans le Sud de la Louisiane* with **Dewey Balfa** and on accompanying soundtrack. Second and third cousin of **Adam** and **Canray Fontenot**.

FONTENOT, CANRAY *Creole.* Fiddle, vocals. Composer. (Born Oct. 16, 1922, L'Anse aux Vaches, near Basile, Evangeline Parish; died July 29, 1995, Welsh, Jefferson Parish.) Highly influential Creole fiddle player often cited as the genre's greatest fiddle instrumentalist and best known for his forty-plus-year partnership with **Bois Sec Ardoin**. Son of influential accordionist **Nonc Adam Fontenot**, began playing a homemade fiddle as a child, learning from **Douglas Bellard**. In the 1930s performed with **Amédé Ardoin** at area house dances and dance halls. After a stint in a string band, began performing with Bois Sec in the late 1940s at local venues, including third cousin **Freeman Fontenot**'s club in Basile. The duo's vast repertoire included songs passed down from his father, Adam, and Amédé Ardoin as well as original compositions such as "Joe Pitre a Deux Femmes" and "Les Barres de la Prison." After an eight-year break from music, performed with Bois Sec at 1966 Newport Folk Festival and gained national prominence. In 1966 recorded LP *Les Blues du Bayou* on Melodeon with Bois Sec. Appeared in 1974 film *Dedans le Sud de la Louisiane* and through the 1980s recorded several albums for Arhoolie, including 1974 LP *La Musique Creole* with Bois Sec and his brothers Gustav, **Morris**, and **Black Ardoin**. In 1986 was awarded NEA National Heritage Fellowship and continued appearing at national festivals into the early 1990s.

FONTENOT, COZ *Cajun.* Accordion, fiddle, harmonica, drums, vocals. Composer. Bandleader. (Born Sept. 23, 1955, Mamou, Evangeline Parish.) Traditional Cajun multi-instrumentalist and exceptional singer was raised in Eunice and began playing harmonica at age 10, soon taking up fiddle and drums as well. After a 10-year stint in Atlanta, returned to Eunice area and continued performing locally with his band and hosting popular weekly jam sessions. Recorded debut CD *Lundi Gras* on Acadiana in 1998 and continued performing in the 2010s, releasing two more CDs, including *Memories of My Past* in 2016. Ill health forced retirement from performing in early 2019.

FONTENOT, CURSEY *Cajun.* Fiddle, vocals. Bandleader. (Born Aug. 23, 1920, Oberlin, Allen Parish; died Dec. 21, 1995, Oberlin, Allen Parish.)[7] Noted Cajun fiddler began playing at age 18, mentored by **Leo Soileau**. After performing around Oberlin and Elton area in the 1940s, joined Oberlin Playboys in 1949. In the mid-1950s formed Louisiana Travelers with **Phil Menard** on accordion and performed with group through the mid-1960s. Also founded Calcasieu Playboys and performed with group for several years. In the 1970s recorded two singles for Big D with **Hadley Fontenot**, including "La Maison Deux Etages."

FONTENOT, FREEMAN (*or* Fremont) *Creole.* Accordion. (Born Apr. 2, 1900, near Eunice, St. Landry Parish; died Apr. 4, 1987, Basile, Evangeline Parish.)[8] Influential early Creole accordionist was raised speaking Creole French and began playing accordion at age 14, learning from second cousin **Nonc Adam Fontenot** and **Amédé Ardoin**. By the 1920s had relocated to Basile area and was playing regularly at la la house dances. In the 1940s retired from performing and began operating popular rural club in Basile which for many years hosted performances by numerous area musicians, including **Bois Sec** and **Morris Ardoin,** third cousin **Canray Fontenot**, and **Clifton Chenier**. Returned to performing in the mid-1970s and recorded selections which appeared on 1978 Smithsonian Folkways LP *Louisiana Creole Music* and 1979 Rounder LP *Zodico: Louisiana Créole Music.* Also mentored **Lawrence "Black" Ardoin** in later years. Older brother of **Bee Fontenot**.

FONTENOT, GEORGE *Cajun.* Fiddle, vocals. Composer. Bandleader. (Born May 2, 1907, Chataignier, Evangeline Parish; died Dec. 17, 1977, Mamou, Evangeline Parish.) Cajun fiddler and singer recorded several singles for Swallow in the mid-1960s and early 1970s with his band the Cajun Four which included **Harrison Fontenot**. Notable songs include "La Gig a George."

FONTENOT, HADLEY *Cajun.* Accordion. (Born July 20, 1909, Mamou, Evangeline Parish; died June 27, 1987, Oberlin, Allen Parish.) Noted Cajun accordion player best known for his work performing and recording with **Dewey Balfa** and the **Balfa Brothers** in the 1960s and 1970s, appearing on numerous acclaimed recordings with the group, including 1967 Swallow LP *Balfa Brothers Play Traditional Cajun Music.* Also recorded two singles for Big D around 1970 with his Hi-Mount Playboys with **Cursey Fontenot**, including "Hi-Mount Two Step." Great-grandfather of **Kevin Naquin**.

FONTENOT, HARRISON *Cajun.* Accordion, vocals. Composer. Bandleader. (Born Aug. 1, 1934, Point Blue, Evangeline Parish; died Jan. 21, 2011, Ville Platte, Evangeline Parish.) Cajun accordion player and builder began learning the instrument in his teens, inspired by **Aldus Roger** and **Austin Pitre**. In the 1960s and 1970s recorded several singles for Swallow with his Cajun Trio and Cajun Four, including "La Cravat" and "Cajun Twist." Also recorded with **Dewey Balfa** and **George Fontenot**.

FONTENOT, ISOM J. *Cajun.* Harmonica, triangle, vocals. Composer. (Born July 28, 1908, Mamou, Evangeline Parish; died Apr. 7, 1972, Mamou, Evangeline Parish.) Cajun harmonica player and singer taught himself to play the instrument as a child and later performed at local house dances. In the late 1950s recorded several traditional French Louisiana songs for folklorist Harry Oster which appeared on 1959 LP *Folksongs of the Louisiana Acadians.* Also appeared on 1966 Arhoolie LP *Cajun Fais Do-Do* and backed **Bois Sec Ardoin** and **Canray Fontenot** on 1966 Melodeon LP *Les Blues du Bayou.* Performed at several national festivals in the 1960s and appeared in 1974 film *Dedans le Sud de la Louisiane.*

FONTENOT, LEO *Cajun.* Accordion, vocals. Composer. Bandleader. (Born Sept. 4, 1915, Point Blue, Evangeline Parish; died Oct. 28, 1996, Ville Platte, Evangeline Parish.) Locally renowned Cajun accordionist and singer performed around Ville Platte area with his Ville Platte Playboys throughout the 1950s, appearing regularly on weekly radio broadcasts. In 1959 recorded single "Jole Basette"/"Ville Platte Playboys Special" for Swallow.

FONTENOT, MERLIN *Cajun.* Fiddle. (Born Sept. 26, 1923, Eunice, St. Landry Parish; died Jan. 10, 2017, Lafayette, Lafayette Parish.) Noted veteran Cajun fiddler and son of local Cajun accordionist Enos Fontenot (1902–1977) began playing fiddle at age seven and by age 15 was performing in local dance halls. After serving in World War II, settled in Florida and toured with country and bluegrass bands. Returned to Lafayette area by 1970 and recorded prolifically in following years, appearing on recordings with **Balfa Brothers**, **Nathan Abshire**, **Ambrose Thibodeaux**, **Jo-El Sonnier**, **D. L. Menard**, and many others. Continued performing into his 90s and served as performer and cultural historian at Lafayette's historic Cajun and Creole village Vermilionville for more than 20 years.

FONTENOT, NONC ADAM *Creole.* Accordion. (Born Jan. 9, 1899, near Mamou, Evangeline Parish; died June 2, 1939, Basile, Evangeline Parish.)[9] Influential early Creole accordionist who was a peer and occasional partner of **Amédé Ardoin**. Performed at local house dances in Basile area in the 1920s and 1930s. Father of **Canray Fontenot**, to whom he passed along his vast repertoire.

FONTENOT, RICHARD/"RICK FONTAINE" *Cajun.* Guitar. (Born July 19, 1935, Jennings, Jeff. Davis Parish; died Nov. 26, 1997, Iota, Acadia Parish.)[10] Cajun guitarist who developed a unique finger-picked playing style inspired by Chet Atkins to adapt traditional Cajun songs such as "Jolie Blon" and "Colinda" for solo guitar. In 1964 recorded single "Diggy Liggy Lo"/"Cajun on the Strings" for **J. D. Miller**'s Zynn label under the name Rick Fontaine. Later released LP *Cajun Country Guitar* on Folkways in 1978 under given name produced by French researcher Gerard Dole.

FONTENOT, RODNEY *Cajun.* Fiddle. (Born Jan. 7, 1914, Chataignier, Evangeline Parish; died May 1, 2005, Eunice, St. Landry Parish.) Early Cajun fiddler was inspired to play at age 10 after seeing **Dennis McGee** perform with his father at local house dances. Began learning McGee's style at age 15 and within a year was playing professionally. Continued performing until retiring from music in 1936. Began performing again five decades later and recorded CD *Cajun Fiddle the Way It Was* in 2001.

FORD, CLARENCE *Rhythm and blues, jazz.* Saxophone, clarinet. (Born Dec. 16, 1929, New Orleans, Orleans Parish; died Aug. 9, 1994, New Orleans, Orleans Parish.)[11] New Orleans saxophonist worked with jazz groups in the 1940s, including Eureka Brass Band and **Wallace Davenport**'s Be-Bop Jockeys. From the 1950s through 1970s appeared on dozens of rhythm and blues sessions with **Fats Domino**, Little Richard, **Guitar Slim**, **Dave Bartholomew**, **Roy Brown**, **Smiley Lewis**, **Professor Longhair**, **Earl King**, and many others. Between 1955 and 1970 was member of Domino's touring band. Father of **Louis Ford**.

FORD, DEE DEE (Wrecia Holloway) *Rhythm and blues.* Vocals, organ. Composer. (Born 1936, Minden, Webster Parish; died 1972, New Orleans, Orleans Parish.) Noted soulful rhythm and blues singer-songwriter and organist best known for her 1962 hit "I Need Your Lovin'" with Don Gardner. Moved to New Jersey in the early 1950s and began playing organ in church. In 1960 joined Gardner's band as organist and co-singer and in 1962 had major hit with "I Need Your Lovin'" on Fire. Singles followed on ABC-Paramount, KC, Ludix, and Red Top as well as several European tours and two LPs on Sonet in the mid-1960s. In 1965 wrote "Let Me Down Easy," which was a hit for soul singer Bettye LaVette. Left music business shortly afterwards, reportedly suffering from severe depression.

FORD, FRANKIE (Vincent Francis Guzzo Jr.) *Rhythm and blues.* Piano, vocals. Composer. Bandleader. (Born Aug. 4, 1939, Gretna, Jefferson Parish; died Sept. 28, 2015, Gretna, Jefferson Parish.) Renowned New Orleans rhythm and blues singer and pianist best known for his 1959 hit "Sea Cruise." Began singing in talent shows at age five and formed first band while in high school. In 1958 was signed to Ace Records and made recording debut with "Cheatin' Woman." The following year Ace producer Johnny Vincent overdubbed Ford's vocals on previously recorded track titled "Sea Cruise," written and recorded by **Huey "Piano" Smith**, which became his biggest hit. Several minor hits followed through the early 1960s on Ace and Imperial, the latter produced by **Dave Bartholomew**. Performed mainly in Bourbon Street clubs from the mid-1960s through 1980 and in next several decades toured extensively nationally and overseas. Cofounded record label Briarmeade in the mid-1970s and released multiple recordings through 2009.

FORD, LOUIS *Jazz.* Clarinet, saxophone. Bandleader. (Born Sept. 28, 1962, New Orleans, Orleans Parish.) Son of saxophone and clarinet player **Clarence Ford**, New Orleans jazz multi-instrumentalist studied under **Kidd Jordan** at Southern University. Upon graduation in the 1980s began working with various brass bands—including Onward, Liberty, and Tuxedo—as well as **Doc Paulin**'s group. Throughout the years also performed with many traditional jazz and rhythm and blues musicians and made several recordings as leader, including *Just TRAD-itional.* In the 2010s led his band the New Orleans Flairs and performed with Preservation Hall Jazz Band.

FORESTIER, BLACKIE (Firmin Ledel Forestier) *Cajun.* Accordion, vocals. Composer. Bandleader. (Born Oct. 28, 1928, Cankton, St. Landry Parish; died Nov. 19, 2001, Lake Charles, Calcasieu Parish.) Noted traditional Cajun accordion player, singer, and bandleader began playing in the mid-1950s and in 1957 formed the Cajun Aces. In the late 1960s recorded several singles for Swallow, including "Big Pine Waltz," and released debut LP *Cajun French Music* on La Louisianne which featured **Jay Stutes** and **Rufus Thibodeaux**. More releases followed on La Louisiana, Circle D, Country Star, and Kajun through the late 1970s. In the late 1970s and 1980s appeared on releases by **Sheryl Cormier** and **D. L. Menard**. Continued performing through 2000 with several more recordings on La Louisianne, including *Réunion sur la Butte* in 1999.

FORET, L. J. (Lawrence Joseph Foret) *Cajun.* Guitar, fiddle, drums, vocals. Composer. Bandleader. (Born June 30, 1930, Houma, Terrebonne Parish; died Sept. 12, 2002, Houma, Terrebonne Parish.) Locally popular country-influenced Cajun multi-instrumentalist and singer-songwriter began performing in his early teens in his father's band the Town Serenaders. Formed his band the Country Boys around 1960 and released numerous singles on Houma, Ciro, Arelro, Starbarn, Ajae's, and La Louisianne, including "Fille de Houma." In 1973 released LP *Cajun Country Singer* on La Louisianne. Succumbed to cancer at age 72. Father of musician Ronnie Foret.

FORET, WAYNE *Swamp pop. Piano, vocals.* Composer. Bandleader. (Born Oct. 29, 1948, Westwego, Jefferson Parish.) Born on a houseboat near Westwego, popular swamp pop singer and piano player formed his band the Rockin' 50s in 1973 and made debut recording in the mid-1980s. Released three CDs on CSP in 2000s, including *Still Going Strong!* in 2007, and continued performing throughout south Louisiana in the 2010s.

FOSTER, ABBEY "CHINEE" *Jazz.* Drums, slide whistle, vocals. (Born Mar. 20, 1902, New Orleans, Orleans Parish; died Sept. 7, 1962, New Orleans, Orleans Parish.)[12] Renowned early jazz drummer was playing professionally by age eight and performed with **John Robichaux** and **Manuel Perez** early on. Also worked with **Jack Carey**, **Chris Kelly**, **Buddy Petit**, **Frankie Duson**, and **Punch Miller** in following years. By the early 1920s had replaced **Henry Zeno** in **Papa Celestin**'s Original Tuxedo Band and recorded with Celestin in 1927. In the 1930s worked throughout southwest Louisiana with **Gus Fontenette**'s Banner Orchestra and **Evan Thomas**'s Black Eagles Band, often with **Bunk Johnson**. Continued performing with various groups throughout the 1940s and 1950s, performing at Preservation Hall shortly before his death.

FOSTER, GEORGE "POPS" *Jazz.* Double bass, tuba. (Born May 19, 1892, McCall, Ascension Parish; died Oct. 30, 1969, San Francisco.)[13] Highly accomplished New Orleans jazz bass pioneer who recorded prolifically and worked with many of the greatest figures in early jazz. Moved to New Orleans with family around 1902 and began performing professionally in 1906. Worked early on with **Frankie Duson**'s Eagle Band, **Jack Carey**, **King Oliver**, **Kid Ory**, **Armand Piron**, **Freddie Keppard**, **Buddy Petit**, Tuxedo Jazz Band, and others. In the late 1910s worked regularly on riverboats with **Fate Marable** and in 1923 performed in California with Ory and **Mutt Carey**, followed by several years on riverboats in St. Louis. Moved to New York in 1929 and in following decade worked and recorded with Luis Russell and **Louis Armstrong**, among others. During the New Orleans jazz revival of the 1940s worked and recorded with **Sidney Bechet**, Mezz Mezzrow, and others, and toured nationally and overseas. After stints with **Papa Celestin** in New Orleans and Sammy Price in Europe, relocated to San Francisco in 1956 and worked with Earl Hines, Eddie South, and others through the early 1960s. In 1966 made last tour of Europe with the New Orleans All Stars. Brother Willie Foster was a jazz guitarist who worked with **King Oliver**, **Sidney Desvigne**, and **Fate Marable** in the 1910s and 1920s.

FOUCHÉ, EARL *Jazz.* Saxophone, clarinet. (Born Feb. 5, 1903, New Orleans, Orleans Parish; died after 1962, possibly Santa Barbara, California.) Highly regarded but enigmatic early New Orleans jazz saxophonist returned to New Orleans in the mid-1920s after studying music in New York and joined **Isaiah Morgan**'s Young Morgan Band as saxophonist. Continued performing with group after **Sam Morgan** took over band and stayed through end of decade, appearing on Morgan's famed 1927 recording sessions for Columbia. Tutored several noted musicians, including **Harold Dejan** and **Andrew Morgan**. Also performed with **Bébé Ridgley**'s Young Tuxedo Orchestra and reportedly toured with **Don Albert**'s band in the late 1930s. After World War II, relocated to Santa Barbara, California, and continued performing locally into the 1960s.

FOUNTAIN, DENNIS *Rhythm and blues.* Vocals. Bandleader. (Born July 5, 1958, Tallulah, Madison Parish.) Mississippi-based soul-blues singer and bandleader began performing on the Jackson and Vicksburg, Mississippi, blues scene in the 1980s. Performed regularly at Jackson's famed Subway Lounge and appeared in the film *The Last of the Mississippi Jukes* in 2003.

FOUNTAIN, PETE *Jazz.* Clarinet. Composer. Bandleader. (Born July 3, 1930, New Orleans, Orleans Parish; died Aug. 6, 2016, New Orleans, Orleans Parish.) Highly popular clarinetist who helped traditional New Orleans jazz gain national exposure through regular appearances on Lawrence Welk's and Johnny Carson's television shows, starting in the late 1950s. At age 12 began learning clarinet, influenced largely by **Irving "Faz" Fazola** and Benny Goodman. By age 18 was member of Junior Dixieland Band and made recording debut with **Phil Zito**'s band for Columbia in 1950. In the 1950s worked with Basin Street Six and later formed Pete Fountain and His Three Coins. Also worked with **Tony Almerico**, **Sharkey Bonano**, and **Al Hirt**, and held seven-month engagement in 1955 with Dukes of Dixieland in Chicago. Appeared regularly on the *Lawrence Welk Show* from 1957 to 1959 and began long association with Coral Records. In 1960 opened his popular French Quarter club and performed there regularly throughout next several decades. Appeared numerous times throughout the 1970s and 1980s on Carson's *Tonight Show.* Continued performing in clubs, parades, and festivals into the early 2010s and released more than 100 albums throughout career. Gave last public performance at New Orleans Jazz & Heritage Festival in 2013 before retiring.

FOWLER, SAM *See* Harp Blowin' Sam.

FRAN, CAROL (*born* **Carol Anthony**) *Rhythm and blues, swamp pop.* Piano, vocals. Composer. Bandleader. (Born Oct. 23, 1933, Lafayette, Lafayette Parish.) Renowned rhythm and blues singer-songwriter began playing piano as a child and at age 14 toured the Gulf Coast with the Don Conway Orchestra. In the late 1940s worked with **Joe Lutcher**'s band around Lake Charles before relocating to New Orleans with musician husband Robert Francois. Through the mid-1950s performed regularly at various local clubs, including famed Dew Drop Inn, and worked with **Earl King**, **Guitar Slim**, Big Joe Turner, **Cousin Joe**, and others. Returned to Lafayette area in 1957 and began recording for producer **J. D. Miller**, releasing four singles on Excello, including regional hit "Emmitt Lee." In the late 1950s worked with Guitar Slim's band, which included at times Nappy Brown, **Lee Dorsey**, and Joe Tex, and throughout the 1960s had singles on Lyric, Port, and Roulette, notably "Crying in the Chapel" in 1964. Married Texas blues guitarist Clarence Hollimon in 1983, and the two began performing and recording together, releasing three albums through 2000, including *Soul Sensation* on Black Top in 1992. After Hollimon's death in 2000, recorded CD *Fran-Tastic* for Sound of New Orleans and continued performing at clubs and festivals into her 80s, often with **Lil' Buck Sinegal** or **Major Handy**. Appeared in 2015 film *I Am the Blues.*

FRANCIS, MORRIS (**Albert Morris Francis**) *Zydeco, rhythm and blues.* Accordion, bass, rubboard, vocals. Composer. Bandleader. (Born Mar. 2, 1942, Cypress Island, St. Martin Parish.) Noted Lafayette-based zydeco and rhythm and blues singer and multi-instrumentalist worked as bassist with **Little Bob**, **Rockin' Sidney**, **Rockin' Dopsie**, **Lynn August**, and others. From the 1970s through 1980s had singles as leader on Blue Black, Caillier, and Maison de Soul and recorded LP *Fun in Acadiana* for Maison de Soul in 1986 and *Pass the Salt* for Vidrine in 1995. Throughout the 1990s and 2000s toured and recorded extensively as member of Creole Zydeco Farmers on vocals, bass, and accordion.

FRANK, ALCIDE *Jazz.* Violin. Bandleader. (Born Apr. 1868, New Orleans, Orleans Parish; died 1942, New Orleans, Orleans Parish.)[14] Early New Orleans jazz violinist performed in bands of **Edward Clem** and **Buddy Bolden** in the early 1900s before leading Golden Rule Orchestra starting in 1905, regarded as one of the hottest bands in the city. Around 1913 began working with **John Robichaux** and continued leading Golden Rule Orchestra into the 1920s. Brother of **Gilbert "Bab" Frank**.

FRANK, CARLTON *Creole.* Fiddle, guitar, piano, vocals. Composer. (Born Mar. 5, 1930, Oberlin, Allen Parish; died Feb. 6, 2005, Oberlin, Allen Parish.) Noted Creole fiddle player was raised in a family of musicians dating back several generations. Performed with nephew **Preston Frank**'s Swallow Band with **Leo "the Bull" Thomas** for many years starting in the 1970s and recorded with group for Arhoolie in 1981. Later performed with Preston's Family Zydeco Band with grand-niece Jennifer and grand-nephews Brad and **Keith Frank**, recording with group for Lanor in 1991 and Soulwood in 2002. Also recorded CD *The Creole Connection* with family band produced by Keith on Louisiana Red Hot Records in 2001.

FRANK, EDWARD *Rhythm and blues, jazz.* Piano. Composer. Bandleader. (Born June 14, 1932, New Orleans, Orleans Parish; died Feb. 13, 1997, New Orleans, Orleans Parish.) Remarkable New Orleans piano player who appeared on hundreds of rhythm and blues recordings throughout the 1950s and 1960s with artists such as **Smiley Lewis**, **Fats Domino**, **Lloyd Price**, Little Richard, Big Joe Turner, Elmore James, **Lee Allen**, **Dr. John**, Bobby "Blue" Bland, Junior Parker, and many others, despite having a left hand that was partially paralyzed. Later served as arranger and producer on many sessions and performed with traditional jazz groups in the French Quarter and at Preservation Hall. Continued working as session musician throughout the 1980s and 1990s, appearing on numerous releases by **Dr. John**, **Snooks Eaglin**, **Chuck Carbo**, and others. Relative of **Alcide** and **Bab Frank**.

FRANK, GILBERT "BAB" *Jazz.* Piccolo, flute. (Born 1872, New Orleans, Orleans Parish; died June 1933, St. Louis, Missouri.)[15] Noted early New Orleans jazz musician and bandleader led the Peerless Orchestra starting in the early 1900s, often with **Charles McCurdy**. Around 1913 worked with **John Robichaux** and in 1919 relocated to Chicago and briefly performed with **Lawrence Duhé** before reportedly retiring from music. Older brother of **Alcide Frank**.

FRANK, KEITH *Zydeco.* Accordion, guitar, drums, vocals. Composer. Bandleader. (Born Oct. 9, 1972, Soileau, Allen Parish.) Influential contemporary zydeco singer-songwriter and accordion player who helped usher in a new zydeco sound in the early 1990s behind Zydeco Force and **Beau Jocque**, a style dubbed "nouveau zydeco." At age nine began playing drums in his father **Preston Frank**'s band and in his early teens started playing accordion, inspired by his father and **Boozoo Chavis**. Later formed his Soileau Zydeco Band with sister Jennifer on bass and younger brother Brad on drums. In 1992 recorded debut CD *On the Bandstand* on Lanor and soon became one of the most popular zydeco acts in southwest Louisiana. Dubbed the "Zydeco Boss," throughout the next two decades had numerous releases on Zydeco Hound, Maison de Soul, Shanachie, and his own Soulwood label, including *Love, Feared, Respected* in 2008, which included regional hits "Casanova" and "Haterz." In the 2010s continued performing extensively as one of the region's most popular zydeco acts on club and festival circuit with several more releases on Soulwood, including *Return of the King* in 2018.

FRANK, PRESTON *Zydeco.* Accordion, vocals. Composer. Bandleader. (Born Aug. 30, 1947, Oberlin, Allen Parish.) Noted zydeco accordion player and singer and patriarch of the Frank Family Zydeco Band began learning accordion during his mid-20s and in the 1970s formed the Swallow Band with uncle **Carlton Frank** and **Leo "the Bull" Thomas**. In 1981 recorded for Arhoolie with group, cowriting "Why Do You Want to Make Me Cry" with Thomas, which became a zydeco standard. In the 1980s reformed band as Family Zydeco Band featuring children Jennifer, Brad, and **Keith Frank** with releases *Let's Dance* on Lanor in 1991 and *Born in the Country* on Soulwood in 2002. Continued performing occasionally with group in the 2010s.

FRAZIER, JOSIAH "CIÉ" *Jazz.* Drums. (Born Feb. 23, 1904, New Orleans, Orleans Parish; died Jan. 10, 1985, New Orleans, Orleans Parish.) Highly renowned early New Orleans jazz drummer studied with **Louis Cottrell Sr.** in 1913 and through the 1920s worked with **John Robichaux**, **Armand Piron**, **Alcide Frank**, and **Papa Celestin**, the latter with whom he also recorded in 1927. In the 1930s performed with **Sidney Desvigne** and W.P.A. Brass Band. In 1945 recorded as leader with **Wooden Joe Nicholas** and in the 1950s worked with Celestin, **George Williams**, Eureka Brass Band, and others. Throughout the 1960s recorded extensively with numerous artists, including **Sweet Emma Barrett**, **Alvin Alcorn**, **Harold Dejan**, **George Lewis**, **Peter Bocage**, and **Kid Howard**. Appeared regularly at Preservation Hall for more than two decades and continued performing and recording until shortly before his death from pneumonia at age 80. Great-uncle of **Keith** and **Phillip Frazier**.

FRAZIER, KEITH *Jazz.* Bass drum. (Born Oct. 3, 1968, New Orleans, Orleans Parish.) Cofounded Rebirth Brass Band with older brother **Philip Frazier** and **Kermit Ruffins** in 1983. Evacuated to Dallas after Hurricane Katrina in 2005 and continued to perform and record with Rebirth into the 2010s. Grand-nephew of **Josiah "Cié" Frazier**.

FRAZIER, PHILIP, III *Jazz.* Tuba, trombone, vocals. Composer. Bandleader. (Born Feb. 10, 1966, New Orleans, Orleans Parish.) Cofounded Rebirth Brass Band with younger brother **Keith Frazier** and **Kermit Ruffins** in 1983 while still in high school in Tremé. Band quickly gained national attention and throughout the following decades released numerous albums on various labels, including Arhoolie, Rounder, Mardi Gras, Shanachie, and Basin Street. Continued leading Rebirth into the late 2010s, touring nationally and overseas. Grand-nephew of **Josiah "Cié" Frazier**.

FRED, JOHN (John Fred Gourrier) *Swamp pop, rhythm and blues.* Vocals. Composer. Bandleader. (Born May 8, 1941, Baton Rouge, EBR Parish; died Apr. 15, 2005, New Orleans, Orleans Parish.)[16] Popular early swamp pop singer-songwriter and bandleader best known for his late 1960s hit "Judy in Disguise (with Glasses)." Inspired by **Fats Domino**, formed first group in 1956, which soon became known as John Fred and the Playboys. Recorded debut single "Shirley" on Montel with Domino's backing band, which became minor hit in 1959. After several more singles for label signed with Jewel in 1964 and had several regional hits, including "Boogie Children." In 1967 recorded "Judy in Disguise" on Jewel's sister label Paula, which hit number one on the national charts and sold more than a million copies. Released several singles on Uni in 1969–70 and went on to produce recordings for other artists, including **Irma Thomas**. In 1992 recorded with **G. G. Shinn** and **Joe Stampley** as the Louisiana Boys and continued to make festival and club appearances through the mid-2000s until succumbing to complications following a kidney transplant at age 63.

FREDERICK, DON (Frederick Dauterive) *Rhythm and blues.* Vocals. Bandleader. (Born June 10, 1926, Olivier, Iberia Parish; died July 6, 2002, New Iberia, Iberia Parish.)[17] Powerful rhythm and blues vocalist and bandleader best known for his two 1967 singles "Big Boys Cry" and "Little Bit of Soap" on La Louisianne. Led various bands from the 1950s through the early 1990s based in New Iberia.

FRENCH, ALBERT "PAPA" *Jazz.* Banjo, guitar, vocals. Bandleader. (Born Nov. 16, 1910, New Orleans, Orleans Parish; died Sept. 28, 1977, New Orleans, Orleans Parish.)[18] Noted New Orleans jazz banjoist and bandleader joined **Papa Celestin**'s Original Tuxedo Jazz Band in 1950 and took over leadership in 1958, soon earning "Papa" nickname in tribute to his former bandleader. Band held residency at Tradition Hall in the French Quarter and made several recordings under his leadership, including LP *A Night at Dixieland Hall* on Nobility, recorded by **Cosimo Matassa**. Continued leading band until his death at age 66. Father of **Bob** and **George French** and brother of **Alberta French Johnson**.

FRENCH, BOB (Robert French) *Jazz.* Drums, vocals. Bandleader. (Born Dec. 27, 1937, New Orleans, Orleans Parish; died Nov. 12, 2012, New Orleans, Orleans Parish.) Son of **Albert "Papa" French**, traditional New Orleans jazz drummer and bandleader worked mainly with rhythm and blues bands from the 1950s through mid-1960s. In 1965 began performing with jazz groups and joined Original Tuxedo Band in 1971, led by his father. After his father's death in 1977, took over leadership of band and continued through 2011 until retiring due to illness. Released *Marsalis Music Honors Bob French* in 2007 with **Harry Connick Jr.** and **Branford Marsalis**. Brother of **George French.**

FRENCH, GEORGE *Jazz, rhythm and blues.* Bass, vocals. Bandleader. (Born Feb. 23, 1943, New Orleans, Orleans Parish.) Son of **Albert "Papa" French**. Traditional New Orleans jazz and rhythm and blues bassist and singer began playing in his teens and in subsequent years worked and recorded with numerous rhythm and blues musicians, including **Earl King** and **Robert Parker**. Performed and recorded with Original Tuxedo Jazz Band with brother **Bob French** for several decades and led several traditional jazz bands through the 2010s, appearing on numerous recordings as sideman and leader, including *It's a Beginning* in 2000 on Nia. Father of **Gerald French**.

FRENCH, GERALD *Jazz.* Drums, vocals. Bandleader. (Born May 9, 1970, New Orleans, Orleans Parish.) Traditional New Orleans jazz drummer and bandleader started playing drums as a child, learning from uncle **Bob French**. At age 21 began performing at Preservation Hall and went on to work with **Charmaine Neville**, **Harry Connick Jr.**, **Dr. John** and others. In 2011 took over leadership of Original Tuxedo Jazz Band, replacing his uncle Bob who led the band since 1977. Son of **George French**.

FRENCH, MAURICE *Jazz.* Trombone. (Born Sept. 5, 1885, LaPlace, St. John the Baptist Parish; died May 30, 1963, LaPlace, St. John the Baptist Parish.)[19] Highly regarded early New Orleans jazz trombonist began playing professionally around 1908 and throughout his 40-year music career performed with **Kid Rena**, **Buddy Petit**, **Evan Thomas**'s Black Eagles, **Pinchback Touro**, Lyons Brass Band, **Papa Celestin**, and others. Retired from music in the late 1940s.

FREY, JASON *Cajun.* Accordion, fiddle, vocals. Composer. Bandleader. (Born Oct. 28, 1964, Eunice, St. Landry Parish.) Highly regarded Cajun multi-instrumentalist got his start on accordion with **Bee Cormier**'s Church Point Playboys in the mid-1980s, recording a single with group and also appearing on 1987 LP *Belizaire's Cajun Restaurant* on Bee. In 2000 formed traditional Cajun band Lagniappe with **Travis Matte** and recorded acclaimed CD

À la Vielle Manière on La Louisianne. Later collaborated on releases with **Al Berard**, **Courtney Granger**, and **Paul Daigle**. Continued performing in the 2010s with Lagniappe and other bands.

FRUGÉ, ATLAS *Cajun.* Steel guitar, fiddle, accordion, piano. (Born July 15, 1924, Eunice, St. Landry Parish; died Oct. 18, 1990, Lake Charles, Calcasieu Parish.) Highly influential early Cajun steel guitarist who was among the first to play the instrument in a Cajun band and whose innovative style helped modernize Cajun music's sound in the 1940s. Raised in a musical family, began playing accordion at age 10 and by the late 1930s was performing at local house dances. In the early 1940s joined **J. B. Fuselier**'s band on steel guitar, which helped make the instrument extremely popular in Cajun bands due in large part to his inventive playing. Throughout the 1940s and early 1950s performed regularly with **Nathan Abshire**, **Will Kegley**, **Earl DeMary**, and others in such noted bands as the Pine Grove Boys, Musical Aces, and Musical Five, and appeared on recordings on O.T., Hot Rod, and Khoury's. Also worked and recorded with **Tan Benoit**, **Elise Deshotel**, **Wilson Granger**, **Sidney Brown**, **Joe Bonsall**, **Ervin LeJeune**, **Jesse Legé**, and many others through the 1980s.

FRUGÉ, BENNY (Cecil Farrell Frugé) *Cajun, country.* Piano, vocals. (Born Aug. 9, 1932, Basile, Evangeline Parish; died Jan. 11, 2016, Baton Rouge, EBR Parish.) Early postwar Cajun and country pianist performed and recorded with **Jimmy C. Newman** and Lefty Frizzell in the late 1940s and early 1950s. Later relocated to Baton Rouge, became a master piano technician, and operated his own piano retail and repair company for many years.

FRUGÉ, BLACKIE (Lawrence Frugé Jr.) *Cajun.* Fiddle, guitar, drums, vocals. Bandleader. (Born Sept. 20, 1930, Evangeline, Acadia Parish; died Apr. 6, 2015, Lake Arthur, Jeff. Davis Parish.) Noted postwar Cajun fiddler was raised in a family of musicians and recorded with **Lee Sonnier** on Fais-Do-Do in 1947. Also performed with his father Lawrence Frugé Sr. and his band the Country Boys, recording "Country Boy Waltz"/"T Mamou" on TNT in 1953. Later worked with the **Clément Brothers**, **Ronald Frugé**, **Bobby Leger**, and others, and recorded single as leader of Moonlight Serenaders for Khoury's in 1959. In the early 1960s cofounded Hicks Wagon Wheel Ramblers and performed with group throughout the next four decades, recording singles on Cajun Jamboree and Circle D, and two CDs, including *Ramblin' Back in Time* on Lanor in 1998 with son Paul Frugé. Sister Eula Mae Frugé-Young also was a Cajun musician.

FRUGÉ, COLUMBUS "BOY" *Cajun.* Accordion, vocals. Composer. (Born June 6, 1907, Arnaudville, St. Landry Parish; died Oct. 13, 1980, Arnaudville, St. Landry Parish.) Early Cajun accordionist and singer who was among the first to record Cajun music. Began playing accordion as a child and by his teens was performing at local house dances. In Sept. 1929 recorded four solo Cajun sides for Victor in Memphis, including "Bayou Teche" and "Saute Crapaud," using a wooden Coca-Cola crate to stomp out rhythms with his feet.

FRUGÉ, ERNEST *Cajun.* Fiddle, vocals. (Born Sept. 7, 1906, Church Point, Acadia Parish; died Mar. 4, 1975, Lake Charles, Calcasieu Parish.) Highly regarded early Cajun fiddler began playing the instrument as a child, mentored by his father, Joseph, and older brother Lawrence who played local house dances. In the 1920s performed with **Amédée Breaux**, **Joe Falcon**, **Amédé Ardoin**, and others as well as playing second fiddle in trio with **Angelas LeJeune** and **Dennis McGee**. Made a series of landmark recordings with LeJeune for Brunswick in 1929–30. Also recorded numerous important fiddle duets with McGee for Vocalion and Brunswick in 1929–30, including old Cajun ballads and two-steps such as "Lanse des Belaire." After World War II worked with **Joe Bonsall**, **Earl DeMary**, and others. Widely regarded as one of Cajun music's greatest second-fiddle players.

FRUGÉ, RONALD *Cajun.* Drums, vocals. Composer. Bandleader. (Born Apr. 15, 1942, Jennings, Jefferson Davis Parish.) Cajun drummer and singer performed and recorded with **Bobby Leger**'s Lake Charles Playboys from the early 1960s through mid-1970s. In 1976 formed Cajun Aces and performed with group through the early 1980s with singles on Circle D and Bayou Classics, notably "Cherokee Waltz" in 1978. Rejoined Leger's band for several years in the mid-1980s.

FRUGÉ, WADE *Cajun.* Fiddle, vocals. (Born Aug. 27, 1916, Eunice, St. Landry Parish; died June 23, 1992, Eunice, St. Landry Parish.) Revered early Cajun fiddle player and singer learned from his grandfather Napoleon Frugé and early Creole fiddler **Douglas Bellard**. Performed only at local house dances but later made a series of acclaimed recordings for Arhoolie with **Michael Doucet** and **Ann** and **Marc Savoy** which were issued on LP *Old Style Cajun Music* in 1989.

FUSELIER, J. B. (Jean Batiste Fuselier) *Cajun.* Fiddle, accordion, vocals. Composer. Bandleader. (Born Apr. 17, 1901, Chataignier, Evangeline Parish; died Aug. 16, 1976, Lake Charles, Calcasieu Parish.)[20] Influential early Cajun multi-instrumentalist began playing fiddle and then accordion as a child, winning talent contests and playing house dances around Mamou during his teens. By 1920 had relocated with family to Oberlin. In the mid-1930s joined guitar and banjo player Beethoven Miller's Merrymakers with guitarist Preston Manuel and recorded sixteen sides for Bluebird, including his composition "Chère Tout-Toute." Soon took over leadership of band and recorded sixteen sides for Bluebird in 1938, including "Ma Chère Bassett." Continued performing with group in the 1940s, which included numerous notable musicians, including **Atlas Frugé** and **Tonice LaFleur**. Relocated to Lake Charles in 1950 and throughout decade performed with various musicians, including **Nathan Abshire** and **Iry LeJeune**. In 1955 was seriously injured while accompanying LeJeune during his fatal collision after a gig. In the 1960s recorded several singles for Goldband, including "Lake Arthur Two Step," and continued performing in Lake Charles area until his death.

FUSELIER, PERCY *Cajun.* Fiddle, vocals. Bandleader. (Born May 24, 1913, Elton, Jeff. Davis Parish; died Feb. 17, 1985, Elton, Jeff. Davis Parish.)[21] Early Cajun fiddler began playing at age 14 and soon was performing at house dances with father, Mark; brother Claude; and cousin Dewey Fuselier. Also performed with **Nathan Abshire** in the 1930s. In 1947 formed the Elton Playboys with **Lionel Cormier** and performed with group for two years. In 1949 left band, which Cormier subsequently renamed the Sundown Playboys, and continued leading his Elton Playboys into the 1950s.

GABRIEL, CHARLIE "CHARLIE G" *Jazz.* Saxophone, clarinet, vocals. Bandleader (Born July 11, 1932, New Orleans, Orleans Parish.) Noted jazz reedman and fourth-generation member of prestigious Gabriel family of New Orleans jazz. Began playing at age 11 with the Eureka Brass Band and in 1948 relocated to Detroit. Throughout following six decades led bands of his own and also worked with numerous major artists, including Lionel Hampton, Aretha Franklin, and **Joe Simon** before returning to New Orleans in 2009. Continued performing and recording with Preservation Hall Jazz Band into his late 80s. Son of jazz clarinetist Martin "Manny" Gabriel Jr. (1898–1982) and nephew of **Percy Gabriel**.

GABRIEL, JOSEPH *Jazz.* Violin, mandolin. Bandleader. (Born June 20, 1882, Thibodaux, Lafourche Parish; died Nov. 7, 1950, St. Louis, Missouri.)[1] Influential early jazz violinist and bandleader who led the popular Joe Gabriel Orchestra from Thibodeaux in the first two decades of the 1900s. Became Pullman porter in St. Louis in later years.

GABRIEL, PERCY *Jazz.* Double bass. Bandleader. (Born July 11, 1915, New Orleans, Orleans Parish; died Feb. 7, 1993, Farmington Hills, Michigan.) Renowned member of prestigious Gabriel family of New Orleans jazz, began performing in family band with brother Clarence and later worked on boats traveling to New York with **Kid Rena** and **Harold Dejan**. In the late 1930s worked with **Papa Celestin**, **Sidney Desvigne**, and **Armand Piron**, and toured Texas with **Don Albert**. Led his own band through the early 1940s and worked with **Lee Collins** and **Red Allen** in Chicago. From 1944 to 1947 toured and recorded with Jay McShann and later worked with Lucky Millinder and **Danny** and **Blue Lu Barker**. Relocated to Detroit in 1950 and performed with brother Manny Gabriel Jr. in group which later became Gabriel Brothers New Orleans Jazz Band and which recorded in 1977. Son of Martin "Manny" Gabriel Sr. (1875–1932) who was a noted early jazz cornetist and bandleader of National Orchestra of New Orleans from 1913 to 1932. Nephew of Albert "Dude" Gabriel, who was an early jazz and ragtime clarinetist. In the late 2010s the Gabriel family was in its sixth generation of New Orleans brass-band musicians, which dates back to the Civil War era with bassist Narcisse Gabriel (1844–1900).

GABRIEL THE FLOCK-ROCKER (Mitchell Hearns) *Blues.* Trumpet, vocals. Composer. Bandleader. (Born Aug. 11, 1930, Lake Providence, East Carroll Parish; died Oct. 19, 2018, St. Louis, Missouri.) Beloved veteran St. Louis disc jockey and blues artist was raised in East St. Louis, Illinois, and began playing trumpet with local bands while in high school. In 1952 started career in radio, specializing in blues and gospel and continued broadcasting in the St. Louis area throughout the following seven decades. From the mid-1950s through early 1960s recorded singles on Planet, Norman, Tempora, and Royal American, including "After Hours (No. 2)," often backed by guitarist Bennie Smith. Also produced Ike and Tina Turner's first single, "Boxtop," in 1958 on his Tune Town label. Celebrated for his exuberant and unpredictable on-air style, continued hosting his popular weekly radio program until just a few weeks before his death at age 88.

GAINES, LITTLE JOE *Rhythm and blues, gospel.* Vocals. Composer. (Born May 30, 1919, New Orleans, Orleans Parish; died May 16, 1989, New Orleans, Orleans Parish.) Early New Orleans rhythm and blues vocalist joined well established gospel group the New Orleans Humming Four in 1947 and recorded rhythm and blues single "She Won't Leave No More" on Mercury in 1949. In the early 1950s recorded gospel sides with the Humming Four on Imperial for **Dave Bartholomew** and made several rhythm and blues recordings with same group as the Hawks. In 1959 recorded single "Voo Doo Lou" on Arcadia.

GALLATY, BILL, JR. *Jazz.* Trumpet. (Born Oct. 23, 1910, New Orleans, Orleans Parish; died Aug. 1985, Arabi, St. Bernard Parish.)[2] Early jazz trumpeter who worked with **Santo Pecora**'s band as well as several swing bands in the 1930s. Son of noted trombonist **Bill Gallaty Sr.**

GALLATY, BILL, SR. *Jazz.* Trombone. Bandleader. (Born Nov. 9, 1880, New Orleans, Orleans Parish; died Sept. 29, 1943, New Orleans, Orleans Parish.) Early New Orleans jazz trombone player and longtime member of **Papa Jack Laine**'s Reliance Brass Band and whom Laine considered his finest trombonist. Led his own band in the 1910s. Father of **Bill Gallaty Jr.**

GALLEY, BUFORD *Cajun.* Accordion. Composer. Bandleader. (Born July 4, 1940, Rayne, Acadia Parish; died July 3, 2010, Lake Charles, Calcasieu Parish.) Lake Charles–area Cajun accordionist formed his band the Jolly Playboys in the mid-1970s, releasing singles on Nonc Joe, Circle D, and Kajun through the 1980s, including "I'd Like to Try Again" with **Rodney LeJeune** in 1977.

GALLOWAY, CHARLEY "SWEET LOVIN'" *Jazz.* Guitar, fiddle, mandolin. (Born 1864, New Orleans, Orleans Parish; died May 4, 1921, New Orleans, Orleans Parish.)[3] Important very early New Orleans jazz and ragtime guitarist who was crippled by polio as a child and performed on streets for tips as early as the mid-1880s. Eventually became a popular and highly skilled musician known for his charismatic showmanship. Led his own band in the 1890s which at times included **Buddy Bolden**, **Edward Clem**, and **Frankie Duson**, and his group is often cited as among the first jazz bands. Also performed occasionally in Bolden's band.

GARLAND, ED "MONTUDIE" *Jazz.* String bass, tuba, bass drum. Bandleader. (Born Jan. 9, 1885, New Orleans, Orleans Parish; died Jan. 22, 1980, Los Angeles.)[4] Pioneer of jazz bass and important link to New Orleans pre-jazz era. First performed on streets as a child with **Kid Ory**. At age 13 joined Onward Brass Band and around 1904 began performing regularly with **Buddy Bolden**. Later worked with **Frankie Duson**'s Eagle Band with **Sidney Bechet** and **Bunk Johnson** and performed with numerous brass bands, including Excelsior and Imperial, through 1913. Moved to Chicago in 1914 and worked with **Manuel Perez** and **Freddie Keppard**. After working with **King Oliver** from 1916 to 1921, settled in California and recorded with **Kid Ory** on his historic recordings in 1922. Led his own One-Eleven Band during the Depression, and throughout the 1940s and 1950s worked with Ory, Earl Hines, and others. Continued to perform and record through the 1970s, remaining musically active into his 90s.

GARLOW, CLARENCE "BON TON" *Rhythm and blues, zydeco.* Guitar, accordion, fiddle, vocals. Composer. Bandleader. (Born Feb. 27, 1911, Welsh, Jeff. Davis Parish; died July 24, 1986, Beaumont, Texas.) Highly influential early rhythm and blues and proto-zydeco singer and multi-instrumentalist best known for his 1950 hit "Bon Ton Roula." Son of a Creole musician and raised speaking Creole French, began playing fiddle at age eight and later learned accordion and guitar. Relocated to Beaumont and throughout much of the 1940s worked outside music. Inspired by T-Bone Walker, began performing in Beaumont clubs and in 1949 recorded several sides for Macy's including "Bon Ton Roula," which became a national hit and was the first recording to reference the word "zydeco." Toured extensively and in 1951 recorded singles for Feature and Lyric. In 1953–54 had releases on Aladdin and Flair, notably "New Bon-Ton Roulay" and "Route '90.'" Also operated Bon Ton Drive-In in Beaumont, which featured a young **Clifton Chenier** whom he helped secure his first record deal. In the mid- to late 1950s recorded for producer **Eddie Shuler** as leader and session musician and released several singles on Shuler's Goldband and Folk-Star labels, including early zydeco rocker "Za Belle." Also recorded session for **J. D. Miller** in the late 1950s which was not immediately issued. In the early 1960s recorded single with T-Baby Green on his Bon-Ran label and worked mainly as radio disc jockey into the 1970s. Began performing again in the early 1980s and recorded a single for **Rockin' Sidney**'s Bally Hoo label, making limited local club appearances in the next several years.

GARNER, LARRY *Blues.* Guitar, vocals. Composer. Bandleader. (Born July 8, 1952, New Orleans, Orleans Parish.) Noted blues guitarist and singer-songwriter was raised in a small town outside Baton Rouge, inspired to play guitar as a boy after hearing traveling gospel evangelists **Elder Utah Smith** and **Reverend Charlie Jackson** in church. Performed in gospel and rhythm and blues bands in his teens and later in military bands while stationed in Korea. After working outside music for 20 years, started performing in the early 1980s in Baton Rouge blues clubs such as **Tabby Thomas**'s Blues Box with Thomas, **Henry Gray**, **Silas Hogan**, and others. In the late 1980s became full-time musician and throughout following decades toured extensively throughout the United States and Europe with recordings on JSP, Verve, Ruf, and DixieFrog, notably *You Need to Live a Little* and *Baton Rouge*, all which featured his masterful songwriting.

GARY, ED *Cajun.* Guitar, vocals. Composer. Bandleader. (Born Sept. 7, 1943, Jennings, Jeff. Davis Parish; died June 7, 2017, Basile, Acadia Parish.) Traditional Cajun singer-guitarist joined the Hathaway Playboys in the mid-1960s and performed with group through 1969. In the late 1960s and early 1970s worked and recorded with **Robert Bertrand**, **Ervin LeJeune**, and others before forming his band Louisiana Cajun Aces. Performed with group through the early 1980s and recorded several singles on Kajun, including "Mean Woman." Also worked with **Joe Bonsall**, **Sheryl Cormier**, **Ricky Bearb**, and others in the 1980s. Reformed Cajun Aces in 1990 and continued performing with band for more than two decades, releasing several CDs, including *C'est la Vie* on Lanor in 2002.

GASPARD, BLIND UNCLE (Alcide Gaspard) *Cajun.* Guitar, vocals. Composer. (Born Jan. 29, 1881, Dupont, Avoy. Parish; died Nov. 5, 1937, Cottonport, Avoy. Parish.)[5] Very early Cajun singer and guitarist who recorded for Vocalion in 1929 with fiddler **Delma Lachney** and whose melancholic style and repertoire of older traditional Cajun French ballads preceded the livelier, dance-oriented Cajun music of the day. Nearly blind since age seven from degenerative nerve disease, began playing in string bands with older brothers Amédé and Victor and for many years performed as soloist on streets and at social gatherings throughout Avoyelles Parish. In 1929 recorded sixteen sides on sessions in Chicago and New Orleans for Vocalion, including his best-known work, "Sur Le Borde De L'Eau" (On the Water's Edge). Died of complications from Bright's disease (kidney disease).

GASPARD, EDWARD "T-NEG" *Cajun.* Drums. Bandleader. (Born July 12, 1931, Abbeville, Vermilion Parish; died Dec. 7, 2011, Abbeville, Vermilion Parish.) Noted Cajun drummer who was known for standing while performing on stage, which was rare at the time. Performed and recorded with the **Touchet Brothers** from the late 1960s through early 1980s and worked with various other bands, including **D. L. Menard**'s Louisiana Aces and his group the Abbeville Playboys.

GASPARD, OAK/OKE (Octave Toussaint Gaspard) *Jazz.* String bass, tuba. Bandleader. (Born Nov. 1, 1872, New Orleans, Orleans Parish; died July 1943, New Orleans, Orleans Parish.)[6] Very early ragtime and New Orleans jazz tuba and bass player performed with Piron-Gaspard Orchestra from 1893 to 1902 and with **Bab Frank**'s Peerless Orchestra from around 1903 through 1913. Worked with **John Robichaux** in the mid-1910s and was coleader with brother **Vic Gaspard** of Maple Leaf Orchestra in the late 1910s and 1920s. Lived in Dallas in the late 1920s and recorded with blues singers Lillian Glinn, Billikin Johnson, and Gertrude Perkins. Recorded as string bassist with **Polite Christian**'s Frenchy's String Band in 1928. Younger brother Ed was jazz bass drummer and music teacher.

GASPARD, VIC *Jazz.* Trombone, baritone horn. Bandleader. (Born Apr. 14, 1875, New Orleans, Orleans Parish; died Aug. 27, 1957, New Orleans, Orleans Parish.) Early ragtime and New Orleans jazz trombonist performed with Piron-Gaspard Orchestra in the 1890s and went on to work with Excelsior and Onward brass bands through 1910. In the late 1910s and 1920s worked with brother **Oak Gaspard** as coleader of Maple Leaf Orchestra.

GAYTEN, PAUL *Rhythm and blues.* Piano, vocals. Composer. Bandleader. (Born Jan. 29, 1920, Kentwood, Tangipahoa Parish; died Mar. 26, 1991, Los Angeles.) Highly influential bandleader, producer, and pioneer of New Orleans rhythm and blues in the late 1940s. Settled in New Orleans after World War II and by 1947 was leading one of the most popular rhythm and blues bands in the city. In the next several years had hits on Deluxe and Regal as a leader and with Annie Laurie, **Chubby Newsom**, and **Larry Darnell**, including "Since I Fell For You" with Laurie in 1947. In the early 1950s toured extensively and recorded for OKeh. Worked with Chess Records from the mid-1950s through early 1960s and produced numerous hits for **Clarence "Frogman" Henry**, **Sugar Boy Crawford**, **Bobby Charles**, Chuck Berry, and others. In 1956 recorded biggest hit as leader, "The Music Goes Round & Round." Relocated to California in the 1960s and founded Pzazz label before retiring in the 1970s. Nephew of Joe and **Little Brother Montgomery**.

GEORGE, BARBARA *Rhythm and blues.* Vocals. Composer. (Born Aug. 16, 1942, New Orleans, Orleans Parish; died Aug. 10, 2006, Houma, Terrebonne Parish.) Noted New Orleans rhythm and blues singer best known for her 1961 hit "I Know (You Don't Love Me No More)." Discovered at age 19 by **Jessie Hill**, recorded for **Harold Battiste** on A.F.O., and had major hit with debut recording "I Know," which became a New Orleans standard. After two more singles on A.F.O. had releases on Seven B, Monument, Sue, and Hep' Me. Performed in band with **Sunpie Barnes** in the late 1980s before retiring from music and settling in Houma. Cousin of **Raymond George**.

GEORGE, RAYMOND *Blues.* Guitar, vocals. Composer. Bandleader. (Born July 27, 1940, Chauvin, Terrebonne Parish.) Locally renowned Houma-based blues guitarist and singer began performing in local clubs at age 16, inspired greatly by **Guitar Slim**. Recorded single "If I Should Lose You"/"Soul Sound" for Houma label in the mid-1960s. In the 1960s and 1970s appeared regularly at the Graveyard Inn in Thibodaux. Continued to perform with his band the Blue Flames in Houma area into his late 70s. Cousin of **Barbara George**.

GETREX, LES *Blues.* Guitar, vocals. Composer. Bandleader. (Born Dec. 14, 1950, New Orleans, Orleans Parish.) Self-taught guitarist and singer began performing around New Orleans in the mid-1970s and recorded a single on Bayou Boogie in 1978. In the 1980s and 1990s toured with **Fats Domino** and **Rockin' Dopsie**. Led his own band in following decades and toured internationally, releasing several recordings, including *300 Miles* in 2015.

GIBSON, LOOMIS (Loomis Gipson) *Blues.* Piano. (Born June 1, 1891, Greensburg, St. Helena Parish; died Mar. 10, 1942, Tuskegee, Alabama.)[7] Unrecorded early barrelhouse blues piano player who mentored a very young **Little Brother Montgomery**. Montgomery later reworked Loomis's signature piece into "Crescent City Blues" for Bluebird in 1936, also known as "Loomis Gibson Blues." By 1930 was residing as a disabled veteran in Tuskegee, Alabama, where he later died at age 50.

GILES, EDDIE/EDDY "G" (Elbert Wiggins Giles) *Rhythm and blues, gospel.* Vocals, guitar, bass. Composer. Bandleader. (Born Mar. 17, 1938, Frierson, DeSoto Parish; died Feb. 5, 2019, Shreveport, Caddo Parish.) Renowned Shreveport-based deep soul singer best known for his 1967 recording "Losin' Boy." Began playing on an acoustic guitar as a child and around age 17 moved to Shreveport and soon began performing with local gospel groups, including the Mt. Olive Humming Bees. In the mid-1960s toured as bassist with Chicago-based gospel band the Pilgrim Jubilees. Returned to Shreveport in 1967 and formed soul band the Jive Five and had regional hit with "Losin' Boy" for Murco later that year. Released six more singles on Murco through 1969, followed by releases on Silver Fox, Stax, Alarm, and Custom Sound. By the early 1980s left secular music to rejoin the church and continued serving as pastor of Salem Missionary Baptist Church, performing and recording gospel and hosting his popular gospel radio show into the late 2010s.

GILL, KENNY (Kenneth Guillot) *Jazz, rockabilly, country, swamp pop.* Guitar, bass, fiddle. Composer. Bandleader. (Born Jan. 7, 1936, Bunkie, Avoy. Parish; died Feb. 28, 2010, Gonzales, Ascension Parish.) Highly regarded and versatile guitarist began playing at age seven and by his mid-teens was performing with various bands around Louisiana. In the late 1950s worked regularly with **Rod Bernard**, appearing on hit "This Should Go on Forever." Relocated to Baton Rouge in 1960 and worked as session guitarist for producer **Sam Montel**, appearing on numerous Montel releases, including his own LPs *Fascinating Guitar* and *Guitar Moods*. From 1962 to 1964 worked in Nashville as in-demand session guitarist but returned to Baton Rouge in 1965 and continued working with his jazz quartet. From 1972 to 1997 performed in **Jimmie Davis**'s band before returning to Nashville area in 1998. Continued working as session musician and producer in remaining years.

GILLYARD, DUNNY (Cornelius Gillyard) *Rhythm and blues.* Trombone. (Born Aug. 7, 1938, Shreveport, Caddo Parish; died May 23, 2013, Shreveport, Caddo Parish.) Veteran Shreveport rhythm and blues trombonist who performed in numerous regional bands for several decades and toured nationally with Freddie King, Big Joe Turner, Jimmy Reed, and many others in the 1960s and 1970s.

GILMORE, EDDIE *Jazz.* String bass. (Born Mar. 20, 1895, Verdunville, St. Mary Parish; died July 20, 1960, E. Feliciana Parish, Louisiana.)[8] Early New Orleans jazz bassist began playing professionally after World War I and worked with **Sam Morgan**, Liberty Bell Orchestra, and New Orleans Creole Jazz Band in the 1920s. In the early 1940s was living in Bunkie, Louisiana, and performing at Mac's Boogie Woogie Club.

GLASS, HENRY "BOOKER T" *Jazz.* Bass drum. Bandleader. (Born Aug. 3, 1889, New Orleans, Orleans Parish; died June 25, 1981, New Orleans, Orleans Parish.)[9] Widely regarded as one of the finest and most powerful brass-band bass drummers. Took lessons from **Octave Gaspard**'s brother Ed and started performing with street bands around 1909. Worked with **Wooden Joe Nicholas** and Camelia Brass Band in the 1910s. Went on to work and record with Eureka Brass Band and **Harold Dejan**'s Olympia Brass Band in the 1960s and continued to perform into his 90s until his vision failed.

GLAZE, KANE *Swamp pop.* Keyboards, vocals. Composer. Bandleader. (Born Jan. 16, 1956, Baton Rouge, EBR Parish.) Baton Rouge–based swamp pop singer and leader of band Coozan who recorded a single on Jin and released three CDs in the early 2000s on CSP Records, including *Americajun* in 2002.

GLENN, JERRY *See* Kennedy, Jerry.

GLENNY, ALBERT *Jazz.* Bass, tuba, bass drum, accordion. (Born Mar. 25, 1870, New Orleans, Orleans Parish; died June 11, 1958, New Orleans, Orleans Parish.)[10] Highly renowned very early New Orleans jazz bassist began playing at age 12 on a homemade instrument. Performed through following seven decades and worked regularly with a vast number of prominent jazz musicians, including **Buddy Bolden**, **Charley Galloway**, **Manuel Perez**, **John Robichaux**, **Kid Ory**, **Alphonse Picou**, **Louis** and **Lorenzo Tio**, and **Hypolite Charles**.

GODEAUX, OPHEY VAL *Cajun.* Fiddle. (Born Feb. 25, 1923, Eunice, St. Landry Parish; died Dec. 21, 1999, China, Texas.) Early postwar Cajun fiddler settled in east Texas after World War II and performed with numerous musicians around the Texas Triangle area, including **Iry LeJeune**, **Joe Bonsall**, Cleveland Fontenot, Alvin Meaux, and others. Later recorded two singles with Jimmy Vayon and the Jokers.

GOLDSTON, CHRISTOPHER "BLACK HAPPY" *Jazz.* Drums. (Born Nov. 27, 1894, New Orleans, Orleans Parish; died Mar. 17, 1968, New Orleans, Orleans Parish.) Early New Orleans jazz drummer started playing as a child and performed with **Amos Riley**'s Tulane Orchestra in the mid-1910s, influenced greatly by **Ninesse Trepagnier**. In the late 1910s and 1920s worked with **Jack Carey**, **Punch Miller**, and Golden Leaf Orchestra. Performed with Onward and W.P.A. brass bands in the 1920s and 1930s respectively and with **Papa Celestin** after World War II.

GOOD ROCKIN' BOB (Ed Thomas) *Blues.* Guitar, vocals. Bandleader. (Born Apr. 4, 1924, Opelousas, St. Landry Parish; died Feb. 19, 1979, Angleton, Texas.)[11] Locally renowned bandleader who was a popular performer around Opelousas area in the 1950s and 1960s and whose band included at times **Rudy Richard**, **Leroy Washington**, **Little Bob**, **Roscoe Chenier**, and many others. In 1958 recorded single "Take It Easy, Katy"/"Little One" on Goldband with Little Bob on drums and vocals. Continued performing in area clubs until succumbing to accidental carbon monoxide poisoning in his car at age 54 while in Texas to perform for a trail ride.

GOOD ROCKIN' SAM *See* Sam, Herbert "Good Rockin'."

GOODLY, ANN (Ezolia Ann Goodly) *Zydeco.* Accordion, vocals. Composer. Bandleader. (Born Nov. 28, 1971, Lake Charles, Calcasieu Parish.) One of the first female accordionists to front a zydeco band after **Queen Ida**. Began playing her father's accordion at age nine and at age 11 made her recording debut as "Little Ann Goodly" on **Rockin' Sidney**'s ZBC label with single "Nonc Neg"/"Mama and Daddy's Waltz" in 1982. In the mid-1980s began performing with the band Zydeco Brothers and released two singles on Maison de Soul, including signature song "Zydeco Stomp" in 1988. Also appeared in 1988 film *Zydeco Gumbo.* Released LP *Miss Ann Goodly and the Zydeco Brothers* on Maison de Soul in 1990 and toured nationally and overseas throughout the decade. Appeared on compilation *Santa Claus Wants Some Zydeco* on Louisiana Red Hot Records in 1999 but remained largely musically inactive in following years.

GOODMAN, CHARLES *Zydeco, rhythm and blues.* Bass, vocals. (Born Nov. 27, 1946, Lafayette, Lafayette Parish; died Nov. 27, 2014, Lafayette, Lafayette Parish.) Veteran zydeco bass player who performed and toured with numerous noted musicians throughout his 50-plus-year career, including tenures with **Clifton Chenier**, **Fernest Arceneaux**, **Rockin' Dopsie**, **Big Roger Collins**, and the Creole Zydeco Farmers with **Jockey Etienne** and **Chester Chevalier**.

GOODMAN, SHIRLEY MAE *Rhythm and blues.* Vocals. Composer. Bandleader. (Born June 19, 1936, New Orleans, Orleans Parish; died July 5, 2005, Los Angeles.) Popular New Orleans rhythm and blues singer best known for her work in the 1950s as coleader of Shirley & Lee. Paired with school friend **Leonard Lee**, duo made recording debut on Aladdin in 1952 with "I'm Gone," which reached number two on the R&B charts. Several more releases followed, including the classic hit "Let the Good Times Roll" in 1956. In the late 1950s recorded for Warwick and split with Lee in 1963. After briefly working as a duo with **Jessie Hill**, settled in California around 1965 and did session work. In 1974 had pop hit with "Shame, Shame, Shame" as Shirley & Company and toured for several years before retiring from music in the late 1970s.

GOODSON, BILLIE *See* Pierce, Billie [Notable Musicians Born outside Louisiana].

GORDON, ISSACHER "JUNIOR"/"IZZYCOO" *Rhythm and blues.* Drums. (Born Sept. 13, 1934, New Orleans, Orleans Parish; died July 7, 2007, New Orleans, Orleans Parish.) Soulful rhythm and blues singer who gave **Aaron Neville** his first singing lessons. Joined New Orleans premier vocal group the Spiders in 1955 and toured and recorded with band for several years. As a leader recorded a single each for Ace in 1956 and Jay-Pee in 1962, including "Blow Wind Blow" backed by **Huey "Piano" Smith**'s band.

GORDON, RUSSELL "R.G." *Zydeco, rhythm and blues.* Guitar, accordion, vocals. Composer. Bandleader. (Born Feb. 20, 1943, Cecilia, St. Martin Parish.) Zydeco multi-instrumentalist and bandleader performed and recorded with **Buckwheat Zydeco** and **Rockin' Dopsie** as guitarist in the late 1970s and early 1980s and cut single "Double Booty Bump" as leader on **J. J. Caillier**'s Jay-Cee label with his band Versatile Souls. By the mid-1980s switched to accordion and formed Bayou Zydeco, releasing a single on Voss and 1988 LP *Bayou on Fire* on Takoma. In the early 2000s performed and recorded with **Roy Carrier**.

GORMAN, ISRAEL *Jazz.* Clarinet. Bandleader. (Born Mar. 4, 1895, Oakville, Plaquemines Parish; died Sept. 21, 1965, New Orleans, Orleans Parish.) Highly skilled clarinetist who performed in Storyville District in the mid-1910s and worked with **Chris Kelly**, **Buddy Petit**, **Lee Collins**, **Kid Rena**, and others in the 1920s. During the 1950s performed and recorded with his own band at noted jazz venue Happy Landing Lounge. Appeared regularly at Preservation Hall and recorded with **Kid Howard**, **George Guesnon**, **De De Pierce**, and others in the early 1960s.

GOUDIE, FRANK "BIG BOY" (Francois Gody) *Jazz.* Saxophone, clarinet, cornet. Composer. Bandleader. (Born Sept. 13, 1899, Youngsville, Lafayette Parish; died Jan. 9, 1964, San Francisco.) Internationally renowned early jazz multi-instrumentalist moved to New Orleans with family at age eight and began learning cornet in school. From 1915 to 1921 performed with **Papa Celestin**'s Tuxedo Band, Magnolia Orchestra, and **Jack Carey**. In the early 1920s toured throughout the Southwest, California, and Mexico before moving to France in 1925, becoming one of the first jazz expatriates. Switching mainly to clarinet and saxophone, performed and recorded extensively throughout Europe through 1940, working and/or recording with numerous musicians, including Benny Peyton, Bill Coleman, Noble Sissle, and Django Reinhardt. After several years based in Brazil and Argentina, returned to France in 1946 and continued performing with his own band and others, including **Sidney Bechet** and Coleman Hawkins, and recorded as a leader for Swing and Jazz Time. In 1956 relocated to San Francisco and continued performing locally in remaining years, occasionally working with **Kid Ory** and Earl Hines.

GRACE (of Dale and Grace/Van and Grace) *See* Broussard, Grace.

GRANDPA ELLIOTT/"UNCLE REMUS" (Elliott Small) *Blues.* Guitar, harmonica, vocals. (Born July 10, 1944, New Orleans, Orleans Parish.) Noted street singer who performed in New Orleans French Quarter for several decades. Recorded a handful of singles in the 1960s and 1970s, including "Hate to See You Go" on A.B.S. with arrangement by **Wardell Quezergue**. In the 1980s began performing on the corner of Royal and Toulouse for tips. Gained international recognition in 2009 for appearance in "Playing for Change" viral online video and released debut CD *Sugar Sweet* later that year.

GRANGER, COURTNEY *Cajun, country.* Fiddle, guitar, bass, vocals. (Born July 10, 1982, Eunice, St. Landry Parish.) Acclaimed Cajun and country fiddle player and singer began playing the instrument as a child, greatly influenced by great-uncle **Dewey Balfa**. Made recording debut at age 16 with CD *Un Bal chez Balfa* on Rounder and also toured as member of Balfa Toujours with **Christine Balfa**. In 2008 joined premier Cajun band Pine Leaf Boys and continued performing and recording with group and others in the late 2010s. Released traditional country album *Beneath Still Waters* on Valcour in 2016.

GRANGER, DEAMA *Cajun.* Accordion. (Born Nov. 9, 1904, Lafayette, Lafayette Parish; died Apr. 16, 1963, Lake Charles, Calcasieu Parish.) Early Cajun accordionist played at house dances early on and in the 1940s began performing with **J. B. Fuselier** and the Eunice Playboys. Relocated to Lake Charles area and worked with **Sidney Brown**, **Milton Vanicor**'s Lacassine Playboys, **Robert Bertrand**, and many others in following years.

GRANGER, WILSON "PAGRO" *Cajun.* Fiddle, vocals.

Composer. (Born Jan. 1, 1921, Duralde, Evangeline Parish; died Sept. 3, 2005, Lake Charles, Calcasieu Parish.) Renowned early postwar Cajun fiddle player was raised in a musical family and began playing fiddle at age four, learning from older brother Sidney (1908–1977) and father, Salus (1887–1943). By 1930 was playing house dances and through the early 1940s performed at dance halls around Lake Charles area with Sidney. In the mid-1940s formed Musical Aces with **Earl Demary** and also performed and recorded as member of **Nathan Abshire**'s Pine Grove Boys, appearing with group on 1949 regional hit "Pine Grove Blues." Also recorded single "Bayou Chico Waltz" as leader on Hot Rod in the late 1940s. In the mid-1950s performed with **Iry LeJeune**, appearing on numerous recordings with LeJeune in 1954, including "Duralde Waltz" and "Grand Bosco." Also worked with **Will Kegley**, **Ernest Thibodeaux**, **Robert Bertrand**, and others. In the 1980s performed with Old Timers Band in Lake Charles entertaining residents in nursing homes.

GRAY, HENRY *Blues.* Piano, vocals. Composer. Bandleader. (Born Jan. 19, 1925, Kenner, Jefferson Parish.) Highly regarded blues pianist and singer whose illustrious career spanned more than seven decades as an important figure of the postwar Chicago and Baton Rouge blues scenes. Raised in Alsen, just outside Baton Rouge, began learning piano around age eight and during his teens performed in local blues clubs. After serving in World War II, relocated to Chicago and was mentored by blues piano great Big Maceo Merriweather. In the 1950s worked extensively as session musician and appeared on recordings by **Little Walter**, Jimmy Rogers, Bo Diddley, Muddy Waters, Jimmy Reed, Sonny Boy Williamson (Rice Miller), and many others. Recorded as a leader for Chess and Parrot in the mid-1950s. In 1956 joined Howlin' Wolf's band and performed and recorded with group throughout following 12 years. Returned to Louisiana in 1968 and became prominent member of Baton Rouge blues community with his band the Cats. Throughout following decades toured nationally and overseas with recordings on Blind Pig, Wolf, Hightone, Lucky Cat, Storyville, and other labels, including *Lucky Man* in 1988. In 2006 was recipient of NEA National Heritage Fellowship. Continued to perform locally and tour nationally and abroad into his mid-90s.

GRAYSON, DORI (Doris Lynn Grayson) *Rhythm and blues.* Vocals. (Born June 23, 1950, Shreveport, Caddo Parish.) Shreveport southern soul singer performed as a member of **Eddie Giles**'s Jive Five and recorded two singles as leader for Murco in 1967, "Try Love" and "I Can Fix That For You," and a single for Peermont in 1970. Later left music and continued working in the Shreveport area as a school teacher.

GREELY, DAVID *Cajun.* Fiddle, vocals. Composer. Bandleader. (Born June 12, 1953, Baton Rouge, EBR Parish.) Renowned Cajun fiddler began playing at age 17 and performed in bluegrass and country band Cornbread in the 1970s. After stints in Nashville and Texas, returned to Louisiana in 1986 and cofounded Mamou Playboys with **Steve Riley** in 1988. Toured internationally and appeared on a dozen releases with group through 2011. Released debut recording as a leader *Sud du Sud* in 2009, followed by *Shadows-on-the-Teche* in 2017. Continued performing based in Breaux Bridge as solo artist and as member of several other Cajun bands in the late 2010s.

GREEN, JESSE LEWIS *Blues.* Drums. (Born Aug. 23, 1937, Delhi, Richland Parish.) Chicago blues drummer best known for his work performing and recording with guitarist Otis Rush in the 1960s and 1970s, appearing on several studio and live recordings.

GREEN, RUDY (Rudolph Spencer Green) *Rhythm and blues.* Guitar, vocals. Composer. Bandleader. (Born Sept. 30, 1926, Lake Charles, Calcasieu Parish; died Nov. 1, 1976, Hillsborough County, Florida.)[12] Early rhythm and blues singer and guitarist best known for his 1956 Ember singles "Wild Life" and "Juicy Fruit." Influenced by guitarist T-Bone Walker and jump blues singers such as **Roy Brown**, made recording debut in Nashville in 1946 with three releases for Bullet before relocating to Chicago and cutting three singles for Chance with King Kolax's band in 1953, including "I Had a Feeling." After a single on Club "51," returned to Nashville and cut two releases on Excello in 1956, including "My Mumblin' Baby." After two releases on Ember in 1956, recorded a single for Poncello in 1961 before fading away from the music scene.

GREEN, SONNY (Robert Green) *Rhythm and blues.* Vocals. Composer. Bandleader. (Born Oct. 29, 1941, Monroe, Ouachita Parish.) California-based soul-blues vocalist began singing in church as a child. At age 16 joined blues guitarist Little Melvin Underwood's band as backup singer and following year left to pursue solo career. Toured the South for several years and relocated to Texas, performing there throughout the 1960s. In 1969 moved to Los Angeles and became active on the South Central blues scene. Through 1975 had singles on Whip, Fuller, Mesa, United Artists, Hill, and MHR, notably

"Don't Write a Check with Your Mouth" in 1972. Continued performing in Los Angeles–area nightclubs into the late 2010s.

GRIFFIN, BESSIE (Arlette B. Broil) *Gospel.* Vocals. (Born July 6, 1922, New Orleans, Orleans Parish; died Apr. 10, 1989, Los Angeles.) Widely regarded as one of gospel's greatest voices and was among the first to perform gospel in nightclubs. Began singing in church as a child and in the 1940s performed extensively as member of **Alberta French Johnson**'s Southern Harps, recording two singles with group on King in 1947. Joined the Caravans in Chicago in the early 1950s and recorded for States before relocating to California in the late 1950s and forming the Gospel Pearls. In 1959 starred in first gospel musical, *Portraits in Bronze,* produced by Bumps Blackwell, and continued to record as soloist for numerous labels, including Specialty, Decca, Columbia, Epic, and Savoy in following years. Also appeared on television and in film in the 1960s and 1970s. Made final recordings in 1987, some of which appeared on *Even Me: Four Decades of Recordings* on Spirit Feel in 1989. Succumbed to breast cancer at age 66.

GRIFFIN, CURTIS "JACK"/"C.C." *Blues.* Guitar, drums, vocals. (Born Mar. 17, 1930, Poole, Bossier Parish.) West Coast–based blues guitarist and singer moved to Los Angeles in 1950 to pursue a music career. After a few gigs as drummer, began learning guitar after seeing a performance by **Clarence "Gatemouth" Brown**. In the 1960s had singles on Joyce, Allegro, Movin', and Jewel, notably "I Found Something Better" in 1965. Continued performing on local blues scene in following decades while working full-time as a butcher. In the 1980s recorded with William Clarke and George "Harmonica" Smith and continued performing on L.A.'s South Central blues scene into the 2010s.

GRIFFIN, ROOSEVELT "LITTLE BROTHER" *Blues.* Drums, vocals. Composer. Bandleader. (Born Mar. 21, 1933, Lake Charles, Calcasieu Parish; died Aug. 30, 2009, Lake Charles, Calcasieu Parish.) Lake Charles blues drummer and singer began playing at age 11, mentored by **Bill Parker**. At age 15 started performing locally with **Big Chenier** and in the mid-1950s toured nationally with **Clifton Chenier**. Also performed locally with **Katie Webster**, **Sticks Herman**, and **Marcel Dugas**. From the mid-1950s through the mid-1960s worked as session drummer for **Eddie Shuler**'s Goldband and Folk-Star labels and recorded with numerous artists, including Webster, **Elton Anderson**, **Lonnie Brooks**, **Boozoo Chavis**, **Clarence Garlow**, **Rockin' Sidney**, and Juke Boy Bonner. Later led his band the Nitros around Lake Charles.

GROS, JOHN "PAPA" *Rhythm and blues.* Piano, organ, French horn, vocals. Composer. Bandleader. (Born Sept. 9, 1966, New Orleans, Orleans Parish.) New Orleans funk and rhythm and blues singer-songwriter and piano player began performing with **George Porter Jr.**'s Runnin' Pardners in the 1990s before forming funk band Papa Grows Funk in 2000. Performed with group through 2013, releasing numerous albums, including *Needle in the Groove* in 2012. Continued performing as solo artist in following years, releasing *River's on Fire* in 2016, which was inspired by mentor **Allen Toussaint**.

GROSS, JOHN LEON *See* Archibald.

GUERIN, ROLAND *Jazz, rhythm and blues.* Bass, vocals. Composer. Bandleader. (Born Nov. 15, 1968, Baton Rouge, EBR Parish.) Highly accomplished jazz bassist began playing at age 11, inspired by his mother, who was a blues and zydeco bass player. While attending college performed as member of **Alvin Batiste**'s Jazztronauts and after graduating toured internationally with Mark Whitfield and appeared on recordings with Whitfield, **Ellis Marsalis**, **Allen Toussaint**, and others. From 1994 to 2009 toured as member of Marcus Roberts Trio. Released seven albums as leader, including *Black Coffee* in 2016. Toured as member of Toussaint's band from 2009 until Toussaint's death in 2015. In 2017 became **Dr. John**'s musical director and also continued to lead his own group based in New Orleans.

GUESNON, CREOLE GEORGE *Jazz.* Banjo, guitar, vocals. Composer. (Born May 25, 1907, New Orleans, Orleans Parish; died May 5, 1968, New Orleans, Orleans Parish.) Renowned traditional New Orleans jazz banjo player and prolific songwriter took banjo lessons from **John Marrero** and began performing at the Hummingbird Cabaret before joining **Papa Celestin**'s band in 1928. Toured with **Sam Morgan** in the early 1930s and worked and recorded with **Little Brother Montgomery** in 1936 while based in Jackson, Mississippi. Traveled with Rabbit Foot Minstrels in the late 1930s. In 1940 recorded for Decca and worked with **Jelly Roll Morton** and Trixie Smith in New York. In the 1950s worked with all-star jazz group the Mighty Four and toured with **George Lewis**. Also frequently worked and recorded with **Kid Thomas** through the early 1960s. Performed regularly at Preservation Hall and recorded many of his compositions in the late 1950s and early 1960s.

GUIDRY, ADOLPH "BIXY" *Cajun.* Accordion, vocals.

Composer. (Born Nov. 29, 1904, Scott, Lafayette Parish; died Sept. 28, 1938, Lafayette, Lafayette Parish.)[13] Early Cajun accordionist and singer who recorded eight sides with **Percy Babineaux** for Victor and Bluebird in Nov. 1929, including his influential composition "J'vai Jouer Celea Pour Toi (I'll Play This for You)," which would later be reworked into the Cajun standards "Jai Ete au Bal" and **Iry LeJeune**'s "I Went to the Dance."

GUIDRY, DOC (Oran Guidry) *Cajun.* Fiddle, vocals. Composer. Bandleader. (Born Apr. 28, 1918, Lafayette, Lafayette Parish; died Nov. 10, 1992, Houma, Terrebonne Parish.)[14] Highly regarded and influential early Cajun fiddle player and singer-songwriter started playing fiddle at age 12 and in the late 1930s joined **Happy Fats**'s Rayne-Bo Ramblers, recording with group in 1938 for Bluebird. In 1939 formed Sons of Acadians and recorded 12 sides for Decca. Continued performing extensively with **Happy Fats** from the mid-1940s through 1960s and made numerous recordings for various labels including **J. D. Miller**'s Fais-Do-Do, notably "Chere Cherie" and "Allons Dancer Colinda," which were issued under "Happy, Doc and the Boys." In the 1940s and 1950s performed and recorded extensively with **Jimmie Davis** and also made recordings with **Aldus Roger**, **Lawrence Walker**, **Vin Bruce**, and others through the early 1970s. As a leader released single "Chere Cherie"/"The Little Fat Man" on Decca in 1953 and recorded LP *King of the Cajun Fiddlers* on La Louisianne in 1963. Continued performing throughout the 1970s and 1980s and appeared on LPs with **Gene Rodrigue** and **Marc Savoy**.

GUILBEAU, PRESTON *Zydeco.* Accordion, vocals. Composer. Bandleader. (Born Dec. 25, 1927, Grand Coteau, St. Landry Parish; died Apr. 20, 2001, Opelousas, St. Landry Parish.)[15] Zydeco accordionist who performed in Opelousas and Lafayette area and recorded single "Booze and Women Blues"/"Opelousas Zydeco" on Maison de Soul around 1977.

GUILLORY, CHUCK (Murphy C. Guillory) *Cajun.* Fiddle. Composer. Bandleader. (Born Aug. 16, 1919, Mamou, Evangeline Parish; died Oct. 19, 1998, Alexandria, Rapides Parish.) Popular Cajun string-band fiddle player and bandleader best known for his 1948 recording "Big Texas" whose melody Hank Williams would later use in his 1952 hit "Jambalaya." Began playing fiddle with his father in local clubs as a child and by his teens was leading his own band. After serving in World War II, formed the Rhythm Boys in the mid-1940s, which would include **Milton Molitor**, **Jimmy C. Newman**, and **Papa Cairo** and had releases on Colonial and Modern, including regional hit "Big Texas," which was composed and sung by Cairo. In 1950 recorded two singles for Feature and in the late 1950s appeared on folklorist Harry Oster's 1959 LP *Folk Songs of the Louisiana Acadians.* Worked primarily outside of music in following decades but reformed Rhythm Boys in the late 1980s and recorded LP *Grand Texas* for Arhoolie.

GUILLORY, DELIN T. *Cajun.* Accordion, vocals. Composer. (Born Jan. 7, 1904, Tit Mamou, Evangeline Parish; died Sept. 22, 1948, Pineville, Rapides Parish.)[16] Influential early Cajun accordionist and singer was raised in a musical family and began playing the instrument as a child, learning from a local Creole accordionist. Around 1927 began performing with local fiddler **Lewis LaFleur** at area house dances and dance halls. In Nov. 1929 recorded four influential sides with LaFleur for Victor, including "Quelqu'un est Jalous (Somebody Is Jealous)," which is one of the earliest versions of the Cajun standard "Bosco Stomp." Continued performing in Ville Platte area with LaFleur until the mid-1930s, when he began having epileptic seizures. In late 1936 was committed to Central Louisiana State Hospital, where he later died of tuberculosis at age 44.

GUILLORY, KRISTI *Cajun.* Accordion, guitar, vocals. Composer. Bandleader. (Born Dec. 26, 1978, Lafayette, Lafayette Parish.) Cajun accordionist and singer-songwriter began playing the instrument at age nine and in her early teens cofounded the Cajun band Réveille, inspired greatly by **Zachary Richard**. In the mid-1990s recorded two CDs with band for Swallow, including *The New Cajun Generation* in 1994. After completing graduate school in folklore studies, joined Lafayette Rhythm Devils in the mid-2000s and cofounded all-female Cajun band Bonsoir, Catin. Continued performing and recording with both groups through the 2010s. Granddaughter of Dixie Ramblers guitarist Jesse Duhon, who performed with **Octa Clark** and **Hector Duhon**.

GUITAR GABLE (Gabriel Perrodin Sr.) *Blues, swamp pop.* Guitar. Composer. Bandleader. (Born Aug. 17, 1937, Bellevue, St. Landry Parish; died Jan. 28, 2017, Opelousas, St. Landry Parish.) Influential early swamp blues and swamp pop guitarist and bandleader began playing guitar at age 10 and in his early teens performed at house parties with brother John Clinton on bass. After performing for two years with his band the Swing Master, formed the Musical Kings with **King Karl** and **Jockey Etienne** and began recording for producer **J. D. Miller**

in 1956, releasing numerous singles on Excello, including regional hits "Congo Mombo," "Guitar Rhumba," and seminal swamp pop classic "Irene." Also worked extensively as Miller's session guitarist and bandleader and appeared on numerous recordings by **Slim Harpo**, **Lazy Lester**, **Carol Fran**, **Leroy Washington**, and others. In the mid-1960s performed and recorded with King Karl on La Louisianne and in the 1970s worked regularly with **Little Bob** and **Lynn August**. Appeared on Little Bob's *Back Again* CD on Vidrine in 1990 and performed occasionally through the early 2000s until severe arthritis forced retirement. Father of zydeco guitarist Gabriel "Pandy" Perrodin Jr.

GUITAR JR. *See* Lonnie Brooks.

GUITAR LIGHTNIN' LEE (Leroy Williams) *Blues*. Guitar, harmonica, vocals. Composer. Bandleader. (Born Aug. 23, 1942, New Orleans, Orleans Parish.) Blues singer and guitarist was raised in the Lower Ninth Ward, greatly influenced by Jimmy Reed and **Boogie Bill Webb**. After many years of performing around New Orleans, often with **Polka Dot Slim**, **Little Freddie King**, and **Earl King**, recorded debut CD with his Thunder Band in the early 2000s. Released several more recordings through 2010s, including *Just an Ol' G* in 2013. Also known as "King of St. Claude Avenue" for his long tenure performing in the strip of clubs located on the New Orleans street.

GUITAR RED (Edwin J. Maire) *Rhythm and blues*. Guitar. Bandleader. (Born Jan. 25, 1927, New Orleans, Orleans Parish.) Rhythm and blues guitarist and bandleader recorded single "The Hot Potato"/"The Chili Pot" on Excello in 1956. Also appeared on sessions as sideman with **Champion Jack Dupree**, Papa Lightfoot, and J. D. Horton in the mid-1950s.

GUITAR SLIM JR. (Rodney Armstrong) *Rhythm and blues*. (Born Aug. 24, 1952, New Orleans, Orleans Parish.) Son of influential blues singer, songwriter, and guitarist **Guitar Slim**. New Orleans singer-guitarist began performing rhythm and blues and soul in New Orleans clubs in the 1970s and made recording debut with LP *Story of My Life* for Orleans Records in 1988. Continued to record and perform in clubs and festivals with additional recordings in 1996 and 2010, including *Brought Up the Hardway*.

GUY, BUDDY (George Guy) *Blues*. Guitar, vocals. Composer. Bandleader. (Born July 30, 1936, Lettsworth, Pointe Coupee Parish.) Internationally renowned Chicago blues singer and guitarist whose highly innovative and mercurial playing style influenced several generations of blues and rock musicians from Lurrie Bell to Jimi Hendrix. Began learning guitar on a homemade two-string instrument as a child and by his late teens was performing around Baton Rouge in bands with **Big Papa Tilley** and **Raful Neal**. In Sept. 1957 relocated to Chicago and began performing in local clubs, encouraged early on by mentor Muddy Waters. Through Willie Dixon he recorded two singles for Artistic in 1959 and from 1960 to 1967 served as recording artist and session guitarist for Chess, releasing several singles as a leader, including "Stone Crazy," and backing numerous artists including Muddy Waters, **Little Walter**, and Sonny Boy Williamson (Rice Miller). In the mid-1960s began long partnership performing and recording with harmonica player Junior Wells. Recorded three LPs for Vanguard in late 1960s and toured Europe several times. In the early 1970s cofounded famed South Side blues club the Checkerboard Lounge. In 1989 opened successful Chicago blues club Legends and in 1991 released breakthrough album *Damn Right, I've Got the Blues* on Silvertone, which catapulted his career. Continued to release numerous recordings on Silvertone and RCA through 2010s, including *The Blues Is Alive and Well* in 2018, and remained one of the world's most popular touring blues musicians into his 80s. Older brother of Chicago blues guitarist **Phil Guy**.

GUY, PHIL *Blues*. Guitar, vocals. Composer. Bandleader. (Born Apr. 28, 1940, Lettsworth, Pointe Coupee Parish; died Aug. 20, 2008, Chicago.) Younger brother of **Buddy Guy**, noted Chicago blues guitarist and singer began playing guitar as a child and performed with **Big Papa Tilley** in his teens. In the late 1950s joined **Raful Neal**'s band and continued performing on Baton Rouge blues scene with Neal until relocating to Chicago in the late 1960s to join Buddy's band. In following years worked as sideman with Junior Wells, Son Seals, Albert Collins, Koko Taylor, and others. Formed his own band in the 1980s and released nine recordings on JSP and other labels through the mid-2000s, including *He's My Blues Brother* on Black-Eyed Records in 2006 with Buddy. Continued performing nationally and overseas until succumbing to cancer at age 68.

HADLEY, LEE "LEROY" *Rhythm and blues.* Guitar. Bandleader. (Born Dec. 19, 1941, Raceland, Lafourche Parish.) Rhythm and blues guitarist and singer who was a longtime member of Joe Tex's band from 1961 to 1979 and appeared on numerous recordings with group, including 1967 hit "Skinny Legs and All," in which his name is also mentioned. Also worked with Otis Redding, Johnnie Taylor, Z.Z. Hill, Candi Staton, and others. Later moved to Atlanta area and in the mid-1990s formed NightShift Band, which he continued to lead into the 2010s. Brother Clarence was bassist with Joe Tex.

HAGANS, ROBERT "BUDDY" *Rhythm and blues.* Saxophone. (Born Dec. 18, 1922, Bogalusa, Washington Parish; died June 5, 1980, New Orleans, Orleans Parish.) Early rhythm and blues saxophonist best known for his long tenure with **Fats Domino**. Raised in New Orleans, began playing with Domino in his first band in 1946 and continued touring and occasionally recording with him until 1970, when he sustained serious injuries in an auto accident while on tour.

HALL, EDMOND *Jazz.* Clarinet. Composer. Bandleader. (Born May 15, 1901, Reserve, St. John the Baptist Parish; died Feb. 11, 1967, Boston.) Internationally renowned New Orleans jazz clarinetist began performing in the late 1910s and throughout next several years worked with **Kid Thomas**, **Chris Kelly**, **Lee Collins**, and **Buddy Petit**. From the mid- to late 1920s performed in various bands in Florida and Georgia before settling in New York. Throughout the 1930s and early 1940s worked with Claude Hopkins, Lucky Millinder, Teddy Wilson, Lionel Hampton, **Zutty Singleton**, and **Red Allen**. Recorded as leader in 1941 and cut his best-known work, "Profoundly Blue," featuring electric guitar pioneer Charlie Christian. In the 1940s and early 1950s led his own band with long successful engagements in New York (notably at the prestigious Café Society), Boston, and San Francisco and recorded extensively as leader and sideman. Performed with **Louis Armstrong**'s All Stars from 1955 to 1958. Semiretired from music in the late 1950s but toured Europe sporadically in the early 1960s. Brother of noted jazz clarinetists Robert, Clarence, and **Herb Hall**.

HALL, FRED "TUBBY" *Jazz.* Drums. Bandleader. (Born Oct. 12, 1895, Sellers, St. Charles Parish; died May 11, 1946, Chicago.) Highly regarded early New Orleans jazz drummer began performing in the mid-1910s with **Frankie Duson**'s Eagle Band and Silver Leaf Orchestra. Moved to Chicago shortly before being drafted in 1917 and worked with **King Oliver** after discharge. In the late 1920s and early 1930s worked and recorded with **Louis Armstrong**. Also performed with **Jimmie Noone** and **Johnny Dodds** in the 1930s and led his own band. Older brother of **Ram Hall**.

HALL, GERRI (*born* **Erdirné Bouise**) *Rhythm and blues.* Vocals. (Born Aug. 2, 1934, New Orleans, Orleans Parish.) Best known as the high-spirited female vocalist of **Huey "Piano" Smith**'s band the Clowns but also cut singles as a leader. After briefly working with **Larry Darnell**, **Li'l Millet**, and **Clarence Samuels**, joined Smith's band while working as a barmaid at famed Dew Drop Inn in the mid-1950s. Performed and recorded with Smith's Clowns through the mid-1960s and also had singles as leader on Ace, Hot Line, Rex, Verve, and Atco, including "I Cried a Tear" and "Who Can I Run To." After leaving the Clowns, toured with **Lee Allen** before joining Ray Charles's Raelettes. Retired from music during the disco fad of the 1970s.

HALL, HERB *Jazz.* Clarinet, saxophone. Bandleader. (Born Mar. 28, 1907, Reserve, St. John the Baptist Parish; died

Mar. 5, 1996, San Antonio, Texas.) Prominent member of renowned early jazz family of clarinetists from Reserve. Began playing clarinet and saxophone in the early 1920s and performed around Baton Rouge before moving to New Orleans in 1927. Worked with **Sidney Desvigne** in the late 1920s. Relocated to San Antonio and from 1929 through 1940 performed with **Don Albert**'s band. After a brief stint in Philadelphia moved to New York and worked with Doc Cheatham and toured Europe with Sammy Price in the 1950s. Performed with Don Ewell and Wild Bill Davison's Jazz Giants in the 1960s and with Bob Greene's World of Jelly Roll in the 1970s and 1980s. Made several recordings as leader throughout career, including *Old Tyme Modern* in 1969, and settled in Texas in 1977. Brothers Robert, Clarence, and **Edmond Hall** were also noted jazz clarinetists.

HALL, JOE *Zydeco.* Accordion, vocals. Composer. Bandleader. (Born Dec. 15, 1971, Eunice, St. Landry Parish.) Zydeco accordionist and singer-songwriter with strong traditional Cajun and Creole influences was initially inspired to learn accordion as a child from his grandfather **Clement "King" Ned**. Later learned directly through visits with **Bois Sec Ardoin**, **Carlton Frank**, and **Nolton Semien**. In the mid-2000s formed his band the Cane Cutters and released *Thirty Dobb Special* in 2011 and *Massé Family Two Step* in 2017.

HALL, MINOR "RAM" *Jazz.* Drums. (Born Mar. 2, 1897, Sellers, St. Charles Parish; died Oct. 16, 1959, Los Angeles.) Early New Orleans jazz drummer known for his long association with **Kid Ory**. Began performing in the mid-1910s and worked with **Lawrence Duhé** and Ory. In the early 1920s worked with **King Oliver** in California and later with **Jimmie Noone**. Relocated to California in the late 1920s and performed with **Mutt Carey** for several years. From the 1940s through mid-1950s worked extensively with Ory's band and appeared on several recordings. Younger brother of **Fred "Tubby" Hall**.

HALL, REGGIE *Rhythm and blues.* Vocal, piano. Composer. (Born Dec. 6, 1937, New Orleans, Orleans Parish.) Brother-in-law and sideman of **Fats Domino**, recorded several singles as a leader on Rip, Chess, and White Cliffs in the 1960s, notably "The Joke" in 1962.

HALL, RENÉ *Rhythm and blues, jazz.* Guitar, banjo, trombone. Composer. Bandleader. (Born Sept. 26, 1912, Morgan City, St. Mary Parish; died Feb. 11, 1988, Los Angeles.) Highly accomplished jazz-influenced rhythm and blues guitarist and arranger who appeared on hundreds of rhythm and blues and early rock and roll recordings in the 1950s and 1960s. Began career in the early 1930s as banjoist with **Joe Robichaux**, with whom he first recorded in 1933. From 1935 to 1942 played guitar and trombone with Ernie Fields before joining Earl Hines's band and relocating to New York. In the late 1940s worked as session musician and had singles as a leader on Jubilee, Decca, Domino, and RCA in the early 1950s. Relocated to Los Angeles in 1955 and through 1965 worked extensively as session guitarist with **Plas Johnson** and **Earl Palmer** and appeared on numerous hits by Little Richard, Sam Cooke, **Larry Williams**, Ritchie Valens, Dick Dale, the Coasters, and many others. Also released numerous singles as a leader, including instrumental "Twitchy" on Specialty in 1958. In the late 1960s and 1970s continued working extensively as arranger, notably with Marvin Gaye for Motown.

HALL, TONY (Austin Tony Hall) *Rhythm and blues.* Bass, guitar, drums, vocals. Composer. Bandleader. (Born Dec. 9, 1957, New Orleans, Orleans Parish.) Noted New Orleans funk bass player and multi-instrumentalist began performing at age 10 playing drums with his uncle **Curley Moore**. While in his teens worked with soul singers Candi Staton, Clarence Carter, and the Meters. At age 16 switched to bass and in the mid-1980s recorded unissued session as leader for **Allen Toussaint**. In following years worked extensively as session musician and appeared on recordings by numerous artists, including Bob Dylan, Emmylou Harris, **Neville Brothers**, Linda Ronstadt, and Willie Nelson. Also toured with **Harry Connick Jr.**, **Dr. John**, **Jean Knight**, and others. In 2003 cofounded Dumpstaphunk with **Ivan Neville** and continued performing and recording with various groups, including his New Orleans Soul Stars in the late 2010s. Great-grandson of **Gus Fontenette Sr.** and grandson of Alberta Hall who recorded "Oh! How I Need Your Love" for Specialty in 1955 with **Lloyd Lambert**.

HALL, WILLIE "DRIVE 'EM DOWN" *Blues.* Piano, vocals. Composer. (Born presumably late 1800s, New Orleans, Orleans Parish; died possibly Feb. 4, 1930, New Orleans, Orleans Parish.)[1] Enigmatic influential early barrelhouse blues piano player who performed in New Orleans and mentored **Champion Jack Dupree** in the late 1910s and 1920s. Passed along both his playing style and songs such as "Junker Blues" to Dupree but remained unrecorded. Also influenced **Professor Longhair**.

HAMILTON, GEORGE "POP" *Jazz.* Trumpet, alto horn. Bandleader. (Born Oct. 9, 1888, St. Martinville, St. Martin Parish; died June 12, 1981, New Orleans, Orleans Parish.)[2] Early New Orleans jazz trumpeter and bandleader performed with **Bunk Johnson**, **Lawrence Duhé**, and **Evan Thomas** early in career. Relocated to New Orleans and in the late 1910s and 1920s worked with **Chris Kelly** and **Sam Morgan**. In 1928 led Lyons Brass Band and formed his own orchestra in 1930. Father of jazz trumpeter Lumas Hamilton.

HANDY, MAJOR (Joseph Major Handy) *Zydeco, rhythm and blues.* Guitar, accordion, piano, bass, vocals. Composer. Bandleader. (Born May 15, 1947, Lafayette, Lafayette Parish.) Lafayette-area singer and multi-instrumentalist was raised in St. Martinville speaking Creole French and began performing on bass and guitar while in his teens. After serving in Vietnam, performed with **Rockin' Dopsie** from the mid-1970s through early 1980s and spent a year with **Buckwheat Zydeco**. In the mid-1980s began playing accordion and formed the Louisiana Blues Band, releasing several singles on Caillier and Maison de Soul and LP *Wolf Couchon* on GNP/Crescendo. Released CDs *Zydeco Feeling* on APO in 2009 and *Zydeco Soul* in 2019 and continued performing as bandleader as well as sideman with other blues and zydeco bands.

HANKS, GERVAIS *Cajun.* Accordion. (Born Aug. 3, 1947, Church Point, Acadia Parish; died Nov. 6, 1996, Church Point, Acadia Parish.) Cajun accordionist recorded singles for Bee and Lanor in the 1980s, including "Friendly Lounge Two Step" in 1989. Father Freddie Hanks also was a Cajun musician.

HAPPY FATS (Leroy Joseph LeBlanc) *Cajun.* Guitar, vocals. Composer. Bandleader. (Born Jan. 30, 1915, Bayou Queue de Tortue, Vermilion Parish; died Feb. 23, 1988, Rayne, Acadia Parish.)[3] Highly influential Cajun guitarist, singer-songwriter, and leader of the Rayne-Bo Ramblers who, along with **Luderin Darbone** and **Edwin Duhon** of the Hackberry Ramblers and **Leo Soileau**, was among the most important early Cajun string bandleaders. Began learning guitar as a child, inspired by Jimmie Rodgers, and in the early 1930s performed with **Joe Falcon** and **Amédée Breaux**. In the mid-1930s formed Rayne-Bo Ramblers, which would include at times **Nathan Abshire**, **Harry Choates**, **Joe Werner**, **Papa Cairo**, **Pee Wee Broussard**, and **Doc Guidry**. From 1935 to 1941 recorded more than 50 sides for Bluebird, including regional hit "La Veuve de la Coulee" in 1940. In the early 1940s worked with **Leo Soileau** in Lake Charles before returning to Rayne area and recording several more sides for RCA Victor in 1946 with his Rayne-Bo Ramblers. Formed new band with Guidry and from 1946 to 1950 recorded numerous sides as Happy, Doc and the Boys for **J. D. Miller**'s Fais-Do-Do label, including "Allons Danser Colinda." Continued performing in dance halls throughout the 1950s and hosted popular local radio show. In the 1960s had releases on La Louisianne with Guidry and on Swallow with **Alex Broussard** and Bayou Buckaroos. Also made a series of controversial segregationist recordings for Miller's Reb Rebel label in the late 1960s. Continued performing through the early 1980s with several more releases on various labels until succumbing to diabetes-related health issues at age 73.

HARDESTY, ANTHONY "A.G." *Blues.* Bass. (Born Oct. 5, 1957, Baton Rouge, EBR Parish.) Noted blues bass player who has been a fixture on the Baton Rouge blues scene since the 1980s. Began playing bass as a child and was neighbor of **Slim Harpo**. Performed and recorded with numerous area blues musicians, including **Clarence Edwards**, **Rudy Richard**, **Kenny** and **Raful Neal**, **Chris Thomas King**, and others. Also toured with James Cotton and Fenton Robinson.

HARDESTY, HERB *Rhythm and blues, jazz.* Saxophone, trumpet. Composer. Bandleader. (Born Mar. 3, 1925, New Orleans, Orleans Parish; died Dec. 3, 2016, Las Vegas.) Influential longtime member of **Fats Domino**'s recording and touring band who provided his signature saxophone work on most of Domino's hits. After leading a group in the late 1940s, began working with **Dave Bartholomew** and performed and recorded with Domino from 1949 through the early 1970s. Also appeared on sessions with **Chubby Newsom**, **Lloyd Price**, **Smiley Lewis**, **Tommy Ridgley**, T-Bone Walker, Little Richard, and others. Recorded as a leader in the late 1950s and 1960s with releases on several labels, including Federal. In the 1970s relocated to Las Vegas and worked with Duke Ellington, Count Basie, Ella Fitzgerald, Frank Sinatra, and others. Rejoined Domino's band from 1980 to 2005 and continued performing with his own group and others until 2014.

HARDIN, JOSEPH *Rhythm and blues.* Trumpet, flugelhorn, piano. Composer. Bandleader. (Born Feb. 2, 1947, Plaquemine, Iberville Parish.) Veteran rhythm and blues trumpet player began performing around Baton Rouge in the mid-1960s with **Bobby Powell**, **Buddy Stewart**, and others. After a stint as an Opelousas high-school band director, joined Bobby "Blue" Bland's band in 1971 and remained with group until Bland's death in 2013, serving as musical director from the early 1980s onward. Retired from music in the mid-2010s and settled in Tampa, Florida.

HARDY, EMMETT *Jazz.* Cornet. (Born June 12, 1903, Gretna, Jefferson Parish; died June 16, 1925, New Orleans, Orleans Parish.) Highly regarded early New Orleans jazz cornetist who reportedly influenced Bix Beiderbecke during his very short career. A child prodigy, began performing with top bands while still in his early teens, including **Papa Jack Laine**'s Reliance Band. At age 16 toured with vaudeville performer Bee Palmer along with **Leon Roppolo** and later performed with Carlisle Evans's band on the riverboat Capitol and in Chicago with New Orleans Rhythm Kings. Returned to New Orleans in the early 1920s and worked regularly with **Norman Brownlee**'s orchestra. Died from tuberculosis just after his 22nd birthday.

HARMONICA FATS (Harvey Blackston) *Blues.* Harmonica, vocals. Composer. Bandleader. (Born Sept. 8, 1927, McDade, Bossier Parish; died Jan. 3, 2000, Lynwood, California.) Noted blues harmonica player and singer began playing as a child, influenced early on by Sonny Terry. Relocated to Los Angeles in 1946 and in the mid-1950s began performing with his band the Houserockers on the local blues scene. In 1962 had regional hit with "Tore Up" on Skylark and toured nationally. From the late 1960s through mid-1970s had singles on Dot, In-Sound, Masai, and Normar. In the mid-1980s began working regularly with guitarist Bernie Pearl, touring nationally and releasing four albums throughout the next 15 years, including *Blow, Fat Daddy, Blow!* in 1996 on Bee Bump.

HARP BLOWIN' SAM (Samuel Fowler) *Blues.* Harmonica, vocals. (Born Mar. 10, 1909, possibly Talullah, Madison Parish; died July 27, 1994, St. Louis, Missouri.)[4] Blues harmonica player and singer settled in St. Louis in the early 1930s and began playing harmonica several years later, inspired by John Lee "Sonny Boy" Williamson. Worked regularly with Big Joe Williams and recorded with the guitarist for Baul in 1951–52 and for Vee-Jay in 1956. Remained active on St. Louis blues scene with his band the Houserockers for many years until sidelined by a stroke.

HARRIS, ALLEN "PUDDLER" *Swamp pop, country, rock and roll.* Piano, vocals. (Born June 9, 1936, Jigger, Franklin Parish.) Noted piano player got his start replacing Floyd Cramer on the *Louisiana Hayride* from 1955 to 1960 and toured and recorded with Johnny Horton. Recorded swamp pop single "Wait a Minute" for **J. D. Miller**'s Rocko label in 1960 before relocating to Hollywood and recording with Ricky Nelson, the Ventures, the Lettermen, Paul Revere and the Raiders, and others. Later toured for ten years with Conway Twitty and Loretta Lynn and was member of **Jimmie Davis**'s last band after returning to Louisiana and settling in Lake Charles.

HARRIS, ALPHONSE "ALFONCY" *Blues, jazz.* Vocals, clarinet. (Born Mar. 5, 1876, Napoleonville, Assumption Parish; died Dec. 9, 1942, Lafayette, Lafayette Parish.)[5] Early prewar blues singer who recorded in the late 1920s and early 1930s. By the mid-1910s was living in Lake Charles and performing there with the Royal Orchestra. In 1929 recorded two sides as Harris and Harris for Victor with wife, Bethenea, including "I Don't Care What You Say." Following year recorded six sides in Atlanta for Victor backed by guitarist Blind Willie McTell, but only one record was issued. In 1934 recorded six sides for Vocalion in San Antonio, including "No Good Guy." By 1940 was living back in Lake Charles. Died of chronic kidney disease at Charity Hospital in Lafayette.

HARRIS, JOHNNY RAY *Rockabilly.* Vocals, guitar, banjo. Composer. Bandleader. (Born Jan. 8, 1932, Shreveport, Caddo Parish; died Mar. 19, 1983, Shreveport, Caddo Parish.)[6] Shreveport singer-songwriter best known for his 1960 recording "Cajun Weekend" on Ray. Cut three singles on his own Ray label in 1960 and appeared on the *Louisiana Hayride.* In the early 1960s recorded single "Ripsaw"/"Cajun Blues" on Wanted. Continued performing around Shreveport into the 1970s while working as city fireman.

HARRISON, BIG CHIEF DONALD, SR. *Jazz.* Vocals. Bandleader. (Born Jan. 27, 1933, New Orleans, Orleans Parish; died Dec. 1, 1998, New Orleans, Orleans Parish.) Leader of several Mardi Gras Indian tribes, including Guardians of the Flame. Recorded album *Indian Blues* with son **Donald Harrison Jr.** and **Dr. John** in 1991 and toured internationally.

HARRISON, DONALD, JR. *Jazz, rhythm and blues.* Saxophone. Composer. Bandleader. (Born June 23, 1960, New Orleans, Orleans Parish.) Jazz saxophonist who incorporated elements of rhythm and blues, hip-hop, and Latin rhythms and became known as "The King of Nouveau Swing." Worked early on with Roy Haynes, Jack McDuff, and Art Blakey and in the 1980s formed quintet with **Terence Blanchard**. In 1990 launched solo career and had numerous critically acclaimed releases through the 2010s, including *Spirits of Congo Square* in 2000 on Candid. Son of **Big Chief Donald Harrison Sr.**

HARTMAN, CLYDE *Cajun.* Accordion. Bandleader. (Born Mar. 5, 1942, Lockport, Lafourche Parish.) Traditional Cajun accordionist who formed the Lafourche Cajun Band in 1990 and continued to lead band through the 2010s.

HARTMAN, JOHNNY *Jazz.* Vocals. Bandleader. (Born July 3, 1923, Houma, Terrebonne Parish; died Sept. 15, 1983, New York City.) Renowned jazz vocalist who specialized in ballads and best known for his 1963 collaboration with John Coltrane. Moved to Chicago with family as a child, where he later studied music in high school and at Chicago Musical College. After serving in World War II, worked with Earl Hines, Dizzy Gillespie, and Erroll Garner in the late 1940s. In the early 1950s began solo career and released three LPs throughout decade. In 1963 recorded the classic jazz LP *Johnny Hartman and John Coltrane* on Impulse, which featured only ballads and led to several more releases for the label. Throughout the 1970s had recordings on several labels, including Perception, Capitol, and Musicor and performed regularly in New York and Chicago. In 1980 released highly acclaimed LP *Once in Every Life* on Bee Hive. Died of lung cancer at age 60.

HARTMANN, CHARLES *Jazz.* Trombone. (Born July 1, 1898, New Orleans, Orleans Parish; died Sept. 1, 1982, Springfield, Tennessee.) Traditional jazz trombonist worked with **Johnny Bayersdorffer** and performed and recorded with **Tony Parenti** and **Johnny Wiggs** in the 1920s.

HATHAWAY, MAGGIE *Rhythm and blues.* Vocals, piano. Composer. Bandleader. (Born July 1, 1911, Campti, Natch. Parish; died Sept. 24, 2001, Los Angeles.)[7] Early rhythm and blues singer moved to Los Angeles in 1940 to perform on the thriving Central Avenue music scene and began appearing as extra in films. In 1947 recorded two singles with her band the Bluesmen on Black & White, including "Here Goes a Fool"/"Too Late to Be Good Blues." In 1950 recorded singles as leader on Recorded in Hollywood and as vocalist with the Robins and 2 Sharps and a Natural. Later achieved notoriety as a successful civil rights activist and writer in the film and sports industry, cofounding the Beverly Hills/Hollywood chapter of the NAACP in 1962 with Sammy Davis Jr.

HAWKINS, BARBARA ANN *Rhythm and blues.* Vocals. (Born Oct. 23, 1943, New Orleans, Orleans Parish.) Founding member along with sister **Rosa Lee Hawkins** and cousin **Joan Marie Johnson** of vocal group the Dixie Cups which had several national hits in the mid-1960s such as "Chapel of Love" and the traditional New Orleans classic "Iko Iko." Continued to perform with group into the 2010s.

HAWKINS, DALE (Delmar Allen Hawkins Jr.) *Rockabilly, rock and roll.* Vocals, guitar. Composer. Bandleader. (Born Aug. 22, 1936, Gold Mine Plantation, Richland Parish; died Feb. 13, 2010, Little Rock, Arkansas.) Influential early rockabilly singer and songwriter best known for his 1957 hit "Susie-Q." While in his early teens moved with family to Bossier City. After a stint in the Navy began working at **Stan Lewis**'s record shop in Shreveport and by early 1956 was performing around Shreveport area with teenage guitar ace **James Burton**, inspired by current rhythm and blues hits. Recorded debut single "See You Soon, Baboon," which was released on Checker but failed to chart. In summer of 1957 had major hit with "Susie-Q" and toured nationally. More releases followed on Checker through 1961, including "La-Do-Dada" and "My Babe." Throughout the 1960s had releases on numerous labels, including Tilt, Atlantic, Abnak, and Bell and hosted a teen dance television show. Also worked as successful record producer through the early 1970s. After a twenty-year hiatus released album *Wildcat Tamer* in 1999. Continued performing nationally and abroad for several more years and released final recording *Back Down to Louisiana* in 2006. Younger brother Jerry Hawkins and cousin Ronnie Hawkins were also rockabilly recording artists.

HAWKINS, ROSA LEE *Rhythm and blues.* Vocals. (Born Sept. 24, 1944, New Orleans, Orleans Parish.) Sister of **Barbara Ann Hawkins** and cousin of **Joan Marie Johnson** who together formed vocal group the Dixie Cups in 1963. Had national hits with "Chapel of Love" and "Iko Iko" in 1964–65. Continued to perform with group into the 2010s.

HÉBERT, ADAM *Cajun.* Fiddle, vocals. Composer. Bandleader. (Born Aug. 23, 1923, Church Point, Acadia Parish; died Oct. 11, 2010, Lafayette, Lafayette Parish.) Renowned Cajun fiddler and singer-songwriter began playing on a homemade instrument as a child and by age 13 was playing house dances. In the late 1940s performed and recorded with **Alphée** and **Shirley Bergeron** in Veteran Playboys before forming his Country Playboys in the mid-1950s. Through the mid-1960s recorded numerous singles for Swallow with group, many of which became Cajun standards, including "La Pointe Aux Pins," "Madeleine," and "La Valse de Ma Chérie." Worked largely outside music in following decades but performed occasionally through the early 2000s.

HEBRARD, WARREN *Rhythm and blues.* Saxophone. (Born Apr. 21, 1926, New Orleans, Orleans Parish; died May 5, 1994, Los Angeles.) Rhythm and blues saxophone player and member of **Edgar Blanchard**'s Gondoliers who appeared on numerous sessions in the 1950s with Ray Charles, **Earl King**, Big Joe Turner, and others. Occasionally mis-credited as Warren Hebrew.

HEBREW, WARREN *See* Hebrard, Warren.

HENDERSON, GEORGE *Jazz.* Drums. Bandleader. (Born Sept. 17, 1900, New Orleans, Orleans Parish; died Apr. 15, 1974, New Orleans, Orleans Parish.)[8] Early New Orleans jazz drummer was influenced by **Alec Bigard** and **Louis Cottrell Sr.** and led Black Diamonds Band from 1919 to 1922. Worked with **Sam Morgan** and **Captain John Handy** in the 1930s. In 1951 recorded with **Kid Thomas** and later worked with **Billie** and **De De Pierce**.

HENRY, CHARLES "SONNY" *Jazz.* Trombone. (Born Nov. 17, 1885, Magnolia Plantation, Plaquemines Parish; died Jan. 7, 1960, New Orleans, Orleans Parish.) Early New Orleans jazz trombonist studied music with **Professor Jim Humphrey** and by age 17 was performing with local Eclipse Brass Band. In 1913 moved to New Orleans and in the 1910s and 1920s worked with Excelsior Brass Band, **Hypolite Charles**, and **John Robichaux**. Performed in W.P.A. Brass Band in the 1930s and Young Tuxedo Brass Band in the early 1940s. Member of Eureka Brass Band from 1947 until his death.

HENRY, CLARENCE "FROGMAN" *Rhythm and blues.* Vocals, piano, trombone. Composer. Bandleader. (Born Mar. 19, 1937, New Orleans, Orleans Parish.) Charismatic rhythm and blues performer best known for his 1956 hit "Ain't Got No Home." Influenced by **Professor Longhair** and **Fats Domino**, began sneaking into clubs as a teenager to hear local rhythm and blues acts. Worked with **Bobby Mitchell**'s band the Toppers from 1952 to 1955. Began recording for producer **Paul Gayten** in 1956, which resulted in b-side hit "Ain't Got No Home" on Argo. In 1961 had several more hits on Argo, including "But I Do" and "You Always Hurt the One You Love." Releases followed on Parrot, Dial, and Roulette through the early 1970s and continued performing throughout next several decades including annual appearances at New Orleans Jazz & Heritage Festival into the 2010s.

HENRY, COREY *Jazz.* Trombone, vocals. Composer. Bandleader. (Born July 14, 1975, New Orleans, Orleans Parish.) Born and raised in Tremé, noted trombonist began playing at age 10 and at age 16 joined his uncle **Benny Jones**'s Tremé Brass Band. Led Lil Rascals Brass Band and also worked with Rebirth Brass Band, **Kermit Ruffins**'s BBQ Swingers, and Galactic in the 1990s and 2000s. In 2012 formed Tremé Funktet and released *Lapeitah* on Louisiana Red Hot Records in 2016.

HENRY, OSCAR "CHICKEN" *Jazz.* Trombone, piano. (Born June 8, 1888, New Orleans, Orleans Parish; died Dec. 14, 1984, Los Angeles.)[9] Early New Orleans jazz trombonist began career playing piano in brothels throughout Storyville District around 1905. Switched to trombone in the late 1910s after a hand injury while living in Detroit. Worked in Chicago and on East Coast with various bands and during 1930s joined W.P.A. Brass Band. Also worked regularly with **Kid Howard**. In the 1960s joined Eureka Brass Band and performed and recorded at Preservation Hall.

HENRY, PATRICK *Rhythm and blues.* Vocals. Composer. Bandleader. (Born Feb. 8, 1958, Sunset, St. Landry Parish.) Southern soul singer and bandleader known as "Mr. Excitement" for his high-energy performances. Began singing as a child in church and formed his Liberation Band in 1978, influenced greatly by James Brown and Otis Redding. From the mid-1990s through 2010s had releases on several labels, including Lanor, Hot Box, Lockdowne, and M2K, notably *Come and Get It* in 1995. Continued performing on southern soul circuit in the late 2010s.

HICKS, EDNA (*born* **Edna Landreaux**) *Blues.* Vocals, piano. (Born Oct. 14, 1891, New Orleans, Orleans Parish; died Aug. 16, 1925, Chicago.) Early classic blues singer and half-sister of **Lizzie Miles** and **Herb Morand**, began performing on the black vaudeville circuit in the early 1910s and by 1920 was based in Chicago. In 1923–24 released recordings on Victor, Brunswick, Gennett, Vocalion, Ajax, Columbia, and Paramount, often accompanied by Fletcher Henderson. Died tragically from severe burns sustained in a gasoline-fire accident.

HIGGINBOTHAM, DARREL *Cajun.* Guitar, vocals. (Born Dec. 19, 1938, Church Point, Acadia Parish; died

July 15, 1995, Lake Charles, Calcasieu Parish.) Noted Cajun singer and guitarist began performing in his early teens and worked with **Iry LeJeune** and **Bobby Leger** in the 1950s. From the late 1960s through late 1980s performed and recorded as vocalist and guitarist with Sundown Playboys, appearing on majority of band's recordings in that period.

HILAIRE, ANDREW HENRY *Jazz.* Drums. Bandleader. (Born Feb. 1, 1899, New Orleans, Orleans Parish; died Aug. 3, 1935, Chicago.)[10] Remarkable but under-recorded early jazz drummer moved to Chicago and began performing there in his teens. In the early 1920s worked with Lil Hardin and later performed and recorded with Doc Cook. In late 1926 appeared on famed sessions with **Jelly Roll Morton**'s Red Hot Peppers. Led bands in the early 1930s around Chicago.

HILL, JESSIE *Rhythm and blues.* Vocals, drums. Composer. Bandleader. (Born Dec. 9, 1932, New Orleans, Orleans Parish; died Sept. 17, 1996, New Orleans, Orleans Parish.) Singer-songwriter best known for his 1960 New Orleans rhythm and blues classic "Ooh Poo Pah Doo." Began performing with bands during his teens and in 1951 formed the House Rockers with **Eddie Lang** and **Melvin** and **David Lastie**. In the mid-1950s played drums with **Professor Longhair** and **Huey "Piano" Smith**. Reformed House Rockers in 1958 and recorded hit "Ooh Poo Pah Doo" in 1960 on Minit, produced by **Allen Toussaint**. After several more releases relocated to California in 1962 and worked mainly as songwriter. Recorded for Blue Thumb in the early 1970s and returned to New Orleans in 1977. Performed sporadically throughout following two decades. Grandfather of **James "12"** and **Troy "Trombone Shorty" Andrews** and **Travis "Trumpet Black" Hill**.

HILL, TRAVIS "TRUMPET BLACK" *See* Trumpet Black.

HILLS, JEFFREY *Jazz.* Tuba. Bandleader. (Born Dec. 1, 1975, New Orleans, Orleans Parish.) New Orleans tuba player began performing with Junior Olympia Brass Band during his teens with **Harold Dejan** and **Milton Batiste**. By age 17 was appearing at Preservation Hall with Olympia Brass Band and in following years worked with other brass bands, including Dirty Dozen, Rebirth, Tremé, Lil Rascals, and New Birth. Appeared on recordings with **Ellis Marsalis**, **Leroy Jones**, and **Russell Batiste**, among others. Led Survivors Brass Band in the 2010s.

HIMMEL, KARL T. *Rhythm and blues, rock.* Drums. (Born Aug. 14, 1946, Houma, Terrebonne Parish.) Highly accomplished session drummer who has worked with numerous internationally renowned artists from **Dr. John** to Elvis Presley. Began performing in the mid-1960s in clubs along Bourbon Street before joining Mac Rebennack's (Dr. John) band. Throughout following decades recorded prolifically on sessions with J.J. Cale, Neil Young, Bob Dylan, Elvis Presley, **Bobby Charles**, **Doug Kershaw**, **Clarence "Gatemouth" Brown**, Roy Buchanan, Joe Tex, and countless others. Continued performing and recording in the 2010s.

HINGLE, CAYETANO "TANIO" *Jazz.* Bass drum. (Born Nov. 14, 1969, New Orleans, Orleans Parish.) New Orleans bass drummer began performing with Junior Olympia Brass Band in the early 1990s and later joined Olympia and Tremé brass bands, greatly influenced by **Lionel Batiste** and **Benny Jones**. Worked and recorded with New Birth and Magnificent Seventh brass bands as well as **Allen Toussaint**.

HIRT, AL (Alois Maxwell Hirt) *Jazz.* Trumpet, vocals. Composer. Bandleader. (Born Nov. 7, 1922, New Orleans, Orleans Parish; died Apr. 27, 1999, New Orleans, Orleans Parish.) Internationally renowned trumpeter known for his powerful playing style and one of the most popular instrumentalists of the 1960s. A child prodigy, studied classical trumpet at Cincinnati Conservatory in the early 1940s but was also influenced by Harry James and Roy Eldridge. Later performed with various swing bands, including Tommy and Jimmy Dorsey, before returning to New Orleans in the late 1940s. In the 1950s led his own group which at times included **Pete Fountain** and gained national popularity through Dixieland jazz recordings on Audio Fidelity in the late 1950s. Became one of RCA's best-selling recording artists in the 1960s, notably with the 1964 hit single "Java" and LPs *Honey in the Horn* and *Cotton Candy*, and appeared regularly on television. In 1961 opened popular club on Bourbon Street in which he performed almost exclusively until its closure in 1983. Recorded more than 50 albums throughout career and continued performing until shortly before his death at age 76.

HOFFPAUIR, WALDEN "SLEEPY" *Cajun.* Fiddle. Composer. Bandleader. (Born Jan. 19, 1931, Crowley, Acadia Parish; died Mar. 6, 2007, Lafayette, Lafayette Parish.) Noted Cajun fiddler best known for his long association performing and recording as member of **Belton Richard**'s Musical Aces in the 1960s and 1970s. Also recorded with **Alex Broussard** on La Louisianne and released LP *Fiddles: Traditional Cajun Music* on Swallow in 1976.

HOGAN, CHA CHA (Sumter Joseph Hogan) *Rhythm and blues.* Vocals, piano. (Born Dec. 8, 1920, New Orleans, Orleans Parish; died Nov. 9, 1986, Las Vegas.) Singer, actor, and comedian who recorded a single each for Star Talent in 1950 and Soulville in 1969. Also released comedy album on Laff in 1971 as "The Black Foxx." Relocated to Las Vegas in 1974 and performed in nightclubs. In the 1980s toured with Stanley Morgan's Ink Spots.

HOGAN, SILAS *Blues.* Guitar, vocals. Composer. Bandleader. (Born Sept. 15, 1911, Westover, WBR Parish; died Jan. 9, 1994, Baton Rouge, EBR Parish.) Noted early Baton Rouge swamp blues singer and guitarist best known for his 1960s Excello recordings such as "Airport Blues" and "Dark Clouds Rollin'." Began playing guitar in the mid-1920s, mentored by uncles Robert and Frank Meddy, who were locally renowned musicians. In the mid-1950s formed band the Rhythm Ramblers, which included drummer **Jimmy Dotson** and harmonica player Sylvester Buckley, and in 1959–60 backed Dotson with group on several singles for Zynn and Rocko. From 1962 to 1965 had multiple singles as leader on Excello and in 1970 appeared on LPs on Arhoolie and Blue Horizon. Through the 1980s worked regularly with **Arthur "Guitar" Kelley** and in 1989 released CD *The Godfather* on Blues South West. Father of swamp blues guitarist and drummer Sammy Hogan (1953–).

HOLMES, ELDRIDGE *Rhythm and blues.* Vocals. Composer. (Born June 26, 1941, Violet, St. Bernard Parish; died Nov. 13, 1998, New Orleans, Orleans Parish.)[11] New Orleans soul and funk singer and composer who recorded more than a dozen singles on various labels from the early 1960s through early 1970s. Working mainly with **Allen Toussaint**, released singles on Alon, Jet Set, Sansu, Deesu, Decca, Kansu, Brown Sugar, and Atco, notably "Pop, Popcorn Children" backed by the Meters.

HOOKER, GEORGE *Jazz.* Cornet, baritone horn. (Born July 27, 1877, Algiers, Orleans Parish; died Feb. 25, 1929, New Orleans, Orleans Parish.)[12] One of the original members of Pacific Brass Band of Algiers in 1900. Also worked with Allen Brass Band, **Chris Kelly**, and Tuxedo and Excelsior brass bands in the 1920s.

HOPELESS HOMER (Harvey B. Chambers) *Rockabilly.* Guitar, vocals. Composer. Bandleader. (Born Apr. 25, 1916, Effie, Avoy. Parish; died Jan. 18, 1958, Alexandria, Rapides Parish.)[13] Singer-songwriter best known for his rockabilly single as Hopeless Homer "New Way Rockin'"/"The Girl in the Red Blue Jeans" issued on Goldband in 1957. Died of lung cancer the following year.

HOPKINS, LINDA (Melinda Helen Matthews) *Gospel, jazz, rhythm and blues.* Vocals. Composer. (Born Dec. 14, 1924, New Orleans, Orleans Parish; died Apr. 10, 2017, Milwaukee, Wisconsin.) Renowned gospel and jazz vocalist began singing in church at age three, influenced by **Mahalia Jackson** and Bessie Smith. At age 11 was discovered by Jackson and toured with **Alberta French Johnson**'s Southern Harps for the next 10 years. In the 1950s worked with rhythm and blues bandleader Johnny Otis, singer Little Esther Williams, and Louis Jordan. Recorded for several labels throughout the 1950s and had hit "Shake a Hand" with Jackie Wilson on Brunswick in 1962. From the 1970s through 1990s appeared in several critically acclaimed plays on Broadway including *Purlie, Me and Bessie,* and *Wild Women Blues.* Continued to perform and record until sidelined by a stroke in 2006.

HOT ROD HAPPY *See* Country Jim.

HOUSTON, CLINT *Jazz.* Bass, guitar, piano. Composer. (Born June 24, 1946, New Orleans, Orleans Parish; died June 7, 2000, New York City.) Underrated jazz double-bassist was raised in New York City and began performing in the late 1960s. Through the 1970s and 1980s performed regularly with Nina Simone, Roy Ayers, Stan Getz, Woody Shaw, and others, and had long tenure with Joanne Brackeen from 1978 to 1986. In the late 1970s made two recordings as a leader for Storyville and Timeless, notably *Watership Down.*

HOUSTON, TERRENCE "GROOVE GUARDIAN" *Rhythm and blues.* Drums, vocals. (Born May 14, 1985, Baton Rouge, EBR Parish.) Highly skilled New Orleans funk drummer began playing at age four and by age seven was performing weekly in church. After graduating from Southern University, toured with hip-hop and rock groups before settling in New Orleans and joining **George Porter Jr.**'s band Runnin' Pardners. In 2014 became member of the Funky Meters and continued performing with several popular New Orleans funk bands in the late 2010s.

HOUSTON, WILLIE *Blues.* Guitar, vocals. Composer. Bandleader. (Born Mar. 19, 1927, Grand Cane, DeSoto Parish.) Denver, Colorado–based Louisiana Delta blues guitar player and singer gained local notoriety performing in Denver clubs while in his 70s. Released first CD, *Bluesman Willie Houston,* in 2001 on Fasttrack and continued performing well into his 80s.

HOWARD, AVERY "KID" *Jazz.* Trumpet, cornet, drums. Composer. Bandleader. (Born Apr. 22, 1908, New Orleans, Orleans Parish; died Mar. 28, 1966, New Orleans,

Orleans Parish.) Early New Orleans jazz bandleader and trumpeter began playing drums in his teens with **Chris Kelly** and **Isaiah Morgan** before switching to cornet and trumpet. In the early 1920s performed with Eureka and Tuxedo brass bands and led several bands in the late 1920s. In 1943 recorded with **George Lewis** on Climax, which is widely regarded as his finest work, and in 1946 led Original Zenith Brass Band. Throughout the 1950s and early 1960s worked and recorded regularly with Lewis. Performed at Preservation Hall and Dixieland Hall in the 1960s and made additional recordings as leader for several labels including *Kid Howard at the San Jacinto Hall* in 1965 on GHB.

HOWARD, NOAH *Jazz.* Saxophone. Composer. Bandleader. (Born Apr. 6, 1943, New Orleans, Orleans Parish; died Sept. 3, 2010, Nimes, France.) Noted early free-jazz saxophonist and prolific recording artist began singing in church as a child and was influenced by John Coltrane and later Albert Ayler. After living on the West Coast in the early 1960s, moved to New York City and worked with Sun Ra. Made recording debut with self-titled LP in the mid-1960s on ESP Records and released 35 albums throughout career. Moved to Paris in the early 1970s and spent remainder of life abroad.

HUDSON, JOE (Reynauld Joseph Hudson) *Rhythm and blues.* Drums. Composer. Bandleader. (Born Aug. 28, 1928, Baton Rouge, EBR Parish; died Dec. 22, 1998, Greenville, Mississippi.)[14] Early Baton Rouge blues drummer and bandleader of the Rocking Dukes who were active in the 1950s and 1960s and whose members at times included **Boogie Jake**, **Lazy Lester**, and **Schoolboy Cleve**. Recorded Excello single "Baby Give Me a Chance"/"Hoo-Wee Pretty Baby" in 1957 with **Lester Robertson** on vocals. Also known locally as Rockin' Joe. Relocated to Mississippi around 1970 and continued working as musician and disc jockey. Cousin of Eddie Hudson, who recorded 1958 Excello single "She's Sugar Sweet."

HUG, ARMAND *Jazz.* Piano. Composer. (Born Dec. 6, 1910, New Orleans, Orleans Parish; died Mar. 19, 1977, New Orleans, Orleans Parish.) Highly regarded New Orleans jazz pianist began playing for silent movies as a teenager in local theaters. From the late 1920s through early 1940s worked with **Irving Fazola**, **Sharkey Bonano**, **Louis Prima**, and others. In the 1950s and 1960s performed mainly as soloist in New Orleans hotels and clubs and made over 250 recordings as leader and sideman.

HULIN, T.K. (Alton James Hulin) *Swamp pop, rhythm and blues.* Vocals. Bandleader. (Born Aug. 16, 1943, St. Martinville, St. Martin Parish.) Known as "The Voice with a Tear," popular swamp pop singer formed his band T.K. and the Lonely Knights at age 13 and within a year was performing in local clubs. In 1957 recorded single "Many Nites" on L. and K. and had local success. Continued performing in area clubs and in 1963 had hit with "I'm Not a Fool Anymore," which was released nationally on Smash. Also had regional hit with "As You Pass Me By (Graduation Night)." More releases followed on L. and K. and Crazy Cajun through the early 1970s and had regional hit in 1976 with **Eddy Raven**'s "Alligator Bayou" on Booray. Continued performing in south Louisiana clubs and festivals with his band Smoke through the 2010s with several releases on his T.K. label, including *Larger than Life* in 2007. Worked with brother and drummer Larry "B-Lou" Hulin for almost five decades.

HUMPHREY, EARL *Jazz.* Trombone. (Born Sept. 9, 1902, New Orleans, Orleans Parish; died June 26, 1971, New Orleans, Orleans Parish.) Early New Orleans jazz trombonist studied music with his grandfather **Professor Jim Humphrey** and in 1919 toured in circus band with his father, **Willie Eli Humphrey**. Traveled with tent shows frequently but periodically returned to New Orleans in the 1920s and worked with Eureka and Onward brass bands. Recorded on **Louis Dumaine**'s historic Jazzola Eight session in 1927 and settled in Virginia in the 1930s. Returned to New Orleans in the 1960s. Brother of **Percy** and **Willie James Humphrey Jr.**

HUMPHREY, PERCY *Jazz.* Trumpet, vocals. Bandleader (Born Jan. 13, 1905, New Orleans, Orleans Parish; died July 22, 1995, New Orleans, Orleans Parish.)[15] Noted early New Orleans jazz trumpeter studied under his grandfather, **Professor Jim Humphey**, and performed with Eureka Brass Band and **Kid Howard** in the 1920s. In the late 1940s and early 1950s led and recorded with Eureka Brass Band and from 1951 to 1953 recorded with **George Lewis**. In the 1960s and 1970s led and recorded with Crescent City Joymakers. Performed at Preservation Hall from 1961 through the early 1990s. Son of **Willie Eli Humphrey** and brother of **Earl** and **Willie James Humphrey Jr.**

HUMPHREY, PROFESSOR JIM (James Humphrey) *Jazz.* Trumpet. (Born Nov. 25, 1859, New Orleans, Orleans Parish; died Nov. 25, 1935, New Orleans, Orleans Parish.)[16] Patriarch of important early New Orleans jazz family and one of the city's greatest music teachers. Led Eclipse Brass Band on Magnolia Plantation in the early

1900s and gave music lessons to family members **Willie Eli**, **Earl**, **Percy**, and **Willie James Humphrey Jr.** as well as **Bébé Ridgley**, **Punch Miller**, **Chris Kelly**, and **Sam** and **Isaiah Morgan**, among many others.

HUMPHREY, WILLIE ELI *Jazz.* Clarinet. (Born May 24, 1880, New Orleans, Orleans Parish; died Jan. 8, 1964, New Orleans, Orleans Parish.) Early New Orleans jazz clarinetist was mentored by his father, **Professor Jim Humphrey**, and performed with Eclipse Brass Band from Magnolia Plantation from 1900 to 1910. Worked with Crescent Orchestra in the mid-1910s. Father of **Earl**, **Percy**, and **Willie James Humphrey Jr**.

HUMPHREY, WILLIE JAMES, JR. *Jazz.* Clarinet, vocals. Bandleader. (Born Dec. 29, 1900, New Orleans, Orleans Parish; died June 7, 1994, New Orleans, Orleans Parish.) Renowned early New Orleans jazz clarinetist took lessons from his grandfather **Professor Jim Humphrey** and began performing with Excelsior Brass Band in 1918. Worked with **King Oliver**, **Freddie Keppard**, and **Lawrence Duhé** in Chicago later that year. In the 1920s worked with **Kid Rena** in New Orleans and with **Fate Marable** in St. Louis, and in the 1930s performed and recorded with **Red Allen**. Also worked as music teacher and toured with Lucky Millinder in the mid-1930s. During the 1950s worked and recorded with **Freddie Kohlman** and **Paul Barbarin** as well as Eureka Brass Band and his own group. Toured Europe with **Billie** and **De De Pierce** in 1967 and performed regularly at Preservation Hall from 1961 until May of 1994. Son of **Willie Eli Humphrey Sr.** and brother of **Earl** and **Percy Humphrey**.

HUMPHRIES, MAYLON *Rockabilly.* Vocals. Composer. Bandleader. (Born Mar. 18, 1935, Kelly, Caldwell Parish; died Nov. 3, 2019, Shreveport, Caddo Parish.) Early rockabilly singer best known for his version of "Worried About You Baby" which was mistakenly attributed to **Dale Hawkins** for many years. Raised in Pineville/Alexandria area, moved to Shreveport with family at age 18 and befriended Hawkins and **James Burton**. In 1957 recorded demo of "Worried About You Baby" with Burton on guitar and, on the advice of Chicago label owner Leonard Chess, rerecorded it several more times for producer **Stan Lewis**. Recordings remained unissued until they began appearing on albums credited to Hawkins in the mid-1970s. In 1958 recorded single for Mercury in California with his band the Raiders. Returned to Shreveport and left music business in 1960 but returned for one last single on Paula in 1966, "Gee, I Sure Do Miss You"/"Never Never," under name Maylon D. Witt.

HUNTER, KERRY "FAT MAN" *Jazz.* Snare drum. (Born May 21, 1970, New Orleans, Orleans Parish.) New Orleans brass-band drummer began playing snare drum at age 12 with Roots of Jazz Brass Band led by **Danny Barker**. Later worked with Olympia, Rebirth, Dirty Dozen, and Tornado brass bands. Performed regularly with New Birth Brass Band and at Preservation Hall in the 2010s.

HUNTER, LONG JOHN *Blues.* Guitar, vocals. Composer. Bandleader. (Born July 13, 1931, Ringgold, Bienville Parish; died Jan. 4, 2016, Phoenix, Arizona.) Renowned West Texas blues guitarist, singer, and songwriter began learning guitar at age 22 after moving to Beaumont and seeing B.B. King perform. After working with guitarist **Ervin Charles**, recorded single "She Used to Be My Woman" in 1954, which had regional success on Duke. Relocated to Houston and performed with **Clarence "Gatemouth" Brown**, Albert Collins, and Lightnin' Hopkins. In the late 1950s moved to El Paso and through 1970 was star performer at the famed Lobby Bar in Juarez. Cut several singles for Yucca in 1961–63, including "El Paso Rock" and "Border Town Blues." Continued performing in West Texas and in the early 1990s had releases on Black Magic and Double Trouble. In the mid-1990s recorded two critically acclaimed releases for Alligator, including *Border Town Legend,* and toured extensively. In 1999 recorded and toured as part of Alligator's *Lone Star Shootout* with **Lonnie Brooks** and **Phillip Walker**. Settled in Phoenix in 2003 and released *One Foot in Texas* with brother Tom "Blues Man" Hunter. Recorded final album, *Looking for a Party,* in 2009 and continued performing into the early 2010s.

HUVAL, BRAZOS Cajun. Fiddle, bass, vocals. Composer. Bandleader. (Born June 4, 1979, Breaux Bridge, St. Martin Parish.) Cajun multi-instrumentalist and member of noted Huval family of musicians from Breaux Bridge, which also includes brothers Chad (accordion), Luke (guitar), and Jebb (bass). Longtime member of **Steve Riley**'s Mamou Playboys and Cajun all-star band High Performance. In the 2010s continued performing with Mamou Playboys, High Performance, and Huval Family Band while also operating a music school in Breaux Bridge.

HUVAL FAMILY (of Breaux Bridge) *See* Huval, Brazos.

HYMAN, JOHNNY *See* Wiggs, Johnny.

HYMES, GANEY "POP" *Rhythm and blues.* Drums. (Born July 17, 1954, Natchitoches, Natch. Parish.) Locally renowned rhythm and blues drummer grew up in a musical family and began playing drums during his teens. Performed in numerous bands in Natchitoches area for more than 40 years, working with **Overton Owens**, **B.B. Major**, **Hardrick Rivers**, and many others.

HYPOLITE, HARRY "BIG DADDY" *Blues, zydeco.* Guitar, vocals. Bandleader. (Born Apr. 20, 1937, St. Martinville, St. Martin Parish; died June 22, 2005, Port Allen, WBR Parish.)[17] Renowned zydeco and blues guitarist grew up speaking Creole French and began playing guitar in his teens, inspired by B.B. King, T-Bone Walker, and **Guitar Slim**. After playing for an ailing Guitar Slim on a local show in the mid-1950s, began performing in area clubs. In the early 1980s joined **Clifton Chenier**'s band and toured internationally with group. Recorded a single as leader for La Louisianne in 1985. After Chenier's death in 1987 continued with band under leadership of **C. J. Chenier** until joining nephew **Nathan Williams**'s band Zydeco Cha Chas in 1999. In 2001 released acclaimed CD *Louisiana Country Boy* on APO, which helped launch solo career and international tour. At age 68 was killed in a car accident when his vehicle stalled on Interstate 10 near Baton Rouge.

J

J. MONQUE'D (James Monque Digby) *Blues.* Vocals, harmonica, fife. Composer. Bandleader. (Born Apr. 10, 1946, New Orleans, Orleans Parish.) New Orleans blues singer started playing harmonica as a child, inspired by Jimmy Reed and **Slim Harpo**. Played first gig in 1959 and later learned directly from **Polka Dot Slim**. Released debut CD *Butter Churnin' Man* on Wolf Records in 1994, followed by two more recordings in 2000. Continued performing in clubs and festivals in the 2010s.

JACKSON, AL "LIL FATS" (Alvin E. Jackson) *Rhythm and blues.* Piano, vocals. Composer. Bandleader. (Born Dec. 28, 1973, Bridge City, Jefferson Parish.) Charismatic rhythm and blues singer and piano player best known for his remarkable tributes to **Fats Domino**. Began performing in 1995 and appeared at major U.S. festivals and toured Europe. Released two CDs in the late 1990s and 2000s and starred as Domino in the musical *Walkin' to New Orleans* in 2015.

JACKSON, ALBERT "LOOCHIE" *Jazz.* Trombone. (Born Mar. 13, 1898, New Orleans, Orleans Parish; died Mar. 3, 1978, New Orleans, Orleans Parish.) Early New Orleans jazz trombonist started performing in 1918 with **Kid Thomas** and worked with Tuxedo Brass Band in 1920. Also worked with **Manuel Perez** on occasion. Performed with Young Tuxedo Brass Band from 1932 to 1953 and retired from music.

JACKSON, ARMAND "JUMP" *Blues.* Drums. Bandleader. (Born Mar. 25, 1917, New Orleans, Orleans Parish; died Jan. 31, 1985, Chicago.)[1] Highly regarded blues drummer settled in Chicago in the 1940s, where he led a band and recorded as leader for Columbia, Aristocrat, and Specialty in 1946–47. Through the 1960s appeared on dozens of sessions with numerous blues artists, including **Little Brother Montgomery**, Sunnyland Slim, Roosevelt Sykes, John Lee Hooker, John Lee "Sonny Boy" Williamson, Robert Nighthawk, Tampa Red, and Arthur "Big Boy" Crudup. Toured Europe in 1962 as part of American Folk Blues Festival package.

JACKSON, EDDIE *Jazz.* Bass, tuba. Bandleader. (Born around 1867, New Orleans, Orleans Parish; died 1938, New Orleans, Orleans Parish.) Regarded as an exemplary musician, early New Orleans jazz bass and tuba player began performing with **Edward Clem** around 1907 and worked with Onward Brass Band in the early 1910s. In the 1920s led his own band and worked with Tuxedo Brass Band in the late 1920s. Performed with Young Tuxedo Brass Band in the 1930s.

JACKSON, EMMA L. *Gospel.* Vocals. Composer. Bandleader. (Born Jan. 19, 1910, Ruston, Lincoln Parish; died Oct. 28, 1946, Chicago.)[2] Influential gospel singer and songwriter best known for her 1940s compositions "I'm Going to Die with the Staff in My Hand" and "Don't Forget the Family Prayer." In the late 1920s and early 1930s sold "Gospel Songs" pamphlets in Shreveport as Emma L. Days with husband, Granville Lewis Days. Deciding to further pursue a career in gospel music, relocated to Chicago in the mid-1930s and became one of the city's most celebrated gospel soloists by the early 1940s, operating a successful gospel music studio and publishing house. A close friend of **Mahalia Jackson** and gospel pioneer composer Thomas A. Dorsey, she's credited with introducing Dorsey's "Precious Lord, Take My Hand," to the National Baptist Convention. Toured nationally with her group the Emma L. Jackson Singers. After working in California in 1946 became ill and returned to Chicago, succumbing to an unspecified illness shortly thereafter.

JACKSON, JERRY "COUNT" *See* LaCroix, Jerry.

JACKSON, MAHALIA *Gospel.* Vocals. (Born Oct. 26, 1911,

New Orleans, Orleans Parish; died Jan. 27, 1972, Evergreen Park, Illinois.) Internationally renowned as "The Queen of Gospel" and widely regarded as the greatest and most influential American gospel singer. Raised in New Orleans and influenced by recordings of classic blues singers Bessie Smith and Ma Rainey, relocated to Chicago at age 16 and began singing at Greater Salem Baptist Church and toured with professional gospel group the Johnson Gospel Singers. In the mid-1930s made recordings for Decca and began working with gospel pioneer Thomas A. Dorsey. In 1947 signed with Apollo and the following year released enormous hit "Move On Up a Little Higher," which sold eight million copies and catapulted her to national fame. Began performing in concert halls instead of churches and in 1950 became first gospel artist to perform at Carnegie Hall. Toured Europe for the first time in the early 1950s and signed with Columbia Records in 1954. In the late 1950s and 1960s served as powerful civil rights activist and in 1961 sang at President John F. Kennedy's inaugural ball. Recorded approximately 30 albums and released more than a dozen million-selling singles throughout her career.

JACKSON, PAPA CHARLIE *Blues, jazz.* Vocals, banjo, guitar. Composer. (Born Nov. 10, 1887, New Orleans, Orleans Parish; died May 7, 1938, Chicago.)[3] Exceptional early prewar blues singer, songwriter, and banjoist who recorded prolifically as a leader and accompanist in the mid- to late 1920s and was the first commercially successful solo blues recording artist. Believed to have performed in traveling vaudeville and medicine shows in the 1910s and settled in Chicago's Maxwell Street area in the early 1920s. Recorded extensively for Paramount starting in Aug. 1924 and cut more than 65 sides as a leader through 1930, including "Shake That Thing," "Salty Dog Blues," and "All I Want Is a Spoonful." Also appeared as sideman on recordings with **Freddie Keppard**, Ida Cox, Ma Rainey, Big Bill Broonzy, and Blind Blake. Recorded for OKeh and ARC in 1934–35.

JACKSON, PERVIS *Rhythm and blues.* Vocals. (Born May 17, 1938, New Orleans, Orleans Parish; died Aug. 18, 2008, Detroit.) Original member and bass singer of Detroit-based rhythm and blues group the Spinners, which formed in the late 1950s and had recordings on Tri-Phi and Motown in 1960s and a series of hits on Atlantic in the 1970s, including "Games People Play" and "Then Came You" with Dionne Warwick. Continued performing with group until his death from cancer at age 70.

JACKSON, PRESTON *Jazz.* Trombone. Bandleader. (Born Jan. 3, 1902, New Orleans, Orleans Parish; died Nov. 12, 1983, Blytheville, Arkansas.)[4] Renowned early New Orleans jazz trombonist moved with family to Chicago in 1917. Began performing in the early 1920s and worked with Dave Peyton, Erskine Tate, **Jimmie Noone**, **Johnny** and **Baby Dodds**, **Natty Dominique**, and others. Worked and recorded with **Louis Armstrong**'s band in the early 1930s and recorded with Noone, **Richard M. Jones**, and **Punch Miller**. Led his own bands in the 1940s and 1950s. Returned to New Orleans around 1970 and performed at Preservation Hall. Died while on tour with Preservation Hall Jazz Band.

JACKSON, TONY (Antonio Junius Jackson) *Jazz.* Piano, vocals. Composer. (Born Oct. 25, 1882, New Orleans, Orleans Parish; died Apr. 20, 1921, Chicago.)[5] Highly influential but unrecorded early jazz and ragtime pianist and songwriter who was regarded by many peers as the greatest pianist in New Orleans. Also was a major influence on **Jelly Roll Morton**. Turned professional at age 13 and became the most popular entertainer in Storyville District through the early 1910s, known as the "man of a thousand songs" for his vast repertoire in numerous styles from operatic arias to bawdy blues songs. Moved to Chicago in 1912 and published only a fraction of his many compositions, notably "Pretty Baby," selling the majority outright to others for very small amounts of cash per song. Performed in Chicago until his death at age 39 from liver disease.

JACOB, DONALD (*also* Donnie Jacobs) *Rhythm and blues.* Guitar, vocals. Composer. Bandleader. (Born Dec. 31, 1937, Ville Platte, Evangeline Parish.) Ville Platte area rhythm and blues singer-songwriter and guitarist began performing in local black clubs in the 1960s. In 1966 made recording debut for **Floyd Soileau**'s Jin label with single "If You Want Good Lovin'" followed by "Love Repairman" for the label in 1969. Recorded sporadically throughout the 1970s and 1980s with singles on Maison de Soul, Blues Unlimited, and Lanor, having local success with "She Kept Chewing Gum" in 1988. Also released several full-length albums through the 1990s on Lanor and Vidrine, including *Over the Edge* in 1991.

JACOBS, ERNEST *Swamp pop, rhythm and blues.* Piano, trumpet. Bandleader. (Born July 10, 1934, West Monroe, Ouachita Parish; died Apr. 26, 2010, Lake Charles, Calcasieu Parish.) Noted early swamp pop piano player and bandleader best known for his work as original member of **Cookie** and the Cupcakes. Relocated with family to Lake Charles as a child and began playing with **Simon "Kee-Dee" Lubin** in the Boogie Ramblers in the early 1950s, soon taking over leadership upon Lubin's early departure. Recorded for Goldband with group in the mid-1950s and after addition of **Huey "Cookie" Thierry** eventually changed band name to Cookie and the Cupcakes. Continued leading group until it disbanded in the early 1970s, appearing on all of the band's recordings and on sessions backing **Phil Phillips** ("Sea of Love"), **Carol Fran**, **Lil' Alfred**, and others. In the early 1990s reformed the Cupcakes and performed with group nationally and overseas into the 2000s.

JACQUET, ILLINOIS (Jean Baptiste Illinois Jacquet) *Jazz.* Saxophone, bassoon. Composer. Bandleader. (Born Oct. 30, 1919, Broussard, Lafayette Parish; died July 22, 2004, New York City.) Highly influential jazz tenor saxophonist best known for his groundbreaking solo on Lionel Hampton's 1942 classic "Flying Home" and whose pioneering style of aggressive, full-toned playing punctuated by extreme high and low contrasting notes would serve as a blueprint for rhythm and blues and early rock and roll saxophone. Raised in Houston, began playing in high school and in the late 1930s toured regionally with Milt Larkin Orchestra. In 1940 relocated to Los Angeles with brother **Russell Jacquet** and joined Hampton's band. At age 19 recorded "Flying Home" on his debut session and became internationally renowned. After touring with Hampton for two years, worked with Cab Calloway and Count Basie and appeared at the first *Jazz at the Philharmonic* concert before forming his own group, which at times included brother Russell and Charles Mingus. Began recording extensively as a leader and also appeared in several films in the 1940s including *Jammin' the Blues* with Lester Young. Settled in New York and continued performing and recording, touring Europe with Sarah Vaughan and Coleman Hawkins in 1954. Throughout the 1960s and 1970s performed nationally and abroad mainly as a trio and later toured with Arnett Cobb and Buddy Tate as the Texas Tenors. In the early 1980s formed his Big Band and recorded and toured through the 1990s. Continued performing occasionally in the early 2000s until suffering fatal heart attack at age 81. Brother of jazz drummer Linton and saxophonist Julius.

JACQUET, RUSSELL *Jazz.* Trumpet, vocals. Bandleader. (Born Dec. 4, 1917, Broussard, Lafayette Parish; died Mar. 7, 1990, Los Angeles.)[6] Noted jazz trumpeter began performing with brothers Linton, Julius, and **Illinois Jacquet** in the mid-1930s before relocating with Illinois to Los Angeles in 1940. Performed with his own band in 1940s and from 1945 to 1949 recorded as leader for various labels including Globe, Modern Music, Jewel, Sensation, and King. Also worked and recorded with Illinois through the mid-1950s and then sporadically throughout next several decades.

JAFFE, BEN *Jazz.* Tuba, bass. Composer. (Born Jan. 26, 1971, New Orleans, Orleans Parish.) Son of Preservation Hall founders Allan and Sandra Jaffe. Started managing organization and performing with Preservation Hall Jazz Band in the 1990s on bass and tuba. Continued performing, managing, producing, and recording with group as well as serving as creative director of Preservation Hall in the late 2010s.

JAMES, DANNY (James D. Sonnier) *Swamp pop, rhythm and blues.* Guitar, vocals. Composer. (Born Jan. 26, 1945, Sulphur, Calcasieu Parish; died Aug. 12, 1991, Lake Charles, Calcasieu Parish.)[7] Lake Charles–area guitarist and session player best known for his **Tony Joe White**–inspired 1969 Goldband single "Boogie in the Mud." Began performing in the late 1950s with teen rocker Charles Page and in the 1960s and early 1970s had several singles on Goldband as leader. Also worked as session guitarist for Goldband and other independent labels, recording behind **Rockin' Sidney**, **Jo-El Sonnier**, **Van Preston**, **Tommy McLain**, **Charles Mann**, and others. After a decade away from music, returned in the 1980s and performed with Mann's band Louisiana Pride with **Little Alfred**.

JAMES, JOE *Jazz.* Piano, guitar, banjo, vocals. (Born 1901, Algiers, Orleans Parish; died Oct. 18, 1963, New Orleans, Orleans Parish.) Highly regarded New Orleans jazz pianist who was a key member of **Kid Thomas**'s band for several decades. Began playing piano at age 18 and studied with **Manuel Manetta**. Joined Thomas's band in the 1930s and performed and recorded with group until death, appearing on all of band's recordings during that period. In the early 1960s worked with **Emile Barnes** and recorded with Thomas for Riverside's *Living Legends* series.

JAMES, KERWIN *Jazz.* Tuba. Composer. (Born Dec. 1, 1972, New Orleans, Orleans Parish; died Sept. 26, 2007, Houston.)[8] Noted brass-band tuba player and younger brother of **Philip** and **Keith Frazier**. Began playing at age 11 and joined Junior Olympia Brass Band shortly thereafter. Joined brothers in New Birth Brass Band in the 1990s and composed and arranged many of the group's songs. Suffered a stroke in 2006 and died of complications the following year.

JAMES, LOUIS *Jazz.* Clarinet, string bass, saxophone. Bandleader. (Born Apr. 9, 1890, Thibodaux, Lafourche Parish; died Oct. 26, 1967, New Orleans, Orleans Parish.) Early New Orleans jazz multi-instrumentalist began playing clarinet during his teens with the family band. Moved to New Orleans in the mid-1910s and worked in Storyville District with **Kid Rena**, **Amos Riley**, **Jack Carey**, **Frankie Duson**, and others. From 1920 to 1925 performed with James Brothers Orchestra in Thibodaux before returning to New Orleans to work with **Louis Dumaine** and appearing on his famed Jazzola Eight recordings in 1927. Continued performing with Dumaine off and on through 1949, as bassist in later years. In the 1950s worked regularly with **Percy Humphrey** and led Louis James String Band in the 1960s, recording with group in 1965.

JANO, JOHNNY (John Remie Janot Sr.) *Rockabilly, Cajun, country.* Guitar, vocals. Composer. Bandleader. (Born Sept. 14, 1933, Eunice, St. Landry Parish; died Jan. 23, 1984, Beaumont, Texas.) Early Louisiana rockabilly singer-songwriter began a long career in radio before recording for **J. D. Miller** in the mid-1950s, which resulted in single "Havin' a Whole Lot of Fun" on Excello in 1957. Also recorded for producer **Eddie Shuler** and had singles on Goldband and Hollywood in the late 1950s. In the 1960s and 1970s had releases on Lyric, Jador, Lanor, Select, and Showtime, including several country singles. Later cut traditional Cajun recordings for Goldband and Swallow, notably 1983 LP *Johnny Jano Sings Cajun Pure* on Goldband. Based in Beaumont since the early 1970s, continued performing and hosting weekly Cajun radio show until suffering a fatal heart attack at age 50.

JARDELL, ROBERT *Cajun.* Accordion, vocals. Composer. Bandleader. (Born Apr. 25, 1957, Morse, Acadia Parish.) Traditional Cajun accordionist began playing the instrument at age eight, inspired greatly by **Nathan Abshire** and local accordionist Ozanne Guidry (1926–2010). In the mid-1970s began playing with the **Balfa Brothers** and toured with band for more than 10 years, appearing on several recordings with group and in the 1986 film *The Big Easy.* After five years away from music while recovering from a serious auto accident, formed band Pure Cajun and recorded acclaimed self-titled CD on Swallow in 1995. In 1998 released *Cajun Saturday Night Dance* and continued performing with band on club and festival circuit in the 2010s.

JAY (and the Traveliers) *See* Collins, Jay.

JEAN, ULYSSES *Jazz.* Trumpet. (Born Dec. 29, 1903, New Orleans, Orleans Parish; died Feb. 1970, Baton Rouge, EBR Parish.)[9] Early New Orleans jazz trumpeter toured with **Polo Barnes** in the 1930s and worked with **George Lewis** and **Lawrence Marrero** in the 1940s. Uncle of jazz trumpeter Nelson Jean.

JILES, ALBERT, JR. *Jazz.* Drums. (Born Nov. 7, 1905, Thibodaux, Laforche Parish; died Sept. 3, 1964, New Orleans, Orleans Parish.) Hailing from a family of prominent drummers, noted early New Orleans jazz percussionist moved to New Orleans in 1913 and began playing at age 16. In the 1920s worked with **Chris Kelly** and **Lawrence Toca** and through the early 1940s performed with **Kid Howard**, **Kid Clayton**, and **Captain John Handy**. Led his Original Creole Stompers in the late 1940s and 1950s. Recorded with **Wooden Joe Nicholas** in the late 1940s and with **Billie** and **De De Pierce**, **Charlie Love**, and as a leader in the early 1960s. Also appeared regularly at Preservation Hall. Father, Albert Sr., was also noted drummer with Thibodaux brass bands around 1900–1905. Nephew of **Clay Jiles**.

JILES, CLAY *Jazz.* Drums. (Born 1879, Thibodaux, Lafourche Parish; died June 16, 1927, New Orleans, Orleans Parish.)[10] Renowned early New Orleans jazz bass drummer performed early on with Thibodaux's Youka Brass Band. Around 1905 moved to New Orleans and replaced **John Robichaux** in Excelsior Brass Band and performed with group until his death. Also worked with Onward and Allen brass bands. Brother of noted early jazz drummer Albert Jiles Sr. and uncle of **Albert Jiles Jr.**

JOE L. (Joe Louis Carter) *Rhythm and blues.* Vocals, piano. (Born July 31, 1938, Farmerville, Union Parish.)[11] Remarkable but largely unheralded Detroit deep soul singer best known for his soul-blues labor anthem "Please Mr. Foreman." Moved to Detroit as a child and began performing in his teens. Worked full-time in auto assembly plant in the 1960s and in 1968 wrote and recorded "Please Mr. Foreman" on local Clissac label. In 1971 recorded two singles in Memphis for Hi, including updated version of "Please Mr. Foreman" and the searing "I Can't Stand It." Also had releases on local Detroit labels Audrey, Boss, and Valtone in the late 1960s and early 1970s. In 2007 recorded theme song for documentary *The Water Front.* Often mis-credited as Joe Lee Carter.

JOHN, BILLY (Billy John Babineaux) *Swamp pop.* Drums, vocals. Composer. Bandleader. (Born Jan. 7, 1947, St. Martinville, St. Martin Parish; died May 27, 2002, Lafayette, Lafayette Parish.)[12] Swamp pop singer and drummer who led his band the Continentals in the 1960s and released two singles each on Jin and N-Joy, notably "The Alligator" in 1966. Brother of Continental guitarist and vocalist Bobby Babineaux.

JOHN, MABLE *Rhythm and blues, gospel.* Vocals. Composer. (Born Nov. 3, 1930, Bastrop, Morehouse Parish.) Noted rhythm and blues singer and songwriter was raised in Detroit from age 12 and sang in the family gospel group during her teens. In 1956 began performing in Detroit with Berry Gordon and became the first female solo artist signed to his Motown label Tamla. After several singles on Tamla in the early 1960s performed in Chicago for several years before signing with Stax in 1966. Released seven singles for label, including hit "Your Good Thing (Is About to End)" and "Able Mable." In 1969 joined Ray Charles's band as lead singer of the Raelettes and toured and recorded with group until the late 1970s when she left secular music to join the church. Recorded gospel album in 1993 but later made occasional appearances at blues festivals in the 2010s. Older sister of rhythm and blues singer Little Willie John.

JOHNSON, AL "CARNIVAL TIME" *Rhythm and blues.* Vocals, piano, trumpet. Composer. Bandleader. (Born June 20, 1939, New Orleans, Orleans Parish.) New Orleans rhythm and blues performer and songwriter best known for his 1960 local Mardi Gras hit "Carnival Time." Began playing trumpet and piano around age 11, influenced by **Fats Domino**, **Sugar Boy Crawford**, and other local performers early on. Made first recordings in 1956 for Aladdin. In 1958 signed with Ric Records and released "Carnival Time" in 1960, which became a New Orleans Mardi Gras standard. Continued to perform sporadically around New Orleans through the 2010s, appearing at clubs and festivals resplendent in full Mardi Gras regalia.

JOHNSON, ALBERTA FRENCH *Gospel.* Piano, vocals. Bandleader. (Born 1907, New Orleans, Orleans Parish; died July 7, 1968, New Orleans, Orleans Parish.)[13] Influential early gospel singer and bandleader taught herself piano as a child and performed as singer and organist in church in her youth. In 1934 founded Southern Harps Spiritual Singers, who became one of New Orleans's earliest gospel groups to attain national recognition. Led group for several decades and helped launch the careers of prominent gospel singers **Bessie Griffin** and **Linda Hopkins**, who were early members. In 1947 group recorded several sides for King, including "Standing in the Safety Zone," and in 1948 recorded as the Southern Revivalists of New Orleans for Sittin-In-With. A lifelong resident of New Orleans, continued leading Southern Harps until her death at age 61. Brother of jazz musician **Albert "Papa" French** and aunt of Zion Harmonizers founder **Reverend Benjamin Maxon Jr.**

JOHNSON, ALONZO *Zydeco, blues.* Bass. (Born Mar. 22, 1951, Baton Rouge, EBR Parish.) Veteran zydeco and blues bass player began performing in the early 1970s and worked and recorded with **Clifton Chenier**, **Rockin' Dopsie**, **Lil' Buck Sinegal**, **Fernest Arceneaux**, **Henry Gray**, **Jude Taylor**, and others. Also appeared with Rockin' Dopsie on Paul Simon's *Graceland* album in 1986. Continued performing with various groups in the 2010s, including with **Rockin' Dopsie Jr.**

JOHNSON, ARTHUR "YANK" *Jazz.* Trombone. (Born 1878, New Orleans, Orleans Parish; died 1938, New Orleans, Orleans Parish.) Early New Orleans jazz trombonist worked with Imperial and Superior orchestras before World War I and during the 1920s performed with **Sam Morgan**, **Chris Kelly**, and **Willie Pajeaud**. Also worked with **Papa Celestin**'s Tuxedo Brass Band. Younger brother of **Edward "Buddy" Johnson**.

JOHNSON, BERNARD "BUNCHY" *Rhythm and blues.* Drums. Composer. (Born Sept. 30, 1952, New Orleans, Orleans Parish; died Mar. 21, 2010, New Orleans, Orleans Parish.) Highly regarded rhythm and blues drummer first toured in the early 1970s with Johnny Taylor, **King Floyd**, and Candi Staton. Throughout following decades worked and/or recorded with numerous New Orleans rhythm and blues artists, including **Allen Toussaint**, **Dave Bartholomew**, **Aaron Neville**, **Dr. John**, **Wanda Rouzan**, **Deacon John**, and **James Booker**. Also appeared as actor on stage, television, and film.

JOHNSON, BUNK (William Geary/Gary Johnson) *Jazz.* Cornet, trumpet. Bandleader. (Born Dec. 27, 1889, New Orleans, Orleans Parish; died July 7, 1949, New Iberia, Iberia Parish.)[14] Highly renowned early jazz musician whose rediscovery helped launch the traditional New Orleans jazz revival of the 1940s. Claimed to have performed with **Buddy Bolden**'s band and given young

Louis Armstrong music lessons, although early details remain uncertain due to his many unreliable accounts. Toured with traveling bands to California and Texas in years preceding 1910. In the early 1910s worked in New Orleans with several noted groups, including **Frankie Duson**'s Eagle Band and **Billy Marrero**'s Superior Orchestra. Left New Orleans around 1914 and worked with bands in Mandeville, Bogalusa, and Lake Charles in following years. Toured the country with carnival and minstrel shows and by 1920 had settled in New Iberia. Performed with **Gus Fontenette**'s Banner Orchestra, **Evan Thomas**'s Black Eagles, and other Acadiana jazz groups through the early 1930s. Taught music in W.P.A. program in New Iberia in the 1930s and worked outside music for much of the decade. In the late 1930s was rediscovered by jazz researchers **Bill Russell** and Fred Ramsey. Performed and recorded throughout the 1940s and was hailed as a pioneer of the early jazz era and a direct link to Buddy Bolden and his trumpet style. Worked and recorded with **George Lewis**, **Sidney Bechet**, **Danny Barker**, **Baby Dodds**, and other notable musicians throughout the 1940s. After a series of strokes in late 1948, died the following year.

JOHNSON, CEE PEE (Clifford P. Johnson) *Rhythm and blues.* Vocals, tom-tom drums, guitar. Composer. Bandleader. (Born Feb. 22, 1915, Algiers, Orleans Parish; died after 1954.)[15] Swing and jump blues bandleader and vocalist known as "King of the Tom-Toms," settled in Los Angeles in the mid-1930s with brother trombonist Bert Johnson. Performed in L.A.'s premier jazz clubs and by the early 1940s was leading one of the top big bands on the West Coast. Appeared in several films in the early 1940s, including *Citizen Kane* and *Hellzapoppin'* in 1941, and from 1943 to 1947 recorded for AFRS Jubilee, Black & White, Apollo, and Atomic. Best known release was "The G Man Got the T Man," a veiled reference to marijuana prosecution which became a reality with his 1947 arrest on possession charges. Held two-month engagement in Honolulu in late 1947 and toured South America in 1953. Continued performing on southern California club scene in the mid-1950s but remaining details of life and career are unknown.

JOHNSON, DINK (Ollie Johnson) *Jazz, blues.* Piano, drums, clarinet, vocals. Composer. Bandleader. (Born Oct. 28, 1892, New Orleans, Orleans Parish; died Nov. 29, 1954, Portland, Oregon.)[16] Early New Orleans jazz multi-instrumentalist reportedly performed as a pianist in Storyville as well as the Biloxi, Mississippi, area before relocating to California and working as a drummer in his brother **Bill Johnson**'s Original Creole Orchestra around 1913. Continued performing based in Los Angeles in following years, working as a drummer with brother-in-law **Jelly Roll Morton** and recording as clarinetist on **Kid Ory**'s historic 1922 recordings. Throughout the 1920s led bands in Los Angeles (Five Hounds of Jazz) and Chicago (Los Angeles Six) and performed as house pianist at his sister's club in Las Vegas. Semiretired from music in the early 1940s but made additional recordings as a pianist from 1946 to 1950, notably for producer **Bill Russell**'s American Music label.

JOHNSON, EDDIE *Jazz.* Saxophone. Bandleader. (Born Dec. 11, 1920, Napoleonville, Assumption Parish; died Apr. 7, 2010, Evergreen Park, Illinois.) Highly regarded jazz saxophonist who became one of Chicago's most celebrated jazz musicians in his later career. Moved to Chicago with family at age two and started playing saxophone during his teens. In the early to mid-1940s worked in the bands of Johnny Long and Milt Larkin and performed and recorded with Cootie Williams. In 1947 declined an offer to join Duke Ellington's band to work and record with Louis Jordan's Tympany Five. Recorded as a leader for Chess in 1952 and appeared on sessions with Eddie South and Leo Parker, and later James Moody. Worked largely outside of music from 1959 to 1979 except for a 1964 recording session with Ellington and occasional weekend gigs with Red Saunders. Returned to music in 1980 and quickly became one of the most popular and beloved musicians on the Chicago jazz scene. Recorded several albums as a leader, including *Love You Madly* on Delmark in 1999, and continued performing until retiring in 2004.

JOHNSON, EDWARD "BUDDY" *Jazz.* Trombone. (Born June 1872, Algiers, Orleans Parish; died 1927, New Orleans, Orleans Parish.)[17] Very early New Orleans jazz trombonist performed with Allen and Pacific brass bands around 1900 and worked with **Manuel Perez** several years later. In 1910 worked with Superior Orchestra with **Bunk Johnson** and **Big Eye Louis Nelson**, and through the early 1920s performed with Onward, Tuxedo, and Excelsior brass bands. Around 1925 worked regularly with Perez. Older brother of **Arthur "Yank" Johnson**.

JOHNSON, EDWARD "NOON" *Jazz.* Bazooka, guitar, banjo, harmonica, vocals. (Born Aug. 24, 1903, New Orleans, Orleans Parish; died Sept. 18, 1969, New Orleans, Orleans Parish.)[18] Early New Orleans jazz multi-instrumentalist began performing for tips as a child on the streets in the Storyville District with homemade instruments. Later performed with **Papa Celestin**'s Tuxedo Brass Band. Recorded as vocalist with **Bunk Johnson** in 1945 and on bazooka with **Danny Barker** in 1969. Performed regularly at Preservation Hall in the 1960s.

JOHNSON, ERNIE *Rhythm and blues.* Vocals. Bandleader. (Born Apr. 4, 1939, Winnsboro, Franklin Parish.) Noted veteran soul-blues singer moved to Dallas in the late 1950s and began singing professionally several years later, inspired by Bobby Bland. In the late 1960s formed his band the Soul Blenders and made recording debut with "Loving You" on Ride in 1968. Releases followed on Rowan, Steph and Lee, Paula, and Ronn through the 1980s. In the 1990s and 2000s had releases on Waldoxy, Phat Sounds, and Stairway Ent., notably *In the Mood* in 1995. Continued performing into the 2010s, appearing regularly at R.L.'s Blues Palace in Dallas.

JOHNSON, GWEN "GYPSY BRICK" *Rhythm and blues, jazz.* Vocals. (Born Feb. 21, 1933, New Orleans, Orleans Parish; died Aug. 31, 2007, Runnemede, New Jersey.) Sister of **Ray** and **Plas Johnson**, began singing at age four and performed with family band around New Orleans. Recorded for Peacock in 1952 and settled in California in the mid-1950s, singing backup for Frank Sinatra, Dean Martin, and Nat King Cole. Signed with RCA in 1963 and recorded as studio singer with three-octave range.

JOHNSON, HERMAN E. *Blues.* Guitar, vocals. Composer. (Born Aug. 18, 1909, Scotlandville, EBR Parish; died Feb. 2, 1975, Baton Rouge, EBR Parish.) Baton Rouge–area country blues guitarist and singer-songwriter began playing guitar during his late teens. Worked mainly outside music throughout life but made a series of recordings for folklorist Harry Oster in 1961 which included autobiographical originals such as "Depression Blues" and "Leavin' Blues." Often employed knife blade as a guitar slide to underscore song's melody. Retired from music after suffering a stroke in 1970.

JOHNSON, HUGH *Cajun.* Fiddle, vocals. (Born Apr. 29, 1928, Lake Arthur, Jeff. Davis Parish; died Mar. 4, 2015, Jennings, Jeff. Davis Parish.) Noted Cajun fiddler began playing at age 12 and within a few years was performing at local house dances. From the late 1950s through following decades performed and recorded with numerous Cajun musicians, including **Sidney Brown**, **Joe Bonsall**, **Phil Menard**, **Lesa Cormier**, **Ed Gary**, and **Johnny Jano**.

JOHNSON, J.J. *See* Johnson, Wallace.

JOHNSON, JAMES "CHICKEN SCRATCH" *Blues.* Guitar, bass, vocals. Composer. Bandleader. (Born Apr. 8, 1940, Erwinville, WBR Parish.) Influential early Baton Rouge blues guitarist best known for his long tenure with **Slim Harpo**'s band the King Bees. Began playing guitar in his teens, inspired by a performance by Albert Collins. At age 18 moved to Baton Rouge and performed with **Big Papa Tilley**'s band before joining Harpo the following year. Performed and recorded with Harpo through the late 1960s, appearing on several hits, including "Baby Scratch My Back" on which he provided its signature "chicken scratch" guitar lines. Worked outside music until the mid-1990s and began performing with **Raful Neal** and others. Continued playing primarily around Baton Rouge in subsequent years, releasing first recording as leader, *Stingin' & Buzzin',* in 2014.

JOHNSON, JAMES "STEADY ROLL" *Blues, jazz.* Violin, piano, guitar, vocals. (Born 1888, New Orleans, Orleans Parish; died East St. Louis, Illinois, early 1960s, unconfirmed.) Older brother of **Lonnie Johnson**, learned several instruments from musician father and began performing in family string band. Worked with brother Lonnie in the 1910s and 1920s and recorded for OKeh as sideman and on several sides as leader. In 1927 appeared on sessions for Gennett backing several blues artists, including Henry Johnson and Lizzie Washington. Reportedly continued performing through the 1950s.

JOHNSON, JOAN MARIE *Rhythm and blues.* Vocals. (Born Jan. 15, 1944, New Orleans, Orleans Parish—Oct. 5, 2016, New Orleans, Orleans Parish.) Founding member of New Orleans rhythm and blues vocal trio the Dixie Cups with cousins **Barbara Ann** and **Rosa Lee Hawkins**. Group had several hits in the mid-1960s, including "Chapel of Love" and "Iko Iko." Left group in 1966 due to illness and retired from music.

JOHNSON, JOE *Blues.* Vocals, harmonica. Composer. Bandleader. (Born Jan. 9, 1942, Independence, Tangipahoa Parish.) Swamp blues singer and harmonica player who recorded for **J. D. Miller** in Crowley in 1966–67 with singles on A-Bet and Cry. In the early 1970s led bands in Dallas and east Texas.

JOHNSON, LONNIE (Alonzo Johnson) *Blues, jazz.* Guitar, banjo, violin, piano, vocals. Composer. Bandleader. (Born Feb. 8, 1894, New Orleans, Orleans Parish; died June 16, 1970, Toronto.)[19] One of the most influential guitarists of the twentieth century, who pioneered the modern blues guitar style through the use of phrasing and soloing while incorporating vibrato and string bends. Heavily influenced T-Bone Walker, Robert Johnson, Charlie Christian, B.B. King, and countless others. Learned guitar and violin from his musician father and began performing in his early teens around New Orleans in his family's string band. In the mid-1910s performed in Storyville district, often with brother **James Johnson**. Also worked in duo with **Punch Miller** and in 1917 toured London with musical revue. In the early 1920s worked on riverboats with **Fate Marable** and Charles Creath and toured black theater circuit in the South. Settled in St. Louis and from 1925 to 1932 made well over 100 recordings as leader for OKeh and became a national recording star. Also recorded with **Louis Armstrong**, Duke Ellington, Victoria Spivey, Eddie Lang, and Texas Alexander. Relocated to Chicago and in the late 1930s and 1940s recorded for Decca and Bluebird and worked with **Baby Dodds** and **Kid Ory**. In 1947 signed with King and had series of hits, including "Tomorrow Night." Settled in Philadelphia in the mid-1950s and worked outside music. Enjoyed career resurgence in the 1960s with recordings on Prestige/Bluesville and toured overseas. Died at age 76 while living in Toronto after complications from being struck by a car the previous year.

JOHNSON, PLAS *Rhythm and blues, jazz.* Saxophone, vocals. Composer. Bandleader. (Born July 21, 1931, Donaldsonville, Ascension Parish.) Highly accomplished saxophonist and studio musician whose work has appeared on hundreds of jazz, blues, rock, pop, and soundtrack recordings. Best known for his lead playing on Henry Mancini's "Pink Panther Theme." Began performing in family band in New Orleans as a child and in the late 1940s formed the Johnson Brothers Combo with older brother **Ray Johnson**. Toured with Charles Brown in 1951 and settled in California in 1954. Worked with Johnny Otis in 1955 and went on to become one of the most prolific and sought-after studio musicians in Los Angeles. Throughout the next several decades appeared on sessions with such diverse artists as Ella Fitzgerald, the Beach Boys, B.B. King, Little Richard, Duane Eddy, Sam Cooke, the Platters, Frank Sinatra, T-Bone Walker, Diana Ross, Ray Charles, Marvin Gaye, Elton John, Barbra Streisand, and countless others. Also had numerous releases as a leader on Capitol and other labels and appeared on well over 100 major film and television soundtracks. In the 1970s performed as member of the studio band on *The Merv Griffin Show.* Recorded as a leader and session musician through the late 2000s and continued performing at clubs and festivals in the 2010s. Brother of **Gwen "Gypsy Brick" Johnson**.

JOHNSON, RAY *Rhythm and blues, jazz.* Piano, bass, vocals. Composer. Bandleader. (Born Apr. 3, 1930, New Orleans, Orleans Parish; died Mar. 16, 2013, Los Angeles.) Raised in a musical family in New Orleans, noted blues and jazz pianist began playing at age four and in the late 1940s formed Johnson Brothers Combo with brother **Plas Johnson**, recording for DeLuxe in 1949. In 1953 recorded for Mercury and relocated to Los Angeles the following year. Recorded extensively as session musician throughout next several decades with artists such as T-Bone Walker, Sam Cooke, Nat King Cole, Ricky Nelson, Frank Sinatra, and others. Also recorded as leader for numerous labels in the 1950s and 1960s. Appeared on several television shows in the 1960s, including *The Johnny Otis Show* and *Shindig.* Toured internationally and continued performing through the 2000s. In 2000 released CD *Ray Johnson Bluz* on Goad, which featured duet with sister **Gwen "Gypsy Brick" Johnson**.

JOHNSON, ROBERT "NIGHTHAWK" *Blues, gospel.* Guitar, vocals. Composer. (Born Dec. 5, 1916, Crowley, Acadia Parish; died Feb. 1974, Cleveland, Mississippi.) Mississippi Delta blues and gospel singer and bottleneck slide guitarist who made field recordings for folklorist George Mitchell in 1969, notably "Hold My Body Down." Relocated with family at age three to farming community of Skene, Mississippi, just south of Cleveland, and began playing guitar at age eight. Performed in area juke joints until the early 1950s when he joined the church, performing only gospel music thereafter.

JOHNSON, SMOKEY (Joseph Johnson) *Rhythm and blues.* Drums, trombone. Composer. (Born Nov. 14, 1936, New Orleans, Orleans Parish; died Oct. 6, 2015, New Orleans, Orleans Parish.) Highly regarded and influential drummer who helped define the New Orleans rhythm and blues and early funk sound of the 1960s. Greatly influenced by **Earl Palmer**. Began playing drums around age 12 and during his teens started performing in New Orleans clubs. Worked with **Dave Bartholomew** and spent 28 years as member of **Fats Domino**'s band. Appeared on numerous recording sessions in the 1960s with **Professor Longhair**, **Eddie Bo**, **Earl King**, and others. Cowrote and recorded Mardi Gras brass-band classic "It Ain't My Fault" with **Wardell Quezergue** in 1964. Retired from music in 1993 after suffering a stroke.

JOHNSON, THEARD *Rhythm and blues.* Vocals. Bandleader. (Born Oct. 23, 1927, New Orleans, Orleans Parish; died Sept. 22, 1990, Chalmette, St. Bernard Parish.) Rhythm and blues singer who recorded for Mercury as a leader and also as vocalist with George Miller's Mid-Drifts in 1949. Also worked with **Dave Bartholomew**'s band in the late 1940s.

JOHNSON, WALLACE *Rhythm and blues.* Vocals. Composer. (Born Oct. 8, 1937, Napoleonville, Assumption Parish.) New Orleans soul singer best known for his recordings produced by **Allen Toussaint** in the 1960s and 1990s. Initially inspired by seeing a performance by **Roy Brown**, moved to New Orleans with family to become a recording artist in the late 1950s. Recorded a single for A.F.O. in 1962 but returned soon after to Napoleonville and worked as opening act at Thibodaux's famed club the Sugar Bowl. In 1965 returned to New Orleans and had one release on Booker as J.J. Johnson and recorded several singles produced by Toussaint on Sansu and RCA between 1967 and 1972. Worked outside music in Napoleonville until 1996 when he recorded his first full-length album, *Whoever's Thrilling You,* with Toussaint for NYNO. Continued to work outside music until 2010, when he made a rare appearance at the Ponderosa Stomp in New Orleans.

JOLIVETTE, NAT (Nathaniel A. Jolivette) *Rhythm and blues, zydeco.* Drums. (Born Apr. 18, 1946, Lafayette, Lafayette Parish; died Aug. 13, 2007, Lafayette, Lafayette Parish.) Accomplished rhythm and blues and zydeco drummer began playing drums in high school and throughout his 40-plus-year career worked and/or recorded with **Clifton Chenier**, **Buckwheat Zydeco**, **Rockin' Dopsie**, **Little Buck Sinegal**'s Top Cats, **Little Bob** and the Lollipops, **Jewell Douglas**, and many others.

JONES, BENNY, SR. *Jazz.* Bass drum, snare drum. Bandleader. (Born Aug. 11, 1943, New Orleans, Orleans Parish.) Important and influential brass-band musician and bandleader since the late 1970s. Son of drummer Chester Jones of Onward, Tuxedo, and Eureka brass bands, joined **Danny Barker**'s Fairview Baptist Church Band in the late 1960s. In 1977 formed Dirty Dozen Brass Band, which incorporated funk and rhythm and blues into the standard brass-band repertoire. Worked with Olympia and **Tuba Fats**'s Chosen Few Brass Band in the late 1980s and early 1990s. In 1994 formed Tremé Brass Band and performed on snare with **Uncle Lionel Batiste** on bass drum. Continued to record and perform with Tremé in the late 2010s.

JONES, BOBBY (*also* Bobby Jonz) *Rhythm and blues.* Vocals. Composer. Bandleader. (Born Jan. 2, 1936, Farmerville, Union Parish.) Veteran soul-blues singer moved to Chicago in 1959 and began performing on the local blues scene. In the 1960s had releases on Vee-Jay, U.S.A., TMP-Ting, and Expo, including LP *Talkin' 'Bout Jones* in 1968. Relocated to Florida in the 1970s and had releases on Lionel, Capri, and Adam before returning to Chicago in 1977. In the 1980s changed stage name to Bobby Jonz with releases on Expansion, Dispo, Fantasy, and Kap and began performing in Las Vegas. In the 1990s and 2000s had numerous southern soul releases on Ace, Avanti, Big Bidness, and his own Red Dot label. Returned to his Chicago blues roots with *Comin' Back Hard* on Delta Groove in 2009 and continued performing and recording into the 2010s.

JONES, CONNIE (Conrad Rodman Jones III) *Jazz.* Trumpet, cornet, vocals. Bandleader. (Born Mar. 22, 1934, New Orleans, Orleans Parish; died Feb. 14, 2019, New Orleans, Orleans Parish.) Renowned New Orleans jazz trumpeter began playing on Bourbon Street at age 18 with **Pete Fountain**'s Basin Street Six and later worked with **Santo Pecora**, **Freddie Kohlman**, and Jack Teagarden's last band. Performed regularly with his Crescent City Jazz Band in nightclubs and festivals for several decades and from the 1990s through early 2000s worked as bandleader on Mississippi steamboats. Recorded several albums for Jazzology and Maison Bourbon, including *Yellow Dog Blues* in 2002, and continued performing until announcing his retirement in 2016.

JONES, DAVID "DAVEY" *Jazz.* Saxophone, mellophone. Composer. Bandleader. (Born around 1888, Lutcher, St. James Parish; died around 1956, Los Angeles.) Early New Orleans jazz saxophonist began performing around Lutcher in 1910 with the Holmes Brass Band before moving to New Orleans several years later and working in Storyville District. In the late 1910s and 1920s worked with **Fate Marable** on the steamer *S.S. Capitol* (with **Louis Armstrong**), **King Oliver** in Chicago, and **Bébé Ridgley**. Formed Jones-Collins Astoria Hot Eight with **Lee Collins** in the late 1920s, which made six celebrated recordings in 1929. Later relocated to Los Angeles.

JONES, EDDIE LEE *See* Guitar Slim [Notable Musicians Born outside Louisiana].

JONES, JOE *Rhythm and blues.* Vocals, piano. Composer. Bandleader. (Born Aug. 12, 1926, New Orleans, Orleans Parish; died Nov. 27, 2005, Los Angeles.) Rhythm and blues pianist and bandleader worked with **Roy Brown** in the late 1940s and appeared on Brown's 1947 hit "Good Rocking Tonight." Worked with B.B. King in the early 1950s and recorded for Capital and Roulette later that decade. In 1960 recorded hit "You Talk Too Much" on Ric and in 1963 discovered and managed New Orleans vocal group the Dixie Cups. Settled in California in the early 1970s and worked in music publishing.

JONES, LEROY *Jazz.* Trumpet. Bandleader. (Born Feb. 20, 1958, New Orleans, Orleans Parish.) Noted brass-band trumpeter and bandleader began performing with **Danny Barker**'s Fairview Baptist Church Band at age 12. In 1974 reformed group into Hurricane Brass Band. Toured with Eddie Vinson and Della Reese in the late 1970s and formed Leroy Jones Quintet. Throughout the early 1980s led New Orleans's Finest and toured Europe. In the 1990s and 2000s recorded as leader and worked with **Harry Connick Jr.**, **Dr. John**, and Preservation Hall Jazz Band. Continued to tour internationally in the 2010s.

JONES, LUKE *Rhythm and blues.* Saxophone, clarinet. Bandleader. (Born Oct. 18, 1910, Shreveport, Caddo Parish; died Dec. 27, 1995, Los Angeles.) Noted West Coast jump blues bandleader and saxophonist was raised in Los Angeles from a child. In the late 1930s began performing on L.A.'s Central Avenue music scene with Lionel Hampton and Roy Milton. In the 1940s formed jump blues trio with pianist Betty Hall Jones and recorded numerous sides for Atlas in 1946–47, including "She's My Baby" with vocalist **Clarence Williams**. Recorded a single for Modern in 1949.

JONES, RICHARD M. *Jazz.* Piano, cornet, alto horn, vocals. Composer. Bandleader. (Born June 13, 1889, Donaldsonville, Ascension Parish; died Dec. 8, 1945, Chicago.)[20] Early New Orleans jazz multi-instrumentalist and bandleader best known for his many early jazz and blues compositions, such as "Trouble in Mind" and "Riverside Blues." Around 1902 began performing with Eureka Brass Band and worked in New Orleans from 1908 through 1917, mainly as pianist. Formed group Four Hot Hounds in 1910, which included future jazz "king" **Joe Oliver**. Also worked with **John Robichaux**, **Armand Piron**, and **Papa Celestin**. Moved to Chicago around 1919 and worked with **Clarence Williams** as publisher and record promoter. In the 1920s and 1930s recorded as leader and sideman and served as session organizer for various labels, including Gennett, OKeh, Victor, and Paramount, and produced **Louis Armstrong**'s historic Hot Five early sessions. In the 1940s recorded with **Johnny Dodds** and **Jimmie Noone** and worked as talent scout for Mercury.

JONES, LITTLE SONNY/"SKINNY DYNAMO" (John Jones) *Rhythm and blues.* Vocals. Composer. (Born Apr. 15, 1931, New Orleans, Orleans Parish; died Dec. 17, 1989, New Orleans, Orleans Parish.) New Orleans rhythm and blues vocalist began performing in the late 1940s and from the early 1950s through 1961 worked as warm-up singer for friend **Fats Domino**, who dubbed him "Skinny Dynamo." Recorded for Specialty in 1952, Imperial in 1954 (as Little Sonny Jones), and Marlin in 1955 (as Skinny Dynamo). In the 1960s worked with **David** and **Melvin Lastie** and recorded LP *New Orleans R&B Gems* on Black Magic in 1975. Not to be confused with **T. J. Richardson**, who also recorded as "Skinny Dynamo" for Excello, or George Sanders LeBlanc, who appeared as "Skinny Dynamo" on Aladdin.

JONES, WILL "DUB" *Rhythm and blues, gospel.* Vocals. Bandleader. (Born May 14, 1928, Shreveport, Caddo Parish; died Jan. 16, 2000, Long Beach, California.) Noted early doo-wop and rhythm and blues singer best known for his bass vocal work with the 1950s group the Coasters. Began performing with gospel groups in the late 1940s and had rhythm and blues hit "Stranded in the Jungle" with the Cadets in 1956. Also recorded on sessions with **Richard Berry**, Jesse Belvin, and others. In 1958 joined the Coasters and appeared on numerous recordings, including hits "Yakety Yak," "Charlie Brown," and "Along Came Jones." In later years worked with several gospel groups, including the Mighty Travelers, and performed with various incarnations of the Coasters.

JONZ, BOBBY *See* Jones, Bobby.

JORDAN, KIDD (Edward Jordan) *Jazz, rhythm and blues.* Saxophone. Composer. Bandleader. (Born May 5, 1935, Crowley, Acadia Parish.) Influential avant-garde jazz saxophonist and educator moved to New Orleans in 1955 after majoring in music education at Southern University, influenced greatly by Charlie Parker. In following years worked with numerous musicians including **Guitar Slim**, Big Joe Turner, Ray Charles, Big Maybelle, **Ellis Marsalis Jr.**, Stevie Wonder, and Aretha Franklin. Also recorded as session musician and appeared on recordings with **Professor Longhair**, **Larry Williams**, **Johnny Adams**, and **Hamid Drake**, among many others. As an educator, former students include **Branford** and

Wynton Marsalis, **Charles Joseph**, **Trombone Shorty**, **Brian Quezergue**, and **Big Sam**. Recorded numerous albums as leader or coleader, including *Palm of Soul* with **Hamid Drake** on AUM Fidelity in 2006. Continued performing in his 80s.

JOSEPH, CHARLES *Jazz.* Trombone. (Born Feb. 21, 1955, New Orleans, Orleans Parish.) Noted trombone player performed with Majestic, Hurricane, and Tornado brass bands and was founding member of Dirty Dozen Brass Band in 1977 with brother **Kirk Joseph**. Performed and recorded with the influential group through 1991 and toured internationally. Later worked with Tremé Brass Band. In the 2000s performed with brother's Backyard Groove and in the 2010s worked with Jambalaya Brass Band. Son of **Waldren "Frog" Joseph**.

JOSEPH, KIRK *Jazz.* Sousaphone. Composer. Bandleader. (Born Feb. 16, 1961, New Orleans, Orleans Parish.) Exceptional sousaphone player who helped shape the modern New Orleans brass-band sound in the 1970s and 1980s. Son of **Waldren "Frog" Joseph**, began playing sousaphone in his teens, inspired by **Tuba Fats**. Worked first gig at age 13 with older brother **Charles Joseph** in Majestic Brass Band. In 1977 was founding member of Dirty Dozen Brass Band and performed with group through 1991. Later worked with Tremé and Forgotten Souls brass bands. In 2000s founded Backyard Groove and continued to record and perform with group into the 2010s. In 2017 reunited with Dirty Dozen Brass Band for group's 40th anniversary.

JOSEPH, OZMA "PAPA JOHN" *Jazz, rhythm and blues.* String bass, clarinet, guitar, saxophone. Bandleader. (Born Nov. 27, 1879, St. James Parish, Louisiana; died Jan. 22, 1965, New Orleans, Orleans Parish.)[21] Raised in a large family of musicians, early New Orleans jazz multi-instrumentalist moved to New Orleans in 1906 and performed in Storyville District. Worked with numerous top jazz musicians in New Orleans, including **King Oliver**, **Kid Ory**, **Louis Dumaine**, **Armand Piron**, and **Manuel Manetta** and in the mid- to late 1910s performed in rural Louisiana with **Gus Fontenette**'s Banner Band, **Evan Thomas**'s Black Eagles, and **Claiborne Williams**'s orchestra. Returned to performing after 20-year break in the 1940s and through the 1960s recorded with jazz and rhythm and blues artists **Smiley Lewis**, **George Lewis**, **Punch Miller**, **Kid Thomas**, and others. Gained fame in later years as beloved elder statesman of jazz. Died on stage at Preservation Hall after performing "When the Saints Go Marching In." Older brother of **Willie Joseph**.

JOSEPH, WALDREN "FROG" *Jazz, rhythm and blues.* Trombone, piano, drums. Bandleader. (Born Sept. 12, 1918, New Orleans, Orleans Parish; died Sept. 19, 2004, New Orleans, Orleans Parish.) Patriarch of noted New Orleans jazz family, toured South with **Joe Robichaux** in the late 1930s. In the 1940s worked with **Sidney Desvigne**, **Octave Crosby**, and **Papa Celestin**'s Tuxedo Brass Band. In the 1950s toured with rhythm and blues artist **Lee Allen** and recorded with **Dave Bartholomew**, **Earl King**, **Smiley Lewis**, and Big Joe Turner. Throughout the 1960s worked and recorded with numerous noted jazz musicians, including **Paul Barbarin**, **Papa French**, and **Louis Cottrell Jr.** Performed regularly with New Camelia Jazz Band in the 1980s and early 1990s. Father of musicians Gerald, **Charles**, and **Kirk Joseph**.

JOSEPH, WILLIE SIMON "KAISER" *Jazz.* Clarinet. (Born Sept. 28, 1887, St. James Parish; died Nov. 2, 1951, Orleans Parish, Orleans Parish.)[22] Early New Orleans jazz clarinetist performed in Storyville District through its closure in 1917 and in the 1920s worked with **Bébé Ridgley**'s Tuxedo Orchestra. In 1927 recorded with **Louis Dumaine**'s Jazzola Eight and **Ann Cook** and in the 1930s worked with **Percy Humphrey** and **Willie Pajeaud**. Younger brother of **Papa John Joseph**.

JULES, JIMMY "PISTOL" (Charley Julien) *Rhythm and blues.* Vocals, piano. Composer. Bandleader. (Born Mar. 25, 1937, New Orleans, Orleans Parish.) New Orleans soul singer and songwriter who had recordings in the 1960s and 1970s on Atlantic, Gamble, Abet, Carnival, and Jim Gem, notably "Talk About You" and "Ten Carat Fool." Worked with Marvin Gaye, Otis Redding, and Little Willie John and wrote songs for Johnny Taylor, Archie Bell, Etta James, and others. In 1977 released LP *Jimmy Jules & the Nuclear Soul System* on Jim Gem. Continued to perform occasionally in the 2010s.

K

KAT (Ida Mae Irvin) *Rhythm and blues.* Vocals. Composer. Bandleader. (Born Mar. 27, 1944, Carencro, Lafayette Parish; died Oct. 15, 1999, Lafayette, Lafayette Parish.) Lafayette area rhythm and blues singer who led her band Kat and the Kittens in the 1980s and 1990s. Released two singles on Blues Unlimited, including "Yes, I've Been Crying" in 1980. Also appeared as vocalist on a single each with **Fernest Arceneaux** and **Buckwheat Zydeco**'s Ils Sont Partis band on Blues Unlimited. Suffered fatal stroke while performing at the New Blue Angel Club at age 55. Brother Peter Irvin Jr. (1941–2018) was a longtime drummer with **Roscoe Chenier**.

K-DOE, ERNIE (Ernest Kador Jr.) *Rhythm and blues.* Vocals, drums. Composer. Bandleader. (Born Feb. 22, 1936, New Orleans, Orleans Parish; died July 5, 2001, New Orleans, Orleans Parish.)[1] Beloved New Orleans rhythm and blues performer and singer-songwriter known for his 1961 hit "Mother-In-Law" who in later years became an iconic cultural figure celebrated for his flamboyant and eccentric style. Began performing at talent shows during his teens and recorded for Specialty in 1955 and Ember in 1958. In the early 1960s worked with **Allen Toussaint** for Minit and reached number one on *Billboard*'s pop and R&B charts with "Mother-In-Law." Numerous singles followed on Minit and Instant, including minor hit "Te-Ta-Te-Ta-Ta." In the mid- to late 1960s had numerous releases on Duke and in the 1970s released singles on Sansu, Janus, and Island. Worked as a local radio disc jockey but remained musically inactive for much of the 1980s. In the 1990s enjoyed career resurgence and opened famed Mother-In-Law Lounge in the city's historic Tremé neighborhood, often performing in colorful attire complete with gold crown and cape as the self-proclaimed "Emperor of the Universe."

KEGLEY, WILL (Wilson Kegley) *Cajun.* Fiddle, guitar, vocals. Composer. Bandleader. (Born Apr. 2, 1917, Evangeline, Acadia Parish; died Jan. 20, 1985, Lafayette, Lafayette Parish.) Renowned early postwar Cajun fiddler best known for his long association with **Nathan Abshire** as founding member of the Pine Grove Boys. Began playing on a homemade fiddle around age five and performed at house dances in the 1930s before forming Lake Charles Playboys with **Ernest Thibodeaux** and **T-Boy Esthay** in 1938. After World War II, renamed band Pine Grove Boys and soon added Abshire on accordion. Performed and recorded with group until the mid-1950s when convicted of stabbing bandmate **Atlas Frugé** and served a year in prison. Also performed with **Iry LeJeune** and **Lawrence Walker** and later worked with **Andrew Cormier**, **Rodney LeJeune**, and **Shorty Sonnier**. Continued performing until retiring from music in the early 1980s, based in Crowley in later years. Older sister Ozide Kegley (1914–1984) was a drummer with Lake Charles Playboys and Pine Grove Boys.

KELLEY, ARTHUR "GUITAR" *Blues.* Guitar, vocals. Composer. (Born Nov. 14, 1922, Clinton, E. Feliciana Parish; died Sept. 17, 2001, Baton Rouge, EBR Parish.) Noted Baton Rouge swamp blues guitarist and singer best known for his long association with **Silas Hogan**. Began playing guitar as a child and performed in church during his teens. Started playing house parties in the 1940s and in 1950s worked regularly in local clubs with **Lightnin' Slim**, who was a major influence. From the mid-1960s through 1980s performed regularly with Hogan. In 1970 recorded several sides for Arhoolie LP *Louisiana Blues* and recorded a single for Excello. Toured Europe several times and appeared regularly at **Tabby Thomas**'s Blues Box in the 1980s and 1990s.

KELLY, CHRIS *Jazz.* Cornet. Bandleader. (Born Oct. 18, 1890, Deer Range, Plaquemines Parish; died Aug. 19, 1929, New Orleans, Orleans Parish.)[2] Highly regarded but unrecorded early New Orleans jazz cornetist and bandleader studied under **Professor Jim Humphrey** at age 16. Moved to New Orleans with family in 1915. After serving in World War I, replaced **Edward Clem** in Magnolia Orchestra in the late 1910s. Led popular bands throughout the 1920s and was regarded as among the best cornetists in New Orleans. His bluesy and highly emotive playing style influenced **De De Pierce**, **Lawrence Toca**, and **Kid Howard**. Died of multiple organ failure due to alcoholism.

KELLY, GUY *Jazz.* Trumpet, vocals. (Born Nov. 22, 1906, Scotlandville, EBR Parish; died Feb. 24, 1940, Chicago.) Noted early New Orleans jazz trumpeter influenced greatly by **Louis Armstrong**. Regarded as one of New Orleans's top players in the late 1920s, along with **Red Allen** and **Lee Collins**. Worked regularly with **Papa Celestin** after arriving in New Orleans in 1927 and recorded with Celestin in 1928. Following year moved to Chicago and worked with **Jimmie Noone**, **Little Brother Montgomery**, Dave Peyton, Tiny Parham, and others. Appeared on recordings with Noone (notably "The Blues Jumped a Rabbit"), Albert Ammons, Frankie "Half-Pint" Jaxon, and Art Tatum in the 1930s.

KENNE' WAYNE (Kenneth Wayne Landry) *Rhythm and blues.* Vocals. Composer. Bandleader. (Born Sept. 3, 1966, Crowley, Acadia Parish.) Southern soul singer-songwriter began performing during his teens and made recording debut with *Old Fashioned Love* on Master-Trak in 1996, which contained regional hit "Innocent Until Proven Guilty." More releases followed on Master-Trak as well as G Street and Goodtime. Continued performing on southern soul circuit in the 2010s, having some local success with zydeco-infused "Ride It Like a Cowboy," featuring **Leon Chavis.**

KENNEDY, JERRY/"JERRY GLENN" *Rockabilly, country, rhythm and blues.* Guitar, vocals. Composer. Bandleader. (Born Aug. 10, 1940, Shreveport, Caddo Parish.) Highly accomplished guitarist and producer who appeared on numerous recordings by artists such as **Jerry Lee Lewis**, Bob Dylan, Elvis Presley, Johnny Hallyday, Roy Orbison, Ruth Brown, and many others. Began playing guitar around age eight, originally inspired by performers on the *Louisiana Hayride* such as Tillman Franks and later by guitarists Scotty Moore and Chuck Berry. At age 11 was signed to RCA and recorded debut single under name Jerry Glenn in 1953. Continued working as session guitarist while in high school and in 1958 recorded single "Teenage Love Is Misery" for Decca. After touring with *Louisiana Hayride* package shows in the late 1950s moved to Nashville and signed with Mercury as recording artist and session guitarist. In the 1960s and 1970s released recordings on Mercury and Smash as a leader and with Tommy Tomlinson as Tom and Jerry. Also worked extensively as successful producer with Mercury for artists such as Lewis, Tom T. Hall, Roger Miller, Reba McIntire, and others. Husband of country singer Linda Brannon, who recorded for **Mira Smith**'s RAM label.

KENNEDY, WILLIE MAE *Gospel.* Vocals. (Born Sept. 8, 1936, Natchitoches, Natch. Parish.) Locally renowned gospel singer who was member of the Gospelrettes of Natchitoches for more than 50 years, touring Louisiana, Texas, and Arkansas. Continued to sing in churches and at special events into her 80s.

KENNER, CHRIS *Rhythm and blues.* Vocals. Composer. (Born Dec. 25, 1928, Kenner, Jefferson Parish; died Jan. 28, 1976, New Orleans, Orleans Parish.)[3] New Orleans rhythm and blues singer and influential songwriter best known for his compositions such as "Sick and Tired" and "Something You Got." Began singing as a child in church and later joined the Harmonizing Four gospel group. Made recording debut in 1956 for Baton and following year had first hit with "Sick and Tired" on Imperial, which was later covered by **Fats Domino**. After singles on Ron and Pontchartrain in the late 1950s, worked with **Allen Toussaint** for Instant in the 1960s and released hits "I Like It Like That," "Something You Got," and "Land of 1000 Dances." Released several more singles on small local labels and performed sporadically through the mid-1970s before succumbing to a fatal heart attack at age 48.

KENT, LUTHER (Kent Rowell) *Rhythm and blues.* Vocals, drums, piano. Bandleader. (Born June 23, 1948, New Orleans, Orleans Parish.) Known for leading large, horn-based New Orleans rhythm and blues bands, popular blue-eyed soul singer began performing professionally at age 14 and made recording debut with "I Wanna Know" for Montel as "Dynamic Duke Royal" in the mid-1960s. Worked as lead singer with Blood, Sweat & Tears in the mid-1970s. Formed Trick Bag in the late 1970s and performed with group through the late 1990s, releasing several recordings, including *It's in the Bag* on Renegade in 1987. Continued performing in the 2010s as leader of own group and as occasional guest vocalist with reformed traditional jazz band Dukes of Dixieland.

KEPPARD, FREDDIE *Jazz.* Cornet, violin, mandolin, accordion, guitar. Bandleader. (Born Feb. 27, 1889, New Orleans, Orleans Parish; died July 15, 1933, Chicago.)[4] Highly renowned early New Orleans jazz multi-instrumentalist and bandleader who succeeded **Buddy Bolden** as the "king" of cornet players and is believed to have performed closely in Bolden's influential style. Brother of **Louis Keppard**, began playing cornet at age 16 and by 1907 was leading Olympia Orchestra, which at times included **Alphonse Picou**, **Sidney Bechet**, **George Baquet**, **Jimmie Noone**, and **King Oliver**. In 1914 moved to Los Angeles at the request of **Bill Johnson** and toured for several years with Original Creole Orchestra, settling in Chicago by 1918. Led bands in Chicago in the 1920s and also worked with Noone, Doc Cooke, **Tony Jackson**, and **Johnny Dodds**. Recorded sporadically from 1923 to 1926 as sideman and also as leader with his Jazz Cardinals. Contracted tuberculosis in the late 1920s and eventually succumbed to the disease in 1933.

KEPPARD, LOUIS *Jazz.* Guitar, tuba. Bandleader. (Born Feb. 2, 1888, New Orleans, Orleans Parish; died Feb. 18, 1986, New Orleans, Orleans Parish.)[5] Noted early New Orleans jazz guitarist began playing professionally in 1906 and in following years worked with Magnolia Orchestra, which included **King Oliver** and **Honoré Dutrey**. Also performed occasionally in brother **Freddie Keppard**'s Olympia Orchestra in the Storyville District through the early 1910s. Worked briefly with **Lawrence Duhé** in Chicago in 1917. Performed on tuba with various brass bands in following decades and recorded with **Wooden Joe Nicholas** in the late 1940s. Reportedly retired from music in the 1960s.

KERR, CLYDE, JR. *Jazz.* Trumpet. Composer. Bandleader. (Born July 27, 1943, New Orleans, Orleans Parish; died Aug. 6, 2010, New Orleans, Orleans Parish.) New Orleans jazz trumpeter and highly regarded music educator for more than 40 years whose former students include **Trombone Shorty**, **Irvin Mayfield**, and **Nicholas Payton**. Released his only recording, *This Is Now!* in 2009. Father Clyde Kerr Sr. was also a jazz bandleader and noted music teacher.

KERSHAW, DOUG (Douglas James Kershaw) *Cajun, country.* Fiddle, accordion, guitar, piano, vocals. Composer. Bandleader. (Born Jan. 24, 1936, Tiel Ridge, Cameron Parish.) Dubbed "the Ragin' Cajun," singer-songwriter and master fiddle player best known for his high-energy performances and popular country-tinged Cajun hits such as "Louisiana Man" and "Diggy Liggy Lo." Raised in a large musical family speaking Cajun French, began playing fiddle at age five and by age nine was performing professionally. After relocating to Lake Arthur with family in the mid-1940s, performed with brothers Pee Wee (1930–2017) and **Rusty Kershaw** in the Continentals in the mid- to late 1940s and early 1950s. In the early 1950s formed duo Rusty and Doug with brother and recorded two singles for **J. D. Miller**'s Feature label, including local hit "No, No, It's Not So." Appeared on the *Louisiana Hayride* and *Grand Ole Opry* and cut numerous singles for Hickory through the early 1960s, including hits "So Lovely, Baby," "Hey Mae," and "Louisiana Man." After singles on RCA, Mercury, and Princess, launched solo career and signed with Warner Bros. in the late 1960s, releasing debut LP *The Cajun Way* in 1969. Toured extensively throughout the 1970s with numerous releases on Warner Bros., including *Alive and Pickin'* in 1975, and made regular appearances on television shows such as *The Ed Sullivan Show* and *The Tonight Show,* which popularized Cajun music with mass audiences. Continued touring in the 1980s with albums on Scotti Bros. and BGM, as well as the single "My Toot Toot" in 1985 with **Fats Domino.** In 2000 released CD *Two Step Fever* on Susie Q and continued performing into his 80s, recording CD *Face to Face* with **Steve Riley** on Valcour in 2014. Mother, Rita (1911–1989); father, Jack (1902–1943); and older brother Edward (1927–1979) were also Cajun musicians.

KERSHAW, RUSTY (Russell Lee Kershaw) *Cajun, country.* Guitar, fiddle, vocals. Composer. Bandleader. (Born Feb. 2, 1938, Tiel Ridge, Cameron Parish; died Oct. 23, 2001, New Orleans, Orleans Parish.) Prominent Cajun and country singer and guitarist best known for his collaboration with older brother **Doug Kershaw** in duo Rusty and Doug. Raised in a musical family, began playing guitar as a child and at age nine joined older brothers Pee Wee (1930–2017) and Doug in the Continentals, performing throughout southwest Louisiana with group. From the early 1950s through early 1960s performed and recorded extensively in duo Rusty and Doug, with numerous releases on Hickory, including "Hey Mae" and "Louisiana Man." Launched solo career in the mid-

1960s and released debut LP, *Cajun in the Blues Country,* on Cotillion in 1970. In 1974 appeared on Neil Young's album *On the Beach.* Recorded final release, *Now and Then,* in 1992 on Domino, which featured Young and **Art Neville**. Continued performing based in New Orleans until suffering fatal heart attack at age 63. Mother, Rita (1911–1989); father, Jack (1902–1943); and older brother Edward (1927–1979) were also Cajun musicians.

KID PUNCH *See* Miller, Ernest.

KID SHEIK/KID SHEIK COLA/KID COLA (George Colar) *Jazz.* Trumpet. Composer. Bandleader. (Born Sept. 15, 1908, New Orleans, Orleans Parish; died Nov. 7, 1996, Detroit.) Early New Orleans jazz trumpeter and bandleader took lessons from **Wooden Joe Nicholas** in the early 1920s and later worked with **Chris Kelly**, **Kid Rena**, and **Buddy Petit**. In the late 1940s worked with **George Lewis** and performed regularly with Eureka Brass Band and **Harold Dejan**'s Olympia Brass Band in the 1950s. Throughout the 1960s performed and recorded with his bands the Swingsters and Storyville Ramblers, which often included **Captain John Handy**, and toured overseas. Performed regularly at Preservation Hall in the 1970s and 1980s. Married jazz pianist Sadie Goodson (1901–2002) in later years.

KID STORMY WEATHER (Edmund Curtis Joseph Jr.) *Blues.* Piano, vocals. Composer. (Born probably Oct. 21, 1911, Garyville, St. John the Baptist Parish; died Sept. 24, 1986, Altadena, California.) Influential New Orleans barrelhouse blues piano player and singer. Performed in French Quarter bars along Bourbon and Burgundy streets. Reportedly also worked in duo with **Captain John Handy**. Recorded three sides for Vocalion in 1935, including "Short Hair Blues," which showcased his lightning-quick right hand. Major influence on **Professor Longhair**.

KID THOMAS (Thomas Valentine) *Jazz.* Trumpet. Bandleader. (Born Feb. 3, 1896, Reserve, St. John the Baptist Parish; died June 16, 1987, New Orleans, Orleans Parish.) Renowned early jazz trumpeter and bandleader who led one of New Orleans's longest-running traditional jazz bands. Began playing trumpet at age eight and often practiced with neighbors **Edmond Hall** and his brothers. At age 14 joined local Pickwick Brass Band, which included his trumpeter father. Moved to Algiers section of New Orleans in the early 1920s and soon began leading his own band, often under the name Algiers Stompers. Made first recordings in 1951 and throughout following decades recorded extensively as a leader and sideman. In the 1960s toured and recorded with **George Lewis**. Performed regularly at Preservation Hall from its inception in 1961 through the mid-1980s and toured with Preservation Hall Jazz Band nationally and abroad. Uncle of **Joe Valentine**.

KILBERT, PORTER *Jazz.* Saxophone. Composer. Bandleader. (Born June 10, 1921, Baton Rouge, EBR Parish; died Oct. 23, 1960, Chicago.) Noted jazz saxophonist began career playing on riverboats with **John Robichaux** in the mid-1930s and in following years performed with Carolina Cotton Pickers, Noble Sissle, and **Illinois Jacquet**. In the mid-1940s worked and recorded with Benny Carter, Roy Eldridge, Coleman Hawkins, and Clarence Samuels. Performed with Fletcher Henderson and Red Saunders in Chicago in the late 1940s. Continued performing in Chicago throughout the 1950s and recorded a single as a leader on Ping in 1957. Joined Quincy Jones's orchestra in 1959 and recorded and toured Europe with group before succumbing to fatal heart attack the following year.

KILGORE, THEOLA *Rhythm and blues, gospel.* Vocals. (Born Dec. 6, 1925, Shreveport, Caddo Parish; died May 15, 2005, Los Angeles.) Noted gospel and early soul singer best known for her two 1963 hits "The Love of My Man" and "This Is My Prayer" on Serock. Began singing gospel in church as a child and relocated to Oakland, California, in the 1940s. In 1955 made recording debut with gospel single "Look to the Hills" on Ajax as featured singer with the Mount Zion Spiritual Choir. In 1960 began partnership with singer-songwriter and producer Ed Townsend with her first secular recording, "The Sound of My Man (Chain Gang)," for Candix. After two hits on Serock, recorded a single each on KT, Scepter, and Mercury through 1966. A recording session for Stax remained unreleased.

KIMBALL, HENRY *Jazz.* String bass. (Born Mar. 2, 1877, New Orleans, Orleans Parish; died Sept. 8, 1934, New Orleans, Orleans Parish.)[6] Early jazz bass pioneer and father of Preservation Hall Jazz Band founding member **Narvin Kimball**. Longtime bassist with **John Robichaux** from 1894 to 1919. In the 1920s toured the Midwest with **Jelly Roll Morton** and worked with **Manuel Perez**, **Fats Pichon**, and **Papa Celestin**, often on riverboats.

KIMBALL, NARVIN *Jazz.* Banjo, string bass, guitar, vocals. Composer. Bandleader. (Born Mar. 2, 1909, New

Orleans, Orleans Parish; died Mar. 17, 2006, Charleston, South Carolina.) Son of **Henry Kimball**, noted early New Orleans jazz banjo player and bassist began learning on a homemade banjo as a child and during his teens worked on riverboats with **Fate Marable**. Performed with **Sidney Desvigne** and **Papa Celestin** in the late 1920s, recording with Celestin in 1928 on Columbia. In 1945 performed as bassist with **Louis Armstrong**. Led Gentlemen of Jazz band in New Orleans for several decades. Also was founding member of Preservation Hall Jazz Band. Husband of jazz pianist **Jeanette Kimball**.

KIMBLE, BOBBY *See* Kimble, Neal.

KIMBLE, NEAL *Rhythm and blues.* Vocals. Composer. (Born Mar. 18, 1933, New Orleans, Orleans Parish; died Dec. 11, 2006, San Francisco.) West Coast–based deep soul singer who recorded under the name Bobby Kimble on early recordings. Performed with gospel groups in New Orleans in the early 1950s before relocating to Oakland and working with the Paramount Singers. Recorded singles for Jab, Fat Fish, and Convoy (as Bobby Kimble) in the mid-1960s, notably "I Have Seniority (Over Your Love)" and "I Can See Everybody's Baby (But I Can't See Mine)." Also had releases on Venture, Maverick, and Tangerine through the early 1970s.

KINCHEN, LITTLE JESSIE *Blues.* Drums. (Born July 28, 1948, Denham Springs, Livingston Parish.) Baton Rouge–area blues drummer best known for his work with **Slim Harpo**'s band the King Bees in the mid- to late 1960s. Later worked with **Bobby Powell**. Son of bass and guitar player T. J. Kinchen, who performed with **Big Papa Tilley** and Slim Harpo in the 1950s. Younger brother of guitarist Simmie Kinchen, who occasionally worked with Slim Harpo and **Big Boe Melvin** and led his own group Simmie and the Uptighters in the 1960s.

KING, AL (Alvin K. Smith) *Rhythm and blues.* Vocals. Composer. Bandleader. (Born Aug. 8, 1923, Monroe, Ouachita Parish; died Jan. 21, 1999, Oakland, California.) Popular West Coast–based soul-blues singer and songwriter best known for his 1965 recording "Think Twice Before You Speak." Settled in San Francisco after serving in World War II and became active on the Bay Area blues scene. In the 1950s and early 1960s had singles on Recorded in Hollywood, Music City, Irma, Art-Tone, and Christy under Al or Alvin Smith. In 1964 began recording as Al King and had success with Lowell Fulson's "Reconsider Me" on Shirley. Following year recorded "Think Twice" for his own Flagg label which became a hit when leased to Sahara. After four more singles on Sahara, recorded two singles each for Modern, Kent, and Ronn in the late 1960s. Continued to perform throughout next three decades, releasing final album, *It's Rough Out Here,* in 1998 on Forevermore shortly before his death.

KING, BNOIS *Blues, jazz.* Guitar, vocals. Composer. Bandleader. (Born Jan. 21, 1943, Delhi, Richland Parish.) Jazz-influenced blues guitarist and singer best known for his long partnership with Texas blues guitarist Smokin' Joe Kubek. Began playing guitar at age eight and during his teens performed with James Moody's large jazz band from New Orleans. Worked with various blues and jazz groups around Texas in the 1960s and 1970s, eventually settling in Dallas and forming band with Kubek in the late 1980s. Toured internationally and had numerous releases on Bullseye Blues/Rounder, Blind Pig, Alligator, and Delta Groove until Kubek's death in 2015. Continued performing with his own group in the late 2010s.

KING, BOBBY (Albert Bobby King) *Rhythm and blues.* Vocals. (Born Sept. 1, 1945, Lake Charles, Calcasieu Parish.) Noted West Coast–based soul singer best known for his long partnership with singer Terry Evans. The son of a minister, began singing in his father's church choir as a child and upon graduating high school relocated to Los Angeles to pursue a singing career, inspired greatly by Sam Cooke. In 1973–74 recorded two singles for Reprise and began working for Warner Bros. as session vocalist, backing up numerous artists, including John Fogerty, George Harrison, Bob Dylan, **Aaron Neville**, and longtime collaborator Ry Cooder through following decade. In 1981 released self-titled LP debut on Warner Bros. before recording *Love in the Fire* for Motown in 1984. Began performing regularly in soul duet with Evans and released acclaimed LP *Live and Let Live!* on Rounder in 1988, followed by *Rhythm, Blues, Soul & Grooves* in 1990. Toured nationally and overseas with Evans in following years and continued with session work, appearing on recordings by Cooder, Bruce Springsteen, John Lee Hooker, Richard Thompson, and others.

KING, CHRIS THOMAS (Chris Thomas) *Blues.* Guitar, bass, piano, drums, vocals. Composer. Bandleader. (Born Oct. 14, 1962, Baton Rouge, EBR Parish.) Internationally renowned blues singer, guitarist, and composer best known for his work in the hit film *O Brother, Where Art Thou?* and accompanying soundtrack. Began playing guitar as a child, performing regularly at his father **Tabby Thomas**'s Baton Rouge club during his teens, influenced by both blues and rock music. In 1986 released debut LP *The Beginning* on Arhoolie (as Chris Thomas) and followed with recordings on Sire, Hightone, and Private Music, being among the first to merge hip-hop with blues as exemplified on *21st Century Blues . . . from Da 'Hood* in 1995. After being based in Europe for several years, returned to Louisiana in 1996 and added King to last name. In following years had numerous releases on Scotti Brothers, Black Top, Blind Pig, and his own 21st Century Blues label. In addition to his high profile work in *O Brother* in 2000, also appeared in several other feature films, including *Ray* in 2004. In 2017 released *Hotel Voodoo,* which continued his formula of mixing both traditional and contemporary blues styles with his original compositions.

KING, EARL (Earl Silas Johnson IV) *Rhythm and blues.* Guitar, vocals. Composer. Bandleader. (Born Feb. 7, 1934, New Orleans, Orleans Parish; died Apr. 17, 2003, New Orleans, Orleans Parish.) Highly influential rhythm and blues guitarist and singer who composed many New Orleans standards. Began playing guitar in his teens, influenced by T-Bone Walker and **Guitar Slim**. Made recording debut in 1953 for Savoy and in 1954 had several releases on Specialty. From 1955 to 1959 recorded numerous sides for Ace and had first national hit with "Those Lonely, Lonely Nights." In the early 1960s worked with **Dave Bartholomew** and recorded signature songs "Come On" and "Trick Bag" for Imperial. Also recorded for Motown, Amy, and Hot Line and wrote songs for **Professor Longhair**, **Fats Domino**, **Willie Tee**, **Lee Dorsey**, and others. In the early 1970s recorded with **Allen Toussaint** and the Meters for LP *Street Parade* and in 1977 released an album on Sonet. Through the 1980s and 1990s had three releases on Black Top and toured internationally. Died from complications of diabetes at age 69.

KING EDWARD (Edward Memphis Antoine) *Blues.* Guitar, vocals. Composer. Bandleader. (Born May 5, 1937, Rayne, Acadia Parish.) Jackson, Mississippi–based blues singer and guitarist began playing during his early teens and at age 18 worked briefly with **Clifton Chenier** while living in Houston. After performing around Orange, Texas, area with brief stints in Denver and Portland, joined brother **Nolan Struck** in Chicago in the early 1960s and worked with Billy Boy Arnold and **Lonnie Brooks**. Continued performing and recording with Struck throughout next several years and also worked as session musician for several small local labels. In the mid-1970s started working with soul vocalist McKinley Mitchell and relocated to Jackson, performing and occasionally recording with Mitchell through the mid-1980s. Recorded as a leader for Ace in 1979 and with Struck in 1995 on *Brother to Brother* for Paula. Continued performing on Jackson blues scene into the 2010s, releasing *50 Years of Blues* on Hit the Road in 2015. Brothers Fulton, Sterling, and Wilton were also musicians.

KING FLOYD *See* Floyd, King, III.

KING, GENE *See* Rodrigue, Gene.

KING IVORY LEE (Ivory Lee Semien Jr.) *Blues.* Drums, piano, vocals. Composer. Bandleader. (Born Sept. 14, 1931, Washington, St. Landry Parish; died Mar. 2, 2002, Houston.) Texas-based blues drummer, singer and label owner relocated to Houston in 1949 and in the early 1950s began performing in local clubs. Recorded four sides for Alameda in the mid-1950s and began working regularly with lap-steel blues guitarist Hop Wilson, cutting several singles with Wilson for **Eddie Shuler**'s Goldband and Trey labels in the late 1950s. In the 1960s formed Ivory label and through the late 1960s released singles as leader and by others such as Wilson, Lightnin' Hopkins and D.C. Bender, notably Wilson's "My Woman Has Got a Black Cat Bone." Continued performing through the mid-1970s before retiring from music.

KING KARL (Bernard Jolivette) *Blues, swamp pop.* Guitar, saxophone, vocals. Composer. (Born Dec. 22, 1931, Grand Coteau, St. Landry Parish; died Dec. 7, 2005, Mesa, Arizona.) Influential early swamp blues and swamp pop singer-songwriter and multi-instrumentalist began performing in the late 1940s and early 1950s with various bands, including a stint with **Lloyd Price** while living in Beaumont. After serving in Korea, joined **Guitar Gable**'s Musical Kings in 1955 as vocalist and began recording for producer **J. D. Miller** with group in 1956, recording such self-penned classics as "Life Problem," "This Should Go On Forever," and "Irene." In the mid-1960s released several singles on Tamm and La Louisianne before retiring from music. In the early 1990s relocated to Arizona for health reasons and from the mid-1990s through early 2000s performed occasionally in Phoenix and Louisiana. Father of blues bassist Larry Jolivette.

KING LEE *See* Lee, Warren.

KING, PETER *Creole.* Accordion. Composer. (Born Sept. 3, 1900, near Opelousas, St. Landry Parish; died May 1976, Lake Charles, Calcasieu Parish.)[7] Creole accordionist and uncle of **Clifton Chenier**. Relocated to Lake Charles by the late 1920s and recorded songs for Arhoolie in 1962, including "Lafayette Zydeco."

KING, SAUNDERS *Rhythm and blues.* Guitar, piano, vocals. Composer. Bandleader. (Born Mar. 13, 1909, Staples, Caddo Parish; died Aug. 31, 2000, San Rafael, California.) Important early West Coast guitarist and singer-songwriter who was an electric guitar pioneer in rhythm and blues in the early 1940s. Raised in Houston, relocated to Oakland with family in the 1920s and began singing and playing piano in his minister father's Pentecostal church. In the mid-1930s sang with gospel group on the radio and began playing guitar several years later. In 1942 recorded for Rhythm and had national hit with "S.K. Blues," one of first rhythm and blues recordings to feature electric guitar. Despite several personal tragedies, had numerous releases on Rhythm, Aladdin, Cava-Tone, and Modern in the 1940s and early 1950s and had hits with "Empty Bedroom Blues" and "Stay Gone Blues" on Rhythm in 1949. After a single for Galaxy in 1961, retired from music and joined the church. Returned briefly in 1979 to appear on son-in-law Carlos Santana's LP *Oneness* on Columbia.

KING SOLOMON *See* Solomon, King.

KIRKPATRICK, BOB *Blues.* Guitar, vocals. Composer. Bandleader. (Born Jan. 10, 1934, Haynesville, Claiborne Parish.) Texas-based blues guitarist and singer began playing guitar as a child. After serving in the Korean War, worked with Ivory Joe Hunter around Monroe in the mid-1950s, being greatly influenced by B.B. King. Relocated to Dallas in 1958 and performed music part-time throughout the 1960s. Appeared at several Newport Folk Festivals in the 1970s and recorded LP *Feeling the Blues* for Folkways in 1973. Recorded *Going Back to Texas* for JSP in 1996 and toured Europe before releasing CD *Drive Across Texas* on Topcat in 2000. Continued performing around Dallas area into the 2010s.

KNIGHT, JEAN (Jean Caliste) *Rhythm and blues.* Vocals. (Born Jan. 26, 1943, New Orleans, Orleans Parish.) New Orleans rhythm and blues and funky soul singer known for her huge crossover hit "Mr. Big Stuff." Started singing around New Orleans while in her late teens and recorded several singles for producer Huey Meaux under given name Jean Caliste. In the early 1970s worked with producer **Wardell Quezerque** and had double-platinum hit with "Mr. Big Stuff" on Stax. In the 1980s had career resurgence with minor hits for Cotillion and Mirage, including a popular cover of **Rockin' Sidney**'s "My Toot Toot." Recorded for Ichiban and Formaldehyde labels in the late 1990s and continued to perform into the 2010s.

KNOX, EMILE *Jazz.* Bass drum, snare drum. (Born May 2, 1902, New Orleans, Orleans Parish; died Aug. 20, 1976, New Orleans, Orleans Parish.) Early New Orleans brass-band drummer who was a longtime member of the Young Tuxedo Brass Band. Also worked with **Paul Barbarin**, **Al Hirt**, **Pete Fountain**, and Olympia and Onward brass bands.

KNOX, HARVEY *Rhythm and blues.* Guitar. Bandleader. (Born Mar. 25, 1937, Tallulah, Madison Parish; died May 16, 2019, Baton Rouge, EBR Parish.) Noted veteran Baton Rouge blues guitarist began playing during his teens, inspired by local performances by B.B. King and **Guitar Slim**. Relocated to Baton Rouge in 1957 to study music at Southern University and began performing on local blues scene, working extensively with numerous area blues musicians, including **Slim Harpo**, **Buddy Stewart**, **Raful Neal**, and many others. Throughout following decades supplemented music with electronics repair and continued performing in local clubs into the late 2010s with his band Soul Spectrum.

KOHLMAN, FREDDIE *Jazz.* Drums, vocals. Bandleader. (Born Aug. 25, 1918, New Orleans, Orleans Parish; died Sept. 29, 1990, New Orleans, Orleans Parish.) Renowned early New Orleans jazz percussionist studied under **Manuel Manetta** and took drumming lessons from **Louis Cottrell Sr.** Started his professional career during his early teens and working with **Armand Piron**, **Joe Robichaux**, **Papa Celestin**, and **Sam Morgan** in the early 1930s. Moved to Chicago in the mid-1930s and worked with Albert Ammons, Earl Hines, and **Lee Collins**. Returned to New Orleans in the early 1940s and led his own band. Recorded LP *Jazz Solos in New Orleans* in the early 1950s and performed with **Louis Armstrong**'s All Stars. In the 1960s worked with **Louis Cottrell Jr.**, Dukes of Dixieland, and Onward and Young Tuxedo brass bands. Regularly toured Europe as bandleader in the 1970s and 1980s.

LABBIE, J. C. (Joseph C. Labbie Jr.) *Cajun.* Accordion, vocals. Bandleader. (Born Apr. 10, 1938, Eunice, St. Landry Parish; died Mar. 9, 2016, Alexandria, Rapides Parish.) Locally popular Cajun accordionist was raised in a musical family speaking Cajun French and began playing accordion at age 23. In the 1980s performed and recorded with **Fred Charlie**'s Acadiana Cajuns and later performed weekly at bar in Mamou for more than two decades.

LACEN, ANTHONY *See* Tuba Fats.

LACHNEY, DELMA *Cajun.* Fiddle, vocals. Composer. (Born June 10, 1896, Egg Bend, Avoy. Parish; died June 25, 1949, Marksville, Avoy. Parish.)[1] Left-handed early Cajun fiddler who recorded with guitarist **Blind Uncle Gaspard** on two sessions for Vocalion in 1929. Began playing as a child, learning traditional French Acadian songs from his musician father. Continued performing around Marksville area, often with brother Philogene, and in 1929 made series of noted recordings with Gaspard as both accompanist and leader, including "La Danseuse (The Dancer)." Reportedly continued performing locally until the mid-1940s. Died at home from coronary heart disease at age 53.

LACOUME, EMILE "STALE BREAD" *Jazz.* Guitar, banjo, zither, piano, bass violin, harmonica, vocals. Bandleader. (Born Sept. 22, 1885, New Orleans, Orleans Parish; died Nov. 19, 1946, New Orleans, Orleans Parish.)[2] Visually impaired multi-instrumentalist who as a child began leading the locally popular Razzy Dazzy Spasm Band and performed "hot music" with group from the mid-1890s through the first decade of the 1900s. Regarded by some as being among the first jazz bands, group consisted of newspaper boys who initially performed on homemade or discarded instruments in the streets of Storyville District for tips. Completely blind by age 15, began performing with more established groups in the 1910s and worked with numerous jazz and society dance bands through the early 1940s, including Halfway House Orchestra and his own Blue Moon Orchestra.

LaCOUR BROTHERS *Creole.* (Born around 1890–1905, Cloutierville, Natch. Parish.) Locally renowned and influential Creole family band which included brothers Yuke (or Youk) (guitar), Duma (fiddle, guitar, saxophone), Sheck (bass fiddle), and Eveck (mandolin, fiddle) who had a very popular early Creole dance band in the Cane River area from the 1920s through 1940s. Performed often at Melrose Plantation. Several descendants continued the family musical legacy in the 2010s, including Katrice and Rainey LaCour with their Natchitoches-based band the LaCour Trio.

LaCROIX, JERRY "COUNT JACKSON" *Rhythm and blues, rock.* Vocals, saxophone. Composer. Bandleader. (Born Oct. 10, 1943, Alexandria, Rapides Parish; died May 7, 2014, Lufkin, Texas.) Highly regarded blue-eyed soul singer best known for his work with the Boogie Kings in the mid-1960s and as member of several 1970s rock groups, including Edgar Winter's White Trash and Blood, Sweat and Tears. Raised in Port Arthur, Texas, since age five; by age 14 was performing across Louisiana border at popular Big Oaks Club in Vinton. In the early 1960s recorded single on Tear Drop as Jerry "Count" Jackson and followed with a release on Vee-Jay. In the mid-1960s toured and recorded as co-vocalist and saxophone player with the Boogie Kings, often sharing duets with **G.G. Shinn** and **Gary Walker**. In the 1970s toured and recorded with Winter; Blood, Sweat and Tears; and Rare Earth and released two solo albums, including *LaCroix* on Epic in 1972. Retired from music in the

1980s but performed occasionally in the late 1990s and 2000s.

LADNIER, TOMMY *Jazz.* Trumpet. Bandleader. (Born May 28, 1900, Mandeville, St. Tammany Parish; died June 4, 1939, Manhattan, New York.) Renowned early New Orleans jazz trumpeter studied under **Bunk Johnson** before moving to Chicago in 1917. In the 1920s worked with **King Oliver**, **Fate Marable**, Lovie Austin, Fletcher Henderson, and others, and recorded behind numerous early classic blues singers, including Bessie Smith, Ida Cox, and **Edna Hicks**. In the late 1920s and early 1930s toured Europe. Relocated to New York in the early 1930s and coled the New Orleans Feetwarmers with **Sidney Bechet** and appeared with group on John Hammond's famed *From Spirituals to Swing* concert series at Carnegie Hall. Recorded with Bechet and Mezz Mezzrow in 1938 before suffering fatal heart attack at age 39.

LaFLEUR, HARRY *Cajun.* Fiddle, guitar, piano, vocals. Composer. Bandleader. (Born Oct. 23, 1933, Swords, St. Landry Parish.) Noted early postwar Cajun fiddle player began playing guitar before switching to fiddle, inspired by his older brother Raymond LeFleur (1927–1982), who played fiddle with **Iry LeJeune**. In the late 1940s joined Pine Grove Boys with **Nathan Abshire** and also performed with LeJeune, **Dennis McGee**, and many others. In the late 1950s and 1960s performed and recorded with **Austin Pitre** and in the late 1970s recorded with **Wallace "Cheese" Read**. Founded Cajun French Music Association in 1984 and continued to perform and record with his band Harry and the Cajuns in 2010s, releasing CD *Kathleen's Crown of Roses* in 2002.

LaFLEUR, LEWIS *Cajun.* Fiddle, vocals. Composer. (Born Jan. 16, 1885, Chataignier, Evangeline Parish; died Oct. 23, 1932, Eunice, St. Landry Parish.)[3] Obscure early Cajun fiddle player who performed with accordionist **Delin T. Guillory** in Ville Platte area from 1927 until his death. In Nov. 1929 recorded four influential sides with Guillory for Victor, including "Alone At Home," which **Iry LeJeune** would later record as "Love Bridge Waltz." Died of gunshot wound to the abdomen.

LaFLEUR, MAYEUS (*or* Maius) *Cajun.* Accordion, vocals. Composer. (Born Aug. 14, 1906, Mamou, Evangeline Parish; died Oct. 28, 1928, Basile, Evangeline Parish.)[4] Renowned early Cajun accordionist best known for his 1928 recording "Mama, Where You At?" with **Leo Soileau**. Performed with childhood friend Soileau throughout the 1920s in Ville Platte, Basile, and Mamou area and in Oct. 1928 recorded four sides with Soileau for Victor, becoming the second Cajun musicians to record after **Joe Falcon** and **Cléoma Breaux**. Recordings included his compositions "Mama, Where You At?" an autobiographical plea to search for his mother who had abandoned him as a baby, and "Ton Pere a Mit D'Eor (Your Father Put Me Out)," which addressed his marital problems. Less than two weeks after recording session he was shot and killed as an innocent bystander during a brawl at a club in Basile.

LaFLEUR, TONICE *Cajun.* Guitar. (Born Apr. 20, 1918, near Oberlin, Allen Parish; died Aug. 19, 2013, Lake Charles, Calcasieu Parish.) Veteran Cajun guitarist began performing at age 14 and worked early on with **J. B. Fuselier**'s Merrymakers, performing with Fuselier from the mid-1930s through mid-1940s. Later performed with **Chuck Guillory** and **Sidney Brown**'s Traveler Playboys. In the 1980s performed and recorded with Old Timers Cajun Band entertaining nursing home residents throughout Calcasieu Parish.

LAINE, PAPA JACK (George Vetiala Laine) *Jazz, ragtime.* Drums, alto horn. Bandleader. (Born Sept. 21, 1873, New Orleans, Orleans Parish; died June 1, 1966, New Orleans, Orleans Parish.) Often cited as the "father of white jazz," pioneering New Orleans bandleader and founder of the popular early marching band Reliance Brass Band which featured many members who later became prominent early jazz musicians. Formed Reliance band in the early 1890s and led group through 1917, although band continued under different leadership into the 1930s. Throughout following decades members included **Tom "Red" Brown**, **Nick LaRocca**, **Sharkey Bonano**, and the **Brunies** brothers, among many others. Although known as a key figure in the development of white jazz, also occasionally defied segregation laws and employed light-skinned Creole and other non-white musicians such as **Achille Baquet** and **Lorenzo Tio Sr.** Retired from music in the late 1910s. Son Alfred "Baby" Laine (1895–1957) was a jazz cornetist and bandleader.

LAMARE, NAPPY (Joseph Hilton Lamare) *Jazz.* Banjo, guitar, vocals. Bandleader. (Born June 14, 1905, New Orleans, Orleans Parish; died May 8, 1988, Los Angeles.)[5] Early New Orleans jazz banjo and guitar player began performing in the mid-1920s and worked around New

Orleans with **Sharkey Bonano**, **Johnny Wiggs**, and **Johnny Bayersdorffer**. Made recording debut in 1927 with **Johnny Hyman**'s Bayou Stompers. Gained fame as original member of Bob Crosby's Bob Cats from the mid-1930s through early 1940s. Relocated to California in the mid-1940s and led his own band and recorded as leader and sideman as well as on film soundtracks through the early 1980s.

LAMBERT, LLOYD *Rhythm and blues, jazz.* Bass, piano, trumpet. Composer. Bandleader. (Born June 4, 1928, Thibodaux, Lafourche Parish; died Oct. 31, 1995, New Orleans, Orleans Parish.)[6] Highly regarded rhythm and blues bassist best known for his long tenure as **Guitar Slim**'s bandleader. Hailing from a musical family, began playing piano with his father in local jazz band at age nine. In the early 1940s switched to trumpet and toured the South with Thibodaux club owner Hosea Hill's band the Serenaders. In the early 1950s switched to bass and in 1953 took over leadership of band and toured with Ray Charles. Later that year began working as bandleader for Guitar Slim and appeared on all of his subsequent recordings for Specialty and the majority for Atlantic. In 1955 had local hit as leader with "Heavy Sugar" on Specialty. After Guitar Slim's death in 1959 worked as bandleader with Nappy Brown and **Carol Fran**. In 1960 relocated to Houston and worked as session musician for Duke Records and performed with jazz saxophonist Arnett Cobb. Returned to New Orleans in the early 1970s and worked with jazz bands along Bourbon Street. From 1981 through the early 1990s led his own jazz band at Maison Bourbon club and appeared on recordings with **James "Thunderbird" Ford** and **Snooks Eaglin**. Younger brother of **Phamous Lambert** and grandfather of **Kipori Woods**.

LAMBERT, PHAMOUS *Jazz, rhythm and blues.* Piano, vocals. (Born July 28, 1918, Thibodaux, Lafourche Parish; died Sept. 16, 2000, New Orleans, Orleans Parish.) Renowned New Orleans jazz pianist worked in Chicago with Miles Davis, Joe Williams, Charlie Parker, and others in the 1940s and 1950s. Returned to New Orleans around 1970 and worked and recorded with Dukes of Dixieland, **Al Hirt**, **Danny Barker**, New Orleans All-Star Stompers, **Thomas Jefferson**, **Wallace Davenport**, and others. Older brother of **Lloyd Lambert** and great-uncle of **Kipori Woods**.

LAMPKINS, DR. ERNEST *Jazz.* Bass. (Born Apr. 12, 1928, Shreveport, Caddo Parish; died Jan. 12, 2018, Shreveport, Caddo Parish.) Locally renowned veteran Shreveport jazz bassist and educator who performed in various jazz groups for more than six decades, including the Polyphonics and the Shreveport Symphony. Also performed with Clark Terry, Kenny Burrell, Nathan Davis, and Isaac Hayes. In 2004 was elected as first African American mayor of Greenwood, Louisiana. Son of Shreveport jazz pianist Major Lampkins.

LANDRENEAU, ADAM *Cajun.* Fiddle. (Born Nov. 4, 1909, Mamou, Evangeline Parish; died Dec. 28, 1972, Mamou, Evangeline Parish.) Noted Cajun fiddler who performed with third cousin **Cyprien Landreneau** in the Mamou Cajun Band. Made recordings for Arhoolie and Swallow with Cyprien in the 1960s, including LP *Cajun Sole* in 1969.

LANDRENEAU, CYPRIEN *Cajun.* Accordion, vocals. (Born Apr. 7, 1903, near Mamou, Evangeline Parish; died Feb. 1, 1981, Mamou, Evangeline Parish.) Noted Cajun accordionist and singer started playing accordion at age seven and soon began performing at local house dances. Formed the Mamou Cajun Band in the 1950s with third cousin **Adam Landreneau**, which became among the first Cajun bands to perform on a national stage during the 1957 National Folk Festival in Oklahoma City. Also performed at other major festivals, including Newport Folk Festival, and toured Europe in the mid-1960s. Recorded for Arhoolie and Swallow in the mid- to late 1960s and in 1975 made recordings for Gerard Dole which appeared on 1977 Folkways LP *Cajun Home Music.*

LANDRY, DEE (Duliss Landry) *Cajun.* Guitar, vocals. Composer. Bandleader. (Born Dec. 31, 1929, Delcambre, Vermilion Parish; died Feb. 22, 1984, Abbeville, Vermilion Parish.) Cajun-country singer and guitarist who had several releases on **J. D. Miller**'s Cajun Classics in the 1960s, notably "Tout le Soir" and "Petite Brun de Campagn."

LANDRY, DICKIE (Richard Landry) *Jazz, rhythm and blues, swamp pop.* Saxophone, flute. Composer. Bandleader. (Born Nov. 16, 1938, Cecilia, St. Martin Parish.) Internationally renowned avant-garde jazz saxophonist and visual artist began playing saxophone at age 10, inspired by West Coast jazz. From the mid-1950s through early 1960s made frequent trips to New York City and studied flute under Arthur Lora. In the mid-1960s performed and recorded with blue-eyed soul band the Swing Kings before relocating to New York City in 1969. From 1970 to 1981 performed and recorded extensively with

Philip Glass Ensemble and released several albums as leader, including *Fifteen Saxophones* on Northern Lights in 1977. Returned to Lafayette area and composed "Mass for Pentecost Sunday" in 1986 and also worked with Laurie Anderson, Bob Dylan, Paul Simon, and others. From the mid-1990s through early 2010s toured and recorded with swamp pop group Lil' Band O' Gold and continued performing as soloist in the late 2010s.

LANDRY, GEORGE *See* Big Chief Jolly.

LANDRY, LULA *Cajun.* Vocals. (Born June 26, 1906, Leroy, Vermilion Parish; died Sept. 18, 1990, Vermilion Parish.) Noted Cajun a cappella singer whose vast repertoire of "home songs" consisted of hundreds of traditional Cajun ballads which dated back many generations. Known for her remarkable ability to memorize entire songs after hearing them one time. Appeared on 1957 Folkways LP *Cajun Songs from Louisiana* as Madame Elie Landry.

LANDRY, RAY *Cajun.* Accordion, guitar, vocals. Composer. Bandleader. (Born Mar. 13, 1945, Lafayette, Lafayette Parish.) Cajun guitarist and accordion player joined **Nonc Allie Young**'s Basile Cajun Band and eventually took over leadership in the mid-1990s when Young retired, releasing CD *La Musique Que Viens du Beaubassin* on Swallow in 1999. In 2008 released *My Cajun Roots Are Deep,* which featured numerous guest musicians, including **Al Berard**, **Sheryl Cormier**, and **Helen Boudreaux**. Continued performing in Lafayette area in the 2010s.

LANDRY, YVETTE *Cajun, swamp pop, country.* Guitar, bass, accordion, fiddle, piano, vocals. Composer. Bandleader. (Born Nov. 30, 1963, Breaux Bridge, St. Martin Parish.) Noted singer-songwriter and multi-instrumentalist was born into a musical family and began playing piano as a child but did not pursue a music career until her early 40s. In the 2000s and 2010s performed as member of several noted Cajun bands, including the Lafayette Rhythm Devils, Balfa Toujours, Bonsoir, Catin, and Les Ferrailles. In 2010 released acclaimed debut CD, *Should Have Known,* and continued to perform internationally and record with her own band as well as other groups, often partnering with **Richard Comeaux**. In 2018 released swamp pop–centric *Louisiana Lovin'* with her band the Jukes, featuring **Roddie Romero**.

LANG, LITTLE EDDIE/"SLY DELL" (Eddie Lee Langois) *Rhythm and blues.* Guitar, vocals. Composer. (Born Jan. 15, 1936, New Orleans, Orleans Parish; died Mar. 10, 1985, Slidell, St. Tammany Parish.) New Orleans rhythm and blues singer and guitarist was greatly influenced by **Guitar Slim**, whom he toured with as band member in the early 1950s. Made recording debut for Bullet in 1951, followed by releases on RPM, Ron, and Flame (as Sly Dell) from 1956 to 1960. In 1967 recorded for Seven B and had regional hit in 1973 with "Food Stamp Blues" on Superdome/Jewel. Toured and recorded in Scandinavia in 1977 but retired from music after suffering stroke two years later. Not to be confused with early jazz guitar pioneer Eddie Lang (Salvatore Massaro).

LAPOINT, EMERY J., SR. *Cajun.* Guitar, vocals. (Born Aug. 14, 1920, Kaplan, Vermilion Parish; died Feb. 15, 1994, Lake Charles, Calcasieu Parish.)[7] Cajun singer-guitarist learned to play the instrument while serving in Italy in World War II and in 1947 formed Elton Playboys with **Lionel Cormier**, which later became Sundown Playboys. Left group in 1952 and continued performing with various groups. In the late 1950s and early 1960s performed and recorded with **Hobo Bertrand** and **Joe Bonsall** and in the early 1970s performed and recorded with the Longshore Playboys with Bertrand. Retired from performing in 1983.

LaROCCA, NICK (Dominic James LaRocca) *Jazz.* Cornet. Composer. Bandleader. (Born Apr. 11, 1889, New Orleans, Orleans Parish; died Feb. 22, 1961, New Orleans, Orleans Parish.) Early jazz cornet player, bandleader, and composer who formed the Original Dixieland Jazz Band, which made the first jazz record in 1917. Began performing around 1905 and worked with **Papa Jack Laine**'s Reliance Brass Band in the early 1910s. Traveled to Chicago in 1916 with **Johnny Stein**'s Dixie Jass Band, but members soon reformed group without Stein into Original Dixieland Jass Band and in 1917 recorded "Livery Stable Blues," which is considered the first jazz recording. (Eventually changed spelling in band name from "Jass" to "Jazz.") Credited as composer of many jazz standards, including "Tiger Rag," which was based on **Jack Carey**'s earlier song. Continued performing with group through the mid-1920s and retired from music in the late 1930s.

LASTIE, DAVID, SR. *Rhythm and blues, jazz.* Saxophone. Bandleader. (Born May 11, 1934, New Orleans, Orleans Parish; died Dec. 5, 1987, New Orleans, Orleans Parish.) Highly regarded rhythm and blues saxophonist and member of New Orleans's renowned family of musicians. From the early 1950s through mid-1980s appeared on dozens of rhythm and blues recording sessions with **Earl King**, **Eddie Bo**, **Snooks Eaglin**, **Sugar Boy Crawford**, **Allen Toussaint**, **Dr. John**, cousin **Jessie Hill**, and others. In the 1980s led Taste of New Orleans band with **George Porter Jr.** Son of **Frank Lastie** and brother of **Melvin** and **Walter Lastie**.

LASTIE, FRANK JOSEPH *Gospel, jazz.* Drums, vocals. (Born July 21, 1902, New Orleans, Orleans Parish; died Apr. 29, 1993, New Orleans, Orleans Parish.)[8] Patriarch of renowned New Orleans family of musicians and father of **David**, **Melvin**, and **Walter Lastie**. A former classmate of **Louis Armstrong** in the mid-1910s, performed mainly as gospel musician and credited as among the first to introduce drumming into black church services in 1927. Ordained deacon by Guiding Star Spiritual Church in the early 1940s. In later years led gospel group the Silver-Haired Song Birds and performed at benefits, schools, churches, and nursing homes.

LASTIE, JOE, JR. *Jazz, gospel.* Drums. (Born Aug. 28, 1958, New Orleans, Orleans Parish.) Best known as longtime drummer with Preservation Hall Jazz Band and toured internationally with group for 27 years. Continued to perform and record with Lastie Family Gospel Singers and lead Joe Lastie's New Orleans Sound in the 2010s. Nephew of **David**, **Melvin**, and **Walter Lastie**.

LASTIE, MELVIN *Jazz, rhythm and blues.* Cornet, trumpet. Composer. Bandleader. (Born Nov. 18, 1930, New Orleans, Orleans Parish; died Dec. 4, 1972, New Orleans, Orleans Parish.) Member of renowned New Orleans jazz family, began performing in his teens and worked with **Paul Barbarin** and **Fats Domino** in the late 1940s. In the early 1950s toured with brother **David Lastie** backing Big Joe Turner and appeared on sessions with **Roy Brown**, **Earl King**, and others. Helped form the A.P.O. label with **Harold Battiste** in 1961 and worked with Sam Cooke in California in 1963. Appeared on numerous jazz and rhythm and blues sessions and also served as producer and arranger through the early 1970s. Oldest son of **Frank Lastie** and brother of **Walter Lastie**.

LASTIE, WALTER "POPEE" *Jazz.* Drums. (Born Sept. 18, 1938, New Orleans, Orleans Parish; died Dec. 28, 1980, New Orleans, Orleans Parish.) Member of prestigious New Orleans jazz family, studied drums in church under his father, **Frank Lastie**. Worked with various rhythm and blues bands, including **Fats Domino** and brother **David Lastie**'s band throughout the 1960s and 1970s. Younger brother of **Melvin Lastie**.

LaTOUR, RAYMOND *Creole.* Accordion, vocals. Bandleader. (Born Aug. 16, 1923, Oberlin, Allen Parish; died Mar. 11, 2004, Sulphur, Calcasieu Parish.)[9] A third-generation Creole accordion player, began playing in his early teens and by age 17 was performing at local la la house dances. Relocated to African American community of Mossville near Sulphur in the mid-1940s and in the mid-1950s formed the Sulphur Playboys. Performed with group throughout southwest Louisiana for several decades, appearing at the 1984 World's Fair in New Orleans to much acclaim.

LaTOUR, WILFRED *Creole.* Accordion, vocals. Bandleader. (Born Sept. 5, 1921, Oberlin, Allen Parish; died Jan. 20, 1994, Lynwood, California.)[10] Noted Creole accordionist began playing the instrument as a child, influenced by **Amédé Ardoin**, and by his teens was performing at la la house dances around Basile. Performed locally on weekends with his band the Travel Aces while working in the farm and oil industries through the early 1980s. Recorded single "Oh Bye Bye" for Maison de Soul in 1976. After retiring in 1982 relocated to Los Angeles and through the early 1990s performed with his bands Louisiana Cajun Trio and Zydeco Goodtime Aces locally and overseas, recording self-released CD *Homage* in 1992.

LAURO, BIG AL *Rhythm and blues.* Drums, vocals. Composer. Bandleader. (Born Oct. 12, 1958, New Orleans, Orleans Parish.) Born and raised in New Orleans, formed Unknown Blues Band in 1996 which eventually reformed as Big Al & the Heavyweights. Continued to tour nationally and overseas into the 2010s with six releases, including *Gumbo Party Music* on Mardi Gras in 2008.

LAZY LESTER (Leslie Johnson) *Blues.* Harmonica, guitar, percussion, vocals. Composer. Bandleader. (Born June 20, 1933, Torras, Pointe Coupee Parish; died Aug. 22, 2018, Paradise, California.) Influential early Baton Rouge blues singer, songwriter, and multi-instrumentalist who helped pioneer the sound of swamp blues with his many early Excello blues recordings such as "Sugar Coated Love," "I Hear You Knockin'," "They Call Me Lazy," and "I'm a Lover, Not a Fighter." Raised in Baton Rouge since age three, began playing guitar around age 11 and picked up harmonica several years later. In his teens performed with **Raful Neal** and later cofounded the Rhythm Rockers, alternating on guitar, harmonica, and drums. In 1956 began recording on harmonica behind **Lightnin' Slim** for producer **J. D. Miller**, which led to numerous recordings on Excello as a leader through the mid-1960s. Also served as a versatile studio musician for Miller and appeared on countless sessions with **Slim Harpo**, **Lonesome Sundown**, **Silas Hogan**, **Katie Webster**, **Nathan Abshire**, and others. Worked primarily outside of music through the late 1970s but reunited with **Lightnin' Slim** briefly in 1971. Returned to music scene in the mid-1980s while living in Detroit and began touring Europe. In 1987 released comeback album, *Lazy Lester Rides Again,* on Blue Horizon and in following decades continued touring nationally and overseas with recordings on Alligator, Antone's, Telarc, APO, and Bluestown. Relocated to California in later years and continued performing until succumbing to cancer at age 85. Brother of blues bassist Huey "Kingfish" Johnson, who recorded with Lightnin' Slim, Katie Webster, **Whispering Smith**, and others.

LEAD BELLY (Huddie William Ledbetter) *Blues, folk.* Guitar, mandolin, fiddle, accordion, piano, harmonica, vocals. Composer. (Born probably Jan. 23, 1888, Jeter Plantation, near Mooringsport, Caddo Parish; died Dec. 6, 1949, New York City.)[11] Profoundly influential blues and folk singer, multi-instrumentalist, and songwriter who was the first to bring authentic African American blues and folk music of the South to national attention. Recorded hundreds of songs of his vast repertoire including "Goodnight, Irene," "Midnight Special," "Rock Island Line," "Cotton Fields," "Bourgeois Blues," "Pick a Bale of Cotton," "Take This Hammer," "Good Morning, Blues," and "Black Betty." Raised in east Texas from age five, began playing accordion as a child before learning guitar. By his early teens was locally renowned as a musician playing at house parties and church. Several years later began performing regularly in Shreveport's notorious red-light district along Fannin Street. After traveling as an itinerant musician throughout the Southwest, relocated to Dallas in the early 1910s and in the following years often partnered with Blind Lemon Jefferson. Also began playing the 12-string guitar, which would become his signature instrument. In 1918 was incarcerated for murder in Texas and was later famously pardoned by the governor in 1925 whom he impressed by singing a pardon song. Performed around Shreveport's Fannin Street in the mid- to late 1920s. In 1933 was discovered by folklorists John and Alan Lomax while incarcerated in Louisiana State Prison in Angola for attempted murder and made dozens of field recordings. After an early release for good behavior in 1934, traveled the South as John Lomax's valet and assistant. Relocated to New York City by 1935 and recorded extensively for Library of Congress and made first commercial recordings for ARC, achieving national fame through prominent newsreel, magazine, and newspaper features. In the late 1930s and 1940s continued recording for Library of Congress and various commercial labels, including Musicraft, Victor, Bluebird, Asch, and Capitol. Also became a leading figure on the burgeoning folk music scene and regularly worked with and mentored younger musicians, including Woody Guthrie and Pete Seeger. While on tour in France in 1949 was diagnosed with ALS and died at Bellevue Hospital later that year.

LeBLANC, CARL *Jazz.* Banjo, guitar, vocals. Composer. Bandleader. (Born May 26, 1955, New Orleans, Orleans Parish.) Traditional New Orleans and avant-garde jazz musician has worked with both Preservation Hall Jazz Band as well as Sun Ra. Began performing in the late 1960s and worked with **Fats Domino**, **Allen Toussaint**, **Ellis Marsalis Jr.**, and others.

LeBLANC, FLOYD *Cajun.* Fiddle, guitar, vocals. Composer. Bandleader. (Born Sept. 17, 1924, Mermentau, Acadia Parish; died Nov. 8, 1975, Lake Charles, Calcasieu Parish.) Noted Cajun swing fiddle player and singer formed the Oklahoma Tornadoes with singer-guitarist Virgil Bozman in the mid-1940s and backed **Iry LeJeune** on his first record, in 1947. In the late 1940s had releases on Opera and Bozman's O.T. label, including "Louisiana Waltz" and "Roseland Two Step." After a hiatus returned to performing in the late 1950s and in following years performed and recorded with **Joe Bonsall**'s Orange Playboys and worked with Lake Charles Playboys, Lake Charles Ramblers, Traveler Playboys, and other groups until his death at age 51.

LeBLANC, LEROY *See* Happy Fats.

LeBLANC, SHORTY (Vorris LeBlanc) *Cajun.* Accordion, guitar, steel guitar, fiddle, drums, vocals. Composer. Bandleader. (Born Dec. 24, 1922, near Lake Arthur, Vermilion Parish; died May 25, 1965, New Orleans, Orleans Parish.)[12] Revered postwar accordion player and multi-instrumentalist began playing various instruments as a child and in the late 1940s joined the Lacassine Playboys. In 1951 replaced **Iry LeJeune** in group on accordion and performed with band through the mid-1950s. In the late 1950s joined **Cleveland Crochet**'s Hillbilly Ramblers and performed and recorded with group for several years, adding his bluesy accordion style to numerous singles, including their 1961 hit "Sugar Bee." Released several singles for Goldband as leader in the early 1960s, including "My Little Cabbage" and "Good Morning Blues." In 1963 formed his Gold Band (later called Acadian Aces) and also recorded on **Jimmy C. Newman**'s acclaimed LP *Folksongs of the Bayou Country* on Decca with **Rufus Thibodeaux**. Continued performing until being hospitalized in New Orleans, where he later succumbed to lung cancer at age 42.

LeBLEU, HORACE "RICKY" (Lloyd Horace LeBleu) *Cajun*. Drums, guitar, bass. Composer. Bandleader. (Born Feb. 4, 1920, Chloe near Iowa, Calcasieu Parish; died Jan. 7, 2004, Alexandria, Rapides Parish.)[13] Postwar Cajun string-band drummer and bandleader formed his Bar X Ramblers in the mid-1940s with brother Albert "Curly" (1927–1989) on fiddle and in following years performed around Lake Charles area. Recorded single "Basile Girl"/"Korea Blues" for Khoury's around 1950. In following decades led several area bands including Ricky and the Hound Dogs and Ricky and the Rockets.

LeBOUEF, RICHARD *Cajun*. Accordion, vocals. Composer. Bandleader. (Born Jan. 24, 1964, Kaplan, Vermilion Parish.) Cajun singer and accordionist and his band Two Step released debut CD, *Again for the First Time,* on La Louisianne in 1997 and had regional success with single "Empty Glass." Continued performing on club and festival circuit through the 2010s with releases *Kickin' in Your Own Backyard* in 2000 and *Longneck Vacation* in 2006.

LEDAY, CLARENCE *Creole, blues*. Guitar, vocals. Composer. (Born Apr. 7, 1929, Fenton, Jeff. Davis Parish; died June 18, 2013, Kinder, Allen Parish.) Blues and Creole guitarist and singer was raised speaking Creole French and spent majority of his life around Kinder. Performed regularly with **Bois Sec**, **Morris** and **Black Ardoin**, and was member of Black's French Band in the 1980s, recording with group on self-titled LP for Arhoolie in 1984. Also worked in trio with Morris and **Mary Jane Broussard**. In the mid-1990s released self-produced album *Miss You Like the Devil* featuring single "Mr. Charlie," which was popular on local radio stations, including KBON in Eunice.

LEDAY, GUYLAND *Zydeco*. Accordion, vocals. Composer. Bandleader. (Born Sept. 29, 1997, Opelousas, St. Landry Parish.) Contemporary zydeco accordionist was a child prodigy and began performing on stage at age four with great-uncle **Jeffery Broussard** in Zydeco Force. At age eight appeared in HBO documentary *The Music in Me* and on several other national television shows and recorded debut CD *Be My Girlfriend* in 2007, produced by **Robby "Mann" Robinson**. After several more releases, including *Teaching the Young* with **Goldman Thibodeaux** in 2010, relocated to Houston in the 2010s and continued performing with his band Zydeco Blazers.

LeDEE, MARSHALL *Swamp pop*. Guitar. (Born Mar. 17, 1926, Lawtell, St. Landry Parish; died June 1, 2012, Lake Charles, Calcasieu Parish.)[14] Noted early swamp pop guitarist best known as an original member of **Cookie** and the Cupcakes. After relocating to Lake Charles after serving in World War II, joined **Simon "Kee-Dee" Lubin**'s Boogie Ramblers in the early 1950s and recorded with band for Goldband in the mid-1950s. Continued performing with group after being renamed Cookie and the Cupcakes through the early 1970s and appeared on all of the band's studio recordings, including swamp pop classic "Mathilda." In the 1990s reunited with Cupcakes and continued performing with group into the 2000s.

LEDET, MORRIS *Zydeco*. Accordion, bass, vocals. Composer. Bandleader. (Born Dec. 27, 1968, Iota, Acadia Parish.) Zydeco multi-instrumentalist began playing accordion in the 1980s, inspired greatly by **Boozoo Chavis**. In the late 1980s formed his band Zydeco Playboys and appeared on Rounder's *Zydeco Shootout at El Sid O's* shortly before releasing *Hot Zydeco Sounds* on Maison de Soul in 1991. In 1994 switched to bass and began performing with wife **Rosie Ledet** leading the band. Toured and recorded extensively with group until the mid-2000s. Formed Zydeco Ramblers and released CD *Swing That Thing* on Maison de Soul in 2012, featuring daughter Kassie. In the late 2010s continued touring and recording as member of **Leroy Thomas**'s Zydeco Roadrunners.

LEDET, ROSIE *Zydeco*. Accordion, vocals. Composer. Bandleader. (Born Oct. 25, 1971, Church Point, Acadia Parish.) Known as the "Zydeco Sweetheart," popular singer-songwriter and accordion player grew up listening to rock music but in her late teens became interested in zydeco after seeing a local performance by **Boozoo Chavis**. In the early 1990s learned to play husband **Morris Ledet**'s accordion and joined his Zydeco Playboys in 1994 with Morris moving to bass. Signed with Maison de Soul later that year and released debut CD *Sweet Brown Sugar.* In following years toured extensively as popular act on national club and festival circuit with numerous releases on Maison de Soul, including *Show Me Something* in 2001 and *Pick It Up* in 2005. Continued touring in the 2010s with several more releases of rock-infused zydeco, including *Come Get Some* on JSP in 2011.

LEE, BONNIE "BOMBSHELL" (Jessie Lee Friels) *Blues.* Vocals, piano. Composer. (Born June 11, 1931, Bunkie, Avoyelles Parish; died Sept. 8, 2006, Chicago.)[15] Renowned Chicago blues singer who was affectionately known as the "Sweetheart of the Blues." Raised in Beaumont, Texas, began singing in church as a child and in her late teens and early 20s performed in Houston clubs and toured with the Famous Georgia Minstrel Show. Relocated to Chicago in 1958 and made recording debut for Ebony in 1960. In the mid-1960s began working regularly with Sunnyland Slim and had releases on his Airway label in 1974, followed by singles on Black Beauty and Big Boy. In the late 1970s began long association with bassist/bandleader Willie Kent and worked as vocalist with band for several decades. Toured Europe in 1982 with Big Time Sarah and Zora Young and appeared on LP *Blues with the Girls* on the Paris Album label. In the 1990s had releases on Wolf and Delmark, notably *Sweetheart of the Blues* in 1995. Continued performing in Chicago clubs mainly with Kent through the mid-2000s.

LEE, JACKIE *See* Nelson, Earl.

LEE, LEONARD *Rhythm and blues.* Vocals. Composer. Bandleader. (Born June 29, 1936, New Orleans, Orleans Parish; died Oct. 23, 1976, New Orleans, Orleans Parish.)[16] Best known as half of New Orleans rhythm and blues vocal duo Shirley & Lee, began singing with classmate **Shirley Goodman** as a teenager. Signed with Aladdin with Goodman in 1952 and had several hits as Shirley & Lee in the next several years, including "I'm Gone," "Feel So Good," and "Let the Good Times Roll." After unsuccessful recordings for Warwick, released two singles as leader for Imperial in early 1963 and split with Goodman. In the late 1960s recorded for **Dave Bartholomew**'s Broadmoor and Trumpet labels.

LEE, WARREN "KING LEE" (Warren Lee Taylor) *Rhythm and blues.* Guitar, vocals. Composer. Bandleader. (Born May 11, 1938, Vacherie, St. James Parish; died Apr. 18, 2014, Marrero, Jefferson Parish.) New Orleans early soul and funk singer and songwriter best known for his 1960s singles "Star Revue" and "Funky Belly." Inspired by **Guitar Slim**, began performing at Dew Drop Inn and other New Orleans area clubs in the late 1950s. From 1960 through 1974 had singles on Ron, Soundex, Nola, Jin, Deesu, Tou-Sea, Pama, Wand, and Choctaw, working with **Eddie Bo**, **Wardell Quezergue**, and **Allen Toussaint**. Continued to lead his band Past, Present and Future until suffering a stroke in 1977 and retiring from the music scene.

LÉGE, JESSE *Cajun.* Accordion, guitar, harmonica, vocals. Composer. Bandleader. (Born Nov. 5, 1951, Gueydan, Vermilion Parish.) Noted Cajun accordionist began playing guitar, harmonica, and accordion during his early teens, inspired greatly by **Marc Savoy**. While in his 20s performed with various bands around southwest Louisiana and east Texas, including substituting for an ailing **Joe Bonsall** in the Orange Playboys before eventually forming his own group the Southern Ramblers. Continued performing in the 1990s and 2000s with several acclaimed releases and toured overseas. In the early 2010s formed Cajun Country Revival with **Joel Savoy** and recorded *The Right Combination* on Valcour in 2011. Continued performing with his own group and other side projects in the late 2010s.

LEGER, ARTHUR *Cajun.* Fiddle, guitar. (Born Mar. 9, 1921, Welsh, Jeff. Davis Parish; died Mar. 17, 2016, Jennings, Jeff. Davis Parish.) Cajun fiddler began playing at age 15 and performed in country bands before relocating to Lake Charles. In the 1960s and 1970s performed and recorded with **Blackie Forestier** and later worked with **Bobby Leger**, **Ronald Frugé**, **Lesa Cormier**, and Texan Cajun Playboys, among others.

LEGER, BOBBY (Elias Leger) *Cajun.* Accordion, vocals. Composer. Bandleader. (Born July 17, 1916, Estherwood, Acadia Parish; died Jan. 21, 2008, Sulphur, Calcasieu Parish.) Veteran Cajun accordionist and bandleader was raised on his family's farm near Church Point and began playing accordion in his teens, inspired by **Lawrence Walker** and later **Iry LeJeune**. Relocated to Lake Charles in 1949 and in the early 1950s joined Lake Charles Playboys with **Jake** and **Robert Bertrand**. By the late 1950s began fronting the band and continued performing with group through the early 1990s with singles on Kajun, Cajun Classics, Bayou Classics, and Swallow in the 1960s and 1970s, including "Trouble's Two Step" and "The Lake Charles Playboys Waltz." Father of Cajun drummer Leroy Leger and nephew of **Martin "Bull" Leger**.

LEGER, ISAAC *Cajun.* Accordion. Bandleader. (Born July 12, 1936, Church Point, Acadia Parish; died Aug. 22, 2018, Hayes, Calcasieu Parish.) Cajun accordionist and bandleader moved to Hayes with family as a child and was soon inspired to play accordion by family friend **Iry LeJeune**. In the mid-1960s formed the Country Cajuns and performed with group for several decades, recording single "Country Cajuns Waltz"/"Cajun Country Special" on Marie in 1975. Father of Cajun bassist Isaac "Tony" Leger Jr.

LEGER, MARTIN "BULL" *Cajun.* Accordion, vocals. Bandleader. (Born Jan. 3, 1900, Bosco, near Church Point, Acadia Parish; died Mar. 19, 1985, Lake Charles, Calcasieu Parish.) Early Cajun accordionist began learning the instrument at an early age from his father and played local house dances. In the mid-1920s moved to Pine Island area and continued performing locally, often playing solo but also occasionally accompanied by nephew **Bobby Leger**, **Leo Soileau**, **Dennis McGee**, and others. After relocating to Lake Charles in the late 1940s, formed band Bull and the Little Bulls and continued performing until his death.

LEGER, WILSON *Cajun.* Accordion, vocals. Composer. (Born Dec. 9, 1913, Branch, Acadia Parish; died Nov. 12, 1988, Branch, Acadia Parish.) Locally renowned Cajun accordionist who was a mentor to nephew **Paul Daigle** and recorded "Ants in My Pants" for Bee in the mid-1980s.

LeJEUNE, ANGELAS *Cajun.* Accordion, vocals. Composer. Bandleader. (Born May 20, 1899, Pointe Noire, near Church Point, Acadia Parish; died June 12, 1974, Opelousas, St. Landry Parish.) Highly influential and important early Cajun accordionist and singer-songwriter whose 1929–30 recordings influenced many generations of musicians, notably his great-nephew **Iry LeJeune**. Raised in a musical family, began playing accordion at age 12 and by the late 1910s was playing at local house dances. Performed often in trio with **Dennis McGee** and **Ernest Frugé** and in 1929–30 recorded 16 sides for Brunswick on two landmark sessions, many of which would become Cajun standards (often under different names) such as "Bayou Pom Pom One Step," "Perrodin Two Step," and "Valse de Pointe Noire." Considered by peers to be one of the greatest accordionists of his era. Continued performing in the following decades at house dances and dance halls, settling in Opelousas in later years and often joined by **Lionel Leleux**.

LeJEUNE, EDDIE *Cajun.* Accordion, vocals. Composer. Bandleader. (Born Aug. 20, 1951, Ardoin Cove, Jeff. Davis Parish; died Jan. 9, 2001, Morse, Acadia Parish.) Renowned traditional Cajun accordionist began playing at age six, two years after his father **Iry LeJeune**'s death, learning initially from watching his maternal grandmother play. Within several years was performing at local house dances with brother **Ervin LeJeune**. Continued performing in local dance halls throughout the 1970s and 1980s, often later as a trio with accordion, fiddle, and guitar with his Morse Playboys. In 1988 made first recording as leader with LP *Cajun Soul* for Rounder followed by *It's in the Blood* in 1991 and *Cajun Spirit* in 1998. Also performed and recorded with **D. L. Menard**. Toured nationally and abroad before succumbing to fatal heart attack at age 49.

LeJEUNE, ERVIN *Cajun.* Accordion, fiddle, vocals. Bandleader. (Born July 2, 1950, Ardoin Cove, Jeff. Davis Parish; died Jan. 26, 2018, Lake Charles, Calcasieu Parish.) Son of Cajun music great **Iry LeJeune**, learned accordion from his grandmother and performed at house dances with brother **Eddie LeJeune** in the 1960s. In the late 1960s and 1970s performed in bands with **Jake** and **Robert Bertrand**, recording several singles as leader with group for Goldband, Jador, and Buck and occasionally billed as "Iry LeJeune Jr." From the late 1970s through mid-1980s performed and recorded with Sundown Playboys before retiring from performing. Also was an accomplished accordion maker.

LeJEUNE, FELTON *Cajun.* Accordion, vocals. Composer. Bandleader. (Born July 11, 1949, Richard, Acadia Parish; died July 5, 2011, Branch, Acadia Parish.) Traditional Cajun accordionist began playing at age eight and turned professional by age 15 under mentorship of **Elton "Bee" Cormier** in Cormier's Church Point Playboys, appearing on LP *The Church Point Playboys Produces Four Accordion Players* in 1973 on Bee. Led popular band the Cajun Cowboys from 1982 until his death, releasing single "Memories of a Broken Heart" on Lanor in 1989. Father of Cajun accordionist Troy LeJeune.

LeJEUNE, IRY (Ira Joseph LeJeune) *Cajun.* Accordion, fiddle, vocals. Composer. Bandleader. (Born Oct. 27, 1928, Pointe Noire, near Church Point, Acadia Parish; died Oct. 8, 1955, near Basile, Evangeline Parish.)[17] Highly influential and important postwar Cajun accordionist and singer-songwriter who was largely responsible for reviving accordion-based Cajun music in the late 1940s and early 1950s. Born legally blind and unable to work in the fields with his sharecropper family, began playing accordion as a child, learning early on from his father, Agnus, and great-uncle **Angelas LeJeune**. Also was greatly influenced by early Creole recordings of **Amédé Ardoin**, both instrumentally and vocally. By the early 1940s was performing throughout south Louisiana, including New Orleans area, and eventually relocated near Lacassine, where he began performing with **Milton Vanicor**'s Lacassine Playboys. Made debut recording, "Love Bridge Waltz"/"Evangeline Special," in Houston in 1947 for Opera with **Floyd LeBlanc** and the Oklahoma Tornadoes, which became a regional sensation. After performing in Houston area, returned to Louisiana and rejoined the Lacassine Playboys. In 1949 began recording for producer **Eddie Shuler** and through 1954 made numerous highly influential recordings, including "Lacassine Special," "I Went to the Dance," "Jolie Catin," "Grande Bosco," "Calcasieu Waltz," and "Teche Special." Continued performing in dance halls throughout south Louisiana until being fatally struck by a car while changing a flat tire along the roadside after a gig at age 26. Father of **Eddie** and **Ervin LeJeune**.

LeJEUNE, RODNEY *Cajun.* Guitar, vocals. Bandleader. (Born July 27, 1935, Church Point, Acadia Parish; died Jan. 25, 2015, Beaumont, Texas.) Texas-based Cajun singer and guitarist began performing in his teens and relocated to east Texas at age 21. In the late 1950s and 1960s performed and recorded with the Rambling Aces, which included at times **Andrew Cormier**, **Dallas Roy**, **Pappy "Tetan" Meaux**, and **Marc Savoy**. In the 1980s and 1990s performed and recorded with the Texas Cajun Playboys before retiring from music in 1998. Cousin of **Iry LeJeune**.

LELEUX, LIONEL *Cajun.* Fiddle. (Born Oct. 28, 1912, Leleux, Vermilion Parish; died June 22, 1996, Kaplan, Vermilion Parish.) Renowned fiddle player and master fiddle maker started playing as a child and in the 1930s began performing with childhood friend **Nathan Abshire** at local house dances and dance halls. Worked outside music as a barber to support his family throughout the 1940s but returned to music in the 1950s. In following decades performed and recorded with **Joe Falcon**, **Lawrence Walker**, **Don Montoucet**, and **Marc Savoy**. Also worked with **Angelas LeJeune**, **Aldus Roger**, **Varise Conner**, and **Walter Mouton** and toured nationally and overseas as performer and fiddle maker. In the early 1990s performed and recorded with **Eddie LeJeune** in the Morse Playboys.

LEVINGSTON, SARAH *Blues.* Vocals. (Born Mar. 31, 1949, Gilbert, Franklin Parish; died Nov. 11, 1989, Oakland, California.) Powerful Oakland, California–based blues singer who began performing in the early 1980s on the Bay Area blues scene. Later toured Europe and performed at the Monterey Jazz Festival and the San Francisco Blues Festival.

LEVY, JOHN *Jazz.* Bass. (Born Apr. 11, 1912, New Orleans, Louisiana; died Jan. 20, 2012, Altadena, California.) Jazz bassist who was the first African American manager in jazz. Raised in Chicago since age five, began playing bass as a teenager, and went on to work with Earl Hines, Tiny Parham, Red Saunders, Stuff Smith, Erroll Garner, Billie Holiday, and others through the late 1940s. In 1951 began managing jazz artists and throughout his prestigious career worked with Wes Montgomery, Cannonball Adderly, Ramsey Lewis, Joe Williams, and Freddie Hubbard, among others.

LEWIS, BETTY *Rhythm and blues, gospel.* Vocals. Composer. Bandleader. (Born Apr. 15, 1952, Shreveport, Caddo Parish.) Noted Shreveport southern soul singer and songwriter began performing in the mid-1980s and worked with various rhythm and blues and gospel groups. Later formed her band the Executives and toured nationally and abroad. Released CD *Live in Deep Elum* in 2001 and continued performing in 2010s.

LEWIS, CLANCY "BLUES BOY" *Blues.* Guitar, vocals. (Born Jan. 23, 1936, Torras, Pointe Coupee Parish.) Blues singer and guitarist began playing in his teens and by late 1960s was performing in New Orleans clubs. In 1970 appeared at the first New Orleans Jazz and Heritage Festival and returned to perform more than 25 times through the late 2000s. Often worked as duo with drummer Edward "Sheba" Kimbrough (1929–2005), who was formerly with **Professor Longhair**.

LEWIS, FATHER AL *Jazz.* Banjo, guitar, vocals. Bandleader. (Born Aug. 9, 1904, Houma, Terrebonne Parish; died Apr. 12, 1992, Galliano, Lafourche Parish.) Charismatic early jazz banjo player moved to New Orleans with family as a child. After attending school in Chicago in the early 1920s, returned to New Orleans and studied music with **Professor Jim Humphrey**. In the late 1920s and 1930s worked on riverboats and toured with **King Oliver**, **Nat Towles**, and others. Worked outside music from the late 1930s to late 1970s. In the 1980s had major career resurgence with several recordings and international tours. Performed regularly with Preservation Hall Jazz Band and New Orleans Joymakers.

LEWIS, FRANKIE JEAN (Terrell) *Rockabilly.* Vocals. (Born Oct. 27, 1944, Jonesville, Catahoula Parish; died July 24, 2016, Ferriday, Concordia Parish.) Younger sister of **Jerry Lee Lewis** who recorded unissued session for Sun in 1960 with sister **Linda Gail Lewis**. Later ran the Lewis Family Museum in Ferriday until her death at age 71.

LEWIS, GEORGE (Joseph Louis Francois Zenon) *Jazz.* Clarinet. Composer. Bandleader. (Born July 13, 1900, New Orleans, Orleans Parish; died Dec. 31, 1968, New Orleans, Orleans Parish.) Highly influential jazz clarinetist who achieved fame in later career as one of the finest traditional New Orleans jazz musicians of the 1940s, 1950s, and 1960s. Started on fife as a child and switched to clarinet during his teens. Played first professional gig in 1917 with **Evan Thomas**'s Black Eagles Band in Mandeville. In the 1920s worked with **Buddy Petit**, **Chris Kelly**, **Kid Rena**, Olympia and Eureka brass bands, and others, and led the New Orleans Stompers. In the early 1930s performed with **Bunk Johnson** in Thomas's Black Eagles and worked irregularly in music throughout rest of decade. Recorded and toured with Johnson from 1942 to 1945 and also cut sessions with **Kid Shots Madison** and as a leader. Recorded signature composition "Burgundy Street Blues" in 1944. In the late 1940s formed George Lewis Ragtime Band and became nationally recognized as major figure in the New Orleans jazz revival by the early 1950s. Toured nationally and overseas, including multiple trips to Japan, in the 1950s and 1960s and appeared regularly at Preservation Hall, performing there from 1961 until just weeks before his death.

LEWIS, JERRY LEE "THE KILLER" *Rockabilly, rock and roll, country.* Piano, guitar, drums, vocals. Composer. Bandleader. (Born Sept. 29, 1935, Ferriday, Concordia Parish.) Highly influential and iconic early rockabilly and rock and roll piano player and singer-songwriter best known for his wild showmanship and late 1950s hits such as "Great Balls of Fire" and "Whole Lotta Shakin' Going On." Began playing piano as a child, often with cousins Mickey Gilley and Jimmy Swaggart, and was greatly influenced by older cousin **Carl McVoy** and blues pianists at local juke joint Haney's Big House. After being expelled from Bible school in the early 1950s, recorded first demo in New Orleans at **Cosimo Matassa**'s studio in 1952 and continued performing around Ferriday and Natchez, Mississippi. After an unsuccessful attempt to break into Nashville music scene, relocated to Memphis in 1956 and began recording as both leader and session musician at Sun Studios, appearing on sessions with Carl Perkins, Johnny Cash, Elvis Presley, Billy Lee Riley, and others. In 1957 had national hits with "Whole Lotta Shakin' Going On" and "Great Balls of Fire" and became an international sensation with his electrifying performances. Several more hits followed, including "Breathless" and "High School Confidential," before his popularity plummeted after news of a recent marriage to his underage cousin. In the 1960s worked mainly as a country artist, reaching the charts numerous times and occasionally working with younger sister **Linda Gail Lewis**. In following decades returned to his rockabilly and rock and roll roots and released recordings on numerous labels, including *Last Man Standing* in 2006 and *Rock and Roll Time* in 2014. Continued performing into his 80s until sidelined by a stroke in 2019.

LEWIS, LINDA GAIL *Rockabilly, country.* Piano, vocals. Composer. Bandleader. (Born July 18, 1947, Ferriday, Concordia Parish.) Rockabilly singer and piano player began touring with older brother **Jerry Lee Lewis** in her early teens as back-up vocalist. In 1960 cut unissued single on Sun with sister **Frankie Jean Lewis** and in 1963 recorded with Jerry Lee for the label. Through the mid-1970s had country releases on Smash, Columbia, and Mercury and had hit with "Don't Let Me Cross Over" with Jerry Lee in 1969. After a long hiatus began performing again with Jerry Lee in the late 1980s before launching solo rockabilly career patterned after his driving piano style. Began touring Europe in the early 1990s and through mid-2010s released over twenty albums on numerous labels, including *You Win Again* with Van Morrison on Virgin in 2000 and *Hard Rockin' Woman* on Lanark in 2015.

LEWIS, ROBERT "SON FEWCLOTHES" *Jazz.* Drums. (Born Mar. 10, 1900, New Orleans, Orleans Parish; died June 24, 1965, New Orleans, Orleans Parish.) Highly respected New Orleans jazz drummer started performing in 1925 with Tulane Brass Band. Also worked with **Chris Kelly**, **Kid Rena**, and from the late 1930s through early 1960s, Eureka Brass Band. Recorded with Eureka in 1951.

LEWIS, ROGER *Jazz, rhythm and blues.* Saxophone. Bandleader. (Born Oct. 5, 1941, New Orleans, Orleans Parish.) Highly regarded saxophonist best known for his long tenure with Dirty Dozen Brass Band. Began playing saxophone at age ten and throughout the 1960s performed in bands of **Deacon John**, **Eddie Bo**, and **Irma Thomas**. In

1971 joined **Fats Domino**'s band and toured with group through the mid-1970s. Became original member of Dirty Dozen Brass Band in 1977 and continued performing and recording with group through the late 2010s. Also performed regularly with Tremé Brass Band.

LEWIS, SMILEY (Overton Amos Lemons) *Rhythm and blues.* Guitar, vocals. Composer. Bandleader. (Born July 5, 1916, Westlake, Calcasieu Parish; died Oct. 7, 1966, New Orleans, Orleans Parish.)[18] Highly influential early New Orleans rhythm and blues singer-songwriter and guitarist best known for his 1950s hits "I Hear You Knocking" and "The Bells Are Ringing." While in his mid-teens hopped a freight train to New Orleans and settled in the city. By the mid-1930s was performing in a jazz band with **Thomas Jefferson**, **Tuts Washington**, and **Noon Johnson**. Formed Smiley Lewis Trio in the mid-1940s with Washington and in next several years performed in New Orleans's most popular clubs, including famed Dew Drop Inn. After cutting two singles for Deluxe in 1947, signed with Imperial in 1950 and recorded prolifically for label with producer **Dave Bartholomew** through the late 1950s, cutting such classics as "Tee Nah Nah," "One Night," "Blue Monday," and "Shame Shame Shame," many of which would be covered by numerous artists, including **Fats Domino** and Elvis Presley. In following years recorded singles for OKeh, Dot, and Loma with little success. Continued performing in local clubs until falling ill and succumbing to stomach cancer at his home in New Orleans.

LEWIS, STEVE J. *Jazz.* Piano. Composer. (Died Mar. 19, 1895, New Orleans, Orleans Parish; died June 16, 1941, Jackson, E. Feliciana Parish.)[19] Early New Orleans jazz piano player and songwriter regarded by peers as one of the finest pianists of his era. Influenced by **Tony Jackson** and **Jelly Roll Morton**, became top entertainer in Storyville District's remaining years. In fall of 1917 toured with **Mary Mack**'s vaudeville act with **Johnny Dodds** and **Mutt Carey**. Worked regularly with **Armand Piron** in the late 1910s and 1920s, recording with Piron in 1923–24. Composed many songs, including Piron's theme, "Purple Rose of Cairo." Worked as soloist and with **Paul Barnes** and **Johnny St. Cyr** in the 1930s. In the late 1930s showed signs of serious mental illness and alcoholism and in Feb. 1940 was committed to the same state hospital where **Buddy Bolden** had passed away a decade earlier. Died at hospital the following year from complications of syphilis.

LEWIS, WALTER *Jazz, blues.* (Born Sept. 21, 1914, Prairieville, Ascension Parish; died June 10, 2002, New Orleans, Orleans Parish.) Early New Orleans piano "professor" who worked with **Claiborne Williams** and **Champion Jack Dupree**. In the 1940s performed with **Papa Celestin** and **Paul Barbarin** and throughout the 1950s worked with **Earl King**, **Guitar Slim**, Big Joe Turner, and others, performing regularly at New Orleans's famed Dew Drop Inn. In later years worked in jazz clubs with **Danny Barker**, **Louis Cottrell Jr.**, and **Placide Adams** and appeared often at Preservation Hall.

LIBERTO, ROY (Anthony) *Jazz.* Trumpet, vocals. Bandleader. (Born Mar. 11, 1928, New Orleans, Orleans Parish; died July 2, 2007, New Orleans, Orleans Parish.) Longtime New Orleans jazz trumpeter and bandleader who performed in clubs on Bourbon Street for many decades. Worked and recorded with **Santo Pecora**'s Tailgaters in the mid-1950s and then formed his band Bourbon Street Six which recorded for United Artists in 1962. In 1977 appeared on LP *Dixieland Plus,* the debut recording of ten-year-old **Harry Connick Jr.**

LIGHTNIN' SLIM (Otis Verries Hicks) *Blues.* Guitar, vocals. Composer. Bandleader. (Born Mar. 13, 1913, Good Pine, LaSalle Parish; died July 27, 1974, Detroit.)[20] Highly influential early swamp blues pioneer whose raw, gutbucket guitar and laid-back singing style helped define the subgenre on his numerous recordings in the 1950s and early 1960s. Began playing guitar as a child, learning from his father and brother Layfield Hicks and largely inspired by Blind Lemon Jefferson and **Lonnie Johnson**. In 1935 was convicted for manslaughter and served a ten-year sentence in Angola Prison. While serving time was injured by lightning strike, which possibly inspired his stage name. After release relocated to Baton Rouge and in the late 1940s began performing on the local blues scene. By the early 1950s was performing with his own group and other local musicians such as **Big Papa Tilley** and **Slim Harpo**. In 1954 began recording for **J. D. Miller**'s Feature label and through 1965 had numerous releases on Excello produced by Miller, including "Rooster Blues," "It's Mighty Crazy," and "Bad Luck and Trouble," the majority featuring **Lazy Lester** on harmonica. Continued to perform around Baton Rouge and southwest Louisiana until relocating to Pontiac, Michigan, in the mid-1960s. In 1971 began performing again by briefly reuniting with Lazy Lester for local folk festival and made additional recordings for Excello. Continued to perform nationally and abroad for several years, often with **Whispering Smith** on harmonica, until succumbing to cancer at age 61.

LI'L MILLET (McKinley James Millet Jr.) *Rhythm and blues.* Vocals, piano, bass. Composer. Bandleader. (Born Oct. 25, 1935, New Orleans, Orleans Parish; died June 29, 1997, New Orleans, Orleans Parish.) New Orleans rhythm and blues musician and songwriter best known for his 1955 Specialty single "Rich Woman." Began performing in the mid-1940s and in early 1950s was founding member of the Hawketts. Left Hawketts early on and formed Li'l Millet and His Creoles, a band discovered by Bumps Blackwell and signed to Specialty. Recorded two sessions for Specialty in 1955–56. Cowrote "All Around the World" for Little Richard. Continued performing occasionally through the 1980s.

LIL' BOB *See* Little Bob.

LIL' NATHAN or **LIL' NATE (Nathan Williams Jr.)** *Zydeco.* Accordion, piano, drums, vocals. Composer. Bandleader. (Born Nov. 18, 1986, Lafayette, Lafayette Parish.) Contemporary zydeco accordionist and singer-songwriter began playing rubboard in his father **Nathan Williams**'s band at age two and several years later started learning accordion, inspired by his father, **Boozoo Chavis**, and **Beau Jocque**. In the early 2000s formed his band Zydeco Big Timers and released debut CD *Zydeco Ballin'* on Mardi Gras in 2002, which incorporated soul, hip-hop, and Latin influences. Continued performing on zydeco club and festival circuit in the 2010s with several releases on family Cha Cha label, having local hit with "That L'Argent" in 2007. Younger brother Naylan is also a zydeco multi-instrumentalist.

LINCOLN, LARRY *See* Bamburg, Larry.

LINDSEY, HERB (*often misspelled* **Lindsay**) *Jazz.* Violin, vocals. Bandleader. (Born Nov. 27, 1888, Algiers, Orleans Parish; died Sept. 1, 1947, Chicago.)[21] Early New Orleans jazz violinist performed in family band with father, brother **John Lindsey**, and **Freddie Keppard** in Storyville District in the early 1910s. Also performed with **Louis Keppard** and dance band Primrose Orchestra. Relocated to Chicago in 1917 and worked with **Lawrence Duhé**. Also brother of jazz bandleader Joe "Kid" Lindsey.

LINDSEY, JOHN (*often misspelled* **Lindsay**) *Jazz.* Trombone, string bass. (Born Aug. 23, 1891, Algiers, Orleans Parish; died July 3, 1950, Chicago.)[22] Highly regarded early New Orleans jazz trombone and bass player began performing with family band as a child. In the early 1910s performed on bass in Storyville with his guitarist father, brother **Herb Lindsey**, and **Freddie Keppard**. Played trombone in military band during World War I and in the late 1910s and early 1920s worked with **John Robichaux**, **Papa Celestin**, and **Armand Piron**, with whom he recorded in 1923–24. In the mid-1920s moved permanently to Chicago and worked with **King Oliver** and Willie Hightower and recorded with **Jelly Roll Morton**. In the early 1930s toured and recorded with **Louis Armstrong** and also appeared on sessions with **Jimmie Noone**, **Richard M. Jones**, **Johnny Dodds**, Harlem Hamfats, and others through 1940, working mainly as bassist. Older brother of Joe "Kid" Lindsey, who is credited with being the first bandleader to hire **Louis Armstrong**, in 1916.

LITTLE ALFRED or **LIL' ALFRED (Alfred F. Babino)** *Swamp pop, rhythm and blues.* Saxophone, vocals. Composer. Bandleader. (Born Jan. 5, 1944, Lake Charles, Calcasieu Parish; died Nov. 14, 2006, Lake Charles, Calcasieu Parish.) Revered swamp pop and Louisiana soul singer best known for his 1960 regional hit "Walkin' Down the Isle." Began singing in church as a child and during his mid-teens started performing professionally with the Whirlwinds as saxophonist and vocalist, earning stage name Little Alfred for his Little Richard covers. In 1960 joined cousin **Simon "Kee-Dee" Lubin**'s band the Berry Cups and had regional hit on Khoury's with "Walkin' Down the Isle." Several more singles followed, including "It Don't Hurt No More" in 1963. After a stint with **Bill Parker**, replaced **Cookie Thierry** as vocalist in the Cupcakes in the mid-1960s and performed and recorded with group for several years. From 1967 to 1969 worked as vocalist for the Boogie Kings and cut a single with group for A&M. Relocated to Chicago in the early 1970s and spent much of decade performing with soul bands. Returned to Lake Charles in 1978 and performed in local clubs through the 1980s and early 1990s, often with **Charles Mann** and **Warren Storm**. In the mid-1990s reunited with Cookie and the Cupcakes and performed overseas. Released first full-length album, *Dealin' with the Feelin',* in 1997 on Jin and continued performing locally until his death at age 62.

LITTLE BOB or **LIL' BOB (Camille Bob Sr.)** *Rhythm and blues, swamp pop.* Drums, vocals. Composer. Bandleader. (Born Nov. 7, 1938, Arnaudville, St. Martin Parish; died July 6, 2015, Opelousas, St. Landry Parish.) Renowned southwest Louisiana soul singer and bandleader best known for his mid-1960s Louisiana classic "I Got Loaded." Began performing in the mid-1950s with **Good Rockin' Bob** as drummer and vocalist and made debut recording with group for Goldband in 1958. In the late 1950s formed his large, horn-driven band the Lollipops and had singles on Decca, Big Wheel, and High-Up before signing with La Louisianne in 1964 and releasing numerous singles and an LP, *Nobody But You.* Toured extensively on Gulf Coast and remained one of the region's most popular rhythm and blues acts through the mid-1970s. In the late 1960s released several singles and LP *Sweet Soul Swinger* on Jin. Throughout the 1970s and early 1980s continued performing in Lafayette area and had singles on Whit, Soul Unlimited, King Creole, and Master-Trak. Made final recording, *Back Again,* for Vidrine in 1990 and continued performing sporadically through the early 2000s until health issues forced retirement.

LITTLE BUCK *See* Sinegal, Lil' Buck.

LITTLE JIM *See* Brown, Sidney.

LITTLE LEO *See* Price, Leo.

LITTLE MISS PEGGY (Mary Wallace Johnson) *Rhythm and blues.* Vocals. Composer. (Born July 18, 1928, New Orleans, Orleans Parish.) Rhythm and blues vocalist who recorded for Goldband with **Bill Parker** in the early 1960s, notably the single "Peggy's Blues." Began singing in mid- to late 1950s after husband was killed serving in Korean War. Toured nationally for many years opening for top rhythm and blues acts such Aretha Franklin, Gladys Knight, Bobby Bland, and others. Eventually settled in Oklahoma City and performed on the local music scene throughout following decades. Continued performing locally into her late 80s at nursing homes and benefits.

LITTLE VICTOR (Victor Phillips) *Rhythm and blues.* Piano, trumpet, vocals. Composer. Bandleader. (Born Feb. 3, 1937, Youngsville, Lafayette Parish; died May 1984, Lafayette, Lafayette Parish.) Exceptional rhythm and blues piano and trumpet player and singer began performing in the Lafayette area in the early 1950s and made recording debut for **J. D. Miller**'s Feature label in 1954 with single "Loc-A-Li." Several years later recorded the scorching Little Richard–inspired single "Papa Lou and Gran" for Richland in 1961. Also recorded single for Lanor in the mid-1960s. In the 1960s and 1970s performed mainly as sideman on piano and trumpet with various local groups, including **Little Buck Sinegal**'s Top Cats. Mentor of **Buckwheat Zydeco**.

LITTLE WALTER (Marion Walter Jacobs) *Blues.* Harmonica, guitar, vocals. Composer. Bandleader. (Born May 1, probably 1925, Marksville, Avoy. Parish; died Feb. 15, 1968, Chicago.)[23] Profoundly influential Chicago blues singer-songwriter and harmonica player whose pioneering use of amplification and highly innovative and virtuosic playing style helped define postwar Chicago blues and modern blues thereafter. Began playing harmonica as a child and in the early 1940s started traveling as an itinerant musician, spending time in New Orleans, Shreveport, Monroe (Louisiana) and Helena (Arkansas), greatly influenced by saxophone player Louis Jordan and blues harmonica player Sonny Boy Williamson (Rice Miller). By the mid-1940s settled in Chicago and busked on Maxwell Street, where he began experimenting with amplification. Released first single on Ora-Nelle in 1947 and followed with recordings for Tempo-Tone, Regal, and Parkway with Muddy Waters, Sunnyland Slim, and others. By 1950 was working regularly with Muddy Waters and recording for Chess as a sideman. In 1952 had major hit with "Juke," which launched highly successful solo career. Through 1958 had fourteen Top 10 hits on the R&B charts, including "My Babe," "You're So Fine," "Blues with a Feeling," "Key to the Highway," and "Mean Old World." Also worked extensively as session musician with numerous artists, including Memphis Minnie, Bo Diddley, John Brim, Jimmy Rogers, and many others. In the 1960s recorded sporadically for Chess and toured Europe twice, but effects of alcoholism led to his serious decline by the late 1960s. Died in his sleep after a street altercation the previous night.

LITTLE WOLF/LITTLE HOWLIN' WOLF (Lee Arthur Solomon) *Blues.* Vocals. Composer. Bandleader. (Born Jan. 17, 1931, Mound, Madison Parish; died Oct. 31, 2005, Chicago.) Chicago blues singer moved to the Windy City in the early 1960s and worked regularly with bassist Willie Kent in the vocal style of his mentor, Howlin' Wolf. Led his own band on the West Side blues scene regularly through the mid-1990s and recorded two sides for the Wolf label in 1989. Older brother of **King Solomon**.

LITTLETON, JOHN *Gospel, opera.* Vocals. (Born June 20, 1920, Tallulah, Madison Parish; died Aug. 24, 1998, Reims, France.)[24] Internationally acclaimed gospel singer began singing as a child in church. Settled in France after serving there during World War II and studied at the National Academy of Music in Paris. Upon graduation spent several years performing and recording opera. Around

1960 began performing American gospel and black spirituals and became internationally renowned, recording more than seventy albums in following decades and being hailed as "the ambassador of the Negro spiritual in France."

THE LONESOME DRIFTER (Thomas Johnson) *Rockabilly.* Guitar, vocals. Composer. Bandleader. (Born Dec. 6, 1931, near Bastrop, Morehouse Parish.) Obscure but highly regarded early rockabilly singer-guitarist best known for his ultra-rare 1958 single "Eager Boy" on K. Raised on a cotton farm near Bastrop, began playing guitar after hearing local blues performers and records by Jimmie Rodgers and Bill Monroe. In 1958 recorded for **Mira Smith**'s RAM label in Shreveport and released "Teardrop Valley"/"Eager Boy" on K subsidiary which became a rockabilly classic. Released one more single as the Lonesome Drifter on RAM in 1959 and performed on the *Louisiana Hayride* program before retiring from music in 1960.

LONESOME SUNDOWN (Cornelius Green) *Blues.* Guitar, vocals. Composer. Bandleader. (Born Dec. 12. 1928, Donaldsonville, Ascension Parish; died Apr. 23, 1995, Gonzales, Ascension Parish.) Influential swamp blues singer and guitarist best known for his late 1950s and early 1960s Excello recordings such as "My Home Is a Prison" and "I'm a Mojo Man." After spending time in New Orleans in the late 1940s, learned guitar and piano and relocated to the Port Arthur area in 1953. In 1955 toured with **Clifton Chenier**'s band and recorded behind Chenier for Specialty. Settled in Opelousas later that year and performed on the local blues scene. In 1956 recorded debut single, "Lost Without Love," for producer **J. D. Miller** on Excello and had regional success. Through 1963 released more than a dozen singles on Excello, some featuring **Lazy Lester** on harmonica. Left music scene in 1966 to join the church but in the late 1970s briefly returned and recorded LP *Been Gone Too Long* for Joliet. After several festival appearances and tours of Sweden and Japan he retired from music permanently.

LONG, JOEY "CURLY" (Joseph Earl Longoria) *Blues, rockabilly.* Guitar, harmonica, vocals. Composer. Bandleader. (Born Dec. 17, 1932, Zwolle, Sabine Parish; died Mar. 21, 1995, Houston.) Noted Texas blues and early rockabilly guitarist began playing guitar as a child while growing up on family farm. In the early to mid-1950s performed with Texas singer-guitarist Sonny Fisher and cut several early rockabilly classics with Fisher for Starday in 1955, notably "Rockin' Daddy." Relocated to Houston and became regular on the local music scene with singles on Azalea, Som, Argo, Running Bear/Tribe, Tear Drop, and Eric in the late 1950s and early 1960s. In the mid-1960s recorded as sideman with Big Walter Price, **Johnny Copeland**, **Clarence "Frogman" Henry**, T-Bone Walker, and others. Released psychedelic rock album *Stoned Age Man* on Scepter in 1970 under name Joseph, followed by two LPs on Crazy Cajun in 1978, *Flyin High* and *The Rains Came.* Continued performing until suffering fatal heart attack at age 62.

LOPEZ, JOE *Cajun.* Fiddle, guitarist. (Born Dec. 14, 1931, New Iberia, Iberia Parish; died Mar. 19, 2014, New Iberia, Iberia Parish.) Renowned Cajun fiddle player began playing at age 16 and from the late 1950s through late 1960s performed and recorded as member of **Elias "Shute" Badeaux**'s Louisiana Aces, appearing on several singles, including the 1962 Cajun classic "The Back Door." Later performed and recorded with **Touchet Brothers** and **Aldus Roger**.

LOPEZ, LOUIS *Cajun.* Accordion, vocals. (Born Nov. 18, 1918, Elton, Jeff. Davis Parish; died Nov. 24, 1976, Lake Charles, Calcasieu Parish.) Unrecorded early postwar Cajun accordionist began playing as a child and by the late 1940s was playing professionally in Lake Charles area with his band Calcasieu Playboys. Known for his exciting showmanship, performed with **Jake** and **Robert Bertrand**, **August Broussard**, **Atlas Frugé**, **Orsy Vanicor**, and others and mentored many young musicians throughout his career. Brother Valentine Lopez was a noted accordion maker under Starling brand.

LOTT, HERMAN "BUZZARD" *Rhythm and blues.* Bass. (Born Dec. 14, 1937, Shreveport, Caddo Parish; died Aug. 13, 2006, Shreveport, Caddo Parish.) Renowned Shreveport soul-blues bassist toured with Ike and Tina Turner, **Eddie Giles**, Johnnie Taylor, and others in the 1960s and performed in backing bands with Freddie King, Z.Z. Hill, and Etta James. In the 1970s and 1980s worked regularly with **Raymond Blakes**, **Elgie Brown**, and Marvin Seals.

LOUISIANA GUITAR RED (Cardell Boyette) *Blues.* Guitar, piano, vocals. Composer. Bandleader. (Born Sept. 1, 1928, Litroe, Union Parish; died Dec. 6, 2001, Los Angeles.)[25] California-based blues singer and guitarist relocated to Los Angeles in 1953 and began playing on the local blues scene as a pianist. Soon switched to guitar, influenced largely by T-Bone Walker. In following decades worked with Walker, Pee Wee Crayton, Johnny "Guitar"

Watson, Lowell Fulson, George "Harmonica" Smith, and others. In the 1990s had releases on Delphine, Video Uptown, and Ocala. Not to be confused with Alabama-born blues guitarist Louisiana Red (Iverson Minter).

LOVE, C. P. (Carollton Pierre Love) *Rhythm and blues.* Vocals, guitar, bass. Composer. Bandleader. (Born May 1, 1945, New Orleans, Orleans Parish.) New Orleans deep soul singer began performing during his teens and worked with **Walter "Wolfman" Washington** in the early 1960s. Made recording debut on **Earl King**'s King Walk label in 1968. In the early 1970s worked with **Wardell Quezergue** and had releases on Chimneyville and Stone, notably "Never Been in Love Before." In the late 1970s through mid-1980s worked in clubs on Bourbon Street and had releases on Polka Dot and Moon Wind. From 1986 to 1999 lived in California Bay Area and toured West Coast, with a release on Orleans in 1990. Returned to New Orleans in 2000 and continued to perform occasionally in the 2010s.

LOVE, CHARLIE *Jazz.* Trumpet. Bandleader. (Born Oct. 6, 1884, Plaquemine, Iberville Parish; died Aug. 7, 1963, New Orleans, Orleans Parish.)[26] Early New Orleans jazz trumpeter began performing as a child and worked with various local bands in the 1910s, including the Plaquemine Brass Band, which occasionally performed in New Orleans. Also performed with Caddo Jazz Band in Shreveport and toured Chicago with group in 1917. In the 1920s worked in New Orleans with Excelsior Brass Band and **Papa Celestin**'s Tuxedo Brass Band and performed with **John Robichaux** at Lyric Theater. Semiretired from music during the 1930s and worked in clubs in the late 1940s and 1950s and in parades with Tuxedo Brass Band. In the early 1960s recorded with **George Lewis**, **Louis Hall Nelson**, **Kid Sheik Cola**, and **Albert Jiles**.

LOVELESS, BOBBY "THE NIGHT OWL" (Bobbie Anthony Lovless) *Swamp pop.* Saxophone, vocals. Composer. Bandleader. (Born May 22, 1940, Donaldsonville, Ascension Parish; died Sept. 18, 2005, Baton Rouge, EBR Parish.)[27] Swamp pop singer-songwriter and saxophone player best known for his 1964 single "Night Owl." In the late 1950s and 1960s performed as saxophonist with **Van Broussard**, **John Fred**, **Jimmy Clanton**, and Johnny Rivers. Recorded several singles on Carmie, Stephanie, and HBR in the mid-1960s and had local hit with "Night Owl." Dubbed "Little **Lee Allen**" after famed New Orleans studio musician for his instrumental prowess.

LOVIN' SAM FROM DOWN IN 'BAM *See* Theard, Samuel.

LUBIN, SIMON "KEE-DEE" *Swamp pop, rhythm and blues.* Drums, vocals. Bandleader. (Born May 16, 1916, Basile, Evangeline Parish; died Oct. 17, 1988, Lake Charles, Calcasieu Parish.)[28] Early rhythm and blues drummer and bandleader relocated to Lake Charles with family in 1920. By the late 1940s was performing in Lake Charles clubs and taverns and in the early 1950s formed the Boogie Ramblers, which included **Ernest Jacobs**, **Marshall LeDee**, and **Shelton Dunaway** (and later became **Cookie** and the Cupcakes). Left group early on and formed the Berry Cups in the late 1950s, recording for Khoury's with vocalists **Terry Clinton** and **Little Alfred**. Performed and recorded with group through the mid-1960s and later worked and recorded with **Marcel Dugas** and **Wild Bill Pitre**.

LUTCHER, JOE (Joseph Woodman Lutcher) *Rhythm and blues, gospel.* Saxophone, vocals. Composer. Bandleader. (Born Dec. 23, 1919, Lake Charles, Calcasieu Parish; died Oct. 29, 2006, Whittier, California.) Noted early jump blues singer, saxophone player and bandleader performed with family band as a child before following sister **Nellie Lutcher** to California in the early 1940s to pursue a music career. After serving in World War II, began performing on Los Angeles's Central Avenue club scene and in 1947 recorded for Specialty and Capitol, having national hits with "Rockin' Boogie" and "Shuffle Woogie." In 1949 released several singles on Modern, including Latin-inspired "Ojai" and his final hit, "Mardi Gras," which would influence **Professor Longhair**'s more famous version. After a single each on London, Peacock, and Master Music in the early 1950s, became evangelical minister and left secular music. In the late 1950s founded gospel label Jordan Records and released several gospel recordings. Also traveled country with Little Richard on religious tour in 1959. Son of Isaac Sr. (1881–1963), who was a veteran Lake Charles musician, and brother of Isaac "Bubba" (1916–1981), who was a noted Lake Charles promoter and disc jockey.

LUTCHER, NELLIE *Rhythm and blues, jazz.* Piano, vocals. Composer. Bandleader. (Born Oct. 15, 1912, Lake Charles, Calcasieu Parish; died June 8, 2007, Los Angeles.) Influential early rhythm and blues singer and pianist best known for her late 1940s hits "Fine Brown Frame," "Hurry On Down," and "He's a Real Gone Guy." Began performing as a child with her bassist father, Isaac Sr., in Clarence Hart's Imperial Orchestra and during her teens worked as pianist with Ma Rainey. In the mid-1930s relocated to Los Angeles and through the 1940s worked at various venues on Central Avenue, later with brother **Joe Lutcher**. In 1947 signed with Capitol and had national hit with debut single, "Hurry On Down." Through 1950 recorded ten more hit singles, including "Lake Charles Boogie" and duet with Nat King Cole on **Paul Gayten**'s "For You My Love." In the early 1950s made several successful tours of England and throughout decade had releases on OKeh, Decca, Imperial, and Liberty, developing a more pronounced jazz style in later years. Continued performing sporadically in following decades before retiring from music in the early 1990s. Brother Isaac "Bubba" (1916–1981) was a Lake Charles promoter and disc jockey.

LYNN, TAMI (*also* Tammi/Tammy/Tamiya) (Gloria Jean Brown) *Rhythm and blues.* Vocals. Composer. (Born Jan. 25, 1943, New Orleans, Orleans Parish.)[29] Noted New Orleans soul singer began performing in gospel groups while in her teens and joined **Red Tyler**'s band around 1960 when Tyler's vocalist **Angel Face** began missing gigs. In the early 1960s recorded singles and an LP for A.F.O. and toured country with house band the Executives. Worked in California and New York in the mid-1960s and recorded "I'm Gonna Run Away from You" on Atco, which was a hit in England when rereleased in 1971 on Mojo. Recorded singles for Atlantic, including "Mojo Hannah" in 1971, which she had previously cut for A.F.O., and released LP on Cotillion in 1972. In the late 1960s and early 1970s sang back-up on sessions for **King Floyd**, **Dr. John**, the Rolling Stones, and others. In 1992 released jazz CD on Liberty self-titled *Tamiya Lynn.* Continued performing occasionally into the 2010s, based in New York and later Florida.

LYONS, BOB *Jazz.* Bass, guitar, banjo. Bandleader. (Born Apr. 20, 1877, New Orleans, Orleans Parish; died June 27, 1948, New Orleans, Orleans Parish.)[30] Renowned early New Orleans jazz and ragtime bassist began performing in the mid-1880s on the streets for tips and in the 1890s worked with **Oscar Duconge**'s band. Performed with **Buddy Bolden** in the first years of the 1900s and **Frankie Duson**'s Eagle Band from 1907 to 1910. Led **Kid Ory**'s band during World War I and formed Bob Lyons Dixie Jazz Band in the late 1910s. Continued performing into the early 1930s but by 1940 was working on a shoeshine stand.

LYONS, PEE WEE (Ronald Ray Lyons) *Cajun.* Steel guitar, vocals. (Born Jan. 18, 1926, Lake Charles, Calcasieu Parish; died Oct. 7, 1981, Abbeville, Vermilion Parish.)[31] Noted early Cajun steel guitarist performed and recorded with **Harry Choates** in the late 1940s, appearing on several notable releases, including "Poor Hobo" and "Harry Choates Special" in 1947. Also performed and recorded with **Jimmie Choates** in the late 1940s. In the 1950s worked and recorded with producer **Eddie Shuler**'s All Star Reveliers.

M

MACK, MARY (McBride) *Jazz, blues.* Vocals. (Born July 28, 1891, Algiers, Orleans Parish; died Jan. 7, 1979, Chicago.)[1] Early black vaudeville performer who toured with husband in the late 1910s and 1920s as Billy and Mary Mack's Merrymakers Revue, which included at times **Johnny Dodds**, **Steve Lewis**, and **Mutt Carey**. Recorded jazz and blues duets with husband for OKeh in 1925–26, occasionally backed by **Punch Miller**. In 1936–37 had recording sessions in Chicago with releases on Bluebird and Vocalion accompanied by Albert Ammons, Big Bill Broonzy, and Black Bob.

MACKIE, FRANK "RED" *Jazz.* Bass, piano, tuba. Bandleader. (Born Apr. 16, 1903, New Orleans, Orleans Parish; died Aug. 11, 1969, New Orleans, Orleans Parish.)[2] Began playing string bass at age 12 and was original member of Invincibles and New Orleans Owls. Founded and recorded with Six and Seven Eights String Band. Older brother of **Dick Mackie**.

MACKIE, RICHARD H. "DICK" *Jazz.* Cornet. (Born Nov. 26, 1906, New Orleans, Orleans Parish; died Nov. 15, 1987, New Orleans, Orleans Parish.)[3] Early jazz cornet player and original member of New Orleans Owls in the early 1920s. Also worked and recorded with Hal Kemp Orchestra. Brother of **Red Mackie**.

MADISON, LOUIS "KID SHOTS" *Jazz.* Trumpet, drums. Bandleader. (Born Feb. 19, 1899, New Orleans, Orleans Parish; died Sept. 28, 1948, New Orleans, Orleans Parish.)[4] Early New Orleans jazz trumpeter was in Colored Waif's Home with **Louis Armstrong** and **Kid Rena** and performed with both in its band as a drummer. Switched to trumpet and worked with **Frankie Duson**'s Eagle Band in the mid-1910s. In the mid-1920s worked and recorded with **Papa Celestin**'s Original Tuxedo Jazz Orchestra. Throughout the 1930s and 1940s performed with W.P.A., Eureka, and Young Tuxedo brass bands. Recorded with **Bunk Johnson** and **George Lewis** in the mid-1940s.

MAIDEN, SIDNEY *Blues.* Harmonica, vocals. Composer. Bandleader. (Born Oct. 7, 1917, Evelyn, DeSoto Parish; died reportedly late 1980s, Arizona.)[5] Country blues harmonica player and singer best known for his long association with guitarist K.C. Douglas. Relocated to California in the early 1940s and after serving in World War II began performing with Douglas in area clubs. Recorded "Mercury Blues" with Douglas in 1948 for Down Town and sang lead on its b-side, "Eclipse of the Sun." In the 1950s had singles on Imperial, Flash, and Dig and in 1961 released LP *Blues an' Trouble* on Prestige/Bluesville backed by Douglas. Also recorded as sideman with pianist Mercy Dee Walton and Douglas on sessions for Arhoolie that year. Reportedly continued to perform around Fresno for several years but details of remaining years remain unclear.

MAIRE, EDWIN *See* Guitar Red.

MAITRE, HUBERT *Cajun.* Guitar, drums, vocals. Composer. Bandleader. (Born Oct. 9, 1940, Lafayette, Lafayette Parish; died Dec. 16, 2017, Scott, Lafayette Parish.) Noted early postwar Cajun guitarist began playing house parties at age nine with his father, Adam Maitre. From the 1950s through 1960s performed with numerous musicians, including **Walter Mouton**, **Joe Falcon**, **Austin Pitre**, and **Lawrence Walker**. After Walker's death in 1968, continued working with Walker's Wandering Aces through the 1980s, touring internationally and recording for Sonet. In the late 1980s and 1990s performed and recorded with **Eddie LeJeune** and **Milton Adams** and mentored **Kevin Naquin** and **Horace Trahan.** Formed Cajun Friends band in 2001 and recorded acclaimed CD

La Vielle Chaudièr Noire on Acadiana. Continued performing into the 2010s.

MAJOR, B.B. (Image Helaire Jr.) *Blues.* Guitar, vocals. Composer. Bandleader. (Born May 24, 1937, near Melrose, Natch. Parish; died Oct. 19, 2008, Natchitoches, Natch. Parish.) Blues guitarist and singer-songwriter began playing guitar in the 1950s, largely inspired by B.B. King. In the mid-1960s started performing with local bands, including with **Overton Owens**. After two decades of working with various groups, formed B.B. Major Blues Band in the mid-1990s and released debut CD, *Evil Woman/Evil Ways,* in 1997 on Cane River. Two years later released *I Ain't Got Nobody* and continued performing at clubs and festivals until succumbing to kidney disease at age 71.

MALBROUGH, FELTON *Blues.* Guitar, vocals. (Born Mar. 12, 1934, Church Point, Acadia Parish.) Blues singer and guitarist recorded numerous sides with **Raymond Randle** for Lanor in the mid-1980s and released single "Boogie Chillun"/"Short Hair Woman Blues" in 1984. Later settled in Lake Charles.

MANETTA, MANUEL "FESS" *Jazz.* Piano, cornet, saxophone, trombone, violin, guitar. (Born Oct. 3, 1889, New Orleans, Orleans Parish; died Oct. 10, 1969, New Orleans, Orleans Parish.)[6] Highly influential early New Orleans jazz master multi-instrumentalist and music teacher. Began performing during his teens and worked with **Tom Albert**, **Buddy Bolden**, **Frankie Duson**, and **Edward Clem** on various brass instruments before 1910. Gained notoriety for his ability to play a trumpet and trombone simultaneously. Performed as solo pianist in Storyville District and with **Papa Celestin**'s Original Tuxedo Jazz Band. Briefly worked in Chicago around 1917 but returned to New Orleans and toured California as violinist with **Kid Ory** in 1919. In the 1920s worked with **Manuel Perez** as saxophonist and Celestin as pianist. Remained a popular music teacher at his home in Algiers for decades, with **Buddy Petit**, **Red Allen**, and **Papa Lemon Nash** among his many students.

MANGIAPANE, SHERWOOD *Jazz.* Bass, tuba, drums, vocals. (Born Oct. 1, 1912, New Orleans, Orleans Parish; died Jan. 23, 1992, New Orleans, Orleans Parish.) Noted New Orleans jazz upright bassist who played "backwards" by performing left-handed. Worked and recorded with **Johnny Wiggs**, **Raymond Burke**, and **Edmond Souchon** in the 1950s and 1960s. Performed regularly at Preservation Hall and later with Louisiana Repertory Jazz Ensemble in the 1980s. Retired from music in 1990 due to illness.

MANN, CHARLES (Charles Louis Domingue) *Swamp pop.* Guitar, vocals. Composer. Bandleader. (Born Nov. 22, 1944, Welsh, Jeff. Davis Parish.) Swamp pop singer best known for his late 1960s cover of Neil Diamond's "Red Red Wine." Began performing around Lake Charles area in 1960 and while member of the Eltradors was signed to Lanor in the mid-1960s. In the next several years released a number of regional hits, including "Keep Your Arms Around Me" and "You're No Longer Mine," before achieving greatest success with "Red Red Wine" in 1969. Continued releasing singles for Lanor through the 1980s and had minor hit with "Walk of Life" in 1988. In 2007 released CD *Pushing Your Luck* on Jin and continued performing with his band Louisiana Pride in 2010s.

MANONE, WINGY (Joseph Manone) *Jazz.* Trumpet, vocals. Composer. Bandleader. (Born Feb. 13, 1900, New Orleans, Orleans Parish; died July 9, 1982, Las Vegas.) Popular one-armed jazz trumpeter, singer, and composer began performing on kazoo for tips on the streets in Storyville as a child. In the 1920s performed on riverboats and recorded with Arcadian Serenaders in 1924. Recorded with his band the Harmony Kings in 1927, Benny Goodman in 1929, and in Chicago with his band the Cellar Boys in 1930. While living in New York had hit with "The Isle of Capri" in 1935 and gained national fame. Recorded many more of his compositions and in the 1940s relocated to Los Angeles and worked in both film and radio with Bing Crosby. Settled in Las Vegas in the 1950s and continued performing through the 1970s.

MANUEL, ABE, SR. *Cajun, country.* Fiddle, banjo, vocals. Composer. Bandleader. (Born June 19, 1926, Mamou, Evangeline Parish; died June 9, 2003, Milton, Tennessee.)[7] Renowned early postwar Cajun-country fiddle player and singer began playing Cajun music as a child with his father, Adam. In the early 1940s performed with **Leo Soileau** and in the late 1940s worked and recorded with **Harry Choates** along with brother Joe Manuel (1922–1959). Also performed and recorded with **Jelly Elliott** in the late 1940s and appeared on brother Joe's singles on Deluxe and Folk-Star. In the early 1950s performed on the *Louisiana Hayride,* toured with Hank Williams and Lefty Frizzell, and made recording debut as a leader with single on O.T. (as Sandy Austin). Around 1953 formed his Louisiana Hillbillies band, which included wife, Dottie, on guitar and vocals and recorded two singles on Feature, including "Hippy-Ti-Yo," in 1955. Continued performing with group in the 1960s and appeared on **Rufus Thibodeaux**'s 1965 Kajun LP *A Tribute to Harry Choates.* By the 1970s was settled in Creole and performing with family band which included Dottie (1935–) and sons Abe Jr. (1963–) on fiddle and accordion and Little Joe (1960–) on guitar. Relocated near Nashville, Tennessee, in 1987 and continued performing and operating a Cajun restaurant until retiring in 2001.

MANUEL, MANSON *Cajun, country.* Fiddle, guitar, vocals. Composer. Bandleader. (Born July 31, 1934, Basile, Evangeline Parish; died Oct. 3, 2014, Lake Charles, Calcasieu Parish.) Began playing guitar and fiddle as a child and performed at house dances with his accordionist father Mauis (1910–1954) and uncles Rodney and Oreus, who were known locally in the Oberlin area as the Manuel Brothers. Later performed and recorded with band Midnight Express with **John Crochet** in Lake Charles and east Texas region.

MANUEL, SHELTON *Cajun.* Fiddle, drums, accordion, guitar, vocals. (Born Nov. 3, 1921, Eunice, St. Landry Parish; died Jan. 4, 2005, Eunice, St. Landry Parish.) Noted early postwar Cajun master multi-instrumentalist began playing fiddle at age 16 and in the 1940s and early 1950s performed and recorded as drummer with **Nathan Abshire**'s band. Also performed with **J. B. Fuselier** and **Papa Cairo** and recorded with **Shirley Bergeron**, **Lawrence Walker**, **Jimmy C. Newman**, and others in the 1950s and early 1960s. After being blinded in hunting accident around 1970, continued performing occasionally and hosting a Cajun music workshops into his early 80s.

MARCANTEL, NANCY TABB *Cajun.* Vocals. (Born Apr. 19, 1951, Jennings, Jeff. Davis Parish.) Cajun-country vocalist began singing as a child and learned voice techniques as a soloist in her church choir. In 1974 formed family band Lagniappe with brothers David, Greg, and Peter and had regional hit with "Ma Louisiane" on Swallow, a Cajun French ode to Louisiana set to John Denver's "Country Roads" melody. Through the mid-1980s toured extensively nationally and overseas and released albums of Cajun, gospel, and children's songs, including LP *Sweetheart of Cajun Country* on Spun Gold in 1979. In the late 1990s resumed singing career after working outside music and released CD *Louisiana Makes Me Smile* in 1999 on Musique Acadie. Continued working as a performer and vocal instructor in the 2010s.

MARCOTTE, LOUIS MARION *Cajun.* Guitar, vocals. Composer. Bandleader. (Born Aug. 15, 1916, Moreauville, Avoy. Parish; died Jan. 21, 1998, Gretna, Jefferson Parish.) Popular Cajun musician and humorist best known for his many comedy recordings about Cajun life. Began playing guitar and writing songs during his early teens and at age 18 moved with family to New Orleans and formed his own band. In 1953 made recording debut on Carnival and in the mid- to late 1950s had several releases on Arcadia as leader and with the Arcadians. In the 1960s and 1970s became internationally renowned as a Cajun French storyteller with numerous recordings on Jin and Swallow, often combining his humor with music.

MARES, PAUL *Jazz.* Cornet, trumpet. Composer. Bandleader. (Born June 15, 1900, New Orleans, Orleans Parish; died Aug. 18, 1949, Chicago.) Early New Orleans jazz trumpeter, who was greatly influenced by **King Oliver**, began performing in **Tom "Red" Brown**'s band during his teens. In the early 1920s relocated to Chicago and helped form New Orleans Rhythm Kings, one of the city's most popular and influential jazz bands. Band recorded from 1922 to 1923, with **Jelly Roll Morton** appearing on several sides during rare interracial early recording session. In 1925 returned to New Orleans and worked outside music until a brief comeback and recording session in the mid-1930s in Chicago. Younger brother Joseph Mares was a jazz clarinetist and founder of Southland Records.

MARLOWE, PETE/PETO *See* Bergeron, Pete.

MARRERO, BILLY *Jazz.* Bass. Bandleader. (Born Aug. 1871, St. Bernard Parish; died Oct. 24, 1919, New Orleans, Orleans Parish.)[8] Early New Orleans jazz bandleader and patriarch of noted Creole family of musicians which includes sons **Eddie**, **John**, **Lawrence**, and **Simon Marrero**. Worked regularly with **Manuel Perez**'s Imperial Orchestra in 1905–10. Led Original Superior Orchestra in the early 1910s with **Bunk Johnson** and **Peter Bocage**. Also worked with Olympia Orchestra. In the late 1910s led band which included **Sam Morgan** until stepping down due to illness.

MARRERO, EDDIE *Jazz.* Bass. (Born Aug. 4, 1902, New Orleans, Orleans Parish; died Feb. 1984, New Orleans, Orleans Parish.)[9] Son of noted bandleader **Billy Marrero**, began playing bass a few months after death of his father. Worked with brother **Lawrence Marrero** in Young Tuxedo Orchestra and also with **Buddy Petit**, **Emile Barnes**, **Wooden Joe Nicholas**, and **Chris Kelly**

in the 1920s but retired from music by end of decade. Also brother of **John** and **Simon Marrero**.

MARRERO, JOHN *Jazz.* Banjo, guitar. Composer. (Born Aug. 20, 1897, New Orleans, Orleans Parish; died Feb. 20, 1942, Manhattan, New York.)[10] Son of early New Orleans jazz bandleader **Billy Marrero** and widely regarded as one of the finest jazz banjo players of the 1920s. Began performing in 1916 as guitarist in band with **Buddy Petit**, **Sidney Bechet**, and brother **Simon Marrero**. In the 1920s started playing banjo and worked with **Kid Rena**, **Armand Piron**, and **Bébé Ridgley**. Spent several years in **Papa Celestin**'s Original Tuxedo Orchestra and appeared on recording sessions with band for OKeh and Columbia in 1925–27. Gave banjo lessons to **Creole George Guesnon**. In the 1930s moved to New York following brother Simon's relocation. Brother of **Eddie** and **Lawrence Marrero**.

MARRERO, LAWRENCE (*or* **Laurence**) *Jazz.* Banjo, guitar, bass drum. (Born Oct. 24, 1900, New Orleans, Orleans Parish; died June 6, 1959, New Orleans, Orleans Parish.) Son of noted bandleader **Billy Marrero**, celebrated early jazz banjo player took music lessons from his brother **John Marrero** and in the late 1910s worked in bands with **Chris Kelly**, **Kid Rena**, and **Wooden Joe Nicholas**. In 1920 formed Young Tuxedo Orchestra. Worked with **Chris Kelly** regularly throughout the 1920s as well as **Papa Celestin**. Gained fame in the 1940s when he recorded and toured with **Bunk Johnson** during his rediscovery period and as member of **George Lewis** Ragtime Band. Retired after suffering a series of strokes in 1955. Brother of **Eddie** and **Simon Marrero**.

MARRERO, SIMON *Jazz.* Bass, bass drum. (Born Aug. 8, 1893, New Orleans, Orleans Parish; died Nov. 25, 1935, Rapides Parish, Louisiana.)[11] Highly regarded upright bassist and oldest son of noted early jazz bandleader **Billy Marrero**. Started performing at age 17 after receiving bass lessons from father. Worked regularly with **Kid Rena** and **Buddy Petit** in the 1920s. Also performed and recorded with **Papa Celestin**. Performed with **King Oliver** in 1931 and worked in New York with Mills Blue Rhythm Boys. Became ill working on steamboat with **Fate Marable** in 1933 and never recovered. Brother of **Eddie**, **John**, and **Lawrence Marrero.**

MARSALIS, BRANFORD *Jazz, classical.* Saxophone. Composer. Bandleader. (Born Aug. 26, 1960, Breaux Bridge, St. Martin Parish.) Internationally renowned jazz and classical saxophonist, composer, and bandleader and oldest son of acclaimed New Orleans jazz pianist and professor **Ellis Marsalis Jr**. After attending Berklee College of Music, toured with Art Blakey's Jazz Messengers (which included brother **Wynton Marsalis**), Herbie Hancock, and Clark Terry in the early 1980s. Performed with Wynton's quintet from 1982 to 1985 and recorded with Ray Drummond, Dizzy Gillespie, and Bobby Hutcherson. In 1984–85 also performed and recorded with Miles Davis and in the late 1980s toured and recorded with rock musician Sting. Served as bandleader on *The Tonight Show with Jay Leno* from 1992 to 1995. Throughout following years recorded extensively and led several bands, including Branford Marsalis Quintet and Buckshot LeFonque, the latter which combined jazz, rock, blues, pop, and hip-hop influences. In 2010 made debut with New York Philharmonic and the following year was recipient of NEA Jazz Masters Award along with father and brothers Wynton, **Delfeayo**, and **Jason Marsalis**. Continued to tour internationally and record, compose, and produce in the 2010s.

MARSALIS, DELFEAYO *Jazz.* Trombone. Composer. Bandleader. (Born July 28, 1965, New Orleans, Orleans Parish.) Son of influential New Orleans jazz icon **Ellis Marsalis Jr.** Began playing trombone as a child and studied music from elementary through graduate school, eventually obtaining a doctorate. Early in career toured with Ray Charles and Art Blakey. In the 1990s launched solo career and had releases on Novus, Evidence, and Troubadour Jass through the 2010s, including *Minions Dominion* in 2006, and worked extensively as sideman and producer. Brother of **Branford**, **Wynton**, and **Jason Marsalis**.

MARSALIS, ELLIS, JR. *Jazz.* Piano. Composer. Bandleader. (Born Nov. 14, 1934, New Orleans, Orleans Parish.) Patriarch of famed New Orleans jazz family and influential musician and professor whose sons **Branford**, **Wynton**, **Delfeayo**, and **Jason Marsalis** became renowned jazz musicians. Began studying music as a child and played first gig in the late 1940s as saxophonist, but soon switched to piano. Influenced by modern jazz musicians of the day, formed American Jazz Quintet with **Harold Battiste** in the mid-1950s and recorded for A.F.O. In the 1960s worked with Cannonball Adderly and **Al Hirt**. Began teaching at New Orleans Center for Performing Arts in the mid-1970s and later served as educator and director at several New Orleans universities. Former pupils include **Harry Connick Jr.**, **Terence Blanchard**, and

Nicholas Payton. Released nearly 20 albums, including *Father and Sons* in 1982 with Branford and Wynton, and continued to perform into his 80s.

MARSALIS, JASON *Jazz.* Drums, vibraphone. Composer. Bandleader. (Born Mar. 4, 1977, New Orleans, Orleans Parish.) Youngest son of noted New Orleans jazz pianist and professor **Ellis Marsalis Jr.** Began studying drums under **James Black** at age six and by age seven was sitting in with his father's band. Studied music at New Orleans Center for Creative Arts and Loyola University and worked as sideman in the mid-1990s with his father and brothers **Branford**, **Wynton**, and **Delfeayo**; **Dr. Michael White**; Lionel Hampton; Marcus Roberts; and others. In 1998 cofounded Latin-jazz group Los Hombres Caliente with **Irvin Mayfield** and drummer Bill Summers. Recorded extensively as a sideman throughout following years. Released several albums on Basin Street as a leader, including *Music in Motion* in 2000, and continued to perform and record in the 2010s.

MARSALIS, WYNTON *Jazz, classical.* Trumpet. Composer. Bandleader. (Born Oct. 18, 1961, New Orleans, Orleans Parish.) Internationally renowned jazz and classical trumpet player, composer, and bandleader and second oldest son of influential New Orleans jazz pianist and professor **Ellis Marsalis Jr.** A child prodigy, at age eight began performing with **Danny Barker**'s Fairview Baptist Church Band and at age 14 performed with New Orleans Philharmonic. Attended Juilliard in the late 1970s and in 1980 toured with Art Blakey's Jazz Messengers with brother **Branford Marsalis**. In following years performed with Sarah Vaughan, Dizzy Gillespie, Herbie Hancock, and Sonny Rollins, among others. Toured extensively with own band from 1981 through the mid-1990s. Cofounded jazz program *Jazz at Lincoln Center* in 1987 in New York City. In 1995 produced PBS television series and NPR radio series and in 1997 became first jazz musician to win the Pulitzer Prize for Music for his composition "Blood on the Fields." Produced more than 80 jazz and classical albums and has written numerous books. In 2005 was awarded the National Medal of the Arts. Continued to perform, record, produce, and compose in the 2010s. Brothers also include **Delfeayo** and **Jason Marsalis**.

MARSHALL, CARL "SOUL DOG" *Rhythm and blues.* Guitar, drums, bass, keyboards, vocals. Composer. Bandleader. (Born Mar. 28, 1950, Independence, Tangipahoa Parish.) Southern soul singer, songwriter, and multi-instrumentalist was partly raised in New Orleans and influenced by local rhythm and blues and funk players, particularly the Meters. Made recording debut as "Soul Dog" in 1976 on Amhurst LP *Movin' On* and followed with singles on Double Hit, T-Jaye, Chantilly, Hep' Me, and Chocolate Cholly. Continued to perform and record extensively through the 2010s with multiple releases on CDS.

MARTIN, CHINK (Martin Abraham Sr.) *Jazz.* Tuba, bass, guitar, banjo. (Born June 10, 1889, New Orleans, Orleans Parish; died July 7, 1981, New Orleans, Orleans Parish.)[12] Noted early New Orleans jazz tuba and bass player joined **Papa Jack Laine**'s Reliance Brass Band in 1910 and worked with various brass bands on tuba through the 1910s. From 1923 to 1925 performed and recorded with New Orleans Rhythm Kings in Chicago. Later worked and recorded with **Sharkey Bonano**, **Johnny Wiggs**, **Santo Pecora**, and others and made one recording as leader in 1963. Performed at Preservation Hall through 1980.

MARTIN, CHUCK (Gerald Charles Martin) *Zydeco, rhythm and blues.* Drums, accordion, vocals. Composer. Bandleader. (Born Nov. 1, 1937, Opelousas, St. Martin Parish; died Apr. 27, 2003, Houston.) Opelousas rhythm and blues singer and drummer began performing in the early 1950s in a duo with **Leroy Washington**. In the late 1950s recorded for producer **J. D. Miller** in Crowley and had a single "Emma Lee"/"Yeah Yeah Yeah!" on Nasco in 1957, followed by a single on Jin in 1960. Switched to accordion and began playing zydeco and throughout the 1980s recorded several singles for Maison de Soul, including local hit "Make It Hot" in 1986. Relocated to Houston around 1990 and released two singles on his own CM label.

MARTIN, LEROY "LEE" *Cajun, swamp pop.* Guitar, bass, vocals. Composer. Bandleader. (Born Aug. 4, 1929, Galliano, Lafourche Parish; died Sept. 12, 2019, Galliano, Lafourche Parish.) Multitalented Cajun and swamp pop guitarist, singer, songwriter, and producer began performing in the mid-1940s with **Dudley Bernard**'s Southern Serenaders. In the mid-1950s formed the Rebels and later worked with cousin **Joe Barry** in the Vikings. In the early 1960s produced hits for Barry, **Vin Bruce**, and Barbara Lynn and had recordings as leader on Jin as Lee Martin, including "Born to Be a Loser." After several more releases on small local labels continued working largely outside music throughout next two decades. Released albums in 1995 and 2012 and continued to make appearances in the 2010s.

MARTINEZ, GREGG *Rhythm and blues, swamp pop.* Vocals. Composer. Bandleader. (Born Aug. 2, 1956, Lafayette, Lafayette Parish.) Noted blue-eyed soul singer began performing in the mid-1970s and in the 1980s toured nationally with several groups including Kingfish and Heat. In the mid-2000s returned to Louisiana and performed and recorded as member of the Boogie Kings as well as with his own band. Released several CDs, including *Soul of the Bayou* on Louisiana Red Hot Records in 2015, and continued performing with his band the Delta Kings in the late 2010s.

MATTE, BILL (Emmitt Matte) *Cajun.* Accordion, drums, vocals. Composer. Bandleader. (Born Oct. 27, 1917, Church Point, Acadia Parish; died Apr. 10, 2000, Lake Charles, Calcasieu Parish.) Cajun drummer and accordion player best known for his 1961 regional hit "Parlez-Vous L'Francais" which was among the first Cajun recordings to incorporate rock and roll guitar. Performed as drummer in early career and in the mid-1940s formed the Veteran Playboys, which soon featured **Adam Hébert** and **Alphée** and **Shirley Bergeron**. After relocating to Lake Charles, worked with **Sidney Brown** and recorded two singles on Goldband in 1957, and in the early 1960s recorded two singles as accordionist for Lanor, including regional hit "Parlez-Vous L'Francais."

MATTE, DORIS (Doris James Matte) *Cajun.* Accordion, vocals. Composer. Bandleader. (Born Apr. 20, 1937, Church Point, Acadia Parish; died Oct. 10, 2011, Lake Charles, Calcasieu Parish.) Noted Cajun accordionist and singer-songwriter began learning the instrument around age 11, inspired early on by recordings of **Lawrence Walker**, **Aldus Roger**, and others. After family relocated to Lake Charles in the late 1950s, started performing with local musicians and in the early 1960s formed Lake Charles Ramblers. In 1962 made recording debut for Swallow and had regional success with "The Tracks of My Buggy." Several more singles followed on Swallow through 1966, including "Waltz of Regret" and "I Want to Dance with You." Continued performing in area clubs and dance halls and making regular local television appearances until retiring from music in the late 1970s.

MATTE, GURVAIS *Cajun.* Guitar, vocals. Composer. Bandleader. (Born Oct. 14, 1933, Church Point, St. Landry Parish; June 2, 2019, Lafayette, Lafayette Parish.) Locally renowned Cajun singer-guitarist formed the Branch Playboys with his father, **Vinest Matte**, in the late 1960s. In the early 1970s recorded several singles on Bee, notably "Scratch the Cajun's Back," and appeared on Sonet LP *The Cajuns Vol. 2* in 1973. Released CD *Authentic French Cajun* in the 2000s and continued performing around Lafayette area and hosting his popular weekly Cajun French radio show *Dimanche Matin* until succumbing to injuries sustained in an automobile accident at age 85.

MATTE, REGGIE *Cajun.* Accordion, guitar, drums, vocals. Composer. Bandleader. (Born Aug. 26, 1954, Church Point, Acadia Parish.) Noted Cajun accordionist and singer began playing the instrument at age eight, learning from his grandfather and inspired by **Aldus Roger** and **Iry LeJeune**. At age 13 started playing professionally and soon joined **Bee Cormier**'s Church Point Playboys, recording numerous singles and remaining with group for two decades. In 1987 joined Jambalaya Cajun Band with **Terry Huval** and continued performing and recording with group through the 2010s, often touring with **D. L. Menard**.

MATTE, TRAVIS *Cajun, zydeco.* Accordion, fiddle, guitar, drums, vocals. Composer. Bandleader. (Born Sept. 18, 1973, Church Point, Acadia Parish.) Contemporary Cajun and zydeco multi-instrumentalist began playing fiddle at age 18 and performed with numerous Cajun musicians in the 1990s and early 2000s, including **Belton Richard**, **Wayne Toups**, **Robert Jardell**, and **Jason Frey**. After winning multiple fiddle contests and awards, concentrated on accordion and released *Dis Ain'tcha Momma's Zodico* in 2004 and started performing with his new band the Zydeco Kingpins in area clubs. Numerous releases followed through the 2010s, including *Zydeco Train* in 2005 and *Pop It* in 2009, having regional success with originals such as "Barbecue and Drink a Few," "Vibrator," and "Mop the Floor." Continued performing on club and festival circuit with the Kingpins in the late 2010s.

MATTE, VINEST *Cajun.* Accordion. (Born Mar. 9, 1913, Church Point, Acadia Parish; died July 22, 1982, Branch, Acadia Parish.) Early Cajun accordionist began playing at age six and performed at local house dances in the 1920s and early 1930s. Retired from music for several decades to raise family and in the late 1960s began performing again with son **Gurvais Matte**'s Branch Playboys, appearing on several releases with group for Bee and Sonet in the mid-1970s. Retired due to illness by 1980.

MATTHEWS, BILL *Jazz.* Drums, trombone. Bandleader.

(Born May 9, 1899, Algiers, Orleans Parish; died June 3, 1964, New Orleans, Orleans Parish.) Highly accomplished early New Orleans jazz drummer and trombonist began performing in the mid-1910s with Excelsior Brass Band and worked in Storyville before its closure in 1917. In the late 1910s worked as drummer with **Buddy Petit**, **Frankie Duson**, **Kid Rena**, **Sam Morgan**, and **John Robichaux** and with Onward Brass Band with **King Oliver**. In the early 1920s switched to trombone and studied with **Vic Gaspard**. Toured with **Nat Towles** in the mid-1920s and performed on steamboat with **Sidney Desvigne**. In the late 1920s worked and recorded with **Papa Celestin**. Led his own band throughout the 1930s and from the mid-1940s through early 1960s worked and recorded with Celestin, **George Lewis**, **Alphonse Picou**, **Alton Purnell**, and many others. Older brothers Bebé and Ramos were also early jazz and brass-band drummers.

MAXEY, MATTHEW "HOGMAN" *Blues.* Guitar, vocals. (Born Jan. 18, 1917, Haynesville, Claiborne Parish; died May 1978, Homer, Claiborne Parish.) Louisiana Delta blues guitarist and singer who was recorded by folklorist Harry Oster while an inmate at Angola Prison in 1959. Selections "Rock Me Mama," "Duckin' and Dodgin'," and "Hard Headed Woman" appeared on LP *Southern Prison Songs* on Tradition in 1965.

MAXON, REVEREND BENJAMIN, JR. *Gospel.* Vocals. (Born Feb. 11, 1924, New Orleans, Orleans Parish; died Aug. 18, 2005, New Orleans, Orleans Parish.) Original member and organizer of New Orleans's longest-running gospel group the Zion Harmonizers, which was founded in 1939 out of teenagers from the Zion City neighborhood. Toured extensively with group for several years until stepping down to devote himself to full-time preaching, handing over leadership of group to **Sherman Washington**. Nephew of Southern Harps' founder **Alberta French Johnson**.

MAYFIELD, IRVIN *Jazz.* Trumpet. Composer. Bandleader. (Born Dec. 23, 1977, New Orleans, Orleans Parish.) New Orleans jazz trumpeter and bandleader began playing in grade school and performed with Algiers Brass Band in the late 1980s, influenced greatly by **Wynton Marsalis**. In 1998 cofounded Latin-jazz group Los Hombres Calientes with childhood friend **Jason Marsalis** and drummer Bill Summers, whose recordings for Basin Street led to national recognition. Founded nonprofit 16-piece jazz ensemble New Orleans Jazz Orchestra in 2002. Following Hurricane Katrina in 2005, performed numerous benefit concerts and helped bring national attention to the city's devastation. In 2009 opened Irvin Mayfield's Jazz Playhouse on Bourbon Street and served on National Council of the Arts from 2010 to 2014. Released numerous albums as leader, notably *Strange Fruit* in 2005 on Basin Street.

MAYFIELD, PERCY *Rhythm and blues.* Vocals, piano. Composer. Bandleader. (Born Aug. 12, 1920, Minden, Webster Parish; died Aug. 11, 1984, Los Angeles.) Highly influential early rhythm and blues singer and songwriter who was known as the "Poet Laureate of the Blues" for his numerous exceptional compositions, including "Please Send Me Someone to Love," "Hit the Road Jack," and "River's Invitation." Began singing in church and writing poetry as a child. After performing for several years in Texas, relocated to Los Angeles in 1942 and in the late 1940s recorded for Gru-V-Tone and Supreme, having regional success with "Two Years of Torture" in 1949. Signed with Specialty in 1950 and throughout next two years had seven Top 10 hits, including "Please Send Me Someone to Love," "Strange Things Happening," and "Lost Love." At height of career in the summer of 1952 was involved in disfiguring near-fatal car accident which briefly sidelined career. Following year continued to record for Specialty and had singles on Chess, Cash, Imperial and 7 Arts through 1961. In 1962 began working with Ray Charles as private songwriter and recorded numerous sides for Charles's Tangerine label, including 1963 hit "River's Invitation." Several albums followed on Brunswick and RCA, as well as minor hit "I Don't Want to Be the President" on Atlantic in 1974. After several years of obscurity made brief comeback in the early 1980s with a live album and documentary film before succumbing to a fatal heart attack one day shy of his 64th birthday.

MAYS, CURLEY *Blues.* Guitar, vocals. (Born Nov. 26, 1938, Maxie, Acadia Parish.) Renowned Texas-based blues singer and guitarist was raised in Beaumont, Texas, and began playing guitar in his teens, inspired by his uncle **Clarence "Gatemouth" Brown**. Relocated to Dallas after high school and from the late 1950s through early 1960s toured with Etta James and also backed T-Bone Walker, Count Basie, Jerry Butler, and others. In the mid-1960s returned to Texas to form his own group and became known for his theatrical performances, often playing guitar behind his head and back or with his toes.

Recorded single "I'm Walkin' On"/"Oh Why" on Carnival in the early 1960s. Continued performing throughout east and central Texas through the 1970s, eventually settling in San Antonio. After several decades of retirement, began occasionally sitting in with local bands in the early 2010s.

McCALL, TOUSSAINT *Rhythm and blues.* Organ, piano, vocals. Composer. Bandleader. (Born Mar. 26, 1939, Delhi, Richland Parish.)[13] Soul-blues organist and singer-songwriter best known for his 1967 classic hit "Nothing Takes the Place of You" on Ronn. Began singing publicly and learning piano while in high school. Also had minor follow-up hit for Ronn with "I'll Do It for You" in 1967. After numerous singles on Ronn, recorded for several small labels and released LP *Make Love to Me* on McCowan in 1976. Also had releases on La Saint and Nu Sound in the 1980s. In 1988 appeared in the film *Hairspray* and continued performing in the 1990s, based in Los Angeles.

McCLAIN, MIGHTY SAM *Rhythm and blues.* Vocals. Composer. Bandleader. (Born Apr. 15, 1943, Monroe, Ouachita Parish; died June 15, 2015, Newmarket, New Hampshire.) Internationally renowned deep soul singer and songwriter began singing gospel in church as a child. While in his early teens left home and joined blues guitarist Little Milton Underwood's band as vocalist, inspired greatly by Bobby Bland. Toured the South for several years and in 1966 had regional hit with Patsy Cline's "Sweet Dreams" on Amy. More releases followed on label through the late 1960s and in the early 1970s had singles on Atlantic and Malaco. After fifteen years of inactivity, which included periods of homelessness, began performing again in the mid-1980s and recorded for Orleans. After a successful tour of Japan with guitarist Wayne Bennett, relocated to New England and staged major comeback with several critically acclaimed releases on Audioquest in the 1990s, notably *Sledgehammer Soul & Down Home Blues* in 1996. Continued to tour internationally with releases on Ruf, Telarc, and his own label Mighty Music into the mid-2010s until sidelined by a stroke in 2015 shortly before his death.

McCLELLAND, JESSE "JUNIOR" *Cajun.* Steel guitar, guitar, fiddle. (Born Dec. 2, 1927, Evangeline, Acadia Parish; died July 6, 1997, Lake Charles, Calcasieu Parish.)[14] Younger brother of **Tilford McClelland**, began learning guitar at age eight from sister Eurshel (1921–1997) and during his teens learned fiddle before settling on steel guitar. In the late 1940s began performing at dance halls and in following decades worked with **Robert Bertrand**, **Isaac Leger**, **Wallace Derouen**, and others.

McCLELLAND, TILFORD *Cajun.* Steel guitar, fiddle. (Born Apr. 9, 1923, Evangeline, Acadia Parish; died May 17, 1994, Lake Charles, Calcasieu Parish.)[15] Early Cajun steel guitarist was raised in a large musical family and began playing fiddle as a child before switching to steel guitar by his teens, mentored by **Papa Cairo**. Performed in family band with siblings Eurshel (1921–1997) and **Jesse McClelland**. Early in career worked in bands with **Tan Benoit** and **Lawrence Walker** and from the 1950s through 1970s performed and/or recorded with numerous musicians, including **Sidney Brown**, **Joe Bonsall**, **Bobby Leger**, **Cleveland Crochet**, and **Buford Galley**.

McCULLUM, GEORGE, JR. *Jazz.* Trumpet. Bandleader. (Born Feb. 22, 1906, New Orleans, Orleans Parish; died Mar. 22, 1938, New Orleans, Orleans Parish.)[16] Son of noted early jazz bandleader and cornetist **George McMullum Sr.** Began performing at age 14, replacing his recently deceased father in **John Robichaux**'s band. Led his own groups in the 1920s and worked with Excelsior and **Papa Celestin**'s Tuxedo Brass Band. In the 1930s worked with W.P.A. Brass Band. Died in an elevator accident at age 32.

McCULLUM, GEORGE, SR. *Jazz.* Cornet. Composer. Bandleader. (Born July 28, 1885, New Orleans, Orleans Parish; died Nov. 14, 1920, New Orleans, Orleans Parish.)[17] Highly regarded early New Orleans jazz cornetist and bandleader who mentored **King Oliver**. Began playing in parades at age 15 and performed in Barnum & Bailey's circus band in 1909. Throughout the 1910s led marching and funeral bands whose members included **Bunk Johnson**, Sam and **Honoré Dutrey**, **Papa Celestin**, **Armand Piron**, **Sweet Emma Barrett**, **Manuel Manetta**, **Willie Cornish**, **Lizzie Miles**, and others. Father of **George McCullum Jr.**

McCURDY, CHARLES (*or* McCurtis) *Jazz.* Clarinet. (Born Dec. 1872, New Orleans, Orleans Parish; died Oct. 11, 1933, New Orleans, Orleans Parish.)[18] Early New Orleans jazz clarinetist worked with **John Robichaux** from the mid-1890s through 1905. Continued as coleader of Peerless Orchestra with **Bab Frank** through the early 1910s and also worked with **Armand Piron** and **Fate Marable**. In the 1920s performed with Robichaux at Lyric Theater for two years and toured with tent shows.

McDEE, STEPHANIE (Stephanie McDermott Sanders) *Rhythm and blues, gospel.* Vocals. Composer. Bandleader. (Born Aug. 9, 1963, New Orleans, Orleans Parish.) Southern soul singer with blues and zydeco influences began performing around Baton Rouge in the 1990s. Released several CDs from 2002 through 2010s and had regional hits with "Call the Police" and "Monkey Talk" from debut release, *Living the Blues.* In 2008 made gospel recording *No Compromise* as Chief Apostle Stephanie A. Sanders. Returned to secular music in the early 2010s and continued touring on southern soul circuit with several more releases, including *Taking Care of Business* in 2015. Also known as "Da Queen."

McGEE, DENNIS *Cajun.* Fiddle, vocals. Composer. (Born Jan. 26, 1893, Bayou Marron, near Chataignier, Evangeline Parish; died Oct. 3, 1989, Eunice, St. Landry Parish.) Extremely influential early Cajun recording artist widely regarded as the greatest fiddle player in Cajun music and whose vast repertoire of Louisiana French songs dated back centuries. Began playing fiddle during his early teens, learning songs from his father, and was soon performing at local house dances. In the mid-1910s taught **Leo Soileau** to play fiddle and throughout the 1920s performed regularly with longtime partner **Sady Courville** as well as **Amédé Ardoin**, **Angelas LeJeune**, Soileau, and others. In Mar. 1929 became one of the first Cajun musicians to record and through 1934 made numerous landmark recordings as leader and on accompaniment with Courville, LeJeune, **Ernest Frugé**, and, most notably, Ardoin, which are considered among the most important recordings in Cajun and Creole music. Many of these would be reworked into Cajun standards in coming decades. From the late 1930s through 1960s worked mainly outside music but had major career resurgence in the 1970s during the Cajun music and culture revival and performed at numerous national festivals, often with Courville. Also made several recordings with Courville, **Michael Doucet** and BeauSoleil, and others, notably 1977 LP *La Vieille Musique Acadienne* on Swallow. In the late 1980s was named honorary dean of Cajun music by University of Southwestern Louisiana (now the University of Louisiana at Lafayette) and continued performing and mentoring students into his 90s. Father of acclaimed guitarist Gerry McGee (1937–2019).

McGEE, JUDGE *Blues.* Guitar, vocals. Composer. Bandleader. (Born May 20, 1945, Ruston, Lincoln Parish.) Locally renowned blues guitarist and singer who performed on the Monroe and Ruston–area blues scene for several decades. Released CD single *Back in the Woods* on AMP in 2011 and continued performing with his band the Jury in the late 2010s.

McLAIN, TOMMY *Swamp pop.* Vocals, bass, guitar, drums, keyboards. Composer. Bandleader. (Born Mar. 15, 1940, Jonesville, Catahoula Parish.) Internationally renowned swamp pop singer-songwriter and multi-instrumentalist best known for his million-selling hit version of "Sweet Dreams." Began playing guitar as a child and by the late 1950s was performing around Alexandria area, joining **Clint West** in the Vel-Tones. In 1965 began recording for Jin and cut successful duet "Try to Find Another Man" with West, both current members of the Boogie Kings. In 1966 had hit with "Sweet Dreams" and toured internationally. Several more releases followed on Jin, including regional hit "Before I Grow Too Old." In the 1970s released numerous singles on Huey Meaux's Crazy Cajun label, including the swamp pop classic "Jukebox Songs," and led his band Mule Train during the next several decades. Continued performing throughout south Louisiana into the 2010s.

McLEAN, ERNEST *Rhythm and blues, jazz.* Guitar, banjo. (Born Mar. 23, 1925, New Orleans, Orleans Parish; died Feb. 24, 2012, Los Angeles.) Highly regarded New Orleans guitarist who appeared on numerous landmark rhythm and blues and early rock and roll recordings in the late 1940s and 1950s. Began playing guitar at age 11, taught by his father, **Richard McLean**. Joined **Dave Bartholomew**'s band in the late 1940s and appeared on hundreds of sessions at **Cosimo Matassa**'s studios through the late 1950s with **Fats Domino**, **Lloyd Price**, **Smiley Lewis**, Little Richard, **Cousin Joe**, **Paul Gayten**, **Shirley & Lee**, Big Joe Turner, and many others. In the late 1950s relocated to Los Angeles and worked with Earl Bostic and appeared on sessions with **Dr. John**, Screaming Jay Hawkins, Lou Rawls, and others. From the early 1960s through late 1990s performed jazz standards at Disneyland's New Orleans Square.

McLEAN, RICHARD *Jazz.* Banjo, guitar, bass (Born Jan. 25, 1896, New Orleans, Orleans Parish; died Sept. 1968, New Orleans, Orleans Parish.) Early New Orleans jazz banjo player began performing in the mid-1920s and worked with **Arnold Depass**, **Kid Rena**, and **Sam Morgan**. In the 1930s performed with W.P.A. Brass Band. After World War II switched to guitar and bass and performed with **Sidney Desvigne** and worked and recorded with **Paul Barbarin**, **Lizzie Miles**, **Johnny St. Cyr**, and others through 1950s. Father of **Ernest McLean**.

McLOLLIE, OSCAR (Oscar Mack Lollie) *Rhythm and blues.* Vocals. Composer. Bandleader. (Born Sept. 22, 1924, Kelly, Caldwell Parish; died July 4, 2008, Oakland, California.) Noted West Coast–based jump blues singer and bandleader known for his 1950s recordings "Roll Hot Rod Roll" and "Hey Girl-Hey Boy." Began singing while serving in World War II and settled in California after the war. Performed on Los Angeles's Central Avenue music scene for several years and cut debut single "I'm Hurt" for Mercury in 1951. Released single "The Honey Jump" on Class in 1953 which was then picked up by Modern. Numerous releases followed on Modern with his band the Honey Jumpers through 1956, including pop hit "Convicted." Recorded for Mercury/Wing in 1956–57 before returning to Class in 1958 with several singles, including minor hit "Hey Girl-Hey Boy" with Jeanette Baker. Throughout the 1960s performed on Los Angeles club circuit and had singles on Libra, Jet, Sahara, and Showtime. In 1973 released self-titled LP on Big 3 in Canada.

McMAHON, ANDREW "BLUEBLOOD" *Blues.* Guitar, bass, vocals. Composer. Bandleader. (Born Apr. 12, 1926, Delhi, Richland Parish; died Feb. 17, 1984, Monroe, Ouachita Parish.) Chicago blues musician and singer-songwriter began playing guitar at age seven and in the late 1930s ran away from home to become an itinerant musician. In the late 1940s settled in Chicago and performed with his own band as well as with J. B. Hutto and Jimmy Dawkins. From 1960 to 1973 worked extensively as member of Howlin' Wolf's band on bass. In 1971 made debut recording for Bea & Baby and cut albums *Blueblood* for Dharma in 1973 and *Go Get My Baby* for MCM in 1976. Returned to Louisiana in 1976 and retired from music.

McPHERSON, REVEREND DR. J GORDON *See* Black Billy Sunday.

McVOY, CARL (Carl Everett Glasscock) *Rockabilly.* Piano, vocals. Composer. Bandleader. (Born Jan. 3, 1931, Epps, West Carroll Parish; died Jan. 3, 1992, Jackson, Mississippi.) Early rockabilly piano player and singer-songwriter who was an early mentor to cousin **Jerry Lee Lewis**. Influenced by boogie-woogie piano players, recorded "You Are My Sunshine" in Memphis in 1957 which was a regional hit on Hi and Phillips International. Several more recordings at Sun Studios followed but remained unreleased. In 1960 bought stake in Hi Records and joined Bill Black's Combo, appearing on numerous recordings with group, including minor hit "Do It-Rat Now." In the early 1960s had singles as leader on Hi and Tri and appeared on Hi LP *Raunchy Sounds* by the Hi-Tones in 1963 before retiring from music several years later.

MEAUX, KLABY *Cajun.* Accordion, vocals. Bandleader. (Born May 21, 1919, Kaplan, Vermilion Parish; died Apr. 2, 1987, Kaplan, Vermilion Parish.) Locally renowned but unrecorded Cajun accordionist and bandleader who was popular in the Kaplan area in the 1960s and 1970s.

MEAUX, LOUIS *Cajun.* Vocals, guitar. Composer. Bandleader. (Born Aug. 17, 1942, Kaplan, Vermilion Parish.) Cajun-country singer-guitarist who recorded two singles for Jin in the mid-1980s, notably "Temporary Thing"/"Louisiana Bound."

MEAUX, PAPPY "TE-TAN" (Tanislas Meaux) *Cajun.* Accordion. Composer. Bandleader. (Born Feb. 22, 1905, Wright, Vermilion Parish; died Nov. 14, 1975, Winnie, Texas.) Texas-based accordion player and bandleader of the Rambling Aces, who recorded several singles on his son Huey Meaux's Crazy Cajun label in the mid-1960s, notably "Moi Tu Sull"/"Winnie Two Step." Brother of **Theresa Falcon** and father of Texas-based producer Huey Meaux.

MEAUX, U. J. (Uray Jules Meaux) *Cajun, swamp pop.* Fiddle, piano, organ, vocals. (Born Feb. 24, 1927, Lyons Point, Acadia Parish; died July 7, 2006, Lafayette, Lafayette Parish.) Renowned Cajun multi-instrumentalist began performing as fiddler with **Lawrence Walker**'s Wandering Aces in the early 1950s, appearing on several recordings, including Cajun standard "Walker Special." In 1958 left Walker's band to join the Krazy Kats as piano player for fellow Walker bandmate **Johnnie Allan** and performed and recorded with Allan for several years. Also recorded with **Abe Manuel**, **Lazy Lester**, **Rufus Thibodeaux**, and **Camey Doucet** in the 1960s and 1970s. In later years performed regularly with **Walter Mouton** and worked and recorded with stepson **Jimmy Breaux**. Continued performing until his death at age 79.

MEDICA, LEON *Rhythm and blues, rock.* Bass, vocals. Composer. Bandleader. (Born Feb. 22, 1946, Alexandria, Rapides Parish.) Noted bass player, songwriter, and producer best known for his work as longtime member of band Louisiana's Le Roux. Began performing around Baton Rouge in the late 1960s and recorded with **Silas Ho-**

gan, **Arthur "Guitar" Kelley**, and **Clarence Edwards**. In the 1970s toured and recorded with **Clarence "Gatemouth" Brown** and cofounded Louisiana's LeRoux. Continued touring and recording with band throughout next several decades and also worked extensively as session musician and/or producer with **Clifton Chenier**, **Zachary Richard**, **Tab Benoit**, Tom Johnston, **Wayne Toups**, and others. In 2015 announced retirement from performing.

MELLO, LEONCE *Jazz.* Trombone. (Born Jan. 23, 1892, New Orleans, Orleans Parish; died Nov. 1, 1948, New Orleans, Orleans Parish.)[19] Noted early New Orleans jazz trombonist with **Papa Jack Laine**'s Reliance Brass Band in the early to mid-1910s. Also worked with **Dominick** and **Joe Barocco**'s band in the late 1920s. Brother of **Manuel** and **Sanford Mello**.

MELLO, MANUEL *Jazz.* Cornet. (Born June 4, 1887, New Orleans, Orleans Parish; died Oct. 31, 1961, New Orleans, Orleans Parish.)[20] Early New Orleans jazz cornetist began performing with brother **Leonce Mello** around 1903 in the Big Five marching band. Later worked regularly with **Papa Jack Laine**'s band. Also brother of **Sanford Mello**.

MELLO, SANFORD (Symphorian) *Jazz.* Trombone, drums. (Born Feb. 16, 1902, New Orleans, Orleans Parish; died June 1976, Arabi, St. Bernard Parish.)[21] Brother of **Leonce** and **Manuel Mello**, performed as a member of **Papa Jack Laine**'s Reliance Brass Band in the 1920s.

MELVIN, BIG BOE (Melvin Boe Hill) *Blues.* Guitar, bass. Composer. Bandleader. (Born Sept. 8, 1940, Jackson, E. Feliciana Parish; died Dec. 24, 1995, Baton Rouge, EBR Parish.) Longtime fixture on the Baton Rouge blues scene, began performing in the mid-1950s with **Big Papa Tilley**'s band, replacing **Buddy Guy**. From the late 1950s through 1960s worked and recorded periodically with **Slim Harpo** and also performed and appeared on sessions with **Boogie Jake**. Formed band the Night Hawks in the early 1960s which he led for several decades, recording several singles and self-titled LP on his Big Boe label in the early 1980s. Father of blues and gospel keyboardist Little Boe Melvin who was also member of the Night Hawks.

MENARD, D. L. (Doris Leon Menard) *Cajun.* Guitar, vocals. Composer. Bandleader. (Born Apr. 14, 1932, Erath, Vermilion Parish; died July 27, 2017, Scott, Lafayette Parish.) Internationally renowned and highly influential Cajun singer-songwriter and guitarist best known for his 1962 Cajun standard "La Porte d'en Arrière" ("The Back Door"), which became one of the most covered songs in Cajun music. Began playing guitar in his mid-teens, greatly inspired by Hank Williams. Joined **Elias "Shute" Badeaux**'s Louisiana Aces and performed with band through the late 1960s, recording four singles with group as vocalist from 1961 to 1964 for Swallow, including "The Back Door." In the early 1970s reunited with Louisiana Aces and performed at 1973 National Folk Festival in Washington, D.C., which led to national acclaim. Recorded self-titled LP with Louisiana Aces for Rounder in 1974 and, in 1976–77, released LPs *Underneath the Green Oak Tree* on Arhoolie and *Made in Louisiana* on Voyager, both with **Dewey Balfa** and **Marc Savoy**. In the 1980s and early 1990s released several albums on Rounder, including *No Matter Where You Go, There You Are* in 1988 with **Blackie Forestier** and **Eddie LeJeune**. Throughout the 1990s and 2000s toured nationally and abroad, often with **Terry Huval** and his band Jambalaya, and released final CD *Happy Go Lucky* on Swallow in 2010. Despite health issues in final years continued performing until three weeks before his death at age 85.

MENARD, PHIL *Cajun.* Accordion, vocals. Composer. Bandleader. (Born Sept. 6, 1923, Cankton, St. Landry Parish; died Oct. 26, 2016, Lake Charles, Calcasieu Parish.) Renowned Cajun accordionist and longtime bandleader was inspired in his youth by hearing **Joe Falcon**, **Dennis McGee**, **Leo Soileau**, and others playing at house dances. Began learning accordion shortly before settling in Lake Charles in 1945. In the 1950s and early 1960s performed with **Cursey Fontenot**'s Louisiana Travelers and in the late 1960s took over leadership of band. From the late 1960s through 1970s had singles on Folk Star, Swallow, Nonc Joe, and Kajun, including local hit "La Sha Chere." Performed at clubs and festivals throughout the 1980s and 1990s with additional recordings on Kajun, Swallow, and Bee, notably "La Valse de Heritage" with band member **Ivy Dugas** on Bee in 1986. Continued to make occasional appearances into his early 90s.

METOYER, BIG AL/AL GATOR (Allen Metoyer) *Rhythm and blues.* Piano, vocals. (Born Jan. 30, 1936, Natchez, Natch. Parish; died Mar. 7, 2005, Natchez, Natch. Parish.) Locally renowned singer and keyboard player began playing music in the late 1940s, mentored by local musicians the **LaCour Brothers**. Led popular band Big Al and the Gators for many years in Natchitoches and surrounding Cane River area.

MICHOT, ANDRÉ *Cajun.* Accordion, lap steel guitar. Composer. Bandleader. (Born Oct. 2, 1975, Baton Rouge, EBR Parish.) Began performing with father Tommy Michot's family band Les Frères Michot (**Michot Brothers**) as a child. Cofounded contemporary Cajun band Lost Bayou Ramblers with brother **Louis Michot** in 1999 and continued performing and recording with group in the 2010s. Also an accomplished accordion builder.

MICHOT BROTHERS *Cajun.* (Born Pilette, Lafayette Parish.) Brothers Rick (fiddle), Tommy (accordion), Bobby (guitar), David (acoustic bass), and Mike (triangle) formed acoustic-based traditional Cajun band Les Frères Michot in 1986. Released debut recording *Elevés à Pilette* on ARZED in 1987, followed by recordings on Swallow, LFM, and Fremeaux. Continued performing locally and touring overseas in the 2010s.

MICHOT, LOUIS *Cajun.* Fiddle, bass, vocals. Composer. Bandleader. (Born Jan. 2, 1979, Baton Rouge, EBR Parish.) Cofounder with brother **André Michot** of contemporary Cajun band Lost Bayou Ramblers, which formed in 1999. Continued to record and perform with group in the 2010s along with other side projects, including Soul Creole. Son of Cajun musician Tommy Michot of family Cajun band Les Frères Michot (**Michot Brothers**), in which he performed early in career.

MILES, FRANKIE (Frank Mailhes) *Cajun.* Fiddle, vocals. Bandleader. (Born Nov. 11, 1918, Abbeville, Vermilion Parish; died Oct. 17, 1973, Abbeville, Vermilion Parish.) Early postwar Cajun fiddler who recorded as vocalist for producer **Eddie Shuler**'s Reveliers on 1946 Goldband single "Mes Cinquantes Sous"/"Jolie Blond."

MILES, LIZZIE (Elizabeth Landreaux) *Blues, jazz.* Vocals. Composer. (Born Mar. 31, 1895, New Orleans, Orleans Parish; died Mar. 17, 1963, New Orleans, Orleans Parish.) Powerful classic blues and jazz vocalist who **Louis Armstrong** once called "the greatest jazz singer of our day." In her teens worked as vocalist with **King Oliver**, **Kid Ory**, **Armand Piron**, **Bunk Johnson**, and others and toured the southern vaudeville circuit. Settled in Chicago around 1920 and worked with Oliver, **Freddie Keppard**, and **Charlie Elgar**. Relocated to New York in 1922 and recorded extensively through 1930, including sessions with Oliver and **Jelly Roll Morton**. In the 1930s appeared in film and worked with **Paul Barbarin** and Fats Waller. After nearly a decade away, staged comeback in the 1950s and toured with **George Lewis** and Bob Scobey in California and Las Vegas. Often singing in Creole French, made numerous recordings in the 1950s, including 1956 Cook LP *Moans & Blues.* Retired from music in New Orleans in 1959. Half-sister of **Edna Hicks** and **Herb Morand**.

MILES, LUKE "LONG GONE" *Blues.* Vocals. (Born May 8, 1925, Lachute, Caddo Parish; died Nov. 22, 1987, Los Angeles.) Country blues singer who worked on a local cotton plantation until moving to Houston in 1952 to study music with Lightnin' Hopkins. Performed and recorded with Hopkins in the 1950s and relocated to Los Angeles in the early 1960s. In 1962 released two singles on Smash, backed by Sonny Terry and Brownie McGhee. Began twenty-year partnership with guitarist Willie Chambers in 1962 and recorded LP *Country Born* for World Pacific in 1964, followed by singles on Two Kings in 1965 and Kent in 1969. After years of absence from the music scene resurfaced in the 1980s and recorded live performance in Venice, California, in 1985 which was issued posthumously in 2008 on CD *Ridin' Around in My V8 Ford* on Conjur Root.

MILLER, BERT *Swamp pop.* Drums, vocals. Bandleader. (Born Aug. 11, 1941, Eunice, St. Landry Parish.) Early swamp pop singer and drummer who was a founding member of the Boogie Kings in 1956 with **Doug Ardoin** and **Harris Miller**. Performed and recorded with Boogie Kings through the mid-1960s, then formed the Swing Kings with Ardoin. Performed with band through the late 1960s and recorded several singles and LP *The Swing Kings in Stereo* on La Louisianne. In the 1990s reunited with original members of Boogie Kings and performed numerous shows into the 2010s.

MILLER, CURLY "BAREFOOT" (George Frank Miller) *Blues.* Vocals, piano. (Born July 23, 1919, New Orleans, Orleans Parish; died May 2, 1999, Dallas.)[22] Charismatic blues singer began performing as a child tap-dancing on New Orleans street corners for tips, eventually dubbed "Barefoot" for dancing without shoes. After several years of traveling the South selling Hadacol patent medicine, settled in Dallas and became fixture at local blues jams, delighting audiences with his song "The Curly Stomp." Made recordings in the early 1990s for TopCat which appeared on CD *Texas Bluesmen.* Although believed to be in his 90s at time of his death, succumbed to a fatal stroke at age 79.

MILLER, HARRIS *Swamp pop.* Guitar, vocals. (Born July 14, 1939, Eunice, St. Landry Parish.) Early swamp pop guitarist and singer who was an original member of the Boogie Kings with **Doug Ardoin** and **Bert Miller**. Joined band in 1956 and performed and recorded with group through 1964. Retired from music shortly afterwards and eventually relocated out west.

MILLER, JAMES "SING" *Jazz.* Vocals, piano, banjo, bass. (Born June 17, 1914, New Orleans, Orleans Parish; died May 18, 1990, New Orleans, Orleans Parish.) Exceptional jazz and blues singer who was also an accomplished piano and banjo player. Began singing with local quartet and playing banjo with **Kid Howard** in the late 1920s. Started teaching himself piano in 1928 and in the 1930s and 1940s worked with **Percy Humphrey**, **Kid Sheik Cola**, and **Creole George Guesnon** and recorded with **Kid Thomas**. Performed regularly at Preservation Hall from the 1960s through 1980s and recorded two albums as a leader in the 1970s.

MILLER, LARRY *Cajun.* Steel guitar, vocals. Composer. (Born Feb. 13, 1932, near Iota, Acadia Paris.) Veteran Cajun steel guitarist began performing in 1948, influenced greatly by **Atlas Frugé**, and in 1949 joined **Lionel Cormier**'s Sundown Playboys, with whom he performed and recorded for more than six decades. Also performed and recorded with **Nathan Abshire** and worked in bands of **Lawrence Walker**, **Rodney LeJeune**, and many others. Continued performing in the 2010s, occasionally with **Lesa Cormier**'s Sundown Playboys.

MILLER, PUNCH/KID PUNCH (Ernest Miller) *Jazz.* Trumpet, vocals. Bandleader. (Born June 10, 1894, Raceland, Lafourche Parish; died Dec. 2, 1971, New Orleans, Orleans Parish.) Renowned early New Orleans jazz trumpeter and bandleader known for his bluesy and fast-fingered playing style. Began studying cornet under **Professor Jim Humphrey** during his teens and in 1917 joined **Jack Carey**'s band. After serving in World War I rejoined Carey in 1919 and took over leadership of band several years later. In the mid-1920s worked with **Buddy Petit**, **Chris Kelly**, and **Manuel Manetta**. Relocated to Chicago in 1926 and worked and/or recorded with **Freddie Keppard**, **Albert Wynn**, **Jelly Roll Morton**, Tiny Parham, Frankie "Half-Pint" Jaxon, and others. Led his own bands and recorded as leader in Chicago and New York through the late 1940s. After touring with circus bands and rhythm and blues revues returned to New Orleans in 1956. Toured Japan with **George Lewis** and performed regularly at Preservation Hall in final years.

MILLER, RODNEY "HOT ROD" *Cajun.* Steel guitar, fiddle, accordion, piano. (Born Sept. 9, 1937, Church Point, Acadia Parish; died Aug. 30, 2015, Youngsville, Lafayette Parish.) Highly influential Cajun steel guitarist began playing professionally at age 13 and in the early 1950s performed with **Walter Mouton** and **Lawrence Walker**. Spent more than fifteen years performing in bands of **Aldus Roger** and **Belton Richard**, recording frequently with Richard. Also worked and recorded with **Geno Thibodeaux** in the 1960s. In the 1980s recorded with **Jim Olivier**, **Jay Cormier**, **Marc Savoy**, and others as well as Cajun Born with **Warren Storm**, **Clint West**, and **Johnnie Allan**. Continued performing with various groups through the 2000s.

MINOR, FRED "H.E." *Jazz.* Guitar, banjo. (Born Dec. 8, 1913, New Orleans, Orleans Parish; died Oct. 1985, New Orleans, Orleans Parish.)[23] Noted jazz guitarist and banjo player worked with **Sidney Desvigne** in 1930s, and throughout the 1950s and 1960s worked regularly with **Paul Barbarin**. Also performed with **Noon Johnson**'s Bazooka Trio in the mid-1960s. Father of jazz clarinetist Donald Minor.

MIRE, CLEVELAND *Cajun.* Accordion, vocals. Composer. Bandleader. (Born Sept. 2, 1910, Mire, Acadia Parish; died Mar. 28, 1968, Lafayette, Lafayette Parish.) Early postwar Cajun accordionist and bandleader was born into a musical family of accordion players and performed at local dance halls throughout the 1940s and 1950s with his band the Jolly Boys. Recorded single "Prison Waltz"/"Hudson Breakdown" for **J. D. Miller**'s Feature label in 1951. Two sides remain unissued and are believed to have been destroyed. Cousin of **Lawrence Walker**.

MISS La-VELL *See* White, Lavelle.

MITCHELL, BOBBY *Rhythm and blues.* Vocals. Bandleader. (Born Aug. 16, 1935, Algiers, Orleans Parish; died Mar. 17, 1989, New Orleans, Orleans Parish.) Early New Orleans rhythm and blues singer best known for his 1957 recording "I'm Gonna Be a Wheel Someday." Cofounded the Toppers with high-school friends in 1950 and in late 1952 signed with Imperial as leader of group through **Dave Bartholomew**. Made recording debut in 1953 and had national hit with "Try Rock 'n' Roll" in 1956. Following year released "Wheel Someday" which gained national exposure and was later famously covered by **Fats Domino**. In the early 1960s had singles on Sho-Biz, Ron, Imperial, and Rip. Remained popular performer in New Orleans for several years before retiring from music.

MITCHELL, CHUCK (Mitchell Johnus Geran) *Rhythm*

and blues. Vocals. (Born July 27, 1941, Baton Rouge, EBR Parish; died Jan. 20, 2003, Baton Rouge, EBR Parish.) Longtime rhythm and blues and deep soul singer on the Baton Rouge blues scene began performing in the 1960s and worked with **Slim Harpo**, **Raful Neal**, **Buddy Stewart**, Robert Milburn, and others. In the mid-1960s recorded single "Her Precious Love" on Stewart's Budix label, backed by Stewart's band the Top Notchers, and a single sharing vocals with **Merle Spears** with Stewart's Herculoids. In remaining years performed sporadically with various musicians around Baton Rouge, including **Kenny Neal**.

MITCHELL, JOEY (Mitchell Joseph Juneau Jr.) *Rhythm and blues, swamp pop.* Vocals. Composer. (Born Jan. 16, 1942, Bunkie, Avoy. Parish; died May 6, 2005, Bunkie, Avoy. Parish.) Blue-eyed soul singer best known for his work as member of the Swing Kings with **Bert Miller** in the 1960s, appearing as vocalist on numerous tracks of 1967 LP *The Swing Kings in Stereo* on La Louisianne, including "I Can't Turn You Loose." Also recorded "No One Else Will Do," which appeared on 1980 Ace LP *The Sound of the Gulf Coast.*

MODELISTE, JOSEPH "ZIGABOO"/"ZIGGY" *Rhythm and blues.* Drums, vocals. Composer. Bandleader. (Born Dec. 28, 1948, New Orleans, Orleans Parish.) Highly innovative New Orleans funk percussionist and pioneer of second-line funk drumming style and founding member of influential New Orleans band the Meters. Largely influenced by **Smokey Johnson**. Began performing during his teens and worked with **Art Neville**, **Lee Dorsey**, **Deacon John**, and others. In the late 1960s helped form the Meters with Neville, **Leo Nocentelli**, and **George Porter Jr.** and made numerous landmark recordings with group throughout the 1970s, including funk classics "Cissy Strut" and "Sophisticated Cissy." In the early 1980s relocated to California and continued as in-demand session drummer on hundreds of recordings and toured with many top performers of rhythm and blues and rock. Released three albums as leader and led several bands of his own, including Foundation of Funk with Porter in the mid-2010s.

MOLITOR, MILTON (Melton Molitor) *Cajun.* Accordion, vocals. (Born Sept. 26, 1908, Church Point, Acadia Parish; died Apr. 6, 1973, Mamou, Evangeline Parish.) Early postwar Cajun accordionist and singer performed with **Chuck Guillory**'s band in the late 1940s and early 1950s, recording with group on vocals and accordion on two singles for Feature in 1950. Also performed regularly with **Austin Pitre**, recording single "Manuel Bar Waltz"/"Midway Two Step" with Pitre in 1957 for producer **Floyd Soileau**'s first label, Big Mamou. In the late 1950s appeared on Prestige LP *Cajun Folk Music* with Pitre and guitarist Lurlin LeJeune, recorded by folklorist Harry Oster.

MONETTE, RAYMOND "SHWANK" *Blues.* Guitar. (Born Dec. 13, 1936, Lafayette, Lafayette Parish; died Jan. 4, 1977, Lafayette, Lafayette Parish.) Locally influential guitarist who mentored many young Lafayette-area blues guitarists in the 1950s and 1960s, including **Lil' Buck Sinegal**, **Jumpin' Joe Morris**, and younger brother Johnny "Sha-Shant" Monette. Performed occasionally with **Clifton Chenier** and appeared on Chenier's 1970 Arhoolie LP *King of the Bayous.* Succumbed to a fatal heart attack at famed local club the Blue Angel.

MONTGOMERY, GRAY *Rockabilly, blues, string band.* Guitar, harmonica, drums, vocals. Composer. (Born Mar. 6, 1927, Security Plantation near Jonesville, Catahoula Parish.) Noted Natchez, Mississippi–area multi-instrumentalist and occasional one-man band began playing guitar in his early teens. In the late 1940s started performing in area juke joints, often with Papa Lightfoot, and in the early 1950s hired **Jerry Lee Lewis** as his band's drummer. In 1962 recorded rockabilly single "Right Now"/"It's All Right" on Beagle. Continued performing in area clubs and juke joints throughout following decades and remained active as a performer into his 90s.

MONTGOMERY, LITTLE BROTHER (Eurreal Wilson Montgomery) *Blues, jazz.* Piano, vocals. Composer. Bandleader. (Born Apr. 18, 1906, Kentwood, Tangipahoa Parish; died Sept. 6, 1985, Chicago.) Highly regarded and influential early blues piano player and singer-songwriter began playing at age five, largely inspired by **Jelly Roll Morton** and **Loomis Gibson**, who performed at his father's barrelhouse. Left home in his early teens to become a professional musician and traveled throughout Louisiana and Mississippi, performing in juke joints and lumber and turpentine camps, often with Big Joe Williams, and worked with jazz musicians **Sam Morgan**, **Buddy Petit**, and **Danny Barker**. In the late 1920s relocated to Chicago and made recording debut in 1930 for Paramount with his signature composition "Vicksburg Blues," inspired by an older piano blues song called "The Forty-Fours." Toured the South and Midwest in the early

1930s with his band the Southland Troubadours and in 1935–36 recorded numerous sides for Bluebird, notably "Crescent City Blues" and "The First Time I Met the Blues" (mistitled as "The First Time I Met You.") In the early 1940s settled permanently in Chicago and worked with **Lee Collins** and **Kid Ory**. Throughout the 1950s and 1960s recorded for numerous labels, including Century, Atlantic, Ebony, Prestige, Folkways, and Riverside and appeared on many sessions backing blues artists, including Otis Rush, Magic Sam, and **Buddy Guy**. Toured and recorded in Europe throughout the 1960s and 1970s and in later years worked regularly with singer Jeanne Carroll. Older brother of pianist Joe Montgomery, who recorded with J. B. Lenoir. Uncle of **Paul Gayten**.

MONTOUCET, DON (Dieu Donné Montoucet) *Cajun.* Accordion. Composer. Bandleader. (Born Oct. 5, 1925, Scott, Lafayette Parish; died Sept. 11, 2016, Maurice, Vermilion Parish.) Influential Cajun accordionist began playing at age five, learning from parents, who both played the instrument. On recommendation of band member **Lionel Leleux**, replaced the late **Lawrence Walker** in the Wandering Aces after his sudden death in 1968 and toured internationally throughout the 1970s, recording LP *Cajun Two Step* for Sonet in 1979. Later performed with Mulate Playboys and became mentor of **Kevin Naquin**, who produced CD *Don Montoucet et Ses Amis* on Swallow in 2007. Also was a renowned triangle maker. Father of Cajun musicians Virgil and Terry Montoucet.

MONTRELL, ROY (Raymond Eustis Montrell) *Rhythm and blues.* Guitar, vocals. Composer. Bandleader. (Born Feb. 27, 1928, New Orleans, Orleans Parish; died May 16, 1979, Amsterdam.)[24] Revered New Orleans rhythm and blues guitarist best known for his 1956 single "(Every Time I Hear) That Mellow Saxophone." As session guitarist, appeared on numerous recordings throughout the 1950s and 1960s by artists such as **Fats Domino**, Little Richard, **Clarence "Frogman" Henry**, **Lee Dorsey**, **Professor Longhair**, and **Larry Williams**. Besides "That Mellow Saxophone" on Specialty, released one other single as leader in 1960 on Minit. Died of a drug overdose at age 51 while on tour with Domino in the Netherlands.

MOORE, CHARLES *Rhythm and blues, classical.* Bass, guitar. (Born June 25, 1951, New Orleans, Orleans Parish.) Brother of **Deacon John** and member of his band the Ivories since 1968. Appeared on recordings with **Allen Toussaint**, **Cyril Neville**, the Wild Magnolias, Deacon John, and others. Released debut recording as a leader, *Classical Guitar, Vol. 1,* in 2009.

MOORE, CURLEY (June Moore) *Rhythm and blues.* Vocals. (Born June 1943, New Orleans, Orleans Parish; died Dec. 14, 1985, Algiers, Orleans Parish.) New Orleans rhythm and blues singer best known as vocalist with **Huey "Piano" Smith**'s Clowns in the 1960s. Also released singles as a leader on Scram, Nola, Sansu, House of the Fox, Instant, and other labels in the 1960s and early 1970s and had local hits with "Soul Train" and "Sophisticated Sissy." In 1979 joined Smith for brief Clowns reunion at New Orleans Jazz & Heritage Festival. After serving time in the early 1980s, was found murdered on the street in Algiers from gunshot wounds at age 42. Uncle of **Tony Hall**.

MOORE, DEACON JOHN *See* Deacon John.

MOORE, JAMES *See* Slim Harpo.

MOORE, NOAH *Blues.* Guitar, vocals. Composer. (Born 1908, Mooringsport, Caddo Parish; died Dec. 12, 1943, New Hebrides, South Pacific.) Prewar blues guitarist and singer learned guitar from his cousin **Lead Belly**. In Oct. 1940 was recorded by folklorists Ruby and John Lomax in Oil City. Selections included "Oil City Blues," "Sittin' Here Thinking," "Jerry's Saloon Blues," and "Just Pickin.'" Died while serving in anti-aircraft weapons battalion during World War II, presumably from drowning after military boat capsized.

MORAND, HERB "KID" *Jazz.* Trumpet, vocals. Bandleader. (Born Dec. 23, 1905, New Orleans, Orleans Parish; died Feb. 23, 1952, New Orleans, Orleans Parish.)[25] Noted New Orleans jazz trumpeter and bandleader who was original member of popular 1930s jazz-blues group Harlem Hamfats. Inspired by **King Oliver**, began playing trumpet at age 11. In the mid-1920s toured Southwest and performed in Mexico's Yucatan Peninsula to rave reviews. In the late 1920s worked with half-sister **Lizzie Miles** in New York and **Chris Kelly** back in New Orleans. Relocated to Chicago and throughout the 1930s recorded extensively with Harlem Hamfats. In the 1940s returned to New Orleans and led his own band and worked and recorded with **George Lewis**. Recorded as leader in 1950 before retiring from music due to illness. Half-brother of **Edna Hicks**.

MORET, GEORGE *Jazz.* Cornet. Bandleader. (Born May 1871, New Orleans, Orleans Parish; died Dec. 27, 1923, New Orleans, Orleans Parish.)[26] Highly respected early jazz cornet player and bandleader. Member of

Excelsior Brass Band in the late 1890s and took over as leader when **Theogene Baquet** retired in 1904. Continued leading band through the early 1920s until succumbing to kidney disease. Brother and father, both named Eugene, were also cornet players.

MORGAN, AL (Albert Morgan) *Jazz, blues.* Bass. Bandleader. (Born Aug. 19, 1908, New Orleans, Orleans Parish; died Apr. 14, 1974, Los Angeles.)[27] Highly accomplished jazz bassist and member of prestigious Morgan jazz family. Studied under bassist **Simon Marrero** in 1919. In the 1920s worked with **Lee Collins**, **Sidney Desvigne**, and **Fate Marable**. From 1932 to 1936 toured and recorded with Cab Calloway and later settled in California. In following years led his own band and recorded extensively with many top jazz and blues artists such as Fats Waller, T-Bone Walker, Coleman Hawkins, Louis Jordan, Jay McShann, and pop star Bing Crosby, among others. Also appeared in films with Calloway and **Louis Armstrong**. In later years worked in duo with pianist Buddy Banks. Brother of noted jazz musicians **Sam**, **Isaiah**, and **Andrew Morgan**.

MORGAN, ANDREW *Jazz.* Clarinet, saxophone. Bandleader. (Born Mar. 13, 1901, Bertrandville, Plaquemines Parish; died Sept. 19, 1972, New Orleans, Orleans Parish.) Early New Orleans jazz multi-instrumentalist began performing in 1924 with Young Superior Band and the following year joined brother **Isaiah Morgan**'s Young Morgan Band, mentored by bandmate **Earl Fouché**. Recorded on group's famed 1927 sessions under brother **Sam Morgan**'s leadership, performing on both clarinet and saxophone. In the 1930s and 1940s worked with **Kid Rena**, **Alphonse Picou**, **Kid Thomas**, and **Herb Morand**. Throughout the 1950s and 1960s recorded with Young Tuxedo, Eureka, and Onward brass bands; **Sweet Emma Barrett**; **Alvin Alcorn**; and others. Performed at Preservation Hall in the 1960s and recorded as a leader in 1969.

MORGAN, ISAIAH "IKE" *Jazz.* Trumpet. Bandleader. (Born Apr. 7, 1897, Bertrandville, Plaquemines Parish; died May 11, 1966, New Orleans, Orleans Parish.) Early New Orleans jazz trumpeter moved to New Orleans while in his teens and by the late 1910s began learning cornet. Formed Young Morgan Band in the early 1920s which included **Big Jim Robinson** and **Sidney Brown**. In 1925 older brother **Sam Morgan** joined group and was renamed Sam Morgan Jazz Band. Made landmark recordings with group in 1927 for Columbia. In 1932 took over leadership after Sam suffered a stroke. Led bands around Biloxi, Mississippi, and eventually settled there in 1940. Retired from music in the mid-1950s. Also brother of **Al** and **Andrew Morgan**.

MORGAN, MOSE/MOISE *Cajun.* Fiddle, accordion. (Born Aug. 2, 1902, Rayne, Acadia Parish; died Apr. 22, 1996, Sulphur, Calcasieu Parish.)[28] Early Cajun fiddle player who frequently performed with **Joe Falcon** and **Cléoma Breaux Falcon** in the 1930s, appearing on Falcon Trio session for Bluebird in 1936. Later settled in Sulphur area.

MORGAN, OLIVER "NOOKIE BOY" *Rhythm and blues.* Vocals. Composer. (Born May 6, 1933, New Orleans, Orleans Parish; died July 31, 2007, Atlanta.) Charismatic New Orleans rhythm and blues singer best known for his 1964 hit "Who Shot the La La," which referenced the 1963 death of **Prince La La**. Made recording debut as "Nookie Boy" on A.F.O. in 1961 and also had several singles on Seven B following "Who Shot the La La" on GNP/Crescendo. Performed locally throughout the next two decades, regularly brandishing his trademark second-line umbrella. In 1998 released first full-length album *I'm Home* on **Allen Toussaint**'s NYNO label. Evacuated to Atlanta after Hurricane Katrina in 2005.

MORGAN, ROCKET (Roderick Clayel Morgan) *Rockabilly, swamp pop.* Vocals. Composer. (Born Nov. 4, 1939, Lake Charles, Calcasieu Parish; died Sept. 9, 2003, Wilson, North Carolina.)[29] Influential early rockabilly and swamp pop singer-songwriter best known for his 1958 single "You're Humbuggin' Me," which has been covered by numerous blues and rock musicians. From 1958 through the early 1960s recorded numerous sides for producer **J. D. Miller** and had multiple releases on Zynn, notably rockabilly classics "You're Humbuggin' Me" and "Tag Along," backed by Miller's studio band, which included drummer **Warren Storm** and pianist **Katie Webster**. Reportedly left music soon afterwards and became an evangelist preacher, eventually settling in eastern North Carolina near Raleigh, where he later passed at age 63.

MORGAN, SAM *Jazz.* Trumpet, cornet. Bandleader. (Born Sept. 18, 1887, Bertrandville, Plaquemines Parish; died Feb. 25, 1936, New Orleans, Orleans Parish.)[30] Highly regarded early New Orleans jazz cornetist whose 1927 recordings are often cited as among the finest of the decade. In the early 1910s began performing in brass bands around Plaquemines Parish. Moved to New Orleans in

1915 and worked with **Billy Marrero** and later led Magnolia Brass Band. After recovering from a stroke in 1924, took over leadership of brother **Isaiah Morgan**'s band, which quickly became one of the city's most popular jazz bands. Made landmark recordings in 1927 for Columbia and continued performing with group until suffering second stroke in 1932. Briefly performed in W.P.A. Brass Band in 1934 before retiring due to failing health in 1935. Also brother of **Al** and **Andrew Morgan**.

MORRIS, EDDIE *Jazz.* Trombone. Bandleader. (Born July 19, 1896, Algiers, Orleans Parish; died 1962, New Orleans, Orleans Parish.) Early New Orleans jazz trombonist began learning the instrument at age 19, inspired by **Vic Gaspard**. From 1920 to 1927 performed regularly with **Punch Miller**. In the late 1920s and early 1930s worked with **Buddy Petit** and **Kid Rena**. Performed with W.P.A. Brass Band in the mid-1930s and later led his band the Serenaders. Worked and recorded with Miller and **Emile Barnes** in the late 1950s and early 1960s.

MORRIS, GENE (Eugene Brouchet) *Zydeco, rhythm and blues.* Drums, vocals. Composer. Bandleader. (Born June 13, 1940, Crowley, Acadia Parish; died Jan. 15, 2015, Lafayette, Lafayette Parish.) Noted zydeco singer-songwriter best known for his mid-1970s regional hit "Going Back to Big Mamou," which became a zydeco standard. Began music career as occasional drummer with **Clifton Chenier** in the mid-1950s and in 1960s and 1970s performed and recorded as vocalist with **Fernest Arceneaux** and **Rockin' Dopsie**. In the mid-1970s recorded numerous singles for Blues Unlimited backed by **Marcel Dugas**'s Entertainers, including "Big Mamou." Also worked with **(Hiram) Sampy** and the Bad Habits and led band Dr. Gene Morris and the Zydeco Surgeons. Continued performing sporadically through the early 2010s despite health issues in later years. Brother of **Jumpin' Joe Morris** and drummer Jerry Brouchet, who both performed with Chenier.

MORRIS, JUMPIN' JOE (Joseph Brouchet) *Zydeco.* Bass, guitar, vocals. (Born Dec. 25, 1933, Crowley, Acadia Parish; died June 27, 2008, Lafayette, Lafayette Parish.) Noted zydeco bassist began playing guitar as a child, inspired by **Clarence "Gatemouth" Brown** and mentored by local blues guitarist **Raymond "Shwank" Monette**. After leading his own band, switched to bass in the mid-1960s to join **Clifton Chenier**'s band and performed and recorded extensively with Chenier through 1978, touring internationally and appearing on numerous releases. Continued performing with various musicians, including **Hiram Sampy**, until illness eventually forced retirement from music. Older brother of **Gene Morris** and drummer Jerry Brouchet.

MORRIS, LEO *Blues.* Guitar, vocals. Composer. Bandleader. (Born May 6, 1933, Lafayette, Lafayette Parish; died Oct. 28, 2010, Houston.) Texas-based blues guitarist and singer performed as gospel singer before relocating to Houston in 1953 and learning guitar. Through the 1970s worked as sideman with various Houston blues artists, including Peppermint Harris and Walter "Thunderbird" Price. In 1962 recorded single "Wanta Know How You Feel"/"I Don't Need You" with **Marcel Dugas**'s band for **Ivory Lee Semien**'s Ivory label. Continued performing in Houston clubs into the 2000s and appeared on Dialtone CD *Texas Southside Kings* with **Oscar O'Bear** in 2006. Not to be confused with New Orleans drummer **Idris Muhhamad**, who was born Leo Morris.

MORRIS, SKIP *See* Stewart, Skip.

MORTON, JELLY ROLL (Ferdinand Joseph Lamothe) *Jazz.* Piano, guitar, vocals. Composer. Bandleader. (Born probably Sept. 20, 1890, New Orleans, Orleans Parish; died July 10, 1941, Los Angeles.)[31] One of the greatest figures in the history of jazz, who helped transform the music from its blues and ragtime origins in the early 1900s. Also regarded as the genre's first important composer as well as one of its finest. Born in historic Faubourg Marigny neighborhood to a Creole family, began playing guitar at age seven before switching to piano by age 10, influenced early on by opera and classical music and later by local musicians such as **Tony Jackson**. By 1905 was performing in some of the finest brothels in the Storyville District, reportedly changing his professional name to Morton to protect his family's identity. Using New Orleans as a base, began traveling widely throughout the South, Midwest, and West and started composing many songs which would become standards and help define early jazz, including "Jelly Roll Blues," "King Porter Stomp," and "New Orleans Blues." In the late 1910s and early 1920s worked extensively in Los Angeles. Relocated to Chicago in 1923 and made influential recordings for Paramount and Gennett. Also recorded in Chicago with popular white jazz band New Orleans Rhythm Kings. From 1926 to 1930 made landmark recordings with his band the Red Hot Peppers, which included at times **Kid Ory**, **Paul Barbarin**, **Zutty Singleton**, and **Johnny** and **Baby Dodds**. In 1928 moved to

New York and worked and recorded there through 1935 with sessions as bandleader, sideman, and solo pianist. Relocated to Washington, D.C., and in 1938 made important recordings and interviews with Alan Lomax for the Library of Congress. In 1938–39 held his last recording sessions, in New York. While suffering from asthma, exasperated by a stabbing several years earlier, died in a Los Angeles hospital amidst plans for a comeback.

MOSLEY, EDGAR *Jazz.* Drums. (Born Nov. 12, 1895, Algiers, Orleans Parish; died Oct. 28, 1961, Los Angeles.)[32] Highly regarded New Orleans jazz drummer performed with **Kid Rena**, **Chris Kelly**, and **George Lewis** in the 1920s and 1930s. Recorded with Lewis and **Bunk Johnson** in the 1940s. Later relocated to California. Brother of **Batiste Mosley**.

MOSLEY, JOHN BATISTE "BAT" *Jazz.* Snare drum. (Born Dec. 22, 1893, Algiers, Orleans Parish; died Aug. 28, 1965, New Orleans, Orleans Parish.) Popular New Orleans brass-band snare drummer during the 1920s and 1930s who worked in the bands of Joe Harris, **Kid Howard**, and **Kid Rena**. Older brother of **Edgar Mosley**.

MOTT, HILRAE *Cajun.* Bass, guitar. (Born Feb. 23, 1936, Lacassine, Jeff. Davis Parish.) Noted early postwar Cajun guitarist and bassist began performing in the early 1950s by sitting in with **Elton Cormier**'s Sundown Playboys, becoming one of the first electric bass players to regularly perform with Cajun accordion bands. In the 1950s and 1960s performed and recorded with **Robert Bertrand**, **Jo-El Sonnier**, and **Dunice Theriot** and continued performing around Lake Charles area into the 2000s.

MOUTON, ALDUS *Cajun.* Accordion, vocals. Composer. Bandleader. (Born Aug. 9, 1941, Cankton, St. Landry Parish.) Cajun accordionist and bandleader of his Wandering Aces recorded singles on Crazy Cajun, Cajun Classics, Swallow, and La Louisianne in the late 1960s and 1970s, including "Cajun at the Fais Do Do" in 1974. Also recorded with **Johnnie Allan** and **Jim Olivier** in the 1980s.

MOUTON, SHINE (Lawrence Mouton) *Cajun.* Accordion. (Born Sept. 25, 1926, Crowley, Acadia Parish; died Jan. 9, 1998, Crowley, Acadia Parish.) Noted accordion player, bandleader, and master accordion maker performed with various musicians in the 1950s. In 1960 began making handmade accordions and soon became one of the premier Cajun instrument builders in the region. His customers included **Aldus Roger** and **Lawrence Walker**, and he served as mentor to **Marc Savoy**.

MOUTON, WALTER *Cajun.* Accordion, vocals. Bandleader. (Born Nov. 30, 1938, Scott, Lafayette Parish.) Renowned veteran Cajun accordion player who led his band the Scott Playboys for more than 65 years. Formed Scott Playboys at age 13 with members **Johnnie Allan**, **Rodney "Hot Rod" Miller**, and **Leeman Prejean** and performed in dance halls throughout southwest Louisiana and east Texas through the following six decades, including a 45-year residency at La Poussiere in Breaux Bridge. Recorded one single, "The Lonely Girl's Waltz"/"Scott Playboys Special," on Cajun Jamboree in 1968. Continued performing occasionally in the late 2010s.

MR. CALHOUN *See* Monroe, Vince [Notable Musicians Born outside Louisiana].

MR. G/GOOGLE EYES *See* August, Joe.

MUHAMMAD, IDRIS (*born* Leo Morris) *Jazz, rhythm and blues.* Drums. (Born Nov. 13, 1939, New Orleans, Orleans Parish; died July 29, 2014, Fort Lauderdale, Florida.) Highly accomplished and eclectic New Orleans jazz and rhythm and blues drummer regarded as one of the most innovative percussionists of the 1960s. A child prodigy, by age 12 was performing with jazz groups and recorded on sessions during his teens. He later worked with numerous jazz and rhythm and blues musicians such as Sam Cooke, Curtis Mayfield, George Benson, Sonny Stitt, Pharoah Sanders, Lou Donaldson, Grant Green, and many others. From 1968 to 1972 performed as percussionist for Broadway production of *Hair.* Recorded prolifically as sideman and released 12 albums as leader which fused jazz, rhythm and blues, and funk, including *Black Rhythm Revolution!* on Prestige in 1971. His influential drumming was sampled frequently by rap and hip-hop artists in the 1980s. Not to be confused with blues guitarist **Leo Morris**.

MYLES, EDGAR "BIG BOY" *Rhythm and blues.* Vocals, trombone. Composer. Bandleader. (Born Mar. 11, 1933, New Orleans, Orleans Parish; died Aug. 10, 1984, Brooklyn, New York.) New Orleans rhythm and blues singer and trombonist and original member of early 1950s group the Sha-Weez. As lead singer with Sha-Weez, recorded for Aladdin in 1952 and had local hit "No One to Love Me." In 1953–54 recorded with Sha-Weez bandmate **Sugar Boy Crawford** for Chess and appeared on

Crawford's New Orleans classic "Jock-A-Mo." Recorded with **Li'l Millet** and as a leader in 1955–56 for Specialty. Also recorded a single on Argo in 1958 with **August "Dimes" Dupont** as Myles and Dupont. In the early 1960s had two releases on Ace with Mac Rebennack (**Dr. John**) and a single each on V-Tone and Pic-One. Later relocated to New York.

MYLES, RAYMOND A. *Gospel.* Vocals, piano. Composer. Bandleader. (Born July 14, 1958, New Orleans, Orleans Parish; died Oct. 11, 1998, New Orleans, Orleans Parish.) Beloved New Orleans gospel singer, composer, and social activist who was known for his high energy and uplifting performances. At age 12 made first recording, which was a protest of the Vietnam War. Later formed RAMS choir and toured extensively throughout the South and Europe. Released critically acclaimed CD *A Taste of Heaven* in 1995. Found murdered in the streets of the French Quarter at age 40.

N

NAQUIN, EDIUS *Cajun.* Fiddle, vocals. Composer. (Born Mar. 16, 1901, Pine Prairie, Evangeline Parish; died Nov. 13, 1985, Reddell, Evangeline Parish.) Early Cajun fiddle player and singer who recorded centuries-old traditional French Louisiana folk songs and early French ballads for Smithsonian Institute folklorist Ralph Rinzler in the mid-1960s, including "Hack a 'Tit Moreau" and "Ou T'ètait Mercredi Passé." Great-grandfather of **Kevin Naquin**.

NAQUIN, KEVIN *Cajun.* Accordion, vocals. Composer. Bandleader. (Born Apr. 5, 1979, Scott, Lafayette Parish.) Traditional Cajun accordionist, singer-songwriter, and bandleader was raised in a Cajun French–speaking family and began learning accordion at age 14. At age 16 formed the Ossun Playboys and began performing around Lafayette, mentored early on by **Don Montoucet** and **Hubert Maitre**. Released recording debut, *Dans le Couer D'Ossun,* with Maitre on Swallow in 1997. Continued performing with Ossun Playboys through the 2010s with numerous releases on Swallow, including highly acclaimed *Jamais Garantie (No Guarantee)* in 2014. Great-grandson of **Edius Naquin** and **Hadley Fontenot**.

NASH, PAPA LEMON *Jazz, blues.* Ukulele, banjo, guitar, mandolin, vocals. Composer. (Born Apr. 22, 1898, Lakeland, Pointe Coupee Parish; died Dec. 27, 1969, New Orleans, Orleans Parish.)[1] Idiosyncratic New Orleans jazz and early blues multi-instrumentalist was raised in New Orleans from two months of age. Began playing guitar at age thirteen and took music lessons from **Manuel Manetta**. Performed occasionally with **Richard "Rabbit" Brown** on street corners. Started playing ukulele in the early 1920s and, through 1940s, traveled extensively with various medicine shows and circuses. Returned to New Orleans in the 1950s and became a fixture on the streets of the French Quarter, performing for tips. Also worked and recorded with **Noon Johnson**. From 1959 to 1961 recorded numerous sides as ukulele soloist for folklorists Dick Allen and Harry Oster.

NATHAN (of the Zydeco Cha Chas) *See* Williams, Nathan.

NEAL, JACKIE *Rhythm and blues.* Vocals. Composer. Bandleader. (Born July 7, 1967, Baton Rouge, EBR Parish; died Mar. 10, 2005, Baton Rouge, EBR Parish.) Daughter of **Raful Neal**, talented southern soul singer made her recording debut with *The Blues Won't Let You Go* on Cititrax in 1995. Released *Money Can't Buy Me Love* on Back Street in 2002 and two years later had regional success with CD *Down in Da Club* on Jazzy with tours on the southern soul circuit. At height of career and while planning first European tour she was fatally shot by an ex-boyfriend during a domestic dispute. Sister of **Kenny** and **Lil' Ray Neal**.

NEAL, KENNY *Blues.* Guitar, bass, harmonica, drums, vocals. Composer. Bandleader. (Born Oct. 14, 1957, New Orleans, Orleans Parish.) Oldest child of Baton Rouge blues patriarch **Raful Neal**. Born in New Orleans's Charity Hospital but raised in Erwinville, began playing harmonica at age three and guitar several years later. During his early teens performed in his father's family band and at age 19 joined **Buddy Guy**'s band in Chicago as bassist. Formed Neal Brothers Blues Band in Toronto in the early 1980s and in 1987 recorded debut LP *Bio on the Bayou* for King Snake, which was subsequently reissued on Alligator as *Big News from Baton Rouge* and which established him nationally as a leading modern blues artist. In the 1990s and 2000s had numerous releases on Alligator, Telarc, Isabel, and other labels and remained one of the most popular touring artists on the international blues circuit. Continued to tour extensively in the 2010s and released several more recordings, including the critically acclaimed *Bloodline* on Cleopatra in 2016. In 2017 opened Neal's Juke Joint in Baton Rouge, which featured local and national acts. Brother of **Lil' Ray** and **Jackie Neal**.

NEAL, LIL' RAY (Raful Neal Jr.) *Blues.* Guitar, vocals. Composer. Bandleader. (Born Mar. 16, 1960, Erwinville, WBR Parish.) Highly regarded Baton Rouge blues guitarist began playing in his father **Raful Neal**'s family band as a child, greatly influenced by B.B. King, whom he would later befriend. In 1979 toured with John Lee Hooker and in following decades worked in touring bands of Big Mama Thornton, Little Milton, Bobby "Blue" Bland, James Cotton, **Buddy Guy**, **Bobby Rush**, and others. In 2010s continued to lead his own band based in Baton Rouge. Brother of **Kenny** and **Jackie Neal**.

NEAL, RAFUL *Blues.* Harmonica, vocals. Composer. Bandleader. (Born June 6, 1936, Chamberlin, WBR Parish; died Sept. 1, 2004, Baton Rouge, EBR Parish.) Renowned swamp blues musician and patriarch of large Baton Rouge blues family whose many children became professional musicians, including Darnell, Noel, Frederick, Ronnie, Larry, Graylon, **Jackie**, **Lil' Ray**, and **Kenny Neal**. Began performing in Baton Rouge in the 1950s in bands with **Lazy Lester** and **Buddy Guy**. Made recording debut in 1958 with single on Peacock and had handful of releases on La Louisianne, Whit, and Fantastic through the early 1980s. Recorded first full-length album, *Louisiana Legend,* in 1987 for King Snake which was reissued on Alligator in 1990. Following year released *I've Been Mistreated* on Ichiban and toured internationally. In 1998 released *Old Friends* on Club Louisianne with children Noel, Darnell, and Jackie. In 2001 recorded CD *The Hoodoo Kings* with **Tabby Thomas** and **Eddie Bo** and appeared on *Superharps II,* both on Telarc.

NEAL, TYREE *Rhythm and blues.* Guitar, bass, drums, keyboards, vocals. Composer. Bandleader. (Born Jan. 14, 1983, Baton Rouge, EBR Parish.) Popular southern soul singer and guitarist began performing at age three, sitting in at blues festivals with various family members. From the late 1990s through mid-2000s served as band director for aunt **Jackie Neal** and later toured with uncle **Kenny Neal**. In 2006 launched solo career and following year released debut recording, *All Grown Up,* on Jazzy. Several more releases followed, including *Still Got the Blues* in 2017, and continued as popular draw on southern soul circuit in the late 2010s. Grandson of **Raful Neal**.

NED, CLEMENT "KING" *Creole.* Accordion, vocals. (Born July 14, 1906, south of Ville Platte, Evangeline Parish; died Nov. 1977, Eunice, St. Landry Parish.) Early Creole accordionist and singer who recorded "Le Valse de Samedi Après Midi" for Library of Congress folklorist Ralph Rinzler in Mamou in 1965. Grandfather of **Joe Hall**.

NELSON, BIG EYE LOUIS (Louis Nelson Delisle) *Jazz.* Clarinet, bass, banjo, accordion. Bandleader. (Born Jan. 20, 1885, New Orleans, Orleans Parish; died Aug. 15, 1949, New Orleans, Orleans Parish.)[2] Regarded as one of the great clarinetists of early New Orleans jazz whose blues-inflected, fluid playing style influenced **Johnny Dodds**, **Jimmie Noone**, and many others. Took lessons from **Lorenzo Tio Sr.** in 1905 and through 1910 performed with **King Oliver**, **Jelly Roll Morton**, **Papa Celestin**, and others. Worked with **Freddie Keppard** in Chicago around 1918 and in the 1920s with **John Robichaux**, **Lee Collins**, and **Sidney Desvigne**. In 1940 recorded with **Kid Rena** and in 1949 had sessions as leader (as Louis Delisle) and with **Wooden Joe Nicholas**. Not to be confused with jazz trombonist **Louis Hall Nelson**.

NELSON, CHICAGO BOB (Robert Lee Nelson) *Blues.* Harmonica, vocals. Bandleader. (Born July 4, 1944, Bogalusa, Washington Parish; died Jan. 17, 2013, Atlanta.) Chicago blues singer began playing harmonica at age eight and was influenced by **Lazy Lester**, **Slim Harpo**, and Sonny Boy Williamson (Rice Miller). Moved to Chicago in the early 1960s and performed with Muddy Waters, **Buddy Guy**, Earl Hooker, Howlin' Wolf, and others. Relocated to Atlanta in 1977 and formed the Heartfixers with guitarist Tinsley Ellis in the early 1980s. In the 1980s and 1990s had recordings on numerous labels, including Southland, High Water, Erwin, Ichiban, and King Snake and led his own band with occasional tours to Europe through the early 2010s.

NELSON, EARL *Rhythm and blues.* Vocals. Composer. Bandleader. (Born Sept. 8, 1928, Lake Charles, Calcasieu Parish; died July 12, 2008, Inglewood, California.) Noted rhythm and blues and early soul singer and songwriter best known for his 1963 hit "Harlem Shuffle" in duo Bob & Earl. Began singing in church as a child and relocated to Los Angeles with family in the late 1930s. Performed with local doo-wop groups in the early 1950s and in the mid-1950s began working and recording with singer Bobby Byrd in various vocal groups, including the Voices and the Hollywood Flames, singing lead on Flames' 1957 hit "Buzz-Buzz-Buzz" on Ebb. Also recorded several singles with Byrd as Bob & Earl which failed to chart. In the early 1960s reformed Bob & Earl with Bob Relf replacing Byrd and had hit with "Harlem Shuffle," which would later be covered by numerous rock, rhythm and blues, and zydeco bands. From 1965 to 1970 had several hits under name Jackie Lee, including "The Duck" on Mirwood in 1965, and in the mid-1970s recorded as "Jay Dee" for Warner Bros. and had minor hit with "Strange Funky Games and Things" in 1974. Continued performing around Los Angeles area into the 1990s.

NELSON, JAY *Rhythm and blues, swamp pop.* Guitar, vocals. Composer. Bandleader. (Born Oct. 11, 1939, Jeanerette, Iberia Parish; died Apr. 22, 1982, Jeanerette, Iberia Parish.) Southwest Louisiana rhythm and blues singer-songwriter and guitarist made his recording debut on Hollywood with "Raise Some San" [*sic*] in 1958 with his band the Jumpers. Also recorded several sides for producer **Eddie Shuler**'s Goldband label, followed by three releases on Excello in 1958–59, including swamp pop single "A Fool That Was Blind" backed with instrumental "Sleepy Time Rock." In the early 1960s recorded several singles for Morgan City–based Drew-Blan. Sustained serious injuries in an auto accident in 1965 but eventually recovered and continued performing for a short time before retiring from music to work in the oil industry. Killed in a work-related helicopter crash at age 42.

NELSON, LAWRENCE *See* Prince La La.

NELSON, LOUIS HALL *Jazz.* Trombone. Bandleader. (Born Sept. 17, 1902, New Orleans, Orleans Parish; died Apr. 5, 1990, New Orleans, Orleans Parish.) Highly regarded New Orleans jazz trombonist who combined the early tailgate style with swing. Throughout the 1920s and 1930s worked with **Kid Rena**, **Sidney Desvigne**, **Fats Pichon**, and **Bébé Ridgley**'s Original Tuxedo Orchestra. In the 1940s and 1950s worked and recorded with **Big Eye Louis Nelson**, **Wooden Joe Nicholas**, **Kid Thomas**, and others. Performed with **Harold Dejan**'s Olympia Brass Band and also toured Europe and Japan with **George Lewis** and as leader. Recorded extensively as sideman and leader throughout the 1960s and 1970s and performed regularly at Preservation Hall from its inception until his death.

NELSON, WALTER, JR. **"Papoose"** *Rhythm and blues.* Guitar, vocals. (Born July 26, 1932, New Orleans, Orleans Parish; died Feb. 28, 1962, Harlem, New York.) Early New Orleans rhythm and blues guitarist best known for his long tenure as **Fats Domino**'s early guitarist. Began working with **Professor Longhair** in the late 1940s and recorded with the pianist in 1951. Throughout the 1950s worked and recorded with Domino, appearing on more than 70 sides, including many hits such as "I'm Walkin'" and "Ain't It a Shame." Died of a heroin overdose while on tour with Domino in the early 1960s. Son of guitarist **Walter Nelson Sr.** and brother of **Prince La La**.

NELSON, WALTER, SR. **"Black Walter"** *Jazz, blues.* Guitar, banjo. (Born Mar. 21, 1908, Verretville [now Verret], St. Bernard Parish; died Feb. 22, 1984, New Orleans, Orleans Parish.)[3] Influential but unrecorded early jazz guitarist and father of **Walter Nelson Jr.** and **Prince La La**. Moved to New Orleans with family around 1914 and studied under **Manuel Manetta**. From the 1920s through 1940s worked with **Herb Morand**, **George Lewis**, **Noon Johnson**, and **Smiley Lewis**, among others. Continued performing through the early 1980s.

NEVILLE, AARON *Rhythm and blues, gospel.* Vocals. Composer. Bandleader. (Born Jan. 24, 1941, New Orleans, Orleans Parish.) Internationally renowned New Orleans rhythm and blues singer known for his work with the Neville Brothers and as a solo performer. Influenced by Sam Cooke and local singers such as **Izzycoo Gordon**. Joined brother **Art Neville**'s band the Hawketts in the mid-1950s. In 1960 started working with **Allen Toussaint** and had local success with "Over You" on Minit. Released several more singles on Minit in the early 1960s and had first major hit with "Tell It Like It Is" for Par-Lo in 1967, which reached number two on the pop charts. In 1976 joined brothers **Art**, **Charles**, and **Cyril Neville** to record with uncle **Big Chief Jolly** and following year formed the Neville Brothers who performed for more than three decades with numerous hit recordings. In the late 1980s and 1990s had hits with vocalist Linda Ronstadt and as solo act, including "Don't Know Much" and "Everybody Plays the Fool." Released numerous albums throughout the 1990s and 2000s, including country and gospel recordings. Relocated to Nashville for several years after Hurricane Katrina and continued performing and recording with critically acclaimed releases on Blue Note and Tell It in the mid-2010s. Father of musicians Jason and **Ivan Neville**.

NEVILLE, ART *Rhythm and blues.* Piano, organ, vocals.

Composer. Bandleader. (Born Dec. 17, 1937, New Orleans, Orleans Parish; died July 22, 2019, New Orleans, Orleans Parish.) Oldest member of prestigious New Orleans rhythm and blues family and founding member of the Meters. Began playing piano as a child, influenced greatly by **Professor Longhair** and **Fats Domino**. As member of the Hawketts in the early 1950s made recording debut for Chess on New Orleans classic "Mardi Gras Mambo." Recorded for Specialty from 1956 to 1958. After military discharge in the early 1960s, released several singles on Instant and Cinderella, including "All These Things" in 1962. In the late 1960s formed Art Neville and the Neville Sounds, which eventually evolved into seminal New Orleans funk group the Meters with **Leo Nocentelli**, **George Porter Jr.**, and **Zigaboo Modeliste**. In the late 1970s formed band the Neville Brothers with **Aaron**, **Charles**, and **Cyril Neville** and had several hit recordings throughout the following two decades. Around 1990 formed Meters spin-off group, the Funky Meters, and continued performing with group through the 2010s as well as with other side projects until announcing his retirement in late 2018. Father of guitarist Ian Neville.

NEVILLE BROTHERS *See* Neville, Aaron; Neville, Art; Neville, Charles; Neville, Cyril.

NEVILLE, CHARLES *Rhythm and blues.* Saxophone, vocals. Composer. Bandleader. (Born Dec. 28, 1938, New Orleans, Orleans Parish; died Apr. 26, 2018, Huntington, Massachusetts.) Second oldest sibling of prominent New Orleans rhythm and blues family of brothers, began playing saxophone before his teens, influenced by Louis Jordan, Charlie Parker, and John Coltrane. In the 1950s toured with numerous rhythm and blues artists such as Johnny Ace, Bobby Bland, James Brown, and Ray Charles. Relocated to New York in the early 1970s and worked with brothers **Aaron** and **Cyril Neville** in Soul Machine. In 1976 returned to New Orleans to join brothers Aaron, Cyril, and **Art Neville** on recording session with uncle **Big Chief Jolly**. Brothers started performing officially as the Neville Brothers the following year. Continued working and recording with Neville Brothers for several decades as well as leading his own bands. Also worked frequently with daughter **Charmaine Neville**. In the 1990s relocated to Massachusetts and in later years performed with sons Talyn and Khalif as the New England Nevilles. Died of pancreatic cancer at age 79.

NEVILLE, CHARMAINE *Rhythm and blues, jazz.* Vocals. (Born Mar. 31, 1956, New Orleans, Orleans Parish.) Daughter of noted saxophonist **Charles Neville**, celebrated jazz and rhythm and blues vocalist started performing during her teens with her father and uncles in Neville Brothers band. In the 1990s became popular weekly draw at premier New Orleans jazz club Snug Harbor. Made several recordings through the 2000s, including her 1992 CD debut, *It's About Time,* on Gert Town.

NEVILLE, CYRIL *Rhythm and blues.* Drums, vocals. Composer. (Born Oct. 10, 1948, New Orleans, Orleans Parish.) Youngest of noted New Orleans rhythm and blues siblings, started performing in brother **Art Neville**'s band in the late 1960s. In 1977 joined brothers Art, **Aaron**, and **Charles Neville** in forming the Neville Brothers and continued with group throughout the following three decades. In 2005 began performing with **Tab Benoit**'s Voice of the Wetland All-Stars and in 2010 joined New Orleans funk band Galactic. Also cofounded blues-rock group Royal Southern Brotherhood in 2012. Appeared on recordings with Bob Dylan, Willie Nelson, **Dr. John**, and others and recorded several albums as leader, including *The Fire This Time* in 1995.

NEVILLE, IVAN *Rhythm and blues.* Vocals, keyboards. Composer. Bandleader. (Born Aug. 19, 1959, New Orleans, Orleans Parish.) Son of **Aaron Neville**, began performing with his father and uncles' band the Neville Brothers during his teens. In the 1980s and 1990s performed and recorded with rock musicians Bonnie Raitt, the Rolling Stones, Keith Richards, Don Henley, and others. Released four albums as a solo artist from 1988 through 2004, including *If My Ancestors Could See Me Now.* In 2003 formed New Orleans funk-rock band Dumpstaphunk with **Tony Hall** and continued to perform and record with group in the 2010s.

NEW ORLEANS SLIM *See* Amos, Ira.

NEWMAN, DWIGHT *Jazz.* Piano. (Born Nov. 13, 1895, New Orleans, Orleans Parish; died July 13, 1941, New Orleans, Orleans Parish.)[4] Early New Orleans jazz pianist began performing with **Lawrence Marrero**'s Young Tuxedo Orchestra in 1920. In 1928 replaced **Steve Lewis** as pianist in **Armand Piron**'s band until Piron disbanded group several months later. Throughout the 1930s worked regularly with **Peter Bocage**'s Creole Serenaders and also performed occasionally with **George Lewis**. Father of trumpeter **Joe Newman**.

NEWMAN, JIMMY C. *Cajun, country.* Guitar, vocals. Composer. Bandleader. (Born Aug. 29, 1927, Mamou, Evangeline Parish; died June 21, 2014, Nashville.) Renowned Cajun and country singer-songwriter began performing in the mid-1940s with **Chuck Guillory**'s

Rhythm Boys before making recording debut as leader for Feature in the early 1950s. After a single on Khoury's, signed with Dot and had hit with "Cry, Cry Darling" in 1954. Throughout next several years performed on the *Louisiana Hayride* and became lifetime member of *Grand Ole Opry,* releasing several more hits, including "A Fallen Star" in 1957 which reached number two on the country charts. By the 1960s had fully developed his Cajun-country sound and through 1970 reached the country charts over 25 times with songs such as "Bayou Talk," "D.J. for a Day," and his signature hit, "Alligator Man." In following two decades released numerous albums, notably 1976 LP *Lache Pas la Patate* on La Louisianne and 1991 CD *The Alligator Man* on Rounder. Continued performing through the mid-2010s, making final appearance on the *Grand Ole Opry* just several weeks before his death at age 86.

NEWMAN, JOE *Jazz.* Trumpet. Bandleader. (Born Sept. 7, 1921, New Orleans, Orleans Parish; died July 4, 1992, New York City.)[5] Noted bebop and swing trumpeter best known for his long tenure with Count Basie from 1943 to 1946 and 1952 to 1961. Also performed in bands of Lionel Hampton, **Illinois Jacquet**, Benny Goodman, and others. Recorded over 25 albums as leader and appeared on recordings with Frank Sinatra, Judy Garland, Tony Bennett, Aretha Franklin, Louis Jordan, and others. Continued to perform until a year before his death. Son of jazz pianist **Dwight Newman**.

NICHOLAS, ALBERT *Jazz.* Clarinet. Bandleader. (Born May 27, 1900, New Orleans, Orleans Parish; died Sept. 3, 1973, Basel, Switzerland.)[6] Highly regarded traditional New Orleans jazz clarinetist whose distinguished career spanned six decades. Studied under both **Lorenzo Tio Sr.** and **Jr.** and began performing during his teens with **Manuel Perez**. In the early 1920s worked with Perez, **Buddy Petit**, and **Arnold DePass** and also led his own band. In the mid-1920s worked in Chicago with **King Oliver** and recorded with Oliver, **Richard M. Jones**, and Luis Russell. After tours of China, Egypt, and Europe, recorded with **Louis Armstrong**, **Red Allen**, Fats Waller, **Jelly Roll Morton**, and **Zutty Singleton** in the late 1920s and 1930s. In the 1940s and 1950s worked with **Bunk Johnson** and **Kid Ory** and recorded with **Sidney Bechet**, **Baby Dodds**, **Mutt Carey**, and others. Relocated to Europe in the mid-1950s and toured and recorded extensively as a leader until his death at age 73. Nephew of **Wooden Joe Nicholas**.

NICHOLAS, WOODEN JOE (Joseph Nicholas) *Jazz.* Cornet, trumpet, clarinet. Bandleader. (Born Sept. 23, 1883, New Orleans, Orleans Parish; died Nov. 17, 1957, New Orleans, Orleans Parish.) Renowned early New Orleans jazz bandleader performed throughout Storyville as clarinetist in the mid-1910s. Worked with **King Oliver**, who influenced his switch to cornet around 1918, and formed his Camelia Orchestra, which included at times **Buddy Petit**, **Billy** and **Lawrence Marrero**, and **Ike Robinson**. Made first recordings in the mid- to late 1940s as a leader and sideman. Uncle of **Albert Nicholas**.

NICHOLSON, J. D. (James Davis Nicholson) *Blues.* Piano, vocals. Composer. Bandleader. (Born Apr. 12, 1917, Monroe, Ouachita Parish; died July 27, 1991, Los Angeles.) Noted early West Coast–based rhythm and blues pianist began playing in church as a child. In 1926 was sent to live with relatives in Los Angeles and in the 1930s began performing on streets, influenced greatly by Memphis Slim. By the early 1940s was performing around the Watts/South Central music scene and soon teamed up with Jimmy McCracklin. From the late 1940s through 1960s had singles as leader on Courtney, Elko, Hollywood, Imco, Timbre, and Blue Moon and worked and/or recorded with numerous musicians, including Pete "Guitar" Lewis, **Clifton Chenier**, Ray Agee, Big Mama Thornton, Jimmy Reed, **Little Walter**, and Big Joe Turner. In the 1970s worked regularly and recorded with George "Harmonica" Smith and Rod Piazza in band Bacon Fat and toured Japan with his group the Soulbenders. Recorded live LP in the 1980s which was released on Action Pac.

NIXON, ELMORE *Blues.* Piano. Bandleader. (Born Nov. 17, 1935, Crowley, Acadia Parish; died Dec. 11, 1973, Houston.)[7] Texas-based blues pianist and singer was raised in Houston after family relocated in 1939. Began playing piano during his early teens and was mentored by local saxophonist and bandleader Henry Hayes. In the late 1940s and early 1950s recorded for Sittin' in With, Peacock, Mercury, and Savoy and had minor hit with "Alabama Blues" for Peacock with Hayes in 1950. After cutting two records for Imperial and Post for **Dave Bartholomew** in 1955, continued performing in Houston blues clubs through the early 1970s. Also worked as session musician from the late 1940s through 1960s with **Clifton Chenier**, Lightnin' Hopkins, Hop Wilson, Peppermint Harris, L.C. Williams, and others.

NOCENTELLI, LEO *Rhythm and blues.* Guitar, vocals. Composer. Bandleader. (Born June 15, 1946, New Orleans, Orleans Parish.) Highly influential rhythm and blues and funk guitar player and songwriter and original member of seminal New Orleans funk band the Meters. Recorded with **Allen Toussaint** as a teenager in the 1960s on sessions with **Lee Dorsey**, **Chris Kenner**, and others. In the late 1960s joined **Art Neville**'s band with **George Porter Jr.** and **Zigaboo Modeliste**, which eventually became the Meters in 1969. Composed many of group's best-known songs, including "Cissy Strut" and "Sophisticated Sissy." After Meters disbanded in the late 1970s, toured with various bands, worked as session musician, and relocated to California. Performed with the Funky Meters in the 1980s and early 1990s before going solo. In 2016 returned to New Orleans and continued to perform as solo artist and with group Icons of Funk.

NOEL, LOUIS *Cajun.* Guitar, vocals. (Born Dec. 26, 1915, Arnaudville, St. Landry Parish; died June 1, 2002, Westwego, Jefferson Parish.)[8] Early postwar Cajun-country singer and guitarist performed and recorded with **Happy Fats** in the late 1940s, appearing as vocalist on "La Cravat," "Gabriel Waltz," and "Don't Hang Around" for Fais-Do-Do in 1946–47 and issued as by "Happy, Doc and the Boys" with **Doc Guidry**. In 1950 formed the Teche Troubadors and performed with the group on radio and in local dance halls. Relocated to Jefferson Parish in the early 1960s.

NOOKIE BOY *See* Morgan, Oliver.

NOONE, JIMMIE *Jazz.* Clarinet, vocals. Composer. Bandleader. (Born Apr. 23, 1895, Stanton, Orleans Parish; died Apr. 19, 1944, Los Angeles.)[9] Highly influential early New Orleans jazz clarinet player who is widely regarded as one of the greatest clarinetists of the 1920s. Began playing clarinet around 1910 and studied with **Lorenzo Tio Jr.** and **Sidney Bechet**. In 1913 performed with **Freddie Keppard** and cofounded Young Olympia Band with **Buddy Petit** in 1914. Also worked with **Kid Ory** and **Papa Celestin** in Storyville in the mid-1910s. Toured Chicago and the Midwest with Keppard's Original Creole Band in 1917, then relocated to Chicago the following year with **King Oliver**, recording with Oliver in 1923. From 1920 to 1926 worked and recorded with Doc Cook's Dreamland Orchestra. In 1926 formed his famed Apex Club Orchestra and made acclaimed recordings for Vocalion in 1928. Led various bands in Chicago through the early 1940s and recorded extensively for Brunswick, Decca, and Bluebird. Relocated to Los Angeles in 1943 and made final recordings for Capitol. Performed with Ory's all-star band which included **Mutt Carey** and **Zutty Singleton** on Orson Welles's radio broadcasts shortly before Noone's death.

NUNEZ, ALCIDE "YELLOW" *Jazz.* Clarinet. Composer. Bandleader. (Born Mar. 17, 1884, New Orleans, Orleans Parish; died Sept. 2, 1934, New Orleans, Orleans Parish.)[10] Early New Orleans jazz clarinetist best known for his work with the Louisiana Five. From around 1905 through the mid-1910s performed in bands of **Papa Jack Laine** and **Tom Brown** and with a trio in Storyville. In 1916 worked with **Johnny Stein**'s Dixie Jass Band in Chicago until members broke off from Stein to form the Original Dixieland Jass Band, but left group before their historic recording session in 1917. Relocated to New York and performed with Bert Kelly. In 1918 joined the Louisiana Five and performed and recorded with group through the early 1920s. Led his own quartet in the mid-1920s before returning to New Orleans and working as a policeman in remaining years.

O'BEAR, OSCAR *Blues.* Guitar, bass, vocals. Composer. Bandleader. (Born June 9, 1942, Ponchatoula, Tangipahoa Parish.) Houston-based blues guitarist and singer moved to the city's Third Ward at age 13 and began playing bass shortly afterwards. At age 16 played first gig behind **Clarence "Gatemouth" Brown**. Inspired by **Leo Morris**, switched to guitar and throughout the 1960s lived in New Orleans and worked with **Ernie K-Doe**, **Earl King**, and others. Returned to Houston in 1969 and worked with various artists, including **Big Roger Collins**, the Americans, and Archie Bell and the Drells. Recorded first single in 1982 and continued to lead his own band on the Houston blues scene in the 2010s, appearing on Dialtone CD *Texas Southside Kings* with Morris in 2006.

ODOM, ANDREW "BIG VOICE"/"B.B." *Blues.* Vocals. Bandleader. (Born Dec. 15, 1936, Denham Springs, Livingston Parish; died Dec. 23, 1991, Chicago.)[1] Highly regarded Chicago blues singer best known for his work as vocalist with blues guitarist Earl Hooker and Jimmy Dawkins. In the mid-1950s relocated to St. Louis and worked with Albert King and Johnny O'Neal before settling in Chicago in 1960. In the mid- to late 1960s worked regularly with Hooker, appearing on the guitarist's acclaimed releases on Arhoolie and Bluesway. Recorded single (as Andre Odom) for Nation in 1967 and LP *Farther on Down the Road* in 1969 for Bluesway, the latter backed by Hooker. In the 1970s worked with Dawkins and appeared as vocalist on Dawkins's *All for Business* LP on Delmark. Recorded LP *Feel So Good* in 1982 for Isabel and made final recording, *Goin' to California,* for Flying Fish in 1991. Suffered fatal heart attack while driving to the Checkerboard Lounge.

OFFLEE, REVEREND BURNELL JAMES *Gospel.* Vocals. Bandleader. (Born Apr. 10, 1913, Baton Rouge, EBR Parish; died July 16, 1998, Baton Rouge, EBR Parish.) Longtime manager and lead singer of Zion Travelers Spiritual Singers of Baton Rouge, which he cofounded in 1946 and remained as a member for five decades. Group performed on live radio broadcasts every Sunday morning in Baton Rouge for more than fifty years and made several recordings.

OGDEN, BOB *Jazz, blues.* Drums. Bandleader. (Born Oct. 16, 1914, New Orleans, Orleans Parish; died Feb. 19, 1991, New Orleans, Orleans Parish.) New Orleans jazz drummer began performing in the late 1930s and toured with Darktown Scandals Revue which starred classic blues singer Ida Cox. Later worked with **Fats Pichon**, **Papa Celestin**, and **Sidney Bechet**. In 1946 formed his own band which backed **Roy Brown** at **Cosimo Matassa**'s studio in 1947 and appeared on Brown's historic recording "Good Rocking Tonight" for DeLuxe, which is often cited as among the first rock and roll records.

OLD CORN MEAL *Early Americana, folk.* Vocals. (Born mid- to late 1700s, presumably New Orleans, Orleans Parish; died May 20, 1842, New Orleans, Orleans Parish.)[2] African American street vendor who sold Indian cornmeal by horse-drawn cart in the streets of New Orleans for several decades in the first half of the 1800s while singing, dancing, and story-telling to attract and entertain his customers. His wide popularity led to groundbreaking appearances in 1837–38 as the first African American to perform in New Orleans theaters. His songs and falsetto singing style influenced blackface minstrelsy and American popular music. Known for his song "Fresh Corn Meal" as well as "Old Rosin the Bow," "My Long Tail Blue," and other crowd favorites. Continued busking in streets and was often celebrated in print by the *Times-Picayune* newspaper in remaining years until his death in 1842 at an unknown advanced age.

OLIVER, JOHN *Cajun.* Accordion, vocals. Composer. Bandleader. (Born June 18, 1915, Mowata, Acadia Parish; died June 13, 2005, Lake Charles, Calcasieu Parish.) Early Cajun accordionist began playing at age 15 and within several years formed the Louisiana Ramblers. In the early 1960s relocated to Lake Charles and continued performing with group, recording several singles for Goldband with **Robert Bertrand** in the late 1960s and early 1970s, including "Tee Mamou Blues" and "The Mowata Waltz." Performed extensively throughout southwest Louisiana and east Texas in following decades and in later years continued playing in Lake Charles area into the 1990s.

OLIVER, JOSEPH "KING" *Jazz.* Cornet. Composer. Bandleader. (Born Dec. 19, 1885, Aben, Ascension Parish; died Apr. 8, 1938, Savannah, Georgia.)[3] One of the most important figures in early New Orleans jazz, and pioneer cornetist who was among the first to use horn mutes, which helped shape the sound of early jazz. Also served as mentor to **Louis Armstrong** and gave Armstrong his first major break. Moved to New Orleans as a child and first studied trombone before switching to cornet. Around 1908 began performing around New Orleans and in Storyville District and worked with the Eagle, Magnolia, and Olympia brass bands and **Richard M. Jones**'s Four Hot Hounds, among others. Also performed with **Sidney Bechet** and in the mid-1910s was member of **Kid Ory**'s band. In 1918 moved to Chicago to front **Bill Johnson**'s Original Creole Orchestra at Royal Gardens to much acclaim. Formed his own group in 1920 which included **Honoré Dutrey**, **Johnny Dodds**, **Ed Garland**, **Minor Hall**, and singer Lil Hardin and quickly became a sensation. In 1922 invited Armstrong to join band as second cornetist and following year made historic recordings as King Oliver's Creole Jazz Band. Recorded several sides with **Jelly Roll Morton** in 1924 and in 1926–27 made additional recordings, notably with his band the Dixie Syncopators. Between 1927 and 1931 performed and recorded extensively based in New York. Toured through the mid-1930s, but the Great Depression and severe dental problems eventually forced his retirement from music by 1937. Settled in Savannah where he died destitute at age 52.

OLIVIER, JIM *Cajun.* Vocals. (Born Jan. 23, 1951, Arnaudville, St. Landry Parish; died Apr. 13, 2008, Carencro, Lafayette Parish.) Lafayette-based Cajun singer and local television personality who recorded five LPs for Swallow from 1980 to 1985 with producer-songwriter **V. J. Boulet**, having several regional hit singles, including "Brasse don le Cush-Cush" and "Marriage a Pic-et-Poc." In 1986 recorded single "Rockin' Zydeco" with **Rockin' Sidney** on Lanor.

ORY, KID (EDWARD ORY) *Jazz.* Trombone, banjo, vocals. Composer. Bandleader. (Born Dec. 25, 1886, LaPlace, St. John the Baptist Parish; died Jan. 23, 1973, Honolulu.) Regarded as the greatest trombone player in early jazz and credited with defining the tailgate style in the 1910s where the trombone plays rhythmic lines underneath the trumpet and cornet players. Started playing banjo at age 10 before switching to trombone at age 14. From 1912 to 1919 led one of the most prominent bands in New Orleans which at times included **King Oliver**, **Louis Armstrong**, **Johnny Dodds**, **Sidney Bechet**, **Jimmie Noone**, **Mutt Carey**, **Ed Garland**, and **Big Eye Louis Nelson**. Moved to California and formed **Kid Ory**'s Original Creole Jazz Band with Carey and Garland which in 1922 became the first African American New Orleans jazz band to record (under the name Spike's Seven Pods of Peppers). Relocated to Chicago in 1925 and joined King Oliver's Dixie Syncopators and appeared on some of the most important jazz recordings of the period with Oliver's Jazz Band, Armstrong's Hot Five, **Jelly Roll Morton**'s Red Hot Peppers, and the New Orleans Wanderers. Returned to California in 1930 and dropped out of music in 1933. Resumed music career in 1942 with **Barney Bigard**'s band in Los Angeles and performed with **Bunk Johnson** throughout 1943. Helped revive interest in New Orleans jazz in the mid-1940s with popular radio appearances on *The Orson Welles Almanac* and continued to lead one of the period's foremost New Orleans jazz bands until retiring to Hawaii in 1966.

OSBORN, JOE *Rhythm and blues, rock and roll, country.* Bass, guitar. (Born Aug. 28, 1937, Mound, Madison Parish; died Dec. 14, 2018, Greenwood, Caddo Parish.) Highly accomplished and influential bass player best known for his extensive work as member of the famed "Wrecking Crew" group of premier studio musicians in Los Angeles in the 1960s and early 1970s. Began playing guitar at age 12 and, after performing and recording with **Dale Hawkins** in Shreveport in the late 1950s, relocated to Los Angeles with **Puddler Harris** and **James Burton**. In 1960 switched to bass and throughout next several years recorded and performed with Ricky Nelson and Johnny Rivers. From 1964 to 1974 worked extensively as studio musician and appeared on hundreds of sessions backing Simon & Garfunkel, the 5th Dimension, the Carpenters, Neil Diamond, T-Bone Walker, and many others. In 1974 relocated to Nashville and through the late 1980s worked extensively as session musician, appearing on more than fifty country hits. Returned to Shreveport area in 1988 and continued performing and recording sporadically throughout following years.

OVERSTREET, REVEREND LOUIS, SR. *Gospel.* Guitar, bass drum, vocals. Composer. Bandleader. (Born Mar. 21, 1921, Lakeland, Pointe Coupee Parish; died Apr. 22, 1980, Phoenix, Arizona.)[4] Powerful gospel singer and guitarist began performing as a street preacher in the mid-1950s with his four young sons, Alvin Sidney, Robert Lee, Albert Lee, and Louis Jr., traveling throughout the South and Southwest. In 1961 settled in Phoenix and founded St. Luke's Powerhouse Church of God in Christ where Arhoolie founder Chris Strachwitz recorded him and sons with congregation in 1962. Continued to preach and perform in church and on the streets until suffering a fatal heart attack in 1980. His sons and wife, Mary, continued to be active in the church in following years.

OWENS, OVERTON "DR. DRIP DROP" *Blues.* Guitar, vocals. Bandleader. (Born Sept. 27, 1924, Natchitoches, Natch. Parish; died Nov. 15, 1998, Natchitoches, Natch. Parish.) Locally renowned veteran blues singer-guitarist and bandleader began playing music in the late 1940s and in the 1950s and 1960s performed throughout north Louisiana with his band the Natchitoches Serenaders. In the late 1960s formed the Mustangs and throughout next several decades gave many aspiring local musicians their start, including **B.B. Major**, **Hardrick Rivers**, and **Gainey "Pop" Hymes**.

OWENS, TONY *Rhythm and blues.* Vocals. Composer. (Born Jan. 11, 1948, New Orleans, Orleans Parish.) New Orleans deep soul singer and songwriter began singing in church as a child and during his teens performed at local talent shows. Made recording debut with "I Got Soul" on Soul Sound in 1967. In 1971 recorded "Confessin' a Feeling," which made the national charts on Cotillion. Throughout the 1970s had singles on Listening Post, Buddah, Island and Sansu. Worked mainly outside music in following decades but made occasional comeback appearances in the 2010s.

PAGE, BOBBY "BOOGAS" (Elwood Dugas) *Swamp pop.* Vocals, trombone. Composer. Bandleader. (Born Dec. 19, 1938, Rayne, Acadia Parish.) Early swamp pop singer best known for his work with Lafayette-area band the Riff Raffs. In the mid-1950s formed the Riff Raffs, whose members at times included **V.J. Boulet**, **Roy Perkins**, and **Harry Simoneaux**, and recorded singles on RAM and Calvert, having regional success with "Loneliness"/"Hippy-Ti-Yo" in 1958. Band also backed Perkins on several recordings for RAM. In the 2000s worked and recorded with Bobby and the Rockers and in the 2010s continued performing at clubs and swamp pop reunions, often with Swamp Pop Express. Boulet's "I Love My Baby" by Page and the Riff Raffs appeared in the 2018 award-winning film *Green Book.*

PAGE, CLEO/"CURLEY PAGE"/"SLY WILLIAMS" *Blues.* Guitar, vocals. Composer. Bandleader. (Born May 25, 1928, near Robeline, Natch. Parish; died Feb. 19, 1979, Inglewood, California.)[1] Largely unheralded and enigmatic blues guitarist and singer-songwriter who recorded the scorching "Boot Hill," which was issued under the pseudonym "Sly Williams" on an early 1960s Jimmy Witherspoon budget LP on Sutton but whose real identity remained a mystery for many decades. After serving in the army in the early 1950s, settled in Los Angeles and in 1955 had a single on Federal and Aladdin (with Rolling Crew) and worked with Johnny Otis as songwriter. In the late 1950s released two singles on Dalton as Curley Page, including "Boot Hill," and in the early 1970s released singles on CB, Wonder, Goodie Train, and Las Vegas, including "Leaving Mississippi." JSP Records later issued his 1970s singles and several unissued recordings on LP *Leaving Mississippi* in 1979.

PAJEAUD, WILLIE (William E. Pajaud) *Jazz.* Cornet, trumpet, vocals. Bandleader. (Born Dec. 17, 1901, New Orleans, Orleans Parish; died May 12, 1960, New Orleans, Orleans Parish.)[2] Noted early New Orleans jazz trumpeter studied under **Manuel Perez** and in 1919 started performing with **Papa Celestin**'s Tuxedo Brass Band. In the 1920s worked regularly with **John Robichaux**, **Sam Morgan**, **Danny Barker**, **Sidney Vigne**, and others. From the mid-1940s until his death was member of Eureka Brass Band and recorded with group and his own band in the 1950s.

PALMER, EARL *Rhythm and blues.* Drums. (Born Oct. 25, 1924, New Orleans, Orleans Parish; died Sept. 19, 2008, Banning, California.) Profoundly influential New Orleans drummer who played a major role in defining the sound of New Orleans rhythm and blues and early rock and roll in the late 1940s and 1950s. Widely cited as the most recorded drummer in history. Born into a family of entertainers, by age five was performing as tap-dancer on southern vaudeville circuit and toured with Ida Cox. After serving in World War II, studied drumming at New Orleans's Grunewald School of Music and joined **Dave Bartholomew**'s band in the late 1940s. From 1949 through 1957 appeared on hundreds of sessions at **Cosimo Matassa**'s famed studios with his signature backbeat drumming style driving numerous hits by **Fats Domino**, Little Richard, **Lloyd Price**, **Smiley Lewis**, **Professor Longhair**, **Shirley & Lee**, and many others. Relocated to Los Angeles in 1957 and worked extensively as in-demand session drummer, appearing on countless recordings by Ray Charles, the Everly Brothers, Sam Cooke, Frank Sinatra, the Beach Boys, Jan and Dean, Nat King Cole, the Supremes, Ike and Tina Turner, and many others. In the 1970s and 1980s recorded with Bonnie Raitt, Randy Newman, Willie Dixon, and Elvis Costello, among others. Also appeared on hundreds of television and film scores. Continued to perform occasionally in the 2000s with several appearances at festivals in New Orleans in remaining years.

PALMER, ROY *Jazz.* Trombone. (Born Apr. 2, 1887, New Orleans, Orleans Parish; died Dec. 2, 1963, Chicago.)[3] Early New Orleans jazz trombonist worked in Storyville District before relocating to Chicago in 1917. Throughout the 1920s worked with **Lawrence Duhé**, **King Oliver**, **Johnny Dodds**, **Jelly Roll Morton**, and others.

PAPA CAIRO (Julius Lamperez) *Cajun.* Steel guitar, guitar, fiddle, vocals. Composer. Bandleader. (Born July 27, 1920, New Orleans, Orleans Parish; died Nov. 13, 1999, Crowley, Acadia Parish.) Influential Cajun steel guitarist and songwriter best known for his recording "Grand Texas." Raised in Crowley, began performing in the mid-1930s as guitarist and made first recordings on sessions with **Joe Werner**'s Louisiana Rounders and **Leo Soileau**'s Rhythm Boys for Decca in 1937. In the early 1940s performed and recorded with **Happy Fats** and after serving in World War II began playing steel guitar and worked with **Harry Choates**. In 1948 joined **Chuck Guillory**'s band and recorded his composition "Grand Texas" with Guillory, the melody of which Hank Williams would later rework as "Jambalaya." In the late 1940s formed his own band and recorded for Colonial in 1949 and Feature in 1952. Continued performing in clubs and dance halls throughout southwest Louisiana and east Texas into the 1990s, reuniting with Guillory on 1988 LP *Grand Texas* on Arhoolie.

PARENTI, TONY *Jazz.* Clarinet. (Born Aug. 6, 1900, New Orleans, Orleans Parish; died Apr. 17, 1972, New York City.) A child prodigy, renowned New Orleans jazz clarinetist began playing professionally in his early teens and in the late 1910s and 1920s worked with **Papa Jack Laine**, **Johnny De Droit**, **Nick LaRocca**, and others. In the mid-1920s formed Liberty Syncopators and recorded for Columbia. Relocated to New York in the late 1920s and worked with Benny Goodman. After a six-year stint with Ted Lewis, led his own bands from the mid-1940s through 1960s and became popular draw at New York jazz clubs with recordings on Circle, Jazzology, and Riverside.

PARKER, BILL/"LEGENDARY BILL PARKER" (Willie Parker Guidry Jr.) *Rhythm and blues.* Drums, piano, vocals. Composer. Bandleader. (Born Sept. 27, 1927, Lake Charles, Calcasieu Parish; died Mar. 11, 2003, Lake Charles, Calcasieu Parish.)[4] Veteran Lake Charles bandleader and label owner performed and recorded with **Clarence Garlow** and Texas blues singer James Freeman in the early to mid-1950s before forming his Show Band which included guitarist **Chester Randle**. Also began working as session musician for **Eddie Schuler**'s Goldband and Folk-Star labels. In 1958 recorded several novelty rhythm and blues sides including single "Sweet Potato" on Hollywood before relocating to Oklahoma City and releasing two singles on his Showboat label in 1960. In the 1960s and early 1970s continued recording for Shuler's Goldband and Anla labels as leader and session player with singles featuring **Katie Webster** and **Little Miss Peggy**, including "Peggie's Blues" in 1962. Relocated to Oakland, California, and in the 1980s formed the Concrete Band and had releases on Jador and his Optune label, producing recordings by several artists, including Carol Shinnette and Theodis Ealey, as well as his own LP *The Things You Do* in 1990. Returned to Lake Charles in the early 1990s.

PARKER, BOBBY (Robert Lee Parker) *Blues.* Guitar, vocals. Composer. Bandleader. (Born Aug. 31, 1937, Lafayette, Lafayette Parish; died Oct. 31, 2013, Bowie, Maryland.) Influential blues guitarist and singer-songwriter best known for his influential 1961 hit "Watch Your Step." Raised in Los Angeles, began playing guitar at age 12 and by age 15 was performing on local shows with Johnny Otis, Little Esther Phillips, and others. Throughout the 1950s toured nationally with various rhythm and blues performers, including Otis Williams, Bo Diddley, Ruth Brown, Hank Ballard, and Paul "Hucklebuck" Williams. In 1958 recorded blues classic "Blues Get Off My Shoulder" for Vee-Jay. Relocated to Washington, D.C., area in the early 1960s and had hit with "Watch Your Step" on V-Tone, which greatly influenced British rockers such as John Lennon and Jimmy Page. Released a single each on Sabu, Southern Sound, Frisky, and Blue Horizon and toured England in the late 1960s. After working outside music for much of the 1980s, launched comeback in the early 1990s and recorded acclaimed releases *Bent Out of Shape* and *Shine Me Up* for Black Top and toured extensively. Continued performing into the early 2010s until suffering a fatal heart attack at age 76. Not to be confused with **Robert "Barefootin'" Parker**.

PARKER, DOLORES (Dolores Parker Morgan) *Jazz.* Vocals. (Born Oct. 25, 1919, New Orleans, Orleans Parish; died Dec. 17, 2018, Akron, Ohio.)[5] Highly accomplished jazz vocalist best known for her tenure with Duke Ellington. Relocated to Chicago with her mother as a teenager and toured with Fletcher Henderson from 1942 to 1945. Married Earl Hines's trumpet player Vernon Smith and joined Hines's band in 1945. In 1947 joined Duke Ellington's band as featured vocalist and recorded with group and toured extensively. Later appeared on television and film and recorded with Herbie Mann in 1960. Settled near Akron, Ohio, with second husband and continued to perform on the Cleveland jazz scene into the 2000s.

PARKER, ROBERT "BAREFOOTIN'" *Rhythm and blues.* Vocals, saxophone. Composer. (Born Oct. 14, 1930, New Orleans, Orleans Parish.) New Orleans rhythm and blues singer best known for his 1966 hit "Barefootin'." Started performing as saxophonist in the late 1940s with **Professor Longhair**'s Shuffling Hungarians and appeared on sessions for Mercury, Talent, and Atlantic in 1949. From the mid-1950s through early 1960s had singles as leader on Ace, Ron, Booker, and Imperial. In 1966 had national hit "Barefootin'" on Nola produced by **Wardell Quezergue** and toured extensively. Recorded several more local hits for Nola through following year and released a single on Silver Fox in 1969. Continued to perform locally through following decades and made occasional festival appearances in the 2010s. Not to be confused with blues singer-guitarist **Bobby Parker**.

PASLEY, FRANK *Jazz, rhythm and blues.* Guitar. (Born Nov. 10, 1904, New Orleans, Orleans Parish; died Dec. 17, 1968, Los Angeles.) Noted jazz guitarist relocated to Los Angeles in the late 1920s and later joined Les Hite's orchestra, appearing with group on steel guitar on T-Bone Walker's "T-Bone Blues" in 1940. In the 1940s and 1950s also recorded with **Bunk Johnson**, **Joe Darensbourg**, Dizzy Gillespie, and West Coast jump blues musicians Joe Liggins, Little Willie Jackson, and Peppy Prince.

PAUL, EMANUEL *Jazz.* Saxophone, violin, banjo. (Born Feb. 2, 1904, New Orleans, Orleans Parish; died May 23, 1988, New Orleans, Orleans Parish.) Regarded as a key figure in establishing the tenor saxophone in traditional New Orleans jazz. Started on violin at age 18 and from the 1920s through mid-1930s performed on banjo with various groups. Began playing saxophone in the mid-1930s and by 1940 was performing on tenor sax. Worked and recorded with Eureka Brass Band and **Kid Thomas** in following decades. Also recorded with **Papa Celestin**, **Emanuel Sayles**, and Olympia Brass Band in the 1950s and 1960s. Performed regularly at Preservation Hall and toured Europe twice in the late 1960s.

PAULIN, ERNEST "DOC" *Jazz.* Trumpet. Bandleader. (Born June 22, 1907, New Roads, Pointe Coupee Parish; died Nov. 20, 2007, Marrero, Jefferson Parish.)[6] Renowned New Orleans jazz trumpeter and bandleader whose music career spanned seven decades. Born in New Roads but raised in Wallace in a large family of musicians, moved to New Orleans in the late 1920s and began performing with local brass bands. Soon formed his own band, which he led through the late 1990s and which would later include six of his sons. Recorded with **Emile Barnes** in the early 1960s and as leader for Folkways in 1980. After his retirement his sons continued on as the Paulin Brothers Brass Band.

PAVAGEAU, ALCIDE "SLOW DRAG" *Jazz.* Bass. (Born May 2, 1889, New Orleans, Orleans Parish; died Jan. 19, 1969, New Orleans, Orleans Parish.)[7] Dubbed "Slow Drag" for his dancing ability in his youth, started playing double bass in the late 1920s and worked with **Buddy Petit**, **Herb Morand**, and **Emile Barnes** in subsequent years. Starting in the early 1940s worked extensively with **George Lewis** and appeared on sessions with Lewis, **Bunk Johnson**, and **Kid Shots Madison**. Continued working with Lewis through the 1950s and in the 1960s performed regularly at Preservation Hall and appeared on numerous sessions with **Kid Sheik Cola**, **Sweet Emma Barrett**, **Kid Thomas**, and others.

PAYNE, RICHARD *Jazz, classical.* Bass, tuba. (Born Sept. 15, 1931, New Orleans, Orleans Parish; died May 17, 2000, New Orleans, Orleans Parish.) Modern jazz bassist joined American Jazz Quintet with **Ellis Marsalis Jr.**, **Harold Battiste**, **Alvin Batiste**, and **Ed Blackwell** in the mid-1950s. In the late 1950s and early 1960s recorded with **Professor Longhair**, **Larry Williams**, **Wallace Davenport**, and **Jessie Hill**. Later became music teacher and performed occasionally with various symphony orchestras. Not to be confused with early New Orleans jazz guitarist Richard Payne (or Pain) of Superior Orchestra around 1910.

PAYTON, NICHOLAS *Jazz.* Trumpet, piano. Composer. Bandleader. (Born Sept. 26, 1973, New Orleans, Orleans Parish.) Son of noted jazz bassist **Walter Payton**, began playing trumpet at age four and started working professionally at age 10 with **Danny Barker**. In the 1990s toured with Marcus Roberts and Elvin Jones. Signed with Verve in 1993 and released six albums through 2001, including the 1997 critically acclaimed *Doc Cheatham & Nicholas Payton.* In the 2000s released recordings on Warner Bros. and Nonesuch and also played on sessions with **Allen Toussaint**, **Dr. John**, Ray Charles, Stanley Jordan, and others. In the 2010s continued to perform and record with numerous releases on his own label.

PAYTON, WALTER *Jazz, rhythm and blues.* Bass, sousaphone. (Born Aug. 23, 1942, New Orleans, Orleans Parish; died Oct. 28, 2010, New Orleans, Orleans Parish.) Popular New Orleans jazz bassist began learning the instrument in the late 1950s. After receiving a degree in music education in the mid-1960s, spent following 25 years as music teacher in New Orleans public schools. Also worked with various brass bands such as Olympia, Eureka, and Tremé and performed regularly at Preservation Hall. In the mid-1960s appeared on rhythm and blues sessions with **Chris Kenner**, **Lee Dorsey**, **Aaron Neville**, and **Robert Parker**. Toured internationally with Preservation Hall Jazz Band until suffering a stroke in early 2010. Father of **Nicholas Payton**.

PECORA, SANTO (Santo Pecoraro) *Jazz.* Trombone. Composer. Bandleader. (Born Mar. 31, 1902, New Orleans, Orleans Parish; died May 29, 1984, New Orleans, Orleans Parish.)[8] Known as "Mr. Tailgate," early New Orleans jazz trombonist began playing in his teens and in 1924 relocated to Chicago and worked and recorded with New Orleans Rhythm Kings for two years. Throughout the 1930s worked with several large swing bands as well as smaller jazz groups led by **Sharkey Bonano**, **Paul Mares**, and **Wingy Manone**. Also briefly worked as studio musician in Hollywood. Returned to New Orleans in the early 1940s and led his own band through the 1970s, making several recordings as leader.

PEJOE, MORRIS (Morris Pujoe) *Blues.* Guitar, fiddle, vocals. Bandleader. (Born Apr. 11, 1924, Palmetto, St. Landry Parish; died July 23, 1982, Ecorse, Michigan.)[9] Noted early postwar Chicago blues singer-guitarist best known for his 1950s recordings backed by **Henry Gray**. Began playing fiddle before moving to Beaumont in 1949 and switching to guitar, influenced by **Clarence "Gatemouth" Brown**. Relocated to Chicago in 1951 and began long association with Gray, releasing singles on Checker, Vee-Jay, Abco, and Atomic-H through 1960. In the 1960s worked regularly with blues singer Mary Lane and cut single with Lane on Friendly Five. Relocated to Detroit area in the early 1970s and continued performing sporadically until his death at age 58 from heart failure.

PELLERIN, MEL "LUV BUG" *Cajun, swamp pop.* Accordion, vocals. Composer. Bandleader. (Born July 22, 1954, Lafayette, Lafayette Parish; died Jan. 16, 2008, Lake Charles, Calcasieu Parish.) Cajun accordionist and singer-songwriter released several singles, notably "The Crawfish Song," and LPs *Louisiana's Best Kept Secret Now Public* and *Watermelon Rock* on Goldband in the early 1980s. Also recorded single "Cajun Way" with Danny Cooley and Cajun Express on Jador.

PENN, SAMMY (Samuel Hughes Penn) *Jazz.* Drums, vocals. Bandleader. (Born Sept. 15, 1902, Morgan City, St. Mary Parish; died Oct. 30, 1969, La Grange, Georgia.)[10] Highly regarded early New Orleans jazz drummer and vocalist best known for his long association with **Kid Thomas**. Began playing drums during his early teens with local groups before moving to New Orleans in the early 1920s. Through the 1940s performed with numerous artists, including **Buddy Petit**, **Chris Kelly**, **Mutt Carey**, **Punch Miller**, **Kid Rena**, and his own band Penn and His Five Pennies. Worked with Kid Thomas's band from the 1940s through 1960s and appeared on most of his recordings. In the 1960s performed regularly at Preservation Hall. Suffered fatal stroke while on tour with Preservation Hall Jazz Band.

PENOUILH, WOODY *Jazz.* Tuba. Bandleader. (Born Dec. 3, 1943, New Orleans, Orleans Parish.) Inspired by **Tuba Fats**, began playing tuba and was founding member of Storyville Stompers Brass Band in the early 1980s. Toured internationally and continued leading band in the 2010s.

PEREZ, MANUEL (Emile Emanuel Perez) *Jazz, ragtime.* Cornet. Bandleader. (Born Dec. 19, 1878, New Orleans, Orleans Parish; died Dec. 5, 1947, New Orleans, Orleans Parish.)[11] A giant of early New Orleans jazz whose popular and highly influential bands played a major role in transforming the genre from its ragtime roots in the early 1900s. His cornet playing greatly influenced **King Oliver**, **Freddie Keppard**, and **Louis Armstrong**. Classically trained on cornet from age 12, the French Creole musician soon began performing in dance and brass bands and by the late 1890s was playing ragtime. Joined Onward Brass Band in 1900 and took over as leader from 1903 through 1930. Also led his Imperial Orchestra from 1901 to 1913. His bands included such influential early jazz musicians as Oliver, **Sidney Bechet**, **Louis** and **Lorenzo Tio**, **Peter Bocage**, **George Baquet**, **Black Benny**, and many others. In the late 1910s briefly relocated to

Chicago but returned to New Orleans and continued performing throughout the 1920s. Retired from music in the 1930s due to ill health. He was a highly respected music teacher, and his students included **Manuel Manetta**, **Kid Rena**, **Sidney Desvigne**, **Willie Pajeaud**, **Alvin Alcorn**, and **Natty Dominique**.

PERKINS, GEORGE *Rhythm and blues, gospel.* Vocals. Composer. (Born Sept. 25, 1942, Denham Springs, Livingston Parish; died Apr. 17, 2013, Hammond, Tangipahoa Parish.) Deep soul and gospel singer best known for his 1970 hit "Cryin' in the Streets." Began singing in gospel group the Silver Stars during his mid-teens and recorded two singles on Golden with quartet in 1968. In 1970 had major hit "Cryin' in the Streets" recorded for Golden and leased to Silver Fox, written as a response to the assassination of Dr. Martin Luther King Jr. Toured nationally and throughout the 1970s had singles on numerous labels, including Ace, Second Line, Soul Power, Red Stick, Royal Shield, and his own GP Records. Performed mainly gospel after 1980.

PERKINS, ROY "BOOGIE BOY" (Ernest Roy Suarez) *Swamp pop.* Piano, bass, vocals. Composer. Bandleader. (Born Apr. 26, 1935, Lafayette, Lafayette Parish.) Lafayette piano player and singer-songwriter who became one of the first white artists to perform and record rhythm and blues in the 1950s which was later dubbed swamp pop. Began playing piano in the 1940s, inspired early on by boogie-woogie blues of Cecil Gant and later **Fats Domino**. By 1953 was playing in swing band the Modernaires and incorporating New Orleans rhythm and blues into sets. Recorded regional hit "You're on My Mind" on Meladee in 1955 which is considered among the first swamp pop recordings. After a short stint in the military in 1956, joined **Bobby Page**'s Riff Raffs as bassist and recorded singles as leader on RAM, Mercury, Dart, and Eric through the early 1960s. Also worked as session musician for producer **J. D. Miller** with **Warren Storm** and others. Continued performing in the 1960s with **Jerry Starr**, **Bert Miller**'s Swing Kings, and **Johnnie Allan** before retiring from music in the early 1970s. In the 2000s and 2010s made special appearances at Ponderosa Stomp showcases in New Orleans.

PERRILLIAT, NAT *Rhythm and blues.* Saxophone. (Born Nov. 29, 1936, New Orleans, Orleans Parish; died Jan. 26, 1971, Sacramento, California.) Noted saxophonist began his professional career while in his teens performing with **Professor Longhair** in the early 1950s and appeared on recordings by **Fats Domino**, **Shirley & Lee**, **Smiley Lewis**, **Roy Brown**, **Champion Jack Dupree**, **Snooks Eaglin**, **Jessie Hill**, **Earl King**, **Eddie Bo**, **Ellis Marsalis Jr.**, and others throughout the 1950s and 1960s. Also toured with Domino, **Roy Montrell**, Joe Tex, and Junior Parker. Died of a brain hemorrhage at age 34.

PETIT, BUDDY (Joseph Crawford) *Jazz.* Cornet. Bandleader. (Born Dec. 23, 1896, White Castle, Iberville Parish; died July 4, 1931, New Orleans, Orleans Parish.)[12] Influential early New Orleans cornetist regarded by many of his peers to be one of the finest players of his era. Moved to New Orleans as a child and took surname of his stepfather, Joseph Petit, who was a jazz trombonist. In 1914 cofounded Young Olympians with **Jimmie Noone**, a group which also included **Sidney Bechet**. Performed briefly in California with **Jelly Roll Morton** in 1918. Returned to New Orleans and through the late 1920s led his own band, which remained extremely popular and whose members included **Edmond Hall** and **George Lewis**. In 1922 performed with **Frankie Duson**'s band in California. Worked on riverboats in the late 1920s and early 1930s but died suddenly from a ruptured blood vessel in the brain. No commercial recordings are known to exist.

PHILLIPS, PHIL (Philip Baptiste) *Swamp pop.* Vocals, guitar. Composer. Bandleader. (Born Mar. 14, 1926, Crowley, Acadia Parish.)[13] Early swamp pop singer and songwriter best known for his 1959 hit "Sea of Love." Began singing in church as a child and in high school joined brothers in gospel group Gateway Quartet, performing around Lake Charles area and cutting several singles for Dot in 1953. After composing "Sea of Love" for a love interest, recorded song for **George Khoury**'s label, backed by members of **Cookie** and the Cupcakes, and reached number one on the R&B charts and number two on the pop charts in 1959 when leased to Mercury. Recorded several more singles through early 1960s for Mercury which failed to chart. In the late 1960s recorded session at Muscle Shoals before cutting two singles on Lanor, including "The Evil Dope." Also worked as radio disc jockey for many years, using moniker "King of the Whole World." Performed rarely in following decades but made notable appearances at the Ponderosa Stomp and New Orleans Jazz & Heritage Festival in the mid-2000s.

PICHON, WALTER "FATS" *Jazz.* Piano, vocals. Composer. Bandleader. (Born Apr. 3, 1906, New Orleans, Orleans Parish; died Feb. 26, 1967, Chicago.)[14] Early New Orleans jazz pianist began playing piano as a child and, after studying music in Boston, returned to New Orleans and worked with **Amos Riley** and **Sidney Desvigne** in the 1920s and toured Mexico, Texas, and New York. In 1929 recorded as a leader and also with **Red Allen**, **King Oliver**, and Hawaiian guitarist Benny Nawahi. Throughout the 1930s and early 1940s led his own band and also worked with Desvigne, **Armand Piron**, and classic blues singer Mamie Smith. Performed as soloist in French Quarter in the 1940s and 1950s and continued to tour through the early 1960s until failing eyesight forced retirement.

PICOU, ALPHONSE *Jazz.* Clarinet, guitar, vocals. Composer. Bandleader. (Born Oct. 19, 1878, New Orleans, Orleans Parish; died Feb. 4, 1961, New Orleans, Orleans Parish.) Highly influential early New Orleans jazz clarinetist whose landmark performance in the standard "High Society" became an important solo in early jazz. By age 16 was performing with dance bands and orchestras and worked with Excelsior and Onward brass bands in the late 1890s. From 1900 through the early 1910s worked regularly with **Freddie Keppard**'s Olympia and Magnolia orchestras with **King Oliver** and **Pops Foster**, and in the bands of **Manuel Perez** and **Papa Celestin**. In the mid-1910s led his own band and worked in Chicago, and in the late 1910s worked with Perez, **Armand Piron**, and **Buddy Petit** before briefly returning to Chicago to record with **King Oliver** in 1923. Throughout the 1920s performed regularly with **John Robichaux**, **Wooden Joe Nicholas**, and **Lee Collins** as well as Excelsior and Tuxedo orchestras. Worked mainly outside music in the 1930s but returned to record with **Kid Rena** in 1940 and performed with Celestin and Eureka brass bands through the 1950s. In remaining years performed regularly on Bourbon Street as well as at his bar and restaurant on Claiborne Avenue.

PIERCE, DE DE (Joseph Lacroix Pierce) *Jazz.* Cornet, vocals. Composer. Bandleader. (Born Feb. 18, 1904, New Orleans, Orleans Parish; died Nov. 23, 1973, New Orleans, Orleans Parish.) Noted New Orleans jazz cornetist best known for his collaborations with wife **Billie Pierce**. Largely self-taught, began playing in the mid-1920s and worked with **Arnold DePass** early on as well as in riverfront saloons. While working with **George Lewis** in the mid-1930s, met jazz and blues pianist Billie Goodson, and they married in 1935. Pair worked together through the early 1950s with stints with classic blues singer Ida Cox and **Alphonse Picou** and held 24-year engagement at Luthjen's dance hall until club was destroyed by fire in 1960. Took hiatus due to health problems in the mid-1950s but later resumed career with Billie in the 1960s with regular performances at Preservation Hall, numerous recordings including 1961 LP *Vocal Blues and Cornet in the Classic Tradition* on Riverside, television appearances, and several European tours through the early 1970s.

PIERSON, EDDIE *Jazz.* Trombone. Bandleader. (Born Aug. 1, 1904, Algiers, Orleans Parish; died Dec. 17, 1958, New Orleans, Orleans Parish.) Early New Orleans jazz trombonist best known for his short tenure as leader of the Original Tuxedo Jazz Band after the death of the band's founder **Papa Celestin**. Began studying trombone with **Bill Matthews** while in his 20s and in the 1930s performed on riverboats with **Sidney Desvigne**. Later worked with Young Tuxedo Brass Band, **Emanuel Sayles**, **Armand Piron**, and others. Joined Tuxedo band in 1951 and assumed leadership after Celestin's death in 1954. Remained with band until his death during a performance in front of Generation Hall at age 54.

PIRON, ARMAND JOHN "A.J." *Jazz.* Violin. Composer. Bandleader. (Born Aug. 16, 1888, New Orleans, Orleans Parish; died Feb. 17, 1943, New Orleans, Orleans Parish.) Renowned early New Orleans jazz violinist and composer who remained one of the Crescent City's most popular bandleaders in the late 1910s and 1920s. Began playing violin at age 12 and within several years was performing with Bloom Philharmonic Orchestra. He later worked with Peerless Orchestra and in the early 1910s succeeded **Freddie Keppard** as leader of Olympia band. Established publishing company with **Clarence Williams** in 1915 and published numerous compositions, many of which became jazz standards. In 1918 formed Piron's New Orleans Orchestra, which included **Peter Bocage**, **Lorenzo Tio Jr.**, **Louis Cottrell Sr.**, and **Steve Lewis**. In the mid-1920s made several successful tours to New York with group and recorded for Victor, Columbia, and OKeh. In the late 1920s formed Moonlight Serenaders and continued performing mainly on riverboats until his death.

PITRE, AUSTIN *Cajun.* Accordion, fiddle, vocals. Composer. Bandleader. (Born Feb. 23, 1918, near Ville Platte, Evangeline Parish; died Apr. 8, 1981, Elton, Jeff. Davis Parish.) Highly influential and popular early postwar Cajun accordionist and singer-songwriter known for his flamboyant showmanship and recordings such as "Evangeline Playboys Special" and "Les Flammes d'Enfer." Began playing accordion at age six and by age 11 was performing at house dances with his father, who played fiddle. During his early teens started playing fiddle and in the 1940s formed the Evangeline Playboys and developed a strong following, reportedly being the first Cajun musician to perform standing up and also play accordion behind his back and over his head. From the late 1940s through mid-1950s had releases on 4-Star, Feature, and French Hits, including "High Point Two Step." In the late 1950s recorded a single for Big Mamou and Prestige LP *Cajun Folk Music,* performing on fiddle with **Milton Molitor**. From 1959 to 1971 had numerous singles on Swallow and in the 1970s recorded LPs for Arhoolie and Sonet. Continued performing locally as well as making several national tours until his death at age 63.

PITRE, WILD BILL *Blues, zydeco.* Guitar, fiddle, vocals. Composer. Bandleader. (Born Feb. 1, 1931, Basile, Evangeline Parish; died June 26, 2003, Beaumont, Texas.) Texas-based blues singer-songwriter and guitarist began playing fiddle as a child and by his mid-teens was performing in local clubs. In the late 1960s recorded session for producer **Eddie Shuler** in Lake Charles with **Marcel Dugas**'s band which resulted in single "Won't Be Your Hound Dog Anymore" on Anla in 1969 and LP *Baby Yum Yum* issued on Flyright in 1970 as by Wild Bill's Blue Washboard Boys. Continued performing in Port Arthur–Beaumont area in following decades. In the late 1990s began working with local harmonica player Paul Orta and in the early 2000s performed in Europe and recorded CD *I Was Raised on a Farm.* "Wild" was his legal first name, and it appears on his gravestone.

PO' HENRY *See* Dorsey, Po' Henry.

POINDEXTER, NORWOOD "PONY" *Jazz.* Saxophone, vocals. Composer. Bandleader. (Born Feb. 8, 1926, New Orleans, Orleans Parish; died Apr. 14, 1988, Oakland, California.) Noted bebop jazz saxophonist performed with **Sidney Desvigne** in his teens before relocating to Oakland. In the late 1940s and 1950s worked with Billy Eckstine, Lionel Hampton, T-Bone Walker, Billie Holiday, and others and led bands of his own. Also appeared on recordings with Wes Montgomery, Eric Dolphy, and mentor Charlie Parker. In the 1960s had six releases as leader, including debut LP, *Pony Express,* on Epic. From 1963 through the late 1970s lived and performed in Europe. Returned to Oakland in 1979 and continued to perform as vocalist after illness prevented him from playing saxophone.

POIRRIER, ULYSSE "TONKIN'" *Cajun.* Steel guitar, vocals. Composer. (Born Apr. 27, 1939, near Coteau, Iberia Parish; died Sept. 5, 2012, New Iberia, Iberia Parish.) Veteran Cajun steel guitarist began performing in the 1960s and throughout his five-decade career performed with many noted Cajun musicians, including **Elias "Shute" Badeaux**, **Aldus Mouton**, **Leeman Prejean**, and **Danny Brasseaux**. In 1984 recorded single "Musician with a Broken Heart" on Belle.

POLITE, WALTER "CREOLE" *Creole, zydeco.* Accordion, vocals. (Born Dec. 25, 1910, St. Martinville, St. Martin Parish; died May 9, 1997, New Iberia, Iberia Parish.) Early Creole accordionist and bandleader started playing at age 11 and within a few weeks was playing local la la house dances. Performed with his band the Red Hot Swinging Dukes for several decades throughout Louisiana and east Texas, making the transition from traditional Creole music to zydeco in the 1950s under the influence of **Clifton Chenier**. Continued performing in St. Martinville area until the late 1980s. Mentor of **John Wilson**.

POLKA DOT SLIM *See* Monroe, Vince [Notable Musicians Born outside Louisiana].

POPULIST, WALTER *Rhythm and blues.* Vocals. Composer. Bandleader. (Born Mar. 9, 1932, Wallace, St. John the Baptist Parish; died Mar. 13, 2015, Slidell, St. Tammany Parish.) New Orleans rhythm and blues vocalist who released "Oh Look at That Girl"/"Come on Back to Me" with his band the Truetones on Flame in 1961.

POREE, ERNEST *Jazz.* Saxophone, vocals. Bandleader. (Born Nov. 9, 1908, New Orleans, Orleans Parish; died May 26, 1993, New Orleans, Orleans Parish.) New Orleans jazz saxophonist worked with various brass bands in the 1940s and 1950s including with **Kid Howard**'s Brass Band and **Papa Celestin**'s Tuxedo Brass Band. In the 1970s toured Europe and released only recording as leader, *New Orleans Saxophone,* on Rampart.

PORTER, GEORGE, JR. *Rhythm and blues.* Bass, vocals. Composer. Bandleader. (Born Dec. 26, 1947, New Orleans, Orleans Parish.) Premier New Orleans funk bassist and original member of the Meters. Began performing on guitar in his teens and backed **Earl King**, **Walter "Wolfman" Washington**, and **Ernie K-Doe**. Soon switched to bass and in the late 1960s joined **Art Neville** and the Neville Sounds, which included childhood friend **Zigaboo Modeliste**. By 1969 the group evolved into highly influential funk group the Meters, who toured and recorded through 1977 and had several national hits. Throughout following years continued as an in-demand session musician with top rock, blues, and jazz artists and performed in various bands, including Joyride, Runnin' Pardners, the Funky Meters, and the George Porter Jr. Trio, into the 2010s.

PORTER, SMOKEHOUSE, AND MISS MAMIE *Blues.* Guitar, vocals. Composers. Bandleaders. (Born Baton Rouge, EBR Parish.) Longtime husband-and-wife team began performing together on the Baton Rouge blues scene in the early 1990s. McKinley "Smokehouse" Porter (1950–) started playing guitar at age 12, inspired by guitarist preacher James Cannon and was later mentored by **William W. Woolfolk**. Vocalist Miss Mamie (1952–) sang gospel in the church as a child and from 1972 to 1983 lived in Chicago and performed with local blues and jazz groups. Pair released recording debut *King & Queen of the Gutbucket Blues* in 2003 and continued performing around Baton Rouge in the late 2010s.

POTIER, HAROLD, JR. *Blues.* Drums. (Born Nov. 29, 1941, New Iberia, Iberia Parish; died Mar. 17, 1985, New Iberia, Iberia Parish.)[15] Renowned blues drummer known for his long association with Bobby Bland, whose band he joined in 1966. Toured with Bland throughout following 16 years and appeared on several noted recordings, including *Together for the First Time* with B.B. King on ABC-Dunhill in 1974. Succumbed to injuries after being fatally shot in the chest at age 39 by his wife during an argument in their home. Older brother of **John Potier**, son of **Mercedes** and **Harold Potier Sr.**, and grandson of **Gus Fontenette** and **Hypolite Potier**.

POTIER, HAROLD, SR. *Jazz.* Trumpet, saxophone. (Born Oct. 22, 1911, Parks, St. Martin Parish; died Dec. 5, 1998, Parks, St. Martin Parish.) Highly regarded Acadiana jazz musician began studying trumpet and saxophone at age 12, influenced by his father, **Hypolite Potier**, and later **Bunk Johnson**. Joined **Gus Fontenette**'s famed Banner Orchestra at age 16 as saxophonist, then trumpeter, and in the following years worked alongside Johnson, **Lawrence Duhé**, **Evan Thomas**, and wife **Mercedes Potier**. Also performed in other area jazz bands, including Thomas's Black Eagles and Crowley-based Yelpin' Hounds. After Banner disbanded in the early 1950s continued freelancing with various bands and later worked as a noted wood sculptor. Father of **John** and **Harold Potier Jr.**

POTIER, HYPOLITE "IRON MAN" *Jazz.* Cornet. (Born Oct. 20, 1882, Parks, St. Martin Parish; died Aug. 1982, Parks, St. Martin Parish.)[16] Early Acadiana jazz cornetist began performing in **Hypolite Charles** Marching Band around 1906 and was an original member of **Gus Fontenette**'s Banner Orchestra starting in 1908. Also performed in **Bunk Johnson**'s New Iberia band and United Brass Band in Parks. Father of **Harold Potier Sr.** and grandfather of **John** and **Harold Potier Jr.**

POTIER, JOHN *Blues, jazz.* Piano, organ, trumpet, vocals. Bandleader. (Born Sept. 27, 1946, New Iberia, Iberia Parish; died Jan. 20, 2017, Parks, St. Martin Parish.) Noted blues and jazz keyboardist began playing professionally at age 10 and worked with Bobby Bland, Joe Tex, the Drifters, and Ike and Tina Turner as well as numerous regional bands such as **Jay Nelson**'s Jumpers throughout his long career, often with brother **Harold Potier Jr.** Son of noted jazz musicians **Mercedes** and **Harold Potier Sr.**, and grandson of **Gus Fontenette** and **Hypolite Potier**.

POTIER, MERCEDES (*born* **Fontenette**) *Jazz.* Piano, organ. (Born Sept. 3, 1914, New Iberia, Iberia Parish; died June 27, 1982, New Iberia, Iberia Parish.) Accomplished Acadiana jazz pianist began playing piano as a child, mentored by her father **Gus Fontenette**. After graduating in music from Xavier University in New Orleans, performed with Fontenette's Banner Orchestra from the mid-1930s through 1951, often with **Bunk Johnson**, **Lawrence Duhé**, and husband **Harold Potier Sr.** Also worked with **Evan Thomas**'s Black Eagles Band and Johnson's New Iberia band. In later years performed gospel in church. Mother of **John** and **Harold Potier Jr.**

POULLARD, DANNY *Creole.* Accordion, vocals. Bandleader. (Born Jan. 10, 1937, near Eunice, St. Landry Parish; died Apr. 27, 2001, Fairfield, California.) Influential California-based Creole accordionist was raised in a musical family in south Louisiana and east Texas, but did not take up accordion until moving to the California Bay Area in the early 1960s. Mentored by **John Semien**, began performing in Semien's band the Opelousas Playboys in the 1960s and in the 1970s performed and recorded with Louisiana Playboys. In the early 1980s formed California Cajun Orchestra and performed with group until his death, producing two albums on Arhoolie, including *Not Lonesome Anymore* in 1991. Mentored countless Bay Area musicians throughout several decades, including **Mark St. Mary**. Shortly before his death recorded CD *Poullard, Poullard & Garnier* with brother **Edward Poullard** and **D'Jalma Garnier**.

POULLARD, EDWARD *Creole.* Fiddle, accordion, guitar, drums, vocals. (Born Mar. 14, 1952, near Eunice,

St. Landry Parish.) Highly renowned Creole multi-instrumentalist was raised in a large musical family in Beaumont from nine months old. Began playing multiple instruments as a child, learning from his father, John Poullard (1910–1994), who was an exceptional accordion player. Performed at local house dances and church halls with family band for many years. After injury to hand began concentrating on fiddle and in the 1990s was mentored by **Canray Fontenot**. Performed and recorded with Fontenot, **Bois Sec** and **Black Ardoin**, **Preston Frank**, **Jesse Legé**, **Cedric Watson**, brother **Danny Poullard**, and others, and in the mid-2010s as member of band Creole United with **Sean Ardoin**.

POWELL, BENNY *Jazz.* Trombone. Composer. Bandleader. (Born Mar. 1, 1930, New Orleans, Orleans Parish; died June 26, 2010, Manhattan, New York.) Noted jazz trombonist and educator best known for his long association with Count Basie. Began playing trombone at age 12 and at age 15 was a founding member of **Dooky Chase**'s jazz band. From 1948 to 1951 worked with Lionel Hampton. Joined Count Basie Orchestra in 1951 and toured and recorded with group through 1963. While living in New York worked on Broadway and in television and spent time in Los Angeles as session musician. In the 1980s returned to New York and led his own band with regular tours to Europe. Also taught music at New School University in New York City.

POWELL, BOBBY *Rhythm and blues, gospel.* Vocals, piano. Composer. Bandleader. (Born July 25, 1943, Winnfield, Winn Parish.) Highly regarded Baton Rouge–based deep soul and gospel singer-songwriter and pianist began singing in church as a child. Blind since birth, relocated to Baton Rouge in the 1950s to attend state school for the blind at Southern University and performed with various gospel groups. From 1965 to 1971 released numerous singles on Whit and Jewel and had hits with "C.C. Rider," "Do Something for Yourself," and "The Bells." In the early 1970s recorded multiple singles and LP *Thank You* for Excello before recording for Hep' Me in the late 1970s and early 1980s. Continued performing mainly gospel in Baton Rouge area occasionally in the 2010s.

POWELL, SHANNON *Jazz.* Drums, vocals. Composer. (Born Apr. 8, 1962, New Orleans, Orleans Parish.) Dubbed "The King of Tremé," New Orleans jazz percussionist was playing drums in church by age six and during his early teens joined **Danny Barker**'s Fairview Baptist Church Band. Worked with numerous jazz and rhythm and blues musicians such as **Wynton Marsalis**, **Dr. John**, Diana Krall, and **Earl King** and recorded with **Harry Connick Jr.**, **Deacon John**, **Johnny Adams**, **Kermit Ruffins**, and **Snooks Eaglin**, among others. In 2005 released debut recording as leader, *Powell's Place.* In the 2010s continued performing with Preservation Hall Jazz Band and leading his own group.

PREJEAN, LEEMAN *Cajun.* Guitar, vocals. Composer. Bandleader. (Born Dec. 6, 1936, Carencro, Lafayette Parish; died Mar. 25, 2011, Lafayette, Lafayette Parish.) Noted Cajun singer and guitarist began performing at age 15 as an original member of the Scott Playboys with **Walter Mouton** and **Johnnie Allan** in 1951. Later formed the Happy Playboys of Scott and led group for 39 years, recording three singles for Swallow in the 1970s, including "Accordion Two Step" and "Happy Playboys Special."

PREJEAN, WARREN (John Warren Prejean Sr.) *Zydeco.* Accordion, vocals. Composer. (Born Aug. 28, 1948, Maurice, Vermilion Parish; died Aug. 3, 2013, Lafayette, Lafayette Parish.) Blues-influenced zydeco accordionist and singer-songwriter began playing accordion at age 8, inspired by **Clifton Chenier** and later mentored by **Fernest Arceneaux**. At age 17 began performing in clubs and later worked with **Little Bob**, **Warren Ceasar**, and others. From the mid-1990s through early 2010s toured and recorded as member of Creole Zydeco Farmers, appearing on four releases with group, including *On the Road* for Maison de Soul in 1999.

PRESTON, VAN (Preston John Vanicor) *Swamp pop, rhythm and blues.* Vocals, harmonica, guitar. Composer. Bandleader. (Born Sept. 30, 1939, Lacassine, Jeff. Davis Parish; died Sept. 24, 2007, Welsh, Jeff. Davis Parish.) Youngest brother of prominent Cajun family of musicians which included **Milton**, **Ellis**, and **Ivy Vanicor**. Swamp pop and blue-eyed soul singer-songwriter was inspired by rhythm and blues and early rock and roll while in his teens and formed his band the Nite Rockers in the late 1950s. In the mid-1960s recorded several singles for Goldband, including minor regional hit "Baby You Got Soul" in 1966. In the late 1960s released Goldband LP *Who Done It? Who Drained the Pool?* and continued performing throughout southwest Louisiana and east Texas into the 2000s. Uncle of **Orsy Vanicor**.

PREVOST, LIONEL/"LIONEL TORRENCE" *Rhythm and blues, swamp pop.* Saxophone. Composer. Bandleader. (Born Dec. 4, 1935, near Franklin, St. Mary Parish; died

Apr. 25, 2002, Port Arthur, Texas.) Highly regarded and influential saxophonist who appeared on hundreds of rhythm and blues and swamp pop recordings in the 1950s and 1960s. Raised in Port Arthur from age 12, began learning saxophone in his early teens, inspired by Louis Jordan and **Illinois Jacquet**. By age 16 was performing with bands throughout east Texas and Louisiana, and from the mid-1950s through early 1960s performed and recorded with **Clifton Chenier**. In 1958 began working as session musician for producer **J. D. Miller**, and through the mid-1960s appeared on hundreds of swamp blues and swamp pop recordings by **Lazy Lester**, **Lonesome Sundown**, **Leroy Washington**, **Warren Storm**, and others. Also released several singles as leader as "Lionel Torrence" for Miller and recorded on sessions for Goldband, appearing on recordings by **Clarence Garlow**, **Charles Sheffield**, and others. As sideman performed with Ray Charles, **Fats Domino**, T-Bone Walker, Etta James, Bobby Bland, and others throughout Southwest. Took hiatus from music from the mid-1960s through mid-1970s and in the 1980s and 1990s performed around Port Arthur area with various groups. Released CD *Gospel Sax* shortly before his death at age 66.

PRICE, BANNY (Clemon Lee Price) *Blues, gospel.* Guitar, vocals. Composer. (Born Apr. 29, 1935, Mansfield, DeSoto Parish; died Dec. 13, 2003, Dallas.)[17] Noted Shreveport-based blues guitarist recorded with **Elgie Brown** for **Mira Smith**'s RAM Records in the early 1960s. In the mid-1960s cut two singles for Jewel backed by Brown, notably the Otis Rush–inspired "You Love Me Pretty Baby." By the 1980s had moved to Dallas and continued performing gospel as lead guitarist in the Full Gospel Holy Temple Church.

PRICE, BOBBY *Zydeco, rhythm and blues.* Vocals. Composer. Bandleader. (Born May 6, 1936, St. Martinville, St. Martin Parish; died Oct. 10, 2005, St. Martinville, St. Martin Parish.) Locally renowned singer and bandleader performed throughout Lafayette area in the 1970s and 1980s. In the late 1970s released two singles on Blues Unlimited and in 1984 recorded LP *Two Trains a' Runnin'* on Blues Unlimited backed by **Fernest Arceneaux**'s band the Thunders, with whom he often performed.

PRICE, LITTLE LEO *Rhythm and blues.* Vocals, drums. Composer. Bandleader. (Born Jan. 9, 1935, Kenner, Jefferson Parish; died Feb. 10, 2016, Florence, South Carolina.) New Orleans rhythm and blues singer-songwriter began playing drums at age eight and toured nationally with older brother **Lloyd Price** in the early 1950s. Cowrote rhythm and blues standard "Send Me Some Lovin'" which was later covered by Little Richard, Otis Redding, Sam Cooke, Brenda Lee, Buddy Holly, and others. In the late 1950s had releases on Meladee as Little Leo, including "What's It All About" and "Handwriting on the Wall." Also recorded for Hull and GMC. Relocated to Florence in the late 1980s.

PRICE, LLOYD *Rhythm and blues.* Vocals, piano, trumpet. Composer. Bandleader. (Born Mar. 9, 1933, Kenner, Jefferson Parish.) Internationally renowned early New Orleans rhythm and blues singer best known for his 1950s hits such as "Lawdy Miss Clawdy" and "Stagger Lee." Formed first band with younger brother **Leo Price** while still in his teens. In 1952 was discovered by **Dave Bartholomew** and had major hit with debut single on Specialty, "Lawdy Miss Clawdy," which featured **Fats Domino** on piano. After several more hits, including "Ain't It a Shame" in 1953, he was drafted and sent to Korea in 1954. After discharge, recorded for ABC-Paramount from 1957 to 1960 and had a dozen songs reach the charts, including major hits "Stagger Lee," "I'm Gonna Get Married," and "Personality," the latter of which earned him the sobriquet "Mr. Personality." In the 1960s recorded for his own labels, Double L and Turntable, and operated a popular New York City nightclub. During the 1970s and 1980s worked largely outside music before returning to the festival and oldies circuit in the early 1990s. In 2017 released *This Is Rock and Roll* on Double L and continued performing into his 80s.

PRIMA, LEON *Jazz.* Trumpet, piano. Bandleader. (Born July 28, 1907, New Orleans, Orleans Parish; died Aug. 15, 1985, Bay Saint Louis, Mississippi.) Older brother of **Louis Prima**, began playing piano before switching to trumpet. In the 1920s worked with **Leon Roppolo**, **Ray Bauduc**, and Jack Teagarden and coled the Melody Masters with **Sharkey Bonano**. Worked in New York with brother Louis's orchestra from 1940 to 1946 and recorded as leader in 1954. Operated several New Orleans nightclubs from the 1930s through 1950s.

PRIMA, LOUIS *Jazz, rhythm and blues.* Trumpet, vocals. Composer. Bandleader. (Born Dec. 7, 1910, New Orleans, Orleans Parish; died Aug. 24, 1978, New Orleans, Orleans Parish.) Extremely popular and influential swing and jump blues trumpeter, bandleader, singer-songwriter and energetic showman best known for his 1950s hits such as "Just a Gigolo/I Ain't Got Nobody," "Jump Jive an' Wail," and "That Old Black Magic." Began playing trumpet in his teens, inspired by older brother **Leon Prima** and influenced by **Louis Armstrong** and **King Oliver**. Performed with his band the New Orleans Gang through the mid-1930s and recorded numerous sides for Brunswick, notably "Sing, Sing, Sing." Held high-profile engagements in New York, Chicago, and Los Angeles into the late 1930s with sessions for Vocalion and Decca. Throughout the early to mid-1940s led a large swing band and recorded for RCA Victor, perfecting his distinctive vocal style which combined jive talking and scat singing, and often incorporating Italian American themes. In 1948 hired vocalist Keely Smith and later downsized band for nightclubs. In the early 1950s married Smith and had several hits on Columbia, including "Oooh-Dahdily-Dah." In 1954 relocated to Las Vegas and hired **Sam Butera** as saxophonist and arranger and became a huge draw. Following year signed with Capitol and had major commercial success with numerous hits, notably from landmark 1956 LP *The Wildest!* and appeared on television and film. Split with Smith in the early 1960s and made several recordings for Dot, soon adding vocalist Gia Malone. In 1967 voiced character King Louie in the Disney film *The Jungle Book.* Continued to perform in Las Vegas and tour nationally through the early 1970s. Returned to performing regularly in New Orleans for several years with Butera before lapsing into a coma in 1975 following brain surgery to remove a tumor and never recovered. Father of musician Louis Prima Jr.

PRINCE CHARLES (Charles Ray Fontenot) *Swamp pop.* Bandleader. (Born Dec. 8, 1941, Ville Platte, Evangeline Parish; died Dec. 15, 2006, Ville Platte, Evangeline Parish.) Early swamp pop bandleader and booking agent of the Rockin' Kings with **Charles Veillon** on vocals, best known for their 1960 single "I Broke Your Heart"/ "Cheryl Ann" on Jin. Not to be confused with **Charles Sheffield**, who recorded a single as "Prince Charles" for Jet Stream.

PRINCE LA LA (Lawrence Nelson) *Rhythm and blues.* Guitar, vocals. Composer. (Born Aug. 30, 1936, New Orleans, Orleans Parish; died Oct. 27, 1963, New Orleans, Orleans Parish.)[18] New Orleans rhythm and blues singer best known for his 1962 hit "She Put the Hurt on Me" on A.F.O. Released only one other single before his death at age 27 from a suspected drug overdose under unclear circumstances. Case was officially classified as "natural death" but remained under investigation. His mystical stage persona and fashion style had a large influence on **Dr. John**. Son of **Walter Nelson Sr.** and brother of **Walter "Papoose" Nelson**.

PROFESSOR LONGHAIR (Henry Roeland "Roy" Byrd)[19] *Rhythm and blues.* Piano, vocals. Composer. Bandleader. (Born Dec. 19, 1918, Bogalusa, Washington Parish; died Jan. 30, 1980, New Orleans, Orleans Parish.) Iconic and extremely influential piano player and singer-songwriter whose Latin-infused idiosyncratic style profoundly shaped the sound of New Orleans rhythm and blues and funk. Moved to New Orleans with his mother at age two and as a child learned to play on discarded upright pianos in alleyways, influenced by local barrelhouse blues players such as **Tuts Washington** and **Kid Stormy Weather**. In the late 1940s formed band the Shuffling Hungarians and became popular draw at local Caldonia Club. Between 1949 and 1953 recorded for several labels, including Mercury and Atlantic, and produced such New Orleans classics as "Mardi Gras in New Orleans," "Bald Head," and "Tipitina." His distinctive "rhumba-boogie" piano style and second-line rhythms directly influenced **Fats Domino**, **Huey "Piano" Smith**, **Allen Toussaint**, **James Booker**, **Dr. John**, and many others. In the late 1950s and early 1960s had singles on Ebb, Ron, and Rip and in 1964 collaborated with **Earl King** on Watch, which produced local hit single "Big Chief." After a period of inactivity, had major career resurgence throughout the 1970s and performed at several major festivals and toured Europe. Recorded final album, *Crawfish Fiesta,* for Alligator in late 1979, just two months before suffering a fatal heart attack at age 61.

PROFESSOR SHORTHAIR (Gerald Tillman) *Rhythm and blues.* Piano. Composer. Bandleader. (Born Mar. 18, 1955, New Orleans, Orleans Parish; died Sept. 15, 1986, New Orleans, Orleans Parish.) Extremely talented New Orleans rhythm and blues and funk piano player and songwriter whose promising career was cut drastically short by illness. The son of saxophonist Joe Tillman, helped form the Meters-inspired funk band Blackmale in the early 1970s and released one single around 1974 on Moneytown. In the late 1970s through mid-1980s performed and recorded with the Neville Brothers. Also collaborated with **Ivan Neville** and **Zigaboo Modeliste** in Zig and Gaboon's Gang and formed the Uptown Allstars in the early 1980s. In 1986 became ill while in California working on a solo project and passed away shortly afterward.

PRUDHOMME, WILLIS *Zydeco.* Accordion, harmonica, vocals. Composer. Bandleader. (Born Sept. 22, 1931, Kinder, Jeff. Davis Parish.) Noted zydeco accordionist and singer-songwriter began playing harmonica during his early teens and worked mainly outside music as a farmer early on. At age 45 began learning accordion, mentored by **Nathan Abshire**, and was soon playing local dances. Performed and recorded with **Leo "the Bull" Thomas** for several years before forming his band Zydeco Express in the mid-1980s and appearing on LP *Zydeco Live!* on Rounder with **John Delafose** in 1988. Recorded single "Zydeco Queen" on Lanor in the late 1980s and throughout the 1990s and 2000s had releases on Maison de Soul, Goldband, Louisiana Red Hot, and Zydeco Gumbo, including *Crawfish Got Soul* in 1991. Brother of zydeco bassist Joseph "Slim" and guitarist Charles Prudhomme, who performed and recorded with Delafose, among others.

PURNELL, ALTON *Jazz.* Piano, vocals. Composer. Bandleader. (Born Apr. 16, 1911, New Orleans, Orleans Parish; died Jan. 14, 1987, Inglewood, California.) Influential New Orleans jazz pianist best known for his work with **Bunk Johnson** and **George Lewis** in the 1940s New Orleans jazz revival. Began playing piano at age 12, studying under **Burnell Santiago** and **Fats Pichon**. Started playing professionally in 1928 and through the early 1940s worked with **Sidney Desvigne**, **Isaiah Morgan**, **Big Eye Louis Nelson**, **Alphonse Picou**, **Cousin Joe**, and others. From the mid-1940s through mid-1950s worked and recorded with Bunk Johnson and George Lewis. Relocated to California in 1957 and worked with **Kid Ory**, **Barney Bigard**, and others, and recorded extensively as leader. In following years led his own band and regularly toured Europe. Brother of jazz saxophonist Ted Purnell.

QUEEN IDA (Ida Lee Lewis Guillory) *Zydeco.* Accordion, vocals. Bandleader. (Born Jan. 15, 1929, Lake Charles, Calcasieu Parish.) Influential West Coast–based zydeco accordionist and singer who was the first prominent female accordion player to front a zydeco band. Raised speaking Creole French in a large musical family, began playing accordion at age 18, learning the rudiments from her mother soon after relocating to San Francisco with family in 1947. After working outside music for two decades, began playing accordion again in the early 1970s and started sitting in with **John Semien**'s Opelousas Playboys and her brother **Al Rapone**'s Barbary Coast Band. Eventually started fronting Rapone's band on a regular basis, renamed as Queen Ida and the Bon Temps Band, a contemporary zydeco band with Caribbean and Latin influences. In 1976 appeared at Monterey Jazz Festival, which led to recording contract with GNP/Crescendo and debut album *Play the Zydeco* later that year. Toured extensively nationally and overseas, including Japan and Africa, throughout following years with numerous releases on GNP/Crescendo and Sonet through the late 1990s, notably the highly acclaimed LP *On Tour* in 1982. In 1999 reunited with Rapone on her final release, *Back on the Bayou,* and continued performing through the late 2000s, often accompanied by son Myrick Guillory and other family members. In 2009 was a recipient of NEA's National Heritage Fellowship.

QUEZERGUE, BRIAN *Jazz.* Bass, piano. Composer. Bandleader. (Born July 5, 1976, New Orleans, Orleans Parish.) Jazz fusion bassist studied music at New Orleans Center for Creative Arts under **Clyde Kerr Jr.** and **Kidd Jordan**. Later toured with **Dr. John**, the Wild Magnolias, **Alvin Batiste**, and others. Released debut recording, *Reflections,* in 2012 and continued to perform as sideman and with his own group. Son of acclaimed producer and arranger **Wardell Quezergue**.

QUEZERGUE, WARDELL *Rhythm and blues.* Trumpet. Composer. Bandleader. (Born Mar. 12, 1930, New Orleans, Orleans Parish; died Sept. 6, 2011, New Orleans, Orleans Parish.) Highly influential bandleader, producer, arranger, and songwriter whose work had a major impact on New Orleans rhythm and blues in the 1960s and 1970s. Began performing with his band Royal Dukes of Rhythm in the late 1950s after military discharge. Soon was hired as arranger by **Dave Bartholomew** with Imperial and worked with **Fats Domino**, **Earl King** ("Trick Bag"), and **Professor Longhair** ("Big Chief") in the early 1960s. Founded Nola label in the mid-1960s and had national hit with **Robert Parker**'s "Barefootin'." In the early 1970s produced major hits for **King Floyd** ("Groove Me") and **Jean Knight** ("Mr. Big Stuff"). Throughout next several decades worked with Willie Nelson, **Dr. John**, **Neville Brothers**, **Clarence "Gatemouth" Brown**, B.B. King, Paul Simon, and many others. Continued writing, arranging, and producing until his death at age 81. Father of **Brian Quezergue**.

R

RAINES, JERRY (Rubin Bergeron) *Swamp pop.* Vocals. Composer. Bandleader. (Born Aug. 8, 1940, Houma, Terrebonne Parish.) Early swamp pop singer and songwriter best known for his 1960 hit "Our Teenage Love." Began performing in Houma bars at age 18 and in 1959 recorded at New Orleans famed **Cosimo Matassa**'s studios, backed by a stellar band which included Mac Rebennack **(Dr. John)**, **Lee Allen**, and **Roy Montrell**. Sessions produced debut hit, "Our Teenage Love," issued on Drew-Blan and leased to Mercury. In the early 1970s and early 1980s had singles on Black Gold, Starbarn, and Haystack. After long hiatus returned to music in 2000 and continued to perform at festivals and swamp pop reunions into the 2010s.

RAMSEY, PAT (James Patrick Ramsey) *Blues, rock.* Harmonica, vocals. Bandleader. (Born July 22, 1953, Shreveport, Caddo Parish; died Nov. 17, 2008, Tallahassee, Florida.) Noted blues harmonica player began playing at age 17 and in the late 1970s recorded with Johnny Winter. In the 1980s performed with band Crosscut Saw and his own group before relocating to Tallahassee and releasing CD *It's About Time* in 1995. Continued to perform on regional blues scene with his band the Blues Disciples and released two live recordings before illness forced retirement shortly before his death at age 55.

RANDALL, JAY (Joseph Jay Noel) *Swamp pop.* Composer. Bandleader. (Born Feb. 11, 1940, Opelousas, St. Landry Parish.) Swamp pop vocalist began singing in the late 1950s at high-school functions and recorded debut single "You're On My Mind"/"Never Have I" in 1959 for Khoury's. From 1960 through the 1980s had singles on various local labels, including Carl, Jin, Lanor, La Louisianne, Bad Weather, Pelican, and Showtime, leading various bands, including the Epics, the Driving Wheels, the Downbeats, the Electras, the Counts, and Whiskey Creek. In 1982 released LP *Cajun Boogie* on Delta.

RANDLE, CHESTER (Chester J. Randall) *Rhythm and blues.* Guitar, vocals. Composer. Bandleader. (Born July 30, 1929, Lafayette, Lafayette Parish; died July 7, 2005, Lake Charles, Calcasieu Parish.) Rhythm and blues guitarist and singer performed in various bands in the Lake Charles area starting in the early 1950s and through late 1960s worked as session musician and bandleader for **Eddie Shuler**'s Goldband label, recording with numerous artists, including James Freeman, **Clarence Garlow**, **Bill Parker**, **Rockin' Sidney**, and Blue Scotty. In the late 1960s formed Chester Randle's Soul Senders and recorded two funk and soul singles for Shuler's Anla label, notably funk classic "Soul Brother's Testify Part 1 & 2."

RANDLE, RAYMOND *Zydeco, blues.* Guitar, vocals. (Born Feb. 23, 1948, Opelousas, St. Landry Parish; died Sept. 18, 2015, Alexandria, Rapides Parish.) Locally renowned guitarist began playing in his father's zydeco band in his early teens and worked with various blues outfits through the 1970s. In the 1980s and 1990s performed mainly with zydeco bands, including with **Jude Taylor** and **Thomas "Big Hat" Fields**, and worked and recorded regularly with **Roy Carrier** for several decades until Carrier's death in 2010. In the mid-1980s recorded various sides with **Felton Malbrough** for Lanor. Later relocated to Alexandria.

RANDOLPH, BROTHER PERCY *Blues.* Harmonica, washboard, vocals. (Born Sept. 19, 1914, New Orleans, Orleans Parish; died Oct. 29, 1991, New Orleans, Orleans Parish.) Noted down-home blues singer and harmonica player who performed mainly on the streets of the French Quarter for several decades. Taught himself harmonica at age 15 and recorded with **Snooks Eaglin** in 1958 and **Billie** and **De De Pierce** on washboard in 1959. Also worked with **Babe Stoval** and **Little Freddie King** and appeared regularly at New Orleans Jazz & Heritage Festival from 1971 until his death.

RANDY (of **Randy and the Rockets**) *See* David, Randy.

RAPONE, AL (Albert John Lewis Sr.) *Zydeco, blues.* Accordion, guitar, vocals. Composer. Bandleader. (Born June 20, 1936, Lake Charles, Calcasieu Parish; died August 30, 2018, Daly City, California.) California-based zydeco multi-instrumentalist began playing accordion in the late 1940s after relocating to San Francisco with family, influenced early on by **John Semien**. Throughout the 1950s and 1960s performed mainly as blues guitarist on Bay Area music scene, often backing touring musicians such as **Clarence "Gatemouth" Brown**, Big Mama Thornton, and Jimmy Reed. In the early 1970s older sister Ida Guillory began sitting in with his Barbary Coast Band, which was soon renamed **Queen Ida** and the Bon Temps Zydeco Band in the mid-1970s when she began fronting the group. Toured and recorded with band as guitarist, producer, and songwriter until forming Zydeco Express and relaunching solo career in 1982. Through the 1990s had releases on Ornament, L+R, JSP, Blind Pig, Traditional Line, and Atomic Theory, notably *Zydeco to Go* in 1990. In 1999 reunited with Queen Ida on her final recording, *Back to the Bayou,* on GNP/ Crescendo. Continued performing into the 2010s.

RAPP, BUTLER "GUYÉ" *Jazz.* Trombone, banjo, guitar. (Born Apr. 7, 1888, St. Bernard Parish, Louisiana; died Apr. 24, 1942, New Orleans, Orleans Parish.)[1] Early New Orleans jazz multi-instrumentalist played trombone with **Manuel Perez**'s Onward Brass Band and banjo with **Sam Morgan** in the early 1920s. In the late 1920s worked with **Chris Kelly** and Magnolia Orchestra. Killed by knife wound to throat after attacking pianist **Walter Decou** following a gig at the Budweiser (Fern) dance hall in the French Quarter.

RAVEN, EDDY (Edward Garvin Futch) *Cajun, country.* Guitar, vocals. Composer. Bandleader. (Born Aug. 19, 1944, Lafayette, Lafayette Parish.) Popular Cajun and country singer-songwriter began playing guitar as a child and by age 13 was performing in local rock and roll band. After a stint in Georgia and cutting self-released single "Once a Fool" in 1962, returned to Lafayette and signed with La Louisianne, releasing numerous singles in the late 1960s, including "Alligator Bayou," and 1969 LP *That Cajun Country Sound.* On recommendation from **Jimmy C. Newman**, relocated to Nashville in the 1970s and wrote hits for Don Gibson, Connie Smith, Roy Acuff, and others and worked as vocalist with **Jimmie Davis**. Through the early 1980s had releases on ABC, Monument, Dimension, and Elektra before achieving major success with a string of country hits through the late 1980s for RCA and Universal, including "I Got Mexico" and "Bayou Boys." Toured extensively throughout following years with recordings on Capitol and several independent labels, including *Cookin' Cajun* with **Jo-El Sonnier** for K-Tel in 1996. Continued performing and recording in the 2010s, releasing *All Grassed Up* with Carolina Road in 2017.

RAY J. (Raymond L. Jones) *Rhythm and blues.* Piano, trumpet, vocals. (Born Aug. 17, 1939, New Orleans, Orleans Parish; died Feb. 6, 2011, New Orleans, Orleans Parish.) Rhythm and blues multi-instrumentalist and arranger began learning piano as a child, taking lessons from neighbor **Edward Frank**. In the 1960s joined a local band and backed touring musicians such as Barbara Lynn, Solomon Burke, and Etta James. As arranger worked on sessions with **Chris Kenner**, **Johnny Adams**, **Eddie Lang**, and others. Released several funk recordings on Hep' Me in the 1970s, some with vocalist Norma Jean, and worked as arranger and writer with label through the mid-1980s.

READ, WALLACE "CHEESE" *Cajun.* Fiddle, vocals. Composer. (Born Aug. 12, 1924, Eunice, St. Landry Parish; died Nov. 15, 1981, Eunice, St. Landry Parish.) Renowned Cajun fiddler began playing in his early teens, influenced by both Cajun and Creole fiddle players. Began performing in bands in his mid-teens and in following years worked with **Dennis McGee**, **Leo Soileau**, **Sady Courville**, **Harry Choates**, **Chuck Guillory**, and others. In the mid- to late 1950s made field recordings for folklorist Harry Oster with **Cyprien Landreneau** and in 1979 recorded acclaimed LP *Cajun House Party C'ez Cheese* for Arhoolie with **Marc Savoy**.

REBENNACK, MAC *See* Dr. John.

REED, AL (Alfred Lloyd Reed Jr.) *Rhythm and blues.* Vocals, piano. Composer. Bandleader. (Born Nov. 10, 1925, Belle Alliance, Assumption Parish; died Mar. 12, 1990, New Orleans, Orleans Parish.)[2] New Orleans rhythm and blues singer-songwriter began playing piano in the early 1950s, influenced primarily by Ray Charles. In following years worked with **Earl King**, **Guitar Slim**,

Smiley Lewis, and others. Recorded debut single, "She's Rolling," on Post in 1955 and had two singles in the early 1960s on Instant. In 1966 started Axe label and released several singles, having regional success with "99 44/100 Pure Love" in 1968.

REED, BOB *Cajun.* Accordion, harmonica. Bandleader. (Born Aug. 31, 1943, Mamou, Evangeline Parish.) Traditional Cajun accordionist was raised near **Bois Sec Ardoin** and would perform on harmonica with Ardoin as a child. In the 1990s performed and recorded with Mamou Prairie Band, joined by son **Mitch Reed** on fiddle for several years. Also performed and recorded with Cajun band T-Mamou.

REED, DALTON *Rhythm and blues.* Vocals, trumpet. Composer. Bandleader. (Born Aug. 23, 1952, Cade, St. Martin Parish; died Sept. 23, 1994, St. Paul, Minnesota.) Noted deep soul singer and songwriter began singing in church as a child and in his teens performed with various rhythm and blues bands around Lafayette, influenced by Ray Charles and Otis Redding. In the mid-1980s had singles on his own Sweet Daddy and Reed Brothers labels. Signed with Rounder in 1990 and released *Louisiana Soul Man* on Bullseye Blues subsidiary to national acclaim. Toured nationally and released follow-up *Willing & Able* for label in 1994. Succumbed to fatal heart attack while on tour at age 42.

REED, JO JO *Zydeco.* Accordion, harmonica, vocals. Composer. Bandleader. (Born May 28, 1970, Eunice, St. Landry Parish.) Locally popular zydeco accordionist and singer-songwriter began performing in high school, influenced by **Boozoo Chavis** and **John Delafose**. After two singles on Lanor, released CD *Funky Zydeco* on Maison de Soul in 1995 and in 1997 had local hit with title cut from *Not Your Baby's Daddy* on Zydeco Hound. After recovering from a serious car accident in the late 1990s, continued performing on southwest Louisiana club and festival circuit in the 2010s with several more releases on Louisiana Red Hot Records and his own Happy Hill label, including *Back on the Scene* in 2000, produced by **Keith Frank**.

REED, LIL' JIMMY (Leon Atkins) *Blues.* Guitar, harmonica, vocals. Composer. (Born July 14, 1938, Hardwood, W. Feliciana Parish.) Longtime Alabama-based blues musician began playing harmonica at age 12 and guitar at age 16 and by his late teens was performing in clubs around Baton Rouge, reportedly earning stage name after filling in for Chicago bluesman Jimmy Reed, who was too inebriated to perform. After serving two decades in the Army and a long career as a barber, began touring nationally as a one-man band in the 1990s, releasing recording debut *School's Out* on Vent in 1996. Continued performing nationally and overseas into his 80s.

REED, MITCH *Cajun.* Fiddle, cello, guitar, vocals. Composer. Bandleader. (Born Feb. 28, 1971, Bayou Vista, St. Mary Parish.) Renowned Cajun fiddle player was raised in Lafayette and began playing the instrument at age 15. By age 17 was playing professionally and in following years worked with **Dewey Balfa**, **D. L. Menard**, **Canray Fontenot**, **Wade Frugé**, **Steve Riley**, and others. Also performed early on with his father **Bob Reed** in Mamou Prairie Band and later cofounded several groups, including Tasso, Charivari, the Racines, and Lafayette Rhythm Devils, often with **Randy Vidrine**. In the 2010s continued working as music teacher and performing with several acclaimed bands, including BeauSoleil avec **Michael Doucet**, which he joined in 2006.

REGGANS, HENRY, SR. *Rhythm and blues.* Piano, vocals. Bandleader. (Born July 27, 1958, Leesville, Vernon Parish.) Locally renowned Leesville-area rhythm and blues singer and keyboard player toured with Little Johnny Taylor early in career. Performed with numerous bands around Leesville and Natchitoches area for several decades, including **Hardrick Rivers** Revue Band, the Moondogs, and his own group Louisiana Sideman.

REININGER, JOHNNY *Jazz.* Clarinet, saxophone. Bandleader. (Born Aug. 19, 1908, New Orleans, Orleans Parish; died Sept. 14, 1999, New Orleans, Orleans Parish.) Popular New Orleans jazz bandleader began performing in the late 1920s and later worked regularly with **Leon Prima**. Throughout the 1940s and 1950s led his own bands which at times included **Jack Delaney**. Spent 20 years as bandleader at Club My-O-My in Lakefront.

RENA, HENRY "KID" *Jazz.* Trumpet. Bandleader. (Born Aug. 30, 1898, New Orleans, Orleans Parish; died Apr. 25, 1949, New Orleans, Orleans Parish.) Noted early New Orleans jazz bandleader and trumpeter began performing with **Louis Armstrong** in Colored Waif's Home band in 1913 and later studied with **Manuel Perez**. In 1919 succeeded Armstrong in **Kid Ory**'s band. Around 1921 formed his own band, which included **George Lewis** and brother Joseph on drums, and toured Chicago several times. Also worked with **Papa Celestin**'s Tuxedo Brass Band and in the late 1920s led Eureka Brass Band. Led various bands in the 1930s and cut his only recording session in 1940. Retired from music due to ill health in 1947.

REVEREND ETHER *See* Barron, Ronnie.

REYNAUD, LLOYD *Rhythm and blues.* Drums, vocals. Composer. Bandleader. (Born Oct. 26, 1936, Opelousas, St. Landry Parish; died June 30, 2012, La Marque, Texas.) Opelousas rhythm and blues bandleader, drummer, and label owner worked with his own trio, and others in the 1950s, including stints with **Lonesome Sundown** and **Duke Stevens**. Around 1961 started Reynaud label and released singles by **Roscoe Chenier**, **Schoolboy Cleve**, **J. J. Caillier**, and others. After working with Lanor Records as talent scout, relocated to Houston in the mid-1960s to work for NASA. Brother of **Sidney "Hot Rod" Reynaud**.

REYNAUD, SIDNEY "HOT ROD" *Rhythm and blues, swamp pop.* Saxophone. (Born July 25, 1935, Opelousas, St. Landry Parish; died Feb. 14, 2009, Lake Charles, Calcasieu Parish.) Rhythm and blues and swamp pop tenor saxophonist best known as longtime member of **Cookie** and the Cupcakes. Recorded extensively in the 1950s and 1960s with group as well as on sessions with **Carol Fran**, **Lil' Alfred**, **Margo White**, and others. Older brother of **Lloyd Reynaud**.

RICH, DON (Donald Joseph Richard) *Swamp pop.* Vocals, piano, organ, guitar, accordion, fiddle, drums. Composer. Bandleader. (Born July 23, 1954, Pierre Part, Assumption Parish.) Popular swamp pop singer-songwriter and multi-instrumentalist began playing professionally at age 13, largely inspired by his musician father Golden Richard and soul singer Otis Redding. In 1992 made his recording debut with *Louisiana's Own* on his Party Time label. Released more than ten CDs on Jin and continued to be a popular draw at clubs and festivals throughout south Louisiana in the late 2010s.

RICHARD, BECKY *Cajun.* Guitar, bass, vocals. Composer. Bandleader. (Born May 23, 1959, Church Point, Acadia Parish.) Cajun-country singer-songwriter and guitarist performed in all-women Cajun band with **Sheryl Cormier** in the 1980s before forming her own band in the late 1980s with her accordion-player father, Patrick Richard. Released several singles and LP *Southern Belle* on Kajun in the late 1980s and early 1990s and appeared on nationally televised program *Cajun Country* hosted by **Doug Kershaw** in 1990.

RICHARD, BELTON *Cajun.* Accordion, drums, guitar, vocals. Composer. Bandleader. (Born Oct. 5, 1939, Rayne, Acadia Parish; died June 21, 2017, Lafayette, Lafayette Parish.) Highly influential Cajun accordionist and singer-songwriter who became one of the most popular Cajun performers and recording artists of the 1960s and 1970s, known for his soulful vocals and swamp pop, rhythm and blues–, and country-influenced style. Began playing accordion as a child, mentored by his father, Claby Richard (1906–1974), who performed and recorded with **Adam Hébert**'s Country Playboys. In 1959 formed the four-piece Musical Aces, which soon expanded to seven pieces and performed throughout southwest Louisiana and east Texas. Recorded for Chamo in the early 1960s and released numerous singles and LP *Belton Richard Meets* Aldus Roger. In the mid-1960s began recording extensively for Swallow and released numerous influential singles and LPs, including *Modern Sounds in Cajun Music Volume 1 and 2*, which included such signature classics as "Un Autre Soir D'Ennui (Another Lonely Night)," "Cajun Fugitive," "Oh Lucille," and "Cajun Stripper." In 1974 had regional hit with Ray Stevens cover "The (Cajun) Streak" and continued recording for Swallow through the late 1970s. Retired from music in the mid-1980s but returned in the mid-1990s and released CD *I'm Back* on Swallow in 1996. Continued performing sporadically at clubs and festivals through the mid-2010s, releasing CD *The Older the Wine, the Finer the Taste!* in 2003. Retired from performing the year before his death at age 77.

RICHARD, FELIX *Cajun.* Accordion, vocals. (Born Mar. 10, 1918, Cankton, St. Landry Parish; died Oct. 13, 1993, Church Point, Acadia Parish.) Highly revered Cajun accordionist and musical disciple of **Iry LeJeune**, who greatly influenced and mentored several area musicians, notably **Zachary Richard** and cousin **Horace Trahan**. Performed locally with band Cankton Express in the 1970s and 1980s which included sons Sterling and Kenneth. Released album *Cankton Express Live Chez Mulates* on Swallow in 1988. Also was a locally renowned *raconteur* (storyteller).

RICHARD, MURPHY (Leon Murphy Richard) *Zydeco.* Accordion, vocals. Bandleader. (Born Feb. 9, 1937, Leonville, St. Landry Parish.) Noted zydeco accordionist began learning the instrument in the early 1980s and soon became a regular performer at **Roy Carrier**'s Offshore Lounge in Lawtell. In 1991 joined Creole Zydeco Farmers and recorded and toured internationally with group until forming his own band, the Zydeco Kings, in 1999.

Recorded CD *Doin' the Zydeco* on Zydeco Hound in 1999 and continued performing sporadically with various groups into the 2010s. Brother Joe Richard was also a zydeco accordionist.

RICHARD, RENALD *Rhythm and blues.* Trumpet, piano. Composer. Bandleader. (Born May 3, 1925, Thibodaux, Lafourche Parish.) Noted rhythm and blues trumpeter best known for his work as bandleader for Ray Charles. Began playing trumpet at age 13 and in the late 1940s and early 1950s worked with cousins **Ray** and **Plas Johnson**, **Guitar Slim**, Ivory Joe Hunter, and others. In the mid-1950s toured with Ray Charles for several years and served as bandleader, cowriting Charles's hit "I Got a Woman." Also wrote "Teenage Letter," which was recorded by **Jerry Lee Lewis** and Big Joe Turner. Retired from teaching music in the early 1990s and continued performing with local jazz bands in South Florida in the late 2010s. Father of **Thaddeus Richard**.

RICHARD, RUDY (Rudolph Valentine Richard Sr.) *Blues, zydeco.* Guitar, accordion, vocals. (Born Sept. 5, 1937, Church Point, Acadia Parish; died Sept. 22, 2014, Baton Rouge, EBR Parish.) Influential early swamp blues guitarist best known for his long tenure in **Slim Harpo**'s King Bees. Began learning guitar on a homemade instrument at age 12 and by the mid-1950s was performing in Opelousas clubs, mentored by **Lonesome Sundown**. In the next several years performed regularly with **Good Rockin' Bob** and also began learning accordion, occasionally sitting in with **Clifton Chenier**. In 1957 joined **Slim Harpo**'s band and relocated to Baton Rouge. Performed and recorded with group until Harpo's death in 1970, appearing on many classic recordings, including "Baby Scratch My Back," "Raining in My Heart," and "Shake Your Hips." In following decades performed with **Raful Neal**, **Major Handy**, and others, and led his own band Zydeco Express in Baton Rouge area. Older brother of Lefty Richard, who was longtime guitarist with **Little Bob** and the Lollipops.

RICHARD, SHUK (Clopha Richard) *Cajun.* Accordion. Bandleader. (Born Nov. 8, 1909, Rayne, Acadia Parish; died Dec. 8, 1976, Lake Charles, Calcasieu Parish.) Early postwar Cajun accordionist learned to play the instrument as a child from his mother. In the mid-1940s formed the Louisiana Aces, which featured singer-guitarist **Marie Falcon** and performed with group in Lake Charles area through the mid-1950s, recording two singles for Khoury's, including "Le Côté Farouche de la Vic." Group also included at times **Will Kegley** and **Crawford Vincent**.

RICHARD, THADDEUS *Rhythm and blues, jazz.* Saxophone, flute, clarinet, piano. Bandleader. (Born May 23, 1950, Thibodaux, Lafourche Parish.) Son of **Renald Richard**, accomplished blues and jazz multi-instrumentalist began performing on the Chitlin Circuit in the late 1960s and worked with Bobby Bland, Joe Tex, Al Green, and others, and served as bandleader for Z.Z. Hill. From 1975 to 1980 performed and recorded with Paul McCartney's band Wings. In the 2000s and 2010s performed and recorded with Preservation Hall Jazz Band and appeared as a recurring character on the HBO television series *Treme* in 2011.

RICHARD, ZACHARY *Cajun.* Accordion, piano, guitar, harmonica, vocals. Composer. Bandleader. (Born Sept. 8, 1950, Scott, Lafayette Parish.) Internationally renowned Cajun singer-songwriter, poet, multi-instrumentalist, author, filmmaker, and cultural ambassador and activist who helped revitalize Cajun music in the 1970s and 1980s by incorporating modern elements of rock, funk, and Afro-Caribbean rhythms. Began playing piano as a child and started performing in bands while attending Tulane University. In the early 1970s signed with Elektra and recorded LP *High Time,* which remained unissued for several decades. Formed folk-rock band Bayou Drifters with cousin **Michael Doucet** before relocating to Quebec. Composed "Réveille" soon afterwards as a rallying cry to preserve the Cajun French language and culture. Through the early 1980s recorded six albums in French, including gold-selling *Mardi Gras* and *Migration.* In 1981 returned to Louisiana and through the 1990s released numerous albums, including *Zack's Bon Ton* on Rounder in 1988, *Women in the Room* on A&M in 1990, and the highly acclaimed *Cap Enragé* on Audiogram in 1996. Continued touring extensively nationally and abroad in the 2000s with several more releases, including *Lumière Dans le Noir* on Warner France Music in 2007. In the 2010s continued recording and performing, releasing *Gombo* in 2017.

RICHARDSON, EDDIE *Jazz.* Trumpet. (Born Apr. 18, 1903, New Orleans, Orleans Parish; died Nov. 1, 1986, New Orleans, Orleans Parish.)[3] Early New Orleans jazz trumpeter began playing with **Kid Rena**'s band in the late 1920s. Also worked with **Earl Foster** in the late 1920s and with W.P.A. Brass Band in the 1930s. Joined Eureka Brass Band in the 1940s and recorded with group in 1951.

RICHARDSON, RODNEY *Jazz.* Bass. (Born Aug. 21, 1917, New Orleans, Orleans Parish; died Oct. 29, 2005, Modesto, California.) Acclaimed jazz bassist known for his tenure with Count Basie's band. Began playing bass during his late teens and worked with regional bands in Tennessee in the late 1930s. In 1942 joined Basie's band and toured and recorded with group through 1946. Also appeared on recordings with **Illinois Jacquet**, Herbie Fields, Lester Young, Roy Eldridge, Billie Holiday, and others. From 1949 to 1950 performed with Tiny Grimes. Later worked with Erroll Garner and **Duke Burrell**'s Louisiana Shakers, and toured Europe. Brother of bassist James "Beans" Richardson.

RICHARDSON, SOKO (Eulis Joseph Richardson) *Rhythm and blues.* Drums. (Born Dec. 8, 1939, New Iberia, Iberia Parish; died Jan. 28, 2004, Los Angeles.) Renowned rhythm and blues drummer began touring the South at age 16 and within several years joined Ike Turner's band, performing and recording with Turner's Kings of Rhythm and later the Ike and Tina Turner Revue through the early 1970s. After a decade performing and recording with John Mayall, relocated to Chicago and worked with Albert Collins, appearing on his 1991 CD *Iceman* on Virgin. Also recorded with **Cookie** and the Cupcakes, **Carol Fran**, Earl Hooker, Bobby Womack, Pee Wee Crayton, and others throughout career. Twin brother of musician Luther "Ching-Ching" and younger brother of **T. J. Richardson.**

RICHARDSON, T. J./"SKINNY DYNAMO" (Theodore Richardson Jr.) *Rhythm and blues, swamp pop.* Drums, guitar, piano, vocals. Composer. Bandleader. (Born Sept. 26, 1932, New Iberia, Iberia Parish; died May 1988, New Iberia, Iberia Parish.) Vocalist and multi-instrumentalist best known for his 1956 swamp pop single "So Long, So Long," recorded by producer **J. D. Miller** and issued under the name Skinny Dynamo on Excello. Not to be confused with **Sonny Jones** or George Sanders LeBlanc, who also recorded as "Skinny Dynamo." Older brother of musicians Luther and **Soko Richardson**.

RIDEAU, STEP (Stephen Joseph Rideau) *Zydeco.* Accordion, vocals. Composer. Bandleader. (Born May 13, 1966, Lebeau, St. Landry Parish.) Popular Texas-based zydeco accordion player and singer began learning the instrument in the mid-1980s after relocating to Houston, inspired greatly by **Boozoo Chavis**. In 1991 formed his band the Zydeco Outlaws, which incorporated elements of rap and modern rhythm and blues early on but eventually developed a more traditional zydeco style. Continued performing in the 2010s throughout Texas and Louisiana with numerous releases, including *A Step Ahead* in 2005.

RIDGLEY, SAMMY *Rhythm and blues.* Vocals. Bandleader. (Born Aug. 6, 1943, Shrewsbury, Jefferson Parish; died Aug. 27, 2016, New Orleans, Orleans Parish.) Younger brother of **Tommy Ridgley** began performing in the 1960s, inspired by Joe Tex. In the 1970s had singles on King's Row, Hit Sound, and Cash in Today. Led band Operation Plus from the late 1960s through 1990s and worked with his brother's band the Untouchables in the 1980s and 1990s. Released CD *Midnight Rendezvous* in 1998 and led Untouchables following his brother's death in 1999.

RIDGLEY, TOMMY *Rhythm and blues.* Vocals, piano. Composer. Bandleader. (Born Oct. 30, 1925, Shrewsbury, Jefferson Parish; died Aug. 11, 1999, New Orleans, Orleans Parish.) Popular early New Orleans rhythm and blues singer, whose career spanned five decades. Influenced by **Roy Brown**, began performing in the late 1940s after sitting in with **Edgar Blanchard**'s band at the Dew Drop Inn. In 1949 joined **Dave Bartholomew**'s band as featured vocalist and recorded for Imperial from 1949 to 1953, garnering local hit with debut single, "Shrewsbury Blues." Throughout the 1950s recorded for Decca, Atlantic, and Herald and formed his band the Untouchables. In the early 1960s had several local hits on Ric, including "In the Same Old Way," and was dubbed "King of the Stroll." Throughout the 1960s and 1970s recorded for numerous local labels and remained a popular singer despite never achieving a national hit. In 1995 released final recording, *Since the Blues Began,* on Black Top. Older brother of **Sammy Ridgley**.

RIDGLEY, WILLIAM "BÉBÉ" *Jazz.* Trombone, bass. Bandleader. (Born Jan. 15, 1882, Metairie, Jefferson Parish; died May 28, 1961, New Orleans, Orleans Parish.) Important early New Orleans jazz trombonist and bandleader who for a time coled the Tuxedo Jazz Band with **Papa Celestin**. Began playing trombone as a child and studied under **Professor Jim Humphrey**. Around 1900 started forming his own bands, once hiring **Buddy Bolden**, and worked with the Silver Leaf Orchestra. In the mid-1910s helped lead two Tuxedo bands, one brass and one orchestral, with Celestin and remained with groups through 1925 when Celestin departed with key members. Subsequently formed Ridgley's Original Tuxedo Jazz Band, which included **Sweet Emma Barrett** and **Kid Shots Madison** and led group successfully for several years. In the early 1930s developed health issues, which led to his retirement after a stroke in 1936.

RILEY, AMOS *Jazz.* Trumpet. Bandleader. (Born 1879, New Orleans, Orleans Parish; died Apr. 6, 1926, New Orleans, Orleans Parish.)[4] Early New Orleans jazz trumpeter and leader of Tulane Orchestra in the 1910s. Worked occasionally with **Papa Celestin**'s Tuxedo Brass Band in the late 1910s and in the late 1920s led band which included **Fats Pichon** and **Willie Humphrey**. Father of **Teddy Riley**.

RILEY, HERLIN *Jazz.* Drums, trumpet. Composer. Bandleader. (Born Feb. 15, 1957, New Orleans, Orleans Parish.) Highly regarded jazz drummer and longtime member of Jazz at Lincoln Center Orchestra. Began playing drums at age three but focused on trumpet before switching back in junior year of college. Toured as member of Ahmad Jamal's band from 1984 to 1987. Worked and recorded extensively with **Wynton Marsalis** from 1988 to 1994. Joined Jazz at Lincoln Center Orchestra in 1992 and also worked with **Dr. John**, George Benson, Marcus Roberts, and others. In 2016 released third recording as leader, *New Direction,* on Mack Avenue.

RILEY, JUDGE (Judge Lawrence Riley) *Blues, jazz.* Drums, bass, vocals. (Born Jan. 1, 1909, New Orleans, Orleans Parish; died Aug. 22, 1977, Chicago.) Highly accomplished early blues and jazz drummer who appeared on hundreds of recordings in the 1940s and 1950s. Began playing drums and piano as a child and performed early on with **Alvin Alcorn**, **Fats Pichon**, and **Papa Celestin** before working on riverboats with **Sidney Desvigne** and others in the 1930s, often with **Ransom Knowling**. After several years in St. Louis, settled in Chicago in 1941 and upon Knowling's recommendation began working as session drummer for RCA-Victor, Columbia, and other labels. Through the 1950s recorded with numerous artists including Arthur Crudup, Big Bill Broonzy, Jazz Gillum, Tampa Red, Memphis Minnie, Roosevelt Sykes, and John Lee "Sonny Boy" Williamson. Continued performing in Chicago clubs, often on bass and in later years with Blind John Davis, until sidelined by a stroke in 1973.

RILEY, KIRBY *Creole.* Accordion, vocals. (Born Aug. 26, 1904, Ville Platte, Evangeline Parish; died May 23, 1992, Opelousas, St. Landry Parish.)[5] Early Creole accordion player and singer who along with partner **Douglas Bellard** were the first Creole musicians in southwest Louisiana to record French la la music, two months ahead of **Amédé Ardoin**'s recording debut. In Oct. 1929 recorded four sides with Bellard for Vocalion, including "La Valse de la Prison." In later years resided in Opelousas.

RILEY, STEVE *Cajun.* Accordion, fiddle, guitar, vocals. Composer. Bandleader. (Born June 14, 1969, Mamou, Evangeline Parish.) Nationally renowned Cajun accordionist and singer-songwriter began playing the instrument at age seven and during his teens won numerous local accordion contests. At age 15 began being mentored by **Dewey Balfa**, performing and touring with him until Balfa's death in 1992. In 1988 formed contemporary Cajun band Mamou Playboys with **David Greely** and released self-titled recording debut on Rounder in 1990, produced by **Zachary Richard**. Throughout following three decades toured extensively nationally and abroad with numerous releases on Rounder, including *La Toussaint* in 1995 and *Bon Rêve* in 2003. In the 2010s continued touring and recording with Mamou Playboys as well as other side projects, including the Racines, the Band Courtbouillon, and High Performance.

RILEY, THEODORE "TEDDY" *Jazz, rhythm and blues.* Trumpet, vocals. Bandleader. (Born May 10, 1924, New Orleans, Orleans Parish; died Nov. 14, 1992, New Orleans, Orleans Parish.) New Orleans jazz trumpeter performed with **George Williams** Brass Band in the 1950s and 1960s and appeared on sessions with **Roy Brown**, **Clarence "Frogman" Henry**, **Earl King**, **Champion Jack Dupree**, **Harry Connick Jr.**, and **Wynton Marsalis**. Also worked with Olympia, Onward, and **Papa Celestin**'s Tuxedo brass bands. Continued to lead various jazz bands in New Orleans until shortly before his death. Son of **Amos Riley**.

RIVERS, HARDRICK *Rhythm and blues.* Saxophone, vocals. Bandleader. (Born Sept. 12, 1956, Natchitoches, Natch. Parish.) Natchitoches-based saxophonist began performing with **Overton Owens**'s band the Mustangs at age 13. In the 1980s and 1990s performed with the Lighthouse Crew with **B.B. Major** and **Pop Hymes** and his own Rivers Revue Band. Toured Italy in 2003 and continued performing in area clubs in the 2010s with his Revue and with Roque's Blues Band, releasing several CDs, including *$20 Tips* in 2010.

RIVERS, JAMES *Jazz, rhythm and blues.* Saxophone, flute, harmonica, bagpipes, piano, vocals. Composer. Bandleader. (Born Apr. 18, 1937, New Orleans, Orleans Parish.) Veteran New Orleans jazz and rhythm and blues multi-instrumentalist worked as session musician in the 1950s and 1960s and appeared on recordings with **Huey "Piano" Smith**, **Eddie Bo**, **Allen Toussaint**, and others. Toured with Sam Cooke, Jackie Wilson, Jimmy Reed, and others and released numerous singles and several LPs as leader on Instant, Kon-Ti, Eight Ball, and J.B.'s from the 1960s through 1980s, including "It's All Over." Formed James Rivers Movement in the 1970s and continued performing with group into the 2010s, often incorporating flute and bagpipes into his jazz performances. Also appeared on soundtracks for several Clint Eastwood films, including *Bird*.

ROBERTS, NEAL *Blues.* Piano, vocals. (Born probably Jan. 1900, Logansport, DeSoto Parish; date and place of death unknown.) Enigmatic early prewar blues pianist and singer who recorded "Frisco Blues"/"Wild Jack Blues" with Billiken Johnson for Columbia in 1928.

ROBERTSON, LESTER *Rhythm and blues.* Vocals. Composer. Bandleader. (Born Jan. 14, 1938, Greensburg, St. Helena Parish; died June 9, 1964, Denver.)[6] Locally popular rhythm and blues singer was raised in Baton Rouge and began performing on the local blues scene in the mid-1950s. Made recording debut as vocalist on **Joe Hudson**'s Excello single "Baby Give Me a Chance" in 1957. Also submitted demo recordings backed by piano that year to Specialty Records, but all were rejected. Began fronting Little Richard's former band the Upsetters and in 1958 had regional hit for producer **Sam Montel** with "My Girl Across Town," Montel's first release. After two more singles on Montel in 1960 and a demo for **Cosimo Matassa** in 1961, continued performing around Baton Rouge as well as making extended regional tours. While staying in Denver and performing in local nightclubs was fatally shot at age 26 during an altercation with his wife and another man at an East Denver apartment complex.

ROBERTSON, SHERMAN *Blues, zydeco.* Guitar, vocals. Composer. Bandleader. (Born Oct. 27, 1948, Breaux Bridge, St. Martin Parish.) Renowned blues and zydeco guitarist and bandleader was raised in Houston from age two and began playing guitar in his early teens. By age 17 was performing in Houston clubs and in the mid- to late 1970s recorded two LPs for local label Lunar #2. In the 1980s toured and recorded with **Clifton Chenier** and **Rockin' Dopsie**, backing Dopsie on Paul Simon's *Graceland* album in 1986. After several years as guitarist with **Terrance Simien**, launched solo career in the early 1990s and released *I'm the Man* on Code Blue in 1994 to national acclaim. Throughout the 1990s and 2000s toured extensively and released three more recordings, including *Going Back Home* on Audioquest in 1998. Continued touring nationally and overseas until suffering a stroke in late 2011.

ROBERTSON, ZUE (Cornelius Alvin Robertson) *Jazz.* Trombone, piano, bass. (Born Mar. 7, 1891, New Orleans, Orleans Parish; died Nov. 22, 1943, New Orleans, Orleans Parish.)[7] Highly regarded early New Orleans jazz trombonist performed throughout Storyville District in the 1910s and worked with **Manuel Perez**, **King Oliver**, **Armand Piron**, **John Robichaux**, and others. Worked in Chicago in the late 1910s with Oliver, **Jelly Roll Morton**, and W. C. Handy and recorded with Morton in 1923. Toured with tent and circus shows and in later years lived and performed in New York and California. Died of heart failure at age 52.

ROBI, PAUL *Rhythm and blues.* Vocals, piano. Composer. (Born Aug. 20, 1931, New Orleans, Orleans Parish; died Feb. 1, 1989, Los Angeles.) Baritone singer of highly successful vocal group the Platters from 1954 through 1965. Appeared on numerous recordings with group, including hits "Only You," "The Magic Touch," and "The Great Pretender." In later years toured with his own version of the Platters.

ROBICHAUX, JOE *Jazz.* Piano. Bandleader. (Born Mar. 8, 1900, New Orleans, Orleans Parish; died Jan. 17, 1965, New Orleans, Orleans Parish.) Early New Orleans jazz piano player was influenced by uncle **John Robichaux** and jazz pianist **Steve Lewis**. In the late 1910s and 1920s worked with **Evan Thomas**, **Papa Celestin**, and **Lee Collins** and recorded with Jones-Collins Astoria Hot Eight in 1929. In 1931 formed New Orleans Rhythm Boys and recorded in 1933. Later expanded to a 15-piece swing band and toured extensively. Throughout the 1940s performed mainly as soloist in the French Quarter. In the 1950s worked as session musician for Imperial and worked regularly with **Lizzie Miles**, **Cousin Joe**, and **Paul Barbarin**. Toured with **George Lewis**'s band in the late 1950s and early 1960s and performed often at Preservation Hall until his death.

ROBICHAUX, JOHN *Jazz.* Drums, violin. Composer. Bandleader. (Born Jan. 16, 1866, Thibodaux, Lafouche Parish; died Oct. 31, 1938, New Orleans, Orleans Parish.)[8] Highly influential and important early New Orleans jazz bandleader who composed more than 350 songs. Moved to New Orleans in 1891 and played bass drum with Excelsior Brass Band from 1893 to 1905. Led various bands of his own from 1893 through his death, predominantly as a violinist. Locally renowned for his orchestra's infamous band competitions with **Buddy Bolden**'s group between Lincoln and Johnson Park as well as being the first group to use a trap drum set with band member **Dee Dee Chandler**'s innovative pedal system. In the spring of 1913 led a 36-piece symphonic orchestra. Uncle of **Joe** and **John Edward Robichaux**.

ROBICHAUX, JOHN EDWARD *Jazz.* Drums, vocals. (Born May 16, 1915, New Orleans, Orleans Parish; died Aug. 29, 2005, New Orleans, Orleans Parish.) Noted New Orleans drummer performed and recorded with New Orleans Ragtime Orchestra for several decades and appeared regularly at Preservation Hall. In the early 1980s performed in musical *One Mo' Time* and in 1999 recorded as coleader with **Lionel Ferbos**. Tragically drowned in home during Hurricane Katrina. Nephew of renowned bandleader **John Robichaux**.

ROBIN, MOISE *Cajun.* Accordion, vocals. Composer. Bandleader. (Born Jan. 4, 1911, near Arnaudville, St. Landry Parish; died Apr. 26, 2000, Arnaudville, St. Landry Parish.) Noted early Cajun accordion player best known for his prewar recordings with **Leo Soileau** in 1929. Began playing accordion at age nine and was soon playing local house dances, often with his accordionist father. In 1929 joined Soileau, replacing his late accordionist **Mayeus Lafleur** who was recently killed, and recorded 14 sides in three sessions for Paramount, Victor, and Vocalion, including "Easy Rider Blues" and "La Valse de la Rue Canal." Performed with Soileau through 1930 and continued playing for several more years before quitting music. In the early 1970s recorded a single each for Cajun Classics and Jador and made occasional festival appearances through the 1980s.

ROBINSON, ALVIN "SHINE" (*also* Al Robinson) *Rhythm and blues.* Guitar, vocals. Composer. (Born Dec. 22, 1937, New Orleans, Orleans Parish; died Jan. 24, 1989, New Orleans, Orleans Parish.) New Orleans deep soul singer and songwriter who had national hit with "Something You Got" in 1964. Worked as session guitarist in the late 1950s and made first recordings as leader for Imperial in 1961. In 1964 had hit covering **Chris Kenner**'s "Something You Got" for Tiger. Also released singles on Red Bird and Blue Cat, including "Down Home Girl," which was covered by the Rolling Stones in 1965. In the late 1960s recorded for Atco and Pulsar and continued working as session guitarist based in Los Angeles. In the 1970s performed and recorded extensively with **Dr. John** and appeared on sessions with **Chuck Carbo** and Big Joe Turner in the 1980s.

ROBINSON, ELZADIE *Blues.* Vocals. Composer. (Born Apr. 24, 1897, Logansport, DeSoto Parish; died probably Jan. 17, 1975, Flint, Michigan.) Noted classic blues vocalist and songwriter who made numerous recordings for Paramount from 1926 to 1929, including "Humming Blues" and "St. Louis Cyclone Blues." Composed the majority of the forty sides she recorded and was accompanied at times by Will Ezell, **Richard M. Jones**, **Johnny St. Cyr**, and Blind Blake. Also had several releases on Broadway label under name Bernice Duke or Bernice Drake and probably as Blanche Johnson on Herwin.

ROBINSON, ISAIAH "BIG IKE" *Jazz.* Trombone, guitar. (Born Mar. 16, 1891, Thibodaux, Lafourche Parish; died 1962, New Orleans, Orleans Parish.)[9] Early New Orleans jazz trombonist worked as guitarist with various bands in Thibodaux throughout the 1910s. Moved to New Orleans in 1920 and switched to trombone and by the mid-1920s was working with **Chris Kelly** and **Wooden Joe Nicholas**. Performed with **Kid Rena** into the 1930s and retired from music by end of decade.

ROBINSON, JAMES "BAT"/"BAT THE HUMMING BIRD" *Blues.* Vocals, piano, drums. Composer. (Born Dec. 25, 1903, Algiers, Orleans Parish; died Mar. 2, 1957, St. Louis, Missouri.) Early blues recording artist was raised in Memphis, Tennessee, and taught piano and drums by his father. In the early 1920s moved to Chicago and worked in clubs as solo pianist and also backed blues singers such as Bertha "Chippie" Hill. Relocated to St. Louis in 1930 and recorded several sides for Champion in 1931, including "Humming Blues," which showcased his unique vocal style. Worked largely outside music through the 1940s and performed sporadically in the 1950s, making one final recording in St. Louis just before his death.

ROBINSON, NATHAN "BIG JIM"/"JIM CROW" *Jazz.* Trombone. Composer. Bandleader. (Born Dec. 25, 1890, Deer Range, Plaquemines Parish; died May 4, 1976, New Orleans, Orleans Parish.)[10] Early New Orleans jazz trombonist best known for his work with **Bunk Johnson** and **George Lewis** in the 1940s and his later appearances at Preservation Hall. Began performing in the Army during World War I and in the late 1910s worked with Golden Leaf and **Papa Celestin**'s Tuxedo brass bands. In the

1920s and early 1930s worked with **Sam Morgan**'s band, recording with group in 1927. Performed with **Kid Howard** and **Captain John Handy** in the 1930s and in the 1940s worked and recorded with **Bunk Johnson**, **George Lewis**, **Kid Rena**, and others. Recorded extensively from the 1950s through mid-1970s as a leader and sideman. Toured nationally and abroad and appeared regularly at Preservation Hall from 1961 through the mid-1970s. Uncle of **Sidney "Jim Little" Brown**.

ROBINSON, ROBBY "MANN" (Junius Lee Robinson) *Zydeco.* Bass, saxophone, vocals. Composer. Bandleader. (Born Apr. 19, 1943, Sulphur, Calcasieu Parish.) Influential contemporary zydeco bass player best known for his work as cofounder of Zydeco Force with **Jeffrey Broussard**. Played saxophone in high school and college but later switched to bass in the early 1980s. Recorded with **Donald Jacobs** in 1988 shortly before forming Zydeco Force with Broussard, which quickly became leading zydeco band with its modern approach of incorporating funk bass lines and groundbreaking double bass drum beat known as "double clutchin'." Performed and recorded with group until joining **Keith Frank**'s band in the mid-1990s. In 2000 reunited with Zydeco Force and performed and recorded with group through end of decade, appearing in 2005 film *Shultze Gets the Blues* with band. Also mentored and produced **Guyland LeDay** in later years. Retired from performing in the early 2010s but continued composing and producing.

ROCKIN' DOPSIE (Alton Jay Rubin Sr.) *Zydeco.* Accordion, vocals. Composer. Bandleader. (Born Feb. 10, 1932, Carencro, Lafayette Parish; died Aug. 26, 1993, Lafayette, Lafayette Parish.) Internationally renowned zydeco accordionist and bandleader began playing at age eight, inspired by his father, and performed at local house dances in his teens. By the mid-1950s began performing in clubs around Lafayette with cousin **Chester Zeno**. Recorded debut single "A Lil Bon Temps" in 1968 on Bon Temps, which would later become a zydeco standard known as "Zydeco Boogaloo." Throughout the 1970s had numerous singles on Blues Unlimited and recorded debut LP, *Doin' the Zydeco,* for Sonet in 1976 which drew international acclaim. In the late 1970s began touring Europe and released five more albums for Sonet through the mid-1980s with sons Tiger (Alton Rubin Jr.) on drums and David (**Rockin' Dopsie Jr.**) on rubboard. Recorded with Paul Simon on 1986 LP *Graceland* and also had releases on Storyville, Maison de Soul, Mardi Gras, and Atlantic, notably *Louisiana Music* in 1991. Continued touring extensively until suffering a fatal heart attack at age 61. Also father of accordionists Anthony Rubin and **Dwayne Dopsie**.

ROCKIN' DOPSIE JR. (David Rubin) *Zydeco.* Rubboard, vocals. Composer. Bandleader. (Born Apr. 25, 1962, Lafayette, Lafayette Parish.) High-energy zydeco singer and bandleader began performing in his teens in various soul and rhythm and blues groups around Lafayette before joining his father **Rockin' Dopsie**'s Zydeco Twisters in the early 1980s. After his father's death in 1993 took over leadership of band with brothers Anthony on accordion and Tiger (Alton Jr.) on drums. In following years released CDs on AIM, Sound of New Orleans, and Mardi Gras, including debut CD, *Feet Don't Fail Me Now,* in 1995. Continued performing in the 2010s and remained popular act on the zydeco club and festival circuit.

ROCKIN' SIDNEY/COUNT ROCKIN' SIDNEY (Sidney Joseph Simien) *Zydeco, rhythm and blues, swamp pop.* Accordion, piano, guitar, harmonica, drums, vocals. Composer. Bandleader. (Born Apr. 9, 1938, Lebeau, St. Landry Parish; died Feb. 25, 1998, Lake Charles, Calcasieu Parish.) Highly influential and successful singer-songwriter and multi-instrumentalist best known for his 1985 international hit "My Toot Toot," which became the most recognized and successful zydeco recording of all time. Inspired by **Guitar Slim**, began playing piano, guitar, and harmonica as a child and by his mid-teens was performing in area clubs. After recording for Goldband and Carl, signed with Jin and from 1957 to 1964 released numerous rhythm and blues and swamp pop singles, including regional hit "You Ain't Nothin' But Fine"/"No Good Woman" in 1962. In 1965 relocated to Lake Charles and through the 1970s recorded numerous sides for Goldband as Count Rockin' Sidney. After performing mainly as solo organist in area clubs and releasing singles on his Bold label, learned accordion in the late 1970s and started recording zydeco on his Bally Hoo label, playing most of the instruments on the tracks. In 1982 signed with Maison de Soul and released numerous recordings in following years, including million-selling hit "My Toot Toot," which would be covered by numerous artists worldwide including **Fats Domino**, **Doug Kershaw**, **Jean Knight**, and John Fogerty. Continued recording for Maison de Soul and his own ZBC label and toured internationally through the early 1990s. In remaining years performed sporadically while operating a radio station and nightclub before succumbing to throat cancer at age 59.

RODRIGUE, EUGENE/GENE/"GENE KING" *Cajun.* Guitar, vocals. Composer. Bandleader. (Born Oct. 21, 1926, Cut Off, Lafourche Parish; died July 29, 1988, Lockport, Lafourche Parish.)[11] Cajun-country singer and songwriter best known for his 1954 recording "Jolie Fille." Began playing guitar in his father's band in the late 1940s. Made recording debut in 1953 for Folk-Star and following year had regional hit with "Jolie Fille" on Mela'dee and appeared on shows with major country artists Hank Williams and Jim Reeves. In 1960 had local hit with the Cajun-rocker "Little Cajun Girl," which was issued on Jin, Rod (as Gene King), and Richland (as Gene Rodgue). Released several more singles on Houma and Starbarn in the mid-1960s before retiring from music.

ROGER, ALDUS *Cajun.* Accordion. Composer. Bandleader. (Born Feb. 10, 1916, Carencro, Lafayette Parish; died Apr. 4, 1999, Lafayette, Lafayette Parish.)[12] Highly influential and popular early postwar Cajun accordion player, songwriter, and bandleader known as "The King of the French Accordion." Raised in a musical family, began playing accordion as a child and was inspired early on by **Lawrence Walker**. In the mid-1940s formed the Lafayette Playboys, which would include such prominent musicians as **Johnnie Allan**, **Doc Guidry**, **Aldus Broussard**, **Phillip Alleman**, **Belton Richard**, and **Fernest "Man" Abshire** throughout the next two decades. Began recording in the early 1950s for **J. D. Miller**'s Feature label and through the late 1960s had numerous releases on Goldband, TNT, Swallow, Cajun Classics, and La Louisianne, including "Hix Wagon Wheel Special," "Lafayette Two Step," and "Mardi Gras Dance." From 1955 to 1970 hosted weekly television show on Lafayette's KLFY, which greatly expanded his popularity. Recorded a single for Lanor in 1981 and slowed down considerably but continued performing occasionally into the 1990s.

ROGERS, BUCK (Lawrence Rodriguez) *Swamp pop.* Vocals. Composer. Bandleader. (Born Nov. 27, 1936, Brusly McCall, Ascension Parish; died Oct. 2, 2013, Prairieville, Ascension Parish.) Donaldsonville-area singer and songwriter best known for his 1959 swamp pop classic "Crazy Baby." Began performing in the mid-1950s and worked in bands the Night Owls and the Rockets. In 1958 formed Buck Rogers and His Jets and released two singles on Montel in 1959–60, including "Crazy Baby." Released several more singles on Carmie, Herald Recording Studio, and Jin in the 1960s and 1970s before switching to gospel in the mid-1980s.

ROGERS, ERNEST *Jazz.* Drums. (Born Apr. 19, 1891, New Orleans, Louisiana; died Aug. 26, 1956, New Orleans, Orleans Parish.) Early New Orleans jazz drummer began performing with **Edward Clem** around 1910 and worked with **Jack Carey**, **Richard M. Jones**, and Silver Leaf Orchestra through the 1910s. In the 1920s and 1930s performed with various brass bands, including Young Tuxedo. Recorded with **Bunk Johnson** in 1942 and **Big Eye Louis Nelson** in 1949.

ROMERO BROTHERS *See* Romero, Ophé.

ROMERO, OPHÉ "BABE" (Joseph Ophé Romero) *Cajun.* Accordion, vocals. (Born Jan. 8, 1925, St. Martinville, St. Martinville Parish; died Oct. 11, 2009, New Iberia, Iberia Parish.) Internationally renowned as the Romero Brothers with sibling and triangle player Lennis (1917–2004) who performed under St. Martinville's historic Evangeline Oak Tree for several decades. Began playing accordion in 1946 and became popular with locals and international tourists alike by singing and telling stories in both French and English.

ROMERO, RODDIE *Cajun, zydeco.* Accordion, guitar, vocals. Composer. Bandleader. (Born Nov. 5, 1975, Lafayette, Lafayette Parish.) Contemporary Cajun multi-instrumentalist and singer-songwriter began playing accordion as a child, inspired early on by **Buckwheat Zydeco**, **Lawrence Walker**, and **Clifton Chenier** and began touring in his early teens. In 1988 started playing slide guitar after hearing **Sonny Landreth**. Released debut CD, *New Kid in Town,* on Swallow at age 15 and soon formed Hub City All-Stars, which included longtime member keyboardist-songwriter Eric Adcock. Continued performing with All-Stars through 2010s with acclaimed releases *The La Louisianne Sessions* in 2007 and *Gulfstream* in 2016. Also worked and recorded with **Yvette Landry**'s Jukes.

ROPPOLO, LEON "RAP" *Jazz.* Clarinet, saxophone, guitar. Composer. (Born Mar. 16, 1902, Lutcher, St. James Parish; died Oct. 5, 1943, New Orleans, Orleans Parish.) Highly regarded and influential early New Orleans jazz clarinetist best known for his work as an early jazz soloist with the New Orleans Rhythm Kings. Moved to New Orleans in the early 1910s and later worked with

Paul Mares and **George Brunies**. Left New Orleans in 1917 to tour vaudeville circuit with Bee Palmer. In the early 1920s helped form New Orleans Rhythm Kings in Chicago and appeared on their landmark early sessions. Worked in New York and Texas before returning to New Orleans in 1925 and recording with Halfway House Orchestra. Shortly afterwards was committed to state mental hospital where he spent the majority of his remaining years.

ROTIS, JOE *Jazz.* Trombone, vocals. (Born Oct. 30, 1917, New Orleans, Orleans Parish; died Apr. 24, 1965, New Orleans, Orleans Parish.) New Orleans jazz trombonist worked with several groups in the 1940s and 1950s, such as **Irving Fazola**'s Dixielanders, Original Basin Street Six, and **Sharkey Bonano**'s Kings of Dixieland.

ROUSE, MORRIS *Jazz.* Piano, vocals. (Born Mar. 14, 1897, New Orleans, Orleans Parish; died Dec. 7, 1982, Los Angeles.)[13] Early New Orleans jazz pianist and singer who recorded with **Louis Dumaine**'s Jazzola Eight in 1927 and also appeared on sessions backing blues singers **Ann Cook**, Ruth Green, and Genevieve Davis.

ROUZAN, WANDA LEE *Rhythm and blues, jazz.* Vocals. Bandleader. (Born Oct. 29, 1947, New Orleans, Orleans Parish.) New Orleans rhythm and blues singer who recorded in the early 1960s as lead member of the Rouzan Sisters. Began singing at age 13 with older sisters Barbara and Laura in churches and talent shows. In 1963 recorded two singles on Frisco with siblings as the Rouzan Sisters, including local hit "Men of War." Also released two singles as leader and toured with **Clarence "Gatemouth" Brown** and **Lee Dorsey** in the 1960s. In the early 1980s joined **David Lastie**'s band Taste of New Orleans and continued leading group after Lastie's death in 1987. Performed in several musicals and released three CDs on her Huckle-Buck label. Continued performing and touring overseas in the 2010s.

ROY, CURZY "PORK CHOP" *Cajun.* Drums. (Born May 4, 1929, Eunice, St. Landry Parish; died Jan. 31, 2009, Ville Platte, Evangeline Parish.) Early postwar Cajun drummer best known for his work as member of **Harry Choates**'s band in the mid- to late 1940s, appearing on numerous Choates recordings, including 1946 hit "Jole Blon." Also performed and recorded with **Jimmy C. Newman**, **Chuck Guillory**, and **Papa Cairo** in the late 1940s and in following decades worked with **Al Terry**, **Hadley J. Castille**, Don Fontenot, and others. In the late 1980s reunited with Guillory on Arhoolie LP *Grand Texas.* Continued performing in the 1990s and early 2000s as member of Basile Cajun Band with **Nonc Allie Young** and **Ray Landry**.

ROY, DALLAS *Cajun.* Guitar, drums, vocals. Composer. Bandleader. (Born Jan. 10, 1928, Duson, Acadia Parish; died Feb. 7, 2016, Nederland, Texas.) Veteran Cajun guitarist and singer-songwriter began learning guitar at age 10 growing up in Rayne. Later relocated to east Texas in the early 1940s where he continued performing for 70-plus years. In the 1960s performed and recorded with the Rambling Aces, which included at times **Rodney LeJeune**, **Marc Savoy**, **Andrew Cormier**, and **Jackie Caillier**, releasing numerous singles, including "Gran Mamou" and "Cajun from Church Point." In 1996 recorded with Caillier and **Ivy Dugas**'s Cajun Cousins on their debut release, *Front Porch Cajun Music,* and continued performing around east Texas into the 2010s.

ROYAL, DYNAMIC DUKE *See* Kent, Luther.

RUFFINS, KERMIT *Jazz.* Trumpet. Composer. Bandleader. (Born Dec. 19, 1964, New Orleans, Orleans Parish.) Highly regarded and charismatic New Orleans jazz trumpeter and bandleader and cofounder of the influential Rebirth Brass Band in the early 1980s. Began playing trumpet during his early teens and was heavily influenced by **Louis Armstrong**. In 1983 formed Rebirth Brass Band with Tremé high-school friends **Phil** and **Keith Frazier**. Toured extensively and recorded with Rebirth until going solo in 1992 and forming his band the Barbecue Swingers. Held popular weekly gig at Vaughan's in the French Quarter for ten years and released debut recording *Held on a String* on Justice in 1993. Released numerous CDs on Basin Street label and toured extensively into the 2010s.

RUSH, BOBBY (Emmett Ellis Jr.) *Rhythm and blues.* Vocals, harmonica, guitar. Composer. Bandleader. (Born Nov. 10, 1936, Homer, Claiborne Parish.)[14] Internationally renowned soul-blues singer and master showman best known for his bawdy, high-energy stage shows throughout a music career which lasted more than 70 years. The son of a preacher, began performing in his early teens with blues guitarist Boyd Gilmore in Pine Bluff, Arkansas. Relocated to Chicago in the 1950s and performed with various musicians, including Freddie King and Luther Allison, and had singles on Jerry-O, Starville, Palos, Checker, ABC, and Salem in the 1960s.

In 1971 had first hit with "Chicken Heads" on Galaxy. Releases followed on On Top, Warner Bros., and Jewel/ Ronn and in 1979 recorded debut album *Rush Hour* for Philadelphia International. Relocated to Jackson, Mississippi, in the early 1980s and recorded five albums for LaJam, notably *Sue* in 1981, the title cut becoming a staple of his live shows. Throughout the 1990s and 2000s toured extensively and expanded audience outside of the Chitlin Circuit with numerous releases on Urgent, Waldoxy, and his own Deep Rush label in his self-described "folk-funk" style. Continued performing nationally and overseas in the 2010s with several critically acclaimed releases, including *Down in Louisiana* on Deep Rush in 2013 and *Porcupine Meat* on Rounder in 2016. Also appeared in several films, including *I Am the Blues* in 2015 and *Dolemite Is My Name* with Eddie Murphy in 2019.

S

SAILOR BOY *See* Spearman, Alex.

SAM, AMBROSE "POTATO" *Zydeco.* Accordion, vocals. Composer. Bandleader. (Born Oct. 2, 1919, Grand Coteau, St. Landry Parish; died Nov. 22, 1995, Opelousas, St. Landry Parish.) Influential early zydeco accordionist began playing the instrument as a child, learning from his father, Moise. In the 1940s relocated to Lake Charles area and performed locally, often playing "Paper in My Shoe," which would be recorded by **Boozoo Chavis** years later. In 1953 relocated to Los Angeles and was among the first zydeco musicians to perform on the West Coast. Returned to Louisiana in the mid-1970s and appeared on Arhoolie LP *Old Time Zydeco* with **Preston Frank** in 1983. Brother of **Hebert "Good Rockin'" Sam** and uncle of **Leon Sam**.

SAM BROTHERS *See* Sam, Leon [Notable Musicians Born outside Louisiana].

SAM, HERBERT "GOOD ROCKIN'" *Zydeco.* Accordion, vocals. Bandleader. (Born Apr. 2, 1924, Grand Coteau, St. Landry Parish; died May 21, 2004, Lawtell, St. Landry Parish.) Zydeco accordionist relocated to Houston and began performing as Good Rockin' Sam, recording for Arhoolie in 1961. In the late 1970s organized his five sons, including **Leon Sam**, to perform as teenaged contemporary zydeco act Sam Brothers Five, who recorded for Arhoolie and became a regional sensation. Brother of **Ambrose Sam**.

SAMPLE, ROOSEVELT *Blues.* Drums. (Born Aug. 9, 1934, Baton Rouge, EBR Parish; died Feb. 15, 2007, Baton Rouge, EBR Parish.) Active drummer on the early Baton Rouge blues scene in the 1950s and 1960s who worked with **Buddy Guy**, **Lightnin' Slim**, **Slim Harpo**, and others. In the 1970s and 1980s performed regularly with **Raful Neal**.

SAMPY, CLAYTON *Zydeco.* Accordion, bass, vocals. (Born Jan. 28, 1949, Carencro, Lafayette Parish.) Revered traditional zydeco piano accordionist was raised in a musical family and learned bass in his late teens. In the 1970s performed with his guitarist brother Eugene in their cousin **Hiram Sampy**'s zydeco band Sampy and the Bad Habits. Inspired by **Clifton Chenier**, began playing accordion in 1980 and soon formed his band the Zydeco Farmers, occasionally filling in for an ailing Chenier at clubs and festivals. In the 1990s recorded behind **Eugene Alfred** for Vidrine label and continued performing with various groups through the 2000s. Son of Eugene Sampy Sr., who was also a respected local accordion player. Mentor of **Sunpie Barnes**, **Jude Taylor**, and **Nathan Williams**.

SAMPY, HIRAM "LOON" *Zydeco.* Accordion, vocals. Composer. Bandleader. (Born Nov. 19, 1926, Carencro, Lafayette Parish; died Nov. 12, 2002, Carencro, Lafayette Parish.) Noted zydeco accordionist and bandleader began playing at age six, inspired by his father, Avery (1899–1968), who performed at local la la house dances. By the 1960s he was performing with his own band, playing rhythm and blues and rock and roll. In 1972 switched to playing soul- and funk-infused zydeco as Sampy and the Bad Habits, which included cousins Eugene and **Clayton Sampy**. From 1975 to 1980 released several singles and LP *Zydeco Gumbo* on Caillier and appeared on Rounder's 1979 LP *Zodico: Louisiana Créole Music* produced by folklorist Nick Spitzer. Continued performing at clubs and festivals through the late 1990s.

SAMS, T. W. (Thomas W. Sams) *Blues.* Vocals. (Born Dec. 21, 1928, Caddo Parish; died Feb. 10, 1995, Los Angeles.) Enigmatic blues singer who recorded several sides for Johnny Otis's Dig label in Los Angeles in 1955, notably

"Springtime Blues" backed by ace guitarist Pete "Guitar" Lewis.

SAMUELS, CLARENCE *Rhythm and blues.* Vocals. Composer. Bandleader. (Born Oct. 30, 1923, Baton Rouge, EBR Parish; died May 21, 2002, Westwego, Jefferson Parish.) Largely unheralded blues shouter best known for his late 1940s and 1950s recordings such as "Chicken Hearted Woman." Began performing in his father's band in Baton Rouge during his teens and in the mid-1940s worked in New Orleans with **Roy Brown** as the Blues Twins. In 1947 was one of the first artists on Chess Brothers' Aristocrat label with jump blues single "Lolly Pop Mama"/"Boogie Woogie Blues." Through the mid-1960s had releases on numerous labels, including Downbeat, Freedom, Park, Lamp, Excello, and Sharon, recording at times with such noted musicians as **Edgar Blanchard**'s Gondoliers, **Dave Bartholomew**, **Johnny Copeland**, and Jay McShann. After a long hiatus staged comeback in 2000 with self-produced release *House of Blues* and several high-profile festival appearances in Europe and New Orleans shortly before his death.

SANFORD, BILLY *Rockabilly, country.* Guitar, mandolin, bass. (Born Jan. 9, 1940, Natchitoches, Natch. Parish.) Highly accomplished guitarist began performing in clubs during his teens and in the late 1950s appeared regularly on Shreveport's *Louisiana Hayride.* In the early 1960s worked in a rockabilly band with Bob Luman and relocated to Nashville. Toured and recorded with Roy Orbison in 1964 and throughout following four decades worked as in-demand session musician, appearing on hundreds of recordings by artists such as Elvis Presley, Waylon Jennings, George Jones, Kenny Rogers, Tammy Wynette, Ray Charles, John Denver, Don Williams, and many others.

SANTIAGO, BURNELL (Louis Prosper Santiago) *Jazz.* Piano. (Born July 17, 1915, New Orleans, Orleans Parish—Jan. 5, 1944, New Orleans, Orleans Parish.)[1] Virtuosic New Orleans boogie-woogie piano player considered by many of his contemporaries to be the greatest pianist of his era. Billed as the "King of Boogie Woogie" in the 1930s and worked as both a soloist and in trios. Made only two known recordings on a primitive home recorder in 1942. Died of kidney infection and septicemia at age 28. Brother of **Lester Santiago** and nephew of **Willie Santiago**.

SANTIAGO, LESTER "BLACKIE" *Jazz.* Piano, vocals. Bandleader. (Born Aug. 14, 1909, New Orleans, Orleans Parish; died Jan. 18, 1965, New Orleans, Orleans Parish.) Older brother of **Burnell Santiago**, began performing in the late 1920s with **Arnold DePass**. Recorded extensively in the 1950s and early 1960s, appearing on sessions with **Paul Barbarin**, **George Lewis**, **Lizzie Miles**, **Thomas Jefferson**, **Louis Cottrell Jr.**, **John Brunious**, **Frog Joseph**, and others and led several bands. Nephew of **Willie Santiago**.

SANTIAGO, WILLIE *Jazz.* Banjo, guitar. (Born Sept. 7, 1885, New Orleans, Orleans Parish; died Nov. 26, 1949, New Orleans, Orleans Parish.)[2] Highly regarded early New Orleans jazz guitarist and banjo player known for his distinctive rhythmic style. Performed with various bands in the Storyville District and reportedly played with **Buddy Bolden**. In the late 1910s worked with Maple Leaf Orchestra and in the 1920s performed with **Louis Armstrong**, Luis Russell, **Peter Bocage**, and **Paul Barbarin**. Recorded with **Kid Rena** in 1940 for Delta. Uncle of **Lester** and **Burnell Santiago**.

SAUNDERS, SYLVESTER "SLIM" *Rhythm and blues.* Vocals. Composer. (Born Dec. 24, 1929, New Orleans, Orleans Parish; died Sept. 14, 1998, New Orleans, Orleans Parish.) New Orleans rhythm and blues singer had a single each on Specialty and Chess in 1953, notably "Let's Have Some Fun." Not to be confused with George Sanders LeBlanc, who recorded as Slim Sanders.

SAVANT, PAT (Patrick Adam Savant) *Cajun.* Accordion. Composer. Bandleader. (Born Sept. 15, 1955, Lake Charles, Calcasieu Parish.) Noted Lake Charles Cajun accordionist joined Sundown Playboys at age 15 after bandleader and accordionist **Lionel Cormier** succumbed to a fatal heart attack. Recorded two singles with band the following year for Kajun, including "Saturday Night Special," which was issued internationally on the Beatles' Apple Records after his unsolicited submission to the label. Continued performing and recording with Sundown Playboys for several years and also recorded single with **Wayne Toups**. In 1980 formed the Louisiana Playboys, featuring **Joe Turner** on vocals, and released a single and LP *Louisiana Cajun Music* on Kajun in 1981. Toured England with group in 1984 and recorded two LPs for JSP, including *Saturday Night Special.* Continued working outside music as a schoolteacher in following years and performed occasionally on weekends and breaks. In 2003 released CD *Cajun Instrumentals à la Nouvelle Mode* on Swallow.

SAVOIE, JEAN *Cajun.* Accordion, drums, vocals. Composer. Bandleader. (Born May 7, 1947, Crowley, Acadia Parish; died Apr. 8, 2001, Crowley, Acadia Parish.) Cajun accordionist and singer began playing at age 18 and performed with **Blackie Frugé** and **Bobby Leger** through the 1970s, recording with Leger for Bayou Classics and Swallow. In the 1980s formed the Bayou Ramblers, with whom he recorded and toured nationally.

SAVOY, ASHTON *Blues, zydeco.* Guitar, vocals. Composer. Bandleader. (Born Oct. 29, 1928, Sunset, St. Landry Parish; died May 15, 2009, Houston.) Noted Texas-based blues guitarist and singer began playing guitar as a child, learning from his Creole father, who played guitar and fiddle. At age 16 relocated to Lake Charles and soon formed his own band, which performed throughout south Louisiana. In the 1950s hired pianist **Katie Webster** and performed with her for several years, recording a single with Webster on Kry (as Ashton Conroy) as well as several sides for Goldband and the single "Denga Denga" for Hollywood in the late 1950s. Relocated to Houston in 1960 and continued performing in area clubs while working a day job. In the 1980s and 1990s worked with local zydeco bands and occasionally led his own blues band until injuring his left hand in electrical accident in 1999, which limited his playing in later years.

SAVOY, JOEL *Cajun.* Fiddle, guitar, bass, drums, vocals. Composer. Bandleader. (Born July 26, 1980, Eunice, St. Landry Parish.) Renowned Cajun fiddle player, singer-songwriter, and producer, and oldest son of internationally acclaimed Cajun musicians **Ann** and **Marc Savoy**. Began playing fiddle as a child, learning directly from local masters such as **Dennis McGee**, **Dewey Balfa**, and **Wade Frugé**, and later toured internationally with Savoy Family Band. In the late 1990s cofounded contemporary Cajun band Red Stick Ramblers and toured and recorded with group for several years. In 2006 started Valcour Records, which became one of the region's premier roots labels. Continued performing and recording in the 2010s with various musicians and projects, including with wife Kelli Jones-Savoy, which resulted in local hit "I'll Be There" in 2014. Brother of Sarah and **Wilson Savoy**.

SAVOY, MARC *Cajun.* Accordion, vocals. Composer. Bandleader. (Born Oct. 1, 1940, Eunice, St. Landry Parish.) Internationally renowned Cajun accordionist, instrument maker, and patriarch of prestigious Cajun family of Eunice which includes wife **Ann**, sons **Joel** and **Wilson**, and daughter Sarah Savoy. Began playing accordion at age 12, inspired by house performances by his grandfather, as well as **Dennis McGee**, Alton and **Cyprien Landreneau**, and other local musicians. Also began repairing accordions at a young age and later graduated to building them, influenced greatly by **Sidney Brown** and **Shine Mouton**. In the 1960s recorded numerous singles with the Rambling Aces and also as leader for Crazy Cajun and opened the Savoy Music Center in Eunice in 1966. Began decades-long association with Chris Strachwitz of Arhoolie Records and recorded with numerous artists, including **Wade Frugé**, **Chuck Guillory**, **Wallace "Cheese" Read**, and the **Balfa Brothers**, among others, as well as several releases as coleader of Savoy-Doucet Cajun Band with wife Ann and **Michael Doucet**. In the early 1990s was featured in documentary film *Marc and Ann* and was recipient of National Endowment for the Arts National Heritage Fellowship. Continued touring internationally with Savoy Family Band in the 2010s with Ann, Joel, and Wilson and operating his music store that holds weekly Saturday morning Cajun jams which attract tourists worldwide. Daughter Sarah Savoy is a Cajun accordionist and singer based in France.

SAVOY, WILSON *Cajun.* Accordion, piano, fiddle, guitar, vocals. Composer. Bandleader. (Born Feb. 1, 1982, Eunice, St. Landry Parish.) Son of renowned Cajun musicians **Ann** and **Marc Savoy**, Cajun multi-instrumentalist began playing piano at age 10, inspired by **Jerry Lee Lewis** and boogie-woogie players such as Pete Johnson and Albert Ammons. Toured regularly with Savoy Family Band and in his late teens started playing accordion, influenced by his father as well as **Amédé Ardoin** and **Iry LeJeune**. In 2004 joined older brother **Joel Savoy** in Red Stick Ramblers and the following year formed highly acclaimed Cajun band the Pine Leaf Boys. Continued touring and recording with Pine Leaf Boys, Savoy Family Band, and other projects in the 2010s, including as member of the acclaimed Band Courtbouillon with **Steve Riley** and **Wayne Toups**. Brother of France-based Cajun musician Sarah Savoy.

SAYLES, EMANUEL *Jazz.* Banjo, guitar, vocals. Composer. Bandleader. (Born Jan. 31, 1907, Donaldsonville, Ascension Parish; died Oct. 5, 1986, New Orleans, Orleans Parish.) Internationally renowned early New Orleans jazz banjo player and guitarist moved to New Orleans with his family in 1915. Around age 10 started taking guitar lessons from his father, **George Sayles**. From 1924 to 1927 performed in Pensacola, Florida, and surrounding area with the Pensacola Jazzers. Returned to New Orleans and worked with **Bébé Ridgley**'s Tuxedo Band and on riverboats with **Sidney Desvigne**, **Fate Marable**, and **Armand Piron** in the late 1920s and appeared on famed Jones-Collins Astoria Hot Eight recordings. Throughout the 1930s worked regularly with Piron and **Peter Bocage** and from 1939 to 1949 led his own band in Chicago. In the late 1950s began performing regularly with **George Lewis** and throughout the next decade worked and recorded extensively on sessions as leader and sideman with Lewis, **Sweet Emma Barrett**, **Peter Bocage**, **Kid Thomas**, **Punch Miller**, and others. Appeared regularly at Preservation Hall in the 1970s and 1980s and starred in PBS documentary *This Cat Can Play Anything* in 1980.

SAYLES, GEORGE *Jazz.* Guitar, banjo. (Born Nov. 13, 1876, New Orleans, Orleans Parish; died Oct. 27, 1955, New Orleans, Orleans Parish.)[3] Early New Orleans jazz guitar and banjo player performed with Silver Leaf Orchestra from the mid-1890s through 1918. After the 1920s worked mainly as porter and played music only occasionally on weekends. Father of **Emanuel Sayles**.

SBARBARO, TONY "TONY SPARGO" *Jazz.* Drums, kazoo. Bandleader. (Born June 27, 1897, New Orleans, Orleans Parish; died Oct. 30, 1969, New York City.) Influential early New Orleans jazz drummer for Original Dixieland Jass Band, which made the first jazz record in 1917. In the early 1910s worked with **Papa Jack Laine** and **Merritt Brunies** and in 1916 moved to Chicago and joined Original Dixieland Jass Band. Following year appeared on ODJB's historic recording session and continued performing and recording in all reformations of the group through the early 1960s. In the late 1930s relocated to New York and worked with Phil Napoleon, Miff Mole, Muggsy Spanier, and others and led his own bands. Recorded with Eddie Condon in 1943 and continued performing until retiring from music in the early 1960s.

SCATTER, BATTLERACK (Battlerac B. Scatter) *Blues.* Guitar, vocals. Composer. Bandleader. (Born Mar. 15, 1943, Holden, Livingston Parish.) Baton Rouge blues guitarist and singer-songwriter who released CD *The Blues Ain't for Everybody* on Cititrax in 1996, containing all original material.

SCHILLING, HAPPY (George Schilling) *Jazz.* Trombone, guitar, bass. Bandleader. (Born Apr. 26, 1886, New Orleans, Orleans Parish; died Feb. 28, 1964, New Orleans, Orleans Parish.) Influential early New Orleans jazz bandleader began performing with **Papa Jack Laine** and led several popular jazz bands in the 1910s and 1920s, including Happy Schilling's Dixie Jazz Band. Retired from music in the mid-1950s. Father of jazz saxophonist George Schilling Jr.

SCHOOLBOY CLEVE (Cleveland White) *Blues.* Harmonica, guitar, vocals. Composer. Bandleader. (Born June 10, 1925, Livingston, Livingston Parish; died Feb. 5, 2008, Daly City, California.) Early swamp blues harmonica player and singer began performing in Baton Rouge around age 12 and was later greatly inspired by a local performance by Sonny Boy Williamson (Rice Miller). Recorded single "She's Gone"/"Strange Letter Blues" for **J. D. Miller**'s Feature label in 1954 and also backed **Lightnin' Slim** on several sessions for Miller. In the late 1950s and early 1960s recorded for Vivid Sound and Reynaud before relocating to the California Bay Area. Resumed performing in the early 1970s and had singles on Blues Connoisseur and his own Cherrie label. In 2006 released first full-length album *South to West: Iron and Gold* on Cherrie which collected his recordings which spanned fifty years.

SCOTT, ARTHUR "BUD" *Jazz.* Guitar, banjo, violin, vocals. (Born Jan. 11, 1890, New Orleans, Orleans Parish; died July 2, 1949, Los Angeles.) Early New Orleans jazz multi-instrumentalist began performing as a child and played with **Buddy Bolden**, **John Robichaux**, and **Freddie Keppard** while in his teens. Around 1913 toured southern vaudeville circuit and in the mid- to late 1910s performed in clubs and theater orchestras in New York. In 1923 moved to Chicago and worked and recorded with **King Oliver**. Worked with **Kid Ory** in California before returning to Chicago in 1927 to record with **Baby Dodds** and **Jelly Roll Morton**. In 1928 performed and recorded with **Jimmie Noone**. Relocated to California in the early 1930s and worked with **Mutt Carey** and led his own trio. Performed with Ory between 1944 and 1948 and appeared in 1947 film *New Orleans* with **Louis Armstrong**. Retired from music after suffering a stroke in 1948. Not to be confused with early jazz musician (Clarence) Bud Scott from Natchez, Mississippi.

SEGURA BROTHERS *See* Segura, Dewey.

SEGURA, CHRIS *Cajun.* Fiddle. Composer. (Born May 22, 1984, Berwick, St. Mary Parish.) Cofounder of acclaimed contemporary Cajun band Feufollet began playing fiddle at age four and in his teens won several prestigious local and state fiddle championships. In the late 1990s began performing and recording with Feufollet and several years later helped form Cajun band Lafayette Rhythm

Devils. Continued performing with various groups and working as violin maker in the 2010s. Relative of **Dewey Segura**.

SEGURA, DEWEY *Cajun.* Accordion, vocals. Composer. Bandleader. (Born Feb. 12, 1902, Delcambre, Vermilion Parish; died Nov. 15, 1987, Delcambre, Vermilion Parish.) Early Cajun accordion player and singer who along with brother Edier were among the first to record Cajun music. Raised in a musical French-speaking family, began playing accordion at age eight and soon was performing at house dances with his father. In Dec. 1928 recorded four sides for Columbia in New Orleans with brother Edier on triangle which were issued as by the Segura Brothers. Following year recorded four sides for Columbia with guitarist Didier Hébert, including "Rosalia." Continued performing around Delcambre area and in 1934 made field recordings with Edier for folklorists John and Alan Lomax. Worked mainly outside music in following years but performed occasionally on part-time basis. In 1975 made final recordings for musicologist Richard K. Spottswood.

SEIBERT, LARRY *Rhythm and blues.* Vocals. Composer. (Born Mar. 1, 1943, Mix, Pointe Coupee Parish.) New Orleans deep soul singer who recorded single "Never Come Back"/"You Said" on Whit around 1963. Worked with **Raful Neal** in the early 1960s before relocating to New Orleans in 1965. Performed with **Eddie Bo** and various local groups before retiring from music in the 1970s.

SELMA, HARRY *See* Anselmi, Harry.

SEMIEN, JOHN *Creole.* Accordion, vocals. Bandleader. (Born Apr. 15, 1918, Lebeau, St. Landry Parish; died May 19, 1983, South San Francisco.) Influential Bay Area accordionist who was among the first to perform the black Creole music of rural southwest Louisiana in Northern California. Raised in a musical family, began playing accordion as a child after family moved to Lawtell. In the late 1940s settled in the Bay Area and performed at house dances through the early 1960s. In 1964 formed the Opelousas Playboys and recorded for Arhoolie. Throughout the 1970s continued performing with band and recorded self-titled LP for La Louisianne. Influenced many Bay Area zydeco musicians, including **Queen Ida**, **Al Rapone**, and **Danny Poullard**. Brother Joe Semien (1923–1999) was also a noted California-based accordion player and singer.

SEMIEN, KING IVORY LEE *See* King Ivory Lee.

SEMIEN, NOLTON "HORSE" *Creole.* Accordion, vocals. (Born June 17, 1939, near Pitreville, Acadia Parish; died May 22, 2019, Eunice, St. Landry Parish.)[4] Noted Creole accordionist and singer was raised in Lawtell, St. Landry Parish, and learned to play the instrument in his early teens, inspired by his father, Willie, who was a locally renowned accordion player. By age 15 was performing at local la la house dances. Later performed regularly with **Calvin Carrière** in the St. Landry Playboys. In 2006 appeared on CD *La Danse Finis Pas: Classic Louisiana Creole Music* with **Joe Hall** and in 2012 released *Oh Lucille* on Fruge Records. Continued performing occasionally at clubs and festivals into his 70s.

SHANNON, MEM *Blues.* Guitar, vocals. Composer. Bandleader. (Born Dec. 21, 1959, New Orleans, Orleans Parish.) New Orleans blues guitarist and singer-songwriter began playing guitar at age 15, greatly inspired by a performance by B.B. King. Performed in several cover bands in the 1970s but throughout the 1980s worked as a cab driver. In the early 1990s formed Mem Shannon and the Membership and performed around New Orleans. In 1995 recorded critically acclaimed CD *A Cab Driver's Blues* which contained his compositions about experiences driving a New Orleans taxi. In 1996 started performing full-time and through the 2010s toured nationally and overseas with releases on Hannibal, Shanachie, and Northern Blues.

SHARIF, JAMIL *Jazz.* Trumpet. Composer. Bandleader. (Born Sept. 11, 1963, New Orleans, Orleans Parish.) Noted jazz trumpeter began playing at age 14 and studied music at Southern University under **Kidd Jordan** and **Alvin Batiste**. In the 1990s and 2000s worked extensively on television and film projects, including the 2004 hit film *Ray.* Also appeared on recordings with B.B. King, **Dr. John**, **Irma Thomas**, **Johnny Adams**, **Wynton Marsalis**, **Neville Brothers**, **Clarence "Gatemouth" Brown**, and others. Released debut CD *Portraits of New Orleans* in 1993 and continued to record and perform into the 2010s. Son of renowned jazz trumpeter **Emery Humphrey Thompson**.

SHARIF, UMAR *See* Thompson, Emery Humphrey.

SHARKEY *See* Bonano, Joseph.

SHARP, WAYNE *Blues.* Piano, organ, vocals. Bandleader. (Born Sept. 4, 1949, Houma, Terrebonne Parish.) Blues pianist and bandleader began performing at age 17 in bars along the Mississippi Gulf Coast. Toured and recorded as member of blues singer-guitarist Michael Burks's band from 2000 until Burks's death in 2012.

Based in Gulfport, continued performing with his band the Sharpshooters in the late 2010s.

SHARRIFF, OMAR (Dave Alexander Elam) *Blues.* Piano, vocals. Composer. Bandleader. (Born Mar. 10, 1938, Shreveport, Caddo Parish; died Jan. 8, 2012, Marshall, Texas.) Master boogie-woogie piano player and singer-songwriter was raised in Marshall, Texas, and named after Shreveport pianist **Black Ivory King** (Dave Alexander). After a stint in the Navy in the late 1950s, settled in Oakland, California, and worked with Big Mama Thornton, Jimmy Witherspoon, L. C. "Good Rockin'" Robinson, **Buddy Guy**, Albert Collins, and others. In 1968 made his first recordings for World Pacific and released critically acclaimed LPs *The Rattler* and *The Dirt on the Ground* on Arhoolie in 1973–74. Throughout the 1970s appeared at major blues festivals, including Ann Arbor and San Francisco, and toured Europe several times. In the mid-1970s changed name and began performing as Omar the Magnificent. After a long recording hiatus released critically acclaimed album *The Raven* on Arhoolie in 1992, widely regarded as a masterpiece of boogie-woogie piano. Three releases followed on Have Mercy! including *Black Widow Spider.* Continued performing around Sacramento area in the 2000s. Relocated back to Marshall to local acclaim shortly before his death of self-inflicted gunshot wound, reportedly after suffering from serious health issues.

SHEPHERD, KENNY WAYNE *Blues-rock.* Guitar, vocals. Composer. Bandleader. (Born June 12, 1977, Shreveport, Caddo Parish.) Internationally renowned blues-rock guitarist began playing at age seven, inspired by Stevie Ray Vaughan. Signed major label record deal with producer Irving Azoff and released *Ledbetter Heights* on Giant in 1995 which was major hit. Successful releases followed on Revolution and Reprise through the 2000s, including *10 Days Out* in 2007, which featured **Clarence "Gatemouth" Brown**, Hubert Sumlin, B.B. King, **Buddy Flett**, and others. In the 2010s continued to tour internationally with releases on Roadrunner and Concord, including *Lay It on Down* in 2017.

SHERMAN, HERMAN E. *Jazz.* Saxophone. Bandleader. (Born June 28, 1923, New Orleans, Orleans Parish; died Sept. 10, 1984, New Orleans, Orleans Parish.) New Orleans jazz saxophonist began performing in the 1940s and worked with various groups in the 1950s, including **George Williams**, Eureka, and Young Tuxedo brass bands. Made recordings with Young Tuxedo in 1959 and 1983 and led his own band from 1972 until his death.

SHIELDS, EDDIE *Jazz.* Piano. (Born Sept. 1, 1896, New Orleans, Orleans Parish; died Aug. 24, 1938, New Orleans, Orleans Parish.)[5] Middle brother of renowned early New Orleans jazz family which included Pat, **Harry**, and **Larry Shields**. In the 1920s worked with **Santo Pecora** and **Leon Roppolo** and performed in **Alcide Nunez**'s band in Chicago.

SHIELDS, HARRY *Jazz.* Clarinet, saxophone. (Born June 30, 1899, New Orleans, Orleans Parish; died Jan. 19, 1971, New Orleans, Orleans Parish.) Youngest brother of prominent early New Orleans jazz family performed with **Johnny Bayersdorffer** and worked and recorded with **Norman Brownlee** in the 1920s. In the 1950s worked with **Johnny Wiggs**, **Sharkey Bonano**, and others, and recorded with **Tom Brown**, **Al Hirt**, and **Armand Hug**. Brother of Pat, **Eddie**, and **Larry Shields**.

SHIELDS, LARRY *Jazz.* Clarinet. Composer. (Born Sept. 13, 1893, New Orleans, Orleans Parish; died Nov. 21, 1953, Los Angeles.) Influential early New Orleans jazz clarinetist and composer who appeared on the first jazz recording as member the Original Dixieland Jass Band (ODJB). Began playing clarinet at age 14 and in following years performed with **Papa Jack Laine**'s Reliance Brass Band and **Nick LaRocca**. In 1915 performed in Chicago with Bert Kelly and toured vaudeville circuit with **Tom Brown** before joining ODJB and appearing on their historic recordings in 1917. Performed and recorded with group through 1921 and toured the UK. Relocated to California by the mid-1920s and worked with various bands before temporarily retiring from music. In the late 1930s performed and recorded with the reformed ODJB. Brother of **Eddie** and **Harry Shields**. Older brother Pat was a jazz guitarist.

SHINN, G.G./GEE GEE (George Shinn) *Swamp pop, rhythm and blues.* Vocals, trumpet. Bandleader. (Born Aug. 25, 1939, Franklin, St. Mary Parish; died Aug. 7, 2018, Monroe, Ouachita Parish.) Renowned swamp pop and blue-eyed soul singer and trumpeter best known for his powerful vocal work with the Boogie Kings in the 1960s. Began performing in the mid-1950s and formed his first band, the Flat Tops, in 1956. In 1963 joined the Boogie Kings and toured and recorded with group through early 1966, often sharing dual lead vocals with **Jerry LaCroix** to much acclaim. In following years performed and recorded with various bands including the Roller Coasters, Chase, and T.S.C. Trucking Company. After stints in Los Angeles and Las Vegas, returned to

Louisiana and continued performing and recording as a solo artist and operated nightclubs in Lafayette, Lake Charles, Monroe, and Alexandria in following decades. Continued performing, reuniting occasionally with the Boogie Kings, until illness forced retirement in late 2017.

SHIPLEY, THOMAS "THOS" *Jazz.* Vocals, drums, piano. Composer. Bandleader. (Born Aug. 5, 1958, Vernon Parish.) Noted New York City–based jazz vocalist and songwriter started playing drums in rock bands during his teens and later toured with various show bands. In the early 1980s began taking jazz vocal lessons and, after stints in Nashville and Atlanta, relocated to New York City and began performing in clubs and in the theater. Released debut CD *My Favorite Things* in 2005 and continued performing in New York City with occasional tours overseas in the 2010s.

SHIRLEY & LEE *See* Goodman, Shirley, *and* Lee, Leonard.

SHORTS, BARBARA ANN *Jazz, rhythm and blues, gospel.* Vocals, piano. (Born Oct. 5, 1949, New Orleans, Orleans Parish.) Powerful New Orleans jazz and blues vocalist began singing in church as a child and spent 12 years with the Gospel Soul Children. In the 1980s performed in musical *One Mo' Time* and recorded traditional jazz album *A Stone for Bessie Smith* in Norway in 1987. Continued touring internationally and performing with her band Blue Jazz in the 2010s.

SHREVE, FLOYD *Cajun.* Guitar, vocals. (Born Feb. 21, 1915, Crowley, Acadia Parish; died Jan. 27, 1957, Baton Rouge, EBR Parish.) Noted early Cajun string-band guitarist and singer performed and recorded extensively with **Leo Soileau**'s bands the Three Aces and Four Aces in the mid-1930s for Bluebird and Decca. Also had a release each on Bluebird and Decca as leader in 1935, notably "Lonesome Blues." Performed and recorded with Hackberry Ramblers on numerous sides for Bluebird in 1937–38 with guitarist brother Danny Shreve (1919–1982). Reportedly retired from music after World War II.

SIMEON, OMER *Jazz.* Clarinet. (Born July 21, 1902, New Orleans, Orleans Parish; died Sept. 17, 1959, New York City.) Highly regarded jazz clarinetist moved to Chicago with family at age 15. Studied music with **Lorenzo Tio Jr.** and began performing in 1920. In the mid-1920s performed with brother Al Simeon's Hot Six and worked with **Charlie Elgar**'s Creole Orchestra. Worked with **Jelly Roll Morton** in 1926 and appeared on Morton's famed Red Hot Peppers recording sessions. In 1928 toured with **King Oliver**'s Dixie Syncopators and worked briefly with Luis Russell. Recorded as leader in Chicago in 1929 and through 1940 performed and recorded with Earl Hines. In the 1940s worked with Jimmie Lunceford and Coleman Hawkins and recorded with **Kid Ory**. Recorded as leader with Omer Simeon Trio in 1945 and worked and recorded extensively with Wilbur De Paris in the 1950s. In 1954 recorded hit instrumental duet "Skokiaan" with **Louis Armstrong** before succumbing to cancer at age 57.

SIMIEN, TERRANCE *Zydeco.* Accordion, piano, vocals. Composer. Bandleader. (Born Sept. 3, 1965, Mallet, St. Landry Parish.) Internationally renowned zydeco singer-songwriter and accordionist began playing the instrument at age 14 and two years later formed his band the Mallet Playboys. After performing locally for two years began touring nationally and had singles on Caillier, Blues Unlimited, Grand Point, and Maison de Soul through the late 1980s. In 1990 recorded acclaimed album debut *Zydeco on the Bayou* and through the 2000s toured extensively nationally and overseas with releases on Black Top, Tone Cool, AIM, and his own label. Continued performing in 2010s and released highly acclaimed CD *The Dockside Sessions* in 2013. Also served as prominent activist for Creole music education and created *Creole for Kidz and the History of Zydeco* performing arts program in 2000.

SIMMONS, HUEY "SONNY" *Jazz.* Saxophone, oboe, English horn. Composer. Bandleader. (Born Aug. 4, 1933, Sicily Island, Catahoula Parish.) Noted avant-garde jazz saxophonist moved to Oakland with his family at age 11 and at age 16 began learning the instrument, inspired by Charlie Parker. Performed throughout the West Coast in the late 1950s and 1960s and made recording debut as a leader with critically acclaimed LP *Staying on the Watch* on ESP-Disk in 1966. Also recorded two albums with Prince Lasha in the 1960s and had releases on Arhoolie and Contemporary. After nearly two decades struggling with homelessness, had career resurgence in the early 1990s and began touring Europe with releases on numerous labels, including Qwest, Parallactic, Jazzaway, and Hello World! through the 2010s. In 2000 cofounded the Cosmosamatics and performed and recorded with group through 2010s.

SIMON, JOE *Rhythm and blues, gospel.* Vocals. Composer. Bandleader. (Born Sept. 2, 1943, Simmesport, Avoy. Parish.) Highly successful soul singer best known for his numerous hits in the 1960s and 1970s such as "The Chokin'

Kind" and "Power of Love." Started singing in church as a child and relocated with family to northern California in the late 1950s. Began performing with a gospel group in the late 1950s and in 1964 launched solo career with several releases on Vee-Jay. Signed with Sound Stage 7 in 1966 and had series of hits including "Teenager's Prayer," "Nine Pound Steel," and "Further on Down the Road." In 1970 began recording for Spring and partnered with noted rhythm and blues songwriters Gamble and Huff. Throughout the decade reached the charts more than 25 times with hits such as "Drowning in the Sea of Love," "Music in My Bones," and "Get Down, Get Down." In the early 1980s gave up performing and became an evangelical minister near Chicago. In the late 1990s and 2000s released several gospel albums including *This Story Must Be Told* in 1998 and continued running his ministries as Bishop Joe Simon in the 2010s.

SIMON, MILFRED *Cajun.* Accordion, vocals. Composer. Bandleader. (Born Sept. 9, 1947, Wright, Vermilion Parish.) Cajun accordionist was raised in a musical family and began playing accordion at age four, sitting in with **Lawrence Walker** six months later. In 1967 joined **Blackie Frugé**'s Hicks Wagon Wheel Ramblers and performed and recorded with group for several decades, releasing CD *Rolling On* in 2003.

SIMONEAUX, HARRY, JR. *Swamp pop.* Saxophone. Composer. Bandleader. (Born July 7, 1936, Golden Meadow, Lafourche Parish; died Dec. 2, 2016, Opelousas, St. Landry Parish.) Revered early swamp pop saxophonist began performing during his teens and worked with **Leroy Martin**, **Gene Rodrigue**, and **Vin Bruce**. In the mid-1950s performed and recorded with the Dukes of Rhythm with **Joe Barry** and **Joe Carl** and appeared on **Bobby Charles**'s 1955 swamp pop classic "Later Alligator." Relocated to Lafayette in the late 1950s and performed and recorded with **Bobby Page** and the Riff Raffs and the Swing Kings, among others, and worked and recorded with **Johnnie Allan** for several decades. Also worked extensively as studio musician for producer **J. D. Miller** in Crowley.

SIMS, CLARENCE "GUITAR" *See* Fillmore Slim.

SINEGAL, BILL (Willie Norman Sinegal) *Rhythm and blues.* Bass, saxophone, vocals. Composer. Bandleader. (Born May 13, 1928, New Orleans, Orleans Parish; died Apr. 14, 2014, New Orleans, Orleans Parish.) New Orleans rhythm and blues singer and bassist best known for his 1964 Mardi Gras classic "Second Line." Started out on saxophone and studied bass at Grunewald School of Music in New Orleans in the 1940s. Performed at Dew Drop Inn and other clubs backing numerous rhythm and blues musicians such as **Guitar Slim**, **Sugar Boy Crawford**, and **Tommy Ridgley** throughout the 1950s. Worked and recorded with **Earl King** in the late 1950s and early 1960s. In 1964 recorded "Second Line" for White Cliffs which became a Mardi Gras standard. Retired from music in the late 1960s.

SINEGAL, LIL' BUCK/"LITTLE BUCK" (Paul Alton Senegal Sr.) *Zydeco, blues.* Guitar, vocals. Composer. Bandleader. (Born Jan. 14, 1944, Lafayette, Lafayette Parish; June 10, 2019, Lafayette, Lafayette Parish.) Highly influential blues and pioneering zydeco guitarist best known for his work as longtime member of **Clifton Chenier**'s Red Hot Louisiana Band. Raised speaking Creole French, began playing guitar as a child, inspired by his mother, Odette, who sang and played guitar. At age 12 was mentored by local blues guitarist **Raymond Monette** and in 1959 formed the Jive Five and began playing at local house parties. In the early 1960s formed Little Buck and the Top Cats, which became one of Lafayette's most popular groups, recording two singles in 1969 for La Louisianne, "Monkey in a Sack" and "Don't Make Me Cry." Joined Chenier's band in 1972 and toured internationally and recorded with group extensively through the early 1980s. Throughout the mid- to late 1980s toured and recorded with **Rockin' Dopsie**, and from the 1990s into early 2010s toured and recorded with **Buckwheat Zydeco**, who was a former member of the Top Cats. Released solo albums *The Buck Starts Here* produced by **Allen Toussaint** in 1999 on NYNO and *Bad Situation* on Lucky Cat in 2002, and continued performing with various groups as well as leading his own blues band until his death at age 75.

SINGLETON, TERRY "T-BONE" *Blues.* Guitar, bass, vocals. Composer. (Born Sept. 10, 1952, New Orleans, Orleans Parish; died Aug. 9, 2005, Baton Rouge, EBR Parish.) Baton Rouge blues guitarist and singer began playing guitar in his teens and performed with local gospel and soul groups. In the mid-1970s worked with **Bobby Powell**'s band the Condors for several years. Throughout the 1980s and 1990s performed in clubs around Baton Rouge with releases on Sidetrack in 1991 and JSP in 1996.

SINGLETON, WAYNE *Zydeco.* Accordion, vocals. Composer. Bandleader. (Born Mar. 17, 1985, Opelousas, St. Landry Parish.) Traditional zydeco accordionist began playing during his teens, mentored by **Roy Carrier** at his famed Offshore Lounge dance hall in Lawtell. In the mid-2000s formed band Same Ol' 2 Step and through the 2010s remained popular act on the zydeco club and festival circuit, releasing numerous CDs, including *I Am the Creole Truth* on Shrimpo in 2013.

SINGLETON, ZUTTY (Arthur James Singleton) *Jazz.* Drums. Bandleader. (Born May 14, 1898, Bunkie, Avoy. Parish; died July 14, 1975, New York City.) Highly regarded and innovative early New Orleans jazz drummer began performing in the city around 1915, working with **Big Eye Louis Nelson**, **John Robichaux**, **Steve Lewis**, and **Papa Celestin**'s Tuxedo Brass Band through 1920. In the early 1920s performed with Celestin, Luis Russell, and **Fate Marable**, making recording debut with Marable in 1924. Relocated to Chicago in 1927 and performed in bands with Doc Cook, **Jimmie Noone** and Clarence Jones. In 1928–29 recorded extensively with **Louis Armstrong**, **Jelly Roll Morton**, and **Barney Bigard**. Throughout the 1930s led various bands in Chicago and through the 1940s worked and recorded with numerous artists, including Pee Wee Russell, **Red Allen**, Lionel Hampton, T-Bone Walker, Slim Gaillard, and **Kid Ory**. In the early 1950s toured Europe and worked with Mezz Mezzrow and Hot Lips Page before settling in New York, where he held long residencies at jazz nightclubs such as Jimmy Ryan's throughout the 1960s. A stroke in 1970 forced retirement.

SKINNY DYNAMO *See* Jones, Sonny, *and* Richardson, T. J.

SLIM HARPO (James Moore) *Blues.* Harmonica, guitar, vocals. Composer. Bandleader. (Born Feb. 11, 1924, Lobdell, WBR Parish; died Jan. 31, 1970, Baton Rouge, EBR Parish.)[6] The most influential and successful swamp blues musician, best known for his many classic recordings, such as "I'm a King Bee," "Raining in My Heart," and "Baby Scratch My Back." Little is known about his musical beginnings or early influences but was later inspired by Chicago bluesman Jimmy Reed. By the mid-1950s was performing in clubs and juke joints around Baton Rouge under the name Harmonica Slim and often appeared with **Lightnin' Slim** or **Lazy Lester**. In 1957 began recording for producer **J. D. Miller**, who renamed him Slim Harpo, and had hit with debut single "I'm a King Bee" on Excello. Continued recording for Miller through the mid-1960s and released numerous singles on Excello, often backed by longtime King Bee band members **Rudy Richard** and **James Johnson**. His distinctive pinched vocal delivery, catchy lyrics, and highly danceable rhythms influenced both blues and popular rock bands of the day and inspired cover versions from the Rolling Stones, the Kinks, and others. After falling out with Miller in 1966, toured nationally and continued recording for Excello with sessions in Memphis, Nashville, Los Angeles, and Baton Rouge and had charted singles with "Tip On In" and "Te-Ni-Nee-Ni-Nu." While on the verge of his first European tour, suffered a fatal heart attack at age 45.

SMILIN' JOE *See* Cousin Joe.

SMITH, ALVIN *See* King, Al.

SMITH, ELDER UTAH *Gospel.* Guitar, vocals. Composer. Bandleader. (Born Feb. 17, 1908, Cedar Grove, Shreveport, Caddo Parish; died Jan. 24, 1965, New Orleans, Orleans Parish.)[7] Highly influential gospel singer, guitarist, and traveling evangelist best known for his recordings of "I Got Two Wings." Began preaching in 1923 and from 1925 until his death traveled throughout the country holding Holy Ghost revivals for the Church of God in Christ. In the late 1930s became one of the first traveling musicians to perform on an electric guitar. Became known as the "Two-Winged Preacher" for the giant white wings worn during his highly theatrical performances. In the mid-1940s and early 1950s recorded several versions of "I Got Two Wings" (or "I Want Two Wings"), which were issued on Manor, Regis, Arco, Kay-Ron, and Checker. Relocated to New Orleans in the mid-1940s and founded the Two Wing Temple Church of God in Christ but continued traveling throughout the next two decades, even in later years when his health and sight deteriorated. Influenced many gospel and blues musicians, including **Rev. Charlie Jackson**, **Lazy Lester**, and **Larry Garner**.

SMITH, ELSIE *Jazz.* Saxophone, clarinet. (Born Dec. 9, 1932, New Iberia, Iberia Parish.) Known as "Queen of the Saxophone," noted jazz musician moved to Los Angeles in the late 1940s and performed with all-women band Queens of Swing, led by Frances Grey. Worked extensively as member of Lionel Hampton's orchestra from 1952 to 1953 and again in the late 1950s, recording with Hampton on a session for Ades in 1958. Relocated to New York and in 1959–60 formed band with female saxophonist Willene Barton. In 1964 released single "Watermelon Man"/"Hi Love" on Open Records as Miss Elsie Smith (The Queen of Sax).

SMITH, HUEY "PIANO" *Rhythm and blues.* Piano, vocals. Composer. Bandleader. (Born Jan. 26, 1934, New Orleans, Orleans Parish.) Highly influential and important early New Orleans rhythm and blues pianist, bandleader, and songwriter best known for his many hits, such as

"Rockin' Pneumonia and the Boogie Woogie Flu" and "Don't You Just Know It." Began playing piano as a child, greatly influenced by **Professor Longhair**. While in his mid-teens began performing in clubs with Eddie Jones (**Guitar Slim**) and appeared on Jones's first recordings in 1951–52 for Imperial and J-B. In 1953 made recording debut as leader for Savoy and also recorded with **Earl King**. Worked prolifically as session musician in the mid-1950s and appeared on recordings by King, Little Richard, **Smiley Lewis**, **Lloyd Price**, **Bobby Marchan**, and others. In 1956 formed his band the Clowns and began long association with Ace Records. Joined by key singers which included Marchan and **Gerri Hall**, released numerous hit singles through 1960, including "Rockin' Pneumonia," "High Blood Pressure," "Don't You Know Yockomo," "Little Liza Jane," and others. In the early 1960s recorded with **Dave Bartholomew** for Imperial before returning to Ace for several more years. Later that decade had singles on Pitter-Pat, White Cliffs, and Instant. In the 1970s recorded for Atlantic and Sansu, but sessions remained unissued for years. In the early 1980s retired from music, relocated to Baton Rouge, and spent two decades in court fighting to recover royalties and songwriting credits which had been denied him.

SMITH, JON R. *Rhythm and blues, rock, jazz, swamp pop.* Saxophone. (Born June 8, 1945, Lake Charles, Calcasieu Parish.) Highly accomplished and renowned saxophonist started playing professionally at age 13, appearing on several sides with **Bobby Charles** in 1958. By his mid-teens was performing in clubs around Vinton and toured with **Dale Hawkins**. In following decades toured and recorded extensively with numerous acts, appearing on notable sessions with **Clarence "Gatemouth" Brown**, **Dr. John**, **Jerry LaCroix**, Sarah Vaughan, Johnny and Edgar Winter, Boogie Kings, Doobie Brothers, Albert Collins, and Boz Scaggs. In 2007 released self-titled CD as a leader on Grand Pointe. Continued performing in the 2010s based in Thibodaux, working regularly with several groups, including a reformed Boogie Kings.

SMITH, KEN *Cajun, country.* Fiddle. (Born Feb. 8, 1961, Kinder, Allen Parish.) Highly renowned Cajun and country fiddle player was raised in a large musical family and began playing at age 11, learning from his father Buford and **Wallace "Cheese" Read**. In the 1970s won numerous prestigious fiddle contests, including Louisiana State Fiddle Championship five times. Released LP *Louisiana State Champion* and toured and recorded with numerous musicians in following years, including **D. L. Menard**, **Eddie LeJeune**, **Paul Daigle**, **Ann** and **Marc Savoy**, **Blackie Forestier**, and **Bruce Daigrepont**. In the early 1990s performed in Le Trio Cadien with Menard and LeJeune and toured extensively nationally and overseas with group, releasing self-titled album on Rounder in 1992. Continued performing and operating his music store in Kinder in the 2010s.

SMITH, MIRA ANN *Rockabilly, rhythm and blues, country.* Guitar. Composer. (Born Oct. 22, 1924, Alexandria, Rapides Parish; died Aug. 29, 1989, Shreveport, Caddo Parish.) Important Shreveport-based guitarist, songwriter, and pioneering female label and studio owner best known for her 1950s and early 1960s blues, rockabilly, swamp pop, and country recordings she produced in her RAM Records studios. Opened RAM studio in 1955 to capitalize on Shreveport's rich music scene and in following years recorded numerous artists, including **T.V. Slim**, **Margaret Lewis**, **Jesse Thomas**, and **Roy "Boogie Boy" Perkins**, often backed by session players **James Burton** or **Joe Osborn**. Also recorded as a leader for RAM under name Grace Tennessee. In the early 1960s relocated to Nashville and became successful songwriter and publisher, often partnering with Lewis and writing or cowriting numerous songs, including "Reconsider Me," which was a hit for **Johnny Adams** in 1969. *See also Smith's entry as producer.*

SMITH, MOSES *See* Whispering Smith [Notable Musicians Born outside Louisiana].

SMITH, O.C. (Ocie Lee Smith) *Rhythm and blues, jazz.* Vocals. Bandleader. (Born June 21, 1932, Mansfield, DeSoto Parish; died Nov. 23, 2001, Los Angeles.) Successful West Coast–based rhythm and blues singer best known for his 1968 hit "Little Green Apples." Raised in Los Angeles, was influenced early on by bebop jazz. Released several singles on Cadence, MGM, and Citation in the mid- to late 1950s before serving as Count Basie's vocalist in the early 1960s. Signed with Columbia in 1966 and through the mid-1970s reached charts eleven times, having major hits with "Little Green Apples" and "Daddy's Little Man." In following years had minor hit singles on Caribou, Shadybrook, Family, Motown, and Rendezvous. In the mid-1980s became pastor and founder of a church but continued performing and recording with several more releases before his death, including *Beach Music Classics & Love Songs* in 2000.

SMITH, WEBSTER *Rhythm and blues.* Saxophone, guitar, drums, piano. Bandleader. (Born Feb. 19, 1946, Houma, Terrebonne Parish.) Rhythm and blues multi-instrumentalist who toured with artists such as Joe Tex for many years, beginning in the late 1960s. In 2012 founded the South Louisiana Music Hall of Fame to honor the vast contributions of African American musicians from the region.

SNAER, ALBERT *Jazz.* Trumpet. Bandleader. (Born Jan. 29, 1903, New Orleans, Orleans Parish; died June 26, 1962, Napa, California.)[8] Highly regarded New Orleans jazz trumpeter began playing in the early 1920s with Excelsior Brass Band and also performed on riverboats for several years. From 1926 to 1928 led Moonlight Serenaders and later worked with **Fate Marable**. Around 1930 relocated to New York and worked with Andy Kirk, Claude Hopkins, and others. Appeared in several films and recorded with **Sidney Bechet** in 1949. Settled in California in the 1950s and occasionally performed with **Big Boy Goudie**.

SOILEAU, ALIUS *Cajun.* Fiddle, vocals. (Born Nov. 8, 1905, St. Landry Parish; died Jan. 7, 1996, Eunice, St. Landry Parish.) Early Cajun fiddler who recorded four sides with **Oscar "Slim" Doucet** which were issued on Victor and Bluebird, including "Bayou Courtebleau," and four sides with his cousin **Leo Soileau** as Soileau Couzens for Victor in Nov. 1929.

SOILEAU, LEO *Cajun.* Fiddle, vocals. Composer. Bandleader. (Born Jan. 19, 1904, Ville Platte, Evangeline Parish; died Aug. 2, 1980, Ville Platte, Evangeline Parish.) Highly influential early Cajun fiddle player, bandleader, and prolific recording artist who was the first Cajun fiddler to record. Also was first Cajun musician to incorporate drums in a Cajun band. Began playing fiddle at age 12, learning from his father and **Dennis McGee**. In the early 1920s began performing regularly with accordionist **Mayeus LaFleur** and in Oct. 1929 duo became second Cajun artists to record, cutting four sides for Victor, including "Mama, Where You At?" After the death of LaFleur several weeks later, teamed up with **Moise Robin** and in 1929 recorded sides for Paramount, Victor, and Vocalion, including local hit "Easy Rider Blues." In the mid-1930s formed Cajun string band Three Aces, which included guitarists **Floyd Shreve** and Dewey Landry and drummer Tony Gonzales, and recorded eight sides for Bluebird in 1935, including regional hit "La Valse de Gueydan." Several months later signed with Decca and recorded extensively with his Four Aces and later the Rhythm Boys through 1937, becoming one of the most influential and popular Cajun bands at the time, along with Hackberry Ramblers and **Happy Fats**'s Rayne-Bo Ramblers. Continued performing extensively throughout Lake Charles, Orange, and Beaumont–Port Arthur area through the mid-1940s. By the late 1940s and early 1950s began performing less frequently due to a resurgence of accordion-based Cajun dance hall music popularized by **Iry LeJeune**, **Nathan Abshire**, and others, and retired from music.

SOLOMON, KING (King Sylvester Lee Melicious Solomon) *Rhythm and blues.* Piano, vocals. Composer. Bandleader. (Born May 8, 1934, Tallulah, Madison Parish; died Nov. 2, 2011, Hemet, California.)[9] West Coast–based soul-blues and funk singer began singing in church as a child and in the early 1950s toured with a gospel quartet based in Jackson, Mississippi. Soon switched to singing blues and relocated to Chicago. Toured with B.B. King, Etta James, and others before settling in Los Angeles and cutting debut recording with Liberty in 1959. In the early 1960s had regional hit with "Non-Support Blues" on Chess and through the 1970s released singles on numerous labels, including Magnum, Resist, Kent, Highland, Cadillac, and Stanson. In 1978 released LP *Energy Crisis* on Celestial. Younger brother of **Little Wolf** (Lee Solomon).

SONNIER, JO-EL *Cajun, country.* Accordion, guitar, vocals. Composer. Bandleader. (Born Oct. 2, 1946, Rayne, Acadia Parish.) Internationally renowned accordionist and singer-songwriter who achieved success in both Cajun and country music fields. A child prodigy who was raised speaking Cajun French, began playing accordion at age three and by age six was performing on local radio shows. From 1960 to 1961 recorded several sides for Swallow with Duson Playboys, notably "Tee Yeaux Bleu," and recorded singles and LPs for Goldband from 1965 to 1972, including several with **Robert Bertrand**. In the 1970s relocated to Los Angeles and worked as session musician and had country releases on Mercury with limited success. Recorded acclaimed LP *Cajun Life* for Rounder in 1980 and in 1987 signed with RCA and released LP *Come On Joe,* which produced two Top 10 country hits, including "Tear-Stained Letter." Toured extensively and worked as session musician and songwriter in the following years and recorded prolifically as a leader, releasing more than 20 albums on numerous labels, including *Cajun Pride* on Rounder in 1997 and

Cajun Mardi Gras on Green Hill in 2004. Continued performing nationally and abroad in the 2010s, releasing *The Legacy* in 2013, which contained 13 original compositions sung in Cajun French.

SONNIER, JOHNNY *Cajun.* Accordion, steel guitar, drums, vocals. Composer. Bandleader. (Born Feb. 29, 1960, Opelousas, St. Landry Parish.) Cajun multi-instrumentalist began playing drums and accordion during his teens and soon formed his first band, Cajun Fugitive. In the 1980s released singles on Lanor and Kajun and had regional hit with "Chere Alice" in 1984. Formed band Cajun Heritage in the late 1980s and continued performing with group through the 2010s with several releases, including *Live at Fred's Lounge* in 1999.

SONNIER, LEE *Cajun.* Accordion. Composer. Bandleader. (Born Nov. 19, 1897, Rayne, Acadia Parish; died Dec. 20, 1984, Rayne, Acadia Parish.) Early postwar Cajun accordion player and leader of the Acadian All Stars who released four singles on his son-in-law **J. D. Miller**'s Fais-Do-Do and Feature labels between 1947 and 1952. Releases included "War Widow Waltz" in 1950, with **Laura Broussard** on vocals, which was Miller's first big seller. Miller reportedly started Fais-Do-Do label to record Sonnier.

SONNIER, LENNIS *Cajun.* Guitar, vocals. (Born Feb. 25, 1917, Vinton, Calcasieu Parish; died Dec. 8, 1993, Lake Charles, Calcasieu Parish.) Renowned early Cajun string-band guitarist and singer best known for his work as longtime member of the Hackberry Ramblers with **Luderin Darbone** and **Edwin Duhon**. Joined band shortly before their Aug. 1935 debut recording session on Bluebird and performed and recorded prolifically with group through 1937, singing on many of the band's French-language recordings, including "Jolie Blonde" in 1936. Also appeared on group's recordings as Riverside Ramblers in 1937. After several-year hiatus rejoined band in the mid-1940s and performed with group until retiring due to health issues in the the 1970s, appearing on numerous recordings with band for Deluxe, Arhoolie, and Goldband throughout the years.

SONNIER, SHORTY (Nelon Sonnier) *Cajun.* Drums, vocals. Bandleader. (Born July 31, 1936, Duson, Acadia Parish.) Cajun drummer and bandleader recorded two singles in the late 1970s and early 1980s on Bayou Classics and Kajun with the Lafayette Playboys, including "La Valse de L'Amusement" with **Will Kegley**. Brother of Cajun accordionist Harold Sonnier and steel guitarist Melvin Sonnier.

SOUCHON, EDMOND "DOC" *Jazz.* Guitar, banjo, vocals. (Born Oct. 25, 1897, New Orleans, Orleans Parish; died Aug. 24, 1968, New Orleans, Orleans Parish.) Early New Orleans jazz guitarist who recorded extensively and was a major figure in the historical preservation of the music. Began playing guitar at age 10 and around 1913 helped form the Six and Seven Eights String Band. Appeared on hundreds of jazz recordings from the 1940s through 1960s. As a physician, routinely offered free medical care to musicians who could not afford it.

SOUL DOG *See* Marshall, Carl.

SOULFUL MARY (Johnson) *Rhythm and blues.* Vocals. (Born Mar. 16, 1939, Vedis, Tensas Parish.) Chicago-based soul singer who recorded single "Reap What You Soe" [*sic*]/"Funky Soul" on Aquarius in 1972.

SOUTH SIDE SLIM (Henry Lee Harris) *Blues.* Guitar, vocals. Composer. Bandleader. (Born Sept. 7, 1957, Mer Rouge, Morehouse Parish.) West Coast–based blues guitarist and singer was raised in Oakland and began performing around Los Angeles in the early 1990s, mentored by local blues musician Ray Bailey. In the late 1990s formed South Side Records and had numerous recordings throughout the next decade, including *More Blues from the South Side,* which featured Smokey Wilson and **Curtis Tillman**. Continued recording and performing into the 2010s with national and overseas tours.

SPAIN, JOHNNY (John Curtis Morvant) *Swamp pop.* Vocals. Bandleader. (Born Oct. 1, 1936, Jennings, Jeff. Davis Parish; died Sept. 11, 2003, Houston.) Early swamp pop singer who led his band the Famous Flames in the late 1950s and 1960s and had minor regional success with 1958 single "I'm in Love"/"Family Rules" on Back Beat, covering **Lonnie Brooks**'s swamp pop classic on the b-side. Performed often in Houston clubs and toured early on with **Rusty** and **Doug Kershaw**.

SPARGO, TONY *See* Sbarbaro, Tony.

SPEARMAN, ALEX/"SAILOR BOY" *Rhythm and blues.* Vocals. Composer. (Born Apr. 28, 1935, Bastrop, Morehouse Parish; died May 27, 1999, New Orleans, Orleans Parish.)[10] Rhythm and blues and deep soul singer recorded debut single, "What Have I Done Wrong," in 1956 which was issued under the name Sailor Boy on Dig and recorded while on leave in the Navy in Los Angeles. After discharge settled in New Orleans and from the early 1960s through the early 1970s had singles on numerous local labels, including Rip, Dover, Choctaw, White Cliffs, Satin, and Rosemont. In later years worked as radio disc jockey at WWOZ in New Orleans.

SPEARS, MERLE *Rhythm and blues, gospel.* Vocals. Bandleader. (Born Oct. 25, 1939, Baton Rouge, EBR Parish; died Oct. 8, 2009, Baton Rouge, EBR Parish.) Baton Rouge soul-blues singer began singing as a child with family gospel quartet. In his late teens started performing in clubs and made first recording on Vin in 1960 as Calvin Spears. In the mid-1960s recorded two singles for Whit, which were both leased to Atlantic, notably "It's Just a Matter of Time." Followed with a single on J-Mer with Johnnie Jackson and the Blazers and also shared vocal duties on "When Something Is Wrong with My Baby" with **Chuck Mitchell** backed by **Buddy Stewart**'s Herculoids. In the late 1970s stopped performing blues and continued singing only in church.

SPELL, LOUIS *Cajun.* Accordion. (Born July 7, 1913, Indian Bayou, Vermilion Parish; died Feb. 3, 1984, Crowley, Acadia Parish.) Enigmatic Cajun accordionist who recorded "The Fifty Cent Song"/"Lover's Waltz" with his French Serenaders for **J. D. Miller**'s Feature label in 1952.

SPENCER, EVANS *Blues, gospel.* Guitar. (Born Jan. 22, 1921, Monroe, Ouachita Parish; died Oct. 12, 2003, Lawton, Michigan.) Blues guitarist moved to Chicago in the late 1930s and in the 1950s worked with harmonica player and singer Kid Thomas. In the 1960s worked as session musician for Willie Dixon and recorded with Homesick James, Victoria Spivey, St. Louis Jimmy Oden, Sunnyland Slim, Koko Taylor, and Washboard Sam. Later performed as gospel musician.

SPO-DEE-O-DEE *See* Theard, Samuel.

ST. CYR, JOHNNY *Jazz.* Guitar, banjo. Bandleader. (Born Apr. 17, 1890, New Orleans, Orleans Parish; died June 17, 1966, Los Angeles.) Highly influential early New Orleans jazz guitar and banjo pioneer who appeared on numerous historic recording sessions of **King Oliver**, **Louis Armstrong**, and **Jelly Roll Morton** in the 1920s. Began performing on homemade instruments and formed a trio around 1905. Performed with **Armand Piron** from 1908 to 1909 and through 1920 worked with Superior and Olympia orchestras and Tuxedo Brass Band as well as **Kid Ory** and **Fate Marable**. In the late 1910s and early 1920s worked regularly on riverboats and in 1923 went to Chicago to record with Oliver's Creole Jazz Band. From 1925 to 1927 appeared on Armstrong's famed Hot Five and Hot Seven recordings as well as Morton's Red Hot Peppers sessions, playing his unique hybrid six-string guitar-banjo. Also worked during this period with Doc Cook and **Jimmie Noone**. In 1930 returned to New Orleans and worked mainly outside music throughout decade. In the 1940s and 1950s performed and recorded extensively with **Paul Barbarin**, **George Lewis**, **Big Eye Louis Nelson**, **Wooden Joe Nicholas**, and **Raymond Burke** and also as a leader. Relocated to Los Angeles in 1955 and from 1961 until his death led Young Men from New Orleans jazz band at Disneyland.

ST. JULIEN, ROBERT *Zydeco.* Drums. (Born Jan. 29, 1948, Lafayette, Lafayette Parish.) Highly influential zydeco drummer best known for his work as longtime band member with **Clifton Chenier**. Began learning drums during his early teens from **Joe Morris**'s brother Jerry Brouchet. Toured and recorded extensively with Chenier from the mid-1960s until Chenier's death in 1987, appearing on more than two dozen LPs, including Arhoolie's *Louisiana Blues and Zydeco* in 1965 and *Bogalusa Boogie* in 1976. In 1969 toured Europe with Chenier as part of the *American Folk Blues Festival* package and also performed with Magic Sam, Earl Hooker, and Carey Bell. In the 1980s relocated to Houston and after Chenier's death performed with various Houston-based zydeco artists, including **L.C. Donatto** and Little Willie Davis before retiring from music in 2012. Often mis-credited as Robert St. Judy, Robert St. Peter, Robert Peter, or Robert Pete. Cousin of noted zydeco drummer Gerard St. Julien.

ST. MARY, MARK "BON TON" *Zydeco.* Accordion, vocals. Composer. Bandleader. (Born July 29, 1956, Lake Charles, Calcasieu Parish.) West Coast–based zydeco accordionist and bandleader relocated to Sacramento, California, area with family as a child and began playing accordion during his early teens, inspired by **Clifton Chenier**. In the mid-1970s was mentored by **Danny Poullard** but later developed a more blues-influenced playing style on piano accordion after touring with Chenier. Released several albums on Goldband in the 1980s, including *Crown Prince of Zydeco,* and performed throughout California and Louisiana. Releases followed on Bad Weather and his own MSM label, including *Zydeco Tonight* in 2008, and continued performing into the 2010s. Brother Kirby and uncles Charlie and Arsene St. Mary were also zydeco musicians.

STAFFORD, CHRIS *Cajun.* Accordion, guitar, vocals. Composer. Bandleader. (Born Aug. 20, 1987, Lafayette,

Lafayette Parish.) Cofounder of contemporary Cajun band Feufollet began playing accordion at age eight, mentored by **Steve Riley**. In the late 1990s performed locally with Les Acadiens before reforming group as Feufollet in 1999 with **Chris Segura** and continued performing and recording with the band into the 2010s. Brother of Feufollet drummer Mike Stafford.

STAFFORD, GREGG *Jazz.* Trumpet, cornet. Bandleader. (Born July 6, 1953, New Orleans, Orleans Parish.) Traditional New Orleans jazz trumpeter began playing in brass bands at age 16, mentored early on by **Danny Barker** in his Fairview Baptist Church Band. Performed regularly with Hurricane, Olympia, Royal, and Excelsior brass bands and led Young Tuxedo Brass Band from 1984 through the 2010s. In 1993 cofounded Black Men of Labor organization to promote and preserve traditional jazz. Released several recordings as leader, including *That Man from New Orleans* on Jazz Crusade in 1998.

STALE BREAD *See* Lacoume, Emile.

STAMPLEY, JOE *Swamp pop, rock, country.* Piano, vocals. Composer. Bandleader. (Born June 6, 1943, Springhill, Webster Parish.) Known primarily as a country artist, singer-songwriter and pianist began career in the early 1960s recording demos for local disc jockey Merle Kilgore in Shreveport. In the mid-1960s formed swamp pop and rock band the Uniques and had numerous releases on Paula from 1965 to 1970, including national hits "Not Too Long Ago" (produced by **Dale Hawkins**) and "All These Things." After the band dissolved in 1970 had numerous hits as country artist, often partnering with Moe Bandy in the 1980s. In the early 1990s formed swamp pop group the Louisiana Boys with **John Fred** and **G.G. Shinn**. Continued performing and recording in the 2010s. Brother of Bobby Stampley, who was bassist in the Uniques.

STANFORD, GERVIS *Cajun.* Fiddle, vocals. Composer. (Born Jan. 20, 1930, Lawtell, St. Landry Parish; died Dec. 30, 2015, Eunice, St. Landry Parish.) Noted Cajun fiddler performed and recorded with **Austin Pitre** and **Chuck Guillory** in the 1970s and 1980s. In the 1980s recorded several singles as a leader on Bee and Lanor, notably "Road of Broken Hearts."

STARR, JERRY (Jerome Verrette) *Swamp pop.* Vocals, piano. Composer. Bandleader. (Born Sept. 29, 1936, New Iberia, Iberia Parish.) Early swamp pop singer and bandleader who recorded several singles in the early 1960s with his band the Clippers, notably "Side Steppin'" on Zynn. Also had singles on Ron, Rocko, Tear Drop, and Eric (with **Roy "Boogie Boy" Perkins**).

STEPHENS, JOSEPH "RAG BABY" *Jazz.* Drums. (Born Mar. 3, 1887, New Orleans, Orleans Parish; died Mar. 31, 1925, Chicago.)[11] Influential early New Orleans jazz and ragtime drummer who was a mainstay in **Papa Jack Laine**'s Reliance Brass Band from around 1905 through mid-1910s. Among the first New Orleans jazz musicians to move to Chicago in the mid-1910s, worked regularly with bandleader Bert Kelly and others into the early 1920s. Father of noted jazz drummer Joe Stephens Jr.

STEVENS, DUKE *Rhythm and blues.* Saxophone, vocals. Bandleader. (Born Mar. 4, 1933, Opelousas, St. Landry Parish.) Opelousas rhythm and blues singer-saxophonist performed with his band the Sputniks in the late 1950s and early 1960s. Recorded single "I've Been Your Fool"/"Nobody Knows (What Tomorrow Will Bring)" on Lanor in 1961. Later worked with various blues and zydeco groups, including **Roscoe Chenier**'s Inner City Blues Band and with **Delton Broussard**.

STEVENSON, GEORGE *See* Blazer Boy.

STEWART, BUDDY (Junius Stewart) *Rhythm and blues, jazz.* Saxophone, vocals. Composer. Bandleader. (Born Apr. 26, 1927, Plaquemine, Iberville Parish; died Sept. 19, 1997, Lake Charles, Calcasieu Parish.)[12] Locally renowned rhythm and blues musician who led popular bands in the Baton Rouge area in the 1950s and 1960s. Began performing with **Claiborne Williams**'s orchestra in the 1940s and settled in Baton Rouge in the early 1950s. Through the mid-1960s led one of the area's top rhythm and blues bands, the Top Notchers, which included his twin nephews Ralph and Roy Stewart. Recorded as backing band on singles for **Chuck Mitchell**, **Lee Tillman**, and **Gene Fairchild**. Also led popular band the Herculoids, who recorded a single featuring Mitchell and **Merle Spears** on vocals. Later served as booking agent for numerous blues musicians, including **Slim Harpo** and **Lightnin' Slim**, and operated a Baton Rouge nightclub and record shop. Suffered fatal heart attack on stage while sitting in with a local jazz band in Lake Charles.

STEWART, SKIP (Maurice Jean Guillory Jr.) *Swamp pop.* Bass, vocals. (Born Jan. 8, 1939, Eunice, St. Landry Parish; died Nov. 4, 2017, Eunice, St. Landry Parish.) Early swamp pop singer and bassist joined the Boogie Kings in 1956 soon after the group was formed by **Doug Ardoin**, **Harris Miller**, and **Bert Miller**. Performed and recorded with band through the early 1960s. In 1962 formed the Shondelles with **Warren Storm** and **Rodney Bernard** and recorded several singles and LP *At the Saturday Hop* on La Louisianne. Continued performing with group until disbanding in 1970. Recorded a single as leader on Tamm and Jin in the mid-1960s. Also known as "Skip Morris."

STICKS HERMAN (Herman Joseph Guidry) *Rhythm and blues, swamp pop.* Drums, vocals. Composer. Bandleader. (Born Sept. 1, 1935, Church Point, Acadia Parish.) Rhythm and blues drummer and vocalist began playing around Church Point in the early 1950s with his saxophonist brother Louis Guidry and **Leroy Washington** in the Honeydrippers. In 1957 recorded session for **Eddie Shuler** backed by **Marcel Dugas** which produced three singles issued on Goldband and Hollywood, including "Long Gone Baby." Released "Give Me Your Love" on Tic Toc in 1961 and settled in Lake Charles, where he later worked outside music.

STINSON, KENNY BILL *Rockabilly, rhythm and blues, country.* Piano, guitar, bass, harmonica, drums, vocals. Bandleader. (Born Nov. 10, 1953, West Monroe, Ouachita Parish.) Highly regarded multi-instrumentalist began teaching himself guitar, then piano, during his early teens, inspired greatly by **Jerry Lee Lewis**. Spent time in Nashville and toured with **Dale Hawkins**, Charlie Rich, Rosanne Cash, and others before returning to West Monroe in the mid-1980s. Appeared in the documentary and soundtrack *The Mississippi: River of Song* in 1998 and released debut CD, *Inspiration,* in 2001. Continued to record and perform mainly in Louisiana through the 2010s, based in West Monroe.

STONE, ROLAND (Roland LeBlanc) *Rhythm and blues.* Vocals, guitar. (Born Aug. 12, 1941, New Orleans, Orleans Parish; died Dec. 22, 1999, New Orleans, Orleans Parish.) New Orleans rhythm and blues singer began playing in high-school band the Jokers in the mid-1950s. Joined Mac Rebennack's (**Dr. John**) band the Skyliners in 1959 and made recording debut with "Preacher's Daughter" on Spinett. In the early 1960s recorded several singles on Ace and had regional hit with "Just a Moment" in 1961. After a single on White Cliffs in the mid-1960s, relocated to Texas until the late 1970s. Returned to New Orleans in 1979 and released two albums on Orleans in the 1990s, including the critically acclaimed *Remember Me* in 1994.

STORM, WARREN (Warren Schexnider) *Swamp pop.* Drums, guitar, vocals. Composer. Bandleader. (Born Feb. 18, 1937, Leroy, Vermilion Parish.) Known as "the Godfather of Swamp Pop," veteran singer, drummer, and session musician began playing drums at age 12, inspired by his father, Simon, who was a Cajun drummer. In the early 1950s was greatly influenced by **Fats Domino** and drummers **Earl Palmer** and **Charles "Hungry" Williams**, often traveling to New Orleans with childhood friend **Bobby Charles** to see them perform. Formed first band, the Wee-Wows, in the mid-1950s and in 1958 recorded debut hit single, "Prisoner's Song"/"Mama, Mama, Mama," on Nasco for producer **J. D. Miller**. Continued recording for Miller as a leader with singles on Rocko and Zynn and also worked extensively as a session musician, appearing on numerous swamp blues recordings by **Lazy Lester**, **Lightnin' Slim**, **Lonesome Sundown**, **Leroy Washington**, **Katie Webster**, and others. In the mid-1960s formed the Shondelles with **Rod Bernard** and **Skip Stewart** and recorded for La Louisianne. Numerous releases followed in the 1970s and 1980s on various labels, including Atco, Jin, Starflite, Crazy Cajun, and Master-Trak, including regional hit "Lord I Need Somebody Bad" in 1974 on Showtime. In the 1980s and early 1990s worked with **Willie Tee** in the band Cypress and released several CDs as leader on Jin. Toured internationally and recorded with Lil' Band O' Gold from the early 2000s through early 2010s and continued performing into his 80s, releasing LP *Taking the World, by Storm* in 2019.

STORMY HERMAN (Herman Colbert Jr.) *Blues.* Vocals, guitar. Composer. Bandleader. (Born Nov. 26, 1922, near Plaquemine, Iberville Parish; died May 15, 1984, Los Angeles.) West Coast–based postwar blues singer who recorded the single "The Jitterbug"/"Bad Luck" on Dootone in 1955 with his band the Midnight Ramblers. Also believed by some to be the vocalist on the Dixie Blues Boys' 1955 single "Monte Carlo"/"My Baby Left Town" on Flair. By the early 1970s reportedly had joined the church and given up performing blues.

STRANGE, TOMMY *Swamp pop.* Vocals, piano. Composer. Bandleader. (Born June 6, 1939, Lecompte, Rapides Parish; died July 19, 1992, Fort Worth, Texas.)[13] Noted early swamp pop singer and piano player who recorded the **Jerry Lee Lewis**–influenced single "Nervous and Shakin' All Over" in 1960 on Rocko. Later formed the Features and relocated to Texas, gaining fame as a traditional country artist with recordings on Shamarie and Ramco. Cousin of **Jay Chevalier**, who was a member of the Features in the early 1960s.

STROGIN, HENRY *Rhythm and blues.* Vocals. Composer. Bandleader. (Born Apr. 1, 1934, Shreveport, Caddo Parish; died Oct. 22, 1980, Los Angeles.)[14] Soulful rhythm and blues singer and songwriter who had releases on several Los Angeles labels in the early to mid-1960s, including Hank, Ball, Ten Star, Dynamic, and Amazon, backed on several releases by doo-wop group the Crowns. Notable songs included "Misery," "I Wanna Love" and "Love Insurance."

STRUCK, NOLAN (Nolton Antoine) *Blues.* Vocals, bass. Composer. Bandleader. (Born June 16, 1940, Duson, Acadia Parish.) Noted blues and soul singer began playing bass in Port Arthur, Texas, with **Lonnie Brooks** in the late 1950s and in 1959 relocated to Chicago with Brooks's band, soon to be joined by brother **King Edward**. Performed and recorded with Brooks for several years before forming Little Nolan and the Soul Brothers with Edward in 1967 and recording singles for Ty-Do and Shama in the late 1960s. Also worked with Tyrone Davis, Otis Taylor, and Denise LaSalle and recorded as session musician for One-derful. In 1973 released single "Welfare Problems" on Inner City Trade. Relocated to Jackson, Mississippi, in the late 1970s and through 1990s had releases on Malaco/Retta's, Ace, Ichiban, and Paula, notably *Brother to Brother* with Edward in 1995. Continued performing nationally and overseas into the 2010s. Brothers Fulton, Sterling, and Wilton were also musicians.

STUTES, JAY (Jessie Lloyd Stutes Sr.) *Cajun.* Steel guitar, guitar, drums, bass, vocals. Composer. Bandleader. (Born Sept. 7, 1933, Morse, Acadia Parish; died May 19, 2000, Jennings, Jeff. Davis Parish.)[15] Influential Cajun steel guitarist and singer best known for his bluesy vocals and playing on **Cleveland Crochet**'s 1961 hit "Sugar Bee." Began playing guitar as a child, influenced by his uncle Roy, and in the 1950s performed with **Iry LeJeune**, Pee Wee, **Rusty**, and **Doug Kershaw**, **Shorty LeBlanc**, and others. In 1957 joined Crochet's Hillbilly Ramblers along with LeBlanc and, after a single on Khoury's, recorded Cajun-rocker "Sugar Bee" in late 1960 for Goldband which became the first Cajun record to appear on *Billboard*'s Top 100. Around 1962 took over leadership of band, which was renamed the Sugar Bees and released several more singles on Goldband and Swallow. After group disbanded in the mid-1960s, went on to perform and record with **Jimmy C. Newman**, **Blackie Forestier**, **Jo-El Sonnier**, **Sheryl Cormier**, and others.

SUMMERFIELD, DORSEY, JR. *Jazz, rhythm and blues.* Saxophone, piano, vocals. Composer. Bandleader. (Born Apr. 26, 1948, Shreveport, Caddo Parish.) Noted jazz saxophonist and bandleader who led his Shreveport-based jazz band the Polyphonics for more than forty years. In the 1960s performed as member of Ray Charles's band, replacing Hank Crawford. Released CD *This Masquerade Is Over* in 2002 and continued performing with the Polyphonics and teaching music in 2010s.

SUMMERS, EDDIE *Jazz.* Trombone. (Born Sept. 15, 1903, New Orleans, Orleans Parish; died Oct. 27, 1977, New Orleans, Orleans Parish.) Early New Orleans jazz trombonist performed with **Albert Snaer**'s Moonlight Serenades in the late 1920s and later with **Armand Piron**. Also worked with **Kid Rena** and Eureka and Young Tuxedo brass bands. In the 1960s worked regularly with **Kid Sheik** and performed at Preservation Hall, including on opening night in 1961.

SWANN, BETTYE (*born* Betty Jean Champion) *Rhythm and blues.* Vocals. Composer. Bandleader. (Born Oct. 24, 1944, Shreveport, Caddo Parish.) Noted West Coast soul singer best known for her 1967 hit "Make Me Yours." Raised in Arcadia, began singing in church as a child, and in 1963 relocated to Los Angeles. Signed with Money Records and had minor hit "Don't Wait Too Long" in 1965. After several more releases on Money, including number-one hit "Make Me Yours," recorded for Capitol from 1966 to 1970 and charted with "Don't Touch Me." In the early to mid-1970s had five hits on Atlantic, including a country-soul version of "Today I Started Loving You Again." Relocated to Las Vegas in 1976 and performed locally until retiring from music in 1980 following the death of her husband.

T-BROUSSARD (Bryant Keith Broussard) *Zydeco.* Accordion, drums, bass, vocals. Composer. Bandleader. (Born Nov. 11, 1972, Jennings, Jeff. Davis Parish.) Contemporary zydeco accordionist and bandleader began playing drums and rubboard behind his mother, **Mary Jane Broussard**, as a child before learning accordion, influenced by great-uncle **Bois Sec Ardoin**. In the early 1990s formed the Zydeco Steppers, releasing debut CD *It's All Good* on Harambee in 1995. Through the 2010s continued performing on the club and festival circuit with several more releases including highly acclaimed CD *Zydeco Lover* in 2007. Great-nephew of **Carlton Frank**.

TALBERT, ELMER "COO COO" *Jazz.* Trumpet, vocals. (Born Aug. 18, 1900, New Orleans, Orleans Parish; died Dec. 13, 1950, New Orleans, Orleans Parish.)[1] Early New Orleans jazz trumpeter best known for his work with **George Lewis** in the late 1940s. Began performing in 1929 in **Arnold DePass**'s band with Lewis. Studied and performed with **Kid Rena** in the early 1930s and in 1935 worked with **Paul Barnes** and **Johnny St. Cyr**. In the late 1940s replaced **Bunk Johnson** in Lewis's band and recorded with group several times in 1949 and 1950. Died following a second stroke at age 50.

TAUZIN, RAYMOND *Cajun.* Guitar, vocals. Composer. Bandleader. (Born Dec. 29, 1935, Breaux Bridge, St. Martin Parish.) Cajun-country guitarist and singer-songwriter best known for his composition "Fais L'Amour dans le Poulailler (Making Love in the Chicken Coop)," which he recorded for Swallow in 1974 and which became a Cajun standard. Also had singles on Booray, Nett, and La Louisianne in the 1970s.

TAYLOR, CURLEY (Jude Taylor Jr.) *Zydeco.* Accordion, drums, vocals. Composer. Bandleader. (Born Nov. 28, 1970, Grand Coteau, St. Landry Parish.) Contemporary zydeco singer-songwriter and accordionist began performing with his father **Jude Taylor**'s Burning Flames as a drummer at age 16. In the following years worked with numerous artists, including **Little Bob**, **Steve Riley**, **Geno Delafose**, **C. J. Chenier**, **Kat**, and his uncle **Lil' Buck Sinegal**. Formed his band Zydeco Trouble in 2003 and continued performing as one of the region's most popular zydeco artists in the 2010s with numerous releases of original material, including *Zydeco Confessions* in 2013.

TAYLOR, JUDE *Zydeco, blues.* Accordion, vocals. Composer. Bandleader. (Born May 14, 1950, Grand Coteau, St. Landry Parish.) Noted zydeco and blues singer and bandleader began playing accordion in the 1980s, mentored by **Clayton Sampy**, and as vocalist performed with brother-in-law **Lil' Buck Sinegal** in Zydeco Blues Incorporated. In 1987 formed the Burning Flames and recorded debut single on King Creole in 1988. In the 1990s released two CDs on Mardi Gras Records, including *Zydeco Bayou* in 1997, and appeared on Rounder's *Zydeco Shootout at El Sid O's* in 1991. Continued performing occasionally as vocalist in various blues and soul bands in 2010s, including with **Lil' Ray Neal** and **Major Handy**. Father of zydeco musician **Curley Taylor**.

TEE, WILLIE (William Trahan) *Swamp pop.* Saxophone, vocals. Bandleader. (Born Mar. 1, 1944, Lafayette, Lafayette Parish.) Early swamp pop singer and saxophonist began performing during his teens with the Cool Cats and **Alvin Dugas**. In the late 1950s formed the Jokers with **Kenny Tibbs** and recorded local hit "I Promise" on Viking. In the 1960s and 1970s worked and recorded with the Boogie Kings, **Tommy McLain**, **Charles Mann**, and others. Formed the band Cypress with **Warren Storm** in 1980 and had releases on Master-Trak with group and also recorded with **Rockin' Sidney** and rock musician John Fogerty. In 1999 released solo debut recording, *I Believe in My Soul,* and continued performing with Cypress into the 2010s with several releases on Jin, including *Swamp Pop Jukebox* in 2013. Not to be confused with New Orleans soul and funk musician **Willie Tee** (Turbinton).

TEE, WILLIE (Wilson Turbinton) *Rhythm and blues.* Piano, saxophone, vocals. Composer. Bandleader. (Born Feb. 6, 1944, New Orleans, Orleans Parish; died Sept. 11, 2007, New Orleans, Orleans Parish.) Highly regarded New Orleans soul and funk piano player and singer known for his work with the Wild Magnolias and as lead member of funk band the Gaturs. Began playing piano around age five and during his teens performed with **Harold Battiste**. In the early 1960s had singles on A.F.O. and Cinderella and in 1964 released "Teasin' You" on Nola, which became a national hit when leased to Atlantic. Around 1970 formed funk group the Gaturs with brother **Earl Turbinton** and released several singles, many of which were later sampled by numerous hip-hop artists. In the early to mid-1970s worked and recorded with the Wild Magnolias on two releases as arranger, musician, and songwriter. In 1988 collaborated with Earl on LP *Brothers for Life* on Rounder. Continued to perform, compose, and record through the mid-2000s. Not to be confused with swamp pop saxophonist **Willie Tee** (Trahan).

TENNESSEE, GRACE *See* Smith, Mira Ann.

TERRY (of **Zydeco Bad Boys**) *See* Domingue, Terry.

TERRY, AL (Allison Joseph Theriot) *Rockabilly, country.* Guitar, vocals. Composer. Bandleader. (Born Jan. 14, 1922, Kaplan, Vermilion Parish; died Nov. 23, 1985, Lafayette, Lafayette Parish.) Noted early rockabilly and country singer-songwriter and guitarist best known for his mid- to late 1950s recordings on Hickory such as "Good Deal, Lucille" and "Watch Dog." Raised in a musical family, formed his first band while still in high school, inspired by **Jimmie Davis** and Gene Autry. In the mid- to late 1940s and early 1950s released singles on Gold Star, Champion, and Feature and also recorded as sideman with **Jimmy C. Newman**. Signed with Hickory in 1954 and had immediate country hit with "Good Deal, Lucille," which he later recut in 1957 as a rockabilly number. Numerous singles followed on Hickory through 1960, including "Money" with **Rusty** and **Doug Kershaw** in 1957. In the 1960s had singles on Dot, Index, and Rice but in later years worked mainly as radio broadcaster. Brother Bob Theriot (1925–2004) was an accomplished steel guitarist and songwriter.

TERRY, GENE (Terry Gene Derouen) *Swamp pop.* Guitar, vocals. Composer. Bandleader. (Born Jan. 7, 1940, Lafayette, Lafayette Parish.) Early swamp pop singer and bandleader was raised in a musical family in Port Arthur, Texas, from age two and began playing guitar during his teens, inspired by **Fats Domino** and Elvis Presley. Formed band the Kool Kats and recorded debut single for Rock-It in 1957. In 1958 relocated to Lake Charles and formed the Down Beats, recording several singles for Goldband, including "Cindy Lou" and "No Mail Today." Also had a release on Savoy. Returned to Texas in 1960 and retired from performing several years later.

TERRY, KENNETH *Jazz.* Trumpet, vocals. Composer. Bandleader. (Born Oct. 5, 1969, New Orleans, Orleans Parish.) Traditional New Orleans brass-band trumpeter started playing at age seven and at age 10 began studying under **Milton Batiste**. In the 1980s was founding leader of Young Olympia Brass Band and went on to perform with New Birth, Jackson Square, Rebirth, Chosen Few, Tremé, and other noted brass bands. Continued to lead his own jazz and brass bands in the 2010s.

THEALL, NED *Swamp pop, rhythm and blues.* Trumpet, saxophone. Composer. Bandleader. (Born Nov. 26, 1937, Abbeville, Vermilion Parish; died Jan. 8, 2010, Lafayette, Lafayette Parish.) Longtime bandleader and arranger of the Boogie Kings who began leading the band in 1965 and continued throughout numerous reunions and reformations from the mid-1970s through late 2000s, as well as on subsequent recordings. Composed two of the Boogie Kings' best-known original songs, "Philly Walk" and "I Love That Swamp Pop Music," and was largely responsible for transforming the band's musical style from swamp pop to blue-eyed soul in the mid-1960s. Continued performing and leading the band until his sudden death from an aneurysm at age 72.

THEARD, SAMUEL "LOVIN' SAM" (*also* "Lovin' Sam from Down in 'Bam" *and* "Spo-Dee-O-Dee") *Blues.* Vocals. Composer. Bandleader. (Born Oct. 10, 1904, New Orleans, Orleans Parish; died Dec. 7, 1982, Los Angeles.) Early blues singer and songwriter began performing in circus shows and on the southern vaudeville circuit in the 1920s. From 1929 through 1941 recorded for Banner, Decca, Vocalion, and Bluebird and had several hits, including "You Rascal You" and "Spo-Dee-O-Dee," often backed by Tampa Red and Cow Cow Davenport. In the 1940s and 1950s recorded with Hot Lips Page, Tiny Parham, and Hal Singer, and his compositions were recorded by Louis Jordan, Count Basie, Wynonie Harris, Eddie "Cleanhead" Vinson, and others. In the 1970s worked in television and film.

THERIOT, DUNICE *Cajun.* Guitar, accordion, fiddle, vocals. Composer. Bandleader. (Born Dec. 23, 1937, Breaux Bridge, St. Martin Parish; died Mar. 28, 1990, Henderson, St. Martin Parish.) Noted Cajun-country singer-songwriter and multi-instrumentalist began performing in his teens and formed his first band in 1953. Worked regularly with **Rufus Thibodeaux** and **Warren Storm** and in the 1970s recorded extensively with his band the Lake Charles Playboys with numerous singles on his own Sportsman label, notably regional hit "Cotton Rows."

THERIOT, MAW MAW (John Wallace Theriot) *Cajun.* Accordion, vocals. Bandleader. (Born Aug. 1, 1952, Lake Charles, Calcasieu Parish; died Feb. 28, 2001, Sulphur, Calcasieu Parish.) Lake Charles–area Cajun singer, accordionist, and leader of his Cajun Commandeaux Band in the 1980s and 1990s. Recorded for Lanor in the 1980s, including single "I Made a Big Mistake" in 1985.

THIBODEAUX, AMBROSE *Cajun.* Accordion, triangle. Bandleader. (Born Oct. 18, 1903, Eunice, St. Landry Parish; died Nov. 15, 1995, Lafayette, Lafayette Parish.) Noted early Cajun accordionist began playing at age 15 and two years later was performing at local house dances. At age 21 quit music to raise a family. In 1960 began performing again and through the late 1970s appeared at festivals throughout the United States, recording four LPs on La Louisianne, including *Authentic French Acadian Music,* and one album on Bee. Also appeared regularly on Revon Reed's radio show broadcast from Fred's Lounge in Mamou. Toured Europe in the late 1970s and continued performing into his 80s.

THIBODEAUX, ERNEST *Cajun.* Guitar, fiddle, vocals. Bandleader. (Born Oct. 9, 1925, Mermentau, Acadia Parish; died Aug. 18, 2006, Lake Charles, Calcasieu Parish.) Renowned early postwar Cajun guitarist began playing at age 10 and in 1938 formed the Lake Charles Playboys with **Will Kegley** and **T-Boy Esthay**. In the mid-1940s renamed band Pine Grove Boys with the addition of **Nathan Abshire** on accordion and performed and recorded extensively with group through 1955, appearing on recordings such as "Pine Grove Blues" and "Big Mamou." Also performed with **Iry LeJeune** and **Lawrence Walker**. After Abshire's death continued leading Pine Grove Boys in the 1980s and recorded single "Robert Special" on Lanor.

THIBODEAUX, EUGENE "GENO" *Cajun.* Accordion, vocals. Composer. Bandleader. (Born July 1, 1938, Rayne, Acadia Parish; died Dec. 15, 2011, Lake Charles, Calcasieu Parish.) Noted accordion player and bandleader began playing at age 22, inspired by **Aldus Roger**, and during his mid-20s performed and recorded with **Cleveland Crochet**. From 1965 to 1970 recorded several singles for Swallow/Cajun Jamboree and in the early 1970s recorded signature song, "No Salt in the Beans," with **Robert Bertrand** for Goldband. Later performed with **Belton Richard**'s Musical Aces when Richard retired as well as with his own group the Musical Kings.

THIBODEAUX, GLADIUS *Cajun.* Accordion. (Born Mar. 29, 1922, Church Point, Acadia Parish; died Oct. 23, 1987, Eunice, St. Landry Parish.) Cajun accordionist who accompanied **Dewey Balfa** and fiddler Vinesse LeJeune (1931–2003) on landmark performance at 1964 Newport Folk Festival, which exposed Cajun music to a mass audience outside of Louisiana and sparked national interest. Appeared on recordings from concert on Vanguard's 1965 LP *Traditional Music at Newport 1964 Part 1.*

THIBODEAUX, GOLDMAN *Creole.* Accordion, vocals. Bandleader. (Born Aug. 5, 1932, Opelousas, St. Landry Parish.) Traditional Creole accordionist and singer was first inspired as a child by seeing **Amédé Ardoin** perform. Decades later while in his 50s began learning accordion from **Delton Broussard** and eventually took over for Broussard in the Lawtell Playboys when he retired in the late 1980s, joining fiddler **Calvin Carrière**. Continued performing and eventually leading the band through the 2010s with several noted releases, including *Les Misères dans le Coeur* with Carrière on Louisiana Radio in 2000.

THIBODEAUX, RUDDLEY *Jazz.* Trumpet. Bandleader. (Born Aug. 21, 1947, Algiers, Orleans Parish.) New Orleans brass-band trumpeter began playing the instrument in his early teens, inspired by **Louis Armstrong**. Worked with rhythm and blues bands and artists such as **Rockie Charles** in the 1970s and early 1980s. In 1987 cofounded Algiers Brass Band and continued to lead group through the 2010s, touring nationally and overseas.

THIBODEAUX, RUFUS *Cajun.* Fiddle, guitar, vocals. (Born Jan. 5, 1934, Ridge, Lafayette Parish; died Aug. 12, 2005, Nashville.) Highly revered and influential Cajun fiddler known for his long association with **Jimmy C. Newman**. Began playing guitar and fiddle as a child and by age 13 was performing in local dance halls and appearing on radio broadcasts with **Happy Fats**. After working with **Papa Cairo** in 1949, began touring and recording with Newman, appearing on Newman's first hit, "Cry Cry Darling," in 1954. In the early 1950s also worked as session player for **J. D. Miller** and through 1970s performed and recorded with numerous country artists such as Bob Wills, George Jones, Lefty Frizzell, and Jim Reeves as well as Cajun musicians **Nathan Abshire**, **Balfa Brothers**, **Blackie Forestier**, **Abe Manuel**, and others. In the 1970s and 1980s recorded with Newman, Neil Young, and **Zachary Richard**, among others, and released two LPs as a leader on La Louisianne, including *The Cajun Country Fiddle of Rufus Thibodeaux.* Continued performing into the early 2000s despite suffering from diabetes-related health issues. Cousin of **Tony Thibodeaux**.

THIBODEAUX, TONY (Antoine Thibodeaux) *Cajun.* Fiddle. Bandleader. (Born June 2, 1938, Lafayette, Lafayette Parish; died Sept. 30, 2010, Lake Charles, Calcasieu Parish.) Renowned Cajun fiddle player began performing in the late 1940s and, after working with **Walter Mouton** in the early 1950s, performed and recorded with **Aldus Roger** from 1955 to the late 1960s and with **Belton Richard** from the late 1960s through the early 1980s. Also worked regularly with **Vin Bruce**, **Paul Daigle** (in Cajun Gold), and others and in later years led his band the Cajun Five. In 1998 recorded *Fiddlin' with Friends* on La Louisianne with cousin **Rufus Thibodeaux**. Brother Leon was also a Cajun fiddle player.

THIBODEAUX, WAYLON *Cajun.* Fiddle, guitar, bass, drums, vocals. Composer. Bandleader. (Born Aug. 12, 1969, Houma, Terrebonne Parish.) Dubbed "Louisiana's Rockin' Fiddler," began performing during his early teens, inspired by **Jo-El Sonnier**, and toured France with mentor **Papa Gene Dusenbery** and family in 1983. Performed and recorded with **Bruce Daigrepont**'s band for several years in New Orleans before forming his own group. Released numerous CDs on Mardi Gras, Rockin' River, and Rabadash and continued performing with his own group and as member of **Tab Benoit**'s Voice of the Wetlands All-Stars in the 2010s.

THIERRY, HUEY "COOKIE" *Swamp pop.* Saxophone, vocals. Composer. (Born Aug. 13, 1936, Roanoke, Jeff. Davis Parish; died Sept. 23, 1997, Lake Charles, Calcasieu Parish.)[2] Pioneering swamp pop singer and songwriter best known for his work with premier swamp pop group Cookie and the Cupcakes and his composition "Mathilda," which became a swamp pop anthem. Raised by parents who were both Creole musicians, began singing during his teens, influenced greatly by **Fats Domino**. In the early 1950s joined **Ernest Jacob**'s Boogie Ramblers as singer and saxophonist, sharing vocal duties with **Shelton Dunaway**. After recording for Goldband in the mid-1950s, band changed name to Cookie and the Cupcakes and performed extensively in south Louisiana and east Texas clubs. In late 1958 recorded "Mathilda" for Lyric which was released nationally when leased to Judd. In following years had releases on Lyric, Mercury, and Chess, including swamp pop classics "Got You on My Mind," "Belinda," and "Betty and Dupree" and became one of the most popular groups touring the Gulf Coast circuit. In the mid-1960s left the band and relocated to California, working mainly outside music through the early 1990s. Reunited with original members of the Cupcakes in the early 1990s and performed nationally and overseas with group until his death at age 61. Older brother of **Terry Clinton**.

THOMAS, BLANCHE *Blues, jazz.* Vocals. (Born Oct. 16, 1922, New Orleans, Orleans Parish; died Apr. 21, 1977, New Orleans, Orleans Parish.)[3] Internationally renowned New Orleans jazz and blues singer began performing at age 14 in clubs on Rampart Street. In the 1940s worked with **Sidney Desvigne**, **Louis Cottrell**, **Alvin Alcorn**, and others. Joined **Dave Bartholomew**'s band as vocalist in the mid-1950s and made recording debut on Imperial with "You Ain't So Such a Much" in 1954. In the 1960s recorded with **Paul Barbarin** and **Albert "Papa" French** and toured on USO circuit in Vietnam and Thailand. Around 1970 made recordings with French's Original Tuxedo Brass Band and also with Alcorn. Performed regularly at Dixieland Hall and Heritage Hall, appeared at Carnegie Hall, and toured Europe before retiring due to illness in the mid-1970s.

THOMAS, CARLTON "GUITAR" *Zydeco.* Guitar, vocals. (Born Mar. 26, 1944, Opelousas, St. Landry Parish; died Sept. 4, 2001, Lake Charles, Calcasieu Parish.) Highly regarded zydeco guitarist best known for his long tenure with **Boozoo Chavis**'s band. Began playing guitar at age four and started performing in clubs while in his teens. Worked with various rhythm and blues musicians, including **Good Rockin' Bob**, **Rudy Richard**, and others. From the early 1980s until Chavis's death in 2001 toured and recorded extensively as member of his band the Magic Sounds.

THOMAS, CHRIS *See* King, Chris Thomas.

THOMAS, CRYSTAL *Rhythm and blues.* Vocals, trombone. Composer. Bandleader. (Born May 25, 1977, Shreveport, Caddo Parish.) Raised in rural Mansfield from age one, southern soul singer and songwriter began playing the trombone in elementary school and while in college performed in the Jackson State University Marching Band. In the late 1990s began performing around the Shreveport area as a singer and trombonist, which led to work with Johnnie Taylor's band in Dallas in 2000. By the mid-2010s began branching out as a bandleader on the southern soul circuit, releasing debut CD *Lyrical Gumbo: The Essence of Blues* on Jones Boyz Ent. in 2016 and appearing on *Texas Queens 5* on Dialtone in 2018.

THOMAS, ED *See* Good Rockin' Bob.

THOMAS, EVAN *Jazz.* Trumpet. Bandleader. (Born Jan. 6, 1894, Crowley, Acadia Parish; died Nov. 21, 1931, Rayne, Acadia Parish.)[4] Renowned early Acadiana jazz trumpeter and bandleader whose famed Black Eagles Band of the late 1910s and 1920s included such notable members as **Bunk Johnson**, **Lawrence Duhé**, **George Lewis**, **Kid Avery**, **Chester Zardis**, **Mercedes** and **Harold Potier Sr.**, and **George "Pop" Hamilton**. Regarded by many peers as an equal to the best New Orleans trumpet players of his time. Performed regularly throughout Louisiana and east Texas with his Black Eagles and occasionally with **Gus Fontenette**'s Banner Orchestra. Stabbed to death by a jealous husband while band was playing "I'll Be Glad When You're Dead You Rascal You" during a dance in Rayne with Johnson and Lewis. Brother Walter Thomas was a jazz drummer and member of the Black Eagles.

THOMAS, IRMA *Rhythm and blues.* Vocals. Composer. Bandleader. (Born Feb. 18, 1941, Ponchatoula, Tangipahoa Parish.) Internationally renowned "Soul Queen of New Orleans" started singing as a teenager in her Baptist church choir. While waitressing at a club in New Orleans in the late 1950s, began sitting in with **Tommy Ridgley** who helped her land a recording contract with Ron Records, which resulted in debut hit "Don't Mess with My Man" in 1960. In early to mid-1960s worked with **Allen Toussaint** and had numerous releases on Minit and Imperial, including such New Orleans soul classics as "Ruler of My Heart," "It's Raining," "Time Is on My Side," and "Wish Someone Would Care." Recorded several singles for Chess in 1967–68 and between 1969 and 1976 relocated to California and had releases on Cotillion, Canyon, Roker, and Fungus. Returned to New Orleans in 1976 and in the early 1980s opened club the Lions Den which she operated until its destruction by Hurricane Katrina in 2005. In the mid-1980s signed with Rounder and had 10 releases on label through the late 2000s, including highly acclaimed *After the Rain* in 2006. Continued to perform and tour internationally in the late 2010s, widely regarded as New Orleans's premier soul singer.

THOMAS, JESSE "BABYFACE" *Blues.* Guitar, bass, vocals. Composer. Bandleader. (Born Feb. 3, 1911, Logansport, DeSoto Parish; died Aug. 13, 1995, Shreveport, Caddo Parish.)[5] Highly regarded blues guitarist and singer whose distinguished music career spanned seven decades. Raised in a musical family, began playing guitar as a child, influenced by brother **Willard "Ramblin'" Thomas** and later **Lonnie Johnson** and pianist **Black Ivory King**. In 1929 recorded four sides for Victor, including "My Heart's a Rolling Stone" and "Blue Goose Blues." Continued performing in Texas and Oklahoma before relocating to Los Angeles in the late 1930s. From 1948 to 1957 had singles on Miltone, Freedom, Modern, Swing Time, Specialty, Elko, Hollywood, and his own Club label. Returned to Shreveport area in the late 1950s and in the mid-1960s released singles on his Red River label. After two decades of obscurity had career resurgence in the early 1990s with appearances at numerous national blues festivals and releases on Red River, Delmark, and Black Top, the last of which was recorded shortly before his death at age 84. Uncle of **Lafayette "Thing" Thomas**.

THOMAS, JESSE (*also* **"Young Jesse")** *Rhythm and blues.* Vocals. (Born Sept. 1, 1937, New Orleans, Orleans Parish.) New Orleans rhythm and blues singer who was a member of **Huey "Piano" Smith**'s Clowns in the late 1950s and 1960s. Made recording debut as a leader on Teem in 1961 and in 1964 released "I'm Boss Yeah" on Ace, both backed by Smith's band. Had a single each on Tail-Gate in 1966 and White Cliffs as "Young Jesse" in 1967. Relocated to New York in 1968 and released CD *Easy in the Apple* on Fedora in 2000. Not to be confused with **Jesse "Babyface" Thomas** or California-based Obie Jessie who recorded as "Young Jessie" in the 1950s.

THOMAS, JOSEPH "BROTHER CORNBREAD" *Jazz.* Clarinet, vocals. Bandleader. (Born Dec. 3, 1902, New

Orleans, Orleans Parish; died Feb. 18, 1981, New Orleans, Orleans Parish.) Early New Orleans jazz clarinetist began performing in the mid-1920s and later worked with **Kid Rena**, **Jack Carey**, and **Chris Kelly**. In 1941 recorded as a leader with a small swing outfit and led bands through the late 1940s. Joined **Papa Celestin**'s Tuxedo Brass Band in 1951 and performed and recorded with group throughout next two decades. Also recorded with **Freddie Kohlman**, **Punch Miller**, and **Paul Barbarin**'s Onward Brass Band in the 1950s and 1960s. In the 1970s toured Europe and recorded with **Kid Sheik** and also performed as member of Legends of Jazz tour for several years.

THOMAS, LEO "THE BULL" *Zydeco.* Drums, guitar, vocals. Composer. Bandleader. (Born Jan. 8, 1937, Elton, Jeff. Davis Parish.) Influential zydeco drummer and singer-songwriter who was the first zydeco musician to lead a band from behind the drums. Known for his signature song, "Why You Wanna Make Me Cry." Began playing guitar in rhythm and blues group the House Rockers around Lake Charles area in the late 1950s. Soon switched to drums and performed and recorded with numerous musicians, including **Wilfred LaTour** and **Preston Frank**, before forming his own band in the 1970s, joined by son **Leroy Thomas** in the early 1980s. In 1985 recorded single for Lanor and in the 1990s had releases on Bad Weather and Maison de Soul, including *I'm Going Blind* in 1997. Continued performing occasionally into his 80s, often sitting in with son Leroy. Father of zydeco drummer Lee Andrus Thomas.

THOMAS, LEROY *Zydeco.* Accordion, drums, vocals. Composer. Bandleader. (Born Dec. 14, 1965, Lake Charles, Calcasieu Parish.) Noted traditional zydeco accordion player and singer-songwriter with country music influences was raised in Elton and began playing drums at age eight and accordion during his early teens. In 1983 joined his father **Leo "the Bull" Thomas**'s band and performed and recorded with group until forming the Zydeco Roadrunners in 1998. Throughout following decade had releases on Bad Weather, Hardcore, and his own Leroy label, including *Jewel of the Bayou* in 2010, having success with songs "Trail Ride," "Judgement Day," and "3 O'Clock in the Morning." Continued performing extensively on club and festival circuit in 2010s, releasing CD *We Love You Leroy!* on Maison de Soul in 2015. Brother of zydeco drummer and singer Lee Andrus Thomas.

THOMAS, RAMBLIN' (Willard Thomas) *Blues.* Guitar, vocals. Composer. (Born 1901, Logansport, DeSoto Parish; died 1944, Memphis.) Influential early prewar blues slide guitarist and singer best known for his recordings on Paramount and Victor such as "Poor Boy Blues," "Ramblin' Mind Blues," and "Ground Hog Blues." Relocated to Dallas in the 1920s and in following years performed around Texas and Oklahoma. Recorded 14 sides during two sessions for Paramount in Chicago in 1928 and four sides for Victor in Dallas in 1932 which influenced Robert Johnson, Black Ace, John Lee Hooker, and others. Reportedly died of tuberculosis in Memphis according to younger brother **Jesse "Babyface" Thomas**. Uncle of **Lafayette "Thing" Thomas**.

THOMAS, ROCKIN' TABBY (Ernest Joseph Thomas) *Blues.* Guitar, piano, vocals. Composer. Bandleader. (Born Jan. 5, 1929, Baton Rouge, EBR Parish; died Jan. 1, 2014, Baton Rouge, EBR Parish.) Renowned Baton Rouge blues musician and club owner who was greatly responsible for the city's blues resurgence in the 1980s. Began performing while in the military and stationed in San Francisco. Upon discharge in 1952 recorded a single for Hollywood label but after disappointing sales returned to Baton Rouge. After singles on Feature, Rocko, and Zynn from 1954 to 1960, recorded several noted releases on Excello in the early to mid-1960s, including the swamp blues classic "Hoodoo Party." In following years had releases on numerous local labels including Blues Unlimited, Maison de Soul, Hip, Jin, and his own Blue Beat Records. In 1979 opened popular club Tabby's Blues Box, which featured local and national blues artists and served as an important training ground for many younger and emerging artists such as **Larry Garner**, **Kenny** and **Lil' Ray Neal**, **Tab Benoit**, **Troy Turner**, and his son **Chris Thomas King**. Released several CDs in the late 1990s and early 2000s, including *Hoodoo Kings* on Telarc with **Eddie Bo** and **Raful Neal**. Relocated club in 2000 due to highway expansion but eventually closed it in late 2004 after suffering a stroke. Continued to host his own radio show and perform sporadically as vocalist for several more years.

THOMAS, WILLIE B. *Blues.* Guitar, kazoo, vocals. (Born May 25, 1912, Bellemont Plantation, Lobdell, WBR Parish; died Nov. 23, 1977, Zachary, EBR Parish.) Country blues guitarist and singer best known for his partnership with fiddler **Butch Cage**. Began playing country suppers in local string bands and in the late 1920s joined with Cage, first on kazoo and then guitar. In 1959–60 the pair was recorded by folklorist Harry Oster and appeared at Newport Folk Festival. Continued to perform together until Cage's death in 1975.

THOMPSON, EMERY HUMPHREY (Umar Sharif) *Jazz.* Trumpet. Composer. Bandleader. (Born Sept. 17, 1927, New Orleans, Orleans Parish; died Oct. 16, 1998, Norcross, Georgia.) Renowned New Orleans jazz trumpeter began playing at age five and studied under his grandfather **Professor Jim Humphrey** and cousin **Willie Humphrey**. In the 1940s worked with Jimmie Lunceford and **Dooky Chase** and led his own swing band. In the mid- to late 1940s toured with road shows and performed with Luis Russell, Fletcher Henderson, Louis Jordan, and Lionel Hampton. Through the early 1950s also worked with **Lonnie Johnson**, Ella Fitzgerald, Frank Sinatra, Joe Turner, and others. Retired from music from 1955 to 1974 and changed name to Umar Sharif. Began performing again in 1975 and appeared in Broadway orchestras in the late 1970s and 1980s. Performed as member of Lincoln Jazz Center Orchestra and continued touring internationally through the 1990s. Father of **Jamil Sharif**.

THREE FIFTEEN (David Blunson/Blunston) *Blues.* Vocals. Composer. Bandleader. (Born possibly Dec. 6, 1909, Franklin Parish; died Oct. 20, 1958, San Mateo County, California; *or* born July 5, 1890, Shreveport, Caddo Parish; died Sept. 15, 1968, Shreveport, Caddo Parish.) Enigmatic early blues singer (and possibly pianist) who was a popular performer in Shreveport in the 1930s. Performed with traveling minstrel and carnival shows throughout the 1930s. Recorded four sides for Vocalion in 1937, notably "Saturday Night on Texas Avenue," which described life along Shreveport's black entertainment district.

TIBBS, KENNY (Kenneth Thibodeaux) *Swamp pop.* Guitar, vocals. Composer. Bandleader. (Born July 17, 1942, Youngsville, Lafayette Parish.) Early swamp pop vocalist performed with **Little Alvin** and the Chipmunks in 1958 before joining **Willie Tee**'s band Willie and the Jokers as vocalist. In 1959 group had local hit with "I Promise" on Viking and soon changed band name to Kenny and the Jokers. Continued performing with band for 40-plus years with several more singles on Viking and Jin, including local novelty hit "(Holly Beach) Under the Boardwalk" in the early 1990s.

TILLEY, JOHN "BIG PAPA" *Blues.* Harmonica, vocals. Bandleader. (Born July 11, 1926, Baton Rouge, EBR Parish; died Feb. 5, 1961, New Orleans, Orleans Parish.)[6] Important but unrecorded early Baton Rouge blues musician and bandleader of the late 1940s and 1950s whose popular bands included many up-and-coming local blues musicians, including **Buddy** and **Phil Guy**, **Lightnin' Slim**, **Slim Harpo**, **Lazy Lester**, **Raful Neal**, **Boogie Jake**, **Big Boe Melvin**, **James Johnson**, and others. Reportedly stopped playing blues in the late 1950s to join the church. Died several days after suffering a stroke at age 34 in New Orleans Charity Hospital.

TILLMAN, CURTIS *Blues.* Bass, vocals. Composer. Bandleader. (Born Aug. 5, 1926, New Orleans, Orleans Parish; died Aug. 25, 2006, Los Angeles.) Blues bass player and singer relocated to Los Angeles and worked as a studio musician throughout the 1960s on sessions with Ray Agee, Lowell Fulson, George "Harmonica" Smith, Ace Holder, Little Joe Blue, Sunnyland Slim, T-Bone Walker Jr., and others. Led bands of his own and also worked regularly with Big Mama Thornton, Freddie King, and others. In 2000 appeared on *More Blues from the South Side* with Smokey Wilson and **South Side Slim** on South Side Records.

TILLMAN, GERALD *See* Professor Shorthair.

TILLMAN, LEE *Rhythm and blues.* Vocals. Composer. Bandleader. (Born Feb. 1, 1936, Denham Springs, Livingston Parish.) Noted Baton Rouge soul-blues singer moved to the city as a youth and began sitting in with **Lester Robertson** before joining **Buddy Stewart**'s Top Notchers in 1960. In 1961 had local success with debut single, "If I Ever"/"Will Travel," on Ron and in the mid-1960s released five singles on Michelle/Montel-Michelle labels. Recorded final single "She's the One I Love" for Whit in 1966, backed by the Secrets. Continued to perform with various Baton Rouge groups for several years, including Stewart's Herculoids with **Harvey Knox**. Worked mainly outside music throughout following decades with only occasional appearances at special events.

TIO, LORENZO, JR. *Jazz.* Clarinet. Bandleader. (Born Apr. 21, 1893, New Orleans, Orleans Parish; died Dec. 24, 1933, Manhattan, New York.) Highly influential early New Orleans jazz clarinetist who also served as an important teacher to many noted jazz musicians. By age nine was performing in parade bands and between 1910 and 1915 worked with **Freddie Keppard**'s Olympia Orchestra and Onward and Tuxedo brass bands. Relocated to Chicago in 1916 and worked with **Charlie Elgar** and **Manuel Perez** throughout the next two years. Returned to New Orleans and from 1918 to 1928 performed regularly with **Armand Piron**'s orchestra and recorded with group in 1923–24. Relocated to New York in 1930 and recorded with **Jelly Roll Morton**. Continued performing in New York jazz clubs until his death. As teacher his students included **Sidney Bechet**, **Jimmie Noone**, **Louis Cottrell Jr.**, **Omer Simeon**, **Harold Dejan**, **Don Albert**, **Barney Bigard**, **Paul Barnes**, and many others. Son of **Lorenzo Tio Sr.** and nephew of **Louis "Papa" Tio**.

T. K. SOUL (Terence Kimble) *Rhythm and blues.* Vocals, guitar, bass, piano, drums. Composer. Bandleader. (Born Aug. 26, 1964, Winnfield, Winn Parish.) Contemporary southern soul singer and multi-instrumentalist spent five years as keyboardist and songwriter with Willie Clayton before launching solo career in 2002 with CD *One Woman Man* on his Soulful label. Continued touring as popular draw on the southern soul circuit into the 2010s with multiple releases, including *The Legacy* in 2016.

TOCA, LAWRENCE (Lawrence Martin) *Jazz.* Trumpet. (Born June 6, 1908, New Orleans, Orleans Parish; died July 2, 1972, New Orleans, Orleans Parish.)[7] New Orleans jazz trumpeter studied under **Chris Kelly** and worked regularly with **Emile Barnes** in the 1940s and early 1950s. Also performed with **George Lewis** and **Sweet Emma Barrett**. Recorded with **De De Pierce** in 1951 and retired from music in the mid-1950s.

TOOKIE *See* Collom, Wayne.

TOOMBS, RUDY (Rudolph Toombs) *Rhythm and blues.* Vocals. Composer. (Born 1914, Monroe, Ouachita Parish; died Nov. 28, 1962, Manhattan, New York.) Recorded as vocalist with Johnny Moore's Blazers in 1954 for Blaze but best known for his many early rhythm and blues and doo-wop compositions, which were recorded by numerous artists, including Etta James, Freddie King, James Brown, Amos Milburn, Wynonie Harris, and Ray Charles. His notable songs include "Teardrops from My Eyes," "One Bourbon, One Scotch, One Beer," "5-10-15 Hours," and "One Mint Julep." Credited with writing more than 500 songs. While returning home was fatally beaten during a mugging in the hallway of his apartment building.

TORRENCE, LIONEL *See* Prevost, Lionel.

TOUCHET, ARCONGE "T-COON" *Cajun.* Guitar, drums. Composer. Bandleader. (Born Jan. 6, 1928, Forked Island, Vermilion Parish; died Dec. 9, 2017, New Iberia, Iberia Parish.) Noted Cajun steel guitarist and founding member of the famed **Touchet Brothers** began playing guitar at age 12 and by age 14 started performing with brothers Iday and Willis in local dance halls, joined by brother Elier and sister Eva several years later. From 1954 to 1967 performed with **Elias "Shute" Badeaux**'s Louisiana Aces and appeared on band's 1960s recordings, including band member **D. L. Menard**'s Cajun classic "The Back Door." Continued recording and performing with the Touchet Brothers through the 2000s.

TOUCHET BROTHERS *Cajun.* (Born Forked Island, Vermilion Parish.) Renowned long-running Cajun family band consisting of four brothers: steel guitarist **Arconge "T-Coon"** (1928–2017), guitarist Iday "Pierre" (1908–2007), fiddle player Willis (1926–2012), accordionist Elier (1914–2001), and after 1947, sister Eva (1932–) on bass and guitar. Band performed from the early 1940s through 2000s and recorded numerous sides for Swallow from 1967 to 2000, including several compositions which became Cajun standards, such as "It's Lonesome in Prison," "The Life I Thought I Wanted," and "Old Fashioned Two Step."

TOUCHET, LINUS *Cajun.* Guitar, vocals. Composer. Bandleader. (Born Dec. 19, 1932, Gueydan, Vermilion Parish; died Nov. 15, 2006, Gueydan, Vermilion Parish.) Cajun steel guitarist and bandleader of the Rainbow Ramblers who recorded several sides for Goldband in 1958, including "Gueydan Two Step." Also recorded with **Ellis Vanicor** and performed with **Milton Adams**'s Midnite Playboys. Wife Theresa was an accomplished Cajun drummer.

TOUCHET, WALLACE "RED" *Cajun.* Fiddle. (Born Nov. 12, 1931, Gueydan, Vermilion Parish.) Noted Cajun fiddler began performing in the late 1940s with **Shorty LeBlanc** before joining **Lionel Cormier**'s Sundown Playboys at age 17. Performed and recorded with group for more than five decades. In the 1980s also performed and recorded with **Pat Savant**'s Louisiana Playboys and later worked with **Rodney LeJeune**'s Texas Playboys. Continued performing occasionally with the Sundown Playboys in the 2010s. Son of Cajun fiddler Edwin "Neg" Touchet (1910–1993).

TOUCHET, WILSON *Cajun.* Accordion, vocals. Composer. Bandleader. (Born Apr. 12, 1943, Cypress Island, St. Martin Parish.) Cajun singer-accordionist and longtime bandleader of New Orleans–based traditional Cajun band La Touché, which he formed in 1987. Band released several recordings in the 1990s, including *On the Bayou* in 1994 on Ralph, and performed weekly at Mulate's in

New Orleans for more than 20 years. Retired from performing in the mid-2010s.

TOUPS, WAYNE *Cajun.* Accordion, vocals. Composer. Bandleader. (Born Oct. 2, 1958, Crowley, Acadia Parish.) Popular contemporary Cajun accordion player and singer-songwriter known for his high-energy performances and his early fusion of Cajun, zydeco, and rock which he dubbed "zydecajun" in the mid-1980s. Began playing accordion at age 13, mentored early on by **Milton Adams** and **Shine Mouton**. In the early 1970s performed with **Camey Doucet** and the Crowley Aces, recording two singles for Kajun in 1973–74. Continued performing and recording with Crowley Aces through the 1970s with several more singles on Kajun and Bayou Classics and LP *Cajun Paradise* on Sonet in 1979. In the mid-1980s signed with Mercury after forming band Zydecajun and released album of same name to national acclaim. Throughout following decade toured extensively nationally and overseas, appeared on numerous film and television soundtracks, and had releases on Mercury/Polygram, Master-Trak, Swallow, and New Blues, including *Back to the Bayou* on Swallow in 1995. In the 2000s had releases on Shanachie and Swallow and in the early 2010s performed and recorded with **Steve Riley** and **Wilson Savoy** as member of the Band Courtbouillon. Continued performing in the late 2010s as a popular act on club and festival circuit and released self-titled label debut for Malaco in 2016.

TOURO, PINCHBACK *Jazz.* Baritone horn, guitar, violin. Bandleader. (Born around 1870, St. James Parish; died early 1940s, St. James Parish.) Enigmatic early jazz bandleader and music teacher who led various bands for decades, including his Lincoln Band and Holy Ghost Band of Napoleonville. In the early 1930s also led W.P.A. Brass Band. His former students included **Andrew Morgan** and **Joseph "Kid Twat" Butler**.

TOUSSAINT, ALLEN *Rhythm and blues.* Piano, vocals. Composer. Bandleader. (Born Jan. 14, 1938, New Orleans, Orleans Parish; died Nov. 10, 2015, Madrid.) Extremely influential songwriter, producer, arranger, and pianist who is widely regarded as one of the most important figures in New Orleans rhythm and blues. Began playing piano as a child, initially inspired by **Professor Longhair** and later **Fats Domino** and **Huey "Piano" Smith**. In the early 1950s formed his first band, the Flamingos, which included **Snooks Eaglin**. In the mid-1950s worked as session musician for **Dave Bartholomew** and appeared on recordings with Domino, **Smiley Lewis**, **Lee Allen**, and others. Recorded LP *The Wild Sound of New Orleans* for RCA under the name Tousan in 1958, which included his composition "Java," which became a national hit for **Al Hirt** in 1964. In the 1960s produced, arranged, and composed numerous hits for **Lee Dorsey**, **Irma Thomas**, **Ernie K-Doe**, **Chris Kenner**, **Aaron Neville**, **Jesse Hill**, **Bennie Spellman**, the Meters, and others and cofounded Sansu Enterprises with producer **Marshall Sehorn**. In the 1970s released several LPs as a leader, including *Southern Nights* on Reprise in 1975, and worked with **Dr. John**, the Neville Brothers, Solomon Burke, the Band, Robert Palmer, Patti LaBelle, Paul McCartney, and many others. In the 1980s and 1990s continued to produce, compose, and collaborate with other artists and started his NYNO recording label in 1996. Relocated to New York for several years after Hurricane Katrina in 2005 and began performing more often as leader, releasing several recordings, including *Songbook* on Rounder in 2013 which showcased many of his classic compositions on solo piano. Suffered fatal heart attack at age 77 following a performance while on tour in Spain. *See also entry as producer with* **Marshall Sehorn**.

TOWLES, NAT *Jazz.* Bass. Bandleader. (Born Oct. 10, 1905, New Orleans, Orleans Parish; died Nov. 29, 1962, Berkeley, California.)[8] Influential New Orleans jazz bassist and bandleader worked with **Buddy Petit** and **Red Allen** in the early 1920s. In 1923 formed Creole Harmony Kings and performed with group through 1927. Also worked with **Fate Marable** in 1925. In the 1930s and 1940s led popular swing bands in Mississippi, Chicago, and throughout the Southwest. Retired from music in 1959 and settled in California.

TOWNS, EFREM *Jazz.* Trumpet, vocals. Composer. (Born Dec. 20, 1960, New Orleans, Orleans Parish.) New Orleans brass-band trumpeter who was an original member of Dirty Dozen Brass Band, which formed in 1977. Continued to tour and record with group into the 2010s and appeared on sessions with Elvis Costello, **Dr. John**, **Buckwheat Zydeco**, Norah Jones, and others.

TRAHAN, ADAM *Cajun.* Accordion, fiddle, vocals. Composer. (Born Sept. 21, 1909, Abbeville, Vermilion Parish; died Apr. 1994, near Kaplan, Vermilion Parish.) Noted early Cajun accordion player and singer who was among the first to record Cajun music. Began playing accordion during his teens and performed at area house dances and dance halls with his trio, which included fiddle and guitar. Inspired by the recent success of **Joe Falcon**'s recordings, cut four sides in Dec. 1928 in New Orleans for Columbia, including "The Pretty Girls Don't Want Me" and "The Acadian Waltz." Quit playing music shortly afterwards but performed occasionally on part-time basis through the late 1940s.

TRAHAN, HORACE *Zydeco, Cajun.* Accordion, vocals. Composer. Bandleader. (Born June 12, 1976, Ossun, Lafayette Parish.) Cajun and zydeco accordionist, singer-songwriter, and bandleader began playing guitar and saxophone before learning Cajun on the accordion at age 15, mentored by his cousin **Felix Richard**. After high school toured and recorded with **D. L. Menard** and released debut CD *Ossun Blues* on Swallow in 1996. After performing with his Cajun band Ossun Express for several years, revamped group in 2000 and began playing zydeco as New Ossun Express, joined by father-in-law **Rodney Bernard**. Multiple acclaimed releases followed through the 2010s, featuring signature compositions such as "That Butt Thing," "Same Knife Cut the Sheep Cut the Goat," and "Keep Walking."

TRAHAN, JOHN *Cajun, country.* Accordion, guitar, fiddle, drums. Composer. Bandleader. (Born Mar. 1, 1962, Abbeville, Vermilion Parish.) Toured nationally with country artists Janie Fricke and **Eddy Raven** and performed with various Cajun musicians around Lafayette area such as **Hadley Castille**, **Merlin Fontenot**, and others in the 1980s and early 1990s. Released acclaimed debut CD, *John Trahan avec le Group Acadiana,* on La Louisianne in 1993 and *My Louisiana* on Acadian in 2010.

TREPAGNIER, ERNEST "NINESSE" *Jazz.* Bass drum. (Born Jan. 2, 1890, New Orleans, Orleans Parish; died June 9, 1951, New Orleans, Orleans Parish.)[9] Highly influential early New Orleans jazz drummer who was known as "King of the Bass Drum." Began playing professionally around 1908 and through the 1920s performed with the Magnolia Orchestra, **Freddie Keppard**'s Olympia Orchestra, **John Robichaux**, **Manuel Perez**, **Vic** and **Oke Gaspard**, and others. Joined **Papa Celestin**'s Tuxedo Brass Band in the mid-1910s and worked with group through the mid-1920s. Performed sporadically with various brass bands throughout the 1930s and worked as bartender in later years. Influenced many early jazz drummers, including **Black Happy Goldston** and **Abbey "Chinee" Foster**.

TROMBONE SHORTY (Troy Andrews) *Jazz, rhythm and blues.* Trombone, trumpet, tuba, organ, drums, vocals. Composer. Bandleader. (Born Jan. 2, 1986, New Orleans, Orleans Parish.) Internationally renowned New Orleans brass-band trombonist and bandleader was born and raised in Tremé and mentored by older brother **James "12" Andrews**. Grandfather **Jessie Hill** was also a major influence. A child prodigy, began playing at age four and became a bandleader by age six, performing in the streets of Tremé and the French Quarter. Worked with Andrews Family Band and Stooges Brass Band, among others. Began recording in his teens and soon achieved international acclaim for his dynamic high-energy performances, which incorporated blues, funk, gospel, rock, and hip-hop into the New Orleans brass-band sound. From 2002 through the late 2010s released recordings on Louisiana Red Hot, Tremé, Verve, and Blue Note, including "Backatown" in 2010 and "Parking Lot Symphony" in 2017. Cousin of **Trumpet Black**.

TROY, DAMON *Cajun.* Accordion, guitar, drums, piano, fiddle, vocals. Composer. Bandleader. (Born Jan. 4, 1982, Carencro, Lafayette Parish.) Contemporary Cajun multi-instrumentalist with zydeco, country, and rock influences began playing drums professionally at age 12 and at age 17 formed his band Louisiana Beat. Recorded self-titled debut CD in 1999 and followed with several more releases through the 2010s, including *Resurfaced* in 2007.

TRUITT, JOHNNY (John Truitt III) *Rhythm and blues.* Vocals. Composer. Bandleader. (Born Apr. 18, 1945, Eunice, St. Landry Parish; died July 31, 2007, Eunice, St. Landry Parish.) Southwest Louisiana deep soul singer began singing in church as a child. In the mid-1960s joined **Bobby Allen**'s Hurricanes as colead vocalist, impressing audiences and band members with his multi-octave vocal range and perfect pitch. Made recording debut as "Little John" on Huey Meaux's Neal label with two singles in 1965, notably the soul ballad "My Love Is Gone." In the mid- to late 1960s released four singles on A-Bet, including "There Goes A Girl" backed by Allen's Hurricanes, "Your Love Is Worth the Pain," and "I'm Thru with You." Cut final single "No Sad Times"/"For the Good Times" on Soul Unlimited in 1973. Also performed as member of **Little Buck Sinegal**'s Top Cats and in the 1970s worked regularly as second vocalist with **Little Bob** and the Lollipops. Later left secular music and returned to the church, serving as a Baptist minister.

TRUMPET BLACK (Travis Hill) *Jazz, rhythm and blues.* Trumpet, vocals. Bandleader. (Born Aug. 7, 1986, New Orleans, Orleans Parish; died May 4, 2015, Tokyo.) Talented New Orleans brass-band trumpet player began performing in cousin **Trombone Shorty**'s band as a child and later worked with New Birth, Lil Rascals, and Hot 8 Brass Band as well as **Corey Henry**'s Tremé Funktet. After serving nine years on an armed robbery conviction during his mid-teens, returned to the music scene and formed his band the Heart Attacks in 2012. Just as his popularity began to spread internationally, he suffered a fatal heart attack caused by a severe tooth infection while on tour in Japan at age 28. Grandson of **Jessie Hill**.

TUBA FATS (Anthony Lacen) *Jazz.* Tuba. Bandleader. (Born Sept. 15, 1950, New Orleans, Orleans Parish; died Jan. 11, 2004, New Orleans, Orleans Parish.) Influential and beloved tuba player and bandleader who helped modernize the brass-band sound in the 1970s and 1980s by employing the tuba as a solo instrument instead of strictly a rhythmic accompaniment. Began performing in brass bands on the streets while in middle high school and worked with **Doc Paulin**, **Sweet Emma Barrett**, **Kid Thomas**, and others, as well as Hurricane, Dirty Dozen, Olympia, and Onward brass bands. Also performed with Fairview Baptist Church Brass Band with **Danny Barker**, who named him Tuba Fats. Formed Tuba Fats & the Chosen Few Brass Band in the early 1980s which performed regularly in the French Quarter's Jackson Square and toured internationally. Succumbed to a fatal heart attack at age 53.

TURBINTON, EARL *Jazz, rhythm and blues.* Saxophone, vocals. Composer. Bandleader. (Born Sept. 23, 1941, New Orleans, Orleans Parish; died Aug. 3, 2007, Baton Rouge, EBR Parish.) Modern jazz saxophonist was greatly influenced by John Coltrane. In the 1960s and 1970s worked on rhythm and blues and funk sessions with **Allen Toussaint**, the Wild Magnolias, and the Gaturs. In the late 1960s and early 1970s toured and recorded with B.B. King. As a leader, released *Brothers for Life* on Rounder with younger brother **Willie Tee** in 1988 and *Dominion and Sustenance* on Progressive International in 1998. Continued performing until 2002, when health issues forced retirement.

TURNER, ANNIE *Blues, gospel.* Vocals. (Born July 4, 1921, New Orleans, Orleans Parish; date and place of death unknown.) Early blues vocalist made four recordings for Bluebird in 1936 with **Little Brother Montgomery** and Walter Jacobs in New Orleans. Later relocated to Chicago and sang gospel.

TURNER, HENRY JR. *Rhythm and blues.* Guitar, vocals. Composer. Bandleader. (Born Dec. 2, 1960, Baton Rouge, EBR Parish.) Reggae-influenced Baton Rouge rhythm and blues singer-guitarist formed his first band in the early 1980s and founded record label Hit City in 1983. Throughout following decades toured nationally and released numerous singles and albums on Hit City, including *Louisiana Funk Buffet* in 2006. In 2014 opened local club the Listening Room and continued performing with his band Flavor in the late 2010s.

TURNER, JOE *Cajun.* Guitar, bass, drums, vocals. Bandleader. (Born Mar. 12, 1939, Maurice, Vermilion Parish.) Veteran Cajun singer and guitarist best known for his work with **Pat Savant**'s Louisiana Playboys, notably the 1980 single "Woodpecker Song" on Kajun. Performed and recorded with **Happy Fats** in the 1960s and 1970s and also worked with **Aldus Roger**, **Aldus Mouton**, **Milton Adams**, and others. Later formed the Little Cajun Band. Not to be confused with Kansas City–born blues shouter Big Joe Turner.

TURNER, TROY *Blues.* Guitar, vocals. Composer. Bandleader. (Born Aug. 25, 1967, Baton Rouge, EBR Parish.) Baton Rouge blues-rock guitarist began singing gospel as a child. As a teenager frequented local clubs such as Tabby's Blues Box, performing often with mentors **Kenny** and **Raful Neal**. In 1990 released debut recording, *Teenage Blues from Baton Rouge,* on King Snake and gained national attention. Releases followed on Ichiban, Telarc, and Evidence, including *Whole Lotta Blues* in 2010, which featured guest musicians Hubert Sumlin, Steve Cropper, Howard Tate, and others. Continued performing in the late 2010s based in New Orleans.

TURNER, WINSTON *Jazz.* Trombone, vocals. Composer. Bandleader. (Born Dec. 8, 1973, New Orleans, Orleans Parish.) New Orleans trombonist and singer began performing in marching bands in high school. Later worked and recorded with the Soul Rebels and in 2010 founded the Brass-A-Holics which combined the New Orleans brass-band tradition with Washington, D.C.'s go-go sounds.

TYLER, ALVIN "RED" *Rhythm and blues, jazz.* Saxophone. Composer. Bandleader. (Born Dec. 5, 1925, New Orleans, Orleans Parish; died Apr. 3, 1998, New Orleans, Orleans

Parish.) Highly influential New Orleans rhythm and blues saxophonist who appeared on hundreds of recordings throughout the 1950s and 1960s. Began playing saxophone in the Army in the mid-1940s and studied at New Orleans's Grunewald School of Music after discharge. In 1949 joined **Dave Bartholomew**'s band and appeared on countless sessions throughout following decades with **Fats Domino**, Little Richard, **Shirley & Lee**, **Professor Longhair**, **Huey "Piano" Smith**, **Allen Toussaint**, Sam Cooke, **Smiley Lewis**, Big Joe Turner, and many others. In the 1980s recorded two jazz albums as leader for Rounder and appeared on recordings with **James Booker**, **Clarence "Gatemouth" Brown**, **Johnny Adams**, and others. In 1994 recorded with **Dr. John**, **Allen Toussaint**, **Earl Palmer**, **Edward Frank**, and **Lee Allen** on *Crescent City Gold* for Highstreet.

TYLER, CHARLES/"DRIFTING CHARLES" *Rhythm and blues.* Guitar, vocals. (Born Aug. 31, 1936, Opelousas, St. Landry Parish; died Jan. 23, 2009, Opelousas, St. Landry Parish.) Blues and zydeco singer-guitarist who recorded several singles for Lanor in the mid-1960s, including "Drifting Cloud"/"Evil Hearted Woman" in 1963 under the name Drifting Charles. Later worked with various blues and zydeco musicians, including **Rockin' Dopsie** and **Roscoe Chenier**.

UNCLE REMUS *See* Grandpa Elliott.

VALDALIA, PATSY (Irving Ale) *Rhythm and blues.* Vocals. Composer. (Born Feb. 27, 1921, Vacherie, St. James Parish; died Aug. 29, 1982, New Orleans, Orleans Parish.) Locally renowned female impersonator who as "Patsy Valdalia" emceed New Orleans's famed Dew Drop Inn from the late 1940s through mid-1960s. Recorded signature songs "Keep Your Hands on Your Heart"/"Baby, Rock Me" for Mercury in 1953 with **Plas Johnson** on saxophone and issued by "Pat Valdeler."

VALENTIN, PUNKIE (Joseph Panquiette Valentin) *Jazz.* Cornet. (Born Sept. 25, 1865, New Orleans, Orleans Parish; died Mar. 12, 1958, Alameda, California.)[1] Highly regarded early New Orleans brass-band cornetist worked with Excelsior, Onward, and Melrose brass bands from 1900 to 1910. Also worked as music teacher in the 1890s. A dentist by profession, relocated to Oakland, California, in the early 1950s. Older brother of trombonist Bouboul Valentin, who worked with **Alphonse Picou** in the late 1890s.

VALENTINE, JOE *Rhythm and blues.* Vocals, piano, saxophone. Composer. Bandleader. (Born Feb. 3, 1937, New Orleans, Orleans Parish; died July 13, 2018, Austin, Texas.)[2] New Orleans–born soul singer best known for his long tenure on the Austin, Texas, music scene. Began performing in his early teens in New Orleans and had singles on Merit, Rachan/Athens, Ronn, and his Austin-based Val label throughout the 1960s, including "I Lost the Only Love I Had." After several years based in Baton Rouge in the early to mid-1960s, settled in Austin in 1967 and led his group the Imperials throughout the next several decades with sporadic releases on Cocoa Studios and Tee Jay. Toured as bandleader with Joe Tex in the early 1970s. In the late 1980s opened the 311 Club in downtown Austin, where he continued to perform regularly through the mid-2010s. Nephew of **Kid Thomas**.

VALENTINE, KID THOMAS *See* Kid Thomas.

VALLIER, GENEVA *Rhythm and blues.* Vocals. (Born Mar. 15, 1918, near Crew Lake, Richland Parish; died Oct. 27, 1982, Los Angeles.) San Francisco–based rhythm and blues vocalist best known for her 1955 answer song to Ray Charles, "You Said You Had a Woman," on Cash. Also recorded a single as leader for RPM and with the Emanon Trio on Swing Time in the mid-1950s.

VANICOR, ELLIS *Cajun.* Fiddle, vocals. Composer. Bandleader. (Born Aug. 14, 1929, near Branch, Acadia Parish.) Master Cajun fiddle player and longtime member of the Lacassine Playboys, which included brothers **Milton** and **Ivy Vanicor**, nephew **Orsy Vanicor**, and **Iry LeJeune**. Mentored by Milton, began playing fiddle in 1946 and soon started performing with Lacassine Playboys, performing and recording with LeJeune in the late 1940s and early 1950s. In the late 1950s and 1960s worked and recorded with **Linus Touchet** and **Bobby Leger**, appearing as vocalist on Leger's "Don't Bury Me" around 1967. Reformed the Lacassine Playboys in the late 1990s with Orsy and continued performing biweekly with group into his late 80s, releasing debut CD, *Don't Bury Me,* in 2010. Announced semiretirement from performing in July 2019. Brother of **Van Preston**.

VANICOR, IVY *Cajun.* Guitar, vocals. (Born Feb. 2, 1934, near Branch, Acadia Parish; died Apr. 27, 1989, Lacassine, Jeff. Davis Parish.) Noted Cajun guitarist and vocalist of the Lacassine Playboys with brothers **Milton** and **Ellis Vanicor** and nephew **Orsy Vanicor.** Recorded and performed with **Iry LeJeune** in the late 1940s and early 1950s. Also toured with **Jimmy C. Newman** and performed and recorded with **Shorty LeBlanc** and the

Sugar Bees through the early 1960s. Brother of **Van Preston**.

VANICOR, MILTON *Cajun.* Fiddle. Bandleader. (Born June 15, 1918, near Branch, Acadia Parish; died June 5, 2015, Welsh, Jeff. Davis Parish.) Highly influential early postwar Cajun fiddle player who was founding member of famed Cajun band Lacassine Playboys which included brothers **Ellis** and **Ivy Vanicor**, brother-in-law Asa LeJeune, and later **Iry LeJeune** and nephew **Orsy Vanicor**. Began learning fiddle on a homemade instrument at age 12, inspired by seeing **Angelas LeJeune** and **Amédé Ardoin** at local house dances. Relocated near Welsh in the late 1930s and in the mid-1940s formed Lacassine Playboys and performed throughout the region. In the late 1940s and early 1950s performed and recorded extensively with Iry LeJeune. Worked mainly outside of music in following decades, playing mainly at home. After the passing of his wife in 2008, began sitting in at **Marc Savoy**'s weekly Cajun jam in Eunice and in 2010s appeared at numerous national festivals and workshops. Continued performing into his mid-90s, recording CD *Un Souvenir de Milton Vanicor* at age 95. Brother of **Van Preston**.

VANICOR, ORSY (*or* R.C.) *Cajun.* Steel guitar, guitar. (Born July 28, 1933, near Branch, Acadia Parish.) Renowned Cajun steel guitarist best known for his work as member of Lacassine Playboys with uncles **Milton** and **Ellis** and **Ivy Vanicor** and **Iry LeJeune** in the late 1940s and early 1950s. In the 1950s also performed with **Lawrence Walker** and **Shorty LeBlanc** and in the 1960s and 1970s performed and recorded with **Bobby Leger**. Throughout the 1980s worked regularly with **Pat Savant**'s Louisiana Playboys, appearing on several recordings and overseas tours with group. Reformed Lacassine Playboys in the late 1990s with Ellis and continued performing with group and others into his 80s. Nephew of **Van Preston**.

VAPPIE, DON *Jazz.* Banjo, guitar, bass, mandolin, vocals. Composer. Bandleader. (Born Jan. 30, 1956, New Orleans, Orleans Parish.) Grandnephew of early jazz great **Papa John Joseph**, traditional New Orleans jazz banjo player, singer, and educator began performing as bassist in funk band Trac One in the early 1970s. By the late 1970s switched to banjo and began studying traditional early jazz, working with **Teddy Riley**, **Danny Barker**, **Lloyd Lambert**, **Wynton Marsalis**, and others throughout following years. Released numerous recordings in the 1990s and 2000s, including *Banjo à la Creole* in 2005. In 2008 appeared on Otis Taylor's release *Recapturing the Banjo.* In the 2010s continued performing as soloist as well as with his bands Creole Trio and Creole Jazz Serenaders nationally and abroad.

VECA, LAWRENCE (*often misspelled* Vega) *Jazz.* Cornet. (Born June 1887, New Orleans, Orleans Parish; died Nov. 5, 1911, New Orleans, Orleans Parish.)[3] Studied under famed music teacher **Manuel Perez** and performed as prominent member of **Papa Jack Laine**'s Reliance Brass Band in the first decade of the 1900s. Died of typhoid fever at age 24. Often cited as the first great white New Orleans jazz cornetist.

VEILLON, CHARLES *Swamp pop.* Vocals. (Born Oct. 12, 1941, Ville Platte, Evangeline Parish.) Early swamp pop singer who was vocalist with **Prince Charles** and the Rockin' Kings and recorded single "I Broke Your Heart"/"Cheryl Ann" on Jin in 1960, credited as Lil' Charles. In the 2010s continued performing at swamp pop reunions as Prince Charles Veillon.

VENABLE, JIMMIE *Cajun.* Accordion, vocals. Composer. Bandleader. (Born Feb. 28, 1948, Church Point, Acadia Parish.) Cajun accordionist and singer was mentored early on by **Bee Cormier** and performed with Cormier in the Church Point Playboys, appearing on LP *The Church Point Playboys Produces Four Accordion Players* in 1973 on Cormier's Bee label.

VENABLE, KERMIT (Joseph Kermit Venable) *Cajun.* Accordion, fiddle, guitar, vocals. Composer. Bandleader. (Born Jan. 3, 1944, Lafayette, Lafayette Parish; died Aug. 2006, New Orleans, Orleans Parish.) Noted accordion player and bandleader recorded a single for Bee with his band the Cankton Playboys in 1986 and hosted several Cajun music radio and television programs. Relocated to New Orleans in the early 1990s and formed Beau Bassin Cajun Band, releasing self-titled CD on Sound of New Orleans in 1996.

VERRET, ERROL *Cajun.* Accordion, vocals. Composer. (Born June 13, 1958, Henderson, St. Martin Parish.) Highly regarded accordion player best known for his work as member of Cajun bands BeauSoleil and the Basin Brothers. Also recorded with **Dennis McGee**, **Canray Fontenot**, **Jo-El Sonnier**, **Sonny Landreth**, and others. In 1997 recorded *C'est dans le Sang Cadjin (It's in the Cajun Blood)* on Swallow with **Al Berard**. Also renowned as a master accordion maker and pirogue (Cajun wooden boat) builder.

VERRETT, HARRISON *Jazz.* Banjo, guitar, piano. Bandleader. (Born Feb. 27, 1907, Napoleonville, Assumption Parish; died Oct. 13, 1965, New Orleans, Orleans Parish.)[4] Noted early jazz multi-instrumentalist moved to New Orleans with his family in the early 1910s and began playing banjo and trumpet at age 15. In the mid-1920s toured with a medicine-show band and through the early 1930s worked on riverboats, occasionally with **Papa Celestin**. Led his own band in the 1930s and in the early 1940s performed in California. After serving in World War II, worked regularly and recorded with Celestin. Also taught brother-in-law **Fats Domino** piano and played guitar for five years in Domino's touring band, recording with group in 1952. Later worked and recorded with **Noon Johnson**'s Bazooka Trio and appeared at Preservation Hall in the early 1960s.

VIDACOVICH, JOHNNY *Jazz, rhythm and blues.* Drums. Bandleader. (Born June 27, 1949, New Orleans, Orleans Parish.) Highly regarded and influential New Orleans drummer and music educator known for his decades-long work as founding member of modern jazz group Astral Project. Began playing drums at age 10, greatly inspired by New Orleans street rhythms and second-line beats. Throughout the 1970s and 1980s worked and recorded with numerous prominent New Orleans musicians such as **Professor Longhair**, **James Booker**, **Red Tyler**, **Al Hirt**, and **Johnny Adams**. Cofounded Astral Project in 1978 and performed and recorded with group in following decades. Held long-running weekly gig at New Orleans's Maple Leaf Bar in the 2000s. Through the 2010s continued to perform as bandleader and sideman and remained one of New Orleans's most sought-after drummers. Nephew of **Pinky Vidacovich**.

VIDACOVICH, PINKY (Irvine Vidacovich) *Jazz.* Clarinet. Bandleader. (Born Sept. 14, 1904, Buras, Plaquemines Parish; died July 5, 1966, New Orleans, Orleans Parish.) Traditional New Orleans jazz clarinetist performed with the Princeton Revellers and New Orleans Owls in the 1920s. In the 1930s led his own band and later hosted a popular radio program. In the 1950s worked with **Sharkey Bonano** and recorded as a leader. Also made comedy records as Cajun Pete. Uncle of **Johnny Vidacovich**.

VIDRINE, RANDY *Cajun.* Guitar, vocals. Composer. Bandleader. (Born Nov. 20, 1954, Ville Platte, Evangeline Parish.) Highly acclaimed Cajun singer and guitarist and longtime collaborator with fiddle player **Mitch Reed**. Performed and recorded with Reed in various traditional Cajun bands, including McCauley Reed Vidrine, Mamou Prairie Band, Tasso, Charivari, and the Lafayette Rhythm Devils since the early 1990s. Continued performing in Lafayette area with various Cajun groups in the 2010s.

VIGNE, JEAN/JOHN *Jazz.* Drums. (Born Dec. 24, 1864, New Orleans, Orleans Parish; died Aug. 31, 1916, New Orleans, Orleans Parish.)[5] Early New Orleans jazz drummer performed with numerous society dance bands between 1900 and 1910, including Olympia, **Bab Frank**'s Peerless, **Alcide Frank**'s Golden Rule, and **Manual Perez**'s Imperial Orchestra. Also worked with **Armand Piron** into the early 1910s.

VIGNE, SIDNEY *Jazz.* Clarinet. (Born Oct. 1888, New Orleans, Orleans Parish; died Jan. 1, 1924, New Orleans, Orleans Parish.)[6] Early New Orleans jazz clarinetist performed with Maple Leaf Orchestra, **Bob Lyon**'s Dixie Jazz Band, and Golden Leaf Orchestra in the early 1920s. Succumbed to injuries sustained when struck by a truck during a hit-and-run on North Claiborne Street while returning home the next morning after performing at a New Year's Eve gig with **Willie Pajeaud**. Died of cerebral hemorrhage and shock en route to Charity Hospital.

VILLERY, LOUIS (*often* Villeri) *Rhythm and blues.* Bass, vocals. Composer. Bandleader. (Born Dec. 25, 1940, St. James Parish.) Rhythm and blues and funk bassist best known for his long tenure with Bobby Bland's band beginning in the 1960s. In the 1970s led New Orleans funk band African Music Machine, recorded for Soul Power label, and worked as a studio musician for producer **Stan Lewis**'s Jewel Records in Shreveport, backing numerous artists, including Fontella Bass, Little Johnny Taylor, and Bobby Patterson. From the 1980s through 2000s continued working as session musician and appeared on releases by **Harry Hypolite**, Eddie C. Campbell, Rufus Thomas, and others. Reformed African Music Machine in the early 2000s and recorded self-titled album for Singular before rejoining Bland and touring extensively with group until Bland's death in 2013.

VINCENT, CAESAR/CESAIRE *Cajun.* Vocals. (Born May 12, 1882, near Abbeville, Vermilion Parish; died Feb. 15, 1970, Maurice, Vermilion Parish.) Cajun ballad singer and *raconteur* (storyteller) whose vast repertoire of traditional French and Acadian songs dated back centuries, some to medieval France. A farmer by profession, recorded 23 songs for folklorist Catherine Blanchet in 1953, followed by several dozen field recordings for folklorist Harry Oster in 1957, notably "Travallier C'est Trop Dur." In 2018, **Zachary Richard**, **Steve Riley**, **Roddie Romero**, **Ann Savoy**, and others recorded a tribute album of his material produced by folklorist Barry Jean Ancelet.

VINCENT, CLARENCE "LITTLE DAD" *Jazz.* Banjo, guitar, mandolin. Bandleader. (Born Sept. 20, 1892, Baton Rouge, EBR Parish; died Apr. 23, 1960, New Orleans, Orleans Parish.)[7] Noted early New Orleans jazz banjo player moved to the Crescent City with his family as a baby and in his teens played mandolin in the family string band. In the late 1910s performed with **Jack Carey**, **Punch Miller**, and **Armand Piron** and led his Liberty Band. In the 1920s worked with **John Robichaux**, **Buddy Petit**, **Chris Kelly**, **Red Allen**, Amos White, and others, and toured the Mexican Yucatan with **Herb Morand**. During the early years of the Depression worked with **Louis Dumaine** and **Octave Crosby** before retiring due to hearing loss. Acquired nickname due to his short stature.

VINCENT, CRAWFORD (*often listed as* **Vincent Crawford)** *Cajun.* Drums, guitar, vocals. (Born Oct. 4, 1921, Gueydan, Vermilion Parish; died Aug. 12, 2005, Baytown, Texas.) Influential early Cajun drummer and singer began performing as member of the Hackberry Ramblers in 1940, becoming one of the first drummers to perform in a Cajun band. Also worked regularly with **Leo Soileau** and **Harry Choates**. In the late 1940s and early 1950s recorded with Choates, **Abe** and **Joe Manuel**, **Shuk Richard**, and others and from 1952 to 1954 recorded two singles as leader with **Will Kegley** for Khoury's. Throughout the 1950s and 1960s performed around Lake Charles area with various musicians and recorded with Hackberry Ramblers for Arhoolie and Goldband. Continued performing occasionally with Hackberry Ramblers through the early 1990s, appearing on CD *Cajun Boogie* in 1992. Father David Vincent (1886–1930) and grandfather Theozime Vincent (1853–1929) were both early Cajun fiddle players.

VINCENT, ERNIE *Rhythm and blues.* Guitar, vocals. Composer. Bandleader. (Born July 12, 1945, Thibodaux, Lafourche Parish.) New Orleans rhythm and blues singer and guitarist best known for his 1972 funk single "Dap Walk." Moved to New Orleans with his family as a child and learned guitar in his late teens. Formed his band the Top Notes in the early 1970s and had local hit with "Dap Walk" on Fordom. In the mid-1980s formed his Kolab label and released recordings as a leader and by other artists. In the 2000s reformed the Top Notes and released CD *Bayou Road Blues* in 2009. Continued performing nationally and overseas in the 2010s.

VINCENT, JULES "CHUN" *Cajun.* Fiddle. (Born July 7, 1904, Creole, Cameron Parish; died July 20, 1980, Creole, Cameron Parish.)[8] Locally renowned early Cameron Parish Cajun fiddler who performed at house dances around Creole and Grand Chenier area in the 1920s and 1930s with guitarist brothers Dallas and Morris. Mother Zellan Rae was a Cajun accordionist, and daughter Dottie was a Cajun singer-guitarist who performed with husband **Abe Manuel** and sons.

VINCENT, LANESE *Cajun.* Vocals. (Born Mar. 17, 1914, Kaplan, Vermilion Parish; died Aug. 31, 1994, Kaplan, Vermilion Parish.) Kaplan resident who made six field recordings with cousin Sidney Richard in 1934 for folklorist John Lomax for the Library of Congress singing traditional Louisiana French ballads which were passed down for many generations and sung in Cajun homes.

WALKER, GARY *Rhythm and blues.* Vocals. (Born Oct. 17, 1946, Jennings, Jeff. Davis Parish; died Oct. 16, 1982, Lafayette, Lafayette Parish.)[1] Highly revered blue-eyed soul singer best known for his work as member of the Boogie Kings in the 1960s. Joined the Boogie Kings in the mid-1960s, sharing vocals for a time with **G.G. Shinn** and **Jerry LaCroix**, who were dubbed "the Three Kings." Recorded several singles on Jin in the mid-1960s, including "Who Needs You So Bad"/"Cry Cry Cry."

WALKER, JOE *Zydeco, rhythm and blues.* Accordion, guitar, piano, drums, vocals. Composer. Bandleader. (Born Dec. 13, 1944, Carencro, Lafayette Parish.) Soulful singer and multi-instrumentalist began playing guitar in his teens with **Rockin' Dopsie** and later worked with **Rockin' Sidney**. Relocated to Lake Charles in the late 1960s and through 1970s backed various touring soul and blues artists. In the late 1980s began playing zydeco with strong southern soul influences and through the mid-1990s had releases on Lanor and Zane, including *Zydeco All Night* in 1991, and toured Europe. Older brother of zydeco multi-instrumentalist Percy Walker Sr.

WALKER, LAWRENCE *Cajun.* Accordion, fiddle, vocals. Composer. Bandleader. (Born Sept. 3, 1908, rural Acadia Parish [near Duson]; died Aug. 15, 1968, Rayne, Acadia Parish.)[2] Highly influential early Cajun accordion player and singer who helped revitalize Cajun music in the 1950s and was regarded by many as among its greatest instrumentalists. Began playing fiddle as a child and later learned accordion, mentored by his father, Allen. Relocated with family to Orange, Texas, and from the early 1920s through mid-1930s performed with his father and brother Elton, recording for Bluebird in 1929 and 1935 as the Walker Brothers. After working outside music throughout the 1940s formed the Wandering Aces and recorded for Khoury's from 1950 to 1955, cutting many Cajun classics, including "Bosco Stomp," "Reno Waltz," and "Keep Your Hands Off It." In the late 1950s and early 1960s recorded for producer **Floyd Soileau**'s Vee-Pee and Swallow and **Carol Rachou**'s La Louisianne labels with regional hits such as "Chere Alice," "Unlucky Waltz," and "Allons Rock and Roll." Remained one of the most popular Cajun dance-hall performers throughout southwest Louisiana and east Texas until suffering a fatal heart attack at age 59.

WALKER, PHILLIP *Blues, zydeco.* Guitar, vocals. Composer. Bandleader. (Born Feb. 11, 1937, Welsh, Jeff. Davis Parish; died July 22, 2010, Palm Springs, California.) Internationally renowned blues guitarist and singer-songwriter was raised on farms in the Welsh and Beaumont–Port Arthur areas and began playing guitar at age 14, inspired by Lightnin' Hopkins, T-Bone Walker, and **Clarence "Gatemouth" Brown**. In the early 1950s joined **Clifton Chenier**'s band and toured country with group for several years, recording with Chenier for Specialty and Checker/Argo in 1955–56. Also backed Etta James, Rosco Gordon, Little Richard, and others while touring with group. In the late 1950s performed in El Paso with his own group before relocating to Los Angeles and cutting two singles for Elko in 1959, notably "Hello My Darling." In the 1960s performed and recorded with wife, Ina Beatrice, and through 1970s had releases on Playboy and Joliet, notably acclaimed LPs *The Bottom of the Top* and *Someday You'll Have These Blues.* Throughout the 1980s and 1990s continued touring nationally and overseas with albums on Rounder, Hightone, JSP, Blue Ace, Black Top, and Alligator, including *Lone Star Shootout* in 1999 which reunited him with former Beaumont–Port Arthur musicians **Lonnie Brooks**, **Long**

John Hunter, and **Ervin Charles**. Continued performing on club and festival circuit through the 2000s, releasing final CD, *Going Back Home,* on Delta Groove in 2007.

WALSH, ELLIS "SLOW" *Rhythm and blues.* Drums, vocals. Composer. (Born Feb. 7, 1903, New Orleans, Orleans Parish; died Oct. 25, 1991, Clark, Nevada.)[3] Jump blues drummer, singer, and songwriter recorded with Eddie Williams and His Brown Buddies in the late 1940s. Cowrote and provided lead vocals on Williams's 1949 release "Saturday Night Fish Fry," a song that was also a major hit for Louis Jordan later that year. Released two singles as leader in 1950 on London Records, including "New Orleans Is My Home." Also worked and recorded extensively with rhythm and blues pianist Floyd Dixon in the late 1940s and early 1950s.

WARREN, ROBERT "BABY BOY" *Blues.* Guitar, vocals. Composer. Bandleader. (Born Aug. 13, 1919, Lake Providence, E. Carroll Parish; died July 1, 1977, Detroit.) Noted early Detroit postwar blues guitarist and singer-songwriter was raised in Memphis and learned guitar from his older brothers. In the 1930s and early 1940s performed in the Memphis and Helena, Arkansas, area with Howlin' Wolf, Robert Lockwood Jr., Johnny Shines, Sonny Boy Williamson (Rice Miller), and others. Relocated to Detroit in 1942 and began performing on the local blues scene, often with **Boogie Woogie Red**. From 1949 to 1954 had singles on Gotham, Staff, Swing Time, Blue Lake, Drummond, JVB, Sampson, and Excello, notably "Sanafee"/"Hello Stranger." Continued performing sporadically in Detroit in the 1960s and early 1970s and toured Europe in 1972 before retiring due to health issues several years later.

WASHINGTON, LEROY *Blues.* Guitar, vocals. Composer. Bandleader. (Born Mar. 1, 1932, Palmetto, St. Landry Parish; died June 30, 1962, Leesville, Vernon Parish.)[4] Revered early swamp blues guitarist and singer began playing in his teens and in the early 1950s started performing locally in a duo with drummer **Chuck Martin**, soon earning the nickname "The Guitar Wizard" for his instrumental prowess. In the mid- to late 1950s performed with various groups, including the Honeydrippers with **Sticks Herman**, and regularly backed touring musicians such as Jimmy Reed, **Clarence Garlow**, and **Roy Brown**. In 1957 began recording for producer **J. D. Miller** and had regional hit with debut single, "Wild Cherry," on Excello, followed by two more releases for the label and one each on Rocko and Zynn through 1960. Continued performing with various groups around Opelousas and Lake Charles area until suffering a fatal heart attack at age 30 after performing with **Good Rockin' Bob** at the Big Casino Club in Leesville.

WASHINGTON, SHERMAN, JR. *Gospel.* Vocals. (Born Dec. 13, 1925, Thibodaux, Lafourche Parish; died Mar. 14, 2011, Boutte, St. Charles Parish.) Leader of New Orleans premier gospel group the Zion Harmonizers for more than six decades. Joined group in the early 1940s and within a few years took over leadership when original organizer **Reverend Benjamin Maxon** stepped down. Also hosted popular weekly gospel radio show for many years. Continued performing and leading group until his death in 2011. Younger brother Nolan Washington sang lead tenor with Zion Harmonizers for several decades until his death in 1997.

WASHINGTON, TUTS (Isidore Washington) *Rhythm and blues, jazz.* Piano, vocals. Composer. (Born Jan. 24, 1907, New Orleans, Orleans Parish; died Aug. 5, 1984, New Orleans, Orleans Parish.) Highly influential early New Orleans barrelhouse and rhythm and blues pianist whose style greatly influenced **Professor Longhair**, **Huey "Piano" Smith**, **Fats Domino**, **James Booker**, and others. Began playing piano around age 10 and studied under **Red Cayou**. Throughout the 1920s and 1930s worked with various jazz and dance bands throughout New Orleans and in the late 1940s and early 1950s worked and recorded with **Smiley Lewis**. Relocated to St. Louis for remainder of decade and worked with Tab Smith before returning to New Orleans, where he performed mainly as a soloist in bars and restaurants throughout the 1960s and 1970s. Recorded one album as leader, *New Orleans Piano Professor,* for Rounder in 1983. Died after suffering fatal heart attack during a performance at the 1984 World's Fair in New Orleans.

WASHINGTON, WALTER "WOLFMAN" (Edward Joseph Washington) *Rhythm and blues, jazz.* Guitar, vocals. Composer. Bandleader. (Born Dec. 20, 1943, New Orleans, Orleans Parish.) Popular New Orleans rhythm and blues and funk guitarist started singing in a gospel band as a child. In his early teens began playing guitar and within several years was working in the house band at New Orleans's famed Dew Drop Inn. Throughout the 1960s and 1970s worked regularly with **Lee Dorsey**, **Irma Thomas**, **David Lastie**, **Johnny Adams**, and others. Formed his band the Roadmasters in the early 1980s and had releases on Hep' Me, Rounder, Bullseye, Point

Blank, Go Jazz, and Zoho through the 2000s. Continued performing nationally and overseas with his Roadmasters and as member of the Joe Crown Trio through 2010s. Released CD *My Future Is My Past* in 2018.

WATKINS, JOE *Jazz.* Drums, piano, vocals. (Born Oct. 24, 1899, New Orleans, Orleans Parish; died Sept. 13, 1969, New Orleans, Orleans Parish.)[5] Renowned New Orleans jazz drummer and vocalist best known for his long tenure with **George Lewis**'s band. Began playing piano but switched to drums in the early 1920s, inspired by **Baby Dodds**. In the early 1930s performed in trio with **Herb Morand** and **Walter Nelson Sr.** but worked outside music for most of Depression years. From 1946 through the mid-1960s performed and recorded extensively with Lewis. Also worked with **Lizzie Miles**, **Punch Miller**, **Kid Howard**, Earl Hines, and others. In the 1960s toured Europe and appeared regularly at Preservation Hall until retiring from music due to health issues in 1966. Nephew of **Johnny St. Cyr**.

WATSON, ERNEST "DOC" *Jazz.* Saxophone. Bandleader. (Born June 2, 1932, New Orleans, Orleans Parish; died Feb. 19, 2010, New Orleans, Orleans Parish.) Traditional New Orleans jazz saxophonist began performing in the 1950s and worked in the bands of **Ellis Marsalis Jr.** and **Li'l Millet**. Performed as member of Young Tuxedo Brass Band throughout the 1960s and in the mid-1970s joined **Harold Dejan**'s Olympia Brass Band and remained with group until it disbanded in the early 2000s. Appeared weekly at Preservation Hall in later years.

WAYNE, RUSS *See* Clay, Joe.

WEBSTER, OTIS *Blues.* Guitar, vocals. Composer. (Born Dec. 2, 1919, Homer, Claiborne Parish; died Feb. 18, 1992, Arcadia, Bienville Parish.) Louisiana Delta blues guitarist and singer who was recorded extensively by folklorist Harry Oster while an inmate at Angola Prison in 1959–60. Songs included "Penitentiary Blues" and "Ball and Chain for Me," which appeared on LP *Southern Prison Blues* on Tradition in 1965.

WELSH, NOLAN/"BARREL HOUSE WELCH" *Blues.* Piano, vocals. Composer. (Born Sept. 10, 1892, Thibodaux, Lafourche Parish; died Mar. 11, 1962, Chicago.)[6] Early prewar blues singer and piano player resided in New Orleans in the mid-1910s before relocating to Chicago by the end of the decade. Made four recordings during two sessions for OKeh in Chicago in 1926, including "St. Peter Blues," backed by **Louis Armstrong** on first session and **Richard M. Jones** on both. In 1928–29 cut three additional sides as solo pianist for Paramount, including "Larceny Woman Blues," issued as by "Barrel House Welch." Worked outside music in the railroad industry in Chicago after World War II.

WERNER, JOE (Joseph Edward Werner) *Cajun.* Guitar, harmonica, vocals. Composer. Bandleader. (Born Sept. 26, 1909, Rayne, Acadia Parish; died June 10, 1978, Fort Worth, Texas.)[7] Early Cajun string-band singer and guitarist best known for the 1937 hit "Wondering" he made while member of **Luderin Darbone** and **Edwin Duhon**'s Hackberry Ramblers. Learned harmonica and guitar in his youth and relocated to Crowley and joined Hackberry Ramblers in late 1936. Specializing in singing the group's English-language songs, recorded numerous sides with band in early 1937, including "Wondering" (issued as by the Riverside Ramblers), which quickly became one of the group's biggest hits. Abruptly left band several months later to form his own Ramblers and through 1938 recorded more than 40 sides for Bluebird and Decca, accompanied by **Happy Fats**, **Doc Guidry**, and **Papa Cairo**. Later worked outside music in the newspaper business and eventually moved to Forth Worth.

WEST, CLINT (Clinton Joseph Guillory) *Swamp pop.* Drums, vocals. Bandleader. (Born Aug. 11, 1938, Vidrine, Evangeline Parish; died June 28, 2016, Opelousas, St. Landry Parish.) Early swamp pop singer and drummer best known for his regional hit "Big Blue Diamonds." Began playing drums as a child and by age 13 was performing with the Vidrine Playboys. In the late 1950s joined Red Smiley's Vel-Tones and made recording debut with single "Take a Ride" on Jin. After a stint with the Roller Coasters, began recording for Jin as a leader with single "Our Love" in 1963 and joined the Boogie Kings the following year, replacing **Bert Miller** and soon taking over leadership of band. Recorded several regional hits, including "Mr. Jeweler" and duet "Try to Find Another Man" with band member **Tommy McLain** before leaving band in early 1965. In the next several years led his band the Fabulous Kings, recording numerous singles for Jin, including his signature swamp pop classic, "Big Blue Diamonds," in 1965. In following decades continued performing throughout southwest Louisiana area, including a 20-year stint at Leroy's in Alexandria. Retired from performing in 2010 due to health issues.

WEST, NORMAN *Rhythm and blues.* Vocals, piano. Composer. Bandleader. (Born Oct. 30, 1940, Lake Providence, E. Carroll Parish.) Noted soul singer began playing piano and singing in church as a child. Later moved to Monroe and in the 1950s began performing at talent shows and sitting in at local clubs. In the early 1960s moved to Memphis and joined the Del-Rios. Recorded several singles as leader for Christy, Hi, M.O.C., and Smash, notably "Words Won't Say," before becoming original member of highly successful vocal group Soul Children in 1968. Throughout following 10 years toured and recorded with group with numerous recordings on Stax and Epic. After the band's breakup in 1979 continued performing as soul and gospel artist. In 2007 reunited with Soul Children, recording with group on CD *Still Standing* in 2008.

WEST, WILLIE (Millard Leon West) *Rhythm and blues.* Vocals. Composer. Bandleader. (Born Dec. 8, 1941, Raceland, Lafourche Parish.) New Orleans deep soul singer and songwriter formed his first band, the Sharks, while in his teens. In the late 1950s and early 1960s had local success with releases on Houma-based Rustone label followed by three more on Frisco, including "Don't Be Ashamed to Cry." Moved to New Orleans in the mid-1960s and performed in bands with **Deacon John** and **Edgar Blanchard**. In the late 1960s and 1970s worked with **Allen Toussaint** and had singles on Deesu, Josie, and Warner Brothers, including "Fairchild," often backed by the Meters. Worked as vocalist with the Meters in the late 1970s and continued performing occasionally throughout following decades. Relocated to Minneapolis area after Hurricane Katrina in 2005 and had releases on CDS and Timmion in the 2010s, including *Lost Soul* in 2014.

WHITE, DANNY *Rhythm and blues.* Vocals. Bandleader. (Born July 6, 1931, New Orleans, Orleans Parish; died Jan. 5, 1996, Capitol Heights, Maryland.) New Orleans rhythm and blues and soul singer and bandleader who had several regional hits in the 1960s. Began performing in the mid-1950s and held five-year engagement at the Golden Cadillac club with his band the Cavaliers, becoming one of New Orleans's most popular acts. In the early 1960s recorded for Frisco and had regional hits with "Kiss Tomorrow Goodbye" and "Lend Me a Handkerchief," the latter written by **Earl King**. In 1962 toured nationally with Jimmy Reed, Otis Redding, and Marvin Gaye and recorded singles for Atlas, ABC, Decca, SSS International, and Kashe through the late 1960s. After managing the Meters for two years relocated to Washington, D.C., area in the early 1970s and largely retired from music.

WHITE, MARGO (Marguerite Wright) *Rhythm and blues, swamp pop.* Vocals. Composer. (Born Jan. 5, 1938, Franklin, St. Mary Parish; died Dec. 13, 2006, Union City, California.)[8] Early southwest Louisiana soul singer and songwriter made her recording debut with swamp pop single "Down By the Sea" for Goldband in 1961 backed by **Cookie** and the Cupcakes. In 1962–63 recorded several singles for Jin, having regional success with "Don't Mess with My Man" and "I'm Not Ashamed." Several years later recorded for producer Huey Meaux, which resulted in a single on Jet Stream in 1967 and compilation LP *I've Got a Right to Lose My Mind* on Crazy Cajun in 1978, issued years after she relocated to California and left the music business.

WHITE, MISS LAVELLE *Rhythm and blues.* Vocals. Composer. Bandleader. (Born July 3, 1929, Amite City, Tangipahoa Parish.) Texas-based rhythm and blues and soul singer-songwriter moved to Houston in her teens and started performing in local clubs with blues guitarist Clarence Hollimon. On **Johnny Copeland**'s recommendation, began recording with Duke Records in 1958 as "Miss La-Vell" and through 1964 had numerous singles on label, including "Run to You" and "Why Young Men Go Wild." Toured with major acts such as Otis Redding, James Brown, B.B. King, Junior Parker, and others. In 1978 relocated to Chicago and through 1987 performed regularly in local clubs with **Lonnie Brooks**, **Buddy Guy**, Junior Wells, and others. Settled in Austin in the early 1990s and had two releases on Antone's through 2003, including *Into the Mystic*. Continued performing at clubs and festivals based in Austin into her 90s.

WHITE, TONY JOE *Swamp rock, rhythm and blues.* Guitar, harmonica, vocals. Composer. Bandleader. (Born July 23, 1943, near Oak Grove, W. Carroll Parish; died Oct. 24, 2018, Leiper's Fork, Tennessee.) Highly regarded and influential singer-songwriter and guitarist known for his moody, blues-infused songs dubbed swamp rock, such as "Polk Salad Annie" and "Rainy Night in Georgia." Known as "the Swamp Fox," his compositions have been covered by Elvis Presley, Brook Benton, **Johnny Adams**, Tina Turner, Ray Charles, Dusty Springfield, George Jones, and many others. Raised on a cotton farm in Goodwill, began playing guitar at age 15 after hearing a Lightnin' Hopkins record. Performed in clubs around Corpus Christi, Texas, in the mid-1960s before relocating to Nashville in 1968. Signed with Monument and had Top 10 hit with "Polk Salad Annie" in 1969. Recorded three albums for Monument through 1970 and had releases on Warner Brothers, 20th Century, Casablanca, and Columbia through the early 1980s. After a hiatus from performing in the mid-1980s, worked and recorded with Tina Turner in 1989. In the 1990s began touring extensively overseas and had releases on Polydor and his own Swamp Records, including *Closer to the Truth* in 1991. Continued recording and touring internationally through the 2010s with numerous live and studio releases, including *Hoodoo* and *Rain Crow* on Yep Roc in the mid-2010s. Suffered fatal heart attack at his home a month after releasing blues album *Bad Mouthin'* on Yep Roc.

WHITTAKER, LEON "PEE WEE" *Blues, jazz.* Trombone, mandolin, guitar, clarinet, vocals. (Born Apr. 29, 1901, Newellton, Tensas Parish; died July 22, 1993, Ferriday, Concordia Parish.)[9] Noted blues trombonist and singer began playing music as a child and performed in the family band while living in Mississippi and Arkansas. In the late 1920s and early 1930s toured with string bands and from the mid-1930s through 1950 traveled with the Rabbit Foot Minstrels, accompanied early on by childhood friend and saxophonist Louis Jordan. Settled in Ferriday in the mid-1950s where he led the house band at famed local juke joint Haney's Big House and hosted his own local radio show. Performed and recorded with Hezekiah Early's Houserockers from the 1960s through early 1990s.

WIGGS, JOHNNY (John Wiggington Hyman) *Jazz.* Cornet. Bandleader. (Born July 25, 1899, New Orleans, Orleans Parish; died Oct. 9, 1977, Metairie, Jefferson Parish.)[10] Renowned early New Orleans jazz cornetist and music teacher was initially inspired to learn the instrument after hearing **King Oliver**. In the 1920s worked with **Norman Brownlee**, **Happy Schilling**, and others. Recorded with his band Bayou Stompers for Victor in 1927 and with **Tony Parenti**'s New Orleanians in 1928. In the 1930s and 1940s worked as music teacher in New Orleans public schools, with **Pete Fountain** and **Sam Butera** among his students. Active in the jazz revival of the late 1940s and 1950s (as Johnny Wiggs) and recorded extensively through the mid-1970s. Also appeared regularly at Preservation Hall.

WILD BILL *See* Pitre, Wild Bill.

WILEY, BERTHA *Blues.* Vocals. (Born possibly 1901, near Belcher, Caddo Parish, or Oct. 1900, Claiborne Parish; died possibly Mar. 30, 1952, Shreveport, Caddo Parish.)[11] Prewar blues singer who performed with pianist husband, Arnold "Doc" Wiley, in the 1920s. Reportedly recorded for Paramount in the late 1920s.

WILKERSON, DON *Jazz, rhythm and blues.* Saxophone. Composer. Bandleader. (Born July 6, 1932, Moreauville, Avoy. Parish; died July 18, 1986, Houston.) Highly regarded "Texas tenor" saxophonist best known for his handful of recordings for Riverside and Blue Note in the early 1960s which featured his expressive style, dubbed soul-jazz. Raised in Houston, made his recording debut with blues pianist Little Willie Littlefield in 1948 and worked with T-Bone Walker, Big Joe Turner, and Amos Milburn through the early 1950s. In the mid- to late 1950s worked and recorded with Ray Charles and Charles Brown. Recorded LP *The Texas Twister* in 1960 for Riverside, followed by three releases for Blue Note in 1962–63 featuring jazz guitarist Grant Green. Also toured Europe with Charles in the early 1960s and recorded with Louis Jordan. In the early 1970s was member of the Sonny Franklin Big Band and worked with Tom Archia, Eddie "Cleanhead" Vinson, and **Clarence "Gatemouth" Brown**, among others. In 1983 appeared on the B.B. King LP *Blues 'n' Jazz.*

WILLIAMS, ALFRED *Jazz.* Drums. Bandleader. (Born Sept. 1, 1900, New Orleans, Orleans Parish; died Apr. 30, 1963, New Orleans, Orleans Parish.) Early New Orleans jazz drummer began performing with **Papa Celestin**'s Tuxedo Brass Band in 1920 and worked with **Sam Morgan**, **Manuel Perez**, and **Armand Piron** throughout the decade. From the mid-1930s through early 1940s led band based in El Paso, Texas. Returned to New Orleans in the 1940s and worked regularly with Eureka Brass Band. Recorded with **Jim Robinson**, **Peter Bocage**, and **Kid Howard** in the early 1960s and appeared at Preservation Hall.

WILLIAMS, BENNY *See* Black Benny.

WILLIAMS, CHARLES "HUNGRY" *Rhythm and blues.* Drums, vocals. Composer. (Born Feb. 12, 1935, New Orleans, Orleans Parish; died May 10, 1986, New York City.) Highly influential New Orleans rhythm and blues and early funk percussionist known for his pioneering double beat or "double-clutching" bass drumming style and his incorporation of Latin rhythms. Mentored early on by **Paul Gayten**, released two singles on Checker as leader in 1955 and 1957. In the late 1950s and 1960s appeared on numerous recordings with **Fats Domino**, **Shirley & Lee**, **Huey "Piano" Smith**, **Smiley Lewis**, **Clarence "Frogman" Henry**, **Allen Toussaint**, **Professor Longhair**, **Bobby Charles**, and others. Resided in New York and battled health issues in later years.

WILLIAMS, CLAIBORNE (Joseph McLellan Williams) *Jazz.* Cornet, violin. Bandleader. (Born Dec. 31, 1868, Valenzuela [near Donaldsonville], Assumption Parish; died Oct. 1, 1952, New Orleans, Orleans Parish.)[12] Very important early jazz bandleader and music professor whose many students included **Papa Celestin** and **Louis Hall Nelson**. Began leading his own bands in the late 1880s around Baton Rouge and Donaldsonville areas and continued through the 1940s with his very popular societal orchestra. Noted band members included **Richard M. Jones**, **Papa John Joseph**, **Walter Lewis**, **Dave Bartholomew**, and **Frank Fields**. As music teacher taught all instruments and traveled by boat through bayous to reach his students, who gathered in groups on plantations for weekly lessons. Fell at his home in Donaldsonville at age 83 and succumbed to a pulmonary embolism five days later.

WILLIAMS, CLARENCE *Blues.* Vocals. (Born Nov. 2, 1918, Alexandria, Rapides Parish; died Mar. 18, 2005, Vancouver, Washington.) Jump blues and ballad singer who recorded as a leader for Modern in 1946 with "I'm Drunk" and cut three sides as vocalist with Luke Jones for Atlas in 1947. Not to be confused with early New Orleans jazz musician and composer **Clarence Williams**.

WILLIAMS, CLARENCE *Jazz.* Piano, vocals. Composer. Bandleader. (Born probably Oct. 8, 1893, Plaquemine, Iberville Parish; died Nov. 6, 1965, Queens, New York.) Renowned early New Orleans jazz musician, producer, publisher, and composer whose many blues and jazz compositions include such standards as "T'ain't Nobody's Business If I Do" and "Royal Garden Blues." At age 12 left home and moved to New Orleans and during his teens toured the South with a minstrel show as singer and dancer. In the mid-1910s began playing piano in New Orleans's Storyville District and worked with **Sidney Bechet**, **Bunk Johnson**, and **Armand Piron**, the latter with whom he also partnered in a publishing company. After a brief stint in Chicago, relocated to New York in 1923 and formed his own publishing company. Started long career with OKeh and other labels and produced hundreds of jazz and blues recordings by Bessie Smith, **Lonnie Johnson**, Sara Martin, Sippie Wallace, wife Eva Taylor, and many others, many famously backed by his "Blue Five" group which at times included Bechet and **Louis Armstrong**. Also recorded extensively as a leader through the early 1940s on more than 300 recordings. Not to be confused with Alexandria-born blues vocalist **Clarence Williams**.

WILLIAMS, DAVE "FAT MAN" *Jazz, rhythm and blues.* Piano, vocals. Composer. Bandleader. (Born Apr. 26, 1920, New Orleans, Orleans Parish; died Mar. 13, 1982, New Orleans, Orleans Parish.) New Orleans jazz and blues pianist, singer, and songwriter began performing in local clubs in the 1940s and worked regularly with **Freddie Kohlman**. In the early 1950s recorded with Kohlman and **Cousin Joe**. Recorded one unissued side as leader for Specialty in 1959. In the 1960s and 1970s worked with **Alvin Alcorn**, **Kid Thomas**, **Little Sonny Jones**, and Preservation Hall Jazz Band and toured and recorded overseas. Released debut album, *I Ate Up the Apple Tree,* on New Orleans Records in 1974 containing many of his compositions, including his signature title song, which became a New Orleans brass-band standard.

WILLIAMS, FRANK "SWEET" *Rhythm and blues.* Piano, drums. (Born June 8, 1906, New Orleans, Orleans Parish; died Dec. 14, 1971, Chicago.) Early New Orleans blues pianist started playing professionally in his early teens and worked with **Chris Kelly** in the early 1920s. Moved to Chicago in the mid-1920s and performed with **Lee Collins**, **Herb Morand**, and **Papa Charlie Jackson**. Recorded two sides for Atlantic in 1951.

WILLIAMS, GEORGE *Jazz.* Bass drum. Bandleader. (Born Oct. 25, 1910, New Orleans, Orleans Parish; died Aug. 27, 1965, New Orleans, Orleans Parish.) Led his popular George Williams Brass Band from the late 1940s until his death in 1965. Also worked regularly in the 1950s with **Bill Matthews**. Not to be confused with early New Orleans jazz cornetist or guitarist of same name, both of whom performed in the 1910s.

WILLIAMS, JOHN "SCARFACE" *Rhythm and blues.* Vocals. Bandleader. (Born Oct. 19, 1938, New Orleans, Orleans Parish; died Mar. 4, 1972, New Orleans, Orleans Parish.) Noted New Orleans rhythm and blues singer best known for his distinctive lead vocal work as member of **Huey "Piano" Smith**'s Clowns in the late 1950s. Adopted as a baby by gospel street singer Della Gatlin Williams, began performing at age 18. In 1957 joined Smith's band and sang lead on several notable recordings with group, including "Rockin' Pneumonia and the Boogie Woogie Flu." Around 1959 left the Clowns and formed the Tick Tocks, who had singles on Rush, Sansu, and Enjoy through 1967 and appeared regularly at the Dew Drop Inn. In 1970 reunited with Smith for recording session for Cotillion but was fatally stabbed during a street altercation two years later.

WILLIAMS, LARRY *Rhythm and blues.* Piano, vocals. Composer. Bandleader. (Born May 10, 1935, New Orleans, Orleans Parish; died Jan. 2, 1980, Los Angeles.)[13] Popular New Orleans rhythm and blues singer and songwriter best known for his late 1950s hits "Bony Moronie," "Short Fat Fannie," and others. Began playing piano at age five and while in his teens moved with his family to Oakland, California, and performed with local rhythm and blues group. In the mid-1950s returned to New Orleans and worked as valet for his cousin **Lloyd Price**. From 1957 through 1959 recorded for Specialty and cut such rhythm and blues classics as "Bony Moronie," "Dizzy Miss Lizzy," and "Slow Down." In the 1960s recorded for Chess and Mercury and collaborated on several releases with Johnny "Guitar" Watson. Also produced two albums for longtime friend Little Richard. Appeared in several films in the 1970s. After decades-long battle with drug addiction, died at his home from a gunshot wound which was ruled as self-inflicted.

WILLIAMS, NATHAN *Zydeco.* Accordion, vocals. Composer. Bandleader. (Born Mar. 24, 1963, St. Martinville, St. Martin Parish.) Internationally renowned zydeco accordionist and singer-songwriter who led his band the Zydeco Cha Chas for more than thirty years. Raised in a Creole French–speaking family, first picked up the accordion in his late teens, inspired by **Clifton Chenier**, **Buckwheat Zydeco**, and **Clayton Sampy**. In the mid-1980s began performing at his brother Sid's club El Sid-O's in Lafayette and in 1987 recorded several singles on his El Sid-O label to local success. Signed with Rounder in the late 1980s and through 2006 released eight albums for the label and toured extensively. In 2013 released *A New Road* on his own Cha Cha label. Continued touring nationally and overseas in the 2010s and remained one of the most popular zydeco acts on the festival circuit. Father of musicians **Lil' Nathan** and Naylan and brother of Zydeco Cha Chas guitarist and visual artist Dennis Paul Williams.

WILLIAMS, ROBERT PETE *Blues.* Guitar, vocals. Composer. (Born Mar. 14, 1914, Zachary, EBR Parish; died Dec. 31, 1980, Baton Rouge, EBR Parish.) Highly distinctive country blues singer and guitarist best known for his poignant songs, often improvised in the moment, about his life in prison and other hardships. Began playing guitar in his teens, inspired by Blind Lemon Jefferson and Peetie Wheatstraw and mentored by local guitarists Robert and Frank Meddy. Throughout the next two decades performed at house parties and other local gatherings while working various manual labor jobs. In 1958 was discovered and recorded by folklorist Harry Oster at Angola Penitentiary while serving a life sentence for murder. In late 1959 was granted a servitude parole on a farm in Denham Springs and recorded for Prestige/Bluesville and Takoma in following years. In the mid-1960s began appearing at national festivals, including the Newport Folk Festival in 1964. Continued performing at major festivals and toured Europe multiple times through the 1970s with recordings on Ahura Mazda, 77, Storyville, Blues Beacon, Southland, and Sonet. Recorded final LP *Santa Fe Blues* for Free Bird in Paris in 1979.

WILLIAMS, SLY *See* Page, Cleo.

WILLIAMS, SPENCER *Jazz.* Piano, vocals. Composer. Bandleader. (Born Oct. 14, 1884, New Orleans, Orleans Parish; died July 14, 1965, Flushing, New York.)[14] Early jazz pianist and singer-songwriter best known for his many compositions which have become jazz standards such as "Basin Street Blues," "I Ain't Got Nobody," "Tishomingo Blues," and "Careless Love." Performed around Chicago in the mid-1910s before relocating to New York and working with **Clarence Williams**. In 1923 recorded with **Lizzie Miles** and through the next several decades performed mainly in Europe, touring with Josephine Baker, Fats Waller, and others. Recorded with **Lonnie Johnson** and Teddy Bunn in 1929–30. Resided in England and Sweden throughout remainder of career before returning to New York shortly before his death.

WILLIAMS, UNCLE JOHNNY (John Antwine Jr.) *Blues.* Guitar, vocals. Composer. (Born May 15, 1906, Alexandria, Rapides Parish; died Mar. 6, 2006, Chicago.) Chicago blues singer and guitarist who was among the city's first generation of electric blues musicians to perform and record following World War II. In the late 1910s moved to Belzoni, Mississippi, following his mother's death, and began learning guitar from his uncle, who performed with the Chatmon brothers and Charley Patton. Relocated to Chicago in 1938 and in the 1940s performed regularly on Maxwell Street, often with cousin Johnny Young, Snooky Pryor, Floyd and Moody Jones, **Little Walter**, and others. In 1947 recorded two singles with Young on Ora-Nelle and in 1948 recorded with Young and Pryor on Planet, all considered among the first postwar Chicago blues recordings. Continued performing in clubs through the 1950s with Young, Pryor, Little Walter, and others and made final recordings with Big Boy Spires in 1953 for Chance. In the late 1950s quit playing blues and joined the church, becoming an ordained minister who presided over many blues artists' funeral services in the following decades.

WILLS, OSCAR *See* T.V. Slim [Notable Musicians Born outside Louisiana].

WILSON, JIMMY (Jimmie Ned Wilson) *Rhythm and blues.* Vocals, bass. Composer. Bandleader. (Born Jan. 21, 1918, Gibsland, Bienville Parish; died Feb. 24, 1966, Dallas.)[15] Noted early rhythm and blues singer-songwriter best known for his 1953 hit "Tin Pan Alley," which has been covered by numerous blues and rock artists. While in a gospel group in Oakland, California, in the late 1940s, began performing with Bob Geddin's Cavaliers and recorded for his Cava-Tone label. After several singles as a leader on Aladdin, had major hit with "Tin Pan Alley" in 1953 on Geddin's Big Town label. More singles followed on Big Town, 7–11, Rhythm, Chart, Rockin', and Irma through 1956. In the late 1950s returned to Louisiana and released four singles on Goldband, notably "Please Accept My Love" in 1958. Recorded two singles for Duke in 1961 before succumbing to lung cancer several years later at age 48.

WILSON, JOHN *Zydeco.* Accordion, harmonica, vocals. Bandleader. (Born Oct. 18, 1963, New Iberia, Iberia Parish.) Locally renowned zydeco accordion player and bandleader began playing at age 12, influenced greatly by **Clifton Chenier** and mentored early on by **Walter "Creole" Polite**. After performing with various local bands, including with **Bobby Price**, formed his band the Zydeco House Rockers in the early 1990s and recorded debut LP *Going Down to Louisiana* in the mid-1990s and toured overseas. Also performed and recorded as member of the Zydeco Hurricanes with **Selwyn Cooper** in the 1990s. Continued performing with Zydeco House Rockers in 2010s.

WILSON, U.P. (Huary Perry Wilson) *Blues.* Guitar, vocals. Composer. Bandleader. (Born Sept. 4, 1934, near Shreveport, Caddo Parish; died Sept. 23, 2004, Paris.) Influential Texas blues guitarist and singer who was known for his wild showmanship and one-handed guitar solos. Raised on a farm outside Shreveport, relocated to Dallas in the mid-1950s and began performing in West Side clubs, influenced by local guitarists Frankie Lee Sims and Zuzu Bollin. Later worked with Robert Ealey and Cornell Dupree and relocated to Fort Worth. Continued performing in area clubs and in the late 1980s recorded for local PeeWee label. Two albums followed on Red Lightnin', including *On My Way* in 1988. Toured nationally and overseas throughout the 1990s with five releases on JSP, including *Boogie Boy: The Texas Guitar Tornado Returns* in 1994. In the late 1990s relocated to Paris and continued performing until succumbing to complications following surgery at age 70.

WIMBERLY, RUFUS "RIP" *Blues.* Guitar, vocals. Composer. Bandleader. (Born Dec. 7, 1926, Arcadia, Bienville Parish; died May 14, 2012, Tallulah, Madison Parish.) North Louisiana Delta blues guitarist and singer began playing guitar as a teen, raised in rural Claiborne Parish and inspired by his father, who played fiddle, mandolin, and guitar. Performed in north-central Louisiana and Vicksburg, Mississippi, area for more than five decades and continued into his 80s. Released album *Highway 80 Blues* on Coon Dog Records in 2000.

WITT, MAYLON D. *See* Humphries, Maylon.

WOOD, BRENTON (Alfred Jesse Smith) *Rhythm and blues.* Vocals, piano. Composer. Bandleader. (Born July 26, 1941, Shreveport, Caddo Parish.) Noted West Coast soul singer and songwriter best known for his 1967 hits "The Oogum Boogum Song" and "Gimme Little Sign." Raised in southern California, began singing and writing songs in his teens, and was later influenced by Sam Cooke and Jesse Belvin. In the mid-1960s had singles on Brent and Wand before achieving hits with "Oogum Boogum" and "Gimme Little Sign" on Double Shot in 1967. After two more hits on Double Shot, recorded for numerous labels into the 1970s, including a duet with **Shirley Goodman**. In 1977 had minor hit with "Come Softly to Me" on Cream. Continued performing in following decades and released several more recordings, including a remake of "Gimme Little Sign" with William Pilgrim in 2014.

WOODS, EDDIE "FACE-O" *Jazz.* Drums. (Born around 1890s, probably New Orleans, Orleans Parish; died 1940s, Galveston, Texas.) Early New Orleans jazz drummer worked regularly with **Buddy Petit** in the early 1920s. Reportedly settled in Galveston while on tour with Petit in 1922 and remained there until his death.

WOODS, JERARD *Gospel.* Vocals. (Born Oct. 2, 1972, Shreveport, Caddo Parish.) Noted contemporary gospel vocalist began singing as a child and has since worked with CeCe Winans, Natalie Grant, Israel Houghton, Donnie McClurkin, and others. In the mid-2000s launched solo career and released debut recording as leader, *I Waited,* on Found Sound Music in 2007.

WOODS, KIPORI "BABY WOLF" *Blues, jazz.* Guitar, vocals. Composer. Bandleader. (Born Sept. 4, 1971, New Orleans, Orleans Parish.) Blues and jazz guitarist was raised and mentored by his grandfather **Lloyd Lambert** and began performing as a child with gospel acts the Zion Harmonizers and **Raymond Myles**. After leading a funk group, switched to playing blues in the mid-1990s, influenced by B.B. King, Albert King, and **Walter "Wolfman" Washington**, to whom his stage name refers. Recorded debut CD, *Blues Man from Down South,* in 1998 and had several releases on Louisiana Red Hot Records through the 2010s.

WOODS, OSCAR "BUDDY"/"THE LONE WOLF" *Blues.* Guitar, vocals. Composer. (Born Apr. 7, 1903, near Natchitoches, Natch. Parish; died Dec. 14, 1955, Shreveport, Caddo Parish.)[16] Highly influential prewar blues bottleneck slide-guitar pioneer and singer best known for his 1936 recording "Lone Wolf Blues." Reportedly developed his lap steel slide-guitar style in the early 1920s, inspired by the current Hawaiian music fad. Around 1925 settled in Shreveport and began performing on the streets and in saloons, forming long partnership with enigmatic guitarist Ed Schaffer. In 1930 recorded two sides with Schaffer as the Shreveport Home Wreckers and in 1932 recorded two sides as Eddie and Oscar, notably "Flying Crow Blues," all for Victor. Also appeared with **Jimmie Davis** on several sessions for Victor from 1930 to 1932 and performed with and mentored Black Ace (B. K. Turner). In 1936 recorded three sides for Decca, including "Lone Wolf Blues," followed by two sessions with his group the Wampus Cats in 1937–38, which resulted in three releases on Vocalion. Made final recordings in 1940 for folklorist John Lomax in Shreveport. Continued performing around Shreveport until his death from atelectasis and shock from an undetermined cause.

WOOLFOLK, WILLIAM W. *Blues.* Drums, vocals. Bandleader. (Born Apr. 26, 1926, Maringouin, Iberville Parish; died Apr. 22, 2005, Baton Rouge, EBR Parish.)[17] Swamp blues drummer who led several bands in the Erwinville/Baton Rouge area in the 1970s and 1980s, including the Silver Spoons. Also worked with **Clarence Edwards** and **Smokehouse Porter**.

WRIGHT, MARVA *Blues, gospel.* Vocals. Composer. Bandleader. (Born Mar. 20, 1948, New Orleans, Orleans Parish; died Mar. 23, 2010, New Orleans, Orleans Parish.) Popular blues singer who was known as "the Blues Queen of New Orleans" spent a majority of her life singing gospel in church, influenced by **Mahalia Jackson**, who was a family friend. At age 39 began singing blues in Bourbon Street clubs and soon formed her BMWs band. Recorded debut album, *Heartbreakin' Woman,* in 1990 and released eleven more albums throughout her career, including *After the Levees Broke* in 2007, which detailed her tragic experiences during Hurricane Katrina. Continued to tour nationally and overseas until suffering two strokes in 2009.

WYNN, ALBERT *Jazz.* Trombone. Composer. Bandleader. (Born July 29, 1907, New Orleans, Orleans Parish; died Jan. 20, 1973, Chicago.)[18] Early jazz trombonist toured with Ma Rainey in the mid-1920s and led his band the Gut Bucket Five for several years in Chicago, recording for OKeh and Vocalion in 1926 and 1928. From 1928 to 1932 worked and recorded in Europe. Returned to Chicago and throughout the 1930s worked with Albert Ammons, **Jimmie Noone**, **Richard M. Jones**, Earl Hines, Fletcher Henderson, and others. Throughout the 1940s and 1950s performed with **Baby Dodds**, **Little Brother Montgomery**, and Lil Armstrong. In the early 1960s toured as member of Gold Coast Jazz Band and recorded with Armstrong and as a leader for Riverside. Retired due to ill health in the mid-1960s.

YATES, DUANE (Claude Duane Yates) *Rhythm and blues.* Vocals, trumpet, guitar. Composer. Bandleader. (Born Apr. 18, 1944, Pineville, Rapides Parish; died May 23, 2009, Alexandria, Rapides Parish.) Highly regarded blue-eyed soul singer best known for his work as member of the Boogie Kings. Began performing during his teens and made first recordings with his band the Capris on N-Joy in 1965. In 1966 joined the Boogie Kings, replacing **G.G. Shinn**, and toured and recorded with group for two years. Also released LP *Sings Otis Redding* on Montel-Michelle. After a stint in **Ned Theall**'s band What's Happening in the late 1960s, worked in Las Vegas and Hollywood during the 1970s. Reunited with Boogie Kings in the 1980s and 1990s and continued performing through the late 2000s, releasing two solo albums, including *Katrina's Foot.*

YOUNG, AUSTIN "BOOTS" *Jazz.* Trombone, string bass. (Born Jan. 3, 1890, Napoleonville, Assumption Parish; died June 30, 1954, New Orleans, Orleans Parish.)[1] Early New Orleans jazz trombonist and bass player started his music career as member of Imperial Orchestra in Napoleonville in the 1910s. Later worked with **Sidney Desvigne** in New Orleans and in the 1930s performed regularly with his brother, saxophonist William "Sport" Young, and **Willie Pajeaud**. In the 1940s recorded as bassist with **Bunk Johnson**, **Big Eye Louis Nelson**, **Wooden Joe Nicholas**, **Ann Cooke**, and **Raymond Burke**. Cousin of jazz saxophone great Lester Young and **Lee Young**.

YOUNG JESSE *See* Thomas, Jesse.

YOUNG, LEE *Jazz.* Drums. Bandleader. (Born Mar. 7, 1914, New Orleans, Orleans Parish; died July 31, 2008, Los Angeles.) Highly accomplished jazz drummer toured the South as a child for several years with his family band in traveling carnivals. After touring with **Mutt Carey** and Ethel Waters, made recording debut behind Fats Waller during his early 20s. In the 1940s and 1950s worked with Lionel Hampton, Les Hite, Billie Holiday, Nat King Cole, Benny Goodman, and many others. Appeared on hundreds of jazz recording sessions throughout his long career and also worked as producer for Vee-Jay, Motown, and ABC/Dunhill Records. Younger brother of influential Mississippi-born jazz saxophonist Lester Young.

YOUNG, MIGHTY JOE *Blues.* Guitar, vocals. Composer. Bandleader. (Born Sept. 23, 1926, Belcher, Caddo Parish; died Mar. 24, 1999, Chicago.)[2] Renowned Chicago blues guitarist and singer moved to Milwaukee in the mid-1940s and in the early 1950s began performing on the local blues scene. In the mid-1950s returned to Shreveport and cut debut single for Jiffy and recorded with **T.V. Slim** before relocating to Chicago in 1958. In the late 1950s and 1960s worked and recorded with numerous musicians such as Billy Boy Arnold, Otis Rush, Albert King, Magic Sam, and Jimmy Rogers and had singles as a leader on Atomic-H, Fire, USA, Webcor, Celtex, and other local labels. In 1971 released LP *Blues with a Touch of Soul* on Delmark, which accurately described his music style, followed by albums for Sonet, Ovation, and Black and Blue. In the late 1980s underwent surgery for a pinched nerve which severely limited his guitar playing. Released final recording, *Mighty Man,* on Blind Pig in 1997 before succumbing to complications after a second corrective surgery at age 72.

YOUNG, NELSON *Cajun.* Fiddle. (Born May 18, 1919, Welsh, Jeff. Davis Parish; died May 20, 1997, Lake Charles, Calcasieu Parish.)[3] Veteran Lake Charles–area Cajun fiddle player performed and recorded with **Sidney Brown** and the Traveler Playboys in the 1950s and early 1960s. Also performed with **Louis Lopez**, **Joe Bonsall**,

Hicks Wagon Wheel Ramblers, Sulphur Playboys, and Higginbotham Playboys in the following years.

YOUNG, NONC ALLIE *Cajun.* Fiddle, vocals. Composer. Bandleader. (Born May 3, 1912, Basile, Evangeline Parish; died Apr. 21, 2003, Basile, Evangeline Parish.) Noted Cajun accordionist and singer began playing the instrument at age eight and within several years was performing at local house dances. In the 1970s performed and recorded with the **Balfa Brothers** for seven years, touring Europe several times with group. In 1984 cofounded the Basile Cajun Band to perform at the World's Fair in New Orleans and recorded several singles, including "Ninety Nine Year Waltz" for Bee in 1987. Continued performing with group into his 80s, appearing on band's CD *La Musique Que Viens du Beaubassin* on Swallow in 1999 with **Ray Landry**.

YOUNG, THEO *Cajun.* Guitar, fiddle. (Born Jan. 8, 1898, Creole, Cameron Parish; died Jan. 5, 1958, Grand Lake, Cameron Parish.)[4] Early Cajun guitarist and fiddle player began performing around the Creole and Lake Arthur areas in the mid-1910s with local musicians Albert and Savin Broussard. In the 1920s joined Black Bayou Band with Ada, Levi, and **Anatole Credeur** and performed at house dances and dance halls in Calcasieu and Cameron Parish, recording as guitarist behind Credeur on four sides for Brunswick in Nov. 1929.

Z

ZARDIS, CHESTER "LITTLE BEAR" *Jazz.* Double bass, tuba. (Born May 27, 1900, New Orleans, Orleans Parish; died Aug. 14, 1990, New Orleans, Orleans Parish.)[1] Renowned early New Orleans jazz double bassist studied under **Billy Marrero** at age 16 and soon began performing with **Buddy Petit**. In the 1920s and 1930s worked with **Chris Kelly**, **Kid Rena**, **Armand Piron**, **Sidney Desvigne**, **Fats Pichon**, **Harold Dejan**, and others. Recorded with **Bunk Johnson** and **George Lewis** in 1942–43. After a decade away from music, began appearing regularly at Preservation Hall in 1965 and toured Europe and Japan. Remained active during the 1980s with tours overseas and as member of the Original Liberty Jazz Band. Continued performing at Preservation Hall until a month before his death at age 90.

ZENO, CHESTER *Zydeco.* Rubboard. (Born July 30, 1921, Lafayette, Lafayette Parish; died Oct. 20, 1988, Lafayette, Lafayette Parish.) Noted early zydeco rubboard player who began performing with his cousin **Rockin' Dopsie** in the mid-1950s. Toured and recorded extensively with **Rockin' Dopsie**'s band the Twisters through the early 1980s and was known for his energetic playing style. Cousin of **Lee Allen Zeno**.

ZENO, HENRY *Jazz.* Snare drum. (Born Dec. 1892, New Orleans, Orleans Parish; died Nov. 3, 1921, New Orleans, Orleans Parish.)[2] Highly regarded and influential early New Orleans jazz snare drummer reportedly worked with **Buddy Bolden**'s band during Bolden's peak in the years before his commitment. Renowned for his early work with brushes and his press rolls, often playing in tandem with **Black Benny** and later **Ninesse Trepagnier**. Also performed with **Edward Clem**, **Frankie Duson**, and **Manuel Manetta**. In the 1910s worked with **Armand Piron**'s Olympia Orchestra and **King Oliver**. Joined **Papa Celestin**'s Original Tuxedo Band for a short time before his death from a heart blockage. Mentor of **Baby Dodds**.

ZENO, LEE ALLEN *Zydeco, rhythm and blues.* Bass, guitar, vocals. Composer. Bandleader. (Born Oct. 6, 1954, Lafayette, Lafayette Parish.) Highly accomplished and extremely versatile bass player best known for his 40-plus-year association with Stanley Dural Jr. (**Buckwheat Zydeco**). Began playing guitar as a child, inspired by **Little Buck Sinegal**, but soon switched to bass. In 1974 joined Buckwheat and the Hitchhikers and continued performing and recording extensively with Dural until Dural's death in 2016. Recorded extensively with numerous artists throughout career, including **Irma Thomas**, **Carol Fran**, **Henry Gray**, **Lazy Lester**, **Dalton Reed**, **Snooks Eaglin**, **Phillip Walker**, **Bobby Parker**, and Solomon Burke. In the 2010s continued performing with his own group as well as with Sinegal, Fran, **Reggie Dural**, **Major Handy**, **Zydeco Ray**, and many others. Cousin of **Rockin' Dopsie**.

ZITO, PHIL *Jazz.* Drums. Bandleader. (Born Aug. 8, 1914, New Orleans, Orleans Parish; died Aug. 2, 1998, Metairie, Jefferson Parish.) Noted Dixieland jazz bandleader and drummer led his New Orleans International City Dixielanders, which included **Pete Fountain**, in the late 1940s and early 1950s. Recorded LP *Dixieland Express* for Columbia in 1950 and toured nationally.

ZYDECO JOE (Joseph Adam Mouton) *Zydeco.* Accordion, guitar, vocals. Composer. Bandleader. (Born Oct. 26, 1943, Lafayette, Lafayette Parish; died Nov. 17, 2007, Lafayette, Lafayette Parish.) Renowned traditional zydeco accordionist and singer-songwriter began playing guitar in his early teens and worked with various bands, including **Rockin' Dopsie**'s Twisters in the 1960s. After a

20-year hiatus from music, began playing accordion in the late 1980s and formed his band Laissez le Bon Ton Rouler. Throughout the 1990s developed loyal following by performing at clubs and festivals throughout south Louisiana, and became known for his powerful performances and improvisational skills singing in Creole French. In 2001 released acclaimed CD *Jack Rabbit* on Maison de Soul, which contained mostly originals sung in both Creole French and English. In the 2000s began touring outside Louisiana and released final CD, *Black Cat,* just shortly before his sudden death at age 64 after a brief bout with pneumonia.

ZYDECO RAY (Raymond Hébert) *Zydeco.* Accordian, vocals. Bandleader. (Born Apr. 15, 1935, Segura, Iberia Parish.) Locally popular Lafayette-area accordionist and bandleader started playing rubboard as a child in the 1940s at la la house dances with his father, Marcel "Seaux" Hébert (1881–1969), who was a renowned but unrecorded local Creole fiddle and accordion player. Began playing accordion in the mid-1980s, inspired by **Clifton Chenier** and **Boozoo Chavis**, and continued performing with his band the Creole Night Riders in the 2010s, often with brother-in-law **Lee Allen Zeno** and St. Martinville guitarist Ramsey "Sha-Me-Noo" Robertson.

II

NOTABLE MUSICIANS BORN OUTSIDE LOUISIANA

ADCOCK, C. C. (Charles Clinton Adcock) *Swamp rock, swamp pop.* Guitar, vocals. Composer. Bandleader. (Born Sept. 9, 1969, Tokyo.) Singer-songwriter, bandleader, and producer was born in Tokyo while his father was stationed at an Air Force base and was raised in Lafayette. Began performing in his teens with a local group before relocating to Los Angeles after high school and playing on the local glam rock scene. After touring with **Buckwheat Zydeco**, returned to Lafayette and released debut album for Island in 1994. In the late 1990s cofounded Cowboy Stew Blues Revue with **Lil' Buck Sinegal** and released solo CD *Lafayette Marquis* on Yep Roc in 2004. From 2000 through the early 2010s toured and recorded with Lil' Band 'O Gold and produced music for film and television, including HBO's *True Blood.* Continued performing with his band Lafayette Marquis in the late 2010s. Brother of piano player and songwriter Eric Adcock, longtime member of **Roddie Romero**'s Hub City All-Stars.

ALLEN, JESSE *Rhythm and blues.* Guitar, vocals. Composer. Bandleader. (Born Sept. 25, 1925, Tallahassee, Florida; died Sept. 14, 1976, Miami.)[1] Postwar rhythm and blues singer and guitarist who cut a series of notable singles in New Orleans throughout the 1950s. Made recording debut in 1951 on Aladdin with "Rock This Morning" before releasing a single each on Coral and Bay'ou. Several releases followed on Imperial, produced by **Dave Bartholomew**, in 1953–54, including the **Lloyd Price**-inspired "Sittin' and Wonderin'." In 1958–59 had singles on Vin and Duplex, notably the raw blues rocker "After a While." After performing around Texas in the early 1960s, settled in Miami area and continued playing in local clubs until succumbing to heart disease at age 50.

ALLEN, LEE (Lee Francis Allen) *Rhythm and blues.* Saxophone. Composer. Bandleader. (Born July 2, 1926, Pittsburg, Kansas; died Oct. 18, 1994, Hawthorne, California.)[2] Highly influential saxophonist whose distinctive and powerful playing style helped define New Orleans rhythm and blues and early rock and roll. Raised in Denver, Colorado, began playing saxophone as a child, influenced by **Illinois Jacquet**, Lester Young, and Louis Jordan. Relocated to New Orleans at age 17 on an athletic scholarship and by 1947 was performing regularly with **Paul Gayten**. Soon began working extensively as a session musician at **Cosimo Matassa**'s studio and became a key member in **Dave Bartholomew**'s famed studio band. Through the early 1960s appeared on countless hits by numerous artists including **Fats Domino**, **Lloyd Price**, **Smiley Lewis**, Little Richard, **Guitar Slim**, **Huey "Piano" Smith**, and **Professor Longhair**. In 1958 had minor hit as leader with instrumental "Walkin' with Mr. Lee" on Ember and toured for several years with own group. Relocated to Los Angeles in 1965 and continued working as session musician and performing in local clubs. Toured with Domino in the 1970s and early 1980s and also recorded with rock bands the Stray Cats and the Blasters. Appeared on album *Crescent City Gold* in 1994 with **Allen Toussaint**, **Dr. John**, **Alvin "Red" Tyler**, and **Earl Palmer** shortly before his death.

ANDERSON, JIMMY *Blues.* Harmonica, guitar, vocals. Composer. Bandleader. (Born Nov. 21, 1934, Woodville, Mississippi; died Oct. 5, 2013, Natchez, Mississippi.) Mississippi-born swamp blues harmonica player and singer-songwriter was raised in Natchez and began playing harmonica as a child, inspired early on by Papa Lightfoot and later Jimmy Reed and **Slim Harpo**. After relocating to Baton Rouge in 1950, formed his band the Joy Jumpers in the late 1950s and performed regularly around Baton Rouge as well as Texas and Mississippi. From 1962 to 1964 recorded for producer **J. D. Miller**, which resulted in singles on Zynn and Excello, notably "Naggin'" and "Going Through the Park." Returned to Natchez in 1969 and worked as popular local disc jockey "Soul Man Lee" for many years. Began performing again in the early 1990s and toured Europe several times. Continued performing in Natchez area into the 2000s.

BALL, MARCIA *Rhythm and blues.* Piano, vocals. Composer. Bandleader. (Born Mar. 20, 1949, Orange, Texas.) Popular rhythm and blues pianist and singer-songwriter was raised in a musical family in Vinton, Louisiana, and began playing piano as a child. In the early 1970s settled in Austin and performed in a country band before launching solo career in 1974 and recording country-rock debut album *Circuit Queen* in 1978 for Capitol. By the early 1980s had begun gradually shifting towards New Orleans rhythm and blues, influenced greatly by **Professor Longhair** and singer **Irma Thomas**. In 1984 signed with Rounder and through the late 1990s released numerous albums on the label, including *Let Me Play with Your Poodle* in 1997 and *Sing It!* with Thomas and Tracy Nelson in 1998. Continued touring extensively nationally and overseas into the 2010s with additional releases on Alligator, including the acclaimed *So Many Rivers* in 2004 and *Shine Bright* in 2018.

BARNES, BRUCE "SUNPIE" *Zydeco.* Accordion, piano, harmonica, vocals. Composer. Bandleader. (Born May 18, 1963, Benton, Arkansas.) The son of a blues harmonica player, internationally renowned zydeco accordionist and bandleader learned harmonica and piano as a child, influenced early on by his father and recordings by Sonny Boy Williamson (Rice Miller). After a year playing in the NFL, moved to New Orleans in 1987 and began playing harmonica with various blues and zydeco bands. In 1989 started learning accordion, mentored by **Clayton Sampy**, and in 1991 formed his zydeco band the Louisiana Sunspots. Through the 2000s released several recordings, including *Lick a Hot Skillet* in 1998 on 2EZ Music, performed extensively nationally and overseas, and appeared in several television shows and documentaries. In the 2010s toured internationally with rock musicians Paul Simon and Sting and continued performing at clubs and festivals.

BELL, REUBEN *Rhythm and blues.* Vocals. Composer. Bandleader. (Born Dec. 11, 1942, Jefferson, Texas; died Apr. 18, 2003, Shreveport, Caddo Parish.)[3] Highly regarded early southern soul singer-songwriter with a hauntingly plaintive vocal style and best known for his late 1960s and 1970s recordings such as "I Hear You Knocking (It's Too Late)." Raised in Shreveport, began performing in the 1960s and recorded debut single "It's Not That Easy" on Murco in 1967. After two more singles for Murco, including "You're Gonna Miss Me" in 1969, worked with producer **Wardell Quezergue** and had releases on House of Orange and Deluxe, including minor hit "I Hear You Knocking" in 1972. Releases followed on Alarm and Port City through 1983, including LP *Blues Get off My Shoulders.* Stopped performing soon afterwards due to frustrations with the music business.

BLACK IVORY KING (Dave Alexander) *Blues, jazz.* Piano, vocals. Composer. (Born Oct. 1895, Stamps, Arkansas; died after 1942, possibly in California.)[4] Enigmatic Shreveport-based early boogie-woogie and barrelhouse blues piano player and singer moved to Shreveport with his family as a child. In the 1920s and 1930s performed regularly around the city's Fannin Street black entertainment district and at local house parties. Billed as the "Black King of the Ivories," influenced many local musicians including **Lead Belly** and **Jesse "Babyface" Thomas**. Recorded four sides in Dallas for Decca in 1937 as Black Ivory King, including "Flying Crow Blues" and "Working for the PWA." By the early 1940s had relocated to South Central Los Angeles and worked at the Tip Top Bar Room downtown, but details of life and music career in remaining years are unknown. **Omar Sharriff** (born Dave Alexander Elam) was named after the pianist by his father who was a close friend. Not to be confused with prewar blues pianist Little David (Alexander), who recorded for Decca in 1936.

BOHREN, SPENCER *Blues, folk.* Guitar, vocals. Composer. Bandleader. (Born April 5, 1950, Casper, Wyoming; died June 8, 2019, New Orleans, Orleans Parish.) New Orleans–based singer-songwriter began performing in his early teens and settled in the Crescent City in the mid-1970s, where he became a fixture on the local music scene. Throughout following decades toured extensively nationally and abroad primarily as a solo artist, releasing well over a dozen albums, including highly acclaimed *The Long Black Line* in 2006, which detailed his family's experiences during Hurricane Katrina. After being diagnosed with stage 4 cancer in late 2018, performed only occasional local gigs before succumbing to the disease at age 69.

CAGE, BUTCH (James Cage) *Blues.* Fiddle, guitar, cane fife. Composer. (Born Mar. 16, 1894, near Hamburg, Mississippi; died Sept. 1975, Zachary, EBR Parish.)[5] Early blues and black string-band musician best known for his work with musical partner **Willie B. Thomas**. Learned fife, guitar, and fiddle as a child and relocated to Louisiana in the late 1920s, eventually settling in Zachary. Performed at local house dances and juke joints and soon began performing with Thomas in a duo. In 1959–60 made acclaimed field recordings with Thomas for folklorist Harry Oster and performed at the Newport Folk Festival. Continued working with Thomas until his death at age 81.

CAGE, ROBERT *Blues.* Guitar, vocals. Composer. Bandleader. (Born Apr. 4, 1937, Percy Creek, Mississippi; died July 23, 2012, Woodville, Mississippi.)[6] Raised in Woodville, Mississippi area, began playing guitar at age 11, influenced by local bluesman Scott Dunbar. Performed in local juke joints in the late 1950s and 1960s. Recorded *Can See What You're Doing* for Fat Possum in 1998 which showcased his raw Mississippi juke joint style. Often partnered with blues drummer Hezekiah Early.

CAILLIER, JACKIE *Cajun.* Accordion. Bandleader. (Born Sept. 27, 1952, Orange, Texas.) Noted Texas-born accordionist best known for his longtime partnership with **Ivy Dugas** in the Cajun Cousins. Began playing accordion in the late 1960s, inspired by **Aldus Roger** and **Belton Richard**, and in the 1970s performed with **Dallas Roy**'s Rambling Aces, making recording debut on single "(I'm Glad to Be a) Cajun from Church Point" in 1973. Later performed with **Lesa Cormier**, **Joe Bonsall**, **Walter Mouton**, and others. In the 1990s formed the Cajun Cousins with Dugas and released several acclaimed albums on Lanor and Swallow in following years, including *Blacktop the Gravel Road* in 1999. Continued performing with band throughout Louisiana and Texas in the 2010s.

CHENIER, C. J. (Clayton Joseph Chenier) *Zydeco.* Accordion, saxophone, piano, flute, vocals. Composer. Bandleader. (Born Sept. 28, 1957, Port Arthur, Texas.) Internationally renowned zydeco accordionist and bandleader and son of zydeco pioneer **Clifton Chenier**. Began playing saxophone as a child and in the 1970s performed in soul and funk bands around Port Arthur. In 1978 joined his father's Red Hot Louisiana Band as saxophonist and toured extensively, eventually learning accordion and opening shows during his father's last years. After his father's death in 1987, took over leadership of band and continued performing. In 1990 toured and recorded with Paul Simon and, following releases on Slash and Arhoolie, signed with Alligator and released *Too Much Fun* in 1994. Toured extensively nationally and overseas in following years with several more releases on Alligator and World Village, including *Can't Sit Down* in 2011. Nephew of **Cleveland Chenier**.

CLAYTON, JAMES "KID" *Jazz.* Cornet. Bandleader. (Born Mar. 1, 1902, Jasper County, Mississippi; died Dec. 17, 1963, New Orleans, Orleans Parish.)[7] Noted jazz cornetist and bandleader moved to New Orleans with his family at age three and settled in the notorious Battlefield neighborhood. Largely self-taught and known for his bluesy style, worked with **Jack Carey** in the 1920s and toured Chicago. Formed Kid Clayton and His Happy Pals in the mid-1920s and made recording debut as leader in 1952 for Folkways featuring **Kid Avery**. Also worked regularly with **Captain John Handy** in later years.

CLEARY, JON *Rhythm and blues.* Piano, guitar, bass, drums, vocals. Composer. Bandleader. (Born Aug. 11, 1962, Kent, England.) British-born piano player and singer-songwriter began playing guitar as a child, inspired early on by New Orleans funk and rhythm and blues. In 1980 relocated to New Orleans and began learning piano, influenced greatly by **James Booker** and **Professor Longhair**. In following years worked as sideman with numerous artists, including **Walter "Wolfman" Washington**, **Earl King**, **Snooks Eaglin**, and **Johnny Adams**. Recorded debut album *Alligator Lips and Dirty Rice* on Oolamalawalla in 1989 and throughout following two decades toured with **Dr. John**, Taj Mahal, Bonnie Raitt, and others. In the 2010s continued performing with his band Absolute Monster Gentlemen with several releases on FHQ, including the critically acclaimed *GoGo Juice* in 2015.

DARNELL, LARRY (Leo Edward Donald Jr.) *Rhythm and blues.* Vocals. Composer. Bandleader. (Born Dec. 17, 1928, Columbus, Ohio; died July 3, 1983, Columbus, Ohio.) Known as "Mr. Heart & Soul," popular early rhythm and blues vocalist started singing gospel at age 11 and in his mid-teens toured as a dancer in a black burlesque show. In the late 1940s settled in New Orleans and began performing regularly at famed Dew Drop Inn backed by **Edgar Blanchard**'s Gondoliers. Signed with Regal in 1949 and through 1951 had multiple national hits, including "I'll Get Along Somehow," "For You My Love," and "I Love My Baby." From 1952 to 1954 recorded numerous sides for OKeh that failed to chart. Throughout the next ten years had releases on Savoy, Deluxe, Map, Warwick, Argo, and Misty before cutting last single, "Son of a Son of a Slave," for Instant in 1969 produced by **Huey "Piano" Smith**. Returned to singing gospel in church in the 1970s before succumbing to lung cancer at age 54.

DAVIS, JAMES "THUNDERBIRD" (James Louis Huston) *Blues.* Vocals. Composer. Bandleader. (Born Nov. 10, 1938, Prichard, Alabama; died Jan. 24, 1992, Saint Paul, Minnesota.) Noted Thibodaux-based blues singer best known for his 1963 recording "Blue Monday" and his association with **Guitar Slim**. Began singing gospel early in career before joining Guitar Slim's band in 1957, touring extensively with group led by **Lloyd Lambert** until Guitar Slim's death in 1959. After working with Lambert's band with Nappy Brown and **Carol Fran**, signed with Duke and released several singles in the early 1960s, including regional hits "Blue Monday" and "Your Turn to Cry" in 1963. In the late 1960s and early 1970s toured with southern soul singers O. V. Wright and Joe Tex. After more than a decade away from music, began performing again and signed with Black Top and recorded acclaimed LP *Check Out Time* in 1989 backed by Lambert, **Earl King**, Clarence Hollimon, and Grady Gaines. Toured nationally on the club and festival circuit until suffering fatal heart attack while performing on stage at age 53.

DONLEY, JIMMY (James Kenneth Donley) *Swamp pop.* Guitar, vocals. Composer. (Born Aug. 17, 1929, Gulfport, Mississippi; died Mar. 20, 1963, Long Beach, Mississippi.) Highly regarded but tragic figure of early swamp pop best known for his heartbreaking compositions such as "Born to Be a Loser," many of which have been covered by artists such as **Fats Domino**, **Jerry Lee Lewis**, **Clarence "Frogman" Henry**, **Johnnie Allan**, and **Eddy Raven**. Began performing and writing songs as a teenager, encouraged by his mother early on. After receiving an undesirable discharge from the military in the late 1940s, returned to the Gulf Coast area and continued performing and composing. In 1957 signed with Decca and through 1960 released numerous singles, including "Born to Be a Loser," "Our Love," and "Radio, Jukebox and TV," backed by top Nashville session players such as Hank Garland, Chet Atkins, and Boots Randolph. In the early 1960s recorded for Huey Meaux's Tear Drop label and cut several notable singles, including "Strange Strange Feeling," "I'm to Blame," and "Just a Game." After struggling with long-term depression, alcoholism, and the recent death of his mother, he took his own life at age 33.

DuBOIS, JOHN (John Julius Joseph Dubois) *Cajun.* Vocals. (Born Nov. 21, 1925, Port Arthur, Texas; died Jan. 8, 2000, New Orleans, Orleans Parish.)[8] Known as "the Cajun Balladeer," noted traditional Cajun singer was born in Port Arthur where his Kaplan, Louisiana–born father's family was temporarily living, but was raised in Kaplan. After decades of working in early television and theater on the East Coast, began promoting Cajun culture in the Boston area and started recording Cajun ballads. In the early 1980s returned to Louisiana and toured nationally and abroad promoting Cajun culture and its traditional songs, recording three albums, including *Bayou Ballads: The Forgotten Songs around 1840–1880* on Chaud Dog Jean in 1998.

DuCONGE, ALBERT *Jazz.* Trumpet. (Born Sept. 1, 1899, Mississippi; died after 1960, probably Chattanooga, Tennessee.)[9] Early New Orleans jazz trumpeter worked on riverboats in the 1920s with **Fate Marable** and **Sidney Desvigne**. Also performed with brothers **Adolphus**, **Earl**, and **Peter DuConge**. By 1928 was living and performing in Chattanooga. Son of **Oscar DuConge**.

DuCONGE, EARL/EARLE *Jazz.* Saxophone. (Born July 17, 1898, Mississippi; died Oct. 11, 1979, Los Angeles.)[10] Early New Orleans jazz saxophonist performed in bands with brothers **Adolphus**, **Albert**, and **Peter DuConge** in the 1920s. Son of **Oscar DuConge** and father of **Wendell DuConge**.

GARNIER, D'JALMA, III *Creole.* Fiddle, guitar, bass, vocals. Composer. Bandleader. (Born Jan. 26, 1954, Ramsey, Minnesota.)[11] Noted Creole fiddle player and multi-instrumentalist was mentored by **Canray Fontenot** and performed and/or recorded with numerous Creole, Cajun, and zydeco musicians, including **Jeffrey Broussard**, **Cedric Watson**, **Joe Hall**, **Ed Poullard**, and **Terrance Simien** as well as his own group. In 2009 published instructional book *Louisiana Creole Fiddle Method.* Older brother of musician Tony Garnier and grandson of early New Orleans jazz musician D'Jalma Thomas Garnier.

GRAEFF, BENNY *Swamp pop, Cajun, rock.* Bass, vocals. Composer. Bandleader. (Born Feb. 24, 1948, Aberdeen, Maryland.) Multitalented southwest Louisiana singer-songwriter, bassist, and bandleader best known for his work as leader of the 1970s group Rufus Jagneaux and its 1971 regional hit "Opelousas Sostan." Born on a military base in Maryland, spent several years in the early

1960s living in his mother's native south Louisiana before family relocated to Japan. Performed in several garage rock bands during high school and upon graduation returned to the United States, eventually settling in Lake Charles. Soon began following swamp pop and rhythm and blues bands such as **Little Bob** and **Clint West** and learned bass. In 1970 formed Lafayette-based band Rufus Jagneaux, which included brother Gary Graeff and keyboardist Victor Palmer and quickly gained local following. In 1971 released "Opelousas Sostan" on Jin, cowritten with Palmer, which quickly became a regional sensation. Several more releases followed on Jin, including "Downhome Music" and a bilingual cover of **D. L. Menard**'s "The Back Door" before group disbanded in the mid-1970s. Continued producing and performing with various musicians and groups in the following years, including Po' Boy Rufus and the Sostan Band, and working as a successful commercial artist on numerous Cajun and swamp pop releases.

GUITAR SLIM (Eddie Lee Jones) *Blues.* Guitar, vocals. Composer. Bandleader. (Born Dec. 10, 1926, Greenwood, Mississippi; died Feb. 7, 1959, Manhattan, New York.) Highly influential blues guitarist and singer-songwriter best known for his 1954 hit "The Things That I Used to Do" and his flamboyant and often acrobatic showmanship. Raised by his grandmother in Hollandale, Mississippi, since age five, began dancing and singing in local juke joints during his teens. After serving in World War II, performed around Arkansas and Louisiana with Delta bluesman Willie D. Warren and began developing his guitar style, which was later greatly influenced by **Clarence "Gatemouth" Brown**. In the late 1940s settled in New Orleans and performed on the streets before branching out into area clubs such as the famed Dew Drop Inn, often with **Huey "Piano" Smith**. In 1951–52 recorded singles for Imperial and J-B before signing with Specialty in 1953 and releasing massive hit "The Things That I Used to Do" in early 1954, one of the most influential blues recordings of the decade. Backed by **Lloyd Lambert**'s ace band, toured extensively in following years and released numerous singles on Specialty, including "The Story of My Life" and "Sufferin' Mind." A wildly popular entertainer, became celebrated for his brightly colored suits, often with matching dyed hair, and pioneering stage theatrics such as employing a several-hundred-foot guitar cord which allowed strolls through the audience and outside clubs while performing. In 1956 began recording for Atco and released several notable singles for the label, including "It Hurts to Love Someone" in 1957. After struggling with severe alcoholism for several years which began affecting both his health and his performances, succumbed to pneumonia while on tour in New York. Father of New Orleans–born blues guitarist **Guitar Slim Jr.**

HAMMOND, STICK-HORSE (Nathaniel Hammond) *Blues.* Guitar, vocals. Composer. (Born Mar. 16, 1896, Palestine, Anderson County, Texas; died May 27, 1964, Shreveport, Caddo Parish.)[12] Obscure Texas-born country blues singer and guitarist was a contemporary of Blind Lemon Jefferson and performed in central and east Texas in the 1930s before settling near Shreveport in the early 1940s. In 1950 recorded six sides, including "Alberta," "Too Late Baby," and "Truck 'Em on Down," which were issued on JOB (Shreveport label, not the Chicago label), Royalty, and Gotham. Died of a stroke at age 68.

HANDY, CAPTAIN JOHN *Jazz.* Saxophone, clarinet. Composer. Bandleader. (Born June 24, 1900, Pass Christian, Mississippi; died Jan. 12, 1971, Manhattan, New York.) Influential early New Orleans jazz saxophonist learned guitar, mandolin, and drums as a child and began performing in the family band during his early teens. In the late 1910s began playing clarinet and performed with **Punch Miller**, **Kid Rena**, and **Isaiah Morgan**. Relocated to New Orleans in 1918 and through the 1920s worked with **Tom Albert**, **Charlie Love**, and **Guy Kelly**. Began playing alto saxophone in the late 1920s and in the early 1930s formed the Louisiana Shakers with brother Sylvester (1903–1973). From the mid-1930s through 1950s worked with **Kid Howard**, **Big Jim Robinson**, **Lee Collins**, **Kid Clayton**, and the Young Tuxedo Brass Band. In 1961 began performing with **Kid Sheik** and throughout the 1960s appeared regularly at Preservation Hall and made several tours overseas. Recorded multiple albums as leader in the mid- to late 1960s for RCA, GHB, and Jazz Crusade, including *New Orleans and the Blues* in 1968, which included his signature song, "Cap'n's Blues." His bluesy, rhythmic style influenced many saxophonists, including Earl Bostic and Louis Jordan.

HART, JOHN *Rhythm and blues, zydeco.* Saxophone. (Born July 17, 1932, Dallas; died Dec. 26, 2003, Opelousas, St. Landry Parish.)[13] Highly regarded blind tenor saxophonist was raised in Chicago and attended high school in Shreveport. Began playing saxophone in his late teens while attending Southern University and later settled in

Opelousas. After touring with Big Joe Turner, performed and recorded with **Little Bob**'s Lollipops in the 1960s, appearing on numerous La Louisianne sides with band as well as cutting single "Rat Race"/"Cat Walk" for the label as a leader in 1963. After touring with O. V. Wright in the late 1960s, joined **Clifton Chenier**'s Red Hot Louisiana Band and toured and recorded extensively with group through the 1970s, appearing on numerous recordings, including LP *Bogalusa Boogie* in 1976 for Arhoolie. In the 1980s and 1990s worked with **Rockin' Dopsie**, **Nathan Williams**, **Fernest Arceneaux**, and others.

HIRSCH, GODFREY *Jazz.* Vibraphone, drums, piano. Bandleader. (Born Feb. 2, 1907, Greenville, Mississippi; died May 9, 1992, New Orleans, Orleans Parish.)[14] Raised in New Orleans from age two, began as a drummer and worked with **Louis Prima** and Richard Himber early in career. In 1960 joined **Pete Fountain**'s New Orleans band as vibraphonist and appeared on numerous recordings. Released two LPs as a leader in the mid-1960s on Coral, including *Live at Pete's.*

HUVAL, TERRY *Cajun.* Fiddle, steel guitar, guitar, bass, mandolin, vocals. Composer. Bandleader. (Born Mar. 21, 1956, Port Arthur, Texas.) Renowned Cajun multi-instrumentalist and master fiddle player best known for his work as longtime leader of Jambalaya Cajun Band. Raised in Breaux Bridge since age two speaking both English and Cajun French, began playing guitar at age 10 before learning fiddle and other instruments, inspired early on by **Belton Richard** and **Aldus Roger**. In 1977 formed Jambalaya Cajun Band with brother Tony on drums and released debut LP *A Buggy Full of Cajun Music* on Swallow in 1979. Joined by **Reggie Matte** in 1987, continued performing with group nationally and overseas into the 2010s with multiple releases on Swallow, including *Lessons Learned* in 1999. Performed and/or recorded with countless prominent Cajun musicians throughout the years, including **D. L. Menard**, **Jimmy C. Newman**, **Doug Kershaw**, **Aldus Roger**, **Jo-El Sonnier**, **Vin Bruce**, and many others. Father of Cajun musicians Luke, Phillip, and André Huval.

IRONING BOARD SAM (Samuel Moore) *Rhythm and blues.* Piano, organ, vocals. Composer. Bandleader. (Born July 17, 1939, Rock Hill, South Carolina.) Idiosyncratic rhythm and blues pianist and singer-songwriter who was a popular entertainer in New Orleans's clubs and festivals for more than 25 years. Known for his outlandish stage theatrics, including performing underwater in an 800-gallon tank at the 1979 New Orleans Jazz & Heritage Festival. Began playing boogie-woogie piano as a child and performed his first gig at age 14. In the late 1950s worked in Miami area and, after losing his Hammond B-3 organ in a fire, built a portable electronic keyboard using an ironing board for a stand, which became his trademark. In the early 1960s performed in Memphis area and released a single on Holiday Inn before relocating to Nashville in the mid-1960s and appearing on variety television show *Night Train.* After stints in Chicago; Waterloo, Iowa; and Los Angeles (where he recorded for Style Tone), relocated to New Orleans in 1974 and became popular draw in local clubs, often backed by drummer **Kerry Brown**. Recorded for **Allen Toussaint**'s Sansu label in the mid-1970s and performed on French Quarter streets for many years. In the 1990s recorded CD *The Human Touch* for Orleans. Relocated to Jackson, Mississippi, in the early 2000s for several years before returning to Rock Hill. Relaunched music career in the early 2010s with releases on Music Maker, Dixie Frog, and Big Legal Mess, including *Super Spirit* in 2015. Toured internationally until suffering a stroke in late 2015 but was able to return to JazzFest for its 50th anniversary in 2019.

JACKSON, REVEREND CHARLIE *Gospel.* Guitar, vocals. Composer. (Born July 11, 1932, near McComb, Mississippi; died Feb. 13, 2006, Baker, EBR Parish.) Renowned Baton Rouge gospel singer-songwriter and guitarist began playing guitar at age 10, alternating between blues and gospel songs early on. After living in Houston and Kenner, settled in Amite, Louisiana, in the mid-1950s and began performing in churches, appearing occasionally on programs with **Elder Utah Smith**, who was a major influence. Relocated to Baton Rouge in the mid-1960s and continued performing gospel at churches, social functions, and on radio broadcasts. In 1970 began recording for Booker, releasing an EP and several singles for the label, including "Wrapped Up and Tangled Up in Jesus," "God's Got It," and "Morning Train." In 1978 recorded two singles on his Jackson label, rerecording "Wrapped Up" and "God's Got It." Performed at several national festivals and traveled overseas in the 1990s. Continued making occasional appearances into the mid-2000s despite suffering a stroke in 2002.

JEFFERSON, THOMAS *Jazz.* Trumpet, vocals. Bandleader. (Born June 19, 1921, Chicago; died Dec. 3, 1986, New Orleans, Orleans Parish.)[15] Noted New Orleans jazz trumpeter moved to the city with family as a child and began playing trumpet by his early teens, influenced greatly by **Louis Armstrong** and tutored by music professor **Peter Davis**. By age 14 was performing with **Billie** and **De De Pierce**, and from the late 1930s through 1950s worked with **Papa Celestin**, **Sidney Desvigne**, **Octave Crosby**, and Eureka Brass Band. Also was member of Young Tuxedo Brass Band for several decades. In the 1960s led his Creole Jazz Band and released several albums as leader, notably *Dreaming Down the River to New Orleans* on Southland in 1962. Also recorded as sideman with **Santo Pecora**, **Paul Barbarin**, **Johnny St. Cyr**, **Raymond Burke**, and others. Performed at the Famous Door on Bourbon Street for thirty years.

JEWELL (Jewell S. Douglas) *Swamp pop, rhythm and blues.* Saxophone, trombone, vocals. Composer. Bandleader. (Born Dec. 27, 1924, Gary, Indiana; died Sept. 8, 2000, Gary, Indiana.)[16] Ville Platte–based rhythm and blues singer-songwriter and saxophonist best known for his 1963 swamp pop recording "Kidnapper." Raised in Gary, studied music at Southern University in Baton Rouge before working as high-school band director in Ville Platte in the 1950s. Formed group Jewell and the Rubies in the early 1960s and recorded several singles for La Louisianne, notably 1963 regional hit "Kidnapper" which was leased to ABC/Paramount. Performed throughout Louisiana for several years before moving back to Gary in 1966 and retiring from music.

JIVIN' GENE (Gene Joseph Bourgeois) *Swamp pop.* Vocals, guitar. Composer. Bandleader. (Born Feb. 9, 1940, Port Arthur, Texas.) Early swamp pop singer-songwriter best known for his 1959 hit "Breaking Up Is Hard to Do." After having regional hit with "Going Out with the Tide" backed by the Jokers for Jin in 1959, recorded "Breaking Up," which became national hit when leased to Mercury. Toured nationally and released several more singles on Mercury, including "Poor Me" in 1961, before cutting singles for Chess, Hall-Way, and TCF-Hall through the mid-1960s. After a two-decade hiatus, returned to performing and began appearing at clubs, festivals, and swamp pop revivals. In 2009 released CD *It's Never Too Late* on Jin with **Warren Storm** and keyboardist Ken Marvel. Continued performing in late 2010s.

JOHNSON, BILL (William Manuel Johnson) *Jazz.* Bass, banjo, guitar, mandolin. Composer. Bandleader. (Born Aug. 10, 1874, Talladega, Alabama; died Dec. 3, 1972, New Braunfels, Texas.)[17] Founder of Original Creole Orchestra and leader of the first jazz band to leave New Orleans on extended tours throughout the country. By the early 1900s was playing string bass with a trio in the Storyville District and within several years began leading his own bands, traveling to Los Angeles around 1908. In the early 1910s formed Original Creole Orchestra, which soon included younger brother **Dink Johnson** and **Freddie Keppard**, and toured the country in following years. In 1918 while based in Chicago, hired **King Oliver** to front his band at the Royal Gardens, which catapulted Oliver's career. Remained an integral part of Oliver's Creole Jazz Band in Chicago in the early 1920s along with **Louis Armstrong** and **Johnny** and **Baby Dodds**. Appeared on numerous recordings through the late 1920s with Oliver, **Johnny Dodds,** Tampa Red, and others, including two sides with his Louisiana Jug Band in 1929. Remained in Chicago until retiring to Texas in the early 1950s. Often cited as the father of the slap-bass for his pioneering and influential style.

KIMBALL, JEANETTE (*born* Jeanette Salvant) *Jazz.* Piano, vocals. (Born Dec. 18, 1906, Pass Christian, Mississippi; died Mar. 28, 2001, Charleston, South Carolina.) Renowned early New Orleans jazz pianist whose illustrious career spanned more than 70 years. Classically trained, began learning piano at age seven and within several years was teaching others. Performed with string bands in the 1920s before relocating to New Orleans and joining **Papa Celestin**'s Original Tuxedo Orchestra in 1926, appearing on several Columbia sessions with group through 1928. Married **Narvin Kimball** in 1929 and, after a break to raise a family, returned to performing in the mid-1940s and worked with **Sidney Desvigne, Dave Bartholomew**, and others before reuniting with Celestin in the 1950s. In the 1960s continued working in Original Tuxedo Band under **Papa French** and appeared regularly at Preservation Hall. Recorded prolifically as session musician with **George Lewis**, **Alvin Alcorn**, **Creole George Guesnon**, **Paul Barbarin**, **Danny Barker**, and others and released several albums as leader, notably *Sophisticated Lady* on New Orleans in 1981. Continued performing into the 1990s, receiving Black Men of Labor Jazz Legacy Award in 1998.

KING, JEWEL *Rhythm and blues.* Vocals. Bandleader. (Born June 21, 1910, Texas; died Nov. 25, 1997, San Antonio, Texas.) Early New Orleans rhythm and blues singer best known for her 1950 hit "3 x 7 = 21." Relocated to New Orleans in the mid-1940s and began performing in local clubs, including the famed Dew Drop Inn. After an unissued session for Deluxe in 1948, signed with Imperial in 1949 and released two singles produced by **Dave Bartholomew**, notably "3 x 7 = 21" which reached number four on *Billboard*'s R&B charts in 1950. Several unsuccessful singles on Imperial followed from sessions in 1950 and 1952. Began working in the band of **Paul Gayton**'s former guitarist Jack Scott, whom she would later marry. In the mid-1950s returned with Scott to Texas and performed throughout the 1960s based in Corpus Christi, working as vocalist with various groups, including occasional gigs with **Clarence "Gatemouth" Brown**.

KING, LITTLE FREDDIE (Fread Eugene Martin) *Blues.* Guitar, vocals. Composer. Bandleader. (Born July 19, 1940, McComb, Mississippi.) Veteran New Orleans blues guitarist and singer-songwriter began playing guitar as a child, learning from his father, whom he often accompanied. By the mid-1950s had settled in New Orleans and began performing locally with various musicians, including **Babe Stovall**, **Polka Dot Slim**, and **Boogie Bill Webb**, eventually earning stage name after performing with blues guitarist Freddie King. In 1971 recorded LP *Rock and Roll Blues* with John "Harmonica" Williams for Ahura Mazda and continued performing in New Orleans clubs and taverns in following years. In 1995 recorded CD *Swamp Boogie* for Orleans which garnered national acclaim and led to international tours. Releases followed on Fat Possum, APO, MadeWright, and Music Maker, including *Gotta Walk with Da King* in 2010. Continued performing nationally and overseas in the late 2010s.

KING LLOYD (Lloyd Palmer Jr.) *Blues.* Guitar, bass, vocals. Bandleader. (Born Nov. 30, 1947, Mississippi; died Mar. 17, 2010, Centreville, Mississippi.) Blues singer-guitarist and bass player began performing on the Baton Rouge blues scene in the 1960s. Worked with **Slim Harpo** in the late 1960s and later led his own band on the local blues scene in the 1980s and 1990s, appearing frequently at the River City/Baton Rouge Blues Festival during that time.

KNOWLING, RANSOM *Jazz, blues.* Bass, tuba. Bandleader. (Born June 24, 1908, Vicksburg, Mississippi; died Oct. 22, 1967, Chicago.)[18] Highly accomplished jazz and blues bassist who appeared on hundreds of landmark recordings from the 1930s through 1950s. Raised by his grandparents in Vicksburg, began playing string bass and tuba as a child and started music career in New Orleans in the late 1920s with **Papa Celestin**, later performing on riverboats with **Sidney Desvigne**. Around 1937 relocated to Chicago and worked extensively as session bassist for RCA-Victor and other labels, appearing on hundreds of sessions in following years, backing numerous blues artists such as Big Bill Broonzy, Memphis Minnie, Arthur Crudup, Big Maceo, Tampa Red, Sonny Boy Williamson, **Little Brother Montgomery**, **Champion Jack Dupree**, Elmore James, Muddy Waters, and Harlem Hamfats. Toured Europe in the 1960s and led his own trio, the Three Buddies, around Chicago in later years.

LANDRETH, SONNY (Clyde Vernon Landreth) *Blues, rock, zydeco.* Guitar, vocals. Composer. Bandleader. (Born Feb. 1, 1951, Canton, Mississippi.) Highly regarded slide guitarist and singer-songwriter was raised in Lafayette from a very early age and started playing guitar soon afterwards, inspired by Scotty Moore, Chet Atkins, and the Ventures. Began playing professionally in the late 1970s with **Clifton Chenier**'s Red Hot Louisiana Band and in the 1980s toured with John Hiatt as well as John Mayall's Bluesbreakers, eventually developing a signature slide-guitar style which incorporated seamless fretting of notes and chords behind the slide. After two LPs as leader on Blues Unlimited in the 1980s, achieved national acclaim in the 1990s with releases *Outward Bound* and *South of I-10* on Zoo Entertainment and toured nationally. Continued working extensively as performer and session guitarist in following years with multiple releases as leader on Sugar Hill, Landfall, and Provogue, including *Recorded Live in Lafayette* in 2017.

LEDET, COREY *Zydeco.* Accordion, drums, guitar, bass, piano, vocals. Composer. Bandleader. (Born Aug. 28, 1981, Houston.) Noted zydeco accordion player and multi-instrumentalist began playing drums professionally at age 10 and two years later started learning accordion, influenced by **Clifton Chenier**, **John Delafose**, and **Boozoo Chavis**. In 2002 relocated to Parks, Louisiana, where he had spent childhood summers visiting with relatives, and formed his zydeco band. In following years performed extensively on zydeco club and festival circuit and released numerous self-produced CDs, including critically acclaimed *Nothing But the Best* in 2012. In 2007 recorded CD *Goin' Down to Louisiana* on Valcour with **Cedric Watson**. Continued performing and recording in the late 2010s.

LEE, BRYAN *Blues, rock.* Guitar, vocals. Composer. Bandleader. (Born Mar. 16, 1943, Two Rivers, Wisconsin.)

Longtime New Orleans–based blues-rock singer and guitarist lost his sight as a child and began performing in his teens, playing rock and roll early on before switching to blues in the 1960s and 1970s, inspired by Muddy Waters, Hubert Sumlin, and Freddie King. In the early 1980s relocated to New Orleans and became a fixture at Bourbon Street's Old Absinthe House Bar for 14 years. In the 1990s and 2000s released numerous recordings on Justin Time, including *Braille Blues Daddy* in 1994. After 30 years in New Orleans, relocated to Pensacola, Florida, in 2013 and continued performing on national club and festival circuit, releasing CD *Play One for Me* on Severn in 2013.

LEWIS, MARGARET (Margaret Lewis Warwick) *Rockabilly, country.* Guitar, vocals. Composer. Bandleader. (Born Apr. 30, 1939, Snyder, Texas; died Mar. 29, 2019, Shreveport, Caddo Parish.) Noted Shreveport-based singer-songwriter and Louisiana music advocate formed rockabilly-inspired band the Thunderbolts in the mid-1950s before relocating to Shreveport by 1958 with vocalist sister Rose and performing as the Lewis Sisters. Appeared regularly as member of the *Louisiana Hayride* throughout the next two years and toured with **Dale Hawkins**. In the late 1950s formed writing partnership with **Mira Smith** and through the early 1960s released several singles on Smith's RAM label, including "Cheaters Can't Win" and "Shake a Leg." Relocated to Nashville with Smith in 1963 and continued successful partnership, writing or cowriting hits for **Johnny Adams**, **Dale Hawkins**, Jeannie C. Riley, Connie Francis, Peggy Scott, and others, notably "Reconsider Me" and "Soul Shake." In 1968 had minor country hit as leader with "Honey (I Miss You Too)" on SSS International. Returned to Shreveport in the early 1980s and continued performing with her band the Thunderbolts into the 2010s, releasing CD *But I Know What I Like* in 1998.

MARABLE, FATE *Jazz.* Piano. Bandleader. (Born Dec. 2, 1890, Paducah, Kentucky; died Jan. 16, 1947, St. Louis, Missouri.) Important early jazz bandleader and pianist began performing on Mississippi riverboats in 1907 and by the late 1910s had formed his own riverboat band, the Kentucky Jazz Band. Though based in St. Louis, regularly hired prominent New Orleans jazz musicians and, from the late 1910s through the 1920s, his various bands such as the Jazz Syncopators and Jazz Maniacs included at times **Louis Armstrong**, **Johnny St. Cyr**, **Johnny** and **Baby Dodds**, **Zutty Singleton**, **Pops Foster**, **Red Allen**, **Al Morgan**, and many others. Recorded only one release, "Frankie and Johnny"/"Pianoflage," on OKeh in 1924. Continued directing bands on riverboats through 1941 and worked in St. Louis clubs in remaining years.

MARCHAN, BOBBY (Oscar James Gibson) *Rhythm and blues.* Vocals. Composer. Bandleader. (Born Apr. 30, 1930, Youngstown, Ohio; died Dec. 5, 1999, Gretna, Jefferson Parish.) Colorful early New Orleans rhythm and blues singer and entertainer began career touring as a female impersonator in the early 1950s. In 1953 settled in New Orleans and started performing regularly at the famed Dew Drop Inn. After a single each on Aladdin and Dot, began working with **Huey "Piano" Smith** in the mid-1950s and recorded several singles for Ace, including regional hit "Chickee Wah-Wah" in 1956. By 1957 had joined Smith's band the Clowns as lead vocalist and performed and recorded with group through 1958, appearing on hits "Rockin' Pneumonia and the Boogie Woogie Flu," "Don't You Just Know It," and "High Blood Pressure." Between 1959 and 1962 recorded several singles for Fire, including number-one hit "There's Something on Your Mind." After singles on Volt and Dial, signed with Cameo in the mid-1960s and had minor hit with "Shake Your Tambourine" in 1966. Throughout the 1970s and 1980s recorded singles for numerous labels, including Ace, Sansu, Mercury, B&B, Manicure, Mass, and Edge and continued performing occasionally as both a drag queen and rhythm and blues singer. In later years operated a hip-hop booking and promotion company until succumbing to liver cancer at age 69.

MASON, REVEREND MOSES *Gospel, folk.* Guitar, banjo, vocals. Composer. (Born possibly Aug. 11, 1871, Chicot County, Arkansas; died possibly July 14, 1934, Lake Providence, E. Carroll Parish.)[19] Enigmatic Lake Providence–based early gospel recording artist who cut eight sides for Paramount in Chicago in 1928, including "John the Baptist" and "Go Wash in That Beautiful Stream." Also recorded secular street-vendor songs "Shrimp Man" and "Molly Man" under name (Red Hot) Old Mose.

METOYER, ARNOLD *Jazz.* Cornet. (Born Oct. 26, 1880, Mexico; died Nov. 22, 1933, New Orleans, Louisiana.)[20] Early jazz cornet player who performed predominantly with traveling tent and circus shows. Based mainly in New Orleans but also spent time in Milwaukee. Worked with **John Robichaux**'s Orchestra and Luis Russell in the mid-1910s and early 1920s in New Orleans. Reportedly died of tuberculosis.

MILLER, TAL (Talton Miller) *Rhythm and blues.* Piano, vocals, Composer. (Born probably June 22, 1927, Dothan, Alabama; died Mar. 23, 1993, Newark, New Jersey.)[21] Rhythm and blues pianist and singer-songwriter spent early years in Florida before settling in Opelousas by the mid-1950s. In late 1957 began recording for producer **Eddie Shuler** and had several releases on Goldband and Hollywood, notably "Life's Journey" and "B-A-B-Y." Also recorded as session musician for **J. D. Miller** in the late 1950s and appeared on recordings backing **Lightnin' Slim**, **Guitar Gable**, **Classie Ballou**, **Lonesome Sundown**, **Leroy Washington**, and others. Reportedly returned to Florida in the 1960s, although details of remaining years are unclear.

MONROE, VINCE/"POLKA DOT SLIM"/"MR. CALHOUN" (Willie Monroe Vincent) *Blues.* Harmonica, vocals. Composer. Bandleader. (Born Dec. 9, 1926, Woodville, Mississippi; died June 22, 1981, Oakland, California.)[22] Mississippi-born swamp blues singer-songwriter and harmonica player began playing the instrument in his teens, inspired by John Lee "Sonny Boy" Williamson. After serving in the military, settled in New Orleans in 1954 before relocating to Baton Rouge and performing on the local blues scene, often with **Lightnin' Slim**. In the late 1950s recorded for producer **J. D. Miller** and had a single each on Excello (as Vince Monroe) and Zynn, notably "Hello Friends, Hello Pal" (as "Mr. Calhoun"). In the 1960s returned to New Orleans and recorded single "Ain't Broke, Ain't Hungry"/"A Thing You Gotta Face" in 1964 on Instant. After a single on Apollo in 1966 continued performing in New Orleans until relocating to Oakland shortly before succumbing to a fatal heart attack at age 54.

NEWSOM, CHUBBY (Velma C. Newsom) *Rhythm and blues.* Vocals. (Born Jan. 27, 1920, Wilburton, Oklahoma; died Sept. 13, 2003, Kansas City, Kansas.)[23] Early rhythm and blues singer best known for her 1949 hit "Hip Shakin' Mama." Raised in Detroit, performed on vaudeville circuit in the 1940s before relocating to New Orleans in 1948. While performing at the famed Dew Drop Inn was discovered by **Paul Gayten** and had national hit with recording debut, "Hip Shakin' Mama," on Deluxe backed by Gayten's band. Also recorded a single for Deluxe backed by **Dave Bartholomew**'s band in 1949. In the early 1950s had several releases on Regal and toured nationally. After an unissued session for Chance in 1953, formed female duo the Bluzettes with Detroit singer Alberta Adams in 1955 and toured together with Tiny Bradshaw. Made final recording for Winley in 1957 before retiring from music.

PIERCE, BILLIE (*born* Wilhelmina Goodson) *Jazz, blues.* Piano, vocals. Composer. (Born June 8, 1907, Marianna, Florida; died Sept. 29, 1974, New Orleans, Orleans Parish.) Renowned early boogie-woogie and jazz pianist and singer best known for her long musical partnership with husband **De De Pierce**. Raised in Pensacola in a prominent family of pianists, which included both parents and five sisters, including Ida (1909–2000) and Sadie Goodson (1901–2002). Started playing piano at age two and performed only gospel early on. Turning professional at age 15, performed with Bessie Smith and Ida Cox in the early 1920s and toured as singer, pianist, and dancer through the early 1930s. Settled in New Orleans in 1930 and worked with various musicians, including **Armand Piron**, **Alphonse Picou**, **George Lewis**, and Pierce, whom she married in 1935. Made recording debut with **Emile Barnes** in 1946 and began recording as leader in 1953. Performed regularly at Preservation Hall and toured extensively nationally and overseas with husband De De through the early 1970s with releases on Riverside, Atlantic, Preservation Hall, and Arhoolie, including *Blues and Tonks from the Delta* in 1961.

PRIME, DOROTHY *Rhythm and blues.* Vocals. Bandleader. (Born Dec. 7, 1950, Valdosta, Georgia.) Known as "North Louisiana's Queen of the Blues," powerful blues and rhythm and blues vocalist began singing in church as a child growing up in Georgia. Started performing in the early 1970s and became regionally popular on the Shreveport and Monroe area blues scene, later based in Homer, where she operated the Prime Time Lounge into the 2010s.

QUINN, ED "SNOOZER" (Edward McIntosh Quinn) *Jazz.* Guitar, violin, banjo, mandolin, vocals. Composer. Bandleader. (Born Oct. 1907, McComb, Mississippi; died Apr. 21, 1949, New Orleans, Orleans Parish.)[24] Unheralded early jazz guitarist who was regarded by many of his peers to be among the greatest of his era. Raised in Bogalusa, Louisiana, began playing guitar and other stringed instruments as a child and by his teens was playing professionally. After high school toured with various jazz groups before settling in New Orleans in 1928. In the late 1920s toured and recorded with the Paul Whiteman Orchestra and also recorded several unissued sides as leader for Victor in 1928. In the 1930s recorded as sideman with **Jimmie Davis** and Bee Palmer, performed with Bing Crosby, and led his own group. In 1948 made numerous recordings for **Johnny Wiggs** in New Orleans's Charity Hospital while suffering from tuberculosis, six months before his death from the disease.

ROBICHEAUX, COCO (Curtis John Arceneaux) *Blues.* Guitar, vocals. Composer. Bandleader. (Born Oct. 25, 1947, Merced, California; died Nov. 25, 2011, New Orleans, Orleans Parish.) Son of a Cajun father from Ascension Parish, noted New Orleans–based blues singer-songwriter and guitarist was raised in Gonzales, Louisiana, from age 13 and performed in rhythm and blues and soul bands in the 1960s. After a short stint in the military and time in California, settled in New Orleans in 1970 and performed in local clubs. In the mid-1990s signed with Orleans and released debut CD *Spiritland* in 1994, followed by *Louisiana Medicine Man* in 1998. Continued performing in area clubs in following years with three releases on his Spiritland label, including *Revelator* in 2010. Appeared in several television shows, including HBO's *Treme,* before suffering fatal heart attack at the Apple Barrel bar, where he had performed for many years.

ROOSTER (Curtis Lee Wheeler) *Blues.* Guitar, vocals. Composer. Bandleader. (Born Oct. 5, 1937, Collins, Mississippi.) Popular New Orleans–based blues guitarist and singer who performed in various clubs along Bourbon Street for more than three decades. After working and performing around Shaw, Mississippi, relocated to New Orleans in 1984 and began playing in clubs on Bourbon with his band the Chickenhawks. Released several CDs, including *Born in Mississippi* on Sound of New Orleans in 2001, which included club favorite "Cell Phone Blues." Continued performing as solo act on Bourbon into his 80s.

SAM, LEON *Zydeco.* Accordion, vocals. Composer. Bandleader. (Born Aug. 20, 1964, Houston.) Highly regarded zydeco accordionist, singer, and bandleader who started performing as a child with brothers Carl (1961–), Rodney (1963–2010), Glen (1966–), and Calvin (1968–) in popular teenage zydeco band Sam Brothers Five. A child prodigy, he began playing accordion at a very early age, mentored by his father, **Herbert "Good Rockin'" Sam**, and greatly influenced by **Clifton Chenier**. Under his father's guidance, brothers formed band in 1974, which quickly became popular throughout Houston area. Family relocated to father's hometown of Opelousas, Louisiana, in 1977 and continued performing on southwest Louisiana club and festival circuit. In 1979 recorded self-titled debut LP on Arhoolie and toured nationally throughout the 1980s with albums on Blues Unlimited and Maison de Soul before disbanding. In the mid-1990s briefly reunited with brothers as Leon Sam and the Sam Brothers and released CD *Leon's Boogie is Back* on Master-Trak in 1996. Returned to Houston later that year and formed the Zydeco Dots, releasing CD *Tribute to Clif* on Klarity in 2000. After disbanding the Dots in 2003, continued performing sporadically into the 2010s, occasionally reuniting with various brothers.

SAVOY, ANN ALLEN *Cajun, country.* Guitar, fiddle, accordion, vocals. Composer. Bandleader. (Born Jan. 20, 1952, St. Louis, Missouri.) Internationally renowned Cajun singer-songwriter, multi-instrumentalist, author, and matriarch of prestigious Cajun family of Eunice with husband **Marc Savoy**, sons **Joel** and **Wilson Savoy**, and daughter Sarah Savoy. Born in St. Louis but raised in Richland, Virginia, began playing guitar at age 12 and moved to Eunice in 1977 after meeting future husband Marc at a folk festival. In the 1980s and 1990s performed and recorded as member of Savoy-Doucet Cajun Band with Marc and **Michael Doucet** and in the 1990s began performing and recording with all-female band the Magnolia Sisters, which she originally formed in the late 1970s with **Mary Jane Broussard** and Jeanie McLerie. In 2002 produced highly acclaimed release *Evangeline Made: A Tribute to Cajun Music* which featured Linda Ronstadt, John Fogerty, Linda and Richard Thompson, Patty Griffin, and others, and in 2006 collaborated again with Ronstadt as the Zozo Sisters on *Adieu False Heart.* Contributed to several film soundtracks and continued performing and recording with multiple groups in the 2010s, including Savoy Family Band, Magnolia Sisters, and her jazz swing band Sleepless Knights.

SHAW, AMANDA *Cajun, rock.* Fiddle, vocals. Composer. Bandleader. (Born August 2, 1990, Fitchburg, Massachusetts.) Classically trained fiddle player and singer was raised in Mandeville, Louisiana, from an early age and began learning the instrument at age four. At age seven performed with the Baton Rouge Symphony and subsequently appeared on several national television shows. Soon began playing Cajun music, influenced by rock, pop and country music, and through the 2010s performed extensively throughout the New Orleans area with national and overseas tours, releasing several CDs including *Please, Call Me Miss Shaw* on Little Fiddle in 2018.

SHEFFIELD, CHARLES "MAD DOG" *Rhythm and blues.* Vocals. Composer. Bandleader. (Born Feb. 16, 1931, Houston, Texas; died Mar. 27, 2010, Beaumont, Texas.)[25] Soulful rhythm and blues singer-songwriter best known for his 1961 Excello single "It's Your Voodoo Working." From 1955 to 1957 recorded more than a dozen sides for producer **Eddie Shuler** backed by **Clarence Garlow**'s band with releases on Folk-Star, Goldband, and Hollywood, including "Mad Dog," which provided his stage name. In the late 1950s and early 1960s recorded for **J. D. Miller** and had singles on Rocko and Excello, including "It's Your Voodoo Working" and "I Would Be a Sinner." After a single each in the mid-1960s on Tear Drop and Jet Stream (on the latter as Prince Charles), eventually faded from the music scene.

SPELLMAN, BENNY *Rhythm and blues.* Vocals. Composer. (Born Dec. 11, 1931, Pensacola, Florida; died June 3, 2011, Pensacola, Florida.) Noted New Orleans rhythm and blues singer-songwriter best known for his early 1960s recordings "Lipstick Traces (On a Cigarette)" and "Fortune Teller." Raised in Pensacola, began singing while attending Southern University in Baton Rouge and relocated to New Orleans in 1959 after meeting **Huey "Piano" Smith**. In 1960 started working with **Allen Toussaint** and released several singles on Minit, including double-sided hit "Lipstick Traces"/"Fortune Teller" in 1962. Singles followed on Watch, Alon, Atlantic, Sansu, and Mor Soul through the late 1960s. Also recorded as back-up vocalist with numerous artists, including **Earl King** and **Ernie K-Doe**. Worked mainly outside music after 1970 and returned to Pensacola after suffering a stroke in the mid-1990s. Father of gospel and rhythm and blues singer Judy Spellman (1955–2016).

STEIN, JOHNNY (John Joseph Philip Hountha) *Jazz.* Drums. Bandleader. (Born June 5, 1891, Biloxi, Mississippi; died Sept. 30, 1962, New Orleans, Orleans Parish.)[26] Early jazz bandleader and drummer formed his Dixie Jass Band, which included **Nick LaRocca** and **Alcide "Yellow" Nunez**, and took group to Chicago for a long nightclub engagement in Mar. 1916. Several months later his members left the band to form Original Dixieland Jass Band. After organizing a new group and fulfilling the performance contract, relocated to New York and from 1918 to 1920 performed and recorded with Jimmy Durante's band. In following decades continued performing in New York and Chicago until returning to New Orleans in 1961 and retiring from music.

STOVALL, BABE (Jewel Stovall) *Blues.* Guitar, banjo, vocals. Composer. (Born Oct. 4, 1907, Tylertown, Mississippi; died Sept. 21, 1974, New Orleans, Orleans Parish.)[27] Mississippi-born country blues guitarist and singer began playing as a child and performed at country suppers with his brother Tom around the Picayune area where they sharecropped. In the 1930s associated with early Mississippi bluesman Tommy Johnson, who was a major influence. After making several field recordings in the late 1950s, relocated to New Orleans in 1964 and recorded self-titled debut LP for Verve. Worked as popular street musician in the French Quarter throughout the 1960s and early 1970s and toured on the folk and blues college circuit. Continued performing around New Orleans, often at Jackson Square, until his death at age 66.

THOMAS, LAFAYETTE "THING"/"L.J." *Blues.* Guitar, vocals. Composer. Bandleader. (Born June 13, 1928, Hallsville, Texas; died May 20, 1977, Brisbane, California.)[28] Highly regarded and influential West Coast–based blues guitarist was mentored early on by his uncle **Jesse "Babyface" Thomas**. In the mid-1940s relocated with family to San Francisco and began concentrating on guitar. After working with several area groups, joined Jimmy McCracklin's band in the late 1940s and performed and recorded with group for over 20 years, notably appearing on McCracklin's hit single "The Walk" on Chess in 1957. Also worked and recorded with **Jimmy Wilson**, appearing on numerous releases, including Wilson's 1953 hit "Tin Pan Alley." Throughout the 1950s recorded singles as leader for Chess, Modern, Trilyte, Jumping, and Savoy, including signature instrumental, "The Thing," in 1955. Continued performing based in Oakland into the 1970s, tutoring numerous aspiring area guitarists and making his last recordings as leader for World Pacific LP *Oakland Blues* in 1968, backed by **Dave Alexander**. Died of a fatal heart attack while working at his factory day job. Nephew of **Willard "Ramblin'" Thomas**.

TIMOTHEA (Beckerman) *Rhythm and blues.* Vocals. Composer. Bandleader. (Born Feb. 17, 1951, Hardin, Kentucky; died Nov. 14, 2006, New York City.) Rhythm and blues singer and songwriter moved to New Orleans with her mother as a child and started singing in clubs during her early teens. In 1966 recorded debut single, "Teenage

Prayer," on Virgel. In the 1980s released three singles on Grand Marshall produced by **Earl King** and toured and recorded with **Walter "Wolfman" Washington**. Released several recordings on her own Blue Soul label in the 1990s and early 2000s, including *I'm Still Standing* in 2003, and toured Europe multiple times.

TIO, LORENZO, SR. *Jazz.* Clarinet. (Born Sept. 28, 1867, Tampico, Mexico; died June 15, 1908, New Orleans, Orleans Parish.)[29] Very early New Orleans jazz master clarinetist and teacher was born in Mexico to native New Orleans "free people of color" and was classically trained before family returned to New Orleans in the late 1870s. In the mid-1880s and 1890s performed with Excelsior Brass Band and was founding member of Lyre Club Symphony Orchestra. In the late 1890s and early 1900s worked with **John Robichaux** and toured with a minstrel show. Also worked as highly influential music teacher, mentoring numerous early jazz musicians into the first years of the 1900s. Father of **Lorenzo Tio Jr.** and brother of **Louis "Papa" Tio**.

TIO, LOUIS "PAPA" *Jazz.* Clarinet. Composer. (Born Feb. 4, 1862, Eureka Colony, Mexico; died July 10, 1922, New Orleans, Orleans Parish.)[30] Very early New Orleans jazz master clarinetist was born to native New Orleans "free people of color" in Mexico and was classically trained along with younger brother **Lorenzo Tio** before family returned to New Orleans in the late 1870s. In the mid-1880s and 1890s performed with Excelsior Brass Band and Lyre Club Symphony Orchestra. In the early 1910s worked with **Manuel Manetta** and **Peter Bocage** at the Tuxedo Dance Hall. Also was a renowned music instructor whose students included brother Lorenzo, **Achille** and **George Baquet**, and **Barney Bigard**. Uncle of **Lorenzo Tio Jr.**

T. V. SLIM (Oscar Walter Wills) *Rhythm and blues.* Guitar, harmonica, vocals. Composer. Bandleader. (Born Feb. 10, 1916, near Bethany, Texas; died Oct. 21, 1969, Kingman, Arizona.)[31] Noted rhythm and blues singer, guitarist, and gifted songwriter best known for his 1957 hit "Flatfoot Sam." Learned harmonica and guitar in his youth and began performing in 1950, inspired by DeFord Bailey, John Lee "Sonny Boy" Williamson, and later **Guitar Slim**. After working as a songwriter in Houston, cut several singles in Shreveport in 1957 for the Speed label before having regional hit with "Flatfoot Sam" on Clif which was then leased to Checker. Rerecorded "Flatfoot Sam" with **Paul Gayten**'s band in New Orleans for Argo soon afterwards which was then issued as by Oscar Wills. Toured nationally and relocated to Los Angeles in 1959. Numerous singles followed on Speed, Excell, Timbre, USA, Ideel, and Pzazz through 1968. Died from injuries sustained in a car accident returning home from a gig in Chicago. Acquired stage name from Shreveport producer **Stan Lewis** in reference to his day job as a television repairman.

WATSON, CEDRIC *Creole, Cajun, zydeco.* Accordion, fiddle, vocals. Composer. Bandleader. (Born Sept. 25, 1983, Bryan, Texas.) Texas-born traditional multi-instrumentalist and singer-songwriter was raised in San Felipe and was greatly inspired by Creole and Cajun music of southwest Louisiana early on. After relocating to Lafayette, joined **Wilson Savoy**'s Pine Leaf Boys in the mid-2000s and performed and recorded with group for several years. In 2006 recorded CDs *Les Amis Creole* on Arhoolie with **Edward Poullard** and *Goin' Down to Louisiana* with **Corey Ledet** on Valcour. Soon formed his band Bijou Creole and released several recordings on Valcour and his own Lache Pas label, including highly acclaimed *L'Esprit Creole* in 2009 which garnered international attention. Continued recording and touring nationally and overseas in the 2010s with his own group as well as other projects.

WEBB, BOOGIE BILL *Blues.* Guitar, vocals. Composer. (Born Mar. 24, 1924, Jackson, Mississippi; died Aug. 22, 1990, New Orleans, Orleans Parish.) Idiosyncratic New Orleans–based blues guitarist and singer-songwriter began playing on a homemade instrument as a child, inspired by bluesman Tommy Johnson, and by his teens was performing at local fish fries and country suppers. After traveling back and forth performing in Jackson and New Orleans, settled in the Crescent City in 1952 and recorded four sides in 1953 for Imperial produced by **Dave Bartholomew**, including the John Lee Hooker–inspired single "Bad Dog." From the mid- to late 1950s worked in Chicago before returning to New Orleans in 1959. In 1968 recorded for folklorist David Evans and appeared on 1972 LP *The Legacy of Tommy Johnson* on Matchbox. Toured Europe in the early 1980s and recorded LP *Drinkin' and Stinkin'* on Flying Fish in 1989 shortly before his death at age 66.

WEBSTER, KATIE (*born* Kathryn Jewel Thorne) *Blues.* Piano, vocals. Composer. Bandleader. (Born Jan. 11, 1936, Houston; died Sept. 5, 1999, League City, Texas.)[32] Internationally renowned swamp blues and boogie-woogie piano player and singer who appeared on hundreds of recordings as studio musician and leader in the 1950s and 1960s for producers **J. D. Miller** and **Eddie Shuler**. Began playing piano as a child and while in her teens moved to south Louisiana to stay with relatives after parents relocated to California. Soon joined **Ashton Savoy**'s band and performed with group throughout the region, making recording debut on Miller's Kry label in 1958. In the late 1950s and early 1960s worked as house pianist for Miller and Shuler and recorded extensively behind numerous artists, including **Lazy Lester**, **Slim Harpo**, **Lightnin' Slim**, **Warren Storm**, **Rocket Morgan**, **Guitar Junior**, **Slim Harpo**, **Clifton Chenier**, and many others. Also cut singles as leader for Goldband, Rocko, Zynn, Spot, Decca, and Action and toured with her band the Uptighters with bassist husband Sherman Webster through the early 1960s. Toured extensively with Otis Redding from 1964 until Redding's death in 1967. In the 1970s performed and recorded sporadically before relaunching career in the early 1980s, touring nationally and overseas with releases on Ornament, Arhoolie, and Schubert in following years. Signed with Alligator in 1988 and released acclaimed LP *The Swamp Boogie Queen,* followed by *Two-Fisted Mama!* in 1989. After releasing final album, *No Foolin',* in 1991, continued touring internationally until suffering a stroke while in Greece in 1993, which limited her performances in remaining years.

WHISPERING SMITH (Moses Smith) *Blues.* Harmonica, vocals. Composer. Bandleader. (Born Jan. 25, 1932, Union Church, Mississippi; died Apr. 28, 1984, Baton Rouge, EBR Parish.) Noted swamp blues harmonica player and singer began playing the instrument at age 14 and relocated to Baton Rouge in the late 1950s. In 1958 joined **Lightnin' Slim**'s band and performed throughout the Baton Rouge area. From 1963 to 1964 recorded several singles for Excello produced by **J. D. Miller**, including "Mean Woman Blues" and "Live Jive," and also recorded as sideman with Silas Hogan. Continued performing with his own group as well as with Lightnin' Slim in following years and in the early 1970s made recordings for Arhoolie and Excello, including LP *Over Easy* in 1971. Also recorded as sideman with **Henry Gray** and **Arthur "Guitar" Kelly** and toured Europe with Lightnin' Slim in the early 1970s. Continued performing on the Baton Rouge blues scene until his death at age 52.

WIMMER, KEVIN *Cajun.* Fiddle, vocals. (Born Feb. 8, 1963, New York City.) Renowned Cajun fiddle player was classically trained on the instrument from age four, raised by parents who were both noted classical musicians. In the mid-1980s met **Dewey Balfa** at a Cajun fiddle workshop and relocated to southwest Louisiana to learn directly from the master fiddler. After Balfa's death in 1992, toured and recorded with Balfa Toujours led by **Christine Balfa**. In following years also performed and recorded with numerous musicians and groups, including **Preston Frank**, Red Stick Ramblers, and the Racines. In 2011 joined **Steve Riley**'s Mamou Playboys, replacing cofounder **David Greely**, and continued performing and recording with the group and others in the late 2010s.

WYATT, GENE (Preston Eugene Wyatt) *Rockabilly.* Vocals, guitar. Composer. Bandleader. (Born July 28, 1937, Lake Village, Arkansas; died Jan. 16, 1979, Shreveport, Caddo Parish.) Noted early rockabilly singer-guitarist was raised in Marthaville, Natch. Parish, from age one. Taught himself guitar as a child and began performing in church and at local dances. In 1952 moved to Shreveport and began performing on the *Louisiana Hayride.* In 1957 cut debut single "Lover Boy" for Ebb, followed by "Prettiest Girl in the Dance" on Lucky Seven and "You Bug Me, Baby" on Aetna. Also had singles on Murco, Dollie, and Mercury. Toured Europe in the mid-1960s and cut seven singles for Paula between 1968 and 1974. Died from self-inflicted gunshot wound at age 41 following the death of his wife.

III

PROMINENT RECORD PRODUCERS BY REGION

Baton Rouge

MONTEL, SAM (S. J. MONTALBANO) (1937–) *Labels: Montel, Montel-Michelle, Michelle, Stephanie, Debbie.* Baton Rouge native started local Montel label and recording studio while attending Louisiana State University in 1958 after discussing recording techniques with **Cosimo Matassa** and Ace Records owner Johnny Vincent. Achieved regional success with debut single, "My Girl Across Town," by **Lester Robertson** and in 1959 garnered first national hit with "Shirley" by **John Fred** and the Playboys. Through the late 1960s produced numerous swamp pop and rhythm and blues recordings by the Boogie Kings, Dale and **Grace**, **Van Broussard**, **James "Sugar Boy" Crawford**, **Luther Kent**, **Jay Chevalier**, and others. Label's greatest success was Dale and Grace's number-one hit "I'm Leaving It Up to You" in 1963.

WHITFIELD, LIONEL T. (1934–1976) *Labels: Whit, El-Tee.* Native Baton Rouge producer, musician, and bandleader started his Whit label in the early 1960s and through the early 1970s recorded numerous rhythm and blues and soul artists, including **Bobby Powell**, **Merle Spears**, **Little Bob**, **Raful Neal**, and **Lee Tillman**. Label's most successful and prolific artist was Powell, who had three charted hits with "C.C. Rider," "Do Something for Yourself," and "The Bells." Also produced releases by Powell and **Whispering Smith** for Excello in the early 1970s.

Lake Charles

KHOURY, GEORGE (1908–1998) *Labels: Khoury's, Lyric.* Lake Charles native and local record store owner began recording Cajun musicians in the late 1940s with releases by **Nathan Abshire**, **Lawrence Walker**, **Elise Deshotels**, and others before achieving greater success with swamp pop musicians in the late 1950s and early 1960s. Notable releases included **Phil Phillips**'s national hit "Sea of Love" and numerous swamp pop standards from **Cookie** and the Cupcakes, including "Mathilda." Other artists who recorded for the label include **Little Alfred**, **Carol Fran**, **Jay Randall**, **Terry Clinton**, and **Simon "Kee-Dee" Lubin**'s Berry Cups. Continued producing until the mid-1960s.

SHULER, EDDIE (1913–2005) Goldband Studios. *Labels: Goldband, Folk-Star, Anla, Jador, Trey, Tic Toc.* Texas-born producer and label and studio owner relocated to Lake Charles in the early 1940s and performed with the Hackberry Ramblers and his own country string band, the All Star Reveliers. In 1945 founded Goldband Records to record his group and soon began recording other musicians, notably **Iry LeJeune**, who was greatly responsible for the revitalization of accordion-based Cajun music in the late 1940s and 1950s. Throughout the 1950s and 1960s recorded numerous Cajun, blues, swamp pop, country, and early zydeco musicians, including **Boozoo Chavis**, **Lonnie Brooks** (as Guitar Jr.), **Clarence Garlow**, **Cleveland Crochet**, **Jay Stutes**, **Sidney Brown**, **Rockin' Sidney**, **Classie Ballou**, **Robert Bertrand**, **Jo-El Sonnier**, **Katie Webster**, Freddy Fender, Juke Boy Bonner, and thirteen-year old Dolly Parton. Landmark recordings include Chavis's "Paper in My Shoe" in 1954, which is often cited as the first zydeco recording; Crochet's "Sugar Bee" in 1960, which was the first Cajun recording to appear on *Billboard*'s Top 100 charts; and LeJeune's entire output for the label, widely considered to be among the greatest and most influential postwar recordings of Cajun music. Continued running operations until retiring to Atlanta in 2004 due to failing health. Son

Wayne Shuler (1936–2017) was also a prominent record producer.

New Orleans

BANASHAK, JOE (1923–1985) *Labels: Minit, Instant, Alon, Seven B.* Baltimore native cofounded Minit in 1959 with Houston radio director Larry McKinley and had minor regional success with its first release, "Bad Luck and Trouble" by **Boogie Jake**. In 1960 signed **Allen Toussaint** as house producer and songwriter and throughout the next several years released numerous New Orleans rhythm and blues hits on Minit and Instant by **Ernie K-Doe**, **Chris Kenner**, **Jessie Hill**, **Irma Thomas**, **Benny Spellman**, and others. After Minit was acquired by Liberty/Imperial in 1963, continued releasing singles on Instant through the mid-1970s by Kenner, **Art** and **Aaron Neville**, **Huey "Piano" Smith**, **Eddie Bo** (who also served as producer and songwriter), and **Skip Easterling**, among others. Label's most successful releases include K-Doe's "Mother-In-Law," Kenner's "I Like It Like That," and Hill's "Ooh Poo Pah Doo."

BATTISTE, HAROLD (1931–2015) *Label: A.F.O.* Native New Orleans jazz and rhythm and blues musician founded the A.F.O. (All for One) label in 1961, New Orleans's first African American musician–owned and–operated recording label. Throughout the next two years released rhythm and blues and jazz recordings by **Prince La La**, **Barbara George**, **Ellis Marsalis**, **Willie Tee**, **Tami Lynn**, and others, having national hits with its first two releases, Prince La La's "She Put the Hurt on Me" and George's "I Know (You Don't Love Me No More)." *See also Battiste's entry as musician.*

BOOKER, REV. ROBERT (1927–1992) *Label: Booker.* Jackson, Mississippi, native arrived in New Orleans in the early 1950s and organized the Booker Gospel Singers. In 1963 started Booker label to record local gospel groups and through the mid-1970s released many dozens of singles by regional singers and groups, including the Booker Singers, **Rev. Charlie Jackson**, Zion Harmonizers, Southern Belles, Rev. Cleveland Williams, Alberta Harris, and Star Light Spiritual Singers. Also occasionally recorded rhythm and blues artists such as **Robert Parker**.

BUCK, GEORGE H., JR. (1928–2013) *Labels: Jazzology, GHB.* New Jersey native founded Jazzology in 1949 to record **Tony Parenti** in New York City and in 1954 started GHB label devoted to recording traditional New Orleans jazz. Throughout following decades released recordings of numerous New Orleans artists, including **Sidney Bechet**, **Baby Dodds**, **Sharkey Bonano**, **Danny Barker**, **Kid Thomas**, **Papa Celestine**, **George Lewis**, **Johnny Wiggs**, **Captain John Handy**, and many others. Later acquired other prominent jazz labels, including Black Swan, Circle, Solo Art, Southland, and **Bill Russell**'s American Music. In the late 1980s moved operations to New Orleans and opened Palm Court Jazz Café, which quickly established itself as a premier jazz venue in the French Quarter. Jazzology continued operating in the late 2010s, remaining the world's oldest independent record label.

JONES, SENATOR (NOLAN JONES) (1934–2008) *Labels: Hep' Me, Black Patch, Shagg, Superdome, Erica, Jenmark, JB's.* Mississippi-born producer, composer, and label owner moved to New Orleans with his family in 1951 and sang in various vocal groups in the 1950s. After recording several singles as leader in the 1960s, formed Black Patch label in 1968 and released the debut single of **Rockie Charles**. Through the mid-1980s produced more than a hundred singles and LPs by numerous New Orleans soul and rhythm and blues artists, including **Johnny Adams**, **Charles Brimmer**, **Barbara George**, **Walter "Wolfman" Washington**, **Tommy Ridgley**, **Ray J.**, **Chris Kenner**, and **Eddie Lang** as well as Baton Rouge's **Bobby Powell**. Notable hits included Lang's "Food Stamp Blues" on Superdome (and leased to Jewel), Stop Inc.'s "Second Line" on JB's, and Brimmer's "Afflicted" on Hep' Me.

MATASSA, COSIMO (1926–2014) J&M, Cosimo, and Jazz City Recording Studios. *Labels: Rex, White Cliffs.* Native New Orleans studio owner, sound engineer, producer, and label owner who operated one of the most important and successful recording studios from the mid-1940s through the early 1970s and played a pivotal role in shaping the sound of early rhythm and blues and rock and roll. Opened J&M Recording Studio on North Rampart Street in the French Quarter in the back of his father's appliance store in 1945 with business partner Joe Mancuso. Throughout the following two decades was responsible for virtually every rhythm and blues and early rock and roll recording that came out of New Orleans on major labels as well as independents, with countless hits by **Fats Domino**, **Roy Brown**, **Lloyd Price**, **Professor Longhair**, Little Richard, Ray Charles, Big Joe Turner,

Smiley Lewis, **Guitar Slim**, **Earl King**, and others, many produced by **Dave Bartholomew** or **Paul Gayten**. Around 1956 relocated and expanded studios to Governor Nicholls Street and continued with sessions in that location through the mid-1960s, often for producers Bartholomew or **Allen Toussaint**, with numerous hits by **Huey "Piano" Smith**, **Lee Dorsey**, **Ernie K-Doe**, **Clarence "Frogman" Henry**, **Irma Thomas**, **Chris Kenner**, **Jessie Hill**, and many others. Also launched Rex label in 1959 with releases by artists such as Mac Rebennack (**Dr. John**), **Lee Dorsey**, and **Gerri Hall**. In 1965 opened Jazz City Recording Studios and continued dominating the New Orleans recording business, founding Dover Records Inc., which handled recording, pressing, distribution, and promotion for dozens of various local independent labels. Despite releasing several hits in remaining years, Dover was forced into bankruptcy in the late 1960s. Continued operating Jazz City for several more years before retiring from the music business.

RUFFINO, JOE (1921–1965) *Labels: Ric, Ron, Vibra, Soundex.* New Orleans native briefly worked in sales for Ace Records before forming the Ric label in 1958, working with **Edgar Blanchard** as music arranger on early recordings. The following year founded Ron and through 1962 produced numerous New Orleans rhythm and blues releases by artists such as **Irma Thomas**, **Professor Longhair**, **Robert Parker**, **Tommy Ridgley**, **Johnny Adams**, **Eddie Bo**, **Joe Jones**, and **Al "Carnival Time" Johnson**. Ric/Ron's most successful national, regional, and local hits included Thomas's "Don't Mess with My Man," Adams's "I Won't Cry" and "A Losing Battle," Professor Longhair's "Go to the Mardi Gras," Johnson's "Carnival Time," and Bo's "Check Mr. Popeye."

RUSSELL, BILL (RUSSELL WILLIAM WAGNER) (1905–1992) *Label: American Music.* Missouri-born jazz historian, writer, and musician-composer launched the American Music label in 1944 to record traditional New Orleans jazz musicians during the early part of the jazz revival of the 1940s, which he largely helped initiate. Through 1957 recorded numerous prominent jazz musicians, including **Bunk Johnson**, **George Lewis**, **Sidney Bechet**, **Kid Thomas**, **Wooden Joe Nicholas**, **Johnny** and **Baby Dodds**, **Paul Barbarin**, **Kid Ory**, **Kid Sheik Cola**, and **Billie** and **De De Pierce**. American Music label was later acquired by producer **George H. Buck Jr.**

SEHORN, MARSHALL (1934–2006) and **ALLEN TOUSSAINT** (1938–2015) SeaSaint Studios. *Labels: Sansu, Deesu, Tou-Sea, Sea-Horn, Janus.* North Carolina native worked as an A&R rep for Bobby Robinson's New York–based Fire and Fury labels in the late 1950s and early 1960s, signing Wilbert Harrison, **Bobby Marchan**, and **Lee Dorsey** to the labels and beginning a long partnership with **Allen Toussaint**. Relocated to New Orleans in the mid-1960s and formed Sansu Enterprises in 1965 with Toussaint, who served as producer, songwriter, arranger, and musician. Throughout the following decade released numerous recordings which helped define New Orleans rhythm and blues of the late 1960s and 1970s by artists such as Marchan, Dorsey, Betty Harris, the Meters, **Diamond Joe**, **Ironing Board Sam**, **Curly Moore**, **Benny Spellman**, **Willie West**, **Tony Owens**, and many others. In 1973 opened SeaSaint Recording Studios with Toussaint, which quickly helped fill the void left by **Cosimo Matassa**'s recent departure from the recording business. *See also Toussaint's entry as musician.*

TAYLOR, AL (1932–) *Label: Rosemont.* Mobile, Alabama, native was raised in New Orleans after the death of his father when he was a child. In the early 1960s began recording various annual musical programs at local churches on a portable unit and soon started Rosemont to issue the recordings. In the mid-1960s built a home recording studio and throughout the following three decades remained one New Orleans's most prolific labels, producing hundreds of singles and LPs by many of the region's most prominent gospel groups and singers, including the Zion Harmonizers, Mighty Chariots, New Orleans Spiritualettes, Gospel Soul Children, Rocks of Harmony, Gospelites of New Orleans, and many others. Although primarily a gospel label, also occasionally recorded rhythm and blues, soul, and funk, including **Willie Tee** and **Alex Spearman**, as well as early hip-hop artists in the 1980s. Continued operating labels and recording studio through the early to mid-1990s.

Shreveport

LEWIS, STAN "THE RECORD MAN" (1927–2018) *Labels: Jewel, Paula, Ronn, Suzy-Q, Gospel Jubilee.* Shreveport native purchased local record store on Texas Street in 1948 and opened Stan's Record Shop, which soon expanded and became a highly successful retail and mail-order operation specializing in blues and gospel records. Throughout the 1950s worked as talent scout for rhythm and blues labels including Chess, Imperial, and

Specialty and helped guide the early recording careers of **Dale Hawkins**, **T.V. Slim**, **Country Jim**, **Jimmy C. Newman**, and others, occasionally as producer using local recording studios. In 1963 founded Jewel Records and throughout following years released recordings by numerous artists, including **Bobby Charles**, **John Fred**, Lightnin' Hopkins, Frank Frost, Peppermint Harris, the Carter Brothers, Ted Taylor, **Bobby Rush**, Buster Benton, Little Johnny Taylor, Blind Boys of Mississippi, the Soul Stirrers, and many others. In 1965 started Paula subsidiary for pop music releases and in 1967 launched Ronn for uptown rhythm and blues and jazz. Label's most successful release was **John Fred**'s "Judy in Disguise (with Glasses)," which reached number one in 1968. After being forced into bankruptcy in 1983, eventually sold entire catalog in the late 1990s.

MARAIS, DEE (Harding Guyon Desmarais) (1921–2008) *Labels: Murco, Hy-Sign, Hy-Tree, Hy-Rock, Hy-Sign Gospel, Peermont.* Minnesota-born producer got his start in the music business working promotions throughout the South for several labels, including Chess and Old Town, in the 1950s. In 1960 purchased producer Shelby Singleton's Bayou record shop in Shreveport with partner Dick Martin. From 1967 to 1973 released more than two dozen singles by artists such as **Reuben Bell**, **Eddie Giles**, and **Dori Grayson**, which helped establish Shreveport as a stronghold of southern soul. Notable releases include Bell's "It's Not that Easy" and "Too Late" and Giles's "Losing Boy," all released on Murco.

SMITH, MIRA ANN (1924–1989) RAM Studio. *Labels: RAM, K, Clif, WLS, Jo.* Shreveport-based producer, composer, musician, and pioneering female label and studio owner opened RAM (Royal Audio Music) Recording Studio in 1955 to capitalize on the thriving local music scene and soon started label of the same name. Through the early 1960s recorded numerous blues, rockabilly, country, and swamp pop musicians for her labels as well as for other independents, including **T.V. Slim**, **Roy "Boogie Boy" Perkins**, **the Lonesome Drifter**, **Margaret Lewis**, **Chico Chism**, **Jesse Thomas**, and Linda Brannon. Studio also provided a training ground for young musicians such as **James Burton** and **Joe Osborn**, who appeared on many sessions. *See also Smith's entry as musician.*

IIIIIIII

Southeast Bayou Region

ROBICHAUX, ELDRIDGE, and **ROD RODRIGUE** R&R Recording Studios. *Labels: Houma, WarPath, Desire, Rampart.* Native Houma saxophonist Eldridge Robichaux started Houma label with local producer Anthony "Rod" Rodrigue in the mid-1960s and later founded R&R Recording Studios. Through the 1970s released more than 50 singles by numerous Cajun, rhythm and blues, swamp pop, and country artists, including **Raymond George**, **Joe Barry**, **Gene Rodrigue**, **Uncle Pott Folse**, **L. J. Foret**, and **Leroy "Lee" Martin**. Robichaux also recorded and performed as "Tony Eldridge."

Southwest Bayou and Prairie Region

LAVERGNE, LEE (1932–1998) *Labels: Lanor, Joker.* Church Point native grew up speaking Cajun French and began producing records in 1960 with his first release by **Shirley** and **Alphée Bergeron**'s Veteran Playboys. Throughout following decades recorded numerous Cajun, swamp pop, zydeco, and rhythm and blues artists, including **Charles Mann**, **Elton Anderson**, **Jo Jo Reed**, **Johnny Sonnier**, **Robby "Mann" Robinson**, **Donald Jacobs**, **Felton LeJeune**, **Phil Phillips**, **Beau Jocque**, **Keith Frank**, **Little Victor**, and **Jackie Caillier**. Successful releases included Anderson's "Life Problem" and Mann's "Red Red Wine" in the mid- to late 1960s. Continued producing and composing from his Church Point studio in later years until his death at age 65.

MILLER, J. D. or **JAY (Joseph Delton Miller)** (1922–1996) Miller Studios, Master-Trak Studios. *Labels: Fais-Do-Do, Feature, "French" Hits, Rocket, Rocko, Kry, Zynn, Spot, Blues Unlimited, Soul Unlimited, Pelican, Kajun, Showtime, Reb Rebel, Cajun Classics, Bayou Classics, Action, Ringo, Swade, Tribute, Master-Trak.* Iota, Louisiana, native relocated to Crowley with his family in 1937 and performed with various local country and Cajun string bands. In 1946 started Fais-Do-Do label to record his father-in-law **Lee Sonnier**, inspired by the recent success of **Harry Choates**'s hit "Jole Blon." After recording several releases by **Happy Fats** and **Doc Guidry** at **Cosimo Matassa**'s studio in New Orleans, began recording in his own Crowley studio in 1947 and in following years had numerous releases on Fais-Do-Do and Feature by Sonnier, **Aldus Roger**, **Austin Pitre**, **Amédée Breaux**, **Papa Cairo**, **Rusty** and **Doug Kershaw**, **Al Terry**, and others. In 1954 began recording blues on Feature with **Lightnin' Slim**, **Clarence Garlow**, and **Schoolboy Cleve** and the following year entered into a production agreement with Ernie Young of Nashville-based Excello Records. Through the mid-1960s produced hundreds of classic blues recordings for Excello, which single-handedly defined what would become known as swamp blues with releases by **Lightnin' Slim**, **Slim Harpo**, **Guitar Gable**, **Lazy Lester**, **Lonesome Sundown**, **Silas Hogan**, **Leroy Washington**, and others. Also released swamp pop, rockabilly, zydeco and early rock and roll recordings by **Rocket Morgan**, **Clifton Chenier**, **Warren Storm**, **Katie Webster**, **Terry Clement**, and others during this time on his Rocket, Rocko, Spot, and Zynn labels. In the 1960s also produced a series of controversial and racist segregationist recordings on his Reb Rebel label despite organizing recordings by mixed-race bands for many years. Son Mark Miller (1953–) continued to operate labels, recording studio, and Modern Music retail store in the late 2010s.

RACHOU, CAROL, SR. (1932–2004) La Louisianne Studio. *Labels: La Louisianne, Tamm, Belle, Jazz at the Music Mart.* New Orleans–born producer and studio owner performed in various bands around Lafayette before opening local record shop the Music Mart in the mid-1950s. In 1958 built La Louisianne recording studio in Lafayette and started label of the same name the following year to record **Alex Broussard**'s "Le Sud de la Louisiane." In the following decades recorded numerous Cajun, swamp pop, rhythm and blues, and country artists and Cajun humorists, including **Lawrence Walker**, **Little Bob**, **Eddy Raven**, **Jimmy C. Newman**, **Jewell** and the Rubies, **Aldus Roger**, **Doc Guidry**, **Johnnie Allan**, **Roddie Romero**, **Vin Bruce**, **Little Buck Sinegal**, and **Ambrose Thibodeaux**. Also produced countless recordings for other labels, notably Dale and **Grace**'s 1963 hit "I'm Leaving It Up to You" for **Sam Montel**. Son David Rachou (1964–) continued operating studio and label in the late 2010s.

SOILEAU, FLOYD (1938–) *Labels: Swallow, Jin, Maison de Soul, Kom-A-Day, Bon Temps, Fame, Vee-Pee, Big Mamou.* Ville Platte producer and studio owner grew up speaking Cajun French and worked as a local disc jockey while still in high school. Around 1956 opened Floyd's Record Shop, which specialized in locally produced music and the following year started first label, Big Mamou, with jukebox and nightclub operator Ed Manuel to record **Austin Pitre** and **Milton Molitor**. After several Cajun releases on Vee-Pee, formed Swallow and Jin labels in 1958–59 and throughout following decades recorded numerous Cajun, swamp pop, and rhythm and blues artists, including **Nathan Abshire**, **Aldus Roger**, **Balfa Brothers**, **Lil' Bob**, **Rockin' Sidney**, **Rod Bernard**, **Belton Richard**, **Lawrence Walker**, **D. L. Menard**, **Tommy McLain**, and **Johnnie Allan** as well as noted groups the Boogie Kings, Rufus Jagneaux, and Jambalaya Cajun Band. In 1974 founded Maison de Soul to record zydeco musicians but also occasionally released rhythm and blues and soul recordings. Artists included **Clifton Chenier**, **Rockin' Sidney**, **John Delafose**, **Donald Jacobs**, **Rockin' Tabby Thomas**, **Lynn August**, **Buckwheat Zydeco**, **Boozoo Chavis**, **Rockin' Dopsie**, **Rosie Ledet**, and Zydeco Force. Label's biggest release was Rockin' Sidney's multi-million-selling zydeco hit "My Toot Toot" in 1985. Also operated Louisiana's only record-pressing plant from 1975 until its closure in 1994 from extensive fire damage. Continued operating labels and online merchandise company in the late 2010s.

NOTES

A

1. U.S. World War II Draft Cards Young Men, 1940–1947.

2. Louisiana, Statewide Death Index, 1819–1964.

3. U.S. World War II Draft Cards Young Men, 1940–1947; U.S. Social Security Applications and Claims Index, 1936–2007.

4. City of New Orleans, Louisiana, Certificate of Death.

5. U.S. Social Security Death Index, 1935–2014.

6. Ibid.

7. U.S. World War I Draft Registration Cards; 1920 U.S. Federal Census; Central Louisiana State Hospital record 13387.

8. Louisiana, Statewide Death Index, 1819–1964.

9. Louisiana Death Certificate 56-0175.

B

1. U.S. World War II Draft Cards Young Men, 1940–1947.

2. 1900 U.S. Federal Census; U.S. Social Security Death Index, 1935–2014.

3. California Death Index, 1905–1939.

4. U.S. World War II Draft Registration Card, 1942.

5. 1850 Census, Ascension Parish, Louisiana. California, Death Index, 1905–1939.

6. Obituary, *Times-Picayune*, Apr. 15, 1981.

7. 1910 U.S. Federal Census.

8. U.S. Social Security Death Index, 1935–2014.

9. New Orleans, Louisiana Birth Records Index, 1790–1899.

10. U.S. World War I Draft Registration Cards 1917–1918 lists date of birth as May 14, 1896.

11. 1930 U.S. Federal Census; U.S. World War II Draft Cards Young Men, 1940–1947 (listed as Douglas Bellar); Louisiana Death Certificate 548. Death certificate lists date of birth as Nov. 6 and age as 48, but year is not written out and suggests 1898. Name misspelled as Douglas Ballard.

12. U.S. Social Security Applications and Claims Index, 1936–2007.

13. U.S. Social Security Death Index, 1935–2014.

14. U.S. Social Security Applications and Claims Index, 1936–2007; Louisiana Death Certificate 503-2073.

15. U.S. Social Security Death Index, 1935–2014.

16. Ibid.

17. Louisiana Death Certificate, listed as Hester Bijou.

18. Louisiana Death Certificate.

19. New Orleans, Louisiana, Death Records Index, 1804–1949; Louisiana Death Certificate.

20. U.S. Social Security Applications and Claims Index, 1936–2007; Obituary, *Times-Picayune*, April 15, 1973.

21. U.S. Social Security Death Index, 1935–2014; 1930 U.S. Census, New Orleans, Orleans, Louisiana.

22. U.S. World War I Draft Registration Cards, 1917–1918.

23. 1900 U.S. Federal Census; U.S. World War I Draft Registration Cards, 1917–1918; U.S. Social Security Death Index, 1935–2014.

24. U.S. Social Security Death Index, 1935–2014.

25. U.S. World War II Draft Registration Cards, 1942.

26. U.S. World War II Draft Cards Young Men, 1940–1947.

27. California Death Index, 1940–1997.

28. World War I Draft Registration Card; Louisiana Death Certificate 670001593; death certificate lists date of birth as June 5, 1883, in Patterson, St. Mary Parish.

29. Louisiana, Statewide Death Index, 1819–1964.

30. U.S. World War II Draft Cards Young Men, 1940–1947; U.S. Social Security Death Index, 1935–2014.

31. U.S. World War II Draft Cards Young Men, 1940–1947.

32. Ibid.

33. Ibid.

34. U.S. Social Security Applications and Claims Index, 1936–2007; Index to Annual Deaths, 1958–2002, Ohio Department of Health, State Vital Statistics Unit, Columbus.

35. U.S. World War II Draft Cards Young Men, 1940–1947.

36. U.S. World War II Draft Registration Cards, 1942.

37. U.S. Social Security Applications and Claims Index, 1936–2007.

38. U.S. World War II Draft Cards Young Men, 1940–1947.

39. U.S. World War II Draft Registration Cards, 1942.

40. New Orleans, Louisiana, Birth Records Index, 1790–1915; U.S. World War I Draft Registration Cards, 1917–1918.

41. U.S. Department of Veterans Affairs BIRLS Death File, 1850–2010.

C

1. U.S. Social Security Applications and Claims Index, 1936–2007.

2. California Death Index, 1940–1997. Carey's World War I draft registration card lists place and date of birth as St. John the Baptist Parish on Sept. 17, 1888.

3. U.S. Social Security Death Index, 1935–2014.

4. Louisiana, Statewide Death Index, 1819–1964.

5. U.S. Social Security Death Index, 1935–2014.

6. California Death Index, 1940–1997.

7. New Orleans, Louisiana, Birth Records Index, 1790–1915; Louisiana Death Certificate 103.

8. U.S. Social Security Death Index, 1935–2014; Obituary, *Times-Picayune,* Dec. 2, 1984.

9. U.S. Social Security Death Index, 1935–2014; U.S. Public Records Index, 1950–1993, vol. 2.

10. 1930 U.S. Federal Census. Although numerous sources cite Church Point as his place of birth, Chavis's family was already living in the Lake Charles area in April 1930, six months prior to his birth.

11. U.S. World War II Draft Cards Young Men, 1940–1947.

12. Date of birth as listed on gravestone. SSDI lists date of birth as June 9, 1916.

13. Texas Death Certificate 63957.

14. Place of birth as listed on baptismal certificate. Other sources cite Abbeville (World War II draft card) and New Iberia (Texas death certificate). Original family name is "Choate," not "Choates."

15. U.S. World War II Draft Cards Young Men, 1940–1947.

16. U.S. Social Security Applications and Claims Index, 1936–2007.

17. Texas Death Certificate 58913.

18. U.S. Social Security Applications and Claims Index, 1936–2007.

19. 1880 Census, 3rd Ward, St James, Louisiana; U.S. World War I Draft Registration Cards, 1917–1918; Louisiana Death Certificate.

20. U.S. Social Security Applications and Claims Index, 1936–2007; Obituary, *Lake Charles American Press,* Feb. 7, 1967.

21. U.S. Social Security Applications and Claims Index, 1936–2007.

22. U.S. World War II Draft Cards Young Men, 1940–1947.

23. 1900 U.S. Federal Census. Previously reported place of birth in St. Francisville appears to be misinterpretation of "Fazeneville" location listed on early census records of family. Fazendeville existed in St. Bernard Parish until 1960s in the area that is now Jean Lafitte National Historical Park.

24. U.S. Public Records Index, 1950–1993, vol. 1.

25. 1940 U.S. Federal Census; U.S. Social Security Applications and Claims Index, 1936–2007; correspondence with granddaughter Eliza Dasher.

26. California, Death Index, 1940–1997.

27. U.S. World War I Draft Registration Cards, 1917–1918; New Orleans, Louisiana, Death Records Index, 1804–1949; Louisiana Death Certificate 1336.

28. 1900 and 1920 U.S. Federal Census.

29. Louisiana Death Certificate 4-113.

30. U.S. Social Security Death Index, 1935–2014.

IIIIIIIII

D

1. Texas Death Certificate 52184.

2. U.S. World War II Draft Cards Young Men, 1940–1947.

3. Ibid.; U.S. Social Security Death Index, 1935–2014.

4. U.S. Social Security Death Index, 1935–2014.

5. Obituary, *Times-Picayune,* Feb. 17, 1986.

6. U.S. World War II Draft Cards Young Men, 1940–1947; Missouri Death Certificate 0003338.

7. U.S. World War II Draft Cards Young Men, 1940–1947; Obituary, *Lake Charles American Press,* Aug. 13, 1980.

8. U.S. Social Security Death Index, 1935–2014.

9. New Orleans, Louisiana, Birth Records Index, 1790–1915; Louisiana Death Certificate 4668.

10. U.S. World War II Draft Cards Young Men, 1940–1947.

11. U.S. World War I Draft Registration Cards, 1917–1918; U.S. Social Security Applications and Claims Index, 1936–2007.

12. California, Death Index, 1940–1997.

13. U.S. Social Security Death Index, 1935–2014.

14. California, Death Index, 1940–1997.

15. 1900 U.S. Federal Census; U.S. World War I Draft Registration Cards, 1917–1918.

16. U.S. World War I Draft Registration Cards, 1917–1918; U.S. World War II Draft Registration Cards, 1942.

17. U.S. Social Security Death Index, 1935–2014; Obituary, *Times-Picayune,* Dec. 3, 1986. Other sources including U.S. Department of Veterans Affairs BIRLS Death File list date of birth as Dec. 24, 1926.

18. U.S. World War II Draft Cards Young Men, 1940–1947; Obituary, *Monroe News Star,* Sept. 7, 2018.

19. U.S. Social Security Death Index, 1935–2014.

20. U.S. World War II Draft Cards Young Men, 1940–1947; U.S. Social Security Death Index, 1935–2014.

21. U.S. Social Security Applications and Claims Index, 1936–2007.

22. 1900 U.S. Federal Census; New Orleans, Louisiana, Death Records Index, 1804–1949.

23. New Orleans, Louisiana, Birth Records Index, 1790–1899; Pennsylvania Death Certificate 54413.

24. Obituary, *Crowley Post Signal,* Dec. 30, 1988.

25. U.S. World War I Draft Registration Cards, 1917–1918; Louisiana, Statewide Death Index, 1819–1964. World War II Draft Registration Card lists date of birth as April 30, 1888, and Louisiana Death Certificate lists date of birth as April 30, 1890.

26. U.S. Social Security Applications and Claims Index, 1936–2007.

27. Louisiana Certificate of Death 8-864.

28. U.S. World War II Draft Cards Young Men, 1940–1947; Obituary, *Abbeville Meridional,* May 30, 1977.

29. U.S. World War I Draft Registration Cards, 1917–1918.

30. Ibid.; Illinois Deaths and Stillbirths Index, 1916–1947.

E

1. 1910 and 1940 U.S. Federal Census; Michigan, Marriage Records, 1867–1952; U.S. World War II Draft Cards Young Men, 1940–1947; U.S. Social Security Death Index, 1935–2014.

2. U.S. Social Security Death Index, 1935–2014.

3. Ibid.

4. U.S. World War I Draft Registration Cards, 1917–1918; Cook County, Illinois Death Index, 1908–1988.

5. U.S. World War II Draft Cards Young Men, 1940–1947.

6. Date of birth listed was estimated by Etienne's family as no birth record was issued. Etienne stated he could have been born as early as 1931 or as late as 1935.

F

1. Obituary, *Crowley Register,* Apr. 9, 1941.

2. Texas Death Certificate 14435.

3. Obituary, Blanchard St. Denis Funeral Home, Natchitoches.

4. Cook County, Illinois Death Index, 1908–1988.

5. U.S. World War I Draft Registration Cards, 1917–1918; Louisiana Death Certificate 670003905.

6. 1910 U.S. Federal Census.

7. U.S. World War II Draft Cards Young Men, 1940–1947.

8. 1900 U.S. Federal Census.

9. U.S. World War I Draft Registration Cards, 1917–1918; 1900 U.S. Federal Census; Louisiana Death Certificate 7676.

10. U.S. Social Security Applications and Claims Index, 1936–2007.

11. U.S. Social Security Death Index, 1935–2014.

12. U.S. World War II Draft Cards Young Men, 1940–1947; Louisiana, Statewide Death Index, 1819–1964.

13. U.S. World War I Draft Registration Cards, 1917–1918; California Death Index, 1940–1997.

14. 1880 U.S. Federal Census; 1900 U.S. Federal Census.

15. 1880 U.S. Federal Census.

16. U.S. Social Security Death Index, 1935–2014; Obituary, *Baton Rouge Advocate,* April 20, 2005.

17. U.S. World War II Draft Cards Young Men, 1940–1947; U.S. Social Security Death Index, 1935–2014.

18. U.S. World War II Draft Cards Young Men, 1940–1947.

19. U.S. World War I Draft Registration Cards, 1917–1918; Obituary, *Times-Picayune,* June 2, 1963.

20. U.S. World War II Draft Cards Young Men, 1940–1947.

21. Ibid.

G

1. Missouri Certificate of Death #38502. World War I and World War II Draft Registration Cards give date of birth as June 20, 1883.

2. U.S. Social Security Death Index, 1935–2014.

3. Louisiana Death Certificate.

4. California Death Index, 1940–1997.

5. U.S. World War I Draft Registration Cards, 1917–1918; Louisiana Death Certificate 13994. Date of birth listed as Dec. 1878 in 1900 U.S. Census. Grave headstone incorrectly lists date of death as Oct. 6, 1937.

6. U.S. World War I Draft Registration Cards, 1917–1918; New Orleans, Louisiana, Death Records Index, 1804–1949.

7. U.S. World War I Draft Registration Cards, 1917–1918; 1930 U.S. Federal Census; Alabama, Deaths and Burials Index, 1881–1974. Last name is hand-signed as "Gipson" on his World War I Draft Card and appears as such in later marriage, military, and death records.

8. U.S. World War I Draft Registration Cards, 1917–1918; U.S. City Directories, 1822–1995; Louisiana, Statewide Death Index, 1819–1964.

9. U.S. World War II Draft Registration Cards, 1942. U.S. Social Security Death Index lists Aug. 31, 1891, as date of birth.

10. Although Glenny gave March 25, 1870, as his date of birth in interviews, he reported March 1865 in the 1900 census.

11. Texas Death Certificate 41385.

12. 1930 U.S. Federal Census; Florida Death Index, 1877–1998.

13. Louisiana Death Certificate 11504.

14. U.S. Social Security Death Index, 1935–2014.

15. U.S. World War II Draft Cards Young Men, 1940–1947.

16. Louisiana Death Certificate 13-206.

H

1. New Orleans, Louisiana, Death Records Index, 1804–1949; Louisiana Death Certificate 1881.

2. U.S. World War II Draft Registration Cards, 1942; U.S. Social Security Death Index, 1935–2014; Obituary, *Times-Picayune,* June 18, 1981.

3. 1920 U.S. Federal Census; Initial research by Wade Falcon.

4. U.S. Social Security Death Index, 1935–2014.

5. U.S. World War I Draft Registration Cards, 1917–1918; Louisiana Death Certificate 865.

6. U.S. Second Draft Registration Cards, 1948–1959.

7. U.S. Social Security Applications and Claims Index, 1936–2007.

8. U.S. Social Security Death Index, 1935–2014.

9. New Orleans, Louisiana, Birth Records Index, 1790–1915; California, Death Index, 1940–1997.

10. U.S. World War I Draft Registration Cards, 1917–1918; Illinois Deaths and Stillbirths, 1916–1947.

11. U.S. Social Security Applications and Claims Index, 1936–2007.

12. U.S. World War I Draft Registration Cards, 1917–1918; New Orleans, Louisiana, Death Records Index, 1804–1949.

13. U.S. World War II Draft Cards Young Men, 1940–1947; Louisiana Statewide Death Index, 1819–1964.

14. 1940 U.S. Federal Census; U.S. Social Security Applications and Claims Index, 1936–2007. U.S. Social Security Death Index and Department of Veterans Affairs BIRLS Death File lists date of birth as Aug. 28, 1927.

15. U.S. Social Security Applications and Claims Index, 1936–2007.

16. 1900 U.S. Federal Census; New Orleans, Louisiana, Death Records Index, 1804–1949.

17. U.S. Public Records Index, 1950–1993, vol. 1.

J

1. New Orleans, Louisiana, Birth Records Index, 1790–1915.

2. 1930 and 1940 U.S. Federal Census; Illinois, Deaths and Stillbirths

Index, 1916–1947. U.S. Census for 1930 lists age of Emma L. Days as 26, suggesting her birth year was 1904.

3. Illinois Deaths and Stillbirths Index, 1916–1947.

4. U.S. Social Security Death Index, 1935–2014.

5. 1900 U.S. Federal Census; Illinois Death Certificate 10404.

6. California, Death Index, 1940–1997; U.S. Social Security Death Index, 1935–2014.

7. U.S. Social Security Applications and Claims Index, 1936–2007.

8. U.S. Social Security Death Index, 1935–2014.

9. Ibid.

10. Louisiana Death Certificate.

11. Communications with son Brandon K. Carter, Dec. 2017.

12. U.S. Social Security Applications and Claims Index, 1936–2007.

13. Obituary, *Times-Picayune,* July 9, 1968.

14. Birth year of 1889 is believed to be probable, although Johnson gave year as 1879 in multiple interviews. Dec. 1889 appears on the 1900 Census and on his 1937 Social Security application. The years 1879 (1930 Census and 1949 marriage application), 1880 (death certificate), 1882 (1918 World War I draft card), and 1885 (1907 and 1949 marriage certificates) also appear in the historical record.

15. Honolulu, Hawaii, Passenger and Crew Lists, 1900–1959.

16. Although he is widely believed to have been born in Biloxi, Johnson's World War I and World War II draft registration cards and Social Security application all list New Orleans as his place of birth. World War I draft card lists Apr. 5, 1892, as date of birth.

17. 1900 U.S. Federal Census.

18. Obituary, *Times-Picayune,* September 20, 1969.

19. Birth year of 1894 is listed on Johnson's passport and given by him in several interviews. Years 1899 and 1900 are also cited in sources but seem unlikely.

20. U.S. World War I Draft Registration Cards, 1917–1918; Illinois, Deaths and Stillbirths Index, 1916–1947.

21. 1880 U.S. Federal Census; U.S. World War II Draft Registration Cards, 1942.

22. U.S. World War II Draft Registration Cards, 1942; U.S. Social Security Applications and Claims Index, 1936–2007.

K

1. U.S. Social Security Death Index, 1935–2014. Kador's Social Security application lists birth year as 1935.

2. U.S. World War I Draft Registration Cards, 1917–1918; Louisiana Death Certificate 15-199. Census of 1900 lists his date of birth as March 1885.

3. U.S. Social Security Death Index, 1935–2014.

4. New Orleans, Louisiana, Birth Records Index, 1790–1915; Cook County, Illinois Death Index, 1908–1988.

5. U.S. Social Security Death Index, 1935–2014.

6. New Orleans, Louisiana, Birth Records Index, 1790–1915; New Orleans, Louisiana, Death Records Index, 1804–1949. World War I Draft Card lists date of birth as Mar. 26, 1877.

7. U.S. World War II Draft Cards Young Men, 1940–1947; U.S. Social Security Death Index, 1935–2014, which lists date of birth as Sept. 3, 1898.

L

1. U.S. World War I Draft Registration Cards, 1917–1918; Louisiana Death Certificate 634.

2. New Orleans, Louisiana, Birth Records Index, 1790–1915; Obituary, *Times-Picayune,* Nov. 20, 1946.

3. Louisiana Statewide Death Index, 1819–1964; Louisiana Death Certificate 11674.

4. Louisiana Death Certificate 12953.

5. U.S. World War II Draft Cards Young Men, 1940–1947; California Death Index, 1940–1997.

6. U.S. World War II Draft Cards Young Men, 1940–1947; U.S. Social Security Death Index, 1935–2014. Gravestone lists date of birth as June 6, 1928.

7. U.S. Social Security Death Index, 1935–2014. Lapoint's World War II Draft Card lists birthplace as Arcadia Parish. First name often misspelled as "Emory."

8. U.S. Social Security Death Index, 1935–2014; Obituary, *Times-Picayune,* May 2, 1993.

9. U.S. World War II Draft Cards Young Men, 1940–1947.

10. Ibid.

11. 1900, 1910, 1920, 1930, and 1940 U.S. Federal Census; U.S. World War II Draft Registration Card, 1942. Ledbetter's birth year of 1888 is listed on 1900, 1910, and 1930 censuses. Census of 1920 (as prisoner under name Walter Boyd) lists 1886, and 1940 Census lists 1889. Other sources cite Jan. 20, 1888, as date of birth.

12. U.S. World War II Draft Cards Young Men, 1940–1947. Louisiana Death Certificate lists date of birth as Dec. 25, 1921.

13. U.S. World War II Draft Cards Young Men, 1940–1947.

14. 1930 U.S. Federal Census.

15. U.S. Social Security Death Index, 1935–2014; Obituary, *Chicago Tribune,* Sept. 13, 2006. Gravestone lists date of death as Sept. 7, 2006.

16. U.S. Social Security Death Index, 1935–2014.

17. U.S. World War II Draft Cards Young Men, 1940–1947; Louisiana Death Certificate 12-318.

18. U.S. World War II Draft Cards Young Men, 1940–1947. U.S. Social Security Death Index files list year of birth as 1918.

19. U.S. World War I Draft Registration Cards, 1917–1918; Louisiana Death Certificate 7664.

20. 1920 U.S. Federal Census; U.S. World War II Draft Cards Young Men, 1940–1947; 1935 Louisiana State Penitentiary Convict Record 25876. Although Hicks claimed in interviews to have been born and raised in St. Louis, census, prison, and military records place his birth and early years in Louisiana.

21. U.S. World War II Draft Registration Cards, 1942; Illinois, Deaths and Stillbirths Index, 1916–1947.

22. U.S. World War I Draft Registration Cards, 1917–1918; U.S. World War II Draft Registration Cards, 1942. Last name is hand-signed with spelling of "Lindsey" on both documents.

23. Although May 1, 1930, has been routinely cited as Jacobs's date of birth, historical documents suggest a much earlier date is probable: 1940 U.S. Federal Census shows 1925; 1940 Application for Social Security Account lists 1923; 1943 Draft Registration Card has 1924; 1948 Selective Service Registration Application shows 1925. The day of May

1 remained consistent in all records. A birth certificate has never been found and is believed not to have been issued.

24. U.S. Social Security Applications and Claims Index, 1936–2007.

25. U.S. Social Security Death Index, 1935–2014. Boyette's 1946 World War II Draft Card Application lists date of birth as June 27, 1928.

26. Louisiana Death Certificate.

27. U.S. Social Security Applications and Claims Index, 1936–2007.

28. 1920 U.S. Federal Census; U.S. World War II Draft Cards Young Men, 1940–1947; Obituary, *Lake Charles American Press,* Oct. 20, 1988.

29. U.S. Public Records Index, 1950–1993, vol. 2.

30. 1910, 1930, and 1940 U.S. Federal Census; Louisiana Death Certificate 1504.

31. U.S. Social Security Death Index, 1935–2014.

M

1. U.S. Social Security Death Index, 1935–2014.

2. New Orleans, Louisiana, Birth Records Index, 1790–1915.

3. U.S. Social Security Death Index, 1935–2014.

4. New Orleans, Louisiana, Death Records Index, 1804–1949.

5. U.S. World War II Draft Cards Young Men, 1940–1947.

6. Obituary, *Times-Picayune,* October 12, 1969.

7. U.S. Social Security Applications and Claims Index, 19362007.

8. 1880 and 1900 U.S. Federal Census; New Orleans, Louisiana, Death Records Index, 1804–1949.

9. U.S. Social Security Death Index, 1935–2014.

10. U.S. World War I Draft Registration Cards, 1917–1918; New York, New York, Death Index, 1862–1948.

11. U.S. World War I Draft Registration Cards, 1917–1918; Louisiana, Statewide Death Index, 1819–1964. Appears as August Marrero in records starting in 1917; both his and his father's middle name was August.

12. U.S. Social Security Death Index, 1935–2014.

13. U.S. Public Records Index, 1950–1993, vol. 1.

14. U.S. Social Security Applications and Claims Index, 1936–2007.

15. Ibid.

16. New Orleans, Louisiana, Birth Records Index, 1790–1915; New Orleans, Louisiana, Death Records Index, 1804–1949.

17. New Orleans, Louisiana, Birth Records Index, 1790–1915. U.S. World War I Draft Registration Cards, 1917–1918, lists date of birth as July 28, 1883.

18. 1900 U.S. Federal Census; New Orleans, Louisiana, Death Records Index, 1804–1949.

19. New Orleans, Louisiana, Birth Records Index, 1790–1915; Obituary, *Times-Picayune,* Nov. 2, 1948.

20. New Orleans, Louisiana, Birth Records Index, 1790–1915; Louisiana, Statewide Death Index, 1819–1964.

21. New Orleans, Louisiana, Birth Records Index, 1790–1915; U.S. Social Security Death Index, 1935–2014.

22. 1920, 1930 and 1940 U.S. Federal Census; U.S. Social Security Applications and Claims Index, 1936–2007.

23. U.S. Social Security Death Index, 1935–2014.

24. U.S. Social Security Applications and Claims Index, 1936–2007.

25. Crew Lists of Vessels Arriving at New Orleans, Louisiana, 1910–1945, from Progreso, Mexico, March 1, 1926; Louisiana, Statewide Death Index, 1819–1964.

26. 1900 U.S. Federal Census; Louisiana Death Certificate.

27. California Death Index, 1940–1997.

28. 1920 U.S. Federal Census.

29. 1940 U.S. Federal Census; North Carolina Death Indexes, 1908–2004.

30. U.S. World War I Draft Registration Cards, 1917–1918.

31. Year of birth from baptismal certificate discovered by jazz scholar/researcher Lawrence Gushee. Morton claimed various dates of birth as early as 1884 throughout his life. Sept. 20 remained consistent with family accounts, although Oct. 20 is listed on baptismal record.

32. California, Death Index, 1940–1997.

N

1. Obituary, *Times-Picayune,* December 29, 1969. Social Security Death Index lists Nash's date of death as December 15, 1969, which is probably incorrect.

2. 1940 U.S. Federal Census; New Orleans, Louisiana, Death Records Index, 1804–1949; Obituary, *Times-Picayune,* August, 17, 1949.

3. U.S. Social Security Death Index, 1935–2014. Obituary, *Times-Picayune,* March 2, 1984.

4. New Orleans, Louisiana, Birth Records Index, 1790–1915; Louisiana Death Certificate.

5. U.S. Social Security Death Index, 1935–2014.

6. Reports of Deaths of American Citizens Abroad, 1835–1974.

7. Texas, Death Certificates, 1903–1982.

8. U.S. Social Security Applications and Claims Index, 1936–2007.

9. U.S. World War I Draft Registration Cards, 1917–1918; U.S. World War II Draft Registration Cards, 1942.

10. U.S. Passport Applications, 1795–1925; New Orleans, Louisiana, Death Records Index, 1804–1949.

O

1. Social Security Death Index gives date of birth as May 30, 1936; U.S. Public Records Index, 1950–1993, shows May 3, 1936; Gravestone lists Dec. 15, 1936.

2. Obituary, *Times-Picayune,* May 22, 1842.

3. 1900 U.S. Federal Census; Oliver's widow confirmed date of birth in interview with Bill Russell on Apr. 22, 1959.

4. U.S. Social Security Death Index, 1935–2014.

P

1. 1930 U.S. Federal Census; California Death Index, 1940–1997.

2. New Orleans, Louisiana, Birth Records Index, 1790–1915; Louisiana, Statewide Death Index, 1819–1964.

3. U.S. World War I Draft Registration Cards, 1917–1918; Cook County, Illinois Death Index, 1908–1988.

4. U.S. Social Security Applications and Claims Index, 1936–2007.

5. Michigan, Marriage Records, 1867–1952.

6. Correspondence with son Philip Paulin.

7. New Orleans, Louisiana, Birth Records Index, 1790–1915.

8. U.S. Social Security Death Index, 1935–2014.

9. Pejoe stated in interviews his real family name was Pejas, but in historical documents, including his father Oscar's World War I and World War II draft card applications, the name is listed as Pujoe/Pujoue/Pugoe.

10. Georgia, Death Index, 1919–1998.

11. New Orleans, Louisiana Birth Records Index, 1790–1899; Louisiana, Statewide Death Index, 1819–1964.

12. U.S. World War I Draft Registration Cards, 1917–1918; New Orleans, Louisiana, Death Records Index, 1804–1949. Several dates of birth between 1890 and 1897 exist in the historical record, including Jan. 1895 (1900 Census).

13. U.S. World War II Draft Cards Young Men, 1940–1947.

14. Cook County, Illinois Death Index, 1908–1988.

15. *Baton Rouge Morning Advocate,* March 20, 1985.

16. U.S. Social Security Death Index, 1935–2014.

17. U.S. Social Security Applications and Claims Index, 1936–2007; Obituary, *Dallas Morning News,* Dec. 18, 2003.

18. Louisiana Death Certificate 6307668.

19. His World War II Draft Card and Social Security Application list name as Roeland Henry Byrd, not Henry Roeland Byrd as routinely cited.

R

1. U.S. World War I Draft Registration Cards, 1917–1918; Louisiana Death Certificate 2457.

2. U.S. Social Security Death Index lists date and place of birth as Nov. 10, 1928, New Orleans.

3. U.S. Social Security Death Index, 1935–2014; Obituary, *Times-Picayune,* Nov. 7, 1986.

4. Tenth Census of the United States, 1880; Louisiana Death Certificate.

5. 1910 U.S. Federal Census; U.S. Social Security Applications and Claims Index, 1936–2007. The 1910 Census lists family living in St. Landry Parish, Police Jury Ward 7, which is present-day Ville Platte, Evangeline Parish.

6. Death notice, *Baton Rouge Morning Advocate,* June 16, 1964; author interviews with Harvey Knox, Lee Tillman, and sister Judy Domingue.

7. U.S. World War I Draft Registration Cards, 1917–1918; Louisiana Death Certificate.

8. Louisiana Death Certificate 2053; New Orleans, Louisiana, Death Records Index, 1804–1949. Census of 1900 lists his date of birth as Jan. 1867. Death Certificate lists age at death as 55, which is highly improbable.

9. U.S. World War I Draft Registration Cards, 1917–1918.

10. U.S. Social Security Death Index, 1935–2014.

11. U.S. Social Security Applications and Claims Index, 1936–2007.

12. Ibid.

13. U.S. Social Security Death Index, 1935–2014.

14. 1940 U.S. Federal Census. Rush has stated in several interviews that his birth year is 1933.

S

1. Louisiana Death Certificate 172.

2. New Orleans, Louisiana, Birth Records Index, 1790–1915; New Orleans, Louisiana, Death Records Index, 1804–1949.

3. Louisiana Death Certificate 6368. Sayles's U.S. World War I Draft Registration Cards lists Oct. 12, 1877, as date of birth.

4. 1940 U.S. Federal Census.

5. New Orleans, Louisiana, Birth Records Index, 1790–1915; Louisiana Death Certificate.

6. Although many sources cite Jan. 11, 1924, as Moore's date of birth, Feb. 11, 1924, appears on both his birth certificate and his headstone.

7. 1930 U.S. Federal Census; U.S. World War II Draft Cards Young Men, 1940–1947; death notice, *New Orleans States-Item,* Jan. 28, 1965. Census for 1940 lists year of birth as 1906 with wife, Essie, being the informant.

8. New Orleans, Louisiana, Birth Records Index, 1790–1915; California, Death Index, 1940–1997.

9. 1940 U.S. Federal Census; 1952 U.S. Draft Card; California public records.

10. U.S. Social Security Applications and Claims Index, 1936–2007.

11. New Orleans, Louisiana, Birth Records Index, 1790–1915; Illinois, Deaths and Stillbirths Index, 1916–1947.

12. U.S. Social Security Death Index, 1935–2014.

13. Ibid.

14. U.S. Social Security Applications and Claims Index, 1936–2007.

15. U.S. Second Draft Registration Cards, 1948–1959.

T

1. U.S. World War I Draft Registration Cards, 1917–1918.

2. U.S. Public Records Index, 1950–1993, vol. 1.

3. Gravestone lists date of birth as Oct. 17, 1923. Other sources cite Oct. 5, 1922.

4. U.S. World War I Draft Registration Cards, 1917–1918; Louisiana Death Certificate 13025.

5. U.S. Social Security Applications and Claims Index, 1936–2007.

6. Louisiana Death Certificate 00931.

7. U.S. World War II Draft Cards Young Men, 1940–1947.

8. California Death Index, 1940–1997.

9. U.S. World War I Draft Registration Cards, 1917–1918; U.S. City Directories, 1822–1995; Louisiana Death Certificate 3580. Previously published death date of Apr. 11, 1968, incorrectly referred to a different Ernest Trepagnier who was born in 1899 and not a musician.

V

1. New Orleans, Louisiana, Birth Records Index, 1790–1915; California Death Index, 1940–1997.

2. U.S. Public Records Index, 1950–1993, vol. 1; Obituary, *Times-Picayune,* July 22, 2018.

3. 1900 U.S. Federal Census; Louisiana Death Certificate 153-542.

4. New Orleans, Louisiana, Death Records Index, 1804–1949.

5. New Orleans, Louisiana, Birth Records Index, 1790–1915; New Orleans, Louisiana, Death Records Index, 1804–1949.

6. 1900 U.S. Federal Census; Louisiana Death Certificate 1855.

7. Louisiana, Statewide Death Index, 1819–1964. Vincent's World War I Draft Registration Card gives birth year as 1893, and his World War II Draft Card gives birth year as 1891.

8. U.S. Social Security Death Index, 1935–2014.

W

1. Obituary, *Jennings Daily News,* Oct. 21, 1982.

2. The 1910 U.S. Federal Census suggests a 1907 birth year, but the 1920, 1930, and 1940 censuses and gravestone all indicate 1908.

3. Nevada Death Index, 1980–2012.

4. Louisiana Death Certificate 10-459.

5. U.S. World War I Draft Registration Cards, 1917–1918. Draft card is hand-signed as "Joe Mitchell Watkins," making reports of real surname being Watson apparently false.

6. 1900 U.S. Federal Census; New Orleans, Louisiana, City Directory, 1916; 1920 U.S. Federal Census; U.S. World War II Draft Registration Cards, 1942; Chicago and North Western Railroad Employment Records, 1935–1970; U.S. Social Security Applications and Claims Index, 1936–2007; Cook County, Illinois Death Index, 1908–1988. The 1900 Census and Social Security Applications list Sept. 1892 and Sept. 10, 1892, as birth dates while World War II Draft Card lists Nov. 10, 1892.

7. Texas Death Certificate 48134.

8. U.S. Social Security Applications and Claims Index, 19362007.

9. U.S. Social Security Death Index, 1935–2014.

10. Obituary, *Times-Picayune,* October 14, 1977.

11. Louisiana Death Certificate 3-30.

12. Louisiana Death Certificate 5833.

13. California, Death Index, 1940–1997.

14. New Orleans, Louisiana, Birth Records Index, 1790–1915; U.S. World War I Draft Registration Cards, 1917–1918.

15. Texas Death Certificate 07979.

16. Louisiana Death Certificate 14-801.

17. U.S. Social Security Applications and Claims Index, 1936–2007.

18. Cook County, Illinois Death Index, 1908–1988.

Y

1. U.S. World War I Draft Registration Cards, 1917–1918; U.S. Social Security Applications and Claims Index, 1936–2007; Louisiana, Statewide Death Index, 1819–1964.

2. U.S. Social Security Applications and Claims Index, 1936–2007.

3. Ibid.

4. U.S. World War I Draft Registration Cards, 1917–1918.

IIIIIIIII

Z

1. U.S. Social Security Applications and Claims Index, 1936–2007.

2. 1900 and 1910 U.S. Federal Census; Louisiana Death Certificate 55-183. Another local "Henry Zeno" who was older and listed as "teamster" in several censuses, city directories, and a New Orleans Police Department Arrest Record, and referenced in several jazz sources, is a different person and not the musician. This confusion may have contributed to the drummer's incorrect estimated earlier year of birth.

Notable Musicians Born outside Louisiana

1. Florida Death Index, 1877–1998.

2. U.S. Second Draft Registration Cards, 1948–1959.

3. Texas Birth Index, 1903–1997.

4. 1900, 1910, and 1930 U.S. Federal Census; U.S. World War II Draft Cards Young Men, 1940–1947; 1942 Social Security Application. Draft Card and Social Security Application lists date of birth as Dec. 25, 1897; earliest census lists Oct. 1895. Social Security records reviewed list no death information.

5. U.S. World War I Draft Registration Cards, 1917–1918.

6. 1940 U.S. Census, Wilkinson, Mississippi. A New Orleans birthplace has been repeatedly reported, but the 1940 census confirms that the family had resided at the same Mississippi residence since 1935.

7. U.S. Department of Veterans Affairs BIRLS Death File, 1850–2010.

8. Texas Birth Certificates, 1903–1932.

9. 1900 U.S. Federal Census; U.S. World War I Draft Registration Cards, 1917–1918.

10. 1900 U.S. Federal Census; U.S. Social Security Death Index, 1935–2014; California Death Index, 1940–1997.

11. Minnesota Birth Index, 1935–1995.

12. 1900 U.S. Federal Census; U.S. World War I Draft Registration Cards, 1917–1918; Louisiana Death Certificate 9-267.

13. U.S. Social Security Applications and Claims Index, 1936–2007.

14. U.S. Social Security Death Index, 1935–2014.

15. Ibid.; Obituary, *Times-Picayune,* Dec. 5, 1986.

16. Indiana Death Certificates, 1899–2011.

17. 1880 U.S. Federal Census; U.S. World War I Draft Registration Cards, 1917–1918. Johnson's Texas Death Certificate lists date of birth as Aug. 10, 1872.

18. 1920 U.S. Federal Census. Although routinely cited as a New Orleans native, Knowling was born in Vicksburg according to his application for Social Security (born June 24, 1908), American Federation of Musicians union membership card (born June 24, 1910), and death certificate (born June 12, 1912). Census of 1920 lists his age as 12 and still residing in Vicksburg. (Research courtesy of Jim O'Neal.)

19. Louisiana Death Certificate 20-7933.

20. U.S. World War I Draft Registration Cards, 1917–1918; New Orleans, Louisiana, Death Records Index, 1804–1949.

21. U.S. World War II Draft Cards Young Men, 1940–1947; Florida, County Marriage Records, 1823–1982; U.S. City Directories, 1822–1995; U.S. Social Security Applications and Claims Index, 1936–2007; author's interview with Carol Fran. World War II draft card lists birthplace as Cleveland, Ohio, but marriage records and Social Security files

indicate Dothan, Alabama.

22. U.S. Social Security Death Index, 1935–2014.

23. Ohio, County Marriage Records, 1774–1993; U.S. Social Security Applications and Claims Index, 1936–2007.

24. Louisiana Death Certificate 2-388.

25. Texas Birth Certificate 14144; U.S. Social Security Death Index, 1935–2014.

26. U.S. World War I Draft Registration Cards, 1917–1918; U.S. World War II Draft Registration Cards, 1942; Louisiana Death Certificate 62-06745. Both draft cards indicate June 5, 1891, Biloxi, Mississippi, as date and place of birth, with World War I card listing "traveling musician" as occupation. Middle name "Joseph" also appears on both documents. Death certificate lists New Orleans as place of birth.

27. U.S. World War II Draft Cards Young Men, 1940–1947; U.S. Social Security Death Index, 1935–2014.

28. Texas, Birth Certificates, 1903–1932; U.S. Social Security Applications and Claims Index, 1936, 2007.

29. Tamaulipas, Mexico, Civil Registration Births, 1860–1948; New Orleans, Louisiana, Death Records Index, 1804–1949.

30. Ibid.

31. U.S. World War II Draft Cards Young Men, 1940–1947.

32. Texas Death Index, 1903–2000.

BIBLIOGRAPHY

Books

Abbott, Lynn. *I Got Two Wings: Incidents and Anecdotes of the Two-Winged Preacher and Electric Guitar Evangelist Elder Utah Smith.* New York: CaseQuarter, 2008.

——. *The Original Blues: The Emergence of the Blues in African American Vaudeville.* Jackson: University of Mississippi Press, 2017.

——. *To Do This, You Must Know How: Music Pedagogy in the Black Gospel Quartet Tradition.* Jackson: University Press of Mississippi, 2013.

Abbott, Lynn, and Doug Seroff. *Ragged but Right: Black Traveling Shows, "Coon Songs," and the Dark Pathway to Blues and Jazz.* Jackson: University of Mississippi Press, 2007.

Alger, Dean. *The Original Guitar Hero and the Power of Music: The Legendary Lonnie Johnson, Music, and Civil Rights.* Denton: University of North Texas Press, 2014.

Allan, Johnnie. *Memories: A Pictorial History of South Louisiana Music, Volume I and II Combined, 1910s–1990s.* Lafayette, La.: JADFEL, 1995.

Ancelet, Barry Jean, and Elemore Morgan Jr. *Cajun and Creole Music Makers.* Rev. ed. Jackson: University Press of Mississippi, 1999.

Armstrong, Louis. *Satchmo: My Life in New Orleans.* 1954. Rpt. New York: Da Capo Press, 1986.

Bernard, Shane K. *Swamp Pop: Cajun and Creole Rhythm and Blues.* Jackson: University Press of Mississippi, 1996.

Berry, Jason, Jonathan Foose, and Tad Jones. *Up from the Cradle: New Orleans Music Since World War II.* Rev. ed. Lafayette: University of Louisiana at Lafayette Press, 2009.

Brasseaux, Ryan André. *Cajun Breakdown: The Emergence of an American-Made Music.* New York: Oxford University Press, 2009.

Brasseaux, Ryan André, and Kevin S. Fontenot, eds. *Fiddles, Accordions, Two Step & Swing: A Cajun Reader.* Lafayette: University of Louisiana at Lafayette Press, 2006.

Brinkman, Shannon, and Eve Abrams. *Preservation Hall.* Baton Rouge: Louisiana State University Press, 2011.

Broussard, Sherry T. *Images of America: Louisiana's Zydeco.* Charleston, S.C.: Arcadia Publishing, 2013.

Broven, John. *Record Makers and Breakers: Voices of the Independent Rock 'n' Roll Pioneers.* Urbana: University of Illinois Press, 2009.

——. *Rhythm and Blues in New Orleans.* Rev. ed. Gretna, La.: Pelican Publishing, 2016.

——. *South to Louisiana: The Music of the Cajun Bayous.* Gretna, La.: Pelican Publishing, 1983.

Burns, Mick. *Keeping the Beat on the Street: The New Orleans Brass Band Renaissance.* Baton Rouge: Louisiana State University Press, 2006.

Caffery, Joshua Clegg. *Traditional Music in Coastal Louisiana.* Baton Rouge: Louisiana State University Press, 2013.

Carter, William. *Preservation Hall: Music from the Heart.* New York: W.W. Norton & Co., 1991.

Charters, Samuel B. *Jazz New Orleans, 1885–1963: An Index to the Negro Musicians of New Orleans.* Rev. ed. New York: Oak Publications, 1963.

Coleman, Rick. *Blue Monday: Fats Domino and the Lost Dawn of Rock 'n' Roll.* New York: Da Capo Press, 2006.

DeWitt, Mark F. *Cajun and Zydeco Dance Music in Northern California: Modern Pleasures in a Post-modern World.* Jackson: University Press of Mississippi, 2008.

Dixon, Robert M. W., John Godrich, and Howard W. Rye. *Blues and Gospel Records, 1890–1943.* 4th ed. Oxford, U.K.: Oxford University Press, 1997.

DjeDje, Jacqueline Cogdell, and Eddie S. Meadows, eds. *California Soul: Music of African Americans in the West.* Berkeley: University of California Press, 1998.

Driggs, Frank, and Harris Lewine. *Black Beauty, White Heat: A Pictorial History of Classic Jazz, 1920–1950.* New York: William Morrow and Co., 1982.

Eagle, Bob, and Eric S. LeBlanc. *Blues: A Regional Experience.* Santa Barbara, Calif.: Praeger Publishing, 2013.

Fancourt, Les, and Bob McGrath. *The Blues Discography, 1943–1970.* Vancouver, B.C.: Eyeball Productions, 2006.

——. *The Blues Discography, 1971–2000.* Vancouver, B.C.: Eyeball Productions, 2011.

Feather, Leonard, and Ira Gitler. *The Biographical Encyclopedia of Jazz*. New York: Oxford University Press, 1999.

Feintuch, Burt. *Talking New Orleans Music: Crescent City Musicians Talk about Their Lives, Their Music, and Their City*. Jackson: University Press of Mississippi, 2015.

Floyd, Samuel A., Jr. *The Power of Black Music: Interpreting Its History from Africa to the United States*. New York: Oxford University Press, 1995.

Ford, Robert. *A Blues Bibliography: The International Literature of an Afro-American Music Genre*. Bromley, U.K.: Paul Pelletier Publishing, 1999.

Ford, Robert, and Bob McGrath. *Zydeco Discography 1949–2010: Louisiana & Texas Creole Music*. Vancouver, B.C.: Eyeball Productions, 2016.

Fusilier, Freida Marie, and Jolene M. Adams. *Hé, Là Bas! A History of Cajun and Zydeco Music in California*. Long Beach, Calif.: Self-published, 1994.

Gart, Galen, ed. *First Pressings: The History of Rhythm and Blues, Volumes 1–9, 1950–1959*. Milford, N.H.: Big Nickel Publications, 1993–2002.

Gioia, Ted. *The History of Jazz*. New York: Oxford University Press, 1997.

Glover, Tony, Scott Dirks, and Ward Gaines. *Blues with a Feeling: The Little Walter Story*. New York: Routledge, 2002.

Goreau, Laurraine. *Just Mahalia, Baby: The Mahalia Jackson Story*. 1975. Rpt. Gretna, La.: Pelican Publishing, 1998.

Govenar, Alan. *Meeting the Blues: The Rise of the Texas Sound*. 1988. Rpt. New York: Da Capo Press, 1995.

——, comp. *The Blues Come to Texas: Paul Oliver and Mack McCormick's Unfinished Book*. College Station: Texas A&M University Press, 2019.

Gushee, Lawrence. *Pioneers of Jazz: The Story of the Creole Band*. New York: Oxford University Press, 2005.

Hannusch, Jeff. *I Hear You Knockin': The Sound of New Orleans Rhythm and Blues*. Ville Platte, La.: Swallow Publications, 1985.

——. *The Soul of New Orleans: A Legacy of Rhythm and Blues*. Ville Platte, La.: Swallow Publications, 2001.

Hardie, Daniel. *Exploring Early Jazz: The Origins and Evolution of the New Orleans Style*. San Jose, Calif.: Writers Club Press, 2002.

Harris, Sheldon. *Blues Who's Who: A Biographical Dictionary of Blues Singers*. 1979. Rpt. New York: Da Capo Press, 1991.

Hawkins, Martin. *Slim Harpo: Blues King Bee of Baton Rouge*. Baton Rouge: Louisiana State University Press, 2016.

Joseph, Pleasant "Cousin Joe," and Harriet J. Ottenheimer. *Cousin Joe: Blues from New Orleans*. Chicago: University of Chicago Press, 1987.

Kernfeld, Barry, ed. *The New Grove Dictionary of Jazz, Vol. 1–3*. 2nd ed. London: Oxford University Press, 2002.

Komara, Edward, ed. *Encyclopedia of the Blues*. New York: Routledge Press, 2006.

Leigh, Nick. *Cajun Records 1946–1989*. 3rd ed. Bedfordshire, U.K.: Self-published, 2018.

Levin, Floyd. *Classic Jazz: A Personal View of the Music and the Musicians*. Berkeley: University of California Press, 2002.

Lomax, Alan. *Mister Jelly Roll: The Fortunes of Jelly Roll Morton, New Orleans Creole and "Inventor of Jazz."* Rev. ed. Berkeley: University of California Press, 2001.

Lornell, Kip, and Tracey E. W. Laird, eds. *Shreveport Sounds in Black and White*. Jackson: University Press of Mississippi, 2008.

Marquis, David M. *In Search of Buddy Bolden: First Man of Jazz*. Rev. ed. Baton Rouge: Louisiana State University Press, 2005.

McGee, Kristin A. *Some Liked It Hot: Jazz Women in Film and Television, 1928–1959*. Middletown, Conn.: Wesleyan University Press, 2009.

McGrath, Bob. *The R&B Indies*. Canada: Eyeball Productions, 2000.

Mitchell, George. *Blow My Blues Away*. Baton Rouge: Louisiana State University Press, 1971.

Montalbano, S. J., with Sam Muffoletto. *I'm Leaving It Up to Me: The Sam Montel Story*. Baton Rouge, La.: Self-published, 2018.

Mouton, Todd. *Way Down in Louisiana: Clifton Chenier, Cajun, Zydeco, and Swamp Pop Music*. Lafayette: University of Louisiana at Lafayette Press, 2015.

Newhart, Sally. *The Original Tuxedo Jazz Band: More Than a Century of a New Orleans Icon*. Charleston, S.C.: The History Press, 2013.

Odum, Howard W., and Guy B. Johnson. *The Negro and His Songs: A Study of Typical Negro Songs in the South*. 1925. Rpt. Hatboro, Pa.: Folklore Associates, Inc., 1964.

Oliver, Paul. *Conversation with the Blues*. 2nd ed. Cambridge, U.K.: Cambridge University Press, 1997.

Olivier, Rick, and Ben Sandmel. *Zydeco!* Jackson: University Press of Mississippi, 1999.

Oster, Harry. *Living Country Blues*. New York: Minerva Press, 1975.

Ramsey, Jr., Guthrie P. *Race Music: Black Cultures from Bebop to Hip-Hop*. Berkeley: University of California Press, 2004.

Rose, Al. *I Remember Jazz: Six Decades Among the Great Jazzmen*. Baton Rouge: Louisiana State University Press, 1987.

——. *Storyville, New Orleans: Being an Authentic, Illustrated Account of the Notorious Red Light District*. Tuscaloosa: University of Alabama Press, 1974.

Rose, Al, and Edmond Souchon. *New Orleans Jazz: A Family Album*. 3rd ed. Baton Rouge: Louisiana University Press, 1984.

Russell, Tony. *Country Music Records: A Discography, 1921–1942*. New York: Oxford University Press, 2004.

Rust, Brian. *Jazz and Ragtime Records, 1897–1942*. Denver: Mainspring Press, 2002.

Sandmel, Ben. *Ernie K-Doe: The R&B Emperor of New Orleans*. New Orleans: Historic New Orleans Collection, 2012.

Savoy, Ann Allen. *Cajun Music: A Reflection of a People, Volume 1*. 3rd ed. Eunice, La.: Bluebird Press, 1988.

Scherman, Tony. *Backbeat: Earl Palmer's Story*. Washington, D.C.: Smithsonian Institution Press, 1999.

Silvester, Peter J. *A Left Hand Like God: A History of Boogie-Woogie Piano*. 1988. Rpt. New York: Da Capo Press, 1989.

Solnit, Rebecca, and Rebecca Snedeker. *Unfathomable City: A New Orleans Atlas.* Berkeley: University of California Press, 2013.

Sonnier, Austin, Jr. *Second Linin': Jazzmen of Southwest Louisiana, 1900–1950.* Lafayette: University of Southwest Louisiana Press, 1989.

Tisserand, Michael. *The Kingdom of Zydeco.* New York: Arcade Publishing, 1998.

Vernon, Paul. *African-American Blues, Rhythm and Blues, Gospel and Zydeco on Film and Video, 1926–1997.* Brookfield, Vt.: Ashgate Publishing, 1999.

Wardlow, Gayle Dean, ed. *Chasin' That Devil Music: Searching for the Blues.* San Francisco, Calif.: Miller Freeman Books, 1998.

Whitburn, Joel. *Top R&B Singles, 1942–1999.* 4th ed. Menomonee Falls, Wis.: Record Research, 2000.

Wilkinson, Christopher. *Jazz on the Road: Don Albert's Musical Life.* Berkeley: University of California Press, 2001.

Wirt, John. *Huey "Piano" Smith and the Rocking Pneumonia Blues.* Baton Rouge: Louisiana State University Press, 2014.

Wolfe, Charles, and Kip Lornell. *The Life & Legend of Leadbelly.* New York: HarperCollins Publishers, 1992.

Wood, Roger. *Texas Zydeco.* Austin: University of Texas Press, 2006.

Wood, Roger, and James Fraher. *Down in Houston: Bayou City Blues.* Austin: University of Texas Press, 2003.

Yule, Ron. *Cajun Dancehall Heyday.* DeRidder, La.: Country Fiddle Publishing, 2017.

———. *My Fiddlin' Grounds.* Lafayette: University of Louisiana at Lafayette Press, 2007.

Selected Periodicals

American Folk Music Occasional
Billboard
Black Music Research Journal
Blues Access
Blues & Rhythm: The Gospel Truth Magazine
Blues Unlimited
Cashbox
DownBeat
Ebony
Gambit Weekly
The Jazz Archivist (Hogan Jazz Archive at Tulane University Library)
Jefferson Magazine
Juke Blues
Living Blues
Louisiana Folklife Journal
No Depression
Offbeat
78 Quarterly
Texas Monthly
Wavelength Magazine

Selected Newspapers (Print and Online)

Baton Rouge Advocate
Chicago Defender
Chicago Sun-Times
Chicago Tribune
Clarion Ledger (New Orleans)
Commercial Appeal (Memphis)
Crowley (La.) *Post Signal*
Crowley (La.) *Register*
Daily Advertiser (Lafayette)
Daily Iberian
Dallas Morning News
The Guardian (U.K.)
Houma Times
Houma Today
Houston Chronicle
The Independent (U.K.)
Jennings (La.) *Daily News*
Lake Charles American Press
Los Angeles Times
Monroe News Star
New Orleans States-Item
New Orleans Times-Democrat
New Orleans Times-Picayune
New York Times
Opelousas Daily World
Shreveport Sun
Shreveport Times
Town Talk (Alexandria, La.)
Washington Post
Weekly Iberian

Selected Websites and Blogs

Acadian Museum. www.acadianmuseum.com/
AllMusic Guide. www.allmusic.com
American Folklife Center. www.loc.gov/folklife/news/
Be Bop Wino. bebopwinorip.blogspot.com/
Black Cat Rockabilly. www.rockabilly.nl/
Brown, Chris. Shreveport Songs. shreveportsongs.blogspot.com/
A Closer Walk. acloserwalknola.com/
Cosimo Code. cosimocode.com/
Daddy B. Nice's Southern Soul R&B. www.southernsoulrnb.com/
Discogs. www.discogs.com/
Falcon, Wade. Early Cajun Music. earlycajunmusic.blogspot.com/
Flat Town Music Company. www.flattownmusic.com/
45cat. www.45cat.com/
Grogan, Larry. Funky 16 Corners. funky16corners.com/
Hanley, Peter. Ragtime, Blues, Hot Piano. doctorjazz.co.uk/

Hogan Jazz Archive. jazz.tulane.edu/

Kelly, Red. Soul Detective. souldetective.com/

Know Louisiana. www.knowlouisiana.org/

Koenig, Dr. Karl. Basin Street Historical Jazz Archive. basinstreet.com/

Library of Congress. www.loc.gov/

McNeese State University Archives. libguides.mcneese.edu/databases/

Mississippi Blues Trail. msbluestrail.org/

Music Rising at Tulane: The Musical Cultures of the Gulf South. musicrising.tulane.edu/

New Orleans Jazz & Heritage Foundation Archive. www.jazzandheritage.org/archive/

O'Neal, Jim. BluEsoterica. bluesoterica.com/

Phillips, Dan. Home of the Groove. homeofthegroove.blogspot.com/

Ponderosa Stomp blog. blog.ponderosastomp.com/

Red Hot Jazz Archive. www.redhotjazz.com/

Red Saunders Research Foundation. redsaunders.com/

Ridley, John. Sir Shambling's Deep Soul Heaven. www.sirshambling.com/

Rimmer, Dave. Soulful Kinda Music. www.soulfulkindamusic.net/

Texas State Historical Association. www.tshaonline.org/

University of Mississippi Archives and Special Collections. The Blues Archive. www.olemiss.edu/depts/general_library/archives/blues/

Wirz, Stefan. American Music. www.wirz.de/music/american.htm/